THE JOSEPH SMITH PAPERS

THE
JOSEPH SMITH
PAPERS

JOURNALS

VOLUME 1: 1832–1839

Dean C. Jessee
Ronald K. Esplin
Richard Lyman Bushman

GENERAL EDITORS

Dean C. Jessee
Mark Ashurst-McGee
Richard L. Jensen

VOLUME EDITORS

THE CHURCH
HISTORIAN'S
PRESS

THE CHURCH HISTORIAN'S PRESS is an imprint of the Church History Department
of The Church of Jesus Christ of Latter-day Saints, Salt Lake City, Utah,
and a trademark of Intellectual Reserve, Inc.

www.josephsmithpapers.org

The Joseph Smith Papers Project is endorsed by
the National Historical Publications and Records Commission.

Art direction: Richard Erickson.
Cover design: Scott Eggers. Interior design: Richard Erickson and Scott M. Mooy.
Typography: Laurie C. Cook and R. Eric Smith.

Library of Congress Cataloging-in-Publication Data

Smith, Joseph, 1805–1844.
Journals series / Dean C. Jessee, Mark Ashurst-McGee, Richard L. Jensen, volume editors.
p. cm. — (The Joseph Smith papers)
Includes bibliographical references.
ISBN 978-1-57008-849-0 (hardbound: alk. paper)
1. Smith, Joseph, 1805–1844—Diaries. 2. Mormon Church—Presidents—Biography.
3. Church of Jesus Christ of Latter-day Saints—Presidents—Biography. 4. Mormon Church—
History—Sources. 5. Church of Jesus Christ of Latter-day Saints—History—Sources.
I. Jessee, Dean C. II. Ashurst-McGee, Mark. III. Jensen, Richard L. IV. Title. V. Series.

BX8695.S6A3 2008   289.3092—dc22   [B]   2008037101

Printed in the United States of America on acid-free paper.
10 9 8 7 6 5 4 3 2 1

Preface

The Joseph Smith Papers are being prepared under the auspices of the office of the historian of The Church of Jesus Christ of Latter-day Saints and published by The Church Historian's Press. Before its completion, the project will involve numerous staff members and many years of scholarly labor. The motivation to engage in this vast project comes from the great respect in which Latter-day Saints hold Joseph Smith as the church's founder and a modern prophet. We believe Joseph Smith will be better understood and appreciated if the documents he produced are available for all to examine.

In that spirit, the editorial staff has sought to present Smith's papers as accurately and completely as possible. We have gathered every known Joseph Smith document, verified each transcript at least three times, and provided extensive annotation on the historical context. The documents shed light on many dimensions of Smith's life and personality, his strengths and weaknesses, and the successes and failures of the movement he led.

Of the thousands of items in the Joseph Smith papers, his revelations are among the most significant and contested. According to his own account, the revelations came in a number of forms: visions, inspired words in the voice of God, what he called "translations," and impressions of the Holy Ghost. Although the revelations have religious meaning to us as Latter-day Saints, we present them in these volumes without comment on their ultimate source. In the tradition of documentary editing, our aim is simply to reproduce the documents and their historical setting so far as we can reconstruct it.

To assure balance and rigorous scholarly standards, we have consulted a national advisory board of distinguished scholars. With their guidance, we have sought to produce volumes on which scholars and Latter-day Saints can rely for accurate information.

The General Editors
Salt Lake City
August 2008

The Joseph Smith Papers

The Joseph Smith Papers: Journals, Volume 1

Contents

Journals, 1832–1839

Reference Material

Illustrations and Maps

Textual Illustrations

Contextual Illustrations

MAPS

OTHER VISUALS

Timeline of Joseph Smith's Life

1805
Born in Vermont.

1816–1817
Family moved to New York.

1820
First vision of Deity.

1823
First vision of angel Moroni.

1827
Married Emma Hale.
Obtained Book of Mormon gold plates.

1829
Bulk of Book of Mormon translated.
Received Aaronic and Melchizedek priesthoods.

1830
Book of Mormon published.
Organized church.
Commenced revision of Bible.

1831
Moved from New York to Ohio.
Revelation locating Mormon gathering place in Missouri.

1833
Concluded revision of Bible.
Book of Commandments printed.

1834
Led military expedition to Missouri to assist exiled Mormons.

1835
Organized Quorum of the Twelve Apostles.
Doctrine and Covenants published.

1836
Temple completed in Ohio.
Visions of Jesus Christ, Moses, Elias, and Elijah.

1837
Sent missionaries to England.
Dissension and financial problems in Kirtland.

1838
Moved from Ohio to Missouri.
Surrendered to Missouri militia.
Incarcerated pending trial.

1839
Allowed to escape.
Relocated to Illinois.
Met with U.S. president Martin Van Buren seeking redress for Missouri grievances.

1841
Commissioned as lieutenant general of Nauvoo Legion of Illinois militia.

1842
Organized Female Relief Society.
Introduced temple endowment ceremony.
Elected mayor of Nauvoo.

1843
Revelation on plural wives and eternal marriage recorded.

1844
Nominated as U.S. presidential candidate.

For a detailed chronology of Joseph Smith's life for the period covered in this volume, see pages 357–363. For the sources of the information presented in this timeline, see the Joseph Smith Papers website.

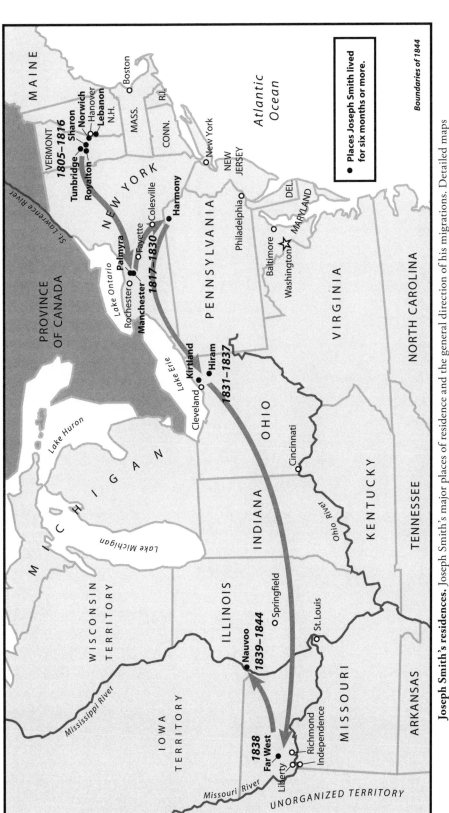

Joseph Smith's residences. Joseph Smith's major places of residence and the general direction of his migrations. Detailed maps relevant to the places mentioned in this volume appear on pages 381–395. (Design by John Hamer.)

Joseph Smith and His Papers

For one who had little schooling, Joseph Smith left an unusually extensive literary record. From 1828, when he began work on the Book of Mormon at age twenty-two, to 1844, when he was killed at age thirty-eight, Smith produced thousands of pages of revelations, translations, correspondence, declarations, discourses, journals, and histories. His records will fill approximately thirty volumes when publication is complete. The goal of the Joseph Smith Papers Project is to publish every extant document written by Smith or by his scribes in his behalf, as well as other records that were created under his direction or that reflect his personal instruction or involvement.

The publication of his papers some two hundred years after his birth opens a window on a life filled with what Joseph Smith called "marvilous experience."[1] His rise from obscurity to prominence as the founder and first prophet of The Church of Jesus Christ of Latter-day Saints did not follow a conventional path. Though he was intelligent and strong willed, no ordinary talent can account for his success. His rise as church leader, city builder, and theologian rested on what he believed was a gift of revelation, by which he meant direct communication from God in the form of visions into heaven, heavenly visitors, or more commonly the words of God coming through direct inspiration. Controversial as his claims were, the revelations were the source of his influence among the tens of thousands of people who joined the church while he was alive and the millions who accepted his teachings after his death. Hundreds of pages of revelations accumulated over his lifetime. His major projects, plans, and doctrines originated in revelation. His followers complied with his often-demanding directions largely because they believed them to be from God. When Joseph Smith asked John Whitmer, an early follower, to be church historian, Whitmer initially refused and finally agreed only if the Lord would "manifest it through Joseph the Seer."[2]

The revelations ranged from mundane directions for keeping a history or opening a store to visions of heaven and the future. One of the most dramatic revelations came in 1832 when Smith and his associate Sidney Rigdon were

---

1. JS History, 1832, 1.
2. Whitmer, History, 24.

puzzling over a biblical passage that raised questions about rewards and punishments in the afterlife.

> And while we meditated upon these things, the Lord touched the eyes of our
> understandings, and they were opened, and the glory of the Lord shone round
> about; and we beheld the glory of the Son, on the right hand of the Father, and
> received of his fulness. . . . And now, after the many testimonies which have been
> given of him, this is the testimony, last of all, which we give of him, that he lives;
> for we saw him, even on the right hand of God; and we heard the voice bearing
> record that he is the only begotten of the Father.[3]

The revelation went on to describe a hereafter divided into three degrees of
glory, more finely graded than the usual heaven-or-hell division and more in
accord with the mixture of good and evil in actual life. The revelations thrilled
believers. William W. Phelps, a New York newspaper editor converted a year
after the church was organized, called the revelation on the three degrees of
glory "the greatest news that was ever published to man."[4] A meeting of Latter-
day Saints making publication plans voted that the revelations "be prized by
this Conference to be worth to the Church the riches of the whole Earth.
speaking temporally."[5]

The revelations derived their credibility partly from the prophetic tradi-
tions of the Bible. Joseph Smith moved into a role well known to Christians.
He was another Moses or Paul. To most Christians, the Bible stood above all
other books precisely because it was the word of God to prophets. Now,
the Mormons claimed, God spoke again. One early convert to the church
approached the preaching of Mormon missionaries skeptically but then
reasoned:

> I found, on searching the Scriptures, that from the commencement of time,
> through every age, God continued to send prophets to the people, and always
> when God had a message for the people, he chose a special messenger to send it by,
> and it was always headed with a "thus saith the Lord." . . . If he supplied every
> other age and people with prophets and special messengers, why not this?[6]

The presence of a modern prophet brought biblical history into the present.

Along with the modern-day revelations that later were compiled into a
book titled the Doctrine and Covenants, Smith produced three major revealed
"translations": the Book of Mormon (from gold plates), the book of Moses
(linked to Genesis), and the book of Abraham (from ancient Egyptian scrolls

---

3. Vision, 16 Feb. 1832, in Doctrine and Covenants 91:3, 1835 ed. [D&C 76:19–23].

4. "Items for the Public," *The Evening and the Morning Star,* July 1832, [6].

5. Minute Book 2, 12 Nov. 1831.

6. Corrill, *Brief History of the Church,* 10.

purchased from a dealer). The three purported to be English renditions of ancient records that, like the Bible, told of events in a distant time and place. Although termed "translations," they were not translations in the ordinary sense. Smith did not understand the languages of the original text and convert the words to English through his own learning. As he put it in the preface to the first edition of the Book of Mormon, "I translated, by the gift and power of God." The resulting "translations" were as much inspired texts, words given him of God, as the revelations in the Doctrine and Covenants.

The persuasiveness of the translations for early converts came partly from the confidence with which Joseph Smith introduced readers into ancient worlds without injecting himself into the story. The Book of Mormon opens with the phrase "I, Nephi, having been born of goodly parents, therefore I was taught somewhat in all the learning of my father"; the book of Moses begins, "The words of God which he spake unto Moses at a time when Moses was caught up into an exceeding high Mountain"; and the book of Abraham starts, "In the land of the Chaldeans, at the residence of my father, I, Abraham, saw that it was needful for me to obtain another place of residence."[7] Readers are transported to remote times and places as they are when reading *Beowulf* or Thucydides—or the Bible. In the book of Moses, the reader learns of Enoch, who conversed with God and built a city that was taken into heaven. In the book of Abraham, the father of nations learns astronomy by consulting a Urim and Thummim. However one accounts for these marvelous narratives, they exceed anything one would expect from a poorly educated rural visionary. They are one reason for Yale literary critic Harold Bloom's comment that Smith was "an authentic religious genius" who "surpassed all Americans, before or since, in the possession and expression of what could be called the religion-making imagination."[8] Latter-day Saints, of course, consider the translations to have come from God.

Origins

The origins of the translations are not easily identified to everyone's satisfaction. Smith had little education and no history of literary experimentation. Indeed, nothing in his background prepared him either to translate or to lead a church. He brought neither wealth, social position, nor education to his work.

---

7. Book of Mormon, 1830 ed., 5 [1 Nephi 1:1]; Old Testament Revision 1, p. 1 [Moses 1:1]; "The Book of Abraham," *Times and Seasons*, 1 Mar. 1842, 3:704 [Abraham 1:1].

8. Bloom, *American Religion*, 96–97.

Joseph Smith's paternal great-grandfather, Samuel Smith, a third-generation New Englander, held local political offices in Topsfield, Massachusetts, a village just north of Salem, but died with his estate insolvent. His son Asael Smith migrated to Vermont and opened farms for his sons, allowing Joseph Smith's father and mother, Joseph Smith Sr. and Lucy Mack, to begin married life with substantial acreage and fair prospects. Joseph Sr. had the enterprise to open a store and export ginseng root to China at the moment when Yankee merchants, released from the constrictions of the British mercantile system, were sending ships around the globe. But by requiring him to go into debt, the trading ventures—and the dishonesty of a business partner—led to his financial downfall. He lost his farm and for the next fourteen years worked rented land to support his family.[9]

Joseph Smith Jr. was born 23 December 1805, in Sharon, Vermont, the fifth of eleven children. The Smith family moved every few years during his boyhood until about 1816, when they migrated to Palmyra, New York, a town along the future route of the Erie Canal. Here they contracted for a farm in the adjacent township of Farmington (later Manchester) and began clearing the land, but even the combined efforts of a large family were insufficient to hold on to the farm. The Smiths made the mistake of beginning a frame house to replace their log house, and when the added expense made it impossible to make payments on their farm, the owners foreclosed.

Because of the family's financial situation, Joseph Jr. acquired no more than a few years of schooling during the rare periods when his family could spare him from work. Indicative of the family's aspirations, his older brother Hyrum attended Moor's Charity School at Dartmouth, but Joseph was not so fortunate in his education. He was further disadvantaged by lacking a church. His parents' families on both sides had lost touch with the Congregational churches of New England. Grandfather Asael Smith, though ostensibly a Congregationalist, sympathized with Universalist doctrines. Joseph Sr. lost confidence in the integrity of churches altogether. He had dreams about wandering in the wilderness in search of peace and salvation. When his wife, Lucy, joined the Presbyterians in Palmyra, he refused to attend.

Lucy Mack Smith was more amenable to churchgoing than was her husband. Her mother, Lydia Gates Mack, was the daughter of a Congregational deacon. Her father, Solomon Mack, though he lived without religion most of his life, finally converted to Christianity in his old age. Her brother Jason became a "seeker," as she called him—one who was searching for true religion.

---

9. On Joseph Smith's ancestry and early life, see Anderson, *Joseph Smith's New England Heritage;* Bushman, *Beginnings of Mormonism,* chap. 1; and Anderson, *Lucy's Book.*

Early in her life, after passing through a distressing illness, Lucy tried to find a church but could not connect with the right pastor. When she finally affiliated with the Presbyterians in Palmyra, three of her children—Hyrum, Sophronia, and Samuel—attended with her. Joseph Jr. stayed home with his father.

In their search for contact with the divine, the Smiths were susceptible to the folk magic still flourishing in rural America in the early nineteenth century. Harboring the perpetual hope of the poor for quick riches, Joseph Smith Sr. searched for lost treasure, often with the help of Joseph Jr. Like many of their neighbors, the family combined the use of divining rods and seer stones with conventional forms of Christian worship. In his early twenties, Joseph Jr. had to extricate himself from the local band of treasure seekers before he could focus on his calling to translate the Book of Mormon.

Even though connected to a church only intermittently, the Smiths were religious. They read the Bible together, and as a young man Joseph Jr. felt the need for personal salvation. He was frustrated by the denominational chaos of the early republic, which was nowhere more confusing than in the highly evangelized "burned-over district" where the Smiths lived. The repeated visits of revival preachers kept religious concern at a high pitch, but the strife of contending voices made it difficult to know where to turn for instruction. The split within the family compounded Joseph Jr.'s confusion.[10] Was he to follow his mother into the Presbyterian church or join his father in abstention? Amid the war of words, he later wrote, he could find no answer to the question "Who of all these parties are right?"[11]

In 1820, in a solitary place where his family had been clearing land, he prayed for an answer. According to his account, he was at first unable to speak as an unseen force nearly overcame him. Then, mustering his strength, he called upon God and saw two persons, the Father and the Son, in "a pillar of light." One told him that he was forgiven of his sins and, in answer to his query, said that he should join none of the churches; they had "a form of Godliness" but lacked godly power.[12] A world overrun with churches was bereft of true religion.

In 1823, three years after his first vision, Joseph Smith was again visited by a messenger from heaven. As Smith retold the story later, while praying for forgiveness one night he noticed a light appearing in his room. In a moment, a white-robed angel stood in the air before him. The angel introduced himself as Moroni and spoke of the record of a people who dwelt anciently on the

---

10. Bushman, "Joseph Smith's Family Background."
11. JS History, vol. A-1, 2.
12. JS History, vol. A-1, 3.

American continents. Moroni, Smith was to learn, was the last in a long line of prophets in the Western Hemisphere who had written their story, just as the prophets in Palestine had written the Bible. Smith would find the book, he was told, inscribed on gold plates buried in a hill near his house in Manchester. His task was to translate the record. In 1827 he obtained possession of the plates, and in 1828 he began the translation with the aid of an interpreting instrument, later called a Urim and Thummim, consisting of two stones set in a bow and attached to a breastplate. His wife, Emma Hale, whom he married in January 1827, was the first to take down his dictation, followed by others such as the young schoolteacher Oliver Cowdery.

The Book of Mormon

In March 1830, Joseph Smith published the 584-page Book of Mormon, an unusual beginning for a life as a minister of the gospel. No other religious career in Smith's time began this way. Others of his generation claimed visions, but none published a "translation" or wrote a parallel Bible. Charles G. Finney, an apprentice lawyer in Adams, New York, claimed to see a vision of Christ at the time of his conversion in 1821, but Finney immediately began preaching; he went on to become the most influential evangelical preacher of his generation.[13] Other budding religious reformers took the same path, moving from visionary to preacher. Joseph Smith, instead of communicating with the world through sermons, made his entrance onto the religious stage with the translation of a large book of ancient records. Though not widely read himself, he instinctively sensed the increasing potency of print in disseminating religious knowledge.

The publication of the Book of Mormon plunged Joseph Smith into immediate controversy. Even before the book was published, his Palmyra neighbors pledged not to purchase it, hoping to discourage printers from finishing the job. The Palmyrans thought the book was a scheme to swindle the gullible. One acquaintance later claimed Smith had put white sand in his frock and told his family it was the gold plates.[14] Smith's refusal to show the plates to curious inquirers encouraged such speculations. Though never able to silence the critics, he did have an answer to their questions about the plates. Eleven of his friends and family members said they saw the plates and agreed to have their testimonies printed in the back of the Book of Mormon.

Apart from its origins, the book itself was contested. Some early readers were enthralled. One convert, Parley P. Pratt, said after obtaining a copy, "I read all day; eating was a burden, I had no desire for food; sleep was a burden

---

13. Finney, *Memoirs*, 1–2, 25.
14. Howe, *Mormonism Unvailed*, 235–236.

when the night came, for I preferred reading to sleep."[15] Others were more skeptical. The Reformed Baptist theologian Alexander Campbell hypothesized that Smith had cobbled the text together from bits and pieces of cultural information swirling about him in Palmyra. Campbell wrote, "This prophet Smith, through his stone spectacles, wrote on the plates of Nephi, in his book of Mormon, every error and almost every truth discussed in New York for the last ten years."[16] Campbell was referring to the book's sermons, prophecies, and discourses on doctrine, but his explanation could not account for the extensive narrative tying the religious passages together.

The Book of Mormon is an elaborate, thousand-year history of a civilization that flourished and then collapsed more than fourteen hundred years before Joseph Smith published the book. In its ambitious scope, the Book of Mormon most resembles the Bible. The first hostile reports immediately called it the "Gold Bible," partly because of the echoes of King James English in the prose. The text begins with the flight of two Israelite families from Jerusalem in about 600 BC and ends with the destruction of their civilization in about AD 421. The text is divided into "books" named for prophets, similar to the prophetic books of the Bible, and tells stories of God's intervention in human affairs. In a reprise of the New Testament, Christ appears to these people after his resurrection and teaches the Christian gospel. Although many New England writers of Smith's generation tried to produce scripture-like writing, the literary historian Lawrence Buell has pointed out that none succeeded in completing more than a few fragments of inspired poetry. "The new Bible did not get written," he says, "unless one counts *The Book of Mormon.*"[17]

Though like the Bible in many respects, the Book of Mormon is not a copy. It introduces scores of distinctive characters and tells dozens of original stories about the struggle to establish a righteous society. The account, which takes place largely in the Western Hemisphere, where the migrating families arrive by ship, re-creates an economy, a culture, a political system, a military, and a church. The complexity of the story and the scene makes it difficult to sustain the hypothesis that the Book of Mormon merely imitates the Bible or that, as Campbell argued, the uneducated Joseph Smith pulled together snatches of theological and political controversy to patch the book together. Considering that Smith dictated the bulk of the book in less than three months, it is perhaps the most notable example of untutored genius in all of American history.

---

15. Pratt, *Autobiography*, 38.

16. Campbell published his analysis in his own newspaper in February 1831 and then in pamphlet form in Boston in 1832. ("Delusions," *Millennial Harbinger*, 7 Feb. 1831, 93; Campbell, *Delusions*, 13.)

17. Buell, *New England Literary Culture*, 183.

To account for the narrative complexity, critics soon began to hypothesize the existence of another author. In 1834, Eber Howe, a newspaper editor writing from Painesville, Ohio, near Mormon headquarters in Kirtland, argued that the Book of Mormon was derived from the work of Solomon Spalding (or Spaulding), a Dartmouth graduate, then dead, who had been fascinated with the history of the American Indians. Spalding had written a romance about a Roman legate to Great Britain who was cast ashore on the North American coast and lived among the native inhabitants for several years. Although Spalding's manuscript was not published, his friends thought they remembered characters resembling those in the Book of Mormon. Howe speculated that Joseph Smith's learned associate Sidney Rigdon had seen Spalding's manuscript, transformed it into the Book of Mormon, and somehow smuggled it to Smith.[18]

The theory fell apart when the Spalding manuscript was discovered in the 1880s and found to bear only a faint resemblance to the Book of Mormon.[19] Josiah Quincy, the Boston Brahmin who visited Joseph Smith in Nauvoo, Illinois, in 1844 and later read Spalding, saw no comparison between Spalding's "tedious romance" and the Book of Mormon.[20] In recent years, the preponderance of non-Mormon scholarly opinion has returned to Campbell's theory of an ingenious Smith writing the book himself.[21]

The debate over the Book of Mormon's origins has partially obscured the actual nature of the text. Critics have been so absorbed in proving or disproving the book's historical authenticity that the literary and theological qualities have been relatively neglected. The authoritative *Cambridge History of American Literature* makes virtually no mention of the book.[22] But even at first glance, it is evident that the Book of Mormon is first and foremost a work of intense piety. Long before Jesus is born, Christ figures in sermons and visions. The urgency of the preaching comes through in passage after passage. Jacob, son of the patriarch in the founding family, exhorts his people to believe:

> Wherefore, my beloved brethren, I beseech of you in words of soberness, that ye would repent, and come with full purpose of heart, and cleave unto God as he cleaveth unto you. . . . Will ye reject the words of the Prophets? and will ye reject

18. Howe, *Mormonism Unvailed*, 278–290.

19. Jackson, *Manuscript Found.*

20. Quincy, *Figures of the Past*, 395–396.

21. See, for example, Riley, *Founder of Mormonism*; Brodie, *No Man Knows My History*; and Vogel, *Making of a Prophet.*

22. Bercovitch and Patell, *Cambridge History of American Literature*, 210. The Book of Mormon is cited primarily as an example of the Israel theory of Indian origins.

all the words which have been spoken concerning Christ, after that so many have spoken concerning him?[23]

The pleading, exhorting, and promising continue down through the final prophet, Moroni, writing four centuries after the birth of Christ:

> Yea, come unto Christ, and be perfected in him, and deny yourselves of all ungodliness; and if ye shall deny yourselves of all ungodliness, and love God with all your might, mind and strength, then is his grace sufficient for you, that by his grace ye may be perfect in Christ.[24]

The text is saturated with Christian faith, a side of Joseph Smith's mentality sometimes overlooked by biographers drawn to the more sensational episodes in his life.

Zion

On 6 April 1830, Joseph Smith organized a handful of followers into the Church of Christ, later named the Church of Jesus Christ of Latter-day Saints. But that was only the first of Smith's complex religious projects. Less than six months after the church's organization, he sent out missionaries to locate a site for a city that the revelations called the "City of Zion" or "New Jerusalem," evoking powerful imagery from the Revelation of John. The city was to be a gathering place for his followers, a refuge from the calamities of the last days, and the place for a temple. Here Christ was to come when he returned to the earth. In summer 1831, Smith traveled to Missouri, on the western edge of American settlement, where a revelation designated the little village of Independence, Jackson County, as the site for the city.

Sometime in that year, Joseph Smith realized it was his mission, at whatever cost, to lay "the foundation" of the city of Zion.[25] In the years to come, he tried in Independence, Missouri, and when defeated, went on to Far West, Missouri, and Nauvoo, Illinois. He pursued the building of the city of Zion to the exclusion of more conventional programs like the construction of chapels for church members in the towns where they already lived. Distributed in smaller numbers, his followers would have been less threatening to their neighbors and probably less subject to persecution. But Smith never constructed a typical meetinghouse for ordinary worship. He gave himself entirely to cities and temples. This vision drove him until the end of his life; and after his death the same vision inspired Mormon settlement in the Great Basin.

---

23. Book of Mormon, 1830 ed., 139–140 [Jacob 6:5, 8].
24. Book of Mormon, 1830 ed., 587 [Moroni 10:32].
25. See Revelation, 1 Aug. 1831, in Doctrine and Covenants 18:3, 1835 ed. [D&C 58:7].

Building cities was a strange mission for a person reared in the rural villages of New England and New York. When Smith drafted a plat for the city of Zion in 1833, it called for fifteen to twenty thousand residents—a major city in those days, considering that St. Louis had fewer than seven thousand residents and Cincinnati, the largest city in the West, fewer than thirty thousand. He envisioned missionaries shepherding converts to Zion, where each family would receive an inheritance of land and have access to the temple for spiritual instruction. His answer to the failings of American society was to gather believers out of the world and organize them into a community where the poor were cared for and everyone stood on an equal material plane. When one city filled up, others were to be laid out until, as he said, the world was filled with cities of Zion.[26]

The Zion project imparted a material, practical side to Joseph Smith's Mormonism that has persisted to the present. The plat drawing specified the width of the streets and the size of the lots for a city that in biblical literature was an ethereal creation of the heavens, descending from the sky at the last day. Smith's faith in scripture was literal in wanting to embody visions that most Christians thought were purely ideals. He had a sense of making heaven on earth. Later in life he said, "That same sociality. which exists amongt us here. will exist among us there only it will be coupled with eternal glory."[27] In that spirit, one revelation specified a dietary code forbidding the use of tobacco and liquor and recommending grains, fresh fruits, and vegetables, coupling these prescriptions with a high promise, in part echoing Isaiah:

> And all saints who remember to keep and do these sayings, walking in obedience
> to the commandments, shall receive health in their navel, and marrow to their
> bones and shall find wisdom, and great treasures of knowledge, even hidden trea-
> sures; and shall run and not be weary, and shall walk and not faint.[28]

His was a religion of the body as well as the spirit.

All of this makes it difficult to situate Joseph Smith's restored gospel among the religions of its time. The gathering to Zion seems to place Joseph Smith among the communitarian reformers. At the same time, he was certainly a millenarian. Because Smith adhered to New Testament organizational patterns, such as appointing twelve apostles, his Church of Christ has been classed with the "restorationist" churches, such as Alexander Campbell's Disciples of Christ, which aimed to strip away every historical accumulation until only a

---

26. Plat of City of Zion, 1833, CHL. For the specifics of the city, see Hamilton, *Nineteenth-Century Mormon Architecture,* chap. 2; see also Olsen, "Mormon Ideology of Place."

27. Instruction, 2 Apr. 1843, in Clayton, Journal, 2 Apr. 1843 [D&C 130:2].

28. Revelation, 27 Feb. 1833, in Doctrine and Covenants 80:3, 1835 ed. [D&C 89:18–20]; Isaiah 40:31.

perfectly reformed New Testament church remained. Although all are applicable in part, no single category is completely satisfactory. While paralleling other restorations in emphasizing faith, repentance, baptism, and the Holy Ghost as fundamentals of salvation, Smith went beyond them in dispensing scripture like Peter or Paul. The claim to revelation appalled Campbell, who sought only to restore the forms and teachings of early Christianity, not the revelatory powers of the first apostles.

Other restorationists were baffled by Joseph Smith's return to Old Testament principles such as priesthood and the gathering of Israel. Most Protestants thought that Old Testament priesthood had ended with Christ, the great high priest of salvation. More immediately, Protestants associated priesthood with Roman Catholicism and the oppressive old regimes of Europe. Heedless of the negative associations, Smith's revelations included ordinations to Aaronic and Melchizedek priesthoods. Male converts to Mormonism could not only be appointed to the office of elder, a New Testament title, but could also be made high priests, a title right out of the Old Testament. Moreover, beginning in 1836, these priesthood holders underwent "washings" and "anointings" in the Kirtland temple, echoing the prescriptions for ordaining priests in Exodus. The revelations spoke of the "restoration of all things," which was interpreted to include not only the New Testament church as Christ established it but the temple and all its associated ordinances. In Nauvoo, the earlier temple rituals evolved into an elaborate course of instruction called the endowment, which led men and women through the course of life from the Creation and Fall to the return to God. All this gave a ritualistic, ceremonial quality to Joseph Smith's restoration quite out of keeping with the radical Protestant background of many converts.

Conflict

Smith's various initiatives—city building, priesthood, and temples—were shaken at regular intervals by devastating persecutions. In 1833, two years after the city of Zion was begun in Independence, Missouri, the Latter-day Saints were expelled and required to start all over. In 1838, Smith and his followers in Kirtland, Ohio, were forced out of that area and moved to Far West, Missouri, where his followers were forming another Zion. In 1838 and 1839, they were expelled when the governor's extermination order compelled Mormon withdrawal. Their next resort, Nauvoo, Illinois, begun in 1839, grew into the largest Mormon city to that point, with ten to twelve thousand inhabitants—until the Mormons were driven out and began the trek to what would become Utah. The pattern was unrelenting: Mormons gathered until their enemies forced them out, requiring them to begin still another city.

One of the perplexities of Mormonism is why a religion formed in America was so constantly in conflict with the society around it. Why could no American community tolerate the Latter-day Saints' presence for more than a few years? In each instance of persecution, particular local complaints contributed to the enmity. The Missourians suspected the predominantly Yankee Mormons of encouraging the immigration of free blacks. Others accused the Saints of conniving with Indians to slaughter white settlers because of Book of Mormon prophecies about the ultimate redemption of America's aborigines. In Illinois, Mormons were accused of counterfeiting, thieving, and being clannishly exclusive.

But one issue underlay all the local concerns: Mormonism and democratic government clashed. Joseph Smith's enemies feared that he thought himself above the law. They believed that because his revelations came first, he would sacrifice obedience to worldly government. He was determined, they were sure, to build his kingdom by force if necessary. There were few specific instances of his actually breaking the law, though he wearied of what he called "vexatious lawsuits" brought for payment of debt and once declared in open meeting that he would stand for it no more.[29] But he went to court anyway, scores of times, assuring government officials he was submissive to legal processes.

Nothing he did could allay suspicion. Smith's claim to revelation by its very nature conflicted with democracy. There was always the question of which took precedence, the voice of the people acting through democratic government or the voice of God speaking through his prophet. Roman Catholics, with their belief in the pope's infallibility, were entangled in the same conflict. Smith assured the world he had no intention of breaking the law, and a revelation admonished his followers to submit to legal proceedings.[30] But the potential for conflict was always there, and in the case of plural marriage, Smith did put his revelation first. A committee of Illinois anti-Mormons summed up the prevailing reasoning. "A certain class of people have obtruded themselves upon us," the committee reported, who have assumed "the sacred garb of Christianity."

> We find them yielding implicit obedience to the ostensible head and founder of this sect, who is a pretended Prophet of the Lord. . . .
>
> We believe that such an individual, regardless as he must be, of his obligations to God, and at the same time entertaining the most absolute contempt for

---

29. JS, Journal, Mar.–Sept. 1838 (undated entry), p. 238 herein; JS, Journal, 30 June 1843, JS Collection, CHL.

30. Revelation, 6 Aug. 1833, in Doctrine and Covenants 85:2, 1835 ed. [D&C 98:4–7]; see also JS, "Church History," *Times and Seasons,* 1 Mar. 1842, 3:710 [Articles of Faith 1:12].

the laws of man, cannot fail to become a most dangerous character, especially when he shall have been able to place himself at the head of a numerous horde, either equally reckless and unprincipled as himself, or else made his pliant tools by the most absurd credulity that has astonished the world since its foundation.[31]

That was the essential anti-Mormon argument: a pretended prophet, who put himself above the law, leading a horde of unprincipled or credulous believers. The political implications were obvious. As Mormon numbers grew, one newspaper editor warned, the Mormons would "give to *Revelation* the balance of power in the District."[32]

Mormons, on the other hand, felt that they had been repeatedly "deprived of our rights & privileges as citizenship driven from town to town place to place State to State, with the sacrifice of our homes & lands & our Blood been shed & many murdered" and never given justice.[33] The Mormons could not forget the long string of abuses they had suffered at the hands of mobs. After their expulsion from Missouri, they vowed that they would never be subjected to such abuses again. In Illinois, they negotiated a strong city charter as a form of protection against further persecution and organized a state-sanctioned militia, the Nauvoo Legion, to withstand attack. Over and over, they rehearsed the horrible tale of their sufferings, certain the manifest injustice of their treatment would evoke sympathy and bring redress. But few came to their aid. Governor Thomas Ford of Illinois explained why. A democratic government, he wrote, is helpless to defend an unpopular group: "The people cannot be used to put down the people."[34]

The Mormons magnified the critics' fears by arming themselves and resorting to judicial maneuvers their enemies considered illegal. It did not help that the temperature of Mormon rhetoric rose to match that of their enemies. Fearing mobs were forming in Illinois like those that had expelled the Mormons from Missouri, Joseph Smith let loose his anger and frustration. He had taken more than he could tolerate. "The time has come when forbearance is no longer a virtue," he declared. "If you are again taken unlawfully you are at liberty to give loose to Blood and Thunder."[35] The Mormons would not attack, but neither would they sit still if mobs came after them again.

This language and the combination of powers bestowed on Mormons by the Nauvoo charter inflamed their enemies. By building up the Nauvoo Legion

---

31. "Great Meeting of Anti-Mormons!" *Warsaw Message,* 13 Sept. 1843, [1].
32. "The Election," *Warsaw Signal,* 6 Sept. 1843, 2.
33. Woodruff, Journal, 30 June 1843.
34. Ford, *History of Illinois,* 249.
35. Woodruff, Journal, 30 June 1843.

to thousands of men, Smith appeared to his enemies as a prophet armed. Using
the Nauvoo Municipal Court to protect himself from arrest made him seem to
set himself above the law. His acquisition of the major offices in the city, the
courts, and the militia, as well as in the church, opened him to charges of
megalomania. By 1844, hundreds of citizens from nearby towns were ready to
invade Nauvoo and drive the Mormons out.

Character

His enemies may have feared Joseph Smith all the more because he was
formidable personally. Josiah Quincy, soon to be the mayor of Boston, visited
Nauvoo in spring 1844 with Charles Francis Adams, son of former American
president John Quincy Adams. Quincy compared Smith to the Rhode Island
congressman Elisha Potter, who had impressed Quincy in Washington. Quincy
said both Smith and Potter "were of commanding appearance, men whom it
seemed natural to obey," who emanated "a certain peculiar moral stress and
compulsion which I have never felt in the presence of others of their
countrymen."[36] Peter Burnett, one of Smith's attorneys in the aftermath of the
Missouri war and later governor of California, saw the steel in his client's character. "He possessed the most indomitable perseverance," Burnett wrote after
watching Smith's conduct in prison. He "deemed himself born to command,
and he did command." By comparison, church counselor Sidney Rigdon,
though a man of superior education and fine appearance, "did not possess the
native intellect of Smith, and lacked his determined will."[37]

Joseph Smith seems rarely to have been intimidated. Howard Coray, one of
the better-educated early converts, was impressed that when Smith entertained
callers "of almost all professions—Doctors, Lawyers Priests," he

> was always equal to the occasion, and perfectly master of the situation; and, pos-
> sessed the power to make every body realize his superiority, which they evinced in
> an unmistakable manner. I could clearly see that Joseph was the captain, no mat-
> ter whose company he was in, Knowing the meagerness of his education, I was
> truly gratified, at seeing how much at ease he always was, even in the company of
> the most scientific, and the ready off hand manner in which he would answer
> their questions.[38]

Joseph Smith may have tried for the upper hand because of a sensitivity to
insult. He came from a social class that bore the onus of contempt almost as a
way of life. Poor tenant farmers like the Smiths were looked down upon as

---

36. Quincy, *Figures of the Past*, 279.
37. Burnett, *Recollections and Opinions*, 39–40.
38. Coray, Reminiscences, 7–8.

shiftless and crude. The ridicule that followed his stories of revelation may have magnified his unease and led him to compensate with abrasive behavior and brave flourishes. He clung to his military title in the Nauvoo Legion as a badge of honor and expected recognition of his standing. When slighted, he would lash back. As Benjamin Johnson, a great admirer, said, "Criticism even by his associates was rarely acceptable & contradiction would rouse in him the Lion at once for by no one of his fellows would he be superseded."[39]

Against his enemies he was adamant. Thomas Sharp, the vitriolic editor of the *Warsaw Signal,* received a hot burst from Smith after publishing an editorial critical of the Mormons. Upon reading the piece, Smith canceled his subscription:

> *Mr. Sharp, Editor of the Warsaw Signal:*
> Sir--You will discontinue my paper--its contents are calculated to pollute me, and to patronize the filthy sheet--that tissue of lies--that sink of iniquity--is disgraceful to any mortal man. Yours, with utter contempt,
>
> Joseph Smith
>
> P.S. Please publish the above in your contemptible paper.[40]

Although Smith was perpetually caught up in controversy, strife pained him. His ideal for the city of Zion was for all to be "of one heart and of one mind."[41] In a letter from the jail in Liberty, he described himself perfectly when he advocated "reproving be-times with sharpness when moved upon by the Holy Ghost and then showing forth afterwords an increas of love." He dreamed of a society filled with love and peace. The anger and hatred the Mormons suffered was exactly the opposite of his own vision. During the expulsion of Mormons from Missouri in winter 1838–1839, he was kept under prison guard for five months, charged with treason for having resisted attack. During those months, Smith meditated on the evils of power—in society and within the church. He had "learned by sad experiance," he wrote to the Saints, "that it is the nature and disposition of almost all men as soon as they get a little auth[o]rity as they [s]uppose they will imediately begin to [e]xercise unritious dominion." He wanted it otherwise.

> [No power or influence] can or ought to be maintained [b]y v[i]rtue of the Priesthood only by persuasion by long suffering by gentleness and meekness and by love unfaigned by kindness by pure knowledge which shall greatly enlarge the soul without hypocrisy and with out guile reproving be-times with sharpness

39. Benjamin F. Johnson to George F. Gibbs, Salt Lake City, UT, 1903, 8, Benjamin Franklin Johnson, Papers, CHL.

40. JS, Nauvoo, IL, to Thomas Sharp, Warsaw, IL, 26 May 1841, *Warsaw Signal,* 2 June 1841, 2.

41. Old Testament Revision 1, p. 16 [Moses 7:18].

when moved upon by the Holy Ghost and then showing forth afterwords an increas of love toward him whom thou hast reproved lest he esteem the[e] [to] be his enimy.[42]

Joseph Smith's overflowing affection for his people was one reason for their loyalty. He entered long exclamations of gratitude in his diary when the Latter-day Saints cut wood for him in the winter, and he often laid his hands on his clerks' heads to give them personal blessings. "Fri[e]ndship," he told his people, "is the gr[a]nd fundamental prniple [principle] of Mormonism, to revolution[ize] [and] civilize the world.— pour forth love."[43] In prison following the Missouri war, chained to six of his companions in two-foot intervals, Smith wrote cheerily to Emma:

> Brother Robison is chained next to me he has a true heart and a firm mind, Brother Whight, is next, Br. Rigdon, next, Hyram, next, Parely, next, Amasa, next, and thus we are bound together in chains as well as the cords of everlasting love, we are in good spirits and rejoice that we are counted worthy to be persicuted for christ sake.

In the same letter he wrote to his wife and children:

> Oh my affectionate Emma, I want you to remember that I am a true and faithful friend, to you and the children, forever, my heart is intwined around you[r]s forever and ever, oh may God bless you all, amen I am your husband and am in bands and tribulation.[44]

Sadly, in the end, the bands between the couple were tried to the breaking point.

At times revelation became a burden as well as a blessing, at no time more than when plural marriage was revealed. Plural marriage was the final component of the logic of restoration. Smith had prayed for an understanding of Old Testament polygamy and was commanded to do the "works of Abraham."[45] Although he hated adultery and was deeply loyal to his wife Emma, he believed he was to take additional wives as had the ancient patriarchs. He went about it carefully, one woman at a time, usually approaching her relatives first and going through a prescribed wedding ceremony. During his lifetime, he was married to approximately thirty women.[46] Although conjugal relations were apparently involved, he spent little time with these women,

---

42. JS et al., Liberty, MO, to the church members and Edward Partridge, Quincy, IL, 20 Mar. 1839, in Revelations Collection, CHL [D&C 121:39, 43].

43. JS, Journal, 23 July 1843, JS Collection, CHL.

44. JS, Richmond, MO, to Emma Smith, Far West, MO, 12 Nov. 1838, CCLA.

45. Revelation, 12 July 1843, in Revelations Collection, CHL [D&C 132:32].

46. Compton, *In Sacred Loneliness.*

the need for secrecy and the demands on his time keeping them apart. At first aghast at what her husband was doing, Emma eventually agreed to a few of the plural marriages but then pulled back. She oscillated between hesitant submission and outright opposition to the practice, but according to Maria Jane Johnston Woodward, who worked for a time as a servant in the Smith household, Emma told her, "The principle of plural marriage is right. . . . [I]t is from our Father in Heaven."[47] After her husband's death, Emma refused to go west, where plural marriage would be practiced. She never admitted to her children that their father had been involved.

To add to his unpopularity, in the final six months of his life Joseph Smith set out on a course of political action that outraged his critics. In January 1844, he announced his candidacy for president of the United States and a few months later organized a shadow government called the Kingdom of God, which may have been envisioned as a prototype of Christ's millennial government of the earth. Whether or not he believed he could win the presidency, he spoke optimistically, as candidates do in the beginning of a campaign. Certainly his patience with government had run out. The Mormons had been abused many times with no compensation for confiscated property from any level of government, and in 1844 they felt the tide of hatred rising again. Smith could not understand why the Constitution did not compel the government to protect the rights of Mormons. His platform defended all downtrodden people of his time: slaves, whom he felt should be purchased from their masters with revenues from public lands; prisoners held under cruel and unsanitary conditions; court-martialed soldiers; and sailors, whose suffering at the hands of tyrannical ship captains was attracting the sympathy of reformers. To all, he promised justice.

One close associate said after a meeting to organize the Kingdom of God, "It seems like heaven began on earth, and the power of God is with us."[48] But Joseph Smith's enemies in the church and the surrounding towns could see nothing noble in his program. A number of onetime believers, some who had been high in the church's hierarchy, took plural marriage as evidence that he had fallen as a prophet. They organized to remove him from office and return the church to its pre-polygamy and pre–Kingdom of God course. When they published a newspaper to rally the opposition, Smith, fearful the paper would incite mob violence, had the press shut down by city authorities and destroyed. Nearby citizens were infuriated. When Smith went to Carthage, the county

---

47. Woodward, "Statement."
48. Clayton, Journal, 18 Apr. 1844.

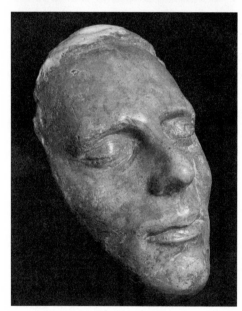

Contemporaneous images of Joseph Smith

Portrait of Joseph Smith by David Rogers, 1842 (above left). On several days in September 1842, Joseph Smith sat for a portrait by a "Brother Rogers" (JS, Journal, 16, 17, and 19–20 Sept. 1842). This painting and a companion portrait of Emma Smith hung in the Mansion House in Nauvoo, Illinois. (Courtesy Community of Christ Library-Archives, Independence, MO. Photograph by Ronald Read.)

Profile of Joseph Smith by Sutcliffe Maudsley, circa 1842 (detail, above right). Joseph Smith's journal records that on 25 June 1842 he "sat for the drawing of his profile. for Lithographing on city chart" by Sutcliffe Maudsley. Several versions of Maudsley's profiles exist, including this one of Smith in a Nauvoo Legion uniform. (Courtesy Church History Museum, Salt Lake City. Photograph by Ronald Read.)

Death mask of Joseph Smith (left). Shortly after the deaths of Joseph and Hyrum Smith, molds of their faces were cast by Arieh C. Brower and George Cannon, from which masks were made. Forensic analysis of the mask shown here indicates that it was made from the original mold. The mask was purchased by Philo Dibble in 1849. (Courtesy Church History Museum, Salt Lake City. Photograph by Alex D. Smith.)

seat, for trial, a mob attacked him in jail. He was shot through an open window, fell to the ground, and died on 27 June 1844.[49]

Joseph Smith's Place in History

From the viewpoint of the present, what is the significance of this charismatic and forceful man? His claims to direct revelation put him too far beyond the pale of conventional Christianity to be taken seriously while he was alive; outside of Latter-day Saint circles, he is scarcely studied as a thinker or a theologian to this day. But he aimed a question at the heart of the culture: Do Christians believe in revelation? If believers in the Bible dismissed revelation in the present, could they defend revelation in the past? By 1830, when Smith came on the religious scene, revelation had been debated in Anglo-American culture for well over a century. Since the first years of the eighteenth century, rational Christians had struggled with deists, skeptics, and infidels over the veracity of miracles and the inspiration of prophets and apostles. In 1829, Alexander Campbell debated the atheist Robert Owen for a full week on the value of religion and the truth of the Bible.[50] Campbell believed he had proven God's presence in the Bible, but doubt lingered on. Over the course of the nineteenth century, belief in revelation eroded among the educated classes, reflecting the notorious disenchantment of the world. At first the loss of confidence in revelation was only dimly perceived by everyday Christians, but in the century to come, the issue divided divinity schools and disturbed ordinary people.

Joseph Smith stood against that rising tide. He received revelation exactly as Christians thought biblical prophets had done. In effect, he reenacted the writing of the Bible before the world's eyes.[51] Most put him aside as an obvious charlatan without bothering to evaluate his doctrine. After one incredulous visitor marveled that the Mormon prophet was "nothing but a man," Smith remarked that "they look upon it as incredible that a man should have any intercourse with his Maker."[52] Smith's historical role, as he understood it, was to give God a voice in a world that had stopped listening.[53] Smith stood on the

---

49. Oaks and Hill, *Carthage Conspiracy,* 12–15, 20–21.

50. See *Debate on the Evidences of Christianity.*

51. This line of reasoning is taken from Givens, *Viper on the Hearth,* 82–93.

52. JS, Journal, 6 Nov. 1835.

53. See Book of Mormon, 1830 ed., 111, 113, 130, 534, 536–537 [2 Nephi 27:23; 28:6; Jacob 4:8; Mormon 8:26; 9:11–20]; Revelation, May 1829–A, in Doctrine and Covenants 37:11, 1835 ed. [D&C 11:23–27]; Givens, *Viper on the Hearth;* and Turner, *Without God, Without Creed.* The philosopher Richard Rorty, representing a modern mentality, said, "The world does not speak. Only we do." (Rorty, *Contingency, Irony, and Solidarity,* 6.)

contested ground between the Enlightenment and Christianity. At a time when the foundations of Christianity were under assault by Enlightenment rationality, he turned Christian faith back toward its origins in revelation.

Mormonism could be categorized as another rearguard action against advancing modernity had not Smith complicated the picture. In the political realm, for example, he thought of himself as democratic. He composed a "motto" for the church that proclaimed: "Exalt the standard of Democracy."[54] He honored the right to free worship: "It is one of the first principles of my life. & one that I have cultivated from my childhood. having been taught it of my father[s], to allow every one the liberty of conscience."[55] One of the first ordinances passed under the Nauvoo charter granted freedom of worship to every denomination, including Roman Catholicism and Islam.[56]

He was, moreover, no enemy of learning. An early revelation explained that "truth is knowledge of things as they are, and as they were, and as they are to come," and his followers were urged to seek that kind of truth. They were to "obtain a knowledge of history, and of countries, and of kingdoms, of laws of God and man, and all this for the salvation of Zion."[57] A revelation commanded them to open a school, where, among other things, the students studied grammar as well as theology. In that same spirit, they established a school at which the students studied Hebrew under the tutelage of a Jewish instructor. "Teach one another," they were enjoined, "words of wisdom; yea, seek ye out of the best books words of wisdom: seek learning even by study, and also by faith."[58] The Nauvoo City Council moved to establish a university soon after the charter was granted.

Godly knowledge, to be sure, outranked secular learning in Smith's thinking, but revelation was not set in opposition to reason. "The glory of God is intelligence," one revelation declared, "or, in other words, light and truth."[59] Among his many superlative qualities, God was the most intelligent of all beings.[60] Church members were told to seek knowledge as part of their salvation. "If a person gains more knowledge in this life through his diligence

---

54. JS, Journal, Mar.–Sept. 1838 (undated entry), p. 238 herein.

55. JS, Journal, 15 Oct. 1843, JS Collection, CHL.

56. Nauvoo City Council Minute Book, 1 Mar. 1841, 13.

57. Revelation, 6 May 1833, in Doctrine and Covenants 82:4, 12, 1835 ed. [D&C 93:24, 53].

58. Revelation, 27 and 28 Dec. 1832 and 3 Jan. 1833, in Doctrine and Covenants 7:36, 1835 ed. [D&C 88:118].

59. Revelation, 6 May 1833, in Doctrine and Covenants 82:6, 1835 ed. [D&C 93:36].

60. "The Book of Abraham," *Times and Seasons*, 15 Mar. 1842, 3:720 [Abraham 3:19].

& obedience than another, he will have so much the advantage in the world to come."[61]

Combining a set of apparently conflicting impulses, Smith left a complex legacy for his people. His revelations sustained a literal belief in scriptural inspiration yet promoted learning and knowledge as if religion and the Enlightenment were compatible. He never wavered in his belief that God had spoken to him but made it an article of faith to let all men "worship how, where, or what they may."[62] While reviving traditional Christian faith, he was equally a prophet of the coming age.

In the fourteen years he led the church, Joseph Smith created a religion and a culture that incorporated these paradoxes into its core beliefs. After his death, Mormons withdrew from the United States to a refuge in the Great Basin, where for a half century they nurtured their faith in relative isolation. Never, however, did they cut themselves off from the world. During this period of consolidation, they carried on a worldwide missionary program that brought tens of thousands of converts to Utah. Although removed from the nation's cultural centers, they founded universities, sent people east for schooling, opened theaters, and gave women the vote, all the while believing that God had revealed himself to their prophet.

Faith in revelation persists to this day among Latter-day Saints. It energizes the church now as it powered Joseph Smith's ascent from obscurity to eminence in the first half of the nineteenth century. The same force that enabled him to build cities and gather thousands of converts motivates ordinary church members today. Modern Mormons believe the Book of Mormon is a revealed translation, solemnly receive priesthood ordination, and consider temples to be houses of God, much as Smith anticipated. The publication of his papers will permit readers to observe the origins of this resilient religious culture and throw light on the achievements—and the complexity—of its intrepid founder.

Joseph Smith and Record Keeping

Joseph Smith's own revelations instructed him to keep a record of the church's rise. At the time of the church's organization in 1830, he was instructed that "there shall be a record kept among you, and in it thou shalt be called a seer, a translator, a prophet, an apostle of Jesus Christ."[63] Smith understood early on that he must keep an account, even though his training did not qualify

---

61. Instruction, 2 Apr. 1843, in Clayton, Journal, 2 Apr. 1843 [D&C 130:19].
62. JS, "Church History," *Times and Seasons,* 1 Mar. 1842, 3:710 [Articles of Faith 1:11].
63. Revelation, 6 Apr. 1830, in Doctrine and Covenants 46:1, 1835 ed. [D&C 21:1].

him to write such a record himself. He had only a modest education and no literary aspirations. He keenly felt the limitations of writing. In a letter to newspaper editor William W. Phelps he wrote: "Oh Lord God deliver us in thy due time from the little narrow prison almost as it were totel darkness of paper pen and ink and a crooked broken scattered and imperfect language."[64] Yet over the years a large collection of documents accumulated. He dictated revelations, prepared translations of ancient documents, and assigned clerks to write letters, his history, and his journals.

Joseph Smith started writing in 1828 when he began dictation of the Book of Mormon in earnest. The first 116 pages were lost through the error of his scribe, but Smith began again, and in the three months between early April and the end of June 1829, he dictated most of what became 584 pages of printed text in the first edition. In that same period, he received more than a dozen revelations and by fall 1830 was preparing them for publication. They appeared first in serial form in the church newspaper *The Evening and the Morning Star,* beginning in June 1832, and later in the Book of Commandments.

For the first two years after the organization of the Church of Christ on 6 April 1830, Smith assigned the work of keeping a history first to Oliver Cowdery and then to John Whitmer, two of the early believers. In 1832, he himself wrote a history of the visions he had received as a young man and in the same year started a personal journal and began to preserve correspondence and other documents in a letterbook.[65] These record-keeping projects soon faltered, however: the history ended after six pages, and the journal keeping lapsed after ten days. Only gradually did Smith establish a pattern of assigning scribes to work on histories, journals, letters, minutes, and other documents. Spotty at first, his record keeping eventually settled into more consistent patterns. By the early 1840s, he and his clerks were composing a comprehensive history, keeping a continuous diary, accumulating minutes from meetings and councils, preserving correspondence, and taking notes of many of his numerous discourses.

Joseph Smith drew upon these materials in 1838, when he again turned his own hand to history. He began by dictating an autobiographical narrative interspersed with revelations, correspondence, and other documents pertaining to his life and the beginnings of the church. When the chronology of the story reached November 1832, the narrative evolved into a day-by-day diary format

---

64. JS, Kirtland, OH, to William W. Phelps, [Independence, MO], 27 Nov. 1832, in JS Letterbook 1, p. 4.

65. More than two dozen main scribes who wrote for Joseph Smith or the church during Smith's lifetime have been identified. In 1843, Smith commented, "For a man to be a great man, he must not dwell upon small things though he may enjoy them," which was explained to mean "a prophet cannot be a scribe." (JS, Journal, 4 Mar. 1843, JS Collection, CHL.)

using Smith's journals as the featured text, supplemented by additional documentary material. Where the journals were written in third person by Smith's scribes, the narrative was changed to first person, and where the journal was deficient it was fleshed out from other sources, which were also edited to maintain the first-person style. When Joseph Smith was killed in June 1844, work on the history had proceeded only as far as 5 August 1838, but his secretary and clerks continued to utilize his journal and other available documents to extend the narrative to the end of his life.

In addition to the published revelations and history, the manuscripts resulting from Smith's record keeping include two volumes of revelations, ten volumes used as journals, two copybooks of correspondence, a half-dozen volumes containing the proceedings of civic and church administrative organizations that he organized, and numerous miscellaneous papers, many of which are legal and business records. The flow of documents sometimes slowed to a trickle during times of stress, and he often required outside impetus to refocus his attention amidst a life teeming with meetings, moves, lawsuits, and persecutions.[66] But record keeping clearly was important to him. As his life went on, he became ever more diligent in collecting the raw materials for his history, accumulating by the end a large trove of papers.

This substantial body of documents does not, however, assure us a clear view of his mind and heart. The reason is that with all of the responsibilities he bore during a tumultuous life, he could not keep a record on his own. Only a tiny proportion of Smith's papers were written by Smith himself, meaning that in most of the documents we come at Joseph Smith through another mind. Though small in number, the autograph writings and the relatively small body of personal writings dictated by him probably offer the best close-up view of his temperament and outlook. They are more direct imprints of his personality than the records of his sermons and speeches. Probably fewer than one-fifth of his sermons were reported in any detail—most from the last years of his life and most in highly abbreviated form by clerks or listeners who took notes. Smith seems never to have spoken from a prepared text or even from an outline. Records of his sermons are at best like class notes taken by students at a lecture, giving only limited access to the speaker's style. His dictated

---

66. One such external impetus was the barrage of falsehoods and misrepresentations that dogged him throughout his life. Smith began his 1838 history with the words: "Owing to the many reports which have been put in circulation by evil disposed and designing persons, in relation to the rise and progress of the Church of Jesus Christ of Latter day Saints, all of which have been designed by the authors thereof to militate against its character, as a church, and its progress in the world, I have been induced to write this history so as to disabuse the publick mind, and put all enquirers after truth into possession of the facts as they have transpired." (JS History, vol. A-1, 1.)

revelations and translations are couched in his plain language, but as Smith documents they are problematic in another way. By his own account, neither the Book of Mormon nor the revelations were his own compositions. "I translated, by the gift and power of God," he said of the Book of Mormon.[67] The revelations stand out as the most interesting and influential of all his recorded words, but they are purportedly not his words at all. They came from him in his special role as revelator.

The large majority of the remaining papers—beyond the revelations, personal writings, dictated documents, and discourses—were not only penned but also composed by his clerks. Smith's scribes must be credited for recording much of what we know about him. Those close associates who wrote his journal, for example, recorded views of his life and work often on a daily basis, especially in the later years. But those same scribes often stand between Joseph Smith and the reader hopeful of capturing his character and magnetism. Even writings issued over Smith's name or written in first person are often the compositions of clerks. Extensive as the papers of Joseph Smith are, they do not afford readers unobstructed access to his mind and heart. In a famous sermon near the end of his life, he said, "You don't know me—you never will,"[68] and the nature of his papers only adds force to that assertion.

History of the Joseph Smith Papers

The work of collecting Joseph Smith's papers, which began during his lifetime, continued after his death. In February 1846, the papers—then in the possession of Brigham Young and other church leaders—were packed into two boxes for the exodus to the West. The papers were unpacked in Salt Lake City in June 1853 and, beginning in April 1854, were used to complete the history Smith started in 1838. Not all the records made it west. John Whitmer retained the history he wrote at Smith's behest, declining to turn it over when requested in 1838. Other significant documents remained with Smith's widow Emma, who stayed in Illinois. These and other documents eventually came under the care of the Community of Christ (formerly the Reorganized Church of Jesus Christ of Latter Day Saints). The relevant items, with the permission of the Community of Christ, will be published in *The Joseph Smith Papers*.

When finished in 1856, nearly two decades after the project was launched, Joseph Smith's history consisted of six large handwritten volumes numbering some twenty-two hundred pages. Publication of the history had commenced in the Nauvoo *Times and Seasons* in 1842 and was continued in church publications

---

67. Preface to Book of Mormon, 1830 ed., iii.
68. JS, Journal, 7 Apr. 1844, JS Collection, CHL.

in territorial Utah and England until 1863. Because of its lengthy serial publication, the history was almost totally inaccessible by the turn of the century. In 1901, Brigham H. Roberts, assistant church historian, was commissioned to make the Smith history available again. Between 1902 and 1912, Roberts edited the previously published installments to produce a six-volume publication titled *History of the Church of Jesus Christ of Latter-day Saints, Period I: History of Joseph Smith, the Prophet, by Himself.* Because of the inclusion of so many complete documents, the *History of the Church* has been widely referred to among Mormons as the "Documentary History of the Church."

As the culmination of Joseph Smith's history-writing endeavor, the *History of the Church* will continue to be an important resource for students of Mormonism, but its limitations detract from its value as a scholarly resource. The chief fault is a failure to distinguish Smith's writings from others whose writings are presented as his own. Although such a practice was acceptable at the time, modern editorial standards require authorship and provenance to be described as fully as possible. *The Joseph Smith Papers* will include an edition of the original manuscript of Smith's history that will identify underlying sources. Other series of the *Papers* will also include numerous items not published in the *History of the Church* and will present exact transcriptions of the originals.

Roots of the current effort to publish Smith's papers extend back to the late 1960s when Truman G. Madsen, then director of the Institute of Mormon Studies at Brigham Young University, invited Dean C. Jessee, then an employee of the Church Historian's Office of The Church of Jesus Christ of Latter-day Saints, to contribute to special issues of *Brigham Young University Studies* focusing on Joseph Smith and early Mormon history. Work on the articles reinforced Jessee's desire to understand and publish the complete documentary record. Jessee's opportunity came following Leonard J. Arrington's 1972 appointment as the official historian of the church. Arrington assigned Jessee to locate, collect, and transcribe Smith's writings. As Jessee developed a methodology, he was aware of the massive documentary editing projects sprouting around the United States following the initiation of *The Papers of Thomas Jefferson* in the 1940s. In response to the publication of Jefferson's early papers, United States president Harry S. Truman had directed the National Historical Publications Commission to promote publication of the papers of America's Founding Fathers. It was said that "no country in the world will have so complete a record of its beginnings."[69] Jessee and Arrington believed that the papers of Joseph Smith were equally essential to the study of Mormon beginnings.

---

69. Malone, "Tapping the Wisdom of the Founding Fathers," 32.

In 1980, the project was transferred from the Church Historian's Office to Brigham Young University in Provo, Utah. There Jessee continued his work as a member of the newly formed Joseph Fielding Smith Institute for Latter-day Saint History, encouraged and aided by institute directors Leonard Arrington and then Ronald K. Esplin. In 1984, Jessee published *The Personal Writings of Joseph Smith* (with a second edition in 2002), containing nearly every document Smith wrote himself and a substantial portion of his dictated writings. This was followed by a broader initiative that resulted in the publication of the two-volume *The Papers of Joseph Smith*—a volume of Smith's autobiographical and historical writings in 1989 and a volume of journals in 1992.

As this work proceeded, a more comprehensive plan for publishing Smith's papers emerged. In 2001, the Joseph Smith Papers Project was established as a collaboration between Brigham Young University and the Archives of The Church of Jesus Christ of Latter-day Saints. Jessee, now general editor, Esplin, now executive editor, and Richard Lyman Bushman, chairman of the Smith Institute's executive committee, took responsibility for coordinating teams of historians serving as editors of various volumes and a central staff of editors and researchers to update, expand, and complete the project. Fortunately, as the expanded project got under way, Larry H. and Gail Miller offered to fund the operation. In 2005, the project returned to the Church Archives, now known as the Church History Library.

The new Joseph Smith Papers Project has adopted an enriched editorial procedure and a new organization of materials. All the material in the two previously published volumes of *The Papers of Joseph Smith* that qualifies for inclusion under new criteria will appear in the new format, with expanded annotation, as part of *The Joseph Smith Papers*. In this edition, we intend to publish, both in paper and electronic form, every extant document to which we can obtain access.[70] Work is under way on six series of Joseph Smith papers:

1. The Journals series will contain the ten volumes of journals kept by Smith and his various scribes and clerks from 1832 through the end of his life in 1844.

2. The Documents series will bring together early versions of revelations, correspondence sent and received, sermons and other addresses, selected minutes

---

70. The only exceptions are routine, repetitive documents, such as the certificates and licenses Smith signed. All will be published online, but only samples will be published in paper. All documents will be calendared. Officials at the Church History Library have given advance permission for a scholarly edition of all Smith papers in their possession. Digitized images of the majority of Smith's documents are available in Richard E. Turley Jr., ed., *Selected Collections from the Archives of the Church of Jesus Christ of Latter-day Saints* (Provo, UT: Brigham Young University Press, 2002). Publication of the relatively few documents in private possession depends on permission of the owners.

and proceedings, editorials and articles in periodicals, official declarations and pronouncements, and other such documents for which Smith was responsible.

3. The History series will publish the entire manuscript history that Smith began in 1838, which was continued by his clerks after his death. The first volume in this series will serve as an introduction chronicling Smith's history-writing initiative that began in 1830 and led up to the larger work begun in 1838.

4. The Legal and Business Records series will reproduce legal papers from the scores of judicial proceedings in which Smith was either a plaintiff, defendant, or witness. The business papers, many of which relate closely to the legal papers, comprise records of Smith's personal or family finances and records relating to Smith's involvement in development efforts and enterprises in behalf of the church. The latter category includes notes and other loan documents; records of purchases, sales, and other transactions relating to land; and store accounts and accounts of church-owned businesses.

5. The Revelations and Translations series will present the earliest manuscript texts of the Joseph Smith revelations and those published during his lifetime. These include the Book of Mormon and the printer's manuscript from which it was produced. In contrast to the Documents series, this series will present the texts of the revelations alone—without other Smith documents interspersed—and will focus mainly on textual, not contextual, annotation.

6. The Administrative Records series will publish minutes and other records pertaining to institutions that were established under Smith's direction and that contain his personal instruction and involvement.

Most of Joseph Smith's papers are located in the Church History Library of The Church of Jesus Christ of Latter-day Saints in Salt Lake City, Utah, while another significant body of his materials is found in the Library-Archives of the Community of Christ in Independence, Missouri. Additional important items have been located in other public and private repositories.

The diversity and expansiveness of this documentary collection stem from Smith's extensive leadership in religious and civic roles. He was a translator, revelator, church president, city builder, mayor, city council member, judge, militia leader, and presidential candidate, and his papers reflect all those roles. These volumes provide essential resources for the study of Joseph Smith's life and times.

Richard Lyman Bushman, Columbia University
Dean C. Jessee, Church History Library

Joseph Smith's journals. Between 1832 and 1844, Joseph Smith and his scribes kept his journals in these books and notebooks. Church History Library, Salt Lake City. (Photograph by Welden C. Andersen and Mark Ashurst-McGee.)

Joseph Smith's Journals

While supervising the recording and copying of his revelations at his residence in Hiram, Ohio, in 1832, Joseph Smith ventured into a new genre. He dictated to his clerk a brief journal entry, which the clerk recorded in a volume that was being used to record revelations. Dated 8 March 1832, the passage reads: "Chose this day and ordained brother Jesse Gause and Broth[er] Sidney [Rigdon] to be my councellers of the ministry of the presidency of th[e] high Pristhood and from the 16th of February up to this date have been at home except a journey to Kirtland on the 29 Feby and returned home one [on] the 4th of March we received a revelation in Kirtland and one since I returned home blessed be the name of the Lord."[1] More than eight months elapsed without any further recording of that nature. On 27 November 1832, Smith's first journal was purchased, and he began it by stating his intention "to keep a minute acount of all things that come under my obsevation."[2] Although useful records resulted, the reality seldom approached this ideal. Many early entries were brief, and there were gaps within journals and between journals. In the 1830s, only for the six months preceding the dedication of the House of the Lord in Kirtland, Ohio, in March 1836 and for part of 1838 were entries relatively sustained and detailed. Diary keeping improved in the 1840s, owing mainly to the diligence and longevity in the task of Willard Richards, who began writing for Joseph Smith in December 1841. And then, on 22 June 1844, Smith's tenth and final journal volume came to an abrupt halt. This volume, kept almost daily by Richards, suddenly ceased amid the mounting trouble that led to Smith being killed within the week.

By the end of Smith's life, he and his scribes produced ten volumes of Joseph Smith journals comprising over 1,500 manuscript pages. Of the total, only about 35 manuscript pages contain autograph writing, where Smith put his own pen to the paper. Internal evidence suggests that he dictated another 250 or so pages. The remaining pages—about 1,300, or more than 80 percent of the total—were primarily the work of five men who were appointed to keep Smith's journals: Warren Parrish, George W. Robinson, James Mulholland,

---

1. Revelation Book 2, pp. 10–11.
2. JS, Journal, 27 Nov. 1832.

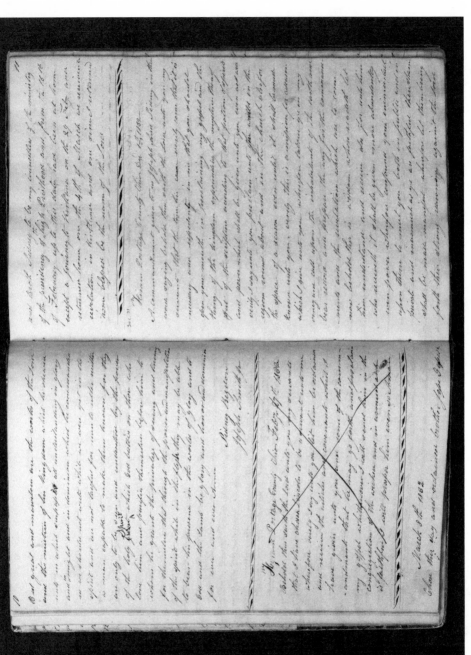

Journal-style note. A note resembling a journal entry in style was recorded in a book used for copying revelations (see 8 March 1832 entry beginning on bottom of page 10 in photograph above). The note predates by several months the beginning of Joseph Smith's first journal. Handwriting of Frederick G. Williams. Revelation Book 2, pp. 10–11, Revelations Collection, Church History Library, Salt Lake City. (Photograph by Welden C. Andersen.)

Willard Richards, and William Clayton. On a few occasions, Sidney Rigdon, Frederick G. Williams, Parley P. Pratt, Eliza R. Snow, and others penned entries.

As with Smith's record keeping in general, his journal-keeping methods developed over time. Before he and his scribes developed a consistent, workable procedure, their efforts, intentionally or not, echoed several genres. The first six journals each bear a title—Book for Record, Sketch Book, Scriptory Book, Memorandum, and Minute Book (all constituting the present first volume of *The Joseph Smith Papers,* Journals series), and Book of the Law of the Lord (the title of the book containing the first journal presented in volume two of the Journals series). These titles, in the end, reflect something of the varied contents and purposes of these journals. The Scriptory Book, for example, contains various written records, or scripts—letters, minutes, revelations, and other transcribed documents—as well as typical journal entries recording daily events. Combining miscellaneous documents with proper journal entries, the book functioned as a repository for information Smith and his scribes wanted to preserve.

Similarly, the record titled "Memorandum" seems to have been intended as a record different from a typical journal. Kept by scribe James Mulholland, the document appears on first inspection to be an example of inept journal keeping. Mulholland's terse entries—"At home all day"; "Saw him early morning"[3]—record almost nothing of interest. But a *memorandum,* in the 1830s as today, is defined as a written reminder or a note of a transaction, a purpose that Mulholland's journal fulfilled. Mulholland apparently began the journal just after Joseph Smith met with legal counsel as difficulties mounted in Missouri—counsel may have recommended that Smith keep a record to verify his whereabouts each day. If we take the title of Mulholland's document at face value, his record accomplishes what we may infer Smith requested.

Early on in the sixth of these variously titled journals, the diary keeping settled into a more predictable pattern. By this time, Joseph Smith had a regular cadre of scribes with better-defined procedures for keeping journals, copying letters, and writing his history. Preeminent among them was Willard Richards, who also inscribed portions of the 1839–1843 letterbook and Nauvoo municipal records and took a leading role in the creation of Smith's history both before and after Smith's death. Although from December 1841 forward Richards inscribed significant parts of the sixth Joseph Smith journal, by 1843 he was Smith's consistent journal keeper. In December 1842, when he began the first of four matching journal volumes, he took an approach that served

---

3. JS, Journal, 16 and 17 Sept. 1838.

him well until the end. The four volumes he kept, each of which he titled "President Joseph Smith's Journal," were one endeavor applied consistently over time.

One benefit to come from Joseph Smith's practice of delegating journal keeping to others is the substantial number of sermons reported in the journals. Smith evidently did not speak from written texts; no such texts survive. An 1830 revelation promised that God would give him "in the very moment" what to say,[4] and Smith relied on that promise. According to a scribe's report, Smith told an audience in 1843 that "his mind was continually ocupied with the business of the day. and he had to depend entirely upon the living God for every thing he said on such occasions."[5] Thus his words to his followers are accessible only through notes kept by others. The four journal volumes written by Willard Richards during the last eighteen months of Smith's life record fifty-nine discourses, twenty-five in substantial detail.

Throughout all Joseph Smith's journals, readers must differentiate between first-person material referring to him and that referring to his scribes. For convenience and brevity, scribes often followed the convention of writing with Joseph Smith as an implied first person. For example, in April 1834, Oliver Cowdery wrote in Smith's journal: "left Kirtland. . . . Travelled to W. W. Williams' . . . took dinner, after which we travelled on."[6] In the first part of this entry, readers must supply Smith as the subject who "left," "Travelled," and "took dinner." Later in the entry, however, Cowdery himself joins in as part of the "we" who "travelled on."

In other cases, assuming Joseph Smith to be the subject creates errors. For example, the documentary *History of the Church,* a work first published serially in church periodicals in the nineteenth century and available since the early twentieth century in six volumes (a seventh volume covers the early administration of Smith's successor, Brigham Young), says that Smith traveled from Commerce to Quincy, Illinois, and back between 14 and 19 May 1839.[7] This is based on a seemingly clear first-person journal entry: "I returned to Quincy so kept no Minute of course, I got back here Sunday ev[en]ing the 19th May."[8] However, other documentary evidence establishes that the "I" in this entry is scribe James Mulholland, who made the entry to explain not having recorded Smith's activities during that week.

---

4. Revelation, July 1830–A, in Doctrine and Covenants 9:3, 1835 ed. [D&C 24:6].
5. JS, Journal, 13 Aug. 1843, JS Collection, CHL.
6. JS, Journal, 18–19 Apr. 1834.
7. *History of the Church,* 3:354–356.
8. JS, Journal, 14–19 May 1839.

The Journals series clarifies other misconceptions stemming from the familiar *History of the Church*. While Joseph Smith's journals were used as the foundation for much of the day-by-day chronological text of the *History*, the early editors and compilers of the *History* inserted a wide variety of other materials into the narrative and then presented the entire work as a seamless first-person account by Smith. The present edition of Smith's journals presents the complete text of the original manuscripts without any of the other material inserted in the *History*, allowing readers to distinguish Smith's journals from other documents.

Through the diverse material in Joseph Smith's journals, readers may follow him on his pursuit of an overarching goal—to "establish Zion" among his people. While the journals fall short of his original intent of providing a "minute acount of all things that come under my obsevation," they do contain over 1,500 pages of material recording his challenges and efforts toward building what he saw as the beginnings of the kingdom of God on earth.

The 1830s Journals

Joseph Smith's foundational spiritual experiences were in the past when he began keeping a journal in November 1832. He had already organized a church in a log home in western New York in April 1830 and set in motion ambitious efforts to preach throughout the world and gather the converted in one location in preparation for the imminent return of the Lord.[1] Seven years later, when the last of the five journals published in this volume concluded, Smith and his followers had built a temple in Kirtland, Ohio, and launched missionary efforts not only in the eastern United States but also in Canada and England. They had weathered internal dissension, external opposition, evacuation of Kirtland, and expulsion from each of the two gathering centers they had established in Missouri, and persisted as a viable religious movement despite repeatedly being forced to leave their homes. By fall 1839, the Latter-day Saints numbered about sixteen thousand, operated with a well-defined leadership and doctrinal structure, and had begun to establish Smith's final and most successful community, Nauvoo, Illinois.

When the first entry in Joseph Smith's first journal was made in 1832, the establishment of a gathering place in Jackson County, Missouri, was well under way. The Book of Mormon, Smith's first published work, prophesied that Gentiles who received the true gospel would assist descendants of the Book of Mormon peoples—usually called "Lamanites" by the Mormons—to build a New Jerusalem, which would be a center for gathering the righteous.[2] Smith announced as early as September 1830 that this city would be located near the western boundaries of the United States.[3] In late 1830, he dispatched missionaries to American Indians living immediately west of Missouri. This mission established a westward trajectory for the Mormons, following the pattern of thousands of other Americans, and would lead to designation of the gathering place in 1831.

On the way west from New York, the missionaries stopped in northeastern Ohio to share their message with Reformed Baptist minister Sidney Rigdon

---

1. Revelation, Sept. 1830–A, in Doctrine and Covenants 10:1–2, 1835 ed. [D&C 29:1–11]; Revelation, 30 Oct. 1831, in Doctrine and Covenants 24, 1835 ed. [D&C 65].

2. Book of Mormon, 1830 ed., 499–501 [3 Nephi 21].

3. Revelation, Sept. 1830–B, in Doctrine and Covenants 51:3, 1835 ed. [D&C 28:9].

and his congregations in Mentor and Kirtland. This apparent diversion had far-reaching effects on the development of Mormonism. Rigdon had long been involved in the Christian restorationist movement and had only recently broken with one of its leading lights, Alexander Campbell. As Rigdon and many of his followers converted to the new faith, Ohio soon became a more promising base of operations than New York, where persecution and the Smith family's financial difficulties thwarted the church's efforts. Revelations in December 1830 and January 1831 mandated gathering the Latter-day Saints to Ohio, where they were to seek sanctification, receive further revelation, and be "endowed with power from on high," all of which would empower them to "go forth among all nations" and play an essential role in the salvation of the house of Israel.[4]

From the time Joseph Smith arrived in Kirtland in February 1831, "the Gathering" knit together Mormon belief and experience. Latter-day Saint converts came to understand the gathering as a divine work of calling out the elect from the world—Babylon—to build communities of believers—Zion and her stakes—who would construct temples and prepare for the imminent return and millennial reign of Christ. Places where the Saints gathered would provide refuge from the destruction expected prior to the Second Coming and function as centers of collective strength from which the word could go forth to warn the world.[5] Gathering made conversion to Mormonism no longer analogous to joining other Christian congregations: Mormonism involved changing location as well as belief.

While the Mormons began moving to Ohio, the missionaries to the Lamanites were scouting a location for the gathering place in Missouri that was envisioned in their original mandate. In July 1831, Smith officially designated the frontier village of Independence, Jackson County—the eastern terminus of the Santa Fe Trail—as the center of Zion and the site for the New Jerusalem.[6] Most Saints who had migrated from New York to Ohio, as well as many of the Ohio converts, moved to Jackson County. Though Smith maintained his headquarters in Kirtland, the Mormon population in Missouri, numbering about eight hundred souls by November 1832, soon exceeded that in Kirtland.[7] Counter to the spirit of freewheeling democratic capitalism

---

4. Revelation, 30 Dec. 1830, in Doctrine and Covenants 58, 1835 ed. [D&C 37]; Revelation, 2 Jan. 1831, in Doctrine and Covenants 12:7, 1835 ed. [D&C 38:31–33].

5. Revelation, 3 Nov. 1831, in Doctrine and Covenants 100:1–3, 1835 ed. [D&C 133:1–16]; Revelation, 1 Aug. 1831, in Doctrine and Covenants 18:15, 1835 ed. [D&C 58:63–65].

6. Revelation, 20 July 1831, in Doctrine and Covenants 27:1, 1835 ed. [D&C 57:1–5].

7. Backman, *Heavens Resound,* 139–140; "The Gathering," *The Evening and the Morning Star,* Nov. 1832, [5]. According to the latter source, the Mormon population of Jackson County included 465 baptized members and 345 unbaptized children, relatives, and friends.

that characterized America at the time, the Latter-day Saints sought to care for the poor collectively, balancing community needs with private stewardship. Temporal concerns were also spiritual, Smith declared. But despite strenuous efforts on the part of Smith and other leaders, the reforms faltered, and the economic blueprint remained a largely unrealized ideal.

These were the circumstances of Joseph Smith and the church when in November 1832 he began keeping his first journal. Covering two momentous years, this fragmentary, personal record provides information about Smith's relationships and attitudes but only a piecemeal narrative of his activities. Evident here are the themes of insufficient resources and competing priorities that surface repeatedly throughout the journals of this volume. Maintaining and developing both Zion in Jackson County and Kirtland in Ohio—more than eight hundred miles apart—with the limited resources of the infant church and the rudimentary transportation and communication systems of the day imposed enormous logistical challenges. Anchored in revelation,[8] both gathering places were indispensable—at least for the present—and yet together they put a nearly unbearable strain on the church.

During the period of this first journal, Smith led the Latter-day Saints toward realization of the promise announced in early 1831 that they would be endowed with divine power in Ohio. For five years, they pursued an "endowment," an anticipated outpouring of spiritual gifts like the Pentecostal experience of the apostles in the New Testament. Smith repeatedly called elders of the church together for instruction and empowerment to help them with their responsibilities in the ministry, but the fulfillment of the promise was not immediate. Revelations in December 1832 and January 1833 mandated the creation of sacred space, "a house of God" for a "school of the prophets" in which to receive instruction, ordinances, and "edification," as part of the longed-for endowment.[9] A revelation in June 1833 chastised the Saints for not having built such a space and dictated the dimensions of the "house" in Kirtland that came to be known as the House of the Lord, or temple.[10] Its construction required a major expenditure of labor and money from a body of the Saints, who at that time numbered only about 150 in Kirtland itself.[11]

---

8. Revelation, 11 Sept. 1831, in Doctrine and Covenants 21:4, 1835 ed. [D&C 64:21]; Revelation, 20 July 1831, in Doctrine and Covenants 27:1, 1835 ed. [D&C 57:1–5].

9. Revelation, 27 and 28 Dec. 1832 and 3 Jan. 1833, in Doctrine and Covenants 7:36, 44–45, 1835 ed. [D&C 88:117–119, 136–139].

10. Revelation, 1 June 1833, in Doctrine and Covenants 95, 1835 ed. [D&C 95]; see also Minute Book 1, 3 June 1833.

11. Backman, *Heavens Resound,* 140.

Joseph Smith envisioned temples—buildings dedicated to God—as key religious and educational centers for the Saints. Three weeks after excavation began for the House of the Lord in Kirtland in June 1833,[12] he sent a plat for an expanded city of Zion to church leaders in Missouri. It provided for twenty-four temples on three central squares and for lots to accommodate an eventual population of fifteen to twenty thousand.[13] He and his presidency mandated the immediate construction of one of these temples in Jackson County.[14]

The Saints' ability to sustain two such costly construction projects was never tested. Conflict with non-Mormon neighbors in Jackson County made it impossible to build any temple there. A cultural chasm divided the Mormons, largely northerners and easterners, from other Missourians, largely southerners and westerners. The fissure corresponded to a growing polarization of the United States in terms of sectional politics and identity. The perceived threat of Mormon economic and political dominance in the region, compounded by the insistence of the Saints that their expansive plans were based on contemporary revelation from God, aroused alarm. Local opposition to the Saints' project of building Zion was inflamed by suspicions that the Mormons would incite rebellion among slaves, ally with Indians, and expand their landholdings and influence by force of arms. Verbal and physical confrontation climaxed with the destruction of the Mormon press at Independence by local vigilantes in July 1833 and the expulsion of the Mormons from the county that November. Most Mormons regrouped north of the Missouri River in Clay County and neighboring counties, awaiting assistance to return to their homes.

"Redeeming Zion" replaced building the temple in Zion as an urgent priority for Joseph Smith and the Latter-day Saints. This meant restoring the Saints to their Jackson County property and swelling their numbers with fellow believers from Kirtland and elsewhere to continue the project of preparing for Christ's second coming. A February 1834 revelation called for the Saints to gather an expeditionary force to escort the exiles back to Jackson County.[15] Expecting that Missouri governor Daniel Dunklin would assist by activating state militia, Smith and an "army" of slightly more than two hundred men marched about eight hundred miles to Clay County in spring 1834 but retreated after state support failed to materialize. Before Smith returned to Ohio, a revelation deferred the Mormons' return to Jackson County until after

---

12. JS History, vol. A-1, 302.

13. Plat of City of Zion, 1833, CHL.

14. JS et al., Kirtland, OH, to Edward Partridge et al., Independence, MO, 25 June 1833, JS Collection, CHL.

15. Revelation, 24 Feb. 1834, in Doctrine and Covenants 101:3–7, 1844 ed. [D&C 103:15–40].

the House of the Lord in Kirtland could be completed and the Saints empowered.[16]

In the ten months that elapsed between the end of Joseph Smith's first journal in 1834 and the start of the second in 1835, the church sought through outreach—proselytizing, fund raising, and attracting additional settlers to both Ohio and Missouri—to achieve their prophet's goals of completing the temple in Kirtland and building a larger population base in areas near Jackson County from which to return to reestablish Zion. To support these efforts and the administration of congregations outside the main gathering places, Smith directed expansion of the church's leadership. At the initial church organization in 1830, the only ecclesiastical officers were Joseph Smith as "first elder" and Oliver Cowdery as "second elder." Within about five years, church leadership included a presidency for Kirtland and the church as a whole, another presidency for Missouri, a patriarch, bishops, high councils, and "quorums" of additional priesthood officers. A Quorum of the Twelve and several members of a Quorum of the Seventy were appointed in February 1835, chosen primarily from the ranks of veterans of the expedition to Missouri. This newly constructed hierarchy administered both local and general jurisdictions, and a lay priesthood that included most adult males and some older youth shared responsibility for the success of the church's activities.

Though self-taught and having little formal education, Joseph Smith cared about learning and promoted education in the Mormon community. In Kirtland's School of the Prophets and its 1835–1836 successor, the Elders School, Smith spearheaded instruction and study in theology, English grammar, and other fields to better qualify himself and the elders of the church for conducting God's work and especially for proselytizing worldwide. As construction of the House of the Lord in Kirtland neared completion and members of the lay ministry gathered from Missouri and elsewhere for training and spiritual preparation, Smith added yet another item to an already full agenda: the study of Hebrew by many of the Mormon ministry under the tutelage of a Jewish scholar.

Joseph Smith's second journal, covering more than six consecutive months from fall 1835 to spring 1836, records the multitude of activities and concerns that filled his days as he prepared his people for a hoped-for Pentecostal season. With daily entries that Smith apparently dictated to scribes, this journal provides a connected and much fuller narrative than the first. It covers institutional and spiritual developments and provides revealing glimpses of Smith's relationships with his family.

---

16. Revelation, 22 June 1834, in Doctrine and Covenants 102, 1844 ed. [D&C 105].

Joseph Smith carefully laid the groundwork during the winter of 1835–1836 for sacred ordinances and spiritual experiences by focusing on discipline, unity, organization, and individual sanctification. From within this highly structured setting, his second journal describes the rituals and spiritual ecstasy experienced in Kirtland from January through early April 1836, culminating in the long-sought endowment in the House of the Lord. The diary concludes with an account of visions that he and Oliver Cowdery experienced in the temple on 3 April 1836. It tells that Jesus Christ appeared and accepted the temple, and Moses, Elias, and Elijah each conferred "keys" upon Smith and Cowdery in anticipation of the advent of the Millennium.

Smith instructed the now empowered Latter-day Saint ministry to go forth as the Spirit directed them. During the two-year gap that separated Smith's second journal from his third, they cast their missionary net widely, establishing the church in the British Isles in 1837. The Saints had initially anticipated an imminent return to Jackson County, perhaps backed by a more impressive Mormon military force than before. Instead, now they sought converts and marshaled resources to help purchase new Missouri land for Mormon settlement.

By summer 1836, the continued influx of Saints into Clay County, Missouri, led the other local residents to insist that the Mormons move elsewhere. Since neither Jackson nor Clay county could serve as their gathering place, the Mormons looked to sparsely settled land to the northeast, where, at the close of 1836, the Missouri legislature created Caldwell County for Mormon settlement. Meanwhile, the Saints continued to build homes and enterprises in Kirtland, where the Mormon population swelled to about two thousand by 1838, eclipsing the local non-Mormon population of about twelve hundred.[17]

Despite continued gathering, growth, and doctrinal development, all was not well. Informed by an Old Testament model of prophetic leaders who exercised a broad scope of leadership powers, Joseph Smith moved increasingly in the direction of theocracy. Some members of the church felt a growing tension between the inspired direction of their prophet and the American value of individual freedom. Vexing to many was Smith's regulation of political and economic matters, especially as economic challenges mounted. Rebellion erupted when a Kirtland banking venture promoted by Smith failed just prior to the nationwide panic of 1837. Mormon enterprises succumbed and the Latter-day Saints struggled as depression engulfed America. Some of Smith's closest associates joined the ranks of the disillusioned, even attempting to depose him as church leader. He rallied support and won votes of confidence from Mormon congregations in both Ohio and Missouri, but dissidents continued their efforts

17. Backman, *Heavens Resound*, 140.

to undermine his leadership. From outside the church, Grandison Newell, a non-Mormon businessman in the Kirtland area, instigated numerous lawsuits against Smith, crippling him financially and constraining his freedom of movement.[18]

As conflict in Kirtland mounted and arrangements for Mormon settlement in Caldwell County, Missouri, were completed, Smith gave renewed emphasis to the imperative to gather to Zion. By late 1837, apostle Brigham Young, fearing for his life, left for Missouri, and Smith himself was planning to move. Facing both threats of physical violence and renewed legal harassment, on 12 January 1838 Joseph Smith and the presidency received a revelation to leave Kirtland as soon as possible for Missouri.[19] Faithful Latter-day Saints were to follow. Smith, Sidney Rigdon, and their families fled to the new Mormon center at Far West in Caldwell County. Other Kirtland Saints immigrated to Missouri throughout the spring, summer, and autumn.

Soon after his arrival in Far West, Smith began a third journal. Incorporating key minutes and correspondence, this first Missouri journal, spanning March to September 1838, documents his reassertion of authority both in Kirtland before his departure and in Missouri, where he set about reestablishing a church headquarters. In a form of documentary history, Smith's clerk copied into this record a series of letters, revelations, and other documents before settling into more traditional journal entries. Operating in crisis mode in early 1838 prior to Smith's arrival in Far West but under his direction, the Latter-day Saints in Caldwell County had already begun to counter the influence of leading dissidents there by removing the Missouri presidency from office and excommunicating two of its members. Upon his arrival in March 1838, Smith ratified these actions and moved against the remaining dissident leaders. David Whitmer, Oliver Cowdery, and other prominent Missouri Saints were excommunicated in Smith's presence that spring. Though Smith had been slow to act against dissenters in Ohio in 1837, now he and his supporters acted decisively to right the ship. In June, Sidney Rigdon publicly denounced excommunicants who still sought to undermine Smith's leadership, and several fled the county in response to threats of physical harm.

As the Mormon population continued to grow, with converts arriving from as far away as Canada, the Latter-day Saints expanded their settlements and moved to establish more. Their hopes for a new Zion, however, were short lived. They came up against the widespread determination of many Missourians

---

18. Adams, "Grandison Newell's Obsession."

19. Revelation, 12 Jan. 1838–C, in Revelations Collection, CHL; see also JS, Journal, 8 July 1838, pp. 283–284 herein.

to confine the Mormons within a small, remote county of their own. The growth of Mormon settlements in neighboring Daviess and Carroll counties especially aroused ire. An August 1838 skirmish between Mormons and Missourians at the Daviess County voting polls triggered a chain of incendiary rumors and responses. Joseph Smith led a large body of armed men across county lines to seek assurances that local Mormons could enjoy their civil rights in peace. For the moment, numbers were now in their favor. Missourians from Jackson and Clay counties had been able to compel the Latter-day Saints to leave their counties where the Saints were a small minority, but the sparsely settled inhabitants of Daviess County could not expel the rapidly immigrating Saints without help from other counties. Vigilantes from Daviess County used the Caldwell County Latter-day Saints' incursion into Daviess as the pretext for soliciting aid from other counties to drive the Mormons out. Legal proceedings against Smith and intervention by state militia to forestall violent confrontation averted a showdown only temporarily.

As the conflict in Missouri escalated, another scribe began Joseph Smith's fourth journal, for September and October 1838. The first week of this set of skeletal notes overlaps the final week of the third journal. The third journal probably ended because Smith or his scribe left Far West to aid endangered Saints in Daviess County. Confining itself to terse reporting of Smith's whereabouts in a five-week period, the fourth journal ends 6 October, just before Smith helped evacuate the Mormon village of De Witt, Carroll County, which was under siege by an overwhelming vigilante force, including many who were among those recently dispersed from Daviess County.[20] No journal was kept during the Mormons' chaotic final weeks in Missouri.

The De Witt debacle demonstrated the futility of Mormon appeals for aid from Missouri governor Lilburn W. Boggs and emboldened a wide-ranging coalition of anti-Mormon volunteers, who regrouped in Daviess County. After two generals in the Missouri militia advised the Latter-day Saints to fight their own battles because the generals' troops could not be relied upon for protection,[21] the Saints started an aggressive counteroffensive. In a preemptive strike, they first drove most of those who did not share their faith out of Daviess County. Immediately south of Caldwell County, a company of Mormon militia defeated and dispersed a unit of Ray County militia that had previously taken Mormon prisoners. Rumors spread quickly that the Mormons had annihilated the entire company. In the midst of this external conflict, two leading apostles denounced Smith, charging him with ruthless aggression to fulfill ambitions

---

20. Baugh, "Call to Arms," 154–155, 163–173.
21. Rigdon, *Appeal to the American People*, 41–44.

for power.[22] The perceived threat of more-widespread Latter-day Saint aggression enraged opponents and alarmed the governor. Vigilantes from Daviess, Livingston, and other nearby counties massacred Mormon villagers in eastern Caldwell County, and Boggs ordered an overwhelming contingent of state militia to restore peace by subduing the perceived insurgency. If necessary, read the governor's order, the Mormons were to be "exterminated or driven from the state."[23] In early November 1838, Missouri's "Mormon War" concluded with the surrender of Far West, the arrest and imprisonment of Joseph Smith and other Mormon leaders, and the beginning of forced exile of all practicing Mormons from the state.

While thousands of Latter-day Saints trudged eastward through bitter cold toward Missouri's boundary at the Mississippi River across from Quincy, Illinois, Smith agonized over the lessons to be learned from the Saints' crushing defeats in Missouri and over the future of their movement. Why had God allowed such an outcome?[24] The practice of gathering together in their own religiously based communities had repeatedly proven hazardous; leaders among the Mormons who had left Missouri questioned whether it should be continued.[25]

Joseph Smith emerged from more than five months in Missouri jails with a tenacious sense of purpose as he rejoined his refugee people in Quincy. He soon established a new gathering place, his last. Smith's 1839 journal, the last in this volume, opens with Smith's escape from Missouri in April 1839. Through 15 October of that year, it reports his activities during the founding of the Mormon community at Commerce (later Nauvoo), Illinois, on a bend on the Mississippi River some fifty miles north of Quincy. Brief entries, mostly from the perspective of the scribe, outline Smith's activities and travels, occasionally conveying the gist of a sermon. Scarcely had the Latter-day Saints begun to regroup in and near their new headquarters before malaria sickened many. Smith extended aid to the suffering and, in a bold move for a difficult time, dispatched some of his most loyal and capable leaders, the Quorum of the Twelve, to the British Isles to find new converts. The gathering was resuming in earnest.

---

22. Thomas B. Marsh and Orson Hyde, Affidavit, Richmond, MO, 24 Oct. 1838, Mormon War Papers, Missouri State Archives, Jefferson City.

23. Lilburn W. Boggs, Jefferson City, MO, to John B. Clark, Fayette, MO, 27 Oct. 1838, Mormon War Papers, Missouri State Archives, Jefferson City.

24. JS et al., Liberty, MO, to the church members and Edward Partridge, Quincy, IL, 20 Mar. 1839, in Revelations Collection, CHL [D&C 121:1–6].

25. Far West Committee, Minutes, 7 Feb. 1839.

Editorial Method

The goal of the Joseph Smith Papers Project is to present verbatim transcripts of Joseph Smith's papers in their entirety, making available the most essential sources of Smith's life and work and preserving the content of aging manuscripts from damage or loss. The papers include documents that were created by Joseph Smith, whether written or dictated by him or created by others under his direction, or that were owned by Smith, that is, received by him and kept in his office (as with incoming correspondence). Under these criteria— authorship and ownership—the project intends to publish, either in letterpress volumes or electronic form, every extant Joseph Smith document to which its editors can obtain access. Certain routine documents, such as some notes and certificates and some legal or business documents, will be calendared and published in their entirety online with only samples published in the letterpress edition. The Journals series of *The Joseph Smith Papers* presents an unaltered and unabridged transcript of each of Smith's known journals.

Rules of Transcription

Because of aging and sometimes damaged texts and imprecise penmanship, not all handwriting is legible or can be fully deciphered. Hurried writers often rendered words carelessly, and even the best writers and spellers left out letters on occasion or formed them imperfectly and incompletely. Text transcription and verification is therefore an imperfect art more than a science. Judgments about capitalization, for example, are informed not only by looking at the specific case at hand but by understanding the usual characteristics of each particular writer. The same is true for deciphering spelling and punctuation. If a letter or other character is ambiguous, deference is given to the author's or scribe's usual spelling and punctuation. Where this is ambiguous, modern spelling and punctuation are favored. Even the best transcribers and verifiers will differ from one another in making such judgments. Interested readers may wish to compare our transcriptions with images of the original manuscripts at the Joseph Smith Papers website, josephsmithpapers.org, to better understand how our transcription rules have been applied to create these transcripts. Viewing the originals also provides other information that cannot be conveyed by typography.

To ensure accuracy in representing the texts, transcripts were verified three times, each time by a different set of eyes. The first two verifications were done using high-resolution scanned images. The first was a visual collation of the journal images with the transcripts, while the second was an independent and double-blind image-to-transcript tandem proofreading. The third and final verification of the transcripts was a visual collation with the original document. At this stage, the verifier employed magnification and ultraviolet light as needed to read badly faded text, recover heavily stricken material, untangle characters written over each other, and recover words canceled by messy "wipe erasures" made when the ink was still wet or removed by knife scraping after the ink had dried. The verified transcripts meet or exceed the transcription and verification requirements of the Modern Language Association's Committee on Scholarly Editions and the National Archives and Records Administration's National Historical Publications and Records Commission.

The approach to transcription employed in *The Joseph Smith Papers* is conservative by historical documentary editing standards. The transcripts render most words letter by letter as accurately as possible, preserving the exact spelling of the originals. This includes incomplete words, variant spellings of personal names, repeated words, and idiosyncratic grammatical constructions. The transcripts also preserve substantive revisions made by the journal keepers. Canceled words are typographically rendered with the strikethrough bar, while inserted words are enclosed within angle brackets. Cancellations and insertions are also transcribed letter by letter when an original word—such as "sparingly" or "attend"—was changed to a new word simply by canceling or inserting letters at the beginning or end of the word—such as "sparing~~ly~~" or "attend⟨ed⟩". However, for cases in which an original word was changed to a new word by canceling or inserting letters in the middle of the word, to improve readability the original word is presented stricken in its entirety, followed by the revised word in its entirety. For example, when "falling" was revised to "failing" by canceling the first "l" and inserting an "i", the revision is transcribed as "~~falling~~ ⟨failing⟩" instead of "fal⟨i⟩ling". Insubstantial cancellations and insertions—those used only to correct spelling and punctuation—are silently emended, and only the final spelling and punctuation are reproduced.

The transcription of punctuation differs from the original in a few other respects. Single instances of periods, commas, apostrophes, and dashes are all faithfully rendered without regard to their grammatical correctness, except that periods are not reproduced when they appear immediately before a word, with no space between the period and the word. Also, in some cases of repetitive punctuation, only the final mark or final intention is transcribed while any other characters are silently omitted. Dashes of various lengths are standardized to a consistent pattern. The short vertical strokes commonly used in early American writing for abbreviation punctuation are transcribed as periods, but abbreviation punctuation is not reproduced when an abbreviation is expanded in square brackets. Flourishes and other decorative inscriptions are not reproduced or noted. Punctuation is never added silently.

Incorrect dates, place names, and other errors of fact are left to stand. The intrusive *sic,* sometimes used to affirm original misspelling, is never employed, although where words or phrases are especially difficult to understand, editorial clarifications or corrections are inserted in brackets. Correct and complete spellings of personal names are supplied in brackets the first time each incorrect or incomplete name appears in a journal entry (unless the correct name cannot be determined). Place names that may be hard to identify are also clarified or corrected within brackets. When two or more words are inscribed together without any intervening space and the words were not a compound according to standard contemporary usage or the scribe's or author's consistent practice, the words are transcribed as separate words for readability. Journal entries appear in their original sequence, retaining the occasional out-of-order or duplicate entry.

Formatting is standardized. Original paragraphing is retained, except that the first paragraph of the journal entry is always run in with the original dateline. Standardized editorial datelines—typographically distinguishable from the text—have also been added before every entry for convenience of use. All paragraphs are given in a standard format, with indention regularized and with blank lines between paragraphs omitted. Block quotations of letters, minutes, revelations, and other similar items within entries are set apart with block indentions, even when, as in a few cases, such items are not set off in the original. Horizontal rules and other devices inscribed between entries to mark them off from each other are not reproduced. Line ends are neither typographically reproduced nor symbolically represented. Because of the great number of words broken across a line at any point in the word, with or without a hyphen, end-of-line hyphens are not transcribed and there is no effort to note or keep a record of such words and hyphens. This leaves open the possibility that the hyphen of an ambiguously hyphenated compound escaped transcription or that a compound word correctly broken across a line ending without a hyphen is mistakenly transcribed as two words. As many end-of-line hyphens have been editorially introduced in the transcripts, a hyphen appearing at the end of a line may or may not be original to the document.

Redactions and other changes made on the manuscript after the original production of the text, such as when later scribes used the journals for drafting history, are not transcribed. Labeling and other forms of archival marking are similarly passed by in silence.

Readers wishing to view those elements not reproduced in the letterpress volumes may consult josephsmithpapers.org. The website will include a detailed "diplomatic" transcript of the journals, including all redactions and other subsequently added elements, along with letter-by-letter presentation of all revisions. For example, Joseph Smith's journal entry for 3 October 1835 is presented in the diplomatic transcript as follows:

> Sate⟨u⟩rday 3d Oct held a⟨a⟩ high council on the case of Elder John Gould for giving credence to false⟨e⟩ and slanderous reports instigated to Injure bro Sidney Rigdon and also Dean Gould for thretning bro Sidney Rigdon and others in authority of the Elders,⟨.⟩ after due deliberation the both confessed and wer acquited,⟨.⟩
>
> In the afternoon waited on the twelve most of them at my house and exhibited to them the ancient reccords in my possession and gave explanation of the same thu⟨i⟩s the day passed off with the blessings of the Lord

The transcript in the letterpress edition gives less detail:

> Saturday 3d Oct held a high council on the case of Elder John Gould for giving credence to false and slanderous reports instigated to Injure bro Sidney Rigdon and also Dean Gould for thretning bro Sidney Rigdon and others in authority of the Elders. after due deliberation the[y] both confessed and wer acquited.
>
> In the afternoon waited on the twelve most of them at my house and exhibited to them the ancient reccords in my possession and gave explanation of the same thus ⟨this⟩ the day passed off with the blessings of the Lord

Transcription Symbols

The effort to render mistakes, canceled material, and later insertions sometimes complicates readability by putting Joseph Smith and his scribes behind the "barbed wire" of symbolic transcription. However, conveying such elements with transcription symbols can aid in understanding the text and the order and ways in which the words were inscribed. Typesetting can never effectively represent all the visual aspects of a document; it cannot fully capture such features as the formation of letters and other characters, spacing between words and between paragraphs, varying lengths of dashes and paragraph indentions, and varying methods of cancellation and the location of insertions. Despite its limitations, a conservative transcription method more faithfully represents the process by which the text was inscribed—especially cancellations and insertions—rather than just the final result.

The following symbols are used to transcribe and expand the text:

/[n]   In documents inscribed by more than one person, the slash mark indicates a change in handwriting. A footnote identifies the previous and commencing scribes.

[roman]	Brackets enclose editorial insertions that expand, correct, or clarify the text. This convention may be applied to the abbreviated or incorrect spelling of a personal name, such as Brigham Yo[u]ng, or of a place, such as Westleville [Wesleyville]. Obsolete or ambiguous abbreviations are expanded with br[acket]s. Bracketed editorial insertions also provide reasonable reconstructions of badly miss[p]elled worsd [words]. Missing or illegible words may be supplied within brackets in cases where the supplied word is based on textual or contextual evidence. Bracketed punctuation is added only when necessary to follow complex wording.
[roman?]	A question mark is added to conjectured editorial insertions, such as where an entire word was [accidentally?] omitted and where it is difficult to maintain the sense of a sentence without some editorial insertion.
[*italic*]	Significant descriptions of the writing medium—especially those inhibiting legibility—and of spacing between the inscriptions are italicized and enclosed in brackets: [*hole burned in paper*], [*leaf torn*], [*blank*], [*9 lines blank*], [*pages 99–102 blank*].
[*illegible*]	An illegible word is represented by the italicized word [*illegible*] enclosed in brackets.
◊	An illegible character within a partially legible word is rendered with a hollow diamond. Repeated diamonds represent the approximate number of illegible characters (for example: sto◊◊◊◊s).
[p. x]	Bracketed editorial insertions indicate the end of an originally numbered manuscript page, regardless of the location of the written page number on the manuscript page.
[p. [x]]	Bracketing of the page number itself indicates that the manuscript page was not originally numbered and that the number of the page is editorially supplied.
underlined	Underlining is typographically reproduced. <u>Individually</u> <u>underlined</u> <u>words</u> are distinguished from <u>passages underlined with one continuous line</u>.
superscript	Superscription is typographically reproduc^{ed}.
~~canceled~~	A single horizontal strikethrough bar is used to indicate any method of cancellation: strikethrough and cross-out, wipe erasure and knife erasure, overwriting, or other methods. ~~Individually canceled words~~ are distinguished from ~~passages eliminated with a single cancellation~~. Characters individually canceled at the begin~~ning~~ or end of a word are distinguished from ~~words canceled in their entirety~~.
⟨inserted⟩	Insertions in the text—whether interlinear, intralinear, or marginal—are enclosed in angle brackets. Letter⟨s⟩ and other characters individual⟨ly⟩ insert⟨ed⟩ at the beginning or end of a word are distinguished from ⟨words⟩ inserted in ⟨their⟩ entirety.
bold	Joseph Smith's handwriting is rendered in boldface type. Bracketed editorial insertions made within passages of **Smith's own h[and]w[riting]** are also rendered in boldface type.

TEXT   The word TEXT begins textual footnotes describing significant details not com-
          prehended by this scheme of symbolic transcription.

| A line break artificially imposed in an original document is rendered as a verti-
          cal line in textual notes.

Annotation Conventions

The Joseph Smith Papers do not present a unified narrative. Annotations—
including historical introductions, editorial notes, and footnotes—supply
background and context to help readers better understand and use the documents. The aim of the annotation is to serve scholars and students of early
Mormon history and American religious history generally, whose familiarity
with these fields may vary widely.

The *Papers* cite original sources where possible and practical. Secondary
sources of sound scholarship are cited when they usefully distill several primary sources. Quotations from primary sources preserve original spelling but
silently emend cancellations and insertions (unless judged highly significant).

Certain conventions simplify the presentation of the annotation. Joseph
Smith is usually referred to by the initials JS. The terms *Saint, Latter-day Saint,*
and *Mormon*—all used by mid-1834 in reference to church members—are
employed interchangeably here. Most sources are referred to by a shortened
citation form, with a complete citation given in the Works Cited. Some documents are referred to by editorial titles rather than by their original titles or the
titles given in the catalogs of their current repositories. These editorial titles are
in some cases similar to informal names by which the documents have come to
be known. The editorial titles are listed in the Works Cited along with the
complete citations by which the documents can be found in repositories. The
most important sources used in annotating a volume are discussed in the Essay
on Sources preceding the Works Cited.

The volumes in this series use a citation style that lists all source citations at
the end of the footnote. Because of the complexity of some footnotes and the
difficulty readers might have in determining which source citations document
particular statements within such footnotes, superscript letters are sometimes
used to key specific statements to their corresponding documentation. Though
it goes beyond conventional citation style, this detailed approach may best
serve researchers using volumes of the Journals series as reference works.

The annotation extensively cites Joseph Smith's revelations. Smith and his
followers at first used the terms *commandments* and *revelations* interchangeably
in referring to these dictations that they viewed as divine communications.
During the mid-1830s, *revelations*—the term used throughout *The Joseph Smith
Papers* to refer to these works—became standard. Many of these revelations

were first collected and published, with numbered chapters and paragraphs (or verses), as the Book of Commandments in 1833. An expanded collection, organized into sections and with new versification, was published in 1835 as the Doctrine and Covenants. In 1844, at the time of his death, Smith was overseeing publication of a revised edition of the Doctrine and Covenants, which was published later that year. Since then, the Doctrine and Covenants has been published in several editions, each including newly canonized revelations or other items.

Source citations in this series identify revelations by their original date and by a citation of an early printed version relevant to the particular instance of annotation (usually the 1835 edition of the Doctrine and Covenants). In cases in which two or more revelations bear the same date, a letter of the alphabet is appended so that each revelation has a unique editorial title—for example, May 1829–A or May 1829–B. Revelation citations also include a bracketed "D&C" reference that provides the Doctrine and Covenants section and verse numbers that have been standard in The Church of Jesus Christ of Latter-day Saints since 1876. For example, the last portion of the revelation that provided a basis for the Mormon health code is cited as Revelation, 27 Feb. 1833, in Doctrine and Covenants 80:3, 1835 ed. [D&C 89:16–21] (see figure).

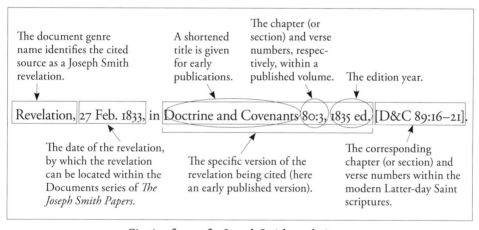

Citation format for Joseph Smith revelations.

Bracketed D&C references are provided for the benefit of Latter-day Saints, who can easily access the revelations in their familiar canon of scriptural works, and other students of early Mormonism who may wish to access the most widely available editions of these revelations. A table titled Corresponding Section Numbers in Editions of the Doctrine and Covenants is provided following the Works Cited to help readers refer from the cited version of a canonized revelation to other published versions of the same revelation. For more information about revelation citations, see the aforementioned table and the introduction to the Works Cited.

Smith's revelations and revelatory translations published outside of the Doctrine and Covenants, such as the Book of Mormon, are referenced in *The Joseph Smith Papers* to an early published or manuscript version, with references to modern Latter-day Saint publications added in brackets. These books of Latter-day Saint scripture are described in more detail in the introduction to the Works Cited. When the Bible is used in annotation, the King James Version—the version read by Smith and his followers and contemporaries as well as by English-speaking Latter-day Saints today—is referenced.

In addition to the annotation in the main body of a volume, several supplementary resources in the back of each volume aid in understanding the text. As many of the places, people, organizations, and terms mentioned in the journals appear more than once, the reference material serves to remove duplicate footnotes and to otherwise systematically reduce the annotation in the main body. To minimize repetition and interruption, only rarely will annotation within the journals directly refer readers to the reference material in the back.

Many of the people whose names appear in the journals in this series have been identified. In most cases, information about these people appears in the Biographical Directory rather than in the notes. Some names have silently been left without identification either because resources did not permit research or because no information was found. Complete documentation for reference material in the back and for the timeline and maps included earlier in the volume will be made available at josephsmithpapers.org, as will other resources, including a complete calendar of Smith's papers and expanded versions of many of the reference resources.

The Journals series will be indexed cumulatively in the final volume of the series. A printable, searchable index for volume 1 is available at josephsmithpapers.org.

JOURNALS
1832–1839

First Ohio journal. Joseph Smith and various scribes kept his first journal in this pocket-size account book. It spans from late 1832 to late 1834. Handwriting of Joseph Smith on cover. JS, Journal, 1832–1834, JS Collection, Church History Library, Salt Lake City. (Photograph by Welden C. Andersen.)

JOURNAL, 1832–1834

Source Note

JS, "Joseph Smith Jrs Book for Record," Journal, Nov. 1832–Dec. 1834; handwriting of Oliver Cowdery, JS, Frederick G. Williams, Parley P. Pratt, Sidney Rigdon, Freeman Nickerson, and six unidentified scribes; 105 pages; JS Collection, CHL. Includes redactions and archival marking.

Pocket-size memorandum book, 5⅞ x 3¾ x ¼ inches (15 x 10 x 1 cm). The text block consists of fifty-four leaves measuring 5⅞ x 3⅝ inches (15 x 9 cm). There are four gatherings of six sheets each of ledger paper. Each sheet is folded so that each gathering has twelve leaves (twenty-four pages). These pages are ruled with sixteen blue horizontal lines—now almost entirely faded—as well as with red vertical lines for recording financial information. The endpapers consist of pastedowns on the inside covers and two free flyleaves in both the front and back. The gatherings are sewn all along on sawn-in cords. The front and back covers of the journal are pasteboard. The ledger has a tight-back case binding with a black calfskin quarter-leather binding. The outside covers are adorned in schrottel marbled paper, with gray body and veins of black and blue. The volume originally had three leather loops—two in the back and one in the front—that were tipped in between the inside covers and the pastedowns. The former presence of the front cover loop, no longer extant, is evident from creasing and staining on the pastedown, which is now detached. The leather loops and their spacing allowed for the book to be fastened by inserting a pencil between all three loops. The vibrant blue veins and the grain of the marbling, now greatly diminished by water damage, are also visible under the now loose front pastedown.

JS wrote "Joseph Smith 1832.(3–4)" on the front cover in black ink that later turned brown. On the front pastedown, "Joseph Smith" is written sideways, running upward near the bottom of the outer edge. Also, "Joseph" is written sideways, running downward near the top of the inside of the same page. The handwriting of these inscriptions has not been identified. The journal entries begin on the recto of the second leaf (the first flyleaf) and end on the recto of the back pastedown, making 105 numbered pages. Regular journal entries, inscribed in various shades of brown (formerly black) ink, continue through page 93. Pages 94 to 102 are blank except for page 98, which has JS's name in graphite pencil at the top in JS's handwriting. Pages 103–105 record subscriptions, which were evidently solicited during JS's 26 February–28 March 1834 New York mission, as well as a note apparently inscribed on 20 April 1834 in preparation for the conference held 20–21 April 1834 at Norton, Ohio. The book has suffered from water and mud damage, evidenced in part by some extremely faded ink on page 2. Glue from tipping in a damaged leaf has also obscured several characters in the gutter of page 2.

The journal's textual redactions and use marks, in graphite pencil, were made by later scribes who used the journal to produce the multivolume manuscript history of the church. This occurred in Nauvoo, indicating the journal remained in JS's possession. The journal is listed in Nauvoo and early Utah inventories of church records, indicating continuous custody.[1]

---

1. Historian's Office, "Schedule of Church Records"; "Historian's Office Catalogue," [7], Catalogs and Inventories, 1846–1904, CHL; Johnson, *Register of the Joseph Smith Collection*, 7.

Historical Introduction

By late November 1832, when this record began, JS had resided in Ohio for nearly two years. Most members of the fledgling church in New York had migrated to Ohio in spring 1831; many had subsequently moved on to Jackson County, Missouri, where they sought to establish a latter-day Zion. As headquarters for the church, Kirtland, Ohio, served as a base for proselytizing missions ranging as far afield as Upper Canada (now Ontario) and the eastern United States. Meanwhile, attempts to create historical records had failed to keep pace with the development of the church. JS had recently prepared a six-page personal history. Now he began keeping a personal journal, documenting his experiences as they occurred and thereby paving the way for writing a more extensive history. Journal writing was a new genre for JS, and in this record, he employed a personal tone quite different from the prophetic voice of his scriptural translations and revelations.

JS's first journal begins 27 November 1832 and ends 5 December 1834, with entries spread unevenly over this period of just over two years. After titling this journal "Joseph Smith Jrs Book for Record," JS recorded his ambitious intention "to keep a minute acount of all things that come under my obsevation &c." However, reality failed to match his expectations. From the outset, the level of detail JS preserved in this record was limited. His pattern of journalizing varied widely. After recording only nine more entries, JS abandoned journal keeping for ten months. Yet his original aspiration to keep a journal occasionally yielded significant information. Sporadic notations followed, with three instances of sustained writing covering a consecutive week or more in the remainder of the journal. The events described in these passages are a proselytizing mission to Canada in October 1833, a fund-raising and recruitment mission to Pennsylvania and New York in March 1834 to prepare for an expedition to help the Mormons in Missouri, and activities in Ohio in April 1834 just before the expedition departed. The journal's most consistent daily entries cover the period from late February to late April 1834. The entire two-year record contains fewer than one hundred entries. It skips over many key developments but provides rare glimpses into the lives of JS and the other leaders of the church during these formative years.

Despite its brevity, this first journal contains more of JS's handwriting than do any of his other journals. Almost half of the entries in the journal were written either entirely or primarily by JS himself; some of the remainder were apparently dictated. His openly expressed hopes and concerns, prayers and blessings, and observations on his own state of mind are a rich source of insight into spiritual and emotional dimensions of JS's personality.

This journal illustrates how closely leadership in the early church was intertwined with record keeping. Trusted associates who served as scribes for JS for key projects in the earliest years soon found themselves called to join JS in church leadership, with continued scribal responsibilities. Oliver Cowdery, primary scribe for JS's Book of Mormon translation, served as second elder beginning in April 1830 and wrote some of the entries for this first journal. Sidney Rigdon, scribe for JS's "translation," or revision, of the Bible beginning in December 1830, served as a counselor to JS beginning in March 1832 and also wrote entries in this journal. Frederick G. Williams, a scribe for JS beginning 20 July 1832[2] and a

---

2. Frederick G. Williams, Statement, no date, Frederick G. Williams, Papers, CHL.

Principal scribes of first Ohio journal. Clockwise from top left: Oliver Cowdery, Frederick G. Williams, and Parley P. Pratt were the principal scribes who assisted Joseph Smith in keeping his first journal. (Williams image courtesy Church History Museum, Salt Lake City. Other images: Church History Library, Salt Lake City.)

counselor to JS by January 1833,[3] recorded JS's concluding revisions to the Bible from July 1832 to July 1833 as well as some entries beginning in November 1833 in this journal. Some of the journal's most revealing moments are JS's candid evaluations of associates Cowdery, Rigdon, and Williams in connection with blessings he pronounced upon them in November and December 1833.

The journal's first ten entries, covering 27 November to 6 December 1832 and all written in JS's handwriting, describe a trip to visit family, a happy return, receipt of a new revelation, and translation work. JS's state of mind is apparent in phrases such as "my mind is calm and serene," "found all well to the Joy and satisfaction of my soul on my return," and "Oh Lord deliver thy servent out of temtations."[4] Yet the seemingly unhurried introspection of these first entries gives way to ten months of silence, a period during which JS became increasingly caught up in church leadership activities.

Revelation persistently nudged JS and his fellow believers toward building communities with a central focus on education and spiritual empowerment. In late December 1832, less than four weeks after this journal lapsed into silence, a new revelation called for a "solemn assembly" of the lay ministry, amplifying a promise in a revelation of January 1831 that in Ohio the Latter-day Saints would be "endowed with power from on high." In preparation for this experience, they were to receive training in spiritual and temporal affairs and a ritual "washing of feet" in a "house of God."[5] A "School of the Prophets" began in January 1833, and in April land was purchased on which to build a structure that would be called the House of the Lord. A subsequent revelation called for the Saints to use this temple as the central reference point around which to develop a substantial community to be known as "the city of the stake of Zion."[6] As for Zion itself, on 25 June 1833 JS and his associates sent plans to church leaders in Jackson County, Missouri, envisioning the purchase of new lands and the expansion of Mormon settlement there, building outward from a cluster of centrally located temples.[7]

But by the time the plans arrived in Jackson County, Zion's future looked bleak. Negotiations in mid-July between Mormon settlers and their unwilling neighbors broke down, and violence erupted. With the 9 August 1833 arrival of Oliver Cowdery in Ohio from Missouri, JS learned for the first time that twelve hundred Jackson County Saints would be forced from their homes by spring 1834. JS dispatched Orson Hyde and John Gould to Missouri to advise the Saints.[8]

When journal keeping resumed on 4 October 1833, much had changed for JS and his followers. The impending eviction of the Jackson County Latter-day Saints and construction of the House of the Lord in Kirtland loom in the background of subsequent journal

---

3. Minute Book 1, 22 Jan. 1833.

4. Entries for 28 and 30 Nov. 1832; 4 Dec. 1832.

5. Revelation, 2 Jan. 1831, in Book of Commandments 40:28 [D&C 38:32]; Revelation, 27 and 28 Dec. 1832 and 3 Jan. 1833, in Doctrine and Covenants 7:19–23, 36–46, 1835 ed. [D&C 88:70–84, 117–141].

6. Revelation, 2 Aug. 1833–B, in Doctrine and Covenants 83:1, 1835 ed. [D&C 94:1].

7. Plat of City of Zion, 1833, CHL.

8. John Whitmer, Independence, MO, to JS and Oliver Cowdery, [Kirtland, OH], 29 July 1833, in JS Letterbook 2, pp. 52–55; Oliver Cowdery with JS postscript, Kirtland Mills, OH, to William W. Phelps et al., [Independence, MO], 10 Aug. 1833, CHL; Knight, Autobiography, 39.

entries. In October 1833, JS and Sidney Rigdon responded to a request from Freeman Nickerson, a Mormon visiting from New York, to join him in proselytizing family members in Canada. JS and Rigdon recorded in this journal their monthlong trip. Three weeks after their return, the journal first mentions explicitly the Saints' Missouri difficulties: JS learned on 25 November 1833 of the vigilante expulsion of the Mormons in Jackson County that month—earlier than the agreed-upon departure—following a series of violent confrontations. Many crossed the Missouri River and found temporary refuge in nearby Clay County.

Most of the subsequent entries of this journal involve either direct or indirect responses to the Missouri problems. By December 1833, the Latter-day Saints had set up a printing press in Kirtland to resume publication efforts that had been halted by the destruction of their print shop in Missouri. A February 1834 revelation instructed the Saints to undertake a paramilitary expedition intended to help the Mormon refugees from Jackson County return to their homes. JS and Parley P. Pratt were one of four pairs of men directed to travel from Kirtland to various locations to solicit volunteers and donations in support of the effort.[9] Journal entries cover the monthlong trip of JS and Pratt through northeastern Pennsylvania and western New York. JS returned from this mission at the end of March, just in time for the opening of a term of the Geauga County Court of Common Pleas. There he testified in a trial against Doctor Philastus Hurlbut, an excommunicant who had threatened his life. Following the trial, JS spent the rest of April preparing for the march to Missouri, which commenced in early May.

JS made no journal entries during the expedition to Missouri. The episode is manifest in the journal as a half page of blank space, almost as if he intended to reserve the space for an entry later on. Although Missouri governor Daniel Dunklin acknowledged the legal right of the Mormons to their Jackson County property, he would not intervene. Based on statements by Dunklin's attorney general, Robert Wells, the Mormons mistakenly assumed that Dunklin was willing to commit state militia to escort them back to Jackson County, and the expedition—later known as "Zion's Camp"—marched with that expectation. As the little army of Mormons neared Missouri, tensions mounted, and Dunklin sought a compromise. But negotiations between the Mormons and their former neighbors in Jackson County failed to resolve major issues that prevented the Mormons' return to their Zion.

The volunteers thus halted near the border of Jackson County, short of their intended destination. A revelation dated 22 June 1834 counseled the Latter-day Saints to prepare themselves more thoroughly and declared that the redemption of Zion must await their empowerment in the House of the Lord at Kirtland. The revelation also directed them to continue to purchase lands in the vicinity of Jackson County.[10] Members of the expedition distributed food and supplies to the refugee Mormons living in nearby Clay County, and JS strengthened local church leadership by appointing a presidency and a "high council" consisting of twelve men. Meanwhile, about sixty-eight of the volunteers, including JS, contracted cholera; thirteen died. After the cholera abated at the end of June, the surviving members were discharged and the expedition officially ended, having failed in its ostensible

---

9. Revelation, 24 Feb. 1834, in Doctrine and Covenants 101, 1844 ed. [D&C 103].
10. Revelation, 22 June 1834, in Doctrine and Covenants 102:3, 8, 1844 ed. [D&C 105:9–13, 27–28].

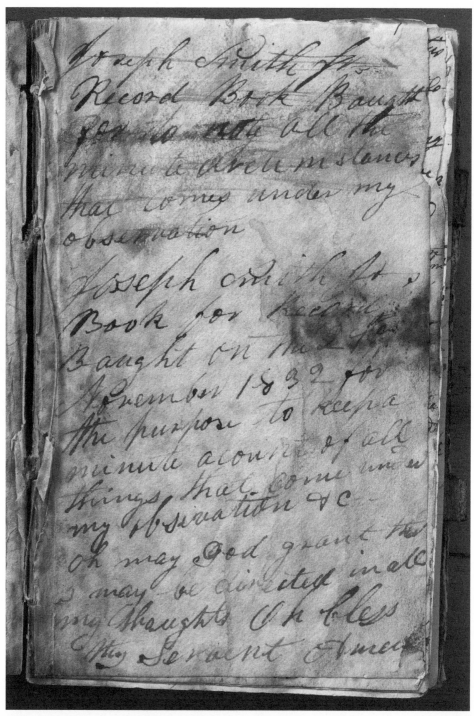

First page of first Ohio journal. Joseph Smith began his first journal expressing the intention "to keep a minute acount of all things that come under my obsevation" and pleading for help from God. Handwriting of Joseph Smith. JS, Journal, 1832–1834, p. 1, JS Collection, Church History Library, Salt Lake City. (Photograph by Welden C. Andersen.)

mission.[11] In early August, JS returned to Kirtland amidst criticism about the expedition. There he faced two heavy financial challenges: to purchase new lands in Missouri and to finish construction of the House of the Lord in Kirtland.

———— ∾ ————

Joseph Smith 1832.⟨3–4⟩ [*front cover*]

~~Joseph Smith Jrs—Record Book Baught for to note all the minute circumstances that comes under my observation~~
Joseph Smith Jrs Book for Record Baught on the 27th of November 1832 for the purpose to keep a minute acount of all things that come under my obsevation &c——
oh may God grant that I may be directed in all my thoughts Oh bless thy Servent Amen[12] [p. 1]

28 November 1832 · Wednesday

November 28th this day I have [spent?] in reading and writing this Evening my mind is calm and serene for which I thank the Lord

29 November 1832 · Thursday

November 29th this day road from Kirtland to Chardon to see my Sister Sopronia [Sophronia Smith Stoddard] and also came to see my Sister Catheri [Katharine Smith Salisbury][13] and[14] found them all [well?]

   this Evening Brother Frederic [Frederick G. Williams] Prophcyed tha[t] next spring I should go to the city of PittsBurg to establish a Bishopwrick and within one year I should go to the city of New York the Lord spare ~~me~~ the life of thy servent Amen[15] [p. 2]

---

11. Kimball, "History," 21–24; Launius, *Zion's Camp*, 110–155.

12. Compare JS's letter to William W. Phelps, written on the day the record book was purchased. Similar to his plea here, "that I may be directed in all my thaughts," JS prayed in his letter to Phelps for the power to "gaze upon Eternal wisdom." (JS, Kirtland, OH, to William W. Phelps, [Independence, MO], 27 Nov. 1832, in JS Letterbook 1, pp. 1–4.)

13. Katharine and her husband, Wilkins Jenkins Salisbury, had apparently settled in the Chardon area, near Calvin and Sophronia Smith Stoddard.

14. TEXT: Faded word rendered as "and".

15. It is unclear whether Williams had accompanied JS or was in Chardon independently. Williams earlier owned property in Chardon and may have had medical patients or other connections there.[a] Williams's prophecy may have been motivated by recent events. A month earlier, JS visited New York City, and Sidney Rigdon had recently organized a branch in Pittsburgh, where he had formerly served as the pastor of a congregation of Regular Baptists.[b] In 1845, Rigdon claimed that while on this mission to Pittsburgh he received a revelation that it would become a gathering center, which would require a bishopric there.[c] (a. Cuyahoga Co., OH, Deeds and Mortgages, 23 Oct. 1828, vol. G-7, 443–444,

30 November 1832 • Friday

November 30th 1830 [1832] this day returned home to Kirtland found all well to the Joy and satisfaction of my soul on my return home stopped at Mr Kings[16] bore testmony to him and Family &c—

1 December 1832 • Saturday

December 1th ⟨bore testimony to mr Gilmore⟩ wrote and corrected revelations &c[17]

2 December 1832 • Sunday

December 2th the sabath went ~~to went~~ to meeting &c

3 December 1832 • Monday

December 3d ordaind Brothe[r] Packherd [Noah Packard] with my own hands[18] also Brother umpry [Solomon Humphrey Jr.] came to see me from the East & braught news from Brother Lyman Johnson and Orson Pratt[19] &c. also held a conference in the Evening Br Jese and Mogan and William Mclelen [William E. McLellin] was excommunicated from the church &c—[20] [p. 3]

---

microfilm, U.S. and Canada Record Collection, FHL. *b.* JS, New York City, NY, to Emma Smith, Kirtland, OH, 13 Oct. 1832, CCLA; Van Wagoner, *Sidney Rigdon,* 26–29, 96. *c.* Sidney Rigdon, "History of Facts," *Messenger and Advocate of the Church of Christ,* 15 June 1845, 235–237; see also "Letters from David and John C. Whitmer," *Saints' Herald,* 5 Feb. 1887, 90.)

16. Possibly David King, who owned property in Chester Township, which bordered Kirtland on the south. (Geauga Co., OH, Duplicate Tax Records, 1831, 31; 1832, 35; 1833, 33, microfilm, U.S. and Canada Record Collection, FHL.)

17. In preparation for the publication of the Book of Commandments (a compilation of JS's revelations), a church conference in November 1831 charged JS to "correct those errors or mistakes which he m[a]y discover by the holy Spirit while reviewing the revelations & commandments & also the fulness of the scriptures." (Minute Book 2, 8 Nov. 1831; see also 30 Apr. 1832; and JS, Hyrum [Hiram, OH], to William W. Phelps, Zion [Independence], MO, 31 July 1832, JS Collection, CHL.)

18. JS ordained Packard a priest at a conference of elders. (Minute Book 1, 3 Dec. 1832.)

19. Earlier revelations assigned Humphrey, Johnson, and Pratt to proselytizing missions, with Johnson and Pratt as partners. (Revelation, 6 June 1831, in Book of Commandments 54:35 [D&C 52:35]; Revelation, 25 Jan. 1832, in Doctrine and Covenants 87:3, 1835 ed. [D&C 75:14].)

20. "Jese" is probably Jesse Gause, JS's counselor in the church presidency, who "denied the faith" sometime earlier in 1832.[a] JS became increasingly frustrated with McLellin throughout 1832. After McLellin failed to carry out a mission in the eastern states with JS's brother Samuel, a January 1832 revelation rebuked him for the "murmurings of his heart" and instructed him to serve a mission in the southern states,[b] which he abandoned as well.[c] Soon thereafter, JS rebuked the Missouri Latter-day Saints for accepting McLellin into their "fellowship & communion."[d] (*a.* Minute Book 2, 30 Apr. 1832; see also Quinn, "Jesse Gause," 492. *b.* Revelation, 25 Jan. 1832, in Doctrine and Covenants 87:2, 1835 ed. [D&C 75:6–8]. *c.* JS, Greenville, IN, to Emma Smith, Kirtland, OH, 6 June 1832, Manuscripts about Mormons

4 December 1832 · Tuesday

December 4ᵗʰ this day I been unwell done but litle been at home all day regulated some of my things this Evening feel better in my mind then I have for a few days back Oh Lord deliver ~~out~~ thy servent out of temtations and fill his heart with wisdom and understanding

5 December 1832 · Wednesday

December 5ᵗʰ this day ~~wrote leters~~ copying letters²¹ and translating²² and in evening held a council to advise with Brother Solomon Humphry [Humphrey Jr.] it was ordered by the council that he should be a companion with Brothe[r] Noah packard in the work of the ministry²³

6 December 1832 · Thursday

December 6ᵗʰ translating and received a Revelation²⁴ explaining the Parable the wheat and the tears [tares] &c [p. 4]

———— ☙ ————

Editorial Note

Ten months passed before JS wrote another entry. In that period he dictated several revelations as he continued revising the Bible, completing his work in July 1833. Organizing and meeting with the School of the Prophets occupied much of his time from January through April. In June, JS and the presidency developed plans for temples in Kirtland and Missouri and for expanded Mormon settlement in each city. In August, JS learned that during the previous month vigilantes had destroyed the church's printing press and store in Jackson County and that the Missouri Latter-day Saints had signed an agreement to evacuate Jackson County by spring 1834. In September, JS helped organize efforts in Kirtland to resume the church's printing operations. JS renewed his journal keeping in October 1833 as he prepared to proselytize in northeastern Pennsylvania, western New York, and Upper Canada. After he returned to Kirtland a month later, journal entries continued for several weeks.

———— ☙ ————

at Chicago History Museum, Research Center, Chicago Historical Society. *d*. JS, Hyrum [Hiram, OH], to William W. Phelps, Zion [Independence], MO, 31 July 1832, JS Collection, CHL.)

21. Probably the three 1829 letters from Oliver Cowdery that JS copied into his first letterbook. (See JS Letterbook 1, pp. 4–8.)

22. On JS's "New Translation," or inspired revision, of the Bible, see Faulring et al., *Joseph Smith's New Translation of the Bible*, 3–13.

23. A council of high priests met at Humphrey's request to ascertain "the will of the Lord respcting him." The council advised Humphrey to go to Parkman, Ohio, to begin a proselytizing mission with Packard. (Minute Book 1, 5 Dec. 1832.)

24. Revelation, 6 Dec. 1832, in Doctrine and Covenants 6, 1835 ed. [D&C 86]. JS's revision of the Bible prompted a number of revelations. (Matthews, "Doctrinal Connections," 27–42.)

4 October 1833 • Friday

October 4[th] ⟨1833⟩ **makeing preperation to go East with Freeman Nickerson**[25]

[26]**A request of Brother David Elliott to call on his Brother in Law Peter Worrin St; kathrine [St. Catharines] upper Cannada**

Cob[o]urg Richard Lyman request of Uncle John [Smith][27]

5 October 1833 • Saturday

5[th] **this day started on a Journy to the East came to Ashtibuly [Ashtabula] ⟨stayed⟩ Lambs tavern**

6–12 October 1833 • Sunday–Saturday

6[th] **arrived at Springfield [Pennsylvania] ⟨on the sabbath⟩ found the Brotheren in meeting Brother Sidney [Rigdon] spake to the people &c—**[28] **and in the [p. 5] ⟨~~Evening~~⟩ held a meeting at Brother Ruds [John Rudd Jr.'s] a had a great congregation paid good attention Oh God Seal our te[s]timony to their hearts Amen** /[29]continued at springfield untill tuesday the 8th Journeyed that day to b[r.] Roundays [Shadrach Roundy's] at Elk creek taried there over night came the next day to a tavern the next day thursday the 10[th] we ar[ri]ved at B[r.] Job Lewises at Westfield the breatheren by a previous appointment met there for meeting we spake to them as the spirite[30] gave [p. 6] utterence they were greatly gratifyed they appeared to be strong in the faith left there friday the 11 and came to the house of an infidel by the Name of Nash[31] reasond with him but to no effect came Saturday the 12th [to?]

---

25. New York Latter-day Saint Freeman Nickerson had traveled to Kirtland, Ohio, and persuaded JS and Sidney Rigdon to accompany him to Mount Pleasant, Upper Canada, to preach to members of his family. Frederick G. Williams explained that JS and Sidney Rigdon had "gone down the Lake to Niagara from thence expect to go into Canada as far as Long point U C and to preach in all the most noted places on the way." (Gates, *Lydia Knight's History*, 16–23; Berrett, *Sacred Places*, 2:249–250; Frederick G. Williams, Kirtland, OH, to "Dear Brethren," Independence, MO, 10 Oct. 1833, in JS Letterbook 1, p. 57.)

26. TEXT: The first part of the entry for 4 October 1833 was initially inscribed in graphite and then retraced in ink—apparently by JS. The following material, written in heavier ink, was apparently inserted at a different time.

27. Richard Lyman, the brother of John Smith's wife, Clarissa Lyman Smith, was apparently residing in Cobourg, Hamilton Township, Upper Canada.

28. This meeting may have been held in the home of Andrews and Elizabeth Comins Tyler. (Tyler, "Recollections of the Prophet," 93; see also Hales, *Windows*, 101.)

29. TEXT: Sidney Rigdon handwriting begins.

30. TEXT: A detached mark at this point could be read as an inserted "s" at the end of "spirite".

31. The 1830 U.S. Census, Portland Township, Chautauque Co., NY, 429, 434, identifies Ruel and Cotton Nash living in Portland, New York, a few miles east of Westfield.

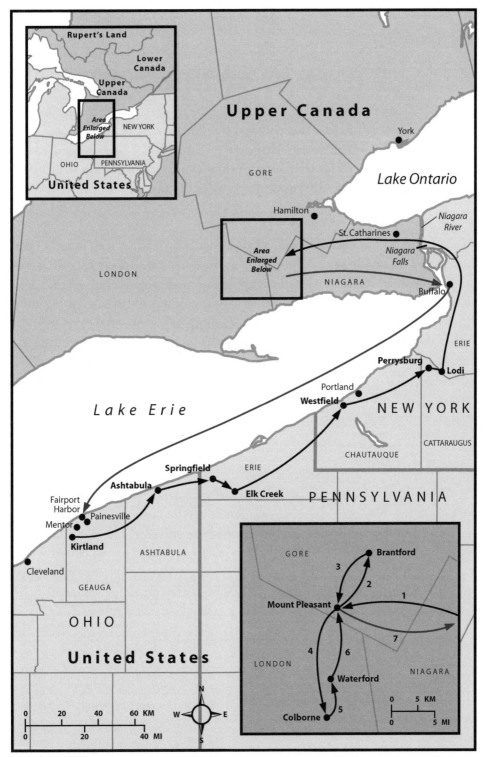

Proselytizing mission, October–November 1833. Joseph Smith and Sidney Rigdon traveled with Freeman Nickerson to Mount Pleasant, Upper Canada, to proselytize Nickerson's relatives, preaching in western New York along the way. (Research by Richard L. Jensen and Mark Ashurst-McGee. Design by John Hamer.)

the house of of father Nickeson [Freeman Nickerson] **I feel very well in my mind the Lord is with us but have much anxiety about my family &c;—**[32]

13 October 1833 • Sunday

Sunday the 13ᵗʰ held a meeting ~~hald~~ **at freeman Nickerson had a large congregation Brother Sidney [Rigdon] preached & I bear record to the people the Lord gave his spirit in** [p. 7] **marvilous man[n]er**[33] **for which I am thankful to the god of Ab[r]aham Lord bless my family and preserve them**

14–18 October 1833 • Monday–Friday

Monday 14ᵗʰ at the same place this day expect to start for Canada Lord be with us on our Journy Amen &c /[34]monday evening arived at Lodi had an appointment preached to a small congregation made an appointment for tuesday at 10 o clock the 15ᵗʰ the meeting was appointed to be held in the Presbeterian meeting house [p. 8] but when the hour arived the man who kept the key of the house refused to open the door the meeting was thus prevented we came immedeately away and left the people in great confusion journeyed till ~~satturday~~ friday 17 [18] Arived at [Eleazer] Freeman Nickerson's[35] in upper Canada having after we came into Canada passed through a very fine country and f well cultivated and had many peculiar feelings in relation to both the country and people we were kindly received at [Eleazer] freeman Nickersons [p. 9]

20–25 October 1833 • Sunday–Friday

On Sunday the 19th [20th] held meeting at brantford on Sunday at 10 o clock to a very attentive congregation at candle lighting the same evening held meeting at mount plesent [Pleasant] where [Eleazer] freeman Nickerson lived to a very large congregation which gave good heed to the things which were spoken what may be the result we cannot tell but the p[r]ospect is flattering this morning Monday the 20 [21]. enjoy pretty good [p. 10] health with good prospects of doing good calculate to stay in Canada till the Monday of

---

32. A revelation dated this day assured JS and Sidney Rigdon of the well-being of their families. (Revelation, 12 Oct. 1833, in Doctrine and Covenants 94, 1835 ed. [D&C 100].)

33. A revelation dated the previous day promised JS and Rigdon that if they would "declare whatsoever things ye declare in my name, in solemnity of heart, in the spirit of meekness," then the "Holy Ghost shall be shed forth in bearing record unto all things whatsoever ye shall say." (Revelation, 12 Oct. 1833, in Doctrine and Covenants 94:2, 1835 ed. [D&C 100:7–8].)

34. TEXT: Sidney Rigdon handwriting begins.

35. Freeman Nickerson; his wife, Huldah Chapman Nickerson; and their son Levi Nickerson accompanied JS and Sidney Rigdon to the home of Freeman and Huldah's sons Eleazer Freeman Nickerson and Moses Nickerson in Mount Pleasant, Upper Canada. Eleazer Freeman Nickerson was often called Freeman. (Gates, *Lydia Knight's History*, 15–16; Goddard, "Mormons in Mount Pleasant," 2–6.)

next week then the Lord willing will start for home. left Mount plesent tuesday and arived at the Village of Coulburn [Colborne] held meeting at candle
lighting the evening was very bad snowing vehemently we were publickly
opposed by a Wesleyen Methodist he was very tumultious but destitute of reason or knawledge he would not [p. 11] give us an oppertunity to reply this
was on the 22nd we find that conviction is resting on the minds of some we
hope that great good may yet be done in canada which O Lord grant for
thy names sake. during our stay at mount plesent we [had?] an interview with
a Mr Wilkeson of the methodist order being a leader in that sect he could not
stand against our words whether he will receive the the truth the Lord only
knows he seemed to [be?] honest [p. 12] Written at Coulburn wednesday morning the 23 at the house of a Mr Bemer[36] left Mr Bemers on thursday 24 came to
watterford [Waterford] held meeting at 1 o clock to spoke to a small congregation being a very wet day after meeting returned to mount plesent and held
meeting at at candle lighting to a large congregation one man [Eleazer]
Freeman Nickerson declared his full beleif in the truth of the work is with his
wife[37] who is also convinced to be baptised on sunday great excitement [p. 13]
prevailes in every place where we have been the result we leave in the hand of
God. written at the house of [Eleazer] Freeman Nickerson in mount plesent on
friday morning the 24th [25th] **[38]this afternoon at Mr Pattricks expect to
hold a Meeting this Evening &c— people very superstitious Oh God
esta[b]lish thy word among this people held a meeting this Evenning had
an attentive conngregation the spirit gave utterance [p. 14]**

26 October 1833 • Saturday

**Saterday 25th [26th] held a meeting at Mount Plasant [Pleasant] the
people very tender**

27–28 October 1833 • Sunday–Monday

/[39]Sunday 26 [27] held a meeting in Mount plesent [Pleasant]. to a large
congregation twelve came forward and was baptized and many more were
deeply impressed appointed a meeting for this day monday the 27 [28] at the
request of some who desires to be baptized at candle lighting held a meeting
for confirmation we broke bread laid on hands for the gift of the holy spirit

---

36. Probably Philip Beemer. (See Moses Nickerson, Wendhom, [Upper Canada], 29 Dec. 1833, letter to the editor, *The Evening and the Morning Star*, Feb. 1834, 134; and Bennett, "Saints in Upper Canada," 96.)

37. Eliza McAlister Nickerson.

38. TEXT: The remainder of this entry and the entry for 26 October were first inscribed in graphite and traced over in ink—apparently by JS.

39. TEXT: Sidney Rigdon handwriting begins.

had a good [p. 15] meeting the spirit was given in great ~~to~~ power to some and the rest had great ~~pease~~ peace may God carry on his work in this place till all shall know him Amen. Held meeting yesterday at 10 o clock after meeting two came forward and were baptized confirmed them at the watters edge held meeting last evening Ordained br E[leazer] F[reeman] Nickerson to the office of Elder had a good meeting one of the sisters[40] got the [p. 16] gift of toungues which made the saints rejoice may God increse the gifts among them for his sons sake this morning we bend our course for home may the Lord prosper our journey Amen

29 October 1833 · Tuesday

Tuesday the 29th **left Mount pleasant for home**

30–31 October 1833 · Wednesday–Thursday

30th continued on our Journy Wensday and on Thirsday 31st arrived at Buffalo

1–4 November 1833 · Friday–Monday

~~Friday 32th~~ **Started from Buffalo** [p. 17] /[41]Friday, November 1. ~~Left~~ ⟨Nove⟩ Buffalo, N. Y. at 8 o'clock A.M. and arrived at home Monday, the 4th at 10, A.M.[42] found my family all well according to the promise of the Lord. for which blessings I feel to thank his holy name; Amen.[43]

5–13 November 1833 · Tuesday–Wednesday

November 13th nothing ~~of~~ of note transpired from the 4th of Noveber u[n]til this day in the morning at 4 Oh clock I was awoke by Brother Davis[44] knocking at ⟨my⟩ door saying Brother Joseph [p. 18] come git ⟨up⟩ and see the signs in the heavens and I arrose and beheld to my great Joy the stars fall from heaven yea they fell like hail stones[45] a litteral

---

40. Possibly Lydia Goldthwaite Bailey. (Gates, *Lydia Knight's History,* 22.)

41. TEXT: Oliver Cowdery handwriting begins.

42. Freeman and Huldah Chapman Nickerson accompanied JS and Sidney Rigdon from Mount Pleasant, Upper Canada, to Buffalo, New York. From Buffalo, the missionaries continued to Kirtland, Ohio, arriving there on 4 November "after a fateagueing journey." (JS, Kirtland Mills, OH, to Moses Nickerson, Mount Pleasant, Upper Canada, 19 Nov. 1833, in JS Letterbook 1, pp. 62–65.)

43. On JS's hopes for his family's well-being and the revealed promise to that effect, see JS, Journal, 6–12 Oct. 1833; and Revelation, 12 Oct. 1833, in Doctrine and Covenants 94:1, 1835 ed. [D&C 100:1].

44. Possibly Marvel Davis. (Kirtland Township Trustees' Minutes and Poll Book, 21 Oct. 1833, 116, microfilm, U.S. and Canada Record Collection, FHL.)

45. This meteor display, caused by debris from comet Tempel-Tuttle, is one of the more spectacular of all recorded Leonid showers. It appears with especial intensity at about thirty-three-year intervals. Newspapers throughout the United States reported the incident. One described it as "a constant

Leonid meteor shower. Newspapers across the United States reported this spectacular display of "falling stars" in the early morning hours of 13 November 1833. Joseph Smith, like many of his contemporaries, viewed it as a sign that Christ's second coming was imminent. Engraving by Adolf Völlmy from a painting by Karl Jauslin, 1888. (Courtesy *Signs of the Times*, Nampa, ID.)

fullfillment of the word of God as recorded in the holy scriptures and a sure sign that the coming of Christ is clost at hand[46] Oh how marvellous are thy works Oh Lord and I thank thee for thy me[r]cy unto me thy servent Oh Lord save me in thy kingdom for Christ sake Amen [p. 19]

14–19 November 1833 · Thursday–Tuesday

November 19th from the 13th u[n]till this date of nothing of note has transpired since the great sign in the heavins this day my ⟨hart⟩ is somewhat sorrowfull but feel to trust in the Lord the god of Jacob I I have learned in my travels that man is trecheous [treacherous] and selfish but few excepted Brother ⟨Sidney [Rigdon]⟩ is a man whom I love but is not capab[le] of that pure and stedfast love for those who are his benefactors as should posess possess the breast of an man a Presedent of the chu[r]ch of Christ [p. 20] this with some other little things such as a selfish and indipendance of mind which to[o] often manifest distroys the confidence of those who would lay down their lives for him but notwithstanding these things he is ⟨a⟩ very great and good man a man of great power of words and can ⟨gain⟩ the friendship of his hearrers very quick he is a man whom god will uphold if he will continue faithful to his calling O God grant that he may for the Lords sake Amen[47] [p. 21] the man who willeth to do well we should extall his virtues and speak not of his faults behind his back a man who willfuly turneth away from his friend without a cause

---

succession of fire balls, resembling sky rockets, radiating in all directions . . . leaving after them a vivid streak of light, and usually exploding before they disappeared. . . . The flashes of light, though less intense than lightning, were so bright as to awaken people in their beds." (Littmann, *Heavens on Fire,* 272; Denison Olmsted, "The Meteors," *Maryland Gazette,* 21 Nov. 1833, 2.)

46. See, for example, Matthew 24:29; and Revelation 6:12–13; see also Revelation, Sept. 1830–A, in Book of Commandments 29:17 [D&C 29:14]; and Revelation, ca. 7 Mar. 1831, in Book of Commandments 48:36 [D&C 45:42]. In the wake of a worldwide cholera epidemic that killed millions, one commentator, referring to Revelation 6:13, considered the meteor shower "a sure *forerunner*—a merciful SIGN of that great and dreadful Day which the inhabitants of earth shall witness when the SIXTH SEAL SHALL BE OPENED!" Like JS, the Missouri Latter-day Saints, who had just been driven from their homes in Jackson County, interpreted the meteor shower within a millenarian framework. ("Meteoric Phenomenon," *Oswego Palladium,* 27 Nov. 1833, [2]; [Edward Partridge], Liberty, MO, to JS, [19] Nov. 1833, JS Collection, CHL; Parkin, "History of the Latter-day Saints in Clay County," 44–47.)

47. A 12 October 1833 revelation appointed Rigdon "a spokesman unto my servant Joseph" with "power to be mighty in testimony" and "in expounding all scriptures." Rigdon had developed a reputation as a talented preacher while a Regular Baptist minister in Pittsburgh and then as a follower of Alexander Campbell, who later described Rigdon as "the great orator of the Mahoning [Reformed Baptist] Association." After joining the Latter-day Saints, Rigdon became their most prominent orator. (Revelation, 12 Oct. 1833, in Doctrine and Covenants 94:3, 1835 ed. [D&C 100:9–11]; Alexander Campbell, "Anecdotes, Incidents, and Facts," *Millennial Harbinger,* Sept. 1848, 523; Van Wagoner, *Sidney Rigdon,* 22–30.)

is not ~~lightly~~ ⟨easily⟩ ~~to be fogiven~~ ⟨forgiven.⟩ the kindness of a man ⟨should⟩ ~~is never to be forgotten~~ that person who never forsaketh his trust should ever have the highest place for regard in our hearts and our love should never fail but increase more and more and this my disposition and sentiment &c Amen [p. 22] Brother Frederick [G. Williams] ~~is a man who~~ is one of those men in whom I place the greatest confidence and trust for I have found him ever full of love and Brotherly kindness he is not a man of many words but is ever wining because of his constant mind he shall ever have place in my heart and is ever intitled to my confidence /⁴⁸He is perfectly honest and upright, and seeks with all his heart to magnify his presidency in the church of ch[r]ist, but fails in many instances, in consequence of a ~~lack~~ ⟨want⟩ of confidence in himself: God grant that he may [p. 23] overcome all evil: Blessed be brother Frederick, for he shall never want a friend; and his generation after him shall flourish. The Lord hath appointed him an inheritance upon the land of Zion. Yea, and his head shall blossom⟨. And he shall be⟩ as an olive branch that is bowed down with fruit: even so; Amen.

And again, blessed be brother Sidney, also, notwithstanding he shall be high and lifted up, yet he shall bow down under the yoke like unto an ass that [p. 24] coucheth beneath his burthen; that learneth his master's ⟨will⟩ by the stroke of the rod: thus saith the Lord. Yet the Lord will have mercy on him, and he shall bring forth much fruit; even as the ~~vin~~ vine of the choice grape when her clusters are ⟨is⟩ ripe, before the time of the gleaning of the vintage: and the Lord shall make his heart merry as with sweet wine because of him who putteth forth his hand and lifteth him up ~~from~~ ⟨out of⟩ deep mire, and pointeth him out the way, and guideth his [p. 25] feet when he stumbles; and humbleth him in his pride. Blessed are his generations. Nevertheless, one shall hunt after them as a man hunteth after an ass that hath strayed in the wilderness, & straitway findeth him and bringeth him into the fold. Thus shall the Lord watch over his generation that they may be saved: even so; Amen.⁴⁹

Retrospective Note regarding Baptisms

/⁵⁰on the 13th and 14th days of October ~~the~~ I baptized the following person in in Mount Pleasant⁵¹ viz [p. 26]

---

48. TEXT: Oliver Cowdery handwriting begins.

49. More extensive transcripts of JS's revelatory-prophetic blessings for Rigdon and Williams, the two men closest to him in church leadership, are recorded in Patriarchal Blessings, 1:13. JS blessed Oliver Cowdery, the other general church leader, on 18 December 1833, as recorded in this journal. Transcriptions of these blessings will be published under their date in *The Joseph Smith Papers,* Documents series.

50. TEXT: Oliver Cowdery handwriting ends; Frederick G. Williams begins.

51. The date of these baptisms is incorrect. On 13 and 14 October, JS was at the home of Freeman

Moses Chapman Nickerson
Ele[a]zer Freeman Nickerson
Prechard Ramon Strowbridge [Richard Ransom Strobridge]
Andrew Rose
Harvey John Cooper
Samuel Mc Alester [McAlister]
Eliza [McAlister] Nickerson
Mary Gates
Mary Birch [Burtch]
Lidia Baeley [Lydia Goldthwaite Bailey]
Elisabeth Gibbs
Phebe Cook
Margrett Birch [Margaret Burtch]
Esthe Birch [Esther Burtch]

25 November 1833 · Monday

25th Nove. Brothe[r] Orson Hyde & John Gould [p. 27] returned from Zion and brough[t] the melencholly intelegen [intelligence] of the riot in Zion with the inhabitants in pers[e]cuting the breth[r]en.[52]

4–6 December 1833 · Wednesday–Friday

the 4th Dec commenced distributing the type. and commenced setting on the 6 and being prepared to ~~commenced~~ commence our Labours in the printing buisness[53] I ask God in the [p. 28] name of Jesus to establish it for ever and

---

Nickerson in Perrysburg, New York. The baptisms referred to here took place on 27 and 28 October at Mount Pleasant, Upper Canada, the residence of Nickerson's son Eleazer Freeman Nickerson. Scribe Frederick G. Williams may have mistakenly dated this list based on the journal entries for the early part of JS's journey, where the name Freeman Nickerson first appears. (See entries for 13 and 27–28 Oct. 1833.)

52. In August 1833, after hearing of the initial depredations in Missouri, JS dispatched Hyde and Gould to Missouri "with advice to the Saints in their unfortunate situation." An October revelation assured JS, who was concerned for the safety of the two messengers, that "inasmuch as they keep my commandments they shall be saved." The pair returned to Kirtland safely but bore the news of vigilantes driving the Latter-day Saint population from Jackson County. (JS History, vol. A-1, 344; Revelation, 12 Oct. 1833, in Doctrine and Covenants 94:4, 1835 ed. [D&C 100:14]; Jennings, "Expulsion of the Mormons"; and Jennings, "Zion Is Fled.")

53. A council held in Kirtland on 11 September 1833, consisting of JS, Frederick G. Williams, Oliver Cowdery, and other members of the United Firm, resolved that a printing office be established there under the firm name of F. G. Williams & Co. to commence a new newspaper, *The Latter Day Saints' Messenger and Advocate.* The council also resolved to continue publication of *The Evening and the Morning Star*—the church newspaper that was printed at Independence, Missouri, prior to the destruction of the press there in July 1833—until it could be moved back to Missouri.[a] They also planned at this time to publish a weekly political paper.[b] Cowdery began printing the first Kirtland issue of the *Star* a week and a half later.[c] The *Messenger and Advocate* superseded the *Star* the following October. The first regular issue

cause that his word may speedely go for[th] t[o] the Nations of the earth to the accomplishing of his great work in bringing about the restoration of the house of Israel[54]

22 November 1833 • Friday

Nov 22[d]— 1833 my brother [Don] Carlos Smith came to live with me and also Learn th[e] printing art [p. 29]

9 December 1833 • Monday

on the 9 of Dec bro Phineas Young came to board with me to board rent & Lodge at one dollar & twenty five cents p[er] week

11 December 1833 • Wednesday

Bro Wilbor [Wilbur] Denton came to board 11 Dec at one Dollar and twenty five cents p[e]r week[55]

18 December 1833 • Wednesday

1833 Dec. 18 This day the Elders assembled togeth[er] in the printing office [p. 30] and then proceded to bow down before the Lord and dedicate the printing press and all that pertains thereunto to God by mine own hand and confirmed by bro Sidney Rigdon and Hyrum Smith and then proceded to take the first proof sheet of the star[56] edited by Bro Oliv Cowdy [Oliver Cowdery] blessed of the Lord is bro Oliver nevertheless there are [p. 31] are two evils in

---

of the political paper, later titled the *Northern Times,* did not appear until February 1835.[d] (*a.* Minute Book 1, 11 Sept. 1833. *b.* See JS, Kirtland, OH, to Edward Partridge, [Liberty], MO, 5 Dec. 1833, in JS Letterbook 1, pp. 65–70. *c.* JS, Journal, 18 Dec. 1833. *d.* See Crawley, *Descriptive Bibliography,* 47–53.)

54. Drawing upon biblical prophecies, many early Americans anticipated a literal gathering of the descendants of the Old Testament patriarch Jacob, also named Israel. Most conceived of this gathering as a return of the Jewish people to Palestine.[a] JS taught that many descendants of the other Israelite tribes—now scattered throughout the earth—would be gathered to Zion, the New Jerusalem, in America. A primary mission of the early Mormon publishing effort was to facilitate a "gathering" through which all who accepted the message of the restored gospel, were baptized and confirmed into the church, and immigrated to Mormon gathering centers would receive the blessings promised to Jacob's descendants.[b] (*a.* Adler, "American Policy toward Zion," 251–259; Whalen, "Millenarianism and Millennialism," 117, 124. *b.* See, for example, Book of Mormon, 1830 ed., 496–501, 566 [3 Nephi 20:11–21:29; Ether 13:4–8]; JS, Kirtland, OH, to N. C. Saxton, Rochester, NY, 4 Jan. 1833, in JS Letterbook 1, pp. 14–18; and JS, "Church History," *Times and Seasons,* 1 Mar. 1842, 3:710 [Articles of Faith 1:10].)

55. Like JS's brother Don Carlos, both Wilbur Denton and Phineas Young had come to work with Oliver Cowdery in the newly established printing operation at Kirtland. (Oliver Cowdery, Kirtland Mills, OH, to Ambrose Palmer, New Portage, OH, 30 Oct. 1833, in Cowdery, Letterbook, 4–5; Oliver Cowdery, Kirtland, OH, to William W. Phelps, [Liberty, MO], 11 Dec. 1833, in Cowdery, Letterbook, 13.)

56. That is, the proof sheet of the first issue of the resuscitated *The Evening and the Morning Star* in Kirtland (December 1833).

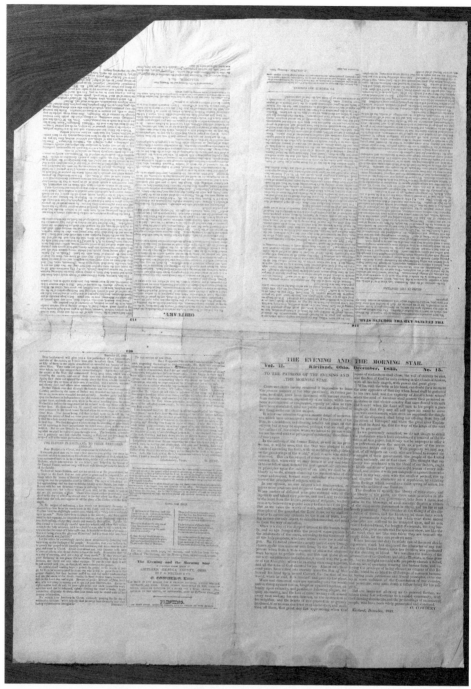

First Ohio issue of *The Evening and the Morning Star.* After the Mormon printing press in Independence, Missouri, was destroyed, the Saints began printing the church newspaper in Kirtland, Ohio. The "first proof sheet of the star" referred to in Joseph Smith's journal entry of 18 December 1833 was an uncut sheet of the December 1833 issue of *The Evening and the Morning Star,* like the one shown here. (Church History Library, Salt Lake City. Photograph by Welden C. Andersen.)

him that he must needs forsake or he cannot altogeth[er] escape the buffettings of the advers[ar]y if he shall forsak these evils he shall be forgiven and shall be made like unto the bow which the Lord hath set in the heavens he shall be a sign and an ensign unto the nations[57] behold he is blessed of the Lord for his constancy [p. 32] and steadfastness in the work of the Lord wherefore he shall be blessed in his generation and they shall never be cut off and he shall be helped out of many troubles and if he keep the ~~commandmend~~ ⟨commandments⟩ and harken unto the ⟨council of the⟩ Lord ~~his and~~ his rest shall be glorious and again blessed of the Lord is my father and also my mother and my brothers and my sisters for they shall [p. 33] yet find redemption in the house of the Lord and their of[f]springs shall be a blessing a Joy and a comfort unto them blessed is my mother for her soul is ever fill[ed] with benevolence and phylanthropy and notwithstanding her age yet she shall receive strength and shall be comforted in the midst of her house and she shall have eternal life and blessed is my father for the hand of the Lord shall be [p. 34] over him for he shall see the affliction ⟨of his children⟩ pass away and when his head is fully ripe he shall behold himself as an olive tree whose branches are bowed down with much fruit he shall also possess a mansion on high blessed of the Lord is my brothe[r] Hyram for the integrity of his heart he shall be girt about with truth and faithfulness shall be the strength of his loins [p. 35] from generation to generation he shall be a shaft in the hand of his God to exicute Judgment upon his enemies and he shall be hid by the hand of the Lord that none of his secret parts shall be discovered[58] unto his hu[r]t his name shall be accounted a blessing among men and when he is in trouble and great tribulation hath come upon him [p. 36] he shall remember the God of Jacob and he will shield him from the power of satan and he shall receive ~~counel~~ ⟨councel⟩ in the house of the most high that he may be streng[t]hened in hope that the goings ⟨of his feet⟩ may be established for ever blessed of the Lord is bro Samuel [Smith] because the Lord shall say unto him Saml., Saml.,[59] therefore he shall be made a teache[r] in [p. 37] the hous of the Lord and the Lord shall mature his mind in Judgment and thereby he shall obtain the esteem and fellowship of his brethren and his soul shall be established and he shall benefit th[e] house of the Lord because he shall obtain answer to prayer in his faithfulness— Bro William [Smith] is as the firce Lion [p. 38] who devideth not the spoil because of his strength and in the pride of his heart he will neglect the more ~~weightier~~ weighty matters until his soul is bowed down in sorrow and then he shall

---

57. See Isaiah 5:26; 11:12; compare Book of Mormon, 1830 ed., 91, 98 [2 Nephi 15:26; 21:12].

58. See Isaiah 3:17.

59. An allusion to 1 Samuel 3:10.

return and call on th[e] name of his God and shall find forgivness and
shall wax valient therefor he shall be saved unto the utter most and as the
[p. 39] roaring Lion of the forest in the midst of his prey so shall the hand of
his generation be lifted up against those who are set on high that fight against
the God of Israel fearless and unda[u]nted shall they be in battle in avenging the
rongs of th[e] innocent and relieving the oppressed therfor the blessings of
the God of Jacob [p. 40] shall be in the midst of his house notwithstanding his
rebelious heart and ⟨now⟩ O God let the residue of my fathers house ever come
up in remembrance before thee that thou mayest save them from the hand of
the oppressor and establish their feet upon the rock of ages that they may have
place in thy house and be saved in thy Kingdom [p. 41] and let all these things
be even as I have said for Christs sake Amen[60]

19 December 1833 • Thursday

Dec 19 This day Bros William Pratt and David Pattin [David W. Patten]
took their Journey to the Land of Zion for the purpose of bearing dispatches to
the Brethren in that place from Kirtland[61] o may God grant it a blessing for
Zion as a kind Angel from heaven Amen [p. 42]

16 January 1834 • Thursday

**January 16ᵗʰ 1834 this night at Brother Jinkins [Wilkins Jenkins]
Salisbury[62] came from home Oh Lord keep us and my Family safe untill I
can return to them again[63] Oh my God have mercy on my Bretheren in
Zion for Christ Sake Amen**

---

60. Oliver Cowdery noted that these blessings were "given by vision and the spirit of prophecy" when
he copied more complete transcripts of the blessings into the first book of patriarchal blessings. However,
the copied transcripts do not mention the weaknesses of Cowdery. Compare the assessment of Cowdery
with similar assessments of JS's counselors Sidney Rigdon and Frederick G. Williams in the blessings they
received a month earlier. (Patriarchal Blessings, 1:8–13; JS, Journal, 14–19 Nov. 1833; transcriptions of these
blessings will be published under their dates in *The Joseph Smith Papers,* Documents series.)

61. Copies of a letter, a revelation, and possibly an earlier letter, all written by JS in response to news
from Missouri, were dispatched to Missouri by way of Pratt and Patten. The documents expressed empa-
thy with the exiled church members and counseled them to remain in Missouri, retain title to their lands
if at all financially possible, collect accounts of the atrocities committed against them, and seek "evry lawful means to obtain redress of your enemies." (JS, Kirtland, OH, to Edward Partridge, [Liberty], MO,
5 Dec. 1833, in JS Letterbook 1, pp. 65–70; JS, Kirtland Mills, OH, to Edward Partridge et al., Liberty,
MO, 10 Dec. 1833, in JS Letterbook 1, pp. 70–75; Revelation, 16 and 17 Dec. 1833, in Doctrine and
Covenants 97, 1835 ed. [D&C 101].)

62. Salisbury and his wife, Katharine Smith Salisbury, JS's sister, lived in the area of Chardon, Ohio.

63. JS apparently returned home to Kirtland within a week. (See "The Elders of the Church in Kirtland,
to Their Brethren Abroad," *The Evening and the Morning Star,* Feb. 1834, 135–136; Mar. 1834, 142–144; Apr.
1834, 152.)

11 January 1834 • Saturday[64]

/[65]January 11, 1834. This evening Joseph Smith Jr, Frederick G. Williams, Newel K. Whitney, John Johnson, Oliver Cowdery, and Orson Hyde united in prayer[66] and asked the Lord to grant the following petition: [p. 43]

Firstly, That the Lord would grant that our lives might be precious in his sight, that he would watch over our persons and give his angels charge concerning us and our families that no evil nor unseen hand might be permitted to harm us.

Secondly, That the Lord would also hold the lives of all the United Firm, and not suffer that any of them shall be taken.

Thirdly, That the Lord would grant that our brother Joseph might prevail over [p. 44] his enemy, even Docter P. [Doctor Philastus] Hurlbut,[67] who has threatened his life, whom brother Joseph has ⟨caused to be⟩ taken with a precept;[68] that the Lord would fill the heart of the Court with a spirit to do

---

64. JS apparently penned the above 16 January entry during his trip away from Kirtland. On JS's return, Oliver Cowdery apparently used notes taken at the previous Sunday's prayer meeting to compose this entry.

65. TEXT: Oliver Cowdery handwriting begins.

66. JS, Williams, Whitney, Johnson, and Sidney Rigdon (not present on this occasion) constituted the Kirtland branch of the United Firm. Cowdery, a member of the Missouri branch of the firm, was appointed four months earlier to represent the other members of that branch.[a] Hyde, appointed a clerk to the church presidency in June 1833, had recently returned from Missouri with the report of the brewing violence there.[b] The economic interests of the firm were reflected in their prayer concerning church debts, the printing operation, and the well-being of the Missouri Latter-day Saints. (*a.* Backman, *Heavens Resound*, 71; Minute Book 1, 11 Sept. 1833. *b.* Minute Book 1, 6 June 1833; see also JS, Journal, 25 Nov. 1833.)

67. Doctor Philastus Hurlbut, a former Latter-day Saint, had worked vigorously to discredit JS and the church. During summer 1833, JS noted that the church was "suffering great persicution on account of" Hurlbut, who was "lieing in a wonderful manner and the peopl are running after him and giveing him mony to brake down mormanism which much endangers our lives."[a] In summer and autumn 1833, Hurlbut traveled in Ohio, Massachusetts, Pennsylvania, and New York to collect statements against JS by his former neighbors and to build a case that the Book of Mormon had been copied from a work of fiction written by Solomon Spalding. On his return in mid-December, Hurlbut defamed JS in lectures and stirred up further persecution.[b] Antagonism against the church in Ohio grew to such proportions that Mormon Heber C. Kimball reported, "Our enemies were raging and threatening destruction upon us, and we had to guard night after night, and for weeks were not permitted to take off our clothes, and were obliged to lay with our fire locks in our arms."[c] (*a.* JS, Kirtland, OH, to William W. Phelps et al., [Independence, MO], 18 Aug. 1833, JS Collection, CHL. *b.* Winchester, *Origin of the Spaulding Story*, 9–11. *c.* Kimball, "History," 11; see also Grua, "Joseph Smith and the 1834 D. P. Hurlbut Case," 35–38.)

68. A "command in writing by a Justice of Peace, or other Officer, for bringing a person or records before him."[a] Hurlbut threatened JS's life. JS's cousin George A. Smith later recalled that "in delivering lectures he [Hurlbut] had said he would wash his hands in Joseph Smith's blood."[b] Kirtland justice of the peace John Dowen later claimed that when Hurlbut said he would "kill" JS, "he meant he would kill Mormonism."[c] On 21 December 1833, JS filed a complaint with the Kirtland justice of the peace, whose decision in a preliminary hearing stated that JS "had reason to fear that Doctor P. Hurlbut would Beat wound or kill him."[d] The justice of the peace then issued a warrant for Hurlbut's arrest.[e] This legal action

justice, and cause that the law of the land may be magnified in bringing him to justice.

Fourthly, That the Lord would provide, in the order of his Providence, the bishop of this Church[69] with means sufficient to discharge every debt that the Firm owes,[70] in due season, that [p. 45] the Church may not be braught into disrepute, and the saints be afflicted by the hands of their enemies.

Fifthly, That the Lord would protect our printing press from the hands of evil men,[71] and give us means to send forth his word, even his gospel that the ears of all may hear it, and also that we may print his scriptures;[72] and also that he would give those who were appointed to conduct the press,[73] wisdom sufficient that the cause [p. 46] may not be hindered, but that men's eyes may thereby be opened to see the truth.

Sixthly, That the Lord would deliver Zion, and gather in his scattered people, to possess it in peace;[74] and also, while in their dispersion, that he would provide for them that they perish not with hunger nor cold. And finally, that God in the name of Jesus would gather his elect speedily, and unveil his face that his saints [p. 47] might behold his glory and dwell with him; Amen.

---

was intended to impede Hurlbut from carrying out the threat. Preliminary evaluation of JS's complaint against Hurlbut began two days later, on 13 January. On the outcome, see 27n78 and 38n127 herein. (*a.* "Precept," in *Law-Dictionary,* 5:271. *b.* George A. Smith, in *Journal of Discourses,* 15 Nov. 1864, 11:8. *c.* John C. Dowen, Statement, 2 Jan. 1885, 3, Manuscripts about Mormons at Chicago History Museum, Research Center, Chicago Historical Society. *d.* Geauga Co., OH, Court of Common Pleas, 31 Mar. 1834, final record bk. P, 432, microfilm, U.S. and Canada Record Collection, FHL. *e.* Dowen, Statement, 2 Jan. 1885, 3.)

69. Newel K. Whitney.

70. Part of the firm's debt stemmed from the purchase of the French farm—the property upon which the House of the Lord was being built. In the coming months, efforts were made to retire church debts. On 20 February 1834, a church council commissioned Orson Hyde and Orson Pratt to raise funds to retire this debt. (Minute Book 1, 20 Feb. 1834.)

71. In a letter to Edward Partridge and others, JS outlined Oliver Cowdery's difficulties returning from New York City with a press and type, "hauling them up in the midst of mobs." (JS, Kirtland, OH, to Edward Partridge et al., Clay Co., MO, 30 Mar. 1834, in Cowdery, Letterbook, 30–36.)

72. Publication of a compilation of revelations, the Book of Commandments, ceased when a mob destroyed the press in Missouri. The mandate to publish the revelations was explicit. A new compilation, the Doctrine and Covenants, was published in 1835. (See Revelation, 4 Dec. 1831, in Doctrine and Covenants 89:4, 1835 ed. [D&C 72:20–23]; and Minute Book 2, 12 Nov. 1831 and 30 Apr. 1832.)

73. A "Literary Firm" had been appointed to conduct the press. Its active members at this time were JS, Cowdery, Sidney Rigdon, and Williams. (Cook, *Law of Consecration,* 43–44.)

74. Less than a month earlier, a revelation promised that the Missouri Latter-day Saints would yet possess their lands in Jackson County: "Zion shall not be moved out of her place, notwithstanding her children are scattered, they that remain and are pure in heart shall return and come to their inheritances." This echoed an earlier revelation that stated, "Zion shall be redeemed, although she is chastened for a little season." (Revelation, 16 and 17 Dec. 1833, in Doctrine and Covenants 97:4, 1835 ed. [D&C 101:17–18]; Revelation, 12 Oct. 1833, in Doctrine and Covenants 94:4, 1835 ed. [D&C 100:13].)

28 January 1834 • Tuesday

On the 13th of March A.D. 1833, Docter P. [Doctor Philastus] Hurlbut came to my house; I conversed with him considerably about the book of Mormon. He was ordained to the office of an elder in this Church under the hand of Sidney Rigdon on the [*blank*] ⟨**18th**⟩ of March in the same year above written.[75] According to my best recollection, I heard him say, in the [p. 48] course of conversing with him, that if he ever became convinced that the book of Mormon was false, he would be the cause of my destruction, &c.

He was tried before a counsel of high priests on the 21ˢᵗ day of June, 1833, and his license restored to him again, ~~it~~ ⟨he⟩ previously having been ~~taken by the Church at~~ ⟨cut off from the⟩ Church by the bishop's court. He was finally cut off from the church [p. 49] a few days after having his license restored,[76] on the 21ˢᵗ of June. /[77]and then saught the distruction of the sainst [saints] in this place and more particularly myself and family and as the Lord has in his mercy Delivered me out of his hand. till the present and also the church that he has not prevailed viz th[e] 28 day of Jany [p. 50] 1834 for which I off[e]r the gratitud of my heart to Allmighty God for the sam[e] and on this night Bro Olivr [Oliver Cowdery] and bro Frederick [G. Williams] and my self bowed before the Lord being agre[e]d and united in pray that God would continu to deliver me and my brethr[e]n from ⟨him⟩ that he may not prevail again[st] us in the law suit that is pending[78] [p. 51] and also that God would soften down the hearts of E[lijah] Smith J[osiah] Jones Lowd [Austin Loud] & [Azariah] Lyman and also [Andrew] Bardsley[79] that they might obey the gospel or if they would not

---

75. See Minute Book 1, 18 Mar. 1833.

76. A "Bishops Council of High Priests" on 3 June 1833 excommunicated Hurlbut from the church for "unchristian conduct with the female sex while on a mission to the east." Hurlbut, who was not present at this council, appealed the decision to a "Presidents council of high priests." The president's council, which met on 21 June 1833, upheld the bishop's council but restored Hurlbut to fellowship after he confessed. Two days later, the council reopened Hurlbut's case. After hearing from two witnesses who testified that Hurlbut had stated "that he had deceived Joseph Smith's God," the council again deprived him of his membership. (Minute Book 1, 3, 21, and 23 June 1833.)

77. TEXT: Oliver Cowdery handwriting ends; Frederick G. Williams begins.

78. The preliminary evaluation of JS's complaint against Hurlbut began two weeks earlier. Justice of the Peace William Holbrook, who heard testimony from 13 to 15 January 1834, found that JS had just cause to issue the complaint and ordered Hurlbut to keep the peace and to appear before the court of common pleas at the start of its next term, 31 March 1834. On 22 January 1834, JS reported to the Missouri Latter-day Saints that Hurlbut's influence had been "pritty much distroyed" as a result of the 13–15 January preliminary hearing. Thus, the "spirit of hostility seams to be broken down in a good degree," and "there is not quite so much danger of a Mob upon us as there has been." (Geauga Co., OH, Court of Common Pleas, 31 Mar. 1834, final record bk. P, 431–432, microfilm, U.S. and Canada Record Collection, FHL; JS et al., Kirtland, OH, to "Brethren scattered from Zion," 22 Jan. 1834, in JS Letterbook 1, p. 81.)

79. These individuals, who never affiliated with the church, owned over forty acres of property in the "Kirtland Flats"—the lowlands in northern and eastern Kirtland. In addition, Loud and Lyman jointly

repent that the lord would send faithful saints to purchase their farms that this stake[80] may be strengthened and ⟨its⟩ ~~the~~ borders enlarged **O Lord grant it for Christ Sake Amen [p. 52]**

31 January 1834 · Friday

/[81]31 Janry 1834 it is my prayer to the Lord that three thousand subscriber may be added to the Star in the term of three yea[rs]

———— ❧ ————

Editorial Note

On 17 February 1834, JS organized a high council, which would serve "the purpose of settling important difficulties which might arise in the church."[82] A week later, on 24 February, the high council met at JS's home to hear a report from Lyman Wight and Parley P. Pratt, envoys representing the Latter-day Saints in Missouri. When Wight and Pratt relayed the plight of their fellow exiles and expressed the desire of the Missouri Saints to return to their Jackson County properties, JS "arose and said that he was going to Zion to assist in redeeming it."[83] A revelation dated the same day instructed eight men to travel east in pairs to solicit funds and recruit volunteers for an expedition to Missouri to reinstate exiled Mormons to their homes and property. The eight "journeyed two and two in different routes."[84] The revelation appointed JS to travel with Parley P. Pratt, Lyman Wight with Sidney Rigdon, Hyrum Smith with Frederick G. Williams, and Orson Hyde with Orson Pratt.[85] Journal keeping resumed in late February as JS began his journey. For the next three weeks, JS and Pratt traveled together through western Pennsylvania and New York. The missionary pairs reunited at a conference in Geneseo, New York, in mid-March.

———— ❧ ————

26–28 February 1834 · Wednesday–Friday

Wensdy ⟨Febuary⟩ 26ᵗʰ Started from home to obtain volenteers for

---

owned a sawmill and a gristmill. Bardsley sold a parcel of land to Latter-day Saint Edmund Bosley on 2 June 1834. Portions of this land were subsequently sold to JS on 23 October 1835 and 2 November 1836. (Geauga Co., OH, Duplicate Tax Records, 1834, "No. 2 Kirtland," 17, 21–22, 25, microfilm, U.S. and Canada Record Collection, FHL; Geauga Co., OH, Deed Records, 2 June 1834, 20:302–303, microfilm, U.S. and Canada Record Collection, FHL; Geauga Co., OH, Deed Records, 23 Oct. 1835, 21:227; 2 Nov. 1835, 22:567–568, microfilm, U.S. and Canada Record Collection, FHL.)

80. Kirtland was designated a "stake to Zion" in 1832; revelations in 1833 spoke of building up the Kirtland stake. (Revelation, 26 Apr. 1832, in Doctrine and Covenants 86:4, 1835 ed. [D&C 82:13]; Revelation, 2 Aug. 1833–B, in Doctrine and Covenants 83:1, 1835 ed. [D&C 94:1]; Revelation, 4 June 1833, in Doctrine and Covenants 96:1, 1835 ed. [D&C 96:1]; see also Minute Book 1, 28 Sept. 1833.)

81. TEXT: Frederick G. Williams handwriting begins.

82. Minutes, 17 Feb. 1834, in Doctrine and Covenants 5, 1835 ed. [D&C 102].

83. Minute Book 1, 24 Feb. 1834.

84. Pratt, *Autobiography,* 117.

85. Revelation, 24 Feb. 1834, in Doctrine and Covenants 101, 1844 ed. [D&C 103].

Zion Thursday 27th ~~startted~~ Started Stayed at Br Roundays [Shadrach Roundy's][86] 28th Stayed at a strangers who entertained us very kindly ⟨⟨in⟩ Westleville [Wesleyville]⟩

1–2 March 1834 · Saturday–Sunday

March 1th arived at Br [Job] Lewis and on the 2d the Sabath Brother Barly [Parley P. Pratt] preached in this place[87] and I preached in the evening had a good [p. 53] meeting there is a small church in this place tha[t] seem to be strong in th[e] faith Oh may God keep them in the faith and save them and lead them to Zion

3 March 1834 · Monday

March 3^d this morning intend to ~~Started~~ on our Journy to ⟨the⟩ east ⟨But did not start⟩[88] O may God bless us with the gift of utterance to accomplish the Journy and the Errand on which we are sent and return s◊◊[89] to the land of Kirtland [p. 54] and ⟨find⟩ my Family all well O Lord bless my little children with health and long life[90] to do good in th◊ generation for Christs ~~sake~~ sake Amen

Notes[91]

/[92]Kirtland	Geauger [Geauga]	Ohio
Thom[p]son	——	——
Springfield	Erie	Pensy
Elk crick [Creek]	^ — —	vania [Pennsylvania]
Westfield		
Laona	Chautauque	N[ew] york
Silver Creek		
Perrysburgh	Cateragus [Cattaraugus]	
Collins	Genesee [actually Erie]	
China		[p. 55]

---

86. At Elk Creek, Pennsylvania.

87. Westfield, New York.

88. TEXT: Insertion in the handwriting of Parley P. Pratt.

89. TEXT: Possibly "save [safe]" or "soon".

90. JS and his wife Emma had lost four of their six children.

91. This table—listing settlements, villages, and townships and identifying them by county and state—apparently charts a proposed itinerary for the recruitment and fund-raising mission. Subsequent journal entries indicate that the men did not actually visit all these locations and that they stopped at others not listed here.

92. TEXT: Unidentified handwriting begins.

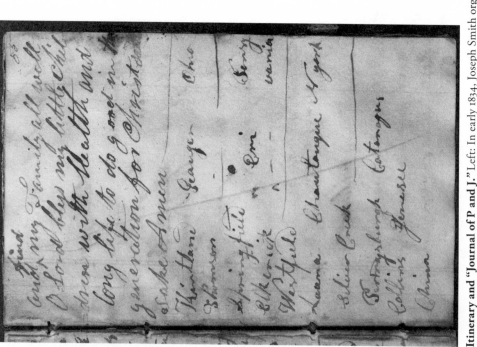

Itinerary and "Journal of P and J." Left: In early 1834, Joseph Smith organized an expedition to Missouri to help reinstate exiled Latter-day Saints on their lands in Jackson County. Smith's journal includes an itinerary of places that he and Parley P. Pratt planned to visit to raise money and recruit for the expedition. Preceding the itinerary is a plea written by Smith for the welfare of his family. Handwriting of Joseph Smith and an unidentified scribe. Right: Following an itinerary of towns to visit are a financial note and the beginning of the "Journal of P and J" —kept by Pratt as a mission journal for both Smith and himself. Handwriting of Parley P. Pratt, Frederick G. Williams, an unidentified scribe, and Joseph Smith. JS, Journal, 1832–1834, pp. 55–56. JS Collection, Church History Library, Salt Lake City. (Photograph by Welden C. Andersen.)

Warsaw

Geneseeo [Geneseo]   Levingston [Livingston]

Sentervill [Centreville]   —— [actually Allegany]

Cattlin [Catlin]   Alleghany [actually Tioga]

Spafford   ~~Spafford~~ ⟨——⟩

                                            Onondaga

/⁹³John Gould payed me on papers—⁹⁴ $ 1.50/⁹⁵

———— ℰℜ ————

Editorial Note

The following section of the journal, through the beginning of the entry for 14 March, was kept by Parley P. Pratt for both JS and himself as they traveled to New York. Pratt's use of "I"—as in "I preached"—evidently refers to himself. Pratt refers to JS as "Brother Joseph" and never refers to himself in the third-person narrative voice.

———— ℰℜ ————

/⁹⁶Journal of P[arley P. Pratt] and J[S]

4–6 March 1834 • Tuesday–Thursday

March 4ᵗʰ took our Journy from Westfield ⟨accompanyed By Br goold [John Gould]⟩ rode 33 miles arrived in [*blank*] ⟨**Vil[l]anova**⟩ staid all night with a Brother [Reuben] Mc Bride,⁹⁷ next morning went 4⁹⁸ m;s [miles] to Br Nicisons [Freeman Nickerson's]⁹⁹ found him and [p. 56] his house hold full of faith and of the holy spirit we cald the church together and Related unto them what had hapened to our Brethren in Zion opened to them the prophesyes and revelations concerning the order of the gethering to Zion¹⁰⁰ and the means of her

---

93. TEXT: Unidentified handwriting ends; Frederick G. Williams begins.

94. Probably a subscription to *The Evening and the Morning Star*. The sum of $1.50 would have paid for eighteen months of the paper. (JS, Journal, 1832–1834 [undated notes], p. 49 herein; Notice, *The Evening and the Morning Star*, Mar. 1834, 144.)

95. TEXT: Frederick G. Williams handwriting ends.

96. TEXT: Parley P. Pratt handwriting begins.

97. Reuben McBride later recalled JS's staying with him. (McBride, Reminiscences, 1.)

98. TEXT: Or "14" or "11".

99. At Perrysburg, New York. (1830 U.S. Census, Perrysburg, Cattaraugus Co., NY, 224.)

100. When the Latter-day Saints were first settling in Missouri, a JS revelation stated that the gathering should "be done in order" by purchasing lands. A revelation dated 16 and 17 December 1833—less than three months before JS departed on his recruitment and fund-raising mission—directed the Saints to continue observing this order by purchasing lands in and around Jackson County. (Revelation, 1 Aug. 1831, in Book of Commandments 59:64–69 [D&C 58:52–56]; Revelation, 16 and 17 Dec. 1833, in Doctrine and Covenants 97, 1835 ed. [D&C 101].)

Redemtion and Brother Joseph Prophesyed to them and the spirit of the Lord
came mightily upon them and with all redyness a the yo[u]ng and mid[d]le aged
volenteered for Zion [p. 57] same evening held 2 meetings 3 or 4 miles Apart.[101]
next day March 6th held another Meeting at Bro Nicisons the few un Believeers
that atended were outragious and the meeting ended in complaet confusion

7 March 1834 · Friday

we March 7 started ~~towds~~ on our Journy accompanyed By Br Nicison
[Freeman Nickerson] Leaving Brs goold [John Gould] and Mathews[102] to Prepare ⟨and gether up⟩ the companys in the churches in that region and meet us
in Ohio Reddy for Zion the first of May we arrived after dark to the [p. 58]
county seat of Cat[t]araugus cald Elicutville [Ellicottville] triyed every tavern
in the place But Being Court time we found no room[103] But were compeled to
ride on in a dark muddy rainy night we found shelter in rideing 1 mile Paid
higher for our fare than tavern price

8 March 1834 · Saturday

March 8th continued our journy came to Palmersville [Farmersville] to
the house of Elder Mc gown [Marcellus McCown] were Invited to go to Esq
_ _ _ _ _ ⟨walkers—⟩[104]— to spend the Evening[105] [p. 59] we found them verry
friendly and somewhat Believeing tarryed all night

9–12 March 1834 · Sunday–Wednesday

sunday 9 held meeting in a school house had great attentian found a few
desyples who were firm in faith and after meeting found many Believeing and
could hardly get a way from them we apointed A meeting in freedom for Monday 10th and are now at Mr Cowderyes [Warren Cowdery's] in the full Enjoyment of ⟨all⟩ the Blessings Both temporal and spiritual [p. 60] of which
we stand in need or are found worthy to receive[106] held meting on [*illegible*]

---

101. JS may have held a meeting in Lodi, New York, approximately four miles to the east of Perrysburg. A subscription to *The Evening and the Morning Star* for Nathan Chase at the West Lodi post office
is recorded in the back of the journal. (See p. 49 herein.)

102. Possibly David Mathews. (Warren Cowdery, Freedom, NY, to Oliver Cowdery, Kirtland, OH,
14 Jan. 1834, *The Evening and the Morning Star*, Jan. 1834, 127; Minute Book 1, 6 June 1835.)

103. Itinerant circuit courts commonly traveled through rural nineteenth-century America, stop-
ping in county seats and important municipalities to bring the state's legal apparatus to its citizens.
(Mahoney, *Provincial Lives*, 178–190.)

104. TEXT: JS inserted "walkers—" over dashed line.

105. 1830 U.S. Census, Farmersville Township, Cattaraugus Co., NY, 149, lists Leonard Walker,
Thomas Walker, and Billings Walker living near Marcellus McCown at Farmersville, New York.

106. Oliver Cowdery's older brother Warren had expressed sympathy with the persecuted Mormons

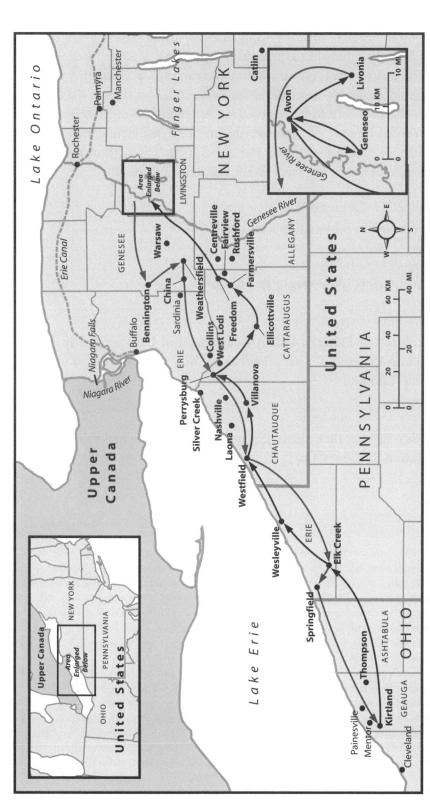

Recruiting mission, February–March 1834. Joseph Smith and Parley P. Pratt traveled to western New York to enlist recruits and raise funds for the expedition to help exiled Latter-day Saints reoccupy their lands in Jackson County, Missouri. (Research by Richard L. Jensen and Mark Ashurst-McGee. Design by John Hamer.)

Monday ~~moved~~ Preach^d to crowd ⟨congregation⟩ at Eve preacht again to a hous crowded full to overflowing after meting I proposed if any wished to obey if they would make it manifest we would stay to administer at another meeting a young man of the methodist order arose and testifie^d his faith in the fulness of ⟨the⟩ gospel and desired to Be Baptised we Appointed another meting and the next [p. 61] day tuesday 11th held meeting and Baptised Heman hide [Hyde]^107 after which we rode 9 m;s [miles] Put up with . . . . ⟨Stewards tavern⟩ next day rode 36 m;s to farthers [Father Edmund] Bosleys.^108

13 March 1834 • Thursday

~~16~~ ⟨13⟩ thursday held meting I Preachd

14 March 1834 • Friday

friday 14th **in F[ather Alvah] Beamans^109**

15 March 1834 • Saturday

March 15th at Father [Alvah] Beamans and Brother Sidny [Sidney Rigdon] and Lyman [Wight] arived at his house to ⟨the⟩ Joy of our Souls in Lyvona [Livonia]^110

16 March 1834 • Sunday

Sunday 16th Brother Sidny [Sidney Rigdon] preached to a very large congregation ⟨in Genes[e]o⟩^111

---

in Missouri; he joined the church within a few months of this visit. (Warren Cowdery, Freedom, NY, to Oliver Cowdery, Kirtland, OH, 14 Jan. 1834, *The Evening and the Morning Star,* Jan. 1834, 127; Warren Cowdery, Freedom, NY, to Oliver Cowdery, Kirtland, OH, 1 Sept. 1834, *The Evening and the Morning Star,* Sept. 1834, 189; see also Revelation, 25 Nov. 1834, in Doctrine and Covenants 99, 1835 ed. [D&C 106].)

107. Parley P. Pratt later recorded that Hyde and "some thirty or forty others, were all baptized and organized into a branch of the Church." (Pratt, *Autobiography,* 117.)

108. At Livonia, New York. (Livingston Co., NY, Deed Records, 1:257, microfilm, U.S. and Canada Record Collection, FHL.)

109. At Avon, New York. Parley P. Pratt later recalled that JS reminisced with Beaman, who "had been intimate with Joseph long before the first organization of the Church." (Noble, Reminiscences, 5; Pratt, *Autobiography,* 118.)

110. JS's history states this somewhat differently: "while at father Beaman's, Elders Rigdon and Wight arrived, much to the joy of their souls, and the Saints in Livona." (JS History, vol. A-1, 447.)

111. Parley P. Pratt later wrote that in Geneseo, he and JS "met with the other Elders who had started from Kirtland on the same mission, and with others who were local, and held a general Conference," at which both JS and Sidney Rigdon "addressed the crowds in great plainness of speech with mighty power." (Pratt, *Autobiography,* 117–118; see also Noble, Reminiscences, 5–7.)

17 March 1834 • Monday

Monday 17 Brother [p. 62] ~~Bro~~ Parly [Parley P. Pratt] preached in the afternoon[112]

18 March 1834 • Tuesday

Tusdy 18ᵗʰ Stayed at Father Boslys [Edmund Bosley's] all day[113]

19 March 1834 • Wednesday

Wensday 19ᵗʰ Started for home arrived at Brother Whitheys [Isaac McWithy's][114] **tarried all night &c**

20 March 1834 • Thursday

Thursday 20ᵗʰ Started on ⟨our⟩ Journy at noon took dinner at Brother Joseph Holbrooks,[115] **and at night tryed three times to git keept in the name of Deciples, and could not be keept, [p. 63] after night we found a man who would keep us for mony thus we see that there ⟨is⟩ more place for mony than for Jesus ⟨Deciples or⟩ the Lamb of God, the name of the man is ~~Wilson Rauben Wilson~~ Reuben Wilson that would not keep us without mony ⟨he lived in China⟩ &c.**[116]

---

112. On this day, JS conducted a conference of elders at Alvah Beaman's home in Avon, New York. The meeting's purposes were to recruit men to "assist in the redemption of Zion according to the commandment" and to raise money to purchase Missouri land and meet debts at Kirtland, Ohio. The conference also reassigned Parley P. Pratt to another companion, voting that JS "go to Kirtland soon" with Rigdon and Wight. JS needed to return to Kirtland to testify against Doctor Philastus Hurlbut. (Minute Book 1, 17 Mar. 1834; see Revelation, 24 Feb. 1834, in Doctrine and Covenants 101:5, 1844 ed. [D&C 103:22–23].)

113. At the conference held the previous day at Avon, New York, Edmund Bosley and others agreed to try to raise two thousand dollars by 1 April 1834 to relieve Kirtland debts. (Minute Book 1, 17 Mar. 1834.)

114. At Bennington, Genesee County, New York. (Genesee Co., NY, Deed Records, 7 Apr. 1832, 29:337, microfilm, U.S. and Canada Record Collection, FHL.)

115. At Wethersfield, Genesee (now Wyoming) County, New York. (*History of the Lafayette Hinckley and Alsina Elisabeth Brimhall Holbrook Families,* 14.)

116. Jesus enjoined his disciples to travel without money, to rely on the hospitality of others, and to condemn those who would not receive them as his representatives. This instruction had been reiterated in revelations for latter-day missionaries, who were not to return to those who rejected them. This may explain why Wilson's name and place of residence were noted. (Matthew 10:9–15; Revelation, July 1830–A, in Book of Commandments 25:28 [D&C 24:18]; Revelation, 22 and 23 Sept. 1832, in Doctrine and Covenants 4:12, 15–16, 1835 ed. [D&C 84:77–78, 86–94]; compare JS, Journal, 26 Mar. 1834.)

21 March 1834 • Friday

March 21ᵗʰ came to a man by the name of Starks 6ᵗʰ miles East of Springville¹¹⁷ [p. 64]

22 March 1834 • Saturday

22ᵈ came and tarri[e]d with Vincen nights [Vinson Knight] in Perrysburg Co— of Cattaraugus

23 March 1834 • Sunday

23ᵈ came to Father [Freeman] Nickersons Perrysburg the same Co NY held a meeting &c.

24 March 1834 • Monday

24ᵗʰ this ⟨day⟩ am not able to start for home but feel determined to go on the morrow morning

25 March 1834 • Tuesday

25ᵗʰ came from Father [Freeman] Nickerson to Father Leweses [Job Lewis's] in [p. 65] Westfield Father Nickerson came with me

26 March 1834 • Wednesday

26ᵗʰ Came from Westfield to Elk kreek [Creek] Stayed with Elder Hunt on free cost

27 March 1834 • Thursday

27ᵗʰ came to springfield found Brother Sidney [Rigdon] and came to within 16 miles from Pain[e]sville

28 March 1834 • Friday

28ᵗʰ Came home found my Family all well and the Lord be praised for this blessing

29 March 1834 • Saturday

29ᵗʰ at home had much [p. 66] Joy with ⟨my⟩ Family

---

117. Probably Joseph Starks of Sardinia, about nine miles east of Springville, New York. (1830 U.S. Census, Sardinia, Erie Co., NY, 205.)

30 March 1834 • Sunday

30th **Sabbath at home and went to hear Brothe[r] Sidney [Rigdon] Preach the word of life &c.**

31 March 1834 • Monday

31th **Monday this day came to Sharden [Chardon] to [at]tend the Court against Docter P Hurlbert [Doctor Philastus Hurlbut] &c**[118]

1 April 1834 • Tuesday

32[d] **Tusday this day at Brother Riders**[119] **and the Court has not braught on our tryal yet we are ingaged in makeing out some supenies [subpoenas] &c for witness**[120] **&c ⟨this⟩ is [p. 67] this Aprel 1st Tusday my Soul delighteth in the Law of the Lord for he forgiveth my sins and ⟨will⟩ confound mine Enimies the Lord shall destroy him who has lifted his heel against me**[121] **even that wicked man Docter P Hrlbert [Doctor Philastus Hurlbut] he ⟨will⟩ deliver him to the fowls of heaven and his bones shall be cast to the blast of the wind ⟨for⟩ he lifted his ⟨arm⟩ against the Almity therefore [p. 68] the Lord shall destroy him**

2–5 April 1834 • Wednesday–Saturday

/[122]Wednesday attended court at Chardon, Thursday the same. Friday morning returned home. Saturday returned to Chardon ⟨as witness for fath[er] [John] Johnson⟩[123] in the evening returned home. Mr. Burse [Lucius Bierce], the State's Att'y for Portage County called on me this evening: He is a gentlemanly appearing man, and treated me with respect.

---

118. Hurlbut had been ordered to appear before the county's court of common pleas at the start of its term, 31 March 1834. The trial commenced on 2 April 1834. (Grua, "Joseph Smith and the 1834 D. P. Hurlbut Case," 44–47.)

119. Probably Ezekiel Rider. (Geauga Co., OH, Duplicate Tax Records, 1833, 95; 1834, 110, microfilm, U.S. and Canada Record Collection, FHL.)

120. JS or his attorney would have filled in witness names on subpoena forms for the court clerk. A week later, when the case was heard, seventeen witnesses attended to testify for JS. (An Act Directing the Mode of Trial in Criminal Cases [7 Mar. 1831], *Acts of a General Nature*, sec. 22; Geauga Co., OH, Court of Common Pleas, Execution Docket 1831–1835, 110, microfilm, U.S. and Canada Record Collection, FHL.)

121. See Psalm 41:9.

122. TEXT: Oliver Cowdery handwriting begins.

123. On 5 April 1834, Johnson was granted a license to keep a tavern in Kirtland. JS testified before the court on Johnson's qualifications. (Geauga Co., OH, Court of Common Pleas, 5 Apr. 1834, final record bk. M, 184, microfilm, U.S. and Canada Record Collection, FHL.)

7–9 April 1834 • Monday–Wednesday

/¹²⁴on the 7th day of April Bros Newel [K. Whitney] Oliver [Cowdery] Frederick [G. Williams] Heber [C. Kimball] and myself meet [p. 69] in the councel room¹²⁵ and bowed down befor the Lord and prayed that he would furnish the means to deliver the firm¹²⁶ from debt and ⟨be⟩ set at liberty and also that I may prevail against that wicked [Doctor Philastus] Hurlbut and that he be put to shame accordingly on the 9 after an impartial trial the Court decided that the said Hurlbut was bound over under 200 dollers [p. 70] bond to keep the peace for six month and pay the cost which amounted to near three hundred dollers all of which was in answer to our prayer for which I thank my heavenly father¹²⁷

Remember to carry the bond between A S— [A. Sidney] Gilbert & NK Whitney¹²⁸ and have them exchaingd when I go to Zion¹²⁹

10 April 1834 • Thursday

on ⟨Thursday⟩ the 10 had a concel [council] [p. 71] of the united firm at which it was agreed that the firm should be desolvd and each one have their stewardship set off to them¹³⁰

---

124. TEXT: Oliver Cowdery handwriting ends; Frederick G. Williams begins.

125. Though council meetings in 1834 generally took place in JS's home, "councel room" probably refers to the upper room in the Newel K. Whitney store where instruction, administrative meetings, and work on the revision of the Bible usually took place. ("Whitney Store," in *Encyclopedia of Mormonism*, 4:1566–1567.)

126. The United Firm. A conference three weeks earlier in Avon, New York, appointed Orson Hyde to remain in the area, preach, and collect money for relieving Kirtland debts, money he was to raise by 1 April. JS had just received Hyde's letter of 31 March reporting his failure to raise the funds. In a letter of reply, JS wrote, "Myself bro Newel Frederick and Oliver retired to the <u>Translating room</u> where prayer was wont to be made and unbosomed our feelings before God and cannot but exercise faith yet that you in the meraculus providence of God will succeed in obtaining help." Otherwise, JS continued, he and the other Kirtland Latter-day Saints would not be able to go with the upcoming expedition to Missouri. (35n112 herein; Minute Book 1, 17 Mar. 1834; JS et al., Kirtland, OH, to Orson Hyde, [Avon, NY], 7 Apr. 1834, in JS Letterbook 1, p. 82.)

127. The court found that JS "had ground to fear" an attack from Hurlbut, who was then ordered to post a $200 bond to keep the peace and pay the court costs of $112.59. (Geauga Co., OH, Court of Common Pleas, 9 Apr. 1834, final record bk. M, 193; 31 Mar. 1834, final record bk. P, 431–432, microfilm, U.S. and Canada Record Collection, FHL; see also "Mormon Trial," *Chardon Spectator and Geauga Gazette*, 12 Apr. 1834, 3; and [Oliver Cowdery], editorial, *The Evening and the Morning Star*, Apr. 1834, 150.)

128. Gilbert and Whitney were the appointed agents for the United Firm, and the bond mentioned here may be related to the dissolution of the United Firm, which was agreed upon the following day. (JS, Journal, 10 Apr. 1834; see also Minute Book 2, 27 and 30 Apr. 1832.)

129. TEXT: A wavy line drawn around the preceding sentence marks it as a personal memorandum.

130. The Missouri branch of the firm had been forcibly removed from its Jackson County property, and the Kirtland branch was in debt to eastern creditors. Two weeks later, a revelation directed that the

Memorandum. Joseph Smith used his "Book for Record" not only to record the events of his life but also to write various notes and memoranda such as the one seen here (enclosed by wavy lines), which follows the entry for 7–9 April 1834. Handwriting of Frederick G. Williams. JS, Journal, 1832–1834, p. 71, JS Collection, Church History Library, Salt Lake City. (Photograph by Welden C. Andersen.)

11 April 1834 • Friday

Fryday 11 atten⟨ded⟩ meeting ⟨and restored Father Tyler[131] to the Church⟩

12 April 1834 • Saturday

Satterday 12 went to the Lake[132] and spent the day in fishing and visiting the brethren in that place and took my horse from Father [John] Johnson and let brothe[r] Frederick [G. Williams] have him to keep

13 April 1834 • Sunday

13 Sunday was sick and could not attend meeting [p. 72]

14 April 1834 • Monday

Monday 14 purch[as]ed som hay and oats and got them home[133]

15–17 April 1834 • Tuesday–Thursday

Tuesday 15 drawed a load of hay & ⟨on Wensday 16⟩ plowed and sowed oats for Broth[er] Frederick [G. Williams] and on Thursday the 17 attended a meeting agreeable to appoint at which time the important subject⟨s⟩ of the deliverence of Zion and the building of the Lords house in [p. 73] Kirtland by bro sidney [Rigdon] after which bro Joseph arose and requested the brethren and sisters to contr[i]bute all the money they could for the deliverence of Zion and receved twenty nine dollers and sixty eight cts

18–19 April 1834 • Friday–Saturday

/[134]April ~~17~~ ⟨18⟩, left Kirtland in company with brothers Sidney Rigdon, Oliver Cowdery, ⟨and⟩ Zebedee Coltrin for New Portage to attend a conference. Travelled to W[illiam] W. Williams' in [p. 74] Newburgh and took dinner, after which we travelled on, and after dark were hailed by a man who desired to ride. We were checked by the Spirit and refused: he professed to be sick; but in a few minutes was joined by two others who followed us hard, cursing and swearing, but we were successful in escaping their hands through

---

firm was to be dissolved in the sense of dividing it into separate Kirtland and Missouri entities. Each member of the Kirtland firm received "stewardship" for an enterprise or a parcel of real estate. (Minute Book 1, 17 Mar. 1834; Revelation, 23 Apr. 1834, in Doctrine and Covenants 98, 1835 ed. [D&C 104].)

131. Probably Andrews Tyler, who lived in Springfield, Erie County, Pennsylvania. Orson Pratt and Lyman Johnson excommunicated a "Bro. Tiler" while traveling in and around Springfield four months earlier. (1830 U.S. Census, Springfield, Erie Co., PA, 337; Pratt, Diary, 5 Dec. 1833.)

132. Lake Erie, about six miles from Kirtland.

133. JS made this purchase for $4.75 with Frederick G. Williams, scribe for this portion of the journal. (See F. G. Williams and Company, Account Book, 6.)

134. TEXT: Frederick G. Williams handwriting ends; Oliver Cowdery begins.

the providence of the Lord, and stayed at a tavern where we were treated with civility. Next morning, 19, started, and arrived at brother Joseph Bozworth's [Bosworth's] ⟨in⟩ [p. 75] Copley, Medina county, where we took dinner. Bro. J. Bozworth was strong in the faith— he is a good man and may, if faithful, do much good. After resting awhile, we left, and soon arrived at brother Johnathan Tayler's [Jonathan Taylor's], in Norton, where we were received with kindness.

We soon retired to the wilderness where we united in prayer and suplication for the blessings of the Lord to be given unto his church: We called upon the Father in the name of Jesus to go with the breth[r]en who were [p. 76] going up to the land of Zion, to give brother Joseph strength, and wisdom, and understanding sufficient to lead the people of the Lord, and to gather back, and establish the saints upon the land of their inheritances, and organize them according to the will of heaven, that they be no more cast down forever.[135] We then united and laid on hands: Brothers Sidney, Oliver, and Zebedee laid hands upon bro. Joseph, and confirmed upon him all the blessings necessary to qualify him to do ⟨stand⟩ before the Lord in his high calling; and [p. 77] he return again in peace and triumph, to enjoy the society of his breth[r]en. Brothers Joseph, Sidney, and Zebedee then laid hands upon bro. Oliver, and confirmed upon him the blessings of wisdom and understanding sufficient for his station; that he be qualified to assist brother Sidney in arranging the church covenants which are to be soon published; and to have intelligence in all things to do the work of printing. Brother Joseph, Oliver, Zebedee then laid [p. 78] hands upon bro. Sidney, and confirmed upon him the blessings of wisdom and knowledge to preside over the church in the abscence of brother Joseph, and to have the spirit to assist bro. Oliver in conducting the Star, and to arrange the Church covenants,[136] and the blessing of old age and peace, till Zion is built up & Kirtland established, till all his enemies are under his feet, and of a crown of eternal life at the ⟨in the⟩ Kingdom of God with us. [p. 79] We, Joseph, Sidney, and Oliver then laid hands upon bro. Zebedee, and confirmed the blessing of wisdom to preach the gospel, even till is ⟨it⟩ spreads to the islands of the seas,

135. Missouri state officials had communicated some willingness to see the expelled Mormons return to Jackson County but with the understanding that Mormons would then be responsible to form legal militia units to prevent a second expulsion. (See Crawley and Anderson, "Political and Social Realities of Zion's Camp.")

136. Following the destruction of the Missouri printing office in July 1833—which interrupted publication of the Book of Commandments—JS, Rigdon, Cowdery, and Frederick G. Williams were assigned to produce in Kirtland an updated compilation of revelations. While JS and Williams traveled to Missouri with the expeditionary force, Rigdon and Cowdery continued to work on the compilation project in addition to sustaining regular publication of *The Evening and the Morning Star* throughout the three-month period. (Minute Book 1, 24 Sept. 1834 and 17 Aug. 1835; see also Woodford, "Development of the Doctrine and Covenants," 1:37–47.)

and to be spared to see th[r]eescore years and ten, and see Zion built up and Kirtland established forever, and even at last to receive a crown of life. Our hearts rejoiced, and we were [p. 80] comforted with the Holy Spirit, Amen.

20 April 1834 • Sunday

~~18~~ 20.th. Sunday, Brother Sidney Rigdon entertained a large congregation of saints, with an interesting discourse upon the "Dispensations of the fulness of times," &c.[137]

21–22 April 1834 • Monday–Tuesday

21. Attended conference and had a glorious time, some few volunteered to go to Zion, and others donated $66.37. for the benefit of the scattered breth[r]en in Zion.[138]

Returned to Kirtland on the 22d and found all well. [p. 81]

23 April 1834 • Wednesday

23. Assembled in council with breth[r]en Sidney [Rigdon], Frederick [G. Williams], Newel [K. Whitney], John Johnson, and Oliver [Cowdery][139] and united in asking the Lord to give bro. Zebedee Coltrin influence over our

---

137. Rigdon preached in Norton, Ohio. A note in the back of the journal was apparently recorded in preparation for the conference at which Rigdon spoke. (Minute Book 1, 21 Apr. 1834; JS, Journal, 1832–1834 [undated note], p. 51 herein.)

138. After recounting the church's foundational historical events to this conference of Latter-day Saints at Norton, Ohio, JS stated, "Without a Zion and a place of deliverance, we must fall, because the time is near when the sun will be darkened, the moon turn to blood, the stars fall from heaven and the earth reel to and fro." JS and Rigdon also spoke on the importance of the construction of the House of the Lord in Kirtland. (Minute Book 1, 21 Apr. 1834.)

139. This 23 April meeting of United Firm members was probably the setting in which a revelation of this date was dictated, though it may be that the meeting was held in response to the revelation. Ratifying the decision made two weeks earlier to "dissolve" the firm,^a the revelation called for it to be divided into two separate firms, one for Kirtland and one for Missouri; gave members of the Kirtland firm individual stewardships for the assets of the firm in that vicinity (enterprises or parcels of real estate); gave them collective responsibility for financing the publication of scriptures; and counseled them to "pay all your debts," which would in some cases require renegotiating the terms or borrowing elsewhere.^b Frederick G. Williams later described another revelation dictated at about this same time, which was not written, requiring certain members of the United Firm "to ballan[ce] all accounts & give up all notes & demands that they had against each other & all be equal which was done." Among these, JS owed the largest amount, $1,151.31.^c After April 1834, neither of the two successor firms outlined in the major 23 April revelation materialized. Instead, church leaders, including several former members of the United Firm, gave general direction to the management of the enterprises and lands involved in Kirtland.^d (a. JS, Journal, 10 Apr. 1834. b. Revelation, 23 Apr. 1834, in Doctrine and Covenants 98:3–11, 13, 1835 ed. [D&C 104:11–13, 19–51, 58–64, 78–85]; see also Revelation Book 2, p. 111. c. Frederick G. Williams, Statement, no date, Frederick G. Williams, Papers, CHL; Balances Due, 23 Apr. 1834, Newel K. Whitney, Papers, BYU. d. Minute Book 1, 24 Sept. 1834; Parkin, "Joseph Smith and the United Firm.")

bro. Jacob Myres [Myers Sr.], and obtain from him the money which he has gone to borow for us, or cause him to come to this place & give it himself.

30 April 1834 · Wednesday

/[140]April 30th this day paid the ~~amount~~ ⟨sum⟩ of fifty dollers on the following memorandom to the [p. 82] following persons viz

Milton Holmes	$15,00
Henry Heriman [Harriman]	7,00
Sylvester Smith	10,00
Wm Smith	5,00
Harvey Stanl[e]y	5,00
William Smith	5,00
N[ewel] K Whitney	3,00
	$50,00

Record of Donations

Money received of the following brethren consecrated for the delivery of Zion

By Lette[r] from East		$10.,,
Do [ditto] "		50,,
Do "		100,,[141] [p. 83]
By Letter		$07,,,
Wm Smith		.5" "
Wm Cahoon		.5" "
Harvey Stanley		.5" "
Received of Martin Har[r]is		47=00
/[142]Recived of Dexter Stillman		10=
Do.	of Lyman Johnson	5=00
Do	of Sophia [Hull] Howe	7=60 /[143]

[8 lines blank] [p. 84]

---

140. TEXT: Oliver Cowdery handwriting ends; Frederick G. Williams begins.

141. This and the previous amount of fifty dollars may have been contributed by a single donor. Wilford Woodruff later recalled that at the end of April 1834, JS received "a letter containing a hundred and fifty dollars, sent to him by sister Voce, of Boston." The donor could have been either Mary (Polly) Vose (1780–1866) or her niece Ruth Vose (1808–1884), both of whom lived in Boston at this time. (Wilford Woodruff, in *Journal of Discourses*, 10 Jan. 1858, 7:101; Compton, *In Sacred Loneliness*, 381–382, 386.)

142. TEXT: Frederick G. Williams handwriting ends; unidentified begins.

143. TEXT: Unidentified handwriting ends.

———— ∽ ————

Editorial Note

JS and other volunteers of the armed expeditionary force that had been recruited for "the restoration and redemption of Zion"[144] departed Ohio for Missouri on 5 May 1834. A smaller contingent started from Pontiac, Michigan, and joined them at Allred settlement, Monroe County, Missouri. After learning on 15 June that Missouri governor Daniel Dunklin would not order the state's militia to escort the Mormons to their Jackson County lands as the Mormons had hoped, JS's company, now numbering some two hundred, nevertheless continued their march to Clay County, Missouri. Their approach prompted negotiations between Mormons exiled from Jackson County—now living in Clay County—and Jackson County residents. Compromise proved impossible given the entrenched positions of both sides: the Mormons insisted on maintaining their rights to return to their property and refused to sell, and Jacksonites refused to have the Mormons live among them. Local residents also prepared for armed confrontation with the advancing Mormons. When questioned about his intentions, JS disavowed any military offensive, and no armed confrontation materialized.

In mid-June a cholera epidemic began to make inroads among JS's company. On 22 June, JS announced a revelation postponing the redemption of Zion "for a little season." Zion would be redeemed only after the Latter-day Saints purchased additional land in Jackson County and vicinity; after their leading elders were "endowed with power from on high" in Ohio; and after the Mormons in Missouri found "favor in the eyes of the people, until the army of Israel becomes very great."[145] Thus JS maintained long-term hopes for a temporarily failed enterprise. The cholera-decimated Mormon troops were dispersed and soon discharged to remain in Clay County or—in most cases—to return eastward to their homes. JS organized a standing high council for the Missouri Mormons and selected a number of Missouri church leaders to be endowed in the House of the Lord then under construction in Kirtland. JS and other members of the expedition, which later became known as Zion's Camp, returned to Ohio in late July. While JS did not keep a personal record during this time, he assigned Frederick G. Williams to send periodic reports of their journey to Oliver Cowdery in Kirtland.[146] However, no such reports have survived. JS later oversaw the creation of a history that drew on others' accounts to create a narrative of the journey.[147]

In the wake of the failure to effect a return of Mormon refugees to Jackson County, the Latter-day Saints' highest priorities became completing the construction of their temple in Kirtland and purchasing land in the vicinity of Jackson County. Both endeavors were understood to be prerequisites to returning to their Zion; both would impose great financial burdens.

———— ∽ ————

144. Revelation, 24 Feb. 1834, in Doctrine and Covenants 101:6, 1844 ed. [D&C 103:29].
145. Revelation, 22 June 1834, in Doctrine and Covenants 102:3, 8, 1844 ed. [D&C 105:9, 13, 26].
146. JS, Richmond, IN, to Emma Smith, Kirtland Mills, OH, 19 May 1834, CCLA.
147. JS History, vol. A-1, 474–527; compare George A. Smith, Autobiography, 14–43; Kimball, "History," 11–24; and Woodruff, Journal, 1 May–1 July 1834.

21 August 1834 • Thursday

/¹⁴⁸August 21ˢᵗ 1834. This day brother Frederick [G.] Williams returned from Cleveland and told us concerning the plague,¹⁴⁹ and after much consultation we agreed that bro. Frederick should go to Cleveland and commence administering to the sick, for the purpose of obtaining ~~means~~ ⟨blessings for them, and⟩ for the ~~work of~~ ⟨glory of⟩ the Lord:¹⁵⁰ Accordingly we, Joseph, Frederick, and Oliver [Cowdery] united in prayer before the Lord for this thing. [p. 85]

Now, O Lord, grant unto us ~~this~~ ⟨those⟩ blessing⟨s⟩, in the name of Jesus Christ, and thy name shall have the glory forever; Amen.

30 August 1834 • Saturday

August 30, 1834. Received of the chu[r]ch by the hand of Jared Carter from the east of consecrated money $3,00¹⁵¹

4 September 1834 • Thursday

Sept. 4, 1834. This day Edward [Edmund] Bosley said that if he could obtain the management of his property in one year he would put it in for the printing of the word of the Lord.¹⁵² [p. 86]

---

148. TEXT: Oliver Cowdery handwriting begins.

149. An epidemic of Asiatic cholera spread through Europe and reached American cities in 1832. Cleveland was revisited with the disease in 1834, and JS and other members of the expeditionary force suffered an outbreak near the end of the Missouri expedition. JS and other Latter-day Saints viewed the epidemic within a framework of millennial judgment. (Chambers, *Conquest of Cholera*, chaps. 1–6; Avery, *History of Cleveland*, 1:145; Kimball, "History," 21–24; JS, Kirtland, OH, to Lyman Wight et al., Missouri, 16 Aug. 1834, in JS Letterbook 1, pp. 84–87; "The Cholera," *The Evening and the Morning Star,* Aug. 1832, [1]; Sept. 1832, [1]; see also JS, Hyrum [Hiram, OH], to William W. Phelps, Zion [Independence], MO, 31 July 1832, JS Collection, CHL.)

150. Before the strikethroughs and revisions, this passage read, "administering to the sick, for the purpose of obtaining means for the work of the Lord", perhaps showing that Williams intended to raise money for the church by charging for medical services. Williams was a practicing botanical physician. (Williams, "Frederick Granger Williams," 244–245, 251–252; George A. Smith, Autobiography, 42; JS History, vol. A-1, addenda, 16n18.)

151. Carter, a member of the committee to raise money for building the House of the Lord in Kirtland, was appointed in April 1834 "to visit the several churches, to receive contributions." (Notice, *The Evening and the Morning Star,* Apr. 1834, 151; see also Minute Book 1, 4 May and 6 June 1833.)

152. Apparently in connection with the church's desire to expand Mormon holdings in Kirtland, Bosley purchased property from Andrew Bardsley on 2 June 1834. Bosley made a formal covenant to give the land to the church. However, because Bosley still owed four hundred dollars for the land, he proposed that he maintain the use and management of the land for one year, presumably allowing him to earn the money to pay his debt. Bosley later refused to honor his agreement, and a church council excommunicated him in July 1835. (Geauga Co., OH, Deed Records, 2 June 1834, 20:302–303; 18:326–327, microfilm, U.S. and Canada Record Collection, FHL; Minute Book 1, 14 July 1835.)

———— ✍ ————

Editorial Note

On 5 September 1834, JS left Kirtland with Oliver Cowdery to attend a conference of elders in New Portage, Ohio.[153] In the second half of October, JS was again away from Kirtland, this time to visit the Latter-day Saints in Pontiac, Michigan. When in Kirtland, he continued to work on the church's printing concerns and on building the House of the Lord.[154]

On the evening of 28 November 1834, the day before this journal resumes, JS attended a high council meeting and heard from members of the Tippets family, who were en route to Missouri. In response to a December 1833 revelation that instructed church branches to "gather together all their moneys" and send "honorable men" to purchase lands in Jackson County, the church in Lewis, New York, had sent the Tippetses with a letter to JS and $848.40 in donations of cash and property. The high council recommended that the migrants winter in Kirtland and requested temporary financial help from them. John Tippets and Caroline Tippets lent $430, to be paid back in the spring when they would resume their journey.[155] This short-term financial assistance brought renewed hope and prompted the recording of prayers and resolutions.

———— ✍ ————

29 November 1834 • Saturday

November 29. 1834. This evening Joseph and Oliver [Cowdery] united in prayer for the continuance of blessings, after giving thanks for the relief which the Lord had lately sent us by opening the hearts of certain brethren from the east to loan us $430.

After conversing and rejoicing before the Lord on this occasion we agreed to enter into the following covenant with the Lord, viz:=

> That if the Lord will [p. 87] prosper us in our business, and open the way before ⟨us⟩ that we may obtain means to pay our debts, that we be not troubled nor brought into disrepute before the world nor his people, that after that of all that he shall give us we will give a tenth, to be bestowed upon the poor in his church, or as he shall command, and that we will be faithful over that which he has entrusted to our care ~~and~~ that we [p. 88] may obtain much: and that our children after us shall remember to observe this sacred and holy covenant: ~~after us:~~ And

153. Oliver Cowdery, Norton, OH, to William W. Phelps, 7 Sept. 1834, *LDS Messenger and Advocate*, Oct. 1834, 1:14; Minute Book 1, 8 Sept. 1834.

154. Minute Book 1, 24 Sept. 1834; JS History, vol. B-1, 557.

155. Revelation, 16 and 17 Dec. 1833, in Doctrine and Covenants 97:10, 1835 ed. [D&C 101:72–73]; Minute Book 1, 28 Nov. 1834; Alvah Tippets, Lewis, NY, to JS, Kirtland, OH, 20 Oct. 1834, in Minute Book 1, pp. 78–80.

that our children and our children's may know of the same we here subscribe our names with our own hands before the Lord:

Joseph Smith Jr

Oliver Cowdery.[156]

And now, O Father, as thou didst prosper our father Jacob, and bless [p. 89] him with protection and prosperity where ever he went from the time he made a like covenant before and with thee; and as thou didst,— even the same night, open the heavens unto him and manifest great mercy and favor, and give him promises,[157] so wilt thou do by us his sons; and as his blessings prevailed above the blessings of his Progenitors into the utmost bounds of the [p. 90] everlasting hills,[158] even so may our blessings prevail above ⟨like⟩ his; and may thy servants be preserved from the power and influence of wicked and unrighteous men; may every weapon formed against us fall upon the head of him who shall form it;[159] may we be blessed with a name and a place among thy saints here, and thy sanctified when they shall rest. Amen. [p. 91]

30 November 1834 • Sunday

Sabbath evening, November 30, 1834. While reflecting upon the goodness and mercy of the Lord, this evening, a prophecy was put into our hearts, that in a short time the Lord would arrange his providences in a merciful manner and send us assistance to deliver us from debt and bondage.[160] [p. 92]

5 December 1834 • Friday

Friday Evening, December 5, 1834. According to the directions of the Holy Spirit breth[r]en Joseph Smith jr. Sidney [Rigdon], Frederick G. Williams, and Oliver Cowdery, assembled to converse upon the welfare of the church, when brother Oliver Cowdery was ordained an assistant President of the High and Holy Priesthood under the hands of brother Joseph Smith jr. Saying, "My brother, in the name of Jesus Christ who died was crucified for the sins of the

---

156. This personal covenant made and signed by JS and Oliver Cowdery preceded by nearly four years the revelation mandating that church members contribute "one tenth of all their interest annually" as tithing. (See Revelation, 8 July 1838–C, in JS, Journal, 8 July 1838, p. 288 herein [D&C 119:4].)

157. See Genesis 28:10–22.

158. See Genesis 49:26.

159. See Isaiah 54:17.

160. In January, donations of Latter-day Saint John Tanner materially improved their situation. Tanner's son Nathan recalled that his father donated over three thousand dollars and saved the mortgage on the temple block from being foreclosed. (Minute Book 1, 18 Jan. 1835; Tanner, Autobiography, 25; compare "Sketch of an Elder's Life," 12–13.)

world, I lay my hands upon thee, and ordain thee an assistant President[161] of the high and holy p[r]iesthood in the church of the Latter Day Saints/[162] [p. 93]

[*pages 94–97 blank*]
Joseph Smith
[*15 lines blank*] [p. 98]
[*pages 99–102 blank*]

———— ❧ ————

Editorial Note

Except for a few notes jotted in the back, this journal ends with the preceding 5 December 1834 entry. "Chapter 1" of JS's 1834–1836 history consisted of a narrative in journal format for 5 and 6 December 1834, recorded by Oliver Cowdery; but that approach was then terminated.[163] Not until late September 1835, nearly ten months later, did JS again keep a journal. Two priorities loomed in the intervening months: the redemption of Zion in Missouri and building a House of the Lord in Kirtland for the promised endowment of power. During the interim, JS also expanded church leadership by forming the Quorum of the Twelve Apostles and another organization called the Quorum of the Seventy, responsible for traveling and preaching. Men who had served in the expedition to Missouri made up most of the initial membership of both entities. When JS's journal keeping resumed, it was more persistent, resulting in a coherent six-month narrative leading up to and including the empowerment in the House of the Lord in Kirtland, which the Latter-day Saints understood to be a prerequisite for the redemption of Zion.

---

161. Cowdery viewed this ordination as fulfillment of an angelic promise. According to JS's history, in May 1829 John the Baptist announced that Cowdery would be second elder, next in authority to JS as first elder, in the church that was yet to be organized.*a* Beginning in April 1830, JS and Cowdery held the positions and titles the angel had specified. But Cowdery was away filling an assignment in Missouri when on 8 March 1832 a presidency was established in Kirtland to lead the church.*b* In Cowdery's absence, Sidney Rigdon and Jesse Gause were appointed counselors to JS.*c* JS had previously been designated "president of the high priesthood of the church" in November 1831 and ordained to that position on 25 January 1832.*d* Frederick G. Williams replaced Gause as a counselor by January 1833.*e* In the history he was keeping for JS at the time, Cowdery recorded a more complete transcription of this 5 December 1834 blessing and reported that although Rigdon and Williams had seniority in office as counselors, Cowdery, in fulfillment of the angel's promise, was now to be first among the three to "assist in presiding over the whole church, and to officiate in the absence of the President." Following Cowdery's ordination, Rigdon and Williams "confirmed the ordinance and blessings by the laying on of hands and prayer, after which each were blessed with the same blessings and prayer." In a meeting the following day, Hyrum Smith and Joseph Smith Sr. were called as additional "assistant presidents," or counselors.*f* (*a*. JS History, vol. A-1, 17–18. *b*. Entry for 5 Dec. 1834, in JS History, 1834–1836, 17. *c*. Revelation Book 2, pp. 10–11. *d*. Revelation, 11 Nov. 1831–B, in Doctrine and Covenants 3:31, 1835 ed. [D&C 107:59–67]. *e*. Minute Book 1, 22 Jan. 1833. *f*. Entries for 5 and 6 Dec. 1834, in JS History, 1834–1836, 17–20.)

162. TEXT: Oliver Cowdery handwriting ends.

163. JS History, 1834–1836, 17–20.

The final three pages of this journal contain notes related to the events recorded in preceding journal entries. Subscriptions to *The Evening and the Morning Star* that were evidently solicited during JS's 26 February–28 March 1834 mission are recorded on these pages. Following the subscriptions, a note was inscribed, apparently in preparation for the conference held 20–21 April 1834 at Norton, Ohio.

———— ℰℐ ————

/[164]Please to send the Paper that Has forme[r]ly Be[e]n sent to John C◊◊p◊◊to◊[165] send it Now to Nathan Chase at West Lodi Cat[t]araugas County NY

/[166]Recieve of Elisha C Hubbard one Dollar for Papers ⟨Perrysburgh [Perrysburg] NY⟩[167]

/[168][*illegible*] [*1/4 page blank*] [p. 103]

/[169]Hazard Andrws [Andrus] 1 paper Fairview Postoffi[ce] Cattara[u]gus County[170]

I have sent the money 25 cents by David Mo◊◊◊◊◊[171] an[d] he was to send the paper to Mis Taylor to Rushford but I wish to have it come in my name as above

/[172]Direct Samuel Mcbride & James Mcbride Papers to Nashville Postoffice Shitauqua [Chautauque] County[173]

I wish you to send me[174] one more Paper monthly and send one Monthly Paper to Eleazer & Samuel & Richard Nickerson South Dennis in the County of Barnstable Masachusetts[175]

F[reeman] Nickerson [p. 104]

----

164. TEXT: Freeman Nickerson handwriting begins.

165. TEXT: Possibly "Carpenton" or "Carpentor".

166. TEXT: Freeman Nickerson handwriting ends; unidentified begins.

167. TEXT: Insertion in graphite in unidentified handwriting. The journal records JS's visit to Perrysburg, New York, 5 and 6 March 1834.

168. TEXT: Unidentified handwriting ends; different unidentified handwriting begins.

169. TEXT: Unidentified handwriting ends; different unidentified handwriting begins—possibly Hazard Andrus.

170. Fairview post office was located in Farmersville Township, New York. The journal records JS's visit to Farmersville on 8 March 1834.

171. TEXT: Possibly "Mathews".

172. TEXT: Unidentified—possibly Hazard Andrus—handwriting ends; Freeman Nickerson begins.

173. The present journal records that JS stayed with Reuben McBride, the brother of Samuel and James, on the night of 4 March 1834.

174. Freeman Nickerson. The present journal records that JS visited Nickerson's home on 5 and 6 March 1834.

175. The 1830 U.S. Census lists Freeman Nickerson's brothers Eleazer, Samuel, and Richard Nickerson in the area of Yarmouth, Barnstable County, Massachusetts—four miles west-northwest of South Dennis. Their subscription was apparently ordered by their brother Freeman Nickerson. (1830 U.S. Census, Yarmouth, Barnstable Co., MA, 375; Dennis, Barnstable Co., MA, 392.)

Note in journal. The final page of the 1832–1834 journal contains a note detailing the order of speakers for one of the meetings in a church conference held at Norton, Ohio, on 20–21 April 1834. Because of aging and damage, some of the penciled characters are not readable, as seen in the left photograph. The image on the right demonstrates the recovery of the text made possible by multispectral imaging. Handwriting of Oliver Cowdery and Joseph Smith. JS, Journal, 1832–1834, p. 105, JS Collection, Church History Library, Salt Lake City. (Photograph on left by Welden C. Andersen.

/[176]The voice of the Spirit is, that brother Sidney [Rigdon] speak to the congregation this day, first, Brother Joseph next, bro. Oliver [Cowdery] next. and if time bro Zebedeee [Zebedee Coltrin].[177]

Joseph Smith Jr Oliver Cowdrey[178] **Oliver Cowdrey** [*1/4 page blank*] [p. 105]

---

176. TEXT: Freeman Nickerson handwriting ends; Oliver Cowdery begins, inscribed in light graphite.

177. Apparently, Rigdon preached on the first day of the conference and Rigdon, Cowdery, and others on the second. (See JS, Journal, 20 Apr. 1834; and Minute Book 1, 21 Apr. 1834.)

178. TEXT: This and the subsequent instance of "Cowdrey" are possibly written "Cowdry".

Second Ohio journal. This journal records Joseph Smith's daily activities during late 1835 and early 1836 as the Latter-day Saints were completing the House of the Lord in Kirtland. The journal culminates with accounts of the dedication of that temple, the long-awaited "solemn assembly," and a vision of the glorified Jesus Christ accepting the building as his house. JS, Journal, 1835–1836, JS Collection, Church History Library, Salt Lake City. (Photograph by Welden C. Andersen.)

JOURNAL, 1835–1836

Source Note

JS, "Sketch Book for the use of Joseph Smith, jr.," Journal, Sept. 1835–Apr. 1836; handwriting of Warren Parrish, an unidentified scribe, Sylvester Smith, Frederick G. Williams, Warren Cowdery, JS, and Oliver Cowdery; 195 pages; JS Collection, CHL. Includes redactions and archival marking.

The text block consists of 114 leaves—including single flyleaves and pastedowns in the front and back—measuring 12¼ x 8 inches (31 x 20 cm). The 110 interior leaves are ledger paper with thirty-four lines in faint—and now faded—black ink that has turned brown. There are nine gatherings of various sizes—each about a dozen leaves per gathering. The text block is sewn all along over cloth tapes. The front and back covers of the journal are pasteboard. The ledger has a tight-back case binding with a brown calfskin quarter-leather binding. The outside covers are adorned in shell marbled paper, with dark green body and veins of light green. The bound volume measures 12⅜ x 8¼ inches (31 x 21 cm) and is ¹³⁄₁₆ inches (2 cm) thick. One cover of the book is labeled "Repentence." in black ink. The first page of ledger paper under that cover contains eight lines of references to the book of Genesis under the heading "Scriptures relating to Repentince". The spine has "No 8" inscribed upside up when the book is standing upright for this side. When the volume is turned upside down and flipped front to back, the other cover is titled "Sabbath Day" with "No 9" written beneath in black ink. The first page of ledger paper under that cover contains two lines of references to the book of Genesis under the heading "Scriptures relating to the Sabbath day". Thus the book was used to simultaneously house two volumes of topical notes on biblical passages. This book was apparently part of a larger series that included at least two other extant volumes—one bearing "Faith" and "10" on the cover, and the other bearing "Second Comeing of Christ" and "No 3" on one cover and "Gift of the Holy Ghost" on the other cover.[1] In late 1835, JS and scribes began using the book to record his journal for 1835–1836, which begins on the recto of the second leaf of ledger paper. Warren Parrish added the title "Sketch Book" to the cover, beneath "Repentence.".

The entire journal is inscribed in black ink that later turned brown. Pages 25, 51, 77, 103, 129, and 154 bear the marks of adhesive wafers that were probably used to attach manuscripts until they were copied into the journal. The journal was used in Nauvoo, Illinois, in 1843 as a major source in composing JS's multivolume manuscript history of the church. At this time, redactions were made in ink and in graphite pencil, and use marks were made in graphite. Also, apparently in Nauvoo, the cover of the journal side of the book was marked with a "D" and then with a larger, stylized "D". At some point a white paper spine label was added with "1835–6 ⟨Kirtland⟩ JOURNAL" hand printed or stenciled in black ink that later turned brown. The insertion "Kirtland" is written in graphite. Also, in the "Repentence" side of the volume, the rectos of the third through eighth leaves of ledger paper are

---

1. "Grammar & Aphabet of the Egyptian Language," Kirtland Egyptian Papers, ca. 1835–1836, CHL; Kirtland Elders Quorum, "A Record of the First Quororum of Elders Belonging to the Church of Christ: In Kirtland Geauga Co. Ohio," 1836–1838, 1840–1841, CCLA.

Kirtland, Ohio. 1907. In this view to the southwest, the east branch of the Chagrin River can be seen in the foreground. The House of the Lord stands out on the horizon. (Church History Library, Salt Lake City. Photograph by George Edward Anderson.)

numbered on the upper right-hand corners as 195, 197, 199, 201, 203, and 205—all written in graphite and apparently redactions. Except with regard to the title "Sketch Book", none of the authors of the inscriptions mentioned previously have been identified. This volume is listed in Nauvoo and early Utah inventories of church records, indicating continuous custody.[2]

Historical Introduction

JS viewed himself as divinely commissioned to gather God's people in the last days and prepare them for Jesus Christ's second coming and millennial reign. By 1835, the House of the Lord, a temple in Kirtland, Ohio, became the centerpiece of this commission and hence of this journal. The Latter-day Saints were commanded in revelations dated as early as December 1832 to establish "a house of God" and were chastised in June 1833 for not having begun the endeavor.[3] Construction began 6 June 1833 after JS and colleagues saw in vision the completed structure.[4] As writing in this journal began, construction was nearing completion. The newly established Quorum of the Twelve and Quorum of the Seventy were returning from preaching assignments and joining with church officers from Ohio and Missouri as well as with traveling elders. All converged on Kirtland to prepare with increasing intensity for the "solemn assembly" to be held in the House of the Lord, where they were to be "endowed with power from on high."[5] Thus empowered, they could better fulfill key elements of their mission: preaching God's message for the last time throughout the world prior to the imminent Second Coming; gathering converts to Missouri, where they would find safety in Zion from the destruction that was to overtake the wicked; and ministering to the Saints. After a hiatus of more than nine months, JS renewed his journal keeping during this period of organization, purification, and preparation.

The longest of any of JS's journals published herein, this volume records his activities in and around Kirtland during the half year from late September 1835 to early April 1836. It is the last journal that contains JS's own handwriting: seven entries—four manuscript pages. Entries were sometimes made one or more days after the fact, but an entry was made for every day from the journal's beginning to its end, providing a continuity lacking in JS's previous journal and reflecting a time of relative stability for the church in Kirtland. JS is not embattled, defending his people and projects against enemies; rather, he is gathering and preparing his people for what they expect to be a pivotal experience. Blessings, rebukes, and counsel recorded here manifest the hopes and expectations of JS and others in church leadership.

While JS, Oliver Cowdery, and Frederick G. Williams penned entries for the first two weeks of the journal, most of the remainder of the journal was kept by Warren Parrish, often mentioned in the journal as "my scribe." Parrish was hired as scribe for JS on 29 October 1835. His duties included keeping JS's journal and minutes of church meetings

---

2. Historian's Office, "Schedule of Church Records"; "Historian's Office Catalogue," [1], Catalogs and Inventories, 1846–1904, CHL; Johnson, *Register of the Joseph Smith Collection*, 7.

3. Revelation, 27 and 28 Dec. 1832 and 3 Jan. 1833, in Doctrine and Covenants 7:36, 1835 ed. [D&C 88:119]; Revelation, 1 June 1833, in Doctrine and Covenants 95:1, 1835 ed. [D&C 95:2–3].

4. Angell, Autobiography, 14–15.

5. Revelation, 22 June 1834, in Doctrine and Covenants 102:3, 1844 ed. [D&C 105:11]. For an account of the solemn assembly, see the journal entry herein for 30 March 1836.

and copying certain materials into JS's 1834–1836 history, which Oliver Cowdery had begun the prior year. Parrish's first recorded journal entry is for 8 October 1835, suggesting that journal keeping was three weeks behind when he started. Parrish inscribed entries covering the next six weeks. The journal was in Parrish's possession during at least part of the time he was inscribing it, and the practice may have been for the assigned scribe to retain possession during his tenure. JS recorded four reflective entries for December 19–22 and indicated in the last of those entries that Parrish was ill. JS then passed the journal to Williams, whose entries covered four days ending 26 December 1835. Parrish resumed scribal duties for four weeks' entries, but then his ill health forced him to relinquish journal keeping to Sylvester Smith, who recorded the next two weeks' entries. On 7 February 1836, Parrish then resumed his work, recording entries for the next eight weeks, with occasional help from an unidentified scribe who copied or kept minutes of church meetings. In early April, Parrish was preparing to leave Kirtland to proselytize, like many others who had sought empowerment in Kirtland for that purpose.[6] Apparently Parrish's scribal responsibilities for the journal and for JS's 1834–1836 history were delegated at this time to Warren Cowdery, older brother of Oliver Cowdery. Cowdery used the first two months of material from the journal, 22 September to 18 November 1835, as the basis for a new section of the 1834–1836 history and also wrote the final two entries in the journal. Parrish's mission departure was delayed until May.[7] It was apparently during this delay that Parrish retrieved the history and the journal from Cowdery and added a final two months of material from the journal, 18 November 1835 through 18 January 1836, to the history—probably before leaving for his missionary assignment. Parrish made no additional entries to the journal before returning it to JS. Thus the journal ended with Cowdery's entries.

Much of the material in the journal seems to have been dictated by JS to the scribe or recorded as JS spoke to various gatherings. For example, the entry for 21 January 1836 is apparently a dictation because it reports a vision seen only by JS. JS may have had the scribe read back his dictations to him in order to make corrections, as he had sometimes done six years earlier in dictating his translation of the Book of Mormon. In the 21 January entry, the scribe writes, "I am mistaken," and a paragraph in the entry corrects a statement made earlier in the entry. A few days later, Parrish wrote to JS that he could not continue to keep the journal for a time. He explained, "Writing has a particular tendency to injure my lungs while I am under the influence of such a cough"—a possible indication that his scribal duties required reading aloud.[8]

The journal reveals aspects not only of the inner spiritual life and the religious fellowship that JS shared with church members and leaders but also of his relations with adherents of other religious persuasions. Various entries describe his interactions with Presbyterians, Methodists, a Baptist, a Universalist, and a Unitarian. The journal records a visit JS received from two followers of the British religious reformer Edward Irving as well as a visit from JS's contemporary Robert Matthews—better known as the Prophet Matthias. During his visit with Matthews, JS shared the foundational religious experiences of his

---

6. Woodruff, Journal, 19 Apr. 1836.
7. Woodruff, Journal, 27 May 1836.
8. JS, Journal, 25 Jan. 1836.

youth, including rare accounts of his visit from the angel Moroni and of his first vision of Deity.

The journal also records several other revelations and visions. Of particular theological significance is the aforementioned 21 January 1836 vision of the "celestial kingdom" of heaven, with its revelation that "all who have died with[out] a knowledge of this gospel, who would have received it, if they had been permitted to tarry, shall be heirs of the celestial kingdom of God."[9] This foreshadows the Latter-day Saint doctrine of redeeming the dead through vicarious ordinances.

A number of entries in this journal relate to JS's revelatory translation of Egyptian writings. In July 1835, JS and associates had purchased from a Michael Chandler four Egyptian mummies and some papyri unearthed at Thebes. Chandler had exhibited the artifacts in Cleveland and other locations and had heard of JS's claims as a translator. This journal provides glimpses of JS's early efforts in transcribing and translating material from the papyri and recounts that JS exhibited the papyri to associates and visitors. Journal entries refer to them as the "records of antiquity," the "Egyptian manuscripts," the "Egyptian records," the "sacred record," the "ancient records," the "records of Abraham," or simply "the records." JS's efforts led to publication in 1842 of a work that he introduced as "purporting to be the writings of Abraham."[10]

The events of this journal, as in JS's 1832–1834 journal, unfold in the shadow of the dual priorities of redeeming Zion and preparing the House of the Lord. A revelation that JS announced in June 1834, prior to the close of the Mormons' armed expedition to Missouri, laid out the course of action the Latter-day Saints were to pursue regarding their future in that state. The "redemption of Zion" in Missouri would not take place until church officers had been further instructed in their duties and empowered in the House of the Lord in Kirtland.[11]

In the third entry in this journal, JS himself recorded further plans and preparations for Missouri. As the time for the promised endowment neared, so did the anticipated return to Jackson County. The dispossessed Missouri Saints were again to petition Governor Daniel Dunklin for support in reoccupying their Jackson County lands. JS and other church officers expressed determination to reenter Jackson County in spring 1836, at the risk of their lives if necessary. JS reported the beginning of efforts that same day to enlist a large volunteer army for this purpose[12]—optimistic plans, fed perhaps by growth in church membership in the two years since their small "Zion's Camp" expedition had failed to accomplish the same goal. Less than two weeks later, he advised members of the Quorum of the Twelve to anticipate moving their families to Missouri.[13]

Latter-day Saints corresponded with Dunklin, asking for his assistance and even suggesting that United States president Andrew Jackson be asked to rectify the Saints' 1833 eviction from their Jackson County property by vigilantes. In January 1836, Dunklin

---

9. JS, Journal, 21 Jan. 1836.

10. "The Book of Abraham," *Times and Seasons,* 1 Mar. 1842, 3:703–706; 15 Mar. 1842, 3:719–722; 16 May 1842, 3:783–784 [Abraham 1–5].

11. Revelation, 22 June 1834, in Doctrine and Covenants 102, 1844 ed. [D&C 105].

12. JS, Journal, 24 Sept. 1835.

13. JS, Journal, 5 Oct. 1835.

effectively foreclosed the possibility of aid from either the state or the federal government in the near future. He ruled out any request for federal intervention on constitutional grounds and again advised the Saints to pursue restoration of their property through the established legal system.[14]

Soon after receiving Dunklin's letter, the Latter-day Saints modified their short-term plans for Missouri. By March 1836, they had apparently dropped the idea of assembling a large army, at least for the present. Church leaders moved their focus for the near future away from Jackson County and instead commissioned agents to find a new location in Missouri and to purchase lands there on which to settle.[15] The church's presidency intended to move to Missouri to direct the relocation.[16]

During the time covered in the journal, the immediate attention of Latter-day Saints was focused on northeastern Ohio. Prerequisite to their major relocation in Missouri, church leaders from Missouri and elsewhere gathered to Kirtland, the site of the temple that bore the name "the House of the Lord," wherein the much-anticipated endowment and solemn assembly were to empower church officers in their ministry. Building the temple in Kirtland—which JS often referred to as the "chapel" or simply "the house"—had been a focal point since summer 1833, when a letter from JS, Sidney Rigdon, and Frederick G. Williams reported that there were only one hundred fifty Saints in Kirtland.[17] In autumn 1834, JS himself helped quarry stone for the building.[18] By late 1835, the nine hundred Mormons in Kirtland, plus the two hundred living nearby, included skilled individuals recruited specifically for the building project, freeing JS to pursue spiritual, educational, and administrative matters. A temple committee composed of JS's brother Hyrum, Reynolds Cahoon, and Jared Carter oversaw construction of the House of the Lord. The construction workers were compensated in part through goods available at the "committee store."

Preparation for the promised endowment required much more than completion of the temple. JS's vision for a church prepared for its expansive mission included an extensive and well-organized priesthood hierarchy. After adding three assistants to the church's presidency in December 1834,[19] JS further expanded his cadre of leaders. Drawn almost exclusively from the ranks of the 1834 expedition to Missouri, the Quorum of the Twelve and the Quorum of the Seventy, organized in February 1835, were assigned primarily to minister outside Ohio and Missouri, the two centers of the church. JS gave the new officers short-term assignments to preach in the East and seek financial support for Zion in Missouri and the temple in Ohio.[20] Beginning in January 1836, JS worked to have every

---

14. Daniel Dunklin, Jefferson City, MO, to William W. Phelps et al., Kirtland, OH, 22 Jan. 1836, in JS History, vol. B-1, addenda, 3nH.

15. Whitmer, History, 83.

16. JS, Journal, 13 Mar. 1836.

17. JS et al., Kirtland, OH, to Edward Partridge et al., Independence, MO, 25 June 1833, JS Collection, CHL.

18. JS History, vol. B-1, 553; Heber C. Kimball, in *Journal of Discourses*, 6 Apr. 1863, 10:165.

19. 48n161 herein; entries for 5 and 6 Dec. 1834, in JS History, 1834–1836, 17–20.

20. JS, Kirtland, OH, to the Quorum of the Twelve Apostles, 4 Aug. 1835, in JS Letterbook 1, pp. 90–93.

House of the Lord. Circa 1875. Joseph Smith's second Ohio journal focuses on the Saints' spiritual and organizational preparation to receive an "endowment of power" in the House of the Lord. (Courtesy Community of Christ Library-Archives, Independence, MO. Photograph by "Faze the Rambling Artist.")

office and organization mentioned in the revelations fully staffed—to "set the different quorems in order."[21] With the entire array of priesthood leadership from both Ohio and Missouri in Kirtland to prepare for empowerment, many of the regular Kirtland council meetings included the Missouri leadership, especially Missouri president David Whitmer and his counselors William W. Phelps and John Whitmer. These three also often joined with the church's presidency in Kirtland—JS, Oliver Cowdery, Sidney Rigdon, Frederick G. Williams, Hyrum Smith, and Joseph Smith Sr.—in a council of presidents that conducted much of the church business.

Preparation of church officials for carrying out their responsibilities required ministerial training. This was accomplished in the Elders School, which was a revival of the earlier School of the Prophets. In early January 1836, an additional school was opened offering two months' intensive study of biblical Hebrew under the tutelage of scholar Joshua Seixas. This instruction ran concurrently with the Elders School and involved many of the same students. JS himself participated as an enthusiastic student of Hebrew.

JS insisted that in addition to being fully staffed and properly organized and trained, the church leadership must have unity and harmony.[22] A prerequisite to the endowment was a sanctification process that in turn required collegiality and love. JS faced significant challenges from within the hierarchy and his own family as he sought to establish this unity. During the apostles' 1835 mission, JS and other leaders in Kirtland chastised the Quorum of the Twelve by letter for offensive statements two of them had made about Sidney Rigdon. The Twelve also had reportedly failed to emphasize donations for temple

---

21. JS, Journal, 30 Jan. 1836.

22. See Revelation, 27 and 28 Dec. 1832 and 3 Jan. 1833, in Doctrine and Covenants 7, 1835 ed. [D&C 88]; and Revelation, ca. Apr. 1835, in Doctrine and Covenants 3:11–12, 1835 ed. [D&C 107:27–33].

construction while seeking funds for Missouri lands and other church needs. JS concluded later that the latter concern, based on a complaint by an observer in New York, was unwarranted. After the Twelve returned to Kirtland there were feelings to reconcile, apologies to make, and clarifications required concerning the role of the Twelve. The flurry of accusations and confessions in council meetings recorded in this journal were meant to heal breaches and promote harmony by airing and then resolving all disagreements.

To JS's great dismay, his confrontations with his volatile younger brother William, an apostle in the church, contrasted starkly with JS's ideals. The two strong-willed Smiths clashed in fall 1835. Harmony was not restored until Joseph Smith Sr. convened a family New Year's gathering to bring about reconciliation. Passages in this diary about their interaction offer revealing insights into the personalities and temperaments of JS and William.

After resolving differences among church leaders, the officers were ready to receive the rituals associated with the temple and the anticipated endowment. This was a new development. The previous fall JS had told members of the Quorum of the Twelve that they were soon to attend the organization of a school of the prophets that would involve a solemn assembly and the ordinance of foot washing—patterned after Jesus's ministration to his disciples after the Last Supper and mandated in the same revelation that first called for a temple to be built.[23] This would have repeated the procedures followed at the organization of the initial School of the Prophets in 1833. Instead, JS organized the Elders School on 3 November 1835 without a solemn assembly, and the foot-washing ordinance was performed during a solemn assembly in the House of the Lord at the conclusion of a set of newly instituted ordinances. Before the Lord could "endow his servants," recorded John Whitmer, "we must perform all the ordinances that are instituted in his house."[24] To this end, washing, anointing, and blessing the presidents of quorums began 21 and 22 January 1836. In the coming weeks, these rituals were administered in hierarchal order to each church officer in the House of the Lord. The ordinances were accompanied by exclamations of "hosanna" in unison. Visions and other spiritual manifestations were noted by numerous participants.

On 27 March 1836, before a general audience of church members, JS dedicated the newly completed House of the Lord. His dedicatory prayer and the accompanying hymns and sermons expressed the vision he and his associates shared for the unfolding of God's plan for the earth and the role they were to play as God's authorized representatives. Not only their worldview and proximate goals but also their perceived challenges and obstacles were delineated in the journal's report.

Two days after the dedication of the House of the Lord, JS and the presidency sought revelation about the proposed move to Missouri. They emerged from an all-night session in the House of the Lord to announce that the key to redeeming Zion lay in proselytizing and gathering converts to Missouri.[25] As for the presidency, their immediate concern was raising funds to purchase Missouri land.[26] Apparently their planned move was postponed until after such purchases could be made.

---

23. JS, Journal, 5 Oct. 1835; Revelation, 27 and 28 Dec. 1832 and 3 Jan. 1833, in Doctrine and Covenants 7:45–46, 1835 ed. [D&C 88:138–141].

24. Whitmer, History, 83.

25. JS, Journal, 29 and 30 Mar. 1836.

26. JS, Journal, 2 Apr. 1836.

Now that the temple was dedicated to the Lord, the long-awaited solemn assembly was finally held. On 30 March 1836, three days after the dedication, about three hundred priesthood officers met in the House of the Lord and received a ritual washing of feet, an ordinance of purification before receiving the endowment of power. JS announced the celebration of a jubilee for the church. While preparing the sacrament of the Lord's Supper to initiate a Passover feast, he instructed the officers that "the time that we were required to tarry in Kirtland to be endued would be fulfilled in a few days." Soon afterward, according to several accounts, many who were gathered in the solemn assembly experienced a powerful spiritual outpouring. They remained in the House of the Lord through the night, prophesying, speaking in tongues, and seeing visions. Many felt that the promise of an endowment of spiritual power had been fulfilled, and elders began leaving Kirtland the following day to perform missions.

For those officers who remained, the jubilee and the Passover were a week of visiting, feasting, prophesying, and pronouncing blessings on one another. During the Sunday worship service held 3 April 1836, the day for which the final entry in the journal was made, JS and Oliver Cowdery secluded themselves behind drawn curtains at the podium of the House of the Lord. There, the journal indicates, they experienced a vision of the resurrected Jesus Christ, who stated that he accepted the edifice as his house. Afterward, according to this account, Moses, Elias, and Elijah also appeared and conferred priesthood keys and authority for essential ministries over which they each had responsibility. The jubilee ended 6 April 1836, the first day of the church's seventh year.

———— ⁓ ————

/²⁷⟨Sketch Book⟩ [*front cover*]

[*Blank flyleaf followed by lined leaf with scriptural references
regarding repentance on the recto*]

/²⁸Sketch Book for the use of

Joseph Smith, jr.²⁹

22 September 1835 • Tuesday

September 22, 1835. This day Joseph Smith, jr. labored with Oliver Cowdery, in obtaining and writing blessings.³⁰ We were thronged a part of the time with

---

27. TEXT: Warren Parrish handwriting begins.

28. TEXT: Warren Parrish handwriting ends; Oliver Cowdery begins.

29. Oliver Cowdery also used "Sketch Book" as a title for his own journal, which he began on 1 January 1836.

30. On this date, 22 September, JS dictated blessings for David Whitmer, John Whitmer, John Corrill, and William W. Phelps. Cowdery copied these blessings on 2 and 3 October 1835 into what became the first book of patriarchal blessings. On the evening of 22 September, Cowdery wrote a prophetic blessing for JS, which he recorded in the same book on 3 October. Additional blessings given in November and December 1833 by JS for Frederick G. Williams, Sidney Rigdon, Cowdery, and JS's parents and siblings

company, so that our labor, in this thing, was hindered; but we obtained many precious things, and our souls were blessed. O Lord, may thy Holy Spirit be with thy servants forever. Amen.

September 23.ᵗʰ [22ⁿᵈ] This day Joseph Smith, Jr. was at home writing blessings for my most beloved Brotheren ⟨I⟩, have been hindered by a multitude of visitors but the Lord has blessed our Souls this day. May God grant ⟨to⟩ continue his mercies unto my house, this ⟨night,⟩ day For Christ sake. This day my Soul has desired the salvation of Brother Ezra, Thay[e]r. Also Brother Noah, Packard. Came to my house and let the Chappel Committee³¹ have one thousand dollers, by loan, for the building the house of the Lord; Oh may God bless him with an hundred fold! even of the ⟨things of⟩ Earth, for this ritious [righteous] act. My heart is full of desire to day, to ⟨be⟩ blessed of the God, of Abraham; with prosperity, untill I will be able to pay all my depts; for it is my ⟨the⟩ delight of my soul to ⟨be⟩ honest. Oh Lord that thou knowes right well! help me and I will give to the poor.

23 September 1835 · Wednesday

September 23ᵈ 1835 This day Brother, ⟨Brothers⟩ William, Tibbets John, and Joseph Tibbets [Tippets] Started for Mosoura [Missouri] the place designated for Zion or the Saints gathering they Came to bid us farewell³² the Brotheren Came in to pray with them and Brother David Whitmer acted as spokesman he prayed in the spirit a glorious time succeded his prayr Joy filled our hearts and we [p. 1] blessed them and bid them God speed and and promiced them a safe Journy and took them ⟨by the hand⟩ and bid them farewell for ⟨a⟩ season Oh! may God grant them long life and good days these blessings I ask ⟨upon them⟩ for Christ sake Amen

were recorded by Cowdery in the book in late September and on 1 and 2 October. (Patriarchal Blessings, 1:8–16; JS, Journal, 14–19 Nov. and 18 Dec. 1833; see also transcriptions of these blessings in *The Joseph Smith Papers,* Documents series [forthcoming], 19 Nov. and 18 Dec. 1833; 22 Sept. 1835.)

31. In June 1833, Hyrum Smith, Reynolds Cahoon, and Jared Carter were appointed as a committee to direct the construction of the House of the Lord in Kirtland. (Minute Book 1, 6 June 1833.)

32. On 28 November 1834, the Kirtland high council met to consider a letter sent by church members in Essex County, New York, and presented by John and Joseph Tippets. The letter listed money and property totaling $848.40 collected to purchase land in Missouri. The two men were advised to remain in Kirtland during the winter and lend part of their money to the church there. At a high council meeting on 24 August 1835, the Tippetses were counseled to resume their journey to Missouri in the fall. This entry marks their departure. (Minute Book 1, 28 Nov. 1834 and 24 Aug. 1835.)

First page of "Sketch Book." Oliver Cowdery inscribed the title for this journal "Sketch Book for the use of Joseph Smith, jr." Together with Oliver Cowdery, Warren Parrish, and other scribes, Smith used it to record daily entries from late September 1835 to early April 1836. On this page: handwriting of Oliver Cowdery and Joseph Smith. JS, Journal, 1835–1836, p. 1, JS Collection, Church History Library, Salt Lake City. (Photograph by Welden C. Andersen.)

24 September 1835 • Thursday

September 24ᵗʰ 1835 This day the high council met at my house to take into conside[r]ation the redeemtion of Zion and it was the voice of the spirit of the Lord that we petition to the Governer³³ that is those who have been driven out ⟨should⟩ to do so to be set back on their Lands next spring³⁴ and we go next season to live or dy to this end so the dy is cast in Jackson County we truly had a good time and Covena[n]ted to strugle for this thing utill [until] death shall desolve this union and if one falls that the rest be not discouraged but pesue [pursue] this object untill it is acomplished which may God grant u[n]to us in the name of Christ our Lord

September 24ᵗʰ 1835 This day drew up an Article of inrollment for the redemtion of Zion that we may obtain volenteers to go we³⁵ next Spring ⟨to Mo [Missouri]⟩³⁶ I ask God in the name of Jesus that we may obtain Eight hundred men ⟨or one thousand⟩ well armed and that they may acomplish this great work even so Amen—— [p. 2]

25 September 1835 • Friday

/³⁷Friday 25th September. This day I remained at home: nothing of note transpired. The twelve all returned from the east to day.

26 September 1835 • Saturday

26th. This evening, the twelve having returned from the east this morning,³⁸

---

33. Daniel Dunklin, governor of Missouri 1832–1836.

34. JS's 1834–1836 history adds: "praying for his [Dunklin's] assistance in his official capacity, in restoring those to their possessions in Jackson County."ᵃ In a November 1834 message to the Missouri legislature, Dunklin made reference to the "outrages" committed against the Mormons and noted that "these unfortunate people are now forbidden to take possession of their homes." A copy of Dunklin's speech arrived in Kirtland in mid-December 1834, reviving hopes that Latter-day Saint losses might be redressed. Following this news, JS counseled the church members in Missouri to "make but little or no stir in that region, and cause as little excitement as possible and endure their afflictions patiently until the time appointed—and the Governor of Mo. fulfils his promise in setting the church over upon their own lands."ᵇ (a. JS History, 1834–1836, 106. b. JS History, vol. B-1, 559, 563; Whitmer, History, 79.)

35. TEXT: Possibly "me".

36. This action reflects JS's firm intention to return to Missouri in spring 1836 with an armed expedition to repossess Mormon property. John Whitmer recorded that at this meeting, a leadership organization for the expedition was established "for the war department, by revelation." (Whitmer, History, 81.)

37. TEXT: Oliver Cowdery handwriting begins.

38. On 12 March 1835, less than a month after it was organized, the Quorum of the Twelve was appointed to a mission to the eastern states to "hold conferences in the vicinity of the several branches of the Church for the purpose of regulating all things necessary for their welfare." The Twelve left 4 May 1835. Six of the Twelve also crossed into Upper Canada and convened a conference at West Loughborough. (Quorum of the Twelve Apostles, Record, 12 Mar. and 4 May 1835; see also Esplin, "Emergence of Brigham Young," 163–170.)

Probable Ohio residence of Joseph Smith. 1884. In February 1834, Smith moved his family from the upper floor of the Newel K. Whitney store to a home north of the temple lot in Kirtland, Ohio. (Courtesy Community of Christ Library-Archives, Independence, MO.)

we met them, and conversed upon some matters of difficulty which ~~was~~ ⟨ware⟩ existing between some of them, and president [Sidney] Rigdon, and all things were settled satisfactorily.[39]

27 September 1835 • Sunday

27th Sunday. Attended meeting: brethren, Thomas B. Marsh, David W. Patten, Brigham Young and Heber C. Kimball[40] preached and broke bread. The Lord poured out his Spirit, and my soul was edified.

28 September 1835 • Monday

28th. High council met and tried brother Gladden Bishop: he was reproved, repented, and was reordained. The next was Lorenzo L. Lewis for fornication: he was cut off from the Church.[41]

29 September 1835 • Tuesday

29th High Council met to-day and tried brother Allen Avery: he was acquited from any charge.[42] Also Brother Phineas H. Young, who was also acquited:[43] also bro. Lorenzo Young, who confessed his error and was forgiven.[44]

---

39. A month and a half earlier, on 4 August 1835, JS and the council of church presidents met to consider a charge that apostles William E. McLellin and Orson Hyde had, while on their mission, "express[ed] dissatisfaction with President Rigdon's school."[a] This was evidently the Kirtland School, a coeducational institution with a secular curriculum, at which McLellin had taught along with Rigdon before leaving Kirtland with the Quorum of Twelve on their mission to the eastern United States.[b] On the date of this entry, McLellin and Hyde "frankly confessed and were forgiven" by the council. The presidencies also considered the "derogatory" reports made by Warren Cowdery, the president of the church conference in Freedom, New York, which the Quorum of the Twelve attended in the course of their mission. Cowdery's charges that the Twelve had not been following JS's commission to raise money for building the House of the Lord were deemed false.[c] (a. JS, Kirtland, OH, to the Quorum of the Twelve Apostles, 4 Aug. 1835, in JS Letterbook 1, pp. 90–93; Minute Book 1, 26 Sept. 1835; Orson Hyde and William E. McLellin, Kirtland, OH, Oct. 1835, letter to the editor, *LDS Messenger and Advocate,* Oct. 1835, 2:204–207. b. "Notice" and William E. McLellin, notice, 27 Feb. 1835, *LDS Messenger and Advocate,* Feb. 1835, 1:80; Kimball, "History," 27. c. Minute Book 1, 26 Sept. 1835; Porter, "Odyssey of William Earl McLellin," 318; Esplin, "Emergence of Brigham Young," 166–170; see also JS, Journal, 16 Jan. 1836.)

40. These were the four oldest members of the Quorum of the Twelve. At this time, seniority in the quorum was based on age. (JS History, vol. B-1, 589.)

41. Francis Gladden Bishop was charged with "advancing heretical doctrines which were derogatory to the character of the Church." Lewis's partial confession was judged unsatisfactory. (Minute Book 1, 28 Sept. 1835.)

42. Avery was charged with rebelling against the decision of the Missouri elders council to take away his elder's license. However, Avery came forward and "complied with the requisitions of the council" and was restored to his office. (Minute Book 1, 29 Sept. 1835.)

43. Phineas Young was charged with "unchristian like conduct" in connection with his sale and distribution of a handful of copies of the Book of Mormon during his 1835 proselytizing journey. (Minute Book 1, 29 Sept. 1835.)

44. Lorenzo Young was charged by William W. Phelps with teaching that "poor men ought not to raise

In all these I acted on the part of the defence for the accused to plead for mercy. The Lord blessed my soul, and the council was greatly blessed, also. Much good will no doubt, result from our labors during the two days in which we were occupied on the business of the Church.

30 September 1835 • Wednesday

30th. Stayed at home and visited many who came to enquire after the work of the Lord.

1 October 1835 • Thursday

October 1, 1835. This after noon labored[45] on the Egyptian alphabet, in company with brsr O[liver] Cowdery and W[illiam] W. Phelps:[46] The system of astronomy was unfolded.[47]

2 October 1835 • Friday

2nd. To-day wrote a letter to be published in the Messenger and Advocate.[48] [p. 3]

3 October 1835 • Saturday

/[49]Saturday 3d Oct held a high council on the case of Elder John Gould for giving credence to false and slanderous reports instigated to Injure bro Sidney Rigdon[50] and also Dean Gould for thretning bro Sidney Rigdon and others

---

up seed or children" but that they might be permitted to marry. After Young "made an humble acknowledgement," the charge was dismissed. (Minute Book 1, 29 Sept. 1835.)

45. The entry for this same date in JS's 1834–1836 history reads "stayed at home and labored."

46. Their efforts apparently included the creation of three documents—nearly identical in content—that include transcripts of Egyptian characters in parallel with material written in English. (Kirtland Egyptian Papers, ca. 1835–1836, 3, 4, 5, CHL; see also Gee, "Eyewitness, Hearsay, and Physical Evidence," 196.)

47. Possibly refers to the astronomical material in three "Egyptian alphabet" documents. Astronomical material also appeared in JS's published "Book of Abraham." (Kirtland Egyptian Papers, ca. 1835–1836, 3, 4, 5, CHL; "The Book of Abraham," *Times and Seasons,* 1 Mar. 1842, 3:703–706; 15 Mar. 1842, 3:719–722 [Abraham 1–5]; see also JS History, vol. B-1, 622; and Gee, "Eyewitness, Hearsay, and Physical Evidence," 197–203.)

48. This was the first in a series of three letters written by JS and published in successive issues of the *LDS Messenger and Advocate* to provide instruction for traveling elders. This first letter provides an account of Mormon settlement in Jackson County and a doctrinal exposition of faith, repentance, baptism, and receiving the gift of the Holy Ghost, which JS considered the foundational principles and ordinances of the restored gospel. (JS, "To the Elders of the Church of Latter Day Saints," *LDS Messenger and Advocate,* Sept. 1835, 1:179–182; see also Nov. 1835, 2:209–212; and Dec. 1835, 2:225–230.)

49. TEXT: Oliver Cowdery handwriting ends; Frederick G. Williams begins.

50. According to council minutes, John Gould was charged with "making expressions which is calculated to do injury to the great cause . . . and manifesting a very strong dissatisfaction against the teachings of the Presidency of the church." (Minute Book 1, 3 Oct. 1835.)

in ~~authority~~ of the Elders. after due deliberation the[y] both confessed and wer acquited.

In the afternoon waited on the twelve most of them at my house and exhibited to them the ancient reccords in my possession and gave explanation of the same ~~thus~~ ⟨this⟩ ~~the~~ day passed off with the blessings of the Lord

4 October 1835 • Sunday

Sunday 4 started early in the mornin with brother J Carrell [John Corrill] to hold a meeting in Perry when about a mile from home we saw two Dears playing in the field which diverted our minds by giving an impatus to our thoughts upon the subject of the creation of God we conversed upon many topicks and the day passed off in a very agreeable manner and the Lord blessed our souls when we arived at Perry we were disappointed of a meeting through misarangements but conversed freely ~~upon~~ with Bro John Correls reletives which allayed much prejudice as we trust may the lord have mercy on their souls

5 October 1835 • Monday

Monday 5th returned home being much fatiegued riding in the rain spent the remainder of the day in reading and meditation &c and [p. 4] in the evening attend[ed] a high councel of the twelve apostles, had a glorious time and gave them many instruction concerning their duties for time to come, told them that it was the will of God they should take their families to Missouri next season, also attend this fall the solemn assembly of the first Elders for the organization of the school of the prophets, and attend to the ordinence of the washing of feet[51] and to prepare their hearts in all humility for an endowment ~~from~~ with power from on high to which they all agreed with one accord, and seamed to be greatly rejoiced may God spare the lives of the twelve with one accord to a good old age for christ the redeemers sake amen

6 October 1835 • Tuesday

Tuesday 6 At home ~~father or~~ Elder Stevens came to my house and loaned

---

51. A December 1832 revelation announced the formation of the School of the Prophets, whose candidates would "be received by the ordinance of the washing of feet." The school was organized in 1833, but foot washing ceased after the initial school term. The Elders School—a successor to the School of the Prophets—was organized in 1834 and again on 3 November 1835. JS frequently referred to it as the School of the Prophets. After the House of the Lord was completed and dedicated, the anticipated solemn assembly was finally held, which included the ordinance of foot washing. (Revelation, 27 and 28 Dec. 1832 and 3 Jan. 1833, in Doctrine and Covenants 7:44–45, 1835 ed. [D&C 88:136–139]; JS, Journal, 29 and 30 Mar. 1836.)

F G Williams and Co six hundred Dollars which greatly releaved us out of our present difficulties[52] may God bless and preserve his soul for ever— Afternoon called to visit my father who was very sick with a fever some better towards evening spent the rest of the day in reading and meditation

7 October 1835 · Wednesday

Wednesday 7 went to visit my fathe[r] find him very low administerd some mild herbs agreeable to the commandment[53] may God grant to restore him immediately to health for christ the redeemers sake Amen This day bro N[ewel] K Whitney and Bro Hyrum Smith started for buffalo to purchace good[s] to replenish the committe store by land in the stage may God grant in the name of Jesus that their lives may [p. 5] be spared and they have a safe Journey and no accident or sickness of the least kind befall them that they may return in health and in safety to the bosom of their families—

Blessed of the lord is bro Whitney even the bishop of the church of the latter day saints,[54] for the bishoprick shall never be taken away from him while he liveth and the time cometh that he shall overcome all the narrow mindedness of his heart and all his covetous desires that so easily besetteth him and ⟨he⟩ shall ~~deliver~~ deal with a liberal hand to the poor and the needy the sick and the afflicted the widow and the fatherless and marviously [marvelously] and miraculously shall the Lord his God provid for him. even that he shall be blessed with ~~a~~ ⟨all the ~~the~~⟩ fullness of the good things of this earth and his seed after him from generation to generation and it shall come to pass that according to to the measure that he meeteth out with a liberal hand unto the poor so shall it be measured to him again by the hand of his God even an hundred fold Angels shall guard ⟨his⟩ house and shall guard the lives of his posterity, and they shall become very great and very numerous on the earth, whomsoever he blesseth they shall be blessed. whomsoever he curseth they shall be cursed. and

---

52. F. G. Williams & Co., the church printing arm, had recently published the first edition of the Doctrine and Covenants, was producing three newspapers, and was preparing its first hymnal. By October 1835, the expenses outlaid for these projects brought the company close to economic collapse. (Crawley, *Descriptive Bibliography*, 47–53, 54–59; Cook, *Law of Consecration*, 47–50.)

53. Apparently a reference to Revelation, 9 Feb. 1831, in Doctrine and Covenants 13:12, 1835 ed. [D&C 42:43]; or Revelation, 27 Feb. 1833, in Doctrine and Covenants 80:2, 1835 ed. [D&C 89:10].

54. Though Whitney was bishop of the church in Kirtland at this time, Edward Partridge was bishop in Missouri; each held regional jurisdictions. In 1847, Whitney was sustained as presiding bishop over the whole church.[a] JS gave Whitney this blessing through the medium of a seer stone.[b] (a. Staker, "Thou Art the Man," 101–103; Quinn, "Evolution of the Presiding Quorums," 32–34, 37. b. Blessing, JS to Newel K. Whitney, 7 Oct. 1835, Newel K. Whitney, Papers, BYU; Blessing, JS to Newel K. Whitney, 7 Oct. 1835, in Patriarchal Blessings, 1:33–34; see also Van Wagoner and Walker, "Gift of Seeing," 62–63; and *The Joseph Smith Papers*, Documents series [forthcoming], 7 Oct. 1835.)

Newel K. Whitney. Joseph Smith appointed Whitney bishop of the Latter-day Saint community centered in Kirtland, Ohio, when the Saints began gathering there in 1831. Whitney's store, located at a crossroads in northwestern Kirtland Township, served for a time as Smith's residence and as church headquarters. (Church History Library, Salt Lake City.)

when his enemies seek him unto his hurt and distruction let him rise up and curse and the hand of God shall be upon his enemies in Judgment [p. 6] they shall be utterly confounded and brought to dessolation, therefor he shall be preserved unto the utmost and his ⟨life⟩ day shall be precious in the sight of the Lord. he shall rise up and shake himself as a lion riseth out of his nest and roareth untill he shaketh the hills and as a lion goeth forth among the Lesser beasts, so shall the goings forth of him ⟨be⟩ whom the Lord hath anointed to exalt the poor and to humble the rich, therefor his name shall be on high and his rest among the sanctified

this afternoon recommenced translating the ancient reccords

8 October 1835 · Thursday

/⁵⁵Thursday 8ᵗʰ at home nothing of note transpired of as we now recollect, ⟨I attended on my Father with feelings of great anxiety—⟩

9 October 1835 · Friday

Friday 9ᵗʰ at home nothing worthy of note transpired ⟨on this day waited on my Father⟩

10 October 1835 · Saturday

Saturday 10ᵗʰ at home⟨, visited the house of my Father found him failing verry fast⟩—

11 October 1835 · Sunday

Sunday 11ᵗʰ visited my Father ⟨again⟩ who was verry sick ⟨in secret prayer in the morning the Lord said my servant thy father shall live⟩ I waited on him all this day with my heart raised to god in the name of Jesus Christ that he would restore him to health again, that I might be blessed with his company and advise esteeming it one of the greatest earthly blessings, to be blessed with the society of Parents, whose maturer years and experience, renders them, capable of administering the most wholsom advise; at Evening Bro. David Whitmer came in we called on the Lord in mighty prayer in the name of Jesus Christ, and laid our hands on him, and rebuked the diseas and God heard and answered our prayers to the great joy and satisfaction of our souls, our aged Father arose and dressed himself shouted and praised the Lord called [p. 7] Br Wᵐ Smith who had retired to rest that he might praise the Lord with us by joining in Songs of praise to the most High

---

55. TEXT: Frederick G. Williams handwriting ends; Warren Parrish begins.

12 October 1835 • Monday

Monday 12th rode to Willoughby in company with my wife to purchase some goods at W. Lyons[56] Store on our return we found a M[r.] Bradly lying across the road he had been thrown ~~from~~ from his waggon was much injured by the fall

13 October 1835 • Tuesday

Tuesday 13th visited my Father who was verry much recovered from his sickness indeed, which caused us ⟨to⟩ marvel at the might power and condesension of our Heavenly Father in answering our prayers in his behalf

14 October 1835 • Wednesday

Wednesday 14th at home

15 October 1835 • Thursday

Thursday 15th Laboured in Fathers orchard gathering apples

16 October 1835 • Friday

Friday 16th was called into the printing ⟨office⟩ to settle some difficulties in that department, at evening on the same day I baptised Ebenezer Robinson the Lord poured out his spirit on us and we had a good time[57]

17 October 1835 • Saturday

Saturday 17th called my family together and aranged my domestick concerns and ~~domestic~~ dismissed my boarders[58]

18 October 1835 • Sunday

Sunday 18th attended meeting in the Chapel confirmed several who had been baptised[59] and blessed several ~~blessings~~ childern with the blessings of the

---

56. Probably Windsor Lyon.

57. Although he worked in the printing office and had boarded with JS, Robinson did not become a member of the church until this day. Robinson later recalled that he requested baptism during lunchtime and, after finishing work for the day, went to the east branch of the Chagrin River for the ordinance. (Ebenezer Robinson, "Items of Personal History of the Editor," *The Return,* May 1889, 74.)

58. JS was boarding men who worked in the printing shop. Ebenezer Robinson, Samuel Brannan, and William W. Phelps were apparently living in the Smith household at this time. Phineas Young, Wilbur Denton, and JS's brother Don Carlos Smith, printers who, as recorded in JS's journal, began boarding with JS in 1833, also may have still been living there. (Robinson, "Items of Personal History," *The Return,* Apr. 1889, 58; Bagley, *Scoundrel's Tale,* 42–44, 144, 193; William W. Phelps, Kirtland Mills, OH, to Sally Phelps, Liberty, MO, 16 Sept. 1835, CHL; JS, Journal, 22 Nov. 1833; 9 and 11 Dec. 1833.)

59. Including Ebenezer Robinson. (Robinson, "Items of Personal History," *The Return,* May 1889, 74–76.)

new and everlasting covenant Elder Parley P. Pratt preachd in the fore noon, and Elder John F. Boynton in the after noon, we had an interesting time

19 October 1835 • Monday

Monday 19ᵗʰ at home, exibited the records of of antiquity to a number who called to see them

20 October 1835 • Tuesday

Tuesday 20ᵗʰ at home, preached at night in the School-house.

21 October 1835 • Wednesday

Wednesday 21ˢᵗ at home nothing [p. 8] of note transpired

22 October 1835 • Thursday

Thursday 22ᵈ at home attending to my domestick concerns

23 October 1835 • Friday

Friday 23ᵈ at home ~~attended the prayer meeting~~⁶⁰

24 October 1835 • Saturday

Saturday 24ᵗʰ Mʳ˙ Goodrich and his lady ~~called~~ called to see the antient Records also called at Doct. F[rederick] G. Williams to see the mummies, Brˢ˙ Hawks & Carpenter from Michigan visited us & taried over Sunday and attended meeting—

25 October 1835 • Sunday

Sunday 25ᵗʰ attended meeting President [Sidney] Rigdon preached in the fore noon, Elder Lyman Johnson in the after noon, after which Elder S. Bronson [Seymour Brunson] joined Br. Wᵐ Perry & Sister Eliza Brown in matrimony,⁶¹ and I blessed them with long life and prosperity in the name of Jesus Christ, at evening I attended prayer meeting opened it and exorted, the brethren & Sister about one hour, the Lord pourd out his spirit and some glorious things, were spoken in the gift of toungs, and interpeted concerning the redemption of Zion

---

60. JS and other church leaders prayed for the redemption of Zion and for relief from church debts. The prayer offered this day was recorded following the entry of 27 November 1835.

61. Brunson—who had obtained a license in Jackson County, Ohio, to solemnize weddings—may have been the only licensed Latter-day Saint at this time. (Bradshaw, "Joseph Smith's Performance of Marriages in Ohio," 40.)

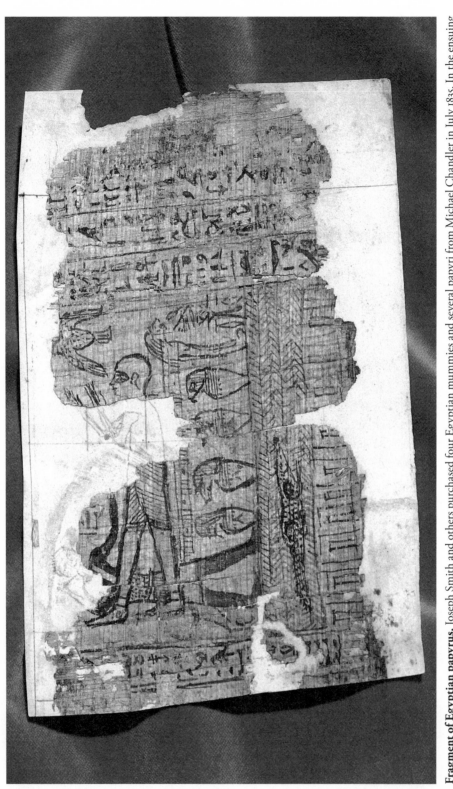

Fragment of Egyptian papyrus. Joseph Smith and others purchased four Egyptian mummies and several papyri from Michael Chandler in July 1835. In the ensuing months, Smith exhibited the artifacts to friends and visitors and began an effort to translate the writings on the papyri. He later published part of his translation as the writings of the biblical patriarch Abraham. (Church History Library, Salt Lake City.)

26 October 1835 • Monday

Monday 26th went to Chardon to attend the county Court in company with Brs Hyrum Samuel & Carloss [Don Carlos] Smith, Br. Samuel was called in question before this Court for not doing military duty,[62] and was fined because we had not our conference minuets with us for testimony to prove that F[rederick] G. Williams was clerk of the conference,— this testimony we should have carried with us had it not been for the neglect of our Council, or Lawyer,[63] who did not put us in possession of this information this we feel was a want of fidelity to his client, and we concider it a base insult ⟨practised⟩ upon us on the account of our faith, that the ungodly might have unlawful power over us and trample us under their unhallowed feet; ⟨&⟩ in consequence of this neglect a fine was imposed on Br Samuel [p. 9] of $20, including costs, for which ~~Lawsuit,~~ he was oblieged to sell his cow, to defray the expenses of the same, and I say in the name of Jesus Christ that the money that they have thus unjustly taken shall be a testimony against them and canker & eat their flesh as fire

27 October 1835 • Tuesday

Tuesday 27th in the morning I was called to visit at Br Samuel Smiths his wife was confined an[d] in a verry dangerous situation, Br. Carloss [Don Carlos Smith] took one of my horses and went to Chardon after Doct. [Frederick G.] Williams I went out into the field and bowed before the Lord and called upon him in mighty prayer in her behalf the word of the Lord came unto me saying my Servant Fredrick shall come and shall have wisdom given him to deal prudently and my handmaden shall be delivered of a living child & be spared, he come in a bout one hour after that and in the course of about 2. hours she was

---

62. As in other states, in Ohio the state militia act required free, white, adult male citizens to serve in the state militia. Fines were levied for failure to attend training. However, the law exempted mail carriers, sailors at sea, and, as in most states, clergymen. Justice of the Peace John C. Dowen originally issued writs against both Samuel Smith and JS for "non-attendance at training" but then excused JS because of his ecclesiastical office. A court of inquiry held 25 September 1833, *George Metcalf, Paymaster of the 1st Brigade, 2nd Regiment, 9th Division, Ohio Militia v. Samuel H. Smith,* fined Samuel Smith $1.75 for failing to attend company and regimental musters in 1833. In this appeal to the county court of common pleas, where Samuel was fined an additional $20 for not bringing the necessary documentation, Samuel argued that he met the legal requirements of an acting minister. (Act for Organizing and Disciplining the Militia [22 Feb. 1831], *Statutes of Ohio,* vol. 1, pp. 1983–2005; John C. Dowen, Statement, 2 Jan. 1885, 2, Manuscripts about Mormons at Chicago History Museum, Research Center, Chicago Historical Society; Geauga Co., OH, Court of Common Pleas, 20 Oct. 1835, final record bk. S, 95–101, microfilm, U.S. and Canada Record Collection, FHL.)

63. Benjamin Bissell. (Geauga Co., OH, Court of Common Pleas, 20 Oct. 1835, final record bk. S, 97, microfilm, U.S. and Canada Record Collection, FHL.)

delivered[64] and thus what God had manifested to me was fulfilled every whit, on the night of the same day I preached in the Schoolhouse to a crowded congregation

28 October 1835 · Wednesday

Wednesday 28th at holm attending to my family concerns &c

29 October 1835 · Thursday

Thursday 29th Br W. Parish [Warren Parrish] commenced writing for me, Father & Mother Smith visit[ed] us and while we set writing Bishop, Partrige [Edward Partridge] passed our window just returned from the East— Br Parish commenced writing for me at $15.00 p[e]r month I paid him $16.00 in advance out of the committee Store Br Parrish agrees to board himself, for which I agree to ⟨allow him⟩ four Dollars more p[e]r. month making $19.00. I was then called to appear before the high Council which was [p. 10] setting to give my testimony in an action brought against Br. David Eliot [Elliott] for whiping his Daughter unreasonably my testimony was in his favour,[65] returned to our writing room, went to Dr. [Frederick G.] Williams after my large journal,[66] made some observations to my scribe concerning the plan of the City which is to be built up hereafter on this ground consecrated for a stake of Zion.[67]

while at the Doct Bishop E, Patrige came in, in company with President [William W.] Phelps, I was much rejoiced to see him, we examined the mumies, returned home and my scribe commenced writing in ⟨my⟩ journal a history of my life, concluding President [Oliver] Cowdery 2d letter to W. W. Phelps,

---

64. The infant was Susanna Bailey Smith, Samuel and Mary Bailey Smith's first child.

65. The high council met at Edmund Bosley's home in Kirtland. William Smith brought charges against both David and Mary Cahoon Elliott for whipping and beating David's teenage daughter from an earlier marriage. The discipline had caused public commotion in Chagrin, where the Elliotts lived. JS had visited with the daughter and her parents in their home, and he testified that "the girl was in the fault, and that the neighbors were trying to create a difficulty." (Minute Book 1, 29 Oct. 1835.)

66. The "large journal," the contents of which are known in the present edition as JS's 1834–1836 history, was a 14 x 9 inch volume in which Oliver Cowdery began recording historical information in 1834. However, Cowdery recorded only brief genealogical information for JS and himself and two journal entries, for 5 and 6 December 1834. Later, Frederick G. Williams began copying into the same volume a series of eight historical and doctrinal letters by Cowdery that had been published in the *LDS Messenger and Advocate* between October 1834 and October 1835. By the date of this journal entry, Williams had copied the first Cowdery letter and most of the second. Parrish finished copying the Cowdery letters into the "large journal." (See JS History, 1834–1836, 9–20, 46–57.)

67. Maps dating from 1833 and 1837 depict Latter-day Saint plans for major expansion in the city of Kirtland. The first map shows 49 square plots, each subdivided into 20 lots; the latter has 225 plots similarly divided. (Plats of Kirtland, Ohio, ca. 1833, ca. 1837, CHL.)

which president Williams had begun[68] Bishop [Newel K.] Whitney & his wife
with his Father & Mother called to Visit us, his parents having lately arived
here from the East[69] called to make enquiry concerning the coming forth of
the book of Mormon, Bishop Partrige & some others came in I then set down
and ~~taught~~ ⟨related to⟩ them the history of the coming forth of the book the
administration of the Angel to me the rudiments of the gospel of Christ &c
they appeared well satisfyed & I expect to baptise them in a few days, or this is
my feelings upon the subject altho they have not made any request of this kind
at present, went to the council, the Presidency arose and adjourned on my
return Elder [John F.] Boynton observed that long debates were had. I replyed
that it was generally the case, that to[o] much, altercation was ~~generally~~
indulged in, on both sides and their debates protracted to an unprofitable
length; we were ~~seated~~ called to sup[p]er, after being seated around the table
Bishop Whitney observed to Bishop Partrige that ⟨the⟩ thought had just
occured to his mind that perhaps in about one yea[r] from this time they might
be seated together around a table ~~in~~ on the land of Zion [p. 11]

Sister Emma ⟨my wife⟩ observed that she hoped it might be the case that
not only they but the rest of the of the company present might be seated
around her table in the land of promise; the same sentiment was reciprocated,
from the company round the table and my heart responded Amen God grant
it, I ask in the name of Jesus Christ, after sup[p]er I went to the high council in
company with my wife and some others that belong to my house hold I was
solicited to take a seat with the presidency and preside in a case of Sister Eliots
[Mary Cahoon Elliott] I did so my Mother was called as testimony and began
to relate circumstances that had been brought before the church and settled I
objected against such testimony the complainant Br. William Smith arose and
accused me of invalidating or doubting my Mothers testimony which I had not
done nor did I desire to do[70] I told him he was out of place & asked him to set
down he refused I repeated my request he become enraged I finally ordered
him to set down he said he would not unless I knocked him down I was agitated in my feeling ~~at~~ on the account of his stubournness and was about to ~~call~~

---

68. See Oliver Cowdery, "Letter II," *LDS Messenger and Advocate,* Nov. 1834, 1:27–32; JS History,
1834–1836, 57.

69. Elizabeth Ann Smith Whitney, with Samuel and Susanna Kimball Whitney from Marlborough,
Windham County, Vermont.

70. The official minute entry for this date indicates that William Smith also brought a second charge,
against Mary Cahoon Elliott only, for "abusing said E[lliott]s daughter as referred to before, and also
abusing the rest of her children." That JS agreed to preside in the case indicates his approval of considering
the new charges. JS ruled that his mother, Lucy Mack Smith, was out of order in presenting testimony
about matters that had already been resolved by the high council earlier in the day. (Minute Book 1,
29 Oct. 1835.)

Emma Hale Smith. Wife of Joseph Smith. Above: Portrait by David Rogers, 1842. Left: With son David Hyrum Smith, circa 1844–1845. (Both images courtesy Community of Christ Library-Archives, Independence, MO. Photograph of Rogers portrait by Ronald Read.)

leave the house, but my Father requsted me not to ⟨do so⟩ I complied the house was brought to order after much debate upon the subject and we proceded to buisness & br. Eliot & his wife were both cleared from the charges prefered against them[71]

30 October 1835 · Friday

Friday 30th at home Mr. Fransis Porter ~~called~~ from Jefferson Co. New York a member of the Methodist Church, called to make some inquiry about lands in this place whether there is any farmes for sale that are valuable and whether [p. 12] a member of our church could move into this vicinity and purchase lands and enjoy his own possessions & property with out making it common Stock, he had been requested to do so by some brethren who live in the town of Leray Jeff [Le Ray, Jefferson] Co N.Y I replyed that ~~he~~ ⟨I⟩ had a valuable farm joining the Temple Lot that ~~he~~ ⟨I⟩ would sell & that there is other lands for sale in this place and that we have no commonstock business among us, that every man enjoys his own property, or can if he is disposed, consecrate liberally or illiberally to the support of the poor & needy, or the building up of Zion,[72] he also enquired how many members there are in this church I told him that there is about five or six hundred who commune at our chapel and perhaps a thousand in this vicinity:—[73] at evening I was presented with a letter from Br. Wm Smith the purport of which is that he is censured by the brethren on the account of what took place at the council last night and wishes to have the matter settled to the understanding of all, that he may not be censured unjustly, concidering that his cause was a just one, and that he had been materially injured; I replied that I thought we parted with the best of feelings, that I am not to blame on the account of the dissatisfaction of others, I invited him to call and talk with me, and that I would ~~give~~ ⟨talk with⟩ him in the

---

71. Minutes of the council state that the Elliotts made confession after the council heard new evidence presented by a "Sister Childs" who had lived in the Elliott home. They were "forgiven, and . . . restored to fellowship." (Minute Book 1, 29 Oct. 1835.)

72. Prior to their 1830 conversion to Mormonism, followers of Sidney Rigdon in Kirtland established a communal society featuring group ownership of property. An 1831 JS revelation mandated establishing a new basis for economic reorganization that featured individual stewardships rather than common ownership. The categorical language in this revelation, "thou shalt consecrate *all* thy properties," was revised by 1835 to read in the Doctrine and Covenants published that year "thou wilt . . . consecrate *of* thy properties." (Revelation, 9 Feb. 1831, in Book of Commandments 44:26, italics added [D&C 42:29–31]; compare Doctrine and Covenants 13:8, 1835 ed., italics added [D&C 42:30]; see also Revelation, 20 May 1831, in Doctrine and Covenants 23:1, 1835 ed. [D&C 51:5]; and Revelation, 30 Apr. 1832, in Doctrine and Covenants 88:1, 1835 ed. [D&C 83:3].)

73. Approximately nine hundred to thirteen hundred Latter-day Saints, including children, lived in Kirtland Township at this time, with two hundred or more in the surrounding area. (Backman, *Heavens Resound,* 139–140.)

spirit of meekness and give him all the satisfaction I could.— this reply was by letter copy retained

31 October 1835 • Saturday

Saturday 31ˢᵗ in the morning br. Hyram [Hyrum] Smith came in and said he had been much troubled all night and had not slept any [p. 13] that something was wrong while talking br. Wᵐ· Smith came in according to my requst last night br. Hyram observed that he must go to the Store I invited him to stay he said he would go and do his business & return he did so while he was gone br. William introduced the subject of our difficulty at the council,⁷⁴ I told him I did not want to converse upon the subject untill Hyrum returned, he soon came in I then proposed to relate the occurrences of the council before named and wherein I had been out of the way I would confess it and ask his forgivness, and then he should relate his story and make confession wherein he had done wrong ~~he said he had not done wrong~~ and then leave it to br. Hyrum Smith & br. Parish [Warren Parrish] to decide the matter between us and I would agree to the decission & be satisfyed there with; he observed that he had not done wrong, and that I was always determined to carry my points whether right or wrong and therefore he would not stand an equal chance with me; this was an insult, but I did not reply to him in a harsh manner knowing his inflamatory disposition, but tryed to reason with him and show him the propriety of a complyance with my request, I finally succeeded with the assistance of br. Hyrum in obtaining his assent to the proposition that I had made. I then related my story and wherein I had been wrong I confessed it and asked his forgivness after I got through he made his statements justifying himself throughout in transgressing the order of the council & treating the authority of the Presidency with contempt; after he had got through br. Hyrum began to make [p. 14] some remarks, in the spirit of meekness, he [William Smith] became enraged, I joined my brother in trying to calm his stormy feelings, but to no purpose he insisted that we intended to add abuse to injury, his passion increased, he arose abruptly and declared that he wanted no more to do with ~~them~~ us or the church and said we might take his licence for he would have nothing to do with us, he rushed out at the door we tryed to prevail on him to stop, but all to no purpose, he went away in a passion, and soon sent his licence to me, he went home and spread the levavin [leaven] of iniquity ~~in~~ among my brethren and especially prejudiced the mind of br. Samuel [Smith] as I soon learned that he was in the streets exclaiming against, me, which no doubt our enemys rejoice at, and where the matter will end I know not, but I pray God to

---

74. See JS, Journal, 29 Oct. 1835.

forgive him and th[e]m, and give them humility and repentance, the feelings of my heart I cannot express on this occasion, I can only pray my heavenly Father to open their eyes that they may discover where they stand, that they may extricate themselves from the snare they have fallen into: after dinner I rode out in company with my wife and children, br. carloss [Don Carlos Smith] & some others, we went to visit br. [Shadrach] Roundy & family who live near Willoughby, we had an interesting visit at br. Roundy as soon as I returned I was called upon to baptise Samuel Whitney & his Wife and Daughter[75] after baptism we returned to their house and offered our thanks, in prayer I obtained a testimony that Br. William would return ~~and~~ to the church and repair the wrong he had done [p. 15]

1 November 1835 · Sunday

Sunday Morning November 1st 1835 Verily thus Saith the Lord unto me, his servant Joseph Smith jun mine anger is kindle[d] against my servant Reynolds Cahoon because of his iniquities his covetous and dishonest principles in himself and family and he doth not purge them away and set his house in order,[76] therefore if he repent not chastisment awaiteth him even as it seemeth good in my sight therefore go and declare unto him ~~this~~ ⟨these⟩ word⟨s⟩ I went imediately and delvired this message according as the Lord commanded me I called him in & read what the Lord had said concerning him, he acknowledged that it was verily so & expressed much humility,— I then went to meeting Elder Carrill [John Corrill] preached a fine discourse, in the after noon President [William W.] Phelps continued the servises of the day by reading the 5th chapt. of Mathew also the laws regulating the High Council[77] and made some remarks upon them after which sacrament was administered I then confirmed a number who had been baptised & blessed a number of children in the name of Jesus Christ with the blessings of the new and everlasting covenant, notice was then given that the Elders School woud commence on the on the morrow, I then dismissed the meeting,

---

75. Kirtland bishop Newel K. Whitney's parents, Samuel and Susanna Kimball Whitney, had recently arrived in Kirtland. Their daughter Caroline probably arrived with them. (JS, Journal, 29 Oct. 1835; Marlborough, VT, Vital Records, 1768–1857, 1:44, microfilm, U.S. and Canada Record Collection, FHL; obituary for Caroline Whitney Kingsbury, *The Wasp,* 29 Oct. 1842, [3].)

76. Less than three months earlier, on 10 August 1835, JS brought charges against Cahoon in a high council meeting for having "failed to do his duty in correcting his children, and instructing them in the way of truth & righteousness." The council agreed with the charges, and Cahoon "confessed the correctness of the decision, and promised to make public acknowledgement before the church." (Minute Book 1, 10 Aug. 1835.)

77. See Minute Book 1, 17 Feb. 1834 [D&C 102].

2 November 1835 · Monday

Monday morning 2ᵈ was engaged in regulating the affairs of the School, I then had my team prepared & Sidney [Rigdon] Oliver [Cowdery] Frederick [G. Williams] ~~and a~~ my scribe and a number of others went to Willoughby to Hear Doct Piexotto [Daniel Peixotto] deliver a lecture on the ~~profession~~ theory & practice of Physic[78] [p. 16] we called at Mr. [Nathan] Cushmans, had our horses put in the Stable took dinner, attended the lecture[79] was treated with great respect, throughout; returned home, Lyman Wight came ~~to~~ from Zion to day;—[80] George [A. Smith] & Lyman Smith also from the East[81] the question was agitated whether Frederick G. Williams or Oliver Cowdery Should go to New York to make arangements respecting a book bindery they refered to me for a decision, and thus came the word of the Lord unto me saying it is not my will that my servant Frederick should go to New York, but inasmuch as he wishes to go and visit his relatives that he may warn them to flee the wrath to come let him go and see them, for that purpose and let that be his only business, and behold in this thing he shall be blessed with power ~~while~~ to overcome their prejudices, Verily thus saith the Lord Amen.[82]

---

78. Peixotto, a public health advocate of national prominence, had revised George Gregory's medical textbook, *Elements of the Theory and Practice of Physic,* and had recently moved from New York City to become a professor at the newly established Willoughby Medical College in Willoughby, Ohio—the only institution for regular medical training in the Western Reserve—where he taught general medicine and obstetrics. (George Gregory, *Elements of the Theory and Practice of Physic, Designed for the Use of Students* [New York: M. Sherman, 1830]; Lake County Historical Society, *Here Is Lake County,* 51; *History of Geauga and Lake Counties,* 40; Wheeler, "Medicine in the Western Reserve," 35; "Peixotto," in *Jewish Encyclopedia,* 9:583.)

79. The lecture impressed church leaders, and Oliver Cowdery planned to insert a copy of it in the church-owned secular newspaper, the *Northern Times.* Soon afterward, Peixotto was invited to provide instruction in Kirtland. (Oliver Cowdery, [Kirtland, OH], to John M. Henderson, Willoughby, OH, 2 Nov. 1835, in Cowdery, Letterbook, 62.)

80. Wight had traveled from Clay County, Missouri, to Kirtland, where he attended the Elders School. He was among the earliest group called by JS to travel to Kirtland to be endowed with "power from on high." (Minute Book 2, 23 June 1834.)

81. Five months earlier, on 5 June 1835, JS's cousin George A. Smith and their second cousin Lyman Smith departed on a proselytizing mission to Ohio, Pennsylvania, and New York. (Historian's Office, "Sketch of the Auto Biography of George Albert Smith," 13, Histories of the Twelve, ca. 1858–1880, CHL.)

82. Cowdery soon left for New York City to "purchase a book-binding establishment and stock, and also a quantity of Hebrew books for the school." He returned within the month. (Oliver Cowdery, Kirtland, OH, to Warren Cowdery, [Freedom, NY], 22 Nov. 1835, in Cowdery, Letterbook, 63; JS, Journal, 20 Nov. 1835.)

3 November 1835 · Tuesday

~~Thus came~~ Tuesday 3ᵈ. Thus came the word of the Lord unto me ~~saying~~ concerning the, Twelve ⟨saying⟩

> behold they are under condemnation, because they have not been sufficiently humble in my sight, and in consequence of their covetous desires, in that they have not dealt equally with each other in the division of the moneys which came into their hands, nevertheless some of them, dealt equally therefore they shall be rewarded, but Verily I say unto you they must all humble themselves before Me, before they will be accounted worthy to receive an endowment to go forth in my name unto all nations, as for my Servant William [Smith] let the Eleven humble themselves in prayer and in faith [p. 17] and wait on me in patience and my servant William shall return, and I will yet make him a polished shaft in my quiver, in bringing down the wickedness and abominations of men and their shall be none mightier than he in his day and generation, nevertheless if he repent not spedily he shall be brought low and shall be chastened sorely for all his iniquities he has commited against me, nevertheless the sin which he hath sined against me is not even now more grevious than the sin with which my servant David W. Patten and my servant Orson Hyde and my servant Wᵐ E. McLellen [McLellin] have sinded against me, and the residue are not sufficiently humble before me, behold the parable which I spake concerning a man having twelve Sons,[83] for what man amon[g] you having twelve Sons and is no respecter to them and they serve him obediantly and he saith unto the one be thou clothed in robes and sit thou here, and to the other be thou clothed in rages [rags] and sit thou there, and looketh upon his sons and saith I am just, ye will answer and say no man, and ye answer truly, therefore Verily thus saith the Lord your God I appointed these twelve that they should be equal in their ministry and in their portion and in their evangelical rights, wherefore they have sined a verry grevious sin, in asmuch as they have made themselves unequal and have not hearkned unto my voice therfor let them repent spedily and prepare their hearts for the solem assembly [p. 18] and for the great day which is to come Verely thus saith the Lord Amen.[84]

---

83. Revelation, 2 Jan. 1831, in Doctrine and Covenants 12:5, 1835 ed. [D&C 38:26].

84. Revelation concerning the Quorum of the Twelve and a charge given to its members soon after its founding warned against disunity and inequality. The twelve apostles met with JS nine days later. Tension between the apostles and other church leaders had been partially resolved more than a month earlier on

I then went to assist in organizing the Elders School called to order and I made some remarks upon the object of this School, and the great necessity there is in ⟨of⟩ our rightly improving our time and reigning up our minds to the a sense of the great object that lies before us, viz, that glorious endowment that God has in store for the faithful I then dedicated the School in the name of the Lord Jesus Christ. after the School was dismissed I attended a patriarchal meeting[85] at Br Samuel Smiths, his wifeses parents were blessed[86] also his child & named Susan[n]ah,[87] at evening I preachd at the School-house to a crowded congregation

4 November 1835 • Wednesday

Wednesday 4th in morning, at home attended school all during the school hours, made rapid progress in our studies, in the evening, lectured on grammar,[88] at home, on this day Br King Follet[t], arived at this place from Zion

5 November 1835 • Thursday

Thursday 5th attended School all day, Isaac Morley came in from the east this morning I was called to visit Thomas Burdick who was sick, I took my scribe with me and we prayed for and laid our hands on him in the ⟨name⟩ of the Lord Jesus and rebuked his affliction—

Wm E. McLellen [McLellin] & Orson Hyde came in and desired to hear the revelation concerning the Twelve, my scribe read to him them they expressed some little dissatisfaction but after examining their own hearts, they accknowledged it to be the word of the Lord [p. 19] and said they were satisfied;[89] after School Brig[h]am Young came in and desired also to hear, it read also after hearing it he appeared perfectly satisfied; in the evening lectured on Grammar

---

their return but was not fully resolved for weeks to come. (Revelation, ca. Apr. 1835, in Doctrine and Covenants 3:11–12, 1835 ed. [D&C 107:27–33]; JS, Journal, 26 Sept. and 12 Nov. 1835; 16 Jan. 1836.)

85. A patriarchal blessing meeting—more commonly called a "blessing meeting"—at which Patriarch Joseph Smith Sr. gave patriarchal blessings. (Compare usage in Woodruff, Journal, 23 May 1837; see also Skinner, "First Patriarch to the Church," 91–96.)

86. Samuel Smith's in-laws Joshua and Susannah Boutwell Bailey.

87. On the birth of Samuel's daughter Susanna Bailey Smith, see JS, Journal, 27 Oct. 1835. In blessing the infant, Joseph Smith Sr. evidently gave her a name. Rather than having their infants baptized and christened, Latter-day Saints were directed to bring their children "unto the elders before the church, who are to lay their hands upon them in the name of Jesus Christ, and bless them in his name." (Revelation, 10 Apr. 1830, in Doctrine and Covenants 2:20, 1835 ed. [D&C 20:70–71].)

88. JS and Sidney Rigdon occasionally instructed in the school, which spent several weeks studying English grammar. (George A. Smith, Autobiography, 81.)

89. The revelation included a rebuke of McLellin and Hyde. (See JS, Journal, 3 Nov. 1835.)

6 November 1835 • Friday

Friday morning 6th at home. attended School during the school hours returned and spent the evening at home I was this morning introduced to a man from the east, after hearing my name he ~~replied~~ remarked that I was nothing but a man: indicating by this expression that he had supposed that a person, ⟨to⟩ who⟨m⟩ the Lord should see fit to reveal his will, must be something more than a man, he seems to have forgotten the saying that fell from the lips of St. James, that Elias was a man of like passions like unto us, yet he had such power with God that He in answer to his prayer, shut the heavens that they gave no rain for the space of three years and six months, and again in answer to his prayer the heavens gave forth rain and the earth brought forth fruit;[90] and indeed such is the darkness & ignorance of this generation that they look upon it as incredible that a man should have any intercourse with his Maker.

7 November 1835 • Saturday

Saturday 7th spent the day at home attending to my domestic concerns; The word ⟨of the Lord⟩ came to me saying, behold I am well pleased with my servant Isaac Morley and my servant Edward Partridge, because of the integrity of their harts in laboring in my vinyard for the salvation of the souls of men,[91] Verily I say unto you their sins are [p. 20] forgiven them, therefor say unto them in my name that it is my will that they should tarry for a little season and attend the school, and also the solem assembly for a wise purpose in me, even so amen

8 November 1835 • Sunday

Sunday 8[th] went to meeting in the morning at the us[u]al hour, Z[erubbabel] Snow preached a verry interesting discourse, in the after noon J[oseph] Young preached; after preaching Isaac Hill came forward to make some remarks by way of confession, he had been previously excommunicated from the church for lying & for an attempt to seduce a female; his confession was not satisfactory to my mind ⟨Uncle⟩ John Smith arose and made some remarks respecting the dealings of the high council on the case of said Hill. that is that he should make a public confession of his crime and have it published in the messenger

---

90. See James 5:17–18.

91. Partridge and Morley had departed on a fund-raising mission to the East almost five months earlier. Partridge returned to Kirtland on 29 October 1835, and Morley on 5 November 1835. They were among a group of Missouri church leaders whom JS appointed in June 1834 to travel to Kirtland to receive the endowment of "power from on high." (JS, Journal, 29 Oct. and 5 Nov. 1835; Partridge, Journal, 2 June and 29 Oct. 1835; Minute Book 2, 23 June 1834.)

and Advocate, he proposed that Mr Hill should now make his confession before the congregation and then immediately observed that he had forgiven Mr Hill, which was in contradiction to the sentiment he first advanced, this I attributed to an error in judgment not in design President [Sidney] Rigdon then arose and verry abruptly militated against ⟨the sentiment of⟩ Uncle John, which had a direct tendency to destroy his influence and bring him into disrepute in the eyes of the church, which was not right, he also misrepresented Mr Hills case and spread darkness rather than light upon the subject a vote ~~was then called~~ of the church was then called on his case and he was restored without any further confession; that he should [p. 21] be received into the church by babtism which was administered acordingly.

after I came home I took up a labour with uncle John and convinced him that he was wrong & he made his confession to my satisfaction; I then went and laboured with President Rigdon and succeded in convincing him also of his error which he confessed to my satisfaction.

The word of the Lord came unto me saying that President [William W.] Phelps & President J[ohn] Whitmer are under condemnation before the Lord, for their iniquities;[92] I also took up a labour with J. Carrill [John Corrill] for ~~leaving the meeting before~~ ⟨not partaking of the⟩ sacrament, he made his confession; also my wife for ~~the same~~ leaving the meeting before sacrament she made no reply, but manifested contrition by weeping

———— ✿ ————

Editorial Note

The following entry describes a visit to JS by Robert Matthews, more commonly known as the Prophet Matthias. In Albany, New York, in 1830 and in Rochester, New York, in 1831, Matthews launched his career as a prophet with attempts to win over recent converts from Charles G. Finney's revivals. In 1832, Matthews converted Elijah Pierson and a few of his Bowery Hill Kingdom disciples in New York City. Following the death of Pierson, Matthews was charged with his murder. Although acquitted, Matthews was jailed for whipping his daughter and for contempt of court. Suffering from internal dissension, public spectacle, and Matthews's four-month incarceration, Matthews's kingdom crumbled.[93] Three months after his release from county jail, Matthews was reported to be traveling in Ohio and asking for directions to Geauga County.[94] A few days later he arrived at the home of JS. His visit prompted JS to relate, as JS characterized it, a "brief history of

---

92. Phelps later inserted here that "they made satisfaction the same day."
93. Johnson and Wilentz, *Kingdom of Matthias*, 79–100, 137–164.
94. See "Matthias," *Western Reserve Chronicle*, 5 Nov. 1835, [2].

the establishment of the Church of Christ in these last days." A visitor later in the week heard a similar recounting, though one recorded in much less detail.[95]

———— ❧ ————

9–11 November 1835 • Monday–Wednesday

Monday morning 9ᵗʰ· after breckfast ~~Sister~~ ⟨Mary⟩ Whitcher[96] came in and wished to see me, ~~she~~ I granted her request she gave a relation of her griveances which were, unfathonable at present, and if true sore indeed, and I pray my heavenly Father to bring the truth of her case to light, that the reward due to evil doers may be given them, and ⟨that⟩ the afflicted & oppressed may be delivered;— while setting in my house between the hours of ~~nine~~ ⟨ten⟩ & ~~10~~ 11 this morning a man came in, and introduced himself to me, calling ⟨himself⟩ ~~self~~ ⟨by the name of⟩ Joshua the Jewish minister,[97] his appearance was some ~~what~~ ⟨thing⟩ singular, having a beard about 3 inches in length which is quite grey, also his hair is long and considerably silvered with age [p. 22] I should think he is about 50 or 55 years old, tall and strait slender built of thin visage blue eyes, and fair complexion, he wears a sea green frock coat, & pantaloons of the same, black fur hat with narrow brim, and while speaking frequently shuts his eyes, with a scowl on his countinance;[98] I made some enquiry after his name but received no definite answer; we soon commenced talking upon the subject of religion and after I had made some remarks concerning the bible I commenced giving him a relation of the circumstances connected with the coming forth of the book of Mormon, as follows— being wrought up in my mind, respecting the subject of religion and looking ~~upon~~ ⟨at⟩ the different systems taught the children of men, I knew not who was right or who was wrong and concidering it of the first importance that I should be right, in matters that involved eternal consequences; being thus perplexed in mind I retired to the silent grove and bowd down before the Lord, under a realising sense that he had said (if the bible be true) ask and you shall receive knock and it shall be opened seek and you shall find and again, if any man lack wisdom let him ask of God who giveth to all men libarally and upbradeth not;[99] information was

95. JS, Journal, 14 Nov. 1835.

96. The entry for 9 November 1835 in JS's 1834–1836 history gives the name as "Whitiker."

97. Robert Matthews. In the early 1820s, Matthews proclaimed himself an Israelite, temporarily identified himself with the Zionist movement of Manuel Mordecai Noah, and came to reject Christianity. (Johnson and Wilentz, *Kingdom of Matthias*, 64–68, 94–95, 103–104.)

98. Matthews was well known for his peculiar costume and appearance. (Johnson and Wilentz, *Kingdom of Matthias*, 106–108.)

99. See Matthew 7:7; Luke 11:9; and James 1:5; compare the account of JS's early religious experience with JS History, 1832, 2; and JS History, vol. A-1, 2.

what I most desired at this time, and with a fixed determination I to obtain it, I called upon the Lord for the first time, in the place above stated or in other words I made a fruitless attempt to pray, my toung seemed to be swolen in my mouth, so that I could not utter,[100] I heard a noise behind me like some person walking towards me, ⟨I⟩ strove again to pray, but could not, the noise of walking seemed to draw nearer, I sprung up on my feet, and [p. 23] and looked around, but saw no person or thing that was calculated to produce the noise of walking, I kneeled again my mouth was opened and my toung liberated, and I called on the Lord in mighty prayer, a pillar of fire appeared above my head, it presently rested down upon my ⟨me⟩ head, and filled me with joy unspeakable, a personage appeard in the midst, of this pillar of flame which was spread all around, and yet nothing consumed, another personage soon appeard like unto the first, he said unto me thy sins are forgiven thee, he testifyed unto me that Jesus Christ is the son of God;[101] ⟨and I saw many angels in this vision⟩ I was about 14. years old when I received this first communication; When I was about 17 years old I saw another vision of angels, in the night season after I had retired to bed I had not been a sleep, when but was meditating upon my past life and experiance, I was verry concious that I had not kept the commandments, and I repented hartily for all my sins and transgression, and humbled myself before Him; ⟨whose eyes are over all things⟩, all at once the room was iluminated above the brightness of the sun an angel appeared before me, his hands and feet were naked pure and white, and he stood between the floors of the room, clothed ⟨with⟩ in purity inexpressible,[102] he said unto me I am a messenger sent from God, be faithful and keep his commandments in all things, he told me of a sacred record which was written on plates of gold, I saw in the vision the place where they were deposited, he said the indians, were the literal descendants of Abraham he explained many things of the prophesies

---

100. JS later explained, "I was siezed upon by some power which entirely overcame me and had such astonishing influence over me as to bind my tongue so that I could not speak. Thick darkness gathered around me and it seemed to me for a time as if I were doomed to sudden destruction." (JS History, vol. A-1, 3; compare Hyde, *Ein Ruf aus der Wüste*, 15–16.)

101. In his 1832 history, JS recorded, "I saw the Lord and he spake unto me saying Joseph my son thy sins are forgiven thee . . . I am the Lord of glory I was crucifyed for the world . . . I come quickly . . . in the glory of my Father." In the 1832 history, JS recorded seeing only Jesus Christ. This journal entry states that he saw two personages, as does the history he began in 1838, his letter to John Wentworth, and other accounts that identify the two personages as the Father and the Son. (JS History, 1832, 3; JS History, vol. A-1, 3; JS, "Church History," *Times and Seasons,* 1 Mar. 1842, 3:706–707; see also, for example, Neibaur, Journal, 24 May 1844.)

102. Oliver Cowdery had recently described the angel as wearing a "garment" that was "perfectly white." JS later clarified that the angel had appeared wearing a "robe of most exquisite whiteness . . . beyond anything earthly I had ever seen." (Oliver Cowdery, "Letter IV," *LDS Messenger and Advocate,* Feb. 1835, 1:79; JS History, vol. A-1, 5.)

to [p. 24] me, one I will mention which is ~~this~~ in Malachi 4 behold the day of the Lord cometh &c;[103] also that the Urim and Thumim,[104] was hid up with the record, and that God would give me power to translate it, with the assistance of this instrument he then gradually vanished out of my sight, or the vision closed, while meditating on what I had seen, the Angel appeard to me again and related the same things and much more, also the third time bearing the same tidings, and departed; during the time I was in this vision I did not realize any thing ~~else~~ around me except what was shown me in this communication: after the vision had all passed, I found that it was nearly day-light, the family soon arose, I got up also:— on that day while in the field at work with my Father he asked me if I was sick I replyed, I had but little strenght, he told me to go to the house, I started and went part way and was finally deprived ~~deprived~~ of my strength and fell, but how long I remained I do not know; the Angel came to me again and commanded me to go and tell my Father, what I had seen and heard, I did so, he wept and told me that it was a vision from God to attend to it[105] I went and found the place, where the plates were, according to the direction of the Angel, also saw them, and the angel as before; the powers of darkness strove hard against me, I called on God, the Angel told me that the reason why I could not obtain the plates at this time was because I was under transgression,[106] but to come again in one year from that time, I did so, but did not obtain them [p. 25][107] also the third and the fourth year, at which time I obtained them, and translated them into the english language; by the gift and power of God and have been preaching it ever since.[108]

---

103. In a later history, JS recounted that the angel also quoted from the books of Isaiah, Acts, and Joel. (JS History, vol. A-1, 6.)

104. Urim and Thummim appears in the Old Testament as a divinatory instrument used by the high priest of Israel. JS here used the phrase to describe an instrument buried with the golden plates, "two stones in silver bows," which he used to translate characters inscribed on the gold plates into English. (Exodus 28:30; Leviticus 8:8; Numbers 27:21; JS History, vol. A-1, 5.)

105. JS's mother later recounted that the angel asked JS why he had not told his father, to which JS responded "he was affraid his father would not beleive him." Whereupon the angel told him his father would "believe every word you say to him." (Lucy Mack Smith, History, 1844–1845, bk. 3, [11]; compare JS History, vol. A-1, 7.)

106. In 1832, JS explained that he attempted to remove the ancient record but was prohibited because he "saught the Plates to obtain riches and kept not the commandment that I should have an eye single to the Glory of God." (JS History, 1832, 4–5; compare JS History, vol. A-1, 7; Lucy Mack Smith, History, 1844–1845, bk. 4, [2]; and Jessee, "Joseph Knight's Recollection," 31.)

107. TEXT: Residue from an adhesive wafer at the top of page 25—as well as some paper residue still stuck to the wafer residue—indicates that a loose leaf had been attached at this point in the journal and suggests that part of the entry for 9–11 November 1835 was probably copied into the journal from an earlier manuscript. The five other instances of wafer residue in this journal appear adjacent to copies of other documents (at the top of manuscript pages 51, 77, 103, 129, and 154).

108. Other JS accounts of the angel, the gold plates, and the translation of the Book of Mormon

An account of Joseph Smith's early visions. On 9 November 1835, Joseph Smith was visited by a man who introduced himself as "Joshua the Jewish minister" and whom the Latter-day Saints soon detected as the infamous Robert Matthews, more commonly known as Matthias the Prophet. Smith related accounts of his earliest visionary experiences to Matthews. Residue from an adhesive wafer and paper residue stuck to the wafer residue (see inset) indicate that part of the entry was probably copied from an earlier loose manuscript. Handwriting of Warren Parrish. JS, Journal, 1835–1836, pp. 24–25, JS Collection, Church History Library, Salt Lake City. (Photograph by Welden C. Andersen.)

me, one I will mention which is [...] in Malachi
4. — behold the day of the Lord cometh &c.
also that the Urim and Thummim, was hid up with
the record and that God would give me power to
translate it, with the assistance of this instrument
he then gradually vanished out of my sight, or
the vision closed, while meditating on what I
had seen. the Angel appeared to me again and
related the same things and much more. also the
third time bearing the same tidings, and departed; during the time I was in this vision I did
not notice any thing [...] around me except
what was shown me in this communication:
after the vision had all passed, I found that it
was nearly day light, the family soon arose, I
got up also:— on that day while in the field at
work with my Father he asked me if I was sick
I replyed, I had but little strenght, he told me
to go to the house, I started and went partway
and was finally deprived [...] of my strength and fell, but how long I remained I do not
know, the Angel came to me again and commanded me to go and tell my Father, what I had
seen and heard, I did so, he wept and told
me that it was a vision from God to attend to it
I went and found the place, where the plates
were according to the direction of the Angel also
saw them, and the angel as before: the powers
of darkness strove hard against me. I called
on God. the Angel told me that the reason
why I could not obtain the plates at this time
was because I was under transgression, but to
come again in one year from that time, I did
so, but did not obtain them

me, on[...]
4 [...]
also tha[...]
the reco[...]
translat[...]

While I was relating this brief history of the establishment of the Church of Christ in these last days, Joshua seemed to be highly entertained after I had got through I observed that, the hour of worship & time to dine had now arived and invited him to tarry, which he concented to,

After dinner the conversation was resumed and Joshua proceded to make some remarks on the prophesies, as follows:

He observed that he was aware that I could bear stronger meat than many others, therefore he should open his mind the more freely;— Daniel has told us that he is to stand in his proper lot, in the latter days according to his vision he had a right to shut it up and also to open it again after many days, or in the latter times;[109] Daniels Image whose head was gold, and body, armes, legs and feet was composed of the different materials described in his vision represents different governments, the golden head was ⟨to represent⟩ Nebuchodnazer King of Babylon, the other parts other kings & forms of government,[110] which I shall not now mention in detail, but confine my remarks, more particularly to the feet of the Image; The policy of the wicked spirit, is to separate what God has joined togather and unite what He has separated, which he has succeded in doing to admiration, in the present state of society, which is like unto Iron and clay, there is confusion in all things, both [p. 26] both Political and religious, and notwithstanding all the efforts that are made to bring about a union, society is remains disunited, and all attempts to ⟨unite her⟩ are as fruitless, as to attemp to unite Iron & Clay.

The feet of the Image, is the government of these united States,[111] other Nations & kingdoms are looking up to her for an example, of union fredom and equal rights, and therefore worship her, like as Daniel saw in the vision, although they are begining to loose confidence in her, seeing the broils and discord that distract, her political & religious horizon this Image is characteristic of all governments and institutions or most of them; as they begin with a head of gold and terminate in the contempible feet of Iron & clay: making a splendid appearance at first, proposing to do much more than the[y] can perform, and finally end in degradation and sink, in infamy; we should not only

provide further details. (See, for example, JS History, 1832, 4–6; and JS History, vol. A-1, 5–34; compare Oliver Cowdery, "Letter IV," *LDS Messenger and Advocate,* Feb. 1835, 1:78–80.)

109. See Daniel 12:4.

110. Matthews drew on Daniel 2, a Bible chapter that was also important in early Mormon eschatology. JS later alluded to Daniel 2:44–45 in his prayer dedicating the House of the Lord. (Whittaker, "Book of Daniel in Early Mormon Thought"; JS, Journal, 27 Mar. 1836, p. 209 herein.)

111. Matthews earlier taught his followers that "President Jackson and his government were the toes of this image" and that "this was the last of the republican governments" and "declared this government at an end." (Stone, *Matthias and His Impostures,* 167.)

start to come out of Babylon but leav it entirely lest we are overthrown in her ruins, we should keep improving and reforming, twenty-fours hours for improvement now is worth as much as a year a hundred years ago; the spirit of the Fathers that was cut down, or those that were under the altar,[112] are now rising this is the first resurection the Elder that fall's first will rise last;[113] we should not form any opinion only for the present, and leave the result of futurity with God: I have risen up out of obscurity, but was look$^{d.}$ up to when but a youth, in temporal things:[114] It is not necessary that God should give us all things at first or in his first commission to us, but in his second. John saw the angel deliver the gospel in the last days,[115] which would not be necessary if [p. 27] it was already in the world this expression would be inconsistent, the small lights that God has given, is sufficient to lead us out of babylon, when we get out we shall have the greater light. I told Johua that I did not understand him concerning the resurection and wishd him to be more explanitory on the subject; he replied that he did not feell impressed by the spirit to unfold it further at present, but perhaps he might at some other time.

I then withdrew to do some buisness with another gentleman that called to see me.

He [Robert Matthews] informed my Scribe that he was born in Washington County Town of Cambridge New York. he says that all the railroads canals and other improvements are performed by spirits of the resurection.

The silence spoken of by John the Revelator which is to be in heaven for the space of half an hour,[116] is between 1830 & 1851, during which time the judgments of God will be poured out after that time there will be peace.[117]

Curiosity to see a man that was reputed to be a jew caused many to call during the day and more particularly at evening suspicions were entertained that said Joshua was the noted Mathias of New York, spoken so much of in the public prints on account of the trials he underwent in that place before a court of justice, for murder manslaughter comtempt of court whiping his Daughter

---

112. A reference to those who were "slain for the word of God" seen in vision by John the Revelator. (Revelation 6:9.)

113. An exegesis of the ultimate reversals prophesied by Jesus. (Matthew 20:16.)

114. Matthews was orphaned in his childhood and later became a farm laborer. However, during his mid- to late twenties he enjoyed a profitable enterprise as a storekeeper. (Johnson and Wilentz, *Kingdom of Matthias,* 57–62.)

115. A paraphrase of Revelation 14:6. Latter-day Saint revelation also used this scripture in a restorationist context. (Revelation, 3 Nov. 1831, in Doctrine and Covenants 100:4, 1835 ed. [D&C 133:36–37].)

116. See Revelation 8:1.

117. In 1830, Matthews marked the beginning of his "Kingdom," then only an idea, by issuing a "Declaration of Judgement." He intended to preach until 1836, after which would follow fifteen years of turmoil before the world burned. (Johnson and Wilentz, *Kingdom of Matthias,* 79–81, 92, 96.)

Robert Matthews ("Joshua the Jewish minister"). Matthews, more commonly known as Matthias the Prophet, visited Kirtland, Ohio, in early November 1835, introducing himself to Joseph Smith as "Joshua the Jewish minister." Warren Parrish recorded Smith's account to Matthews of his early visions. Smith kept Matthews at his home for two days and listened to his teachings. He then denounced Matthews and sent him away. Top: Engraving from the pamphlet *Memoirs of Matthias the Prophet,* 1835. (Courtesy L. Tom Perry Special Collections, Harold B. Lee Library, Brigham Young University, Provo, UT. Photograph by Alex D. Smith.) Bottom: Engraving from the pamphlet *The Prophet!* 1834. (Courtesy Kent State University Department of Special Collections and Archives, Kent, OH.)

&c for the two last crimes he was imprisoned, and came out about 4, months [p. 28] since, after some, equivocating he confessed that he was realy Mathias:[118] after supper I proposed that he should deliver a lecture to us, he did so sitting in his chair; he commenced by saying God said let there be light and there was light,[119] which he dwelt upon through his discource, he made some verry exelent remarks but his mind was evidently filled with darkness, after he dismissed his meeting, and the congregation disperced, he conversed freely upon the circumstances that transpired in New York,

His name is Robert Mathias, he say[s] that Joshua, is his priestly name.[120]

during all this time I did not contradict his sentiments, wishing to draw out all that I could concerning his faith; the next morning Tuesday 10th I resumed the conversation and desired him to enlighten my mind more on his views respecting the resurection, he says that he poss[ess]es the spirit of his fathers, that he is a litteral decendant of Mathias the Apostle that was chosen in the place of Judas that fell[121] and that his spirit is resurected in him, and that this is the way or scheme of eternal life, this transmigration of soul or spirit from Father to Son: I told him that his doctrine was of the Devil that he was in reality in possession of wicked and depraved spirit, although he professed to be the spirit of truth, it self,[122] also that he possesses the soul of Christ; he tarried until Wednesday 11.th, after breckfast I told him, that my God told me that his God is the Devil, and I could not keep him any longer, and he must depart, and so I for once cast out the Devil in bodily shape, & I believe a murderer[123] [p. 29] on monday th[e] 9th Mr. Beeman [Alvah Beman] of [*blank*] N.Y came here to ask advice of me concerning purchasing lands, whether it is best for him to purchase in this vicinity and move into this church, or not, he says that he cannot arrange his buisness so as to go to the Missouri next spring; I advised him to come here, and settle untill he could move to Zion

---

118. In April 1835, Matthews was tried in White Plains, New York, and acquitted of murder and manslaughter, but he was charged with contempt of court for shouting during the proceedings. He was then immediately tried for an alleged assault on his daughter, Isabella Laisdell, and found guilty. He was sentenced to jail for three months on the assault charge and for thirty days for contempt of court. Newspapers covering this widely publicized case expressed astonishment over Matthews's light sentence. (Johnson and Wilentz, *Kingdom of Matthias*, 144–165.)

119. See Genesis 1:3.

120. In his trial held earlier in the year, Matthews declared himself "chief high Priest of the Jews." (Johnson and Wilentz, *Kingdom of Matthias*, 145.)

121. See Acts 1:15–26.

122. On Matthews's claim to be "the spirit of truth," the same spirit that was once within the New Testament apostle Matthias, see Johnson and Wilentz, *Kingdom of Matthias*, 94–95.

123. On parting, Matthews and JS apparently shared a mutual contempt. (See "Prophet Catch Prophet," *Painesville Telegraph*, 20 Nov. 1835, 3.)

11 November 1835 • Wednesday

Wednesday Morning 11th· at home attended School during school Hours, returned home and spent the evening, around my fire-side, teaching my family the science of grammar; it commensed snowing this afternon, the wind is verry heavy indeed

12 November 1835 • Thursday

Thursday 12th attended school again, during school Hours, rain & snow is still falling, it is about one inch in dept[h], the wind is verry heavy, and the weather extremly unpleasant, the labours [laborers] who commenced finishing the out side of the ~~house~~ Chappel were oblieged to brake off from their buisness at the commencement of this storm viz on the 11th·. they commenced plasturing and finishing the out side on Monday the 2. Inst· this job is let to A[rtemus] Millet & L[orenzo] Young, ⟨at $1,000⟩ they have progressed rapidly since they commenced[124]

J[acob] Bump has the job of plastering the inside of the house through, out at $15.00.[125] he commenced on Monday the 9th. and is continueing it notwithstanding the inclemency of the weather. This evening viz the 12th at 6 oclock meet with the council of 12. by their request, 9 of them were present [p. 30] council opened by singing & prayer, and I made some remarks as follows;— I am happy in the enjoyment of this opportunity of meeting with this council on this occasion, I am satisfyed that the spirit of the Lord is here, and I am satisfied with all the breth[r]en present, and I need not say that you have my utmost confidence, and that I intend to uphold, you to the uttermost, for I am well aware that you ~~do and delight in so doing~~ have to sustain my character ~~my charcter~~ against the vile calumnies and reproaches of this ungodly generation and that you delight in so doing:— darkness prevails, at this time as it was, at the time Jesus Christ was about to be crucified, the powers of darkness strove to obscure the glorious sun of righteousness that began to dawn upon the world,[126] and was soon to burst in great blessings upon the heads of the faithful, and let me tell you brethren that great blessings awate us at this time and will soon be poured out upon us if we are faithful in all things, for we are

---

124. Millet, a stonemason, was baptized by Lorenzo Young's brother Brigham. Apparently at Brigham Young's suggestion, Hyrum Smith, a member of the temple committee, wrote to Millet instructing him to move to Kirtland to work on the House of the Lord. Millet's son Joseph later recounted that his father was also asked to donate one thousand dollars toward construction. The contract to plaster the exterior may have functioned as something of a repayment. (See Erekson and Newell, "Conversion of Artemus Millet," 79–81, 91–92.)

125. Bump received fifteen hundred dollars for his labor on the House of the Lord. (JS History, vol. B-1, 684.)

126. See Malachi 4:2; compare Book of Mormon, 1830 ed., 505 [3 Nephi 25:2].

even entitled to greater blessings than they were, because the[y] had the person of Christ with them, to instruct them in the great plan of salvation, his personal presence we have not, therefore we need great faith on account of our peculiar circumstances and I am determined to do all that I can to uphold you, although I may do many things ⟨invertaintly [inadvertently]⟩ that are not right in the sight of God; you want to know many things that are before you, that you may know how ~~how~~ to prepare your selves for the [p. 31] great things that God is about to bring to pass; but there is on[e] great deficiency or obstruction, in the way that deprives us of the greater blessings, and in order to make the foundation of this church complete and permanent, we must remove this obstruction, which is to attend to certain duties that we have not as yet attended to; I supposed I had established this church on a permanent foundation when I went to the Missourie and indeed I did so, for if I had been taken away it would have been enough,[127] but I yet live, and therefore God requires more at my hands:— The item to which I wish the more particularly to call your attention to night is the ordinance of washing of feet, this we have not done as yet but it is necessary now as much as it was in the days of the Saviour,[128] and we must have a place prepared, that we may attend to this ordinance, aside from the world;[129] we have not desired much from the hand of the Lord, with that faith and obediance that we ought, yet we have enjoyed great blessings, and we are not so sensible of this as we should be; When or wher has God suffered one of the witnesses or first Elders of this church ⟨to⟩ fall? never nor nowhere amidst all the calamities and judgments that have befallen the inhabitants of the earth his almighty arm has sustained us, men and Devils have raged and spent the malice in vain. [p. 32] we must have all things prepared and call our solem assembly as the Lord has commanded us, that we may be able to accomplish his great work: and it must be done in Gods own way, the house of the Lord must be prepared, and the solem assembly called and organized in it according to the order of the house of God and in it

---

127. Before leaving on the 1834 military expedition to Missouri, JS established a "high council" for governance of the stake in Kirtland. While in Missouri in July, he similarly organized a high council. In Missouri he also appointed David Whitmer, William W. Phelps, and John Whitmer as a local presidency to preside over the high council, as well as designating David Whitmer as a potential successor in the office of general church president. JS remarked on that occasion that "if he should now be taken away that he had accomplished the great work which the Lord had laid before him." (Minute Book 2, 3 and 7 July 1834; 15 Mar. 1838.)

128. See John 13:4–17; compare New Testament Revision 2, part 2, p. 117 [Joseph Smith Translation, John 13:10].

129. Though JS instituted the washing of feet in the 1833 School of the Prophets, he now prepared to introduce the practice in connection with the House of the Lord. (See Revelation, 27 and 28 Dec. 1832 and 3 Jan. 1833, in Doctrine and Covenants 7:44–46, 1835 ed. [D&C 88:137–141].)

we must attend to the ordinance of washing of feet; it was never intended for any but official members, it is calculated to unite our hearts, that we may be one in feeling and sentiment and that our faith may be strong, so that satan cannot over throw us, nor have any power over us,— the endowment you are so anxious about you cannot comprehend now, nor could Gabriel explain it to the understanding of your dark minds, but strive to be prepared in your hearts, be faithful in all things that when we meet in the solem assembly that is such as God shall name out of all the official members, will meet, and we must be clean evry whit, let us be faithful and silent brethren, ⟨and⟩ if God gives you a manifestation, keep it to yourselves, be watchful and prayerful, and you shall have a prelude of those joys that God will pour out on that day, do not watch for iniquity in each other if you do you will not get an endowment for God will not bestow it on such; but if we are faithful and live by every word that procedes forth from the mouth of God I will venture to prophesy that we shall get a [p. 33] blessing that will be worth remembering if we should live as long as John the Revelator,[130] our blessings will be such as we have not realized before, nor in this generation. The order of the house of God has and ever will be the same, even after Christ comes, and after the termination of the thousand years it will be the same, and we shall finally roll into the celestial kingdom of God and enjoy it forever;— you need an endowment brethren in order that you may be prepared and able to overcome all things, and those that reject your testimony will be damned the sick will be healed the lame made to walk the deaf to hear and the blind to see through your instrumentality;[131]

But let me tell you that you will not have power after the endowment to heal those who have not faith, nor to benifit them, for you might as well expect to benefit a devil in hell as such a⟨n⟩ one, who is possessed of his spirit and are willing to keep it for they are habitations for devils and only fit for his society but when you are endowed and prepared to preach the gospel to all nations kindred and toungs in there own languages you must faithfully warn all and bind up the testimony and seal up the law[132] and the destroying angel will follow close at your heels and execute his tremendeous mission upon the children of disobediance, and destroy [p. 34] the workers of iniquity,[133] while the saints

---

130. Christ told John that he would "tarry till" the Second Coming. (John 21:20–24; see also Revelation, Apr. 1829–C, in Doctrine and Covenants 33, 1835 ed. [D&C 7].)

131. See Mark 16:14–18; compare Book of Mormon, 1830 ed., 514 [4 Nephi 1:5].

132. See Isaiah 8:16; and Revelation, 27 and 28 Dec. 1832 and 3 Jan. 1833, in Doctrine and Covenants 7:23, 1835 ed. [D&C 88:84]; see also JS, Journal, 27 Mar. 1836, p. 208 herein.

133. See Revelation, 27 Feb. 1833, in Doctrine and Covenants 80:3, 1835 ed. [D&C 89:21].

will be gathered out from among them and stand in holy places[134] ready to meet the bridegroom when he comes.—[135]

I feel disposed to speak a few words more to you my brethren concerning the endowment, all who are prepared and are sufficiently pure to abide the presence of the Saviour will see him in the solem assembly.[136]

The brethren expressed their gratifycation for the instruction I had given them, we then closed by prayer,— I then returned home and retired to rest

13 November 1835 • Friday

Friday 13th attended school during school hours, returned home after School; Mr Messenger [George Messinger Jr.] of Bainbridge Chenango Co. N. Y. came in to make some enquiry about H[ezekiah] Peck's family he is a Universalian Minister[137] we entered into conversation upon religious subjects, we went to President [Sidney] Rigdon's and spent the evening in conversation, we preachd the gospel to him, and bore testimony to him of what we had seen and heard, he attempted to raise some objections but, the force of truth bore him down, and he was silent, although unbelieving; returned home and retired to rest

14 November 1835 • Saturday

Saturday morning 14th Thus came the word of the Lord unto me saying:

> verily thus saith the the Lord unto my servant Joseph concerning my servant Warren [Parrish], behold [p. 35] his sins are forgiven him because of his desires to do the works of righteousness therefore in as much as he will continue to hearken unto my voice he shall be blessed with wisdom and with a sound mind even above his fellows, behold it shall come to pass in his day that he shall ⟨see⟩ great things shew forth themselves unto my people, he shall see much of my ancient records,

---

134. See, for example, Matthew 24:15; and Revelation, 16 and 17 Dec. 1833, in Doctrine and Covenants 97:5, 1835 ed. [D&C 101:22].

135. See, for example, Matthew 25:1–13; and Revelation, Oct. 1830–B, in Doctrine and Covenants 55:3, 1835 ed. [D&C 33:17].

136. See Revelation, 2 Nov. 1831, in Doctrine and Covenants 25:3, 1835 ed. [D&C 67:10]; and Matthew 5:8.

137. Messinger was a preacher for the First Universalist Society of Smithville Flats, Chenango County, New York. The Peck family, converts from Chenango County, New York, were living at this time in Clay County, Missouri, where Hezekiah was a Latter-day Saint priest. (James H. Smith, *History of Chenango and Madison Counties,* 303–304; Chenango Co., NY, Deed Records, 20 Mar. 1833, bk. TT, 225–226, microfilm, U.S. and Canada Record Collection, FHL; George Messinger Jr., South Bainbridge, NY, to S. Presson Landers, Prompton, PA, 1 Aug. 1837, Andover-Harvard Theological Library, Cambridge, MA; Whitmer, History, 80–81.)

and shall know of hid[d]en things, and shall be endowed with a knowledge of hid[d]en languages,[138] and if he desires and shall seek it at my
hand, he shall be privileged with writing much of my word, as a scribe
unto me for the benefit of my people, therefore this shall be his calling
until I shall order it otherwise in my wisdom and it shall be said of him
in a time to come, behold Warren the Lords Scribe, for the Lords Seer
whom he hath appointed in Israel; Therefore ⟨if he will⟩ keep my commandments he shall be lifted up at the last day, even so Amen

A Gentleman called this after noon by the name of Erastus Holmes of
Newbury Clemon [Clermont] Co. Ohio, he called to make enquiry about the
establishment of the Church of the latter-day Saints and to be instructed more
perfectly in our doctrine &c I commenced and gave him a brief relation of my
experience while in my [p. 36] juvenile years, say from 6, years old up to the
time I received the first visitation of Angels which was when I was about 14,
years old[139] and also the the visitations that I received afterward, concerning
the book of Mormon, and a short account of the rise and progress of the
church, up to this, date[140] he listened verry attentively and seemed highly gratified, and intends to unite with the Church he is a verry candid man indeed
and I am much pleased with him.

15 November 1835 • Sunday

On Sabath morning the 15th he [Erastus Holmes] went with me to meeting,
which was held in the School-house on account of the Chappel not being finished plastering; President [Sidney] Rigdon preached on the subject of men's
being called to preach the gospel and their qualifications &c we had a fine
discourse it was verry interesting indeed; Mr. Holmes was well satisfied, he
came home with me and dined.

---

138. This foreshadowed Parrish's role as a scribe in the coming weeks for JS's work on the book of
Abraham. Parrish later recounted, "I have set by his side and penned down the translation of the Egyptian
Hieroglyphicks as he claimed to receive it by direct inspiration from Heaven." (Book of Abraham
Manuscripts, ca. 1835–1838, ca. 1841–1843; Kirtland Egyptian Papers, ca. 1835–1836, CHL; Warren Parrish,
Kirtland, OH, 5 Feb. 1838, letter to the editor, *Painesville Republican*, 15 Feb. 1838, [3].)

139. JS may have recounted the traumatic leg operation he underwent at age seven, as he did in a
later history. His recounting of "the first visitation of Angels" corresponds with the vision he described
earlier in the week to Robert Matthews, wherein he saw two "personage[s]" and "many angels" when he
"was about 14." (JS History, vol. A-1, 131nA; JS, Journal, 9–11 Nov. 1835; compare JS History, 1832, 1–3; and
JS History, vol. A-1, 1–4.)

140. In 1832, JS wrote a narrative of the origin of the Book of Mormon and early church history.
(JS History, 1832, 1–6; compare Revelation, 10 Apr. 1830, in Doctrine and Covenants 2:1–2, 1835 ed.
[D&C 20:1–12].)

Said Holmes has been a member of the Methodist Church, and was excommunicated for receiving, the Elders of the church of the latter-day Saints into his house

Went to meeting in the afternon, before partaking of the sacrament Isaac Hills case was agitated again, and settled after much controversy, and he retained in the church by making an humble acknowledement before the church, and concenting to have his confession published in the Messenger and advocate,[141] after which the ordinance of the Lord Supper was administered, and the meeting closed, verry late,— returned home and spent the evening.— [p. 37]

16 November 1835 • Monday

Monday the 16th at home, dictated a letter for the Advocate,[142] also one to Harvey Whitlock. Father Beeman [Alvah Beman] called to council with me Elder Strong[143] and some others

/[144]Copy of a Letter from Harvey Whitloc[k][145]

Dear sir having a few leisure moment I have at last concluded to do what my own Judgment has long dictated would be right but the allurements of many vices has long retarded the hand, that would wield the pen to make intelligent the communication that I wish to send to you: And even now that ambition which is a prevaling and predominant principles among the great mass of natural men even now forbids that plainness of sentiment with which I wish to ~~unbosom my feelings~~, write. For know assuredly sir to you I wish to unbosom my feelings, and unravil the secrets of my heart: as before the omnicient Judge of all the earth.

---

141. Hill's case was first heard the previous Sunday. His confession was never published. (JS, Journal, 8 Nov. 1835.)

142. This was the second in a series of three letters written by JS and published in successive issues of the *LDS Messenger and Advocate* providing instruction for traveling elders. The second letter concerns the gathering of Israel in the last days to Zion, the New Jerusalem, and admonishes elders to proselytize only with the permission of heads of households. (JS, "To the Elders of the Church of Latter Day Saints," *LDS Messenger and Advocate,* Nov. 1835, 2:209–212; see also Sept. 1835, 1:179–182; and Dec. 1835, 2:225–230.)

143. Probably Ezra Strong. (Minute Book 1, 7 Mar. 1835; elder's certificate for Ezra Strong, 31 Mar. 1836, in Kirtland Elders' Certificates, 33.)

144. TEXT: Warren Parrish handwriting ends; Frederick G. Williams begins.

145. Written 28 September 1835, as noted in JS's response, which follows.

Be not surprised when I declare unto you, as the spirit will bear record that my faith is firm and unshaken in the things of the everlasting gospel as it is proclaimed by the servants of the latter-day saint.

Dear brother Joseph (If I may be allowed the expression) when I considder the happy times and peaseful moments, and pleasant seasons I have enjoyed with you, ~~and~~ and this people; contrasted with my now degraded state; together with the high, and important station I have held before [p. 38] God:[146] and the abyss into which I have fallen, is a subject that swells/[147], my heart to[o] big for utterance, and language is overwhelmed with feeling, and looses its power of description.

and as I desire to know the will of God concerning me; Believing it is my duty to make known unto you my real situation.

I shall therefore, dispasionately procede to give a true and untarnished relation; I need not tell you that in former times, I have preached the word; and endeavored to be instant in season out of season, to reprove rebuke exhort and faithfully to discharge that trust reposed in me. But Oh! with what grief & lamentable sorrow and anguish do I have to relate that I have fallen, from that princely station where unto our God, has called me. Reasons why are unnecessary. May the fact suffice; and believe me when I tell you, that I have sunk myself, (since my last separation from this boddy) in crimes of the deepest dye, and that I may the better enable you to understand what my real sins are, I will mention (although pride forbids it) some that I am not guilty of, my ⟨hands⟩ have not been stained with inocent blood; neither have I lain couched around the cottages of my fellow men to seize and carry off the booty; nor have I slandered my neighbor, nor bourn fals testimony, nor taken unlawful hire, nor oppressed the widdow nor fatherless, neither have I persecuted the Saints. But my hands are swift to do iniquity, and my feet are fast running in the paths of vice and folly; and my heart [p. 39] quick to devise wicked imaginations: nevertheless I am impressed with the sure thought that I am fast hast[e]ning into a whole world of disembodied beings, without God & with but one hope in the world; which is to know that to er[r] is human, but to forgive is divine: much I might say in relation to myself and the original difficulties with the church, which I will forbear, and in asmuch as I have been charged with things that ⟨I⟩ was not guilty of I am now more than doubly guilty. and am now willing to forgive and forget only let me know that I am within

---

146. Whitlock was ordained a high priest in 1831. (Minute Book 2, 3 June 1831.)
147. TEXT: Frederick G. Williams handwriting ends; Warren Parrish begins.

the reach of mercy; If I am not I have no reflections to cast, but say that I have sealed my own doom and pronounced my own sentence. If the day is passed by with me may I here beg leave to entreat of those who are still toiling up the rug[g]ed assent to make their way to the realms of endless felicity, and delight, to stop not for anchors here below, follow not ~~the~~ ⟨my⟩ example. but steer your course onward inspite of all the combined powers of earth and hell, for know that one miss step here is only retrievable by a thousand groans and tears before God. Dear Brother Joseph, let me entreat you on the reception of this letter, as you regard the salvation of my soul, to enquire at the hand of the Lord in my behalf; for I this day in the presence of God, do covenant to abide the word that may be given, for I am willing to receive any [p. 40] chastisement that the Lord sees I deserve.

Now hear my prayer and suffer me to break forth in the agony of my soul. O ye Angels! that surround the throne, ⟨of God,⟩ Princes of heaven, that excell in strength, ye who are clothed with transcendant brightness, plead O plead for one of the most wretched of the sons of men. O ye heavens! whose azure arches rise immensely high and strech immeasurably wide, grand ampitheater of nature, throne of the eternal God bow to hear the prayer of a poor wretched bewildered way wanderer to eternity, O thou great Omnicient & omnipresent Jehovah, thou who siteth upon the throne before whom all things are present, thou maker moulder & fashioner of all things visible and invisable breath[e] o breath[e] into the ears of thy servant the Prophet, words sutably adapted, to my case, and situation, speak once more, make known thy will concerning me, which favours I ask in the name of the Son of God Amen

N.B I hope you will not let any buisiness prevent you from answering this letter in hast[e]

Yours Respectfully
Harvey Whitlock

to Joseph Smith [p. 41]

Copy of a Letter sent Harv[e]y Whitlock in answer to his

Kirtland Nov. 16th 1835

Bro Harvey Whitlock

I have recieved your letter of the 28th Sept. 1835, and I have read it twice, and it gave me sensations that are better imagined than described; let it suffice, that I say the verry flood-gates of my heart were broken up: I could not refrain from weeping, I thank God, that it has entered into your heart, to try to return to the Lord, and to his people; if it so be, that he will have mercy upon you.

I have inquired of the Lord concerning your case, these words came to me

Verily thus saith the Lord unto you; let him who was my servant Harvey, return unto me;— and unto the bosom of my Church, and forsake all the sins wherewith he has offended against me and persue from hence forth a virtuous and upright life, and remain under the direction of those whom I have appointed to be pillars, and heads of my Church, and behold, saith the Lord, your God; his sins shall be blotted out from under heaven, and shall be forgotten from among men, and shall not come up in mine ears, nor be recorded as ⟨a⟩ memorial against him, but I will lift [p. 42] him up as out of deep mire, and he shall be exalted upon the high places, and shall be counted worthy to stand ammong princes, and shall yet be made a polished shaft in my quiver, of bringing down the strong holds of wickedness, among those who set themselves up on high, that they may take council against me, and against annointed ones in the last days.

Therefore let him prepare himself speedily and come unto you; even to Kirtland and inasmuch as he shall harken unto all your council from henceforth he shall be restored unto his former state, and shall be saved unto the uttermost, even as the Lord your God liveth Amen.

Thus you see my dear Brother the willingness of our heavenly Father to forgive sins and restore to favour all those who are willing to humble themselves before him, and confess their sins and forsake them, and return to him with full purpose of heart (acting no hypocrisy) to serve him to the end.

Marvle not that the Lord has condescended to speak from the heavens and give you instructions whereby you may learn your duty, he has heard your prayers, and witnessed your humility; and holds forth the hand of paternal affection, for your return; the angels rejoice over you, while the saints are willing to recieve you again into fellowship.

I hope on the recipt of this, you will not loose any no time in coming to [p. 43] Kirtland: for if you get here in season, you will have the privelege of attending the School of the prophets, which has already commenced and, also received instruction in doctrine, and principle, from those whom God has appointed whereby you may be qualified to go forth, and declare the true doctrines of the kingdom according to the ~~true doctrines of the~~ mind and, will of God. and when you come to Kirtland, it will be explained to you why God has condescended to give you a revelation according to your request.

please give my respects to you family, and bee assured I am yours in the bonds of the new and everlasting covenant[148]

Joseph Smith Jun

on this evening, viz the 16ᵗʰ a council was called at my house to council with ~~Father~~ Alva Beeman [Alvah Beman] on the subject of his mooving to the Missourie; I had previously told him that the Lord had said that he had better go to the Missourie, next Spring: however he wished a council, called, the council met President D. Whtmer [David Whitmer] arose and said the spirit manifested to him that it was his duty to go;[149] also others bore the same testimony.

The same night ~~that~~ I received the word of the Lord on Mr. Hlmes [Erastus Holmes] case, he had, desired that I would inquire at the hand of the Lord whether it was [p. 44] his duty to be baptised here, or wait until he returned home;— The word of the Lord came ~~to~~ unto me saying, that Mr. Holmes had better not be baptised here, and that he had better not return by water,[150] also that there were three men that were seeking his destruction, to be ware of his eneys [enemies]

17 November 1835 • Tuesday

Tuesday 17ᵗʰ exibited ⟨the Alphabet⟩ ~~some~~ of the ancient records[151] to Mr. [Erastus] Holmes and some others, went with him to F[rederick] G. Williams to see the Mumies, ~~he~~ we then took the parting hand, and he started for home, being strong in the faith of the gospel of Christ and determined to obey the requirements of the same.[152]

I returned home and spent the day dictating and comparing letters.

This has been a fine pleasant day although cool, this Evening at early candle-light I pr[e]ached at the School-house, returned home and retired to rest,

---

148. Two and a half months later, church leaders resolved that Whitlock be "restored to the church in full fellowship on his being rebaptized and after be ordained to the High Priesthood." (Minute Book 1, 30 Jan. 1836.)

149. See JS, Journal, 9–11 Nov. 1835. Whitmer presided over the Latter-day Saints in Missouri. (Minute Book 2, 3 July 1834.)

150. Holmes lived in Newbury, Clermont County, Ohio, and could return overland or by boat on the canal system or the Ohio River. (JS, Journal, 14 Nov. 1835.)

151. Possibly the "Egyptian alphabet" that JS, Oliver Cowdery, and William W. Phelps apparently worked on seven weeks earlier. (Kirtland Egyptian Papers, ca. 1835–1836, 4, CHL; JS, Journal, 1 Oct. 1835.)

152. There is no evidence that Holmes joined the church.

18 November 1835 • Wednesday

~~Thursday~~ ⟨Wednesday⟩ 18ᵗʰ at home in the fore noon, untill about 11, oclock. I then went to Preserved Harris's, to preach his fathers funeral Sermon,[153] by the request of the family I preached on the subject of the resurection, the congregation were verry attentive My wife my mother and my scribe went with me to the funeral, we rode in a waggon, had a pleasant ride, the weather was pleasant, when we went. but cloudy and cool when we returned [p. 45]

at evening Bishop [Newel K.] Whitney his wife Father and Mother, and ~~wife~~ Sister in law,[154] came in and invited me and my wife to go with them & visit Father Smith & family my wife was unwell and could not go; however I and my Scribe went, when we got there, we found that some of the young Elders, were about engaging in a debate, upon the subject of miracles, the question was this; was or was it not the design of Christ to establish his gospel by miracles,[155]

After an interesting debate of three hours or more, during which time much talent was displayed, it was decided by the presidents of the debate in the negative; which was a righteous descision I discovered in this debate, much warmth displayed, to[o] much zeal for mastery, to[o] much of that enthusiasm that characterises a lawyer at the bar, who is determined to defend his cause right or wrong.[156] I therefore availed myself of this favorable opportunity, to drop a few words upon this subject by way of advise, that they might improve their minds and cultivate their powers of intellect in a proper manner, that they might not incur the displeasure of heaven, that they should handle sacred things verry sacredly, and with a due deference to the opinions of others and with an eye single to the glory of God [p. 46]

---

153. Nathan Harris, father of Preserved and Martin Harris, died the day before at Mentor, Geauga County, Ohio. (Tuckett and Wilson, *Martin Harris Story,* 178.)

154. Bishop Newel K. Whitney was accompanied by his wife, Elizabeth Ann Smith Whitney; his parents, Samuel Whitney and Susanna Kimball Whitney; and probably by Eve Doane Whitney, wife of Newel Whitney's brother Samuel Whitney, who also lived in Kirtland during this time. (Geauga Co., OH, Marriage Records, 26 July 1829, bk. B, 132; Geauga Co., OH, Duplicate Tax Records, 1835, "No. 2 Kirtland," 18–19, microfilm, U.S. and Canada Record Collection, FHL.)

155. The lyceum movement—part of the larger reform movement of Jacksonian America, with its lectures, dramatic performances, class instruction, and debates—contributed significantly to the education of adult Americans in the nineteenth century and provided the cultural context for the schools and debating societies of Kirtland. (See Stevens, "Science, Culture, and Morality," 69–83; and Bode, *American Lyceum.*)

156. JS expressed this view on other occasions. (See JS, Journal, 29 Oct. and 18 Dec. 1835; see also Thompson, "Recollections of the Prophet," 399.)

19 November 1835 • Thursday

Thursday 19th went in company with Doct. [Frederick G.] Williams & my scribe to see how the workmen prospered in finishing the house; the masons on the inside had commenced puting on the finishing coat of plastureing, on my return I met L[l]oyd & Lorenzo Lewis and conversed with them upon the subject of their being disaffected.[157] I found that they were not so, as touching the faith of the church but with some of the members:

I returned home and spent the day in translating the Egyptian records: on this has been a warm & pleasant day—

20 November 1835 • Friday

Friday 20th in morning at home: the weather is warm but rainy, we spent the day in translating, and made rapid progress

At Evening, President [Oliver] Cowdery returned from New York,[158] bringing with him a quantity of Hebrew book's for the benefit of the school, he presented me with a Hebrew bible, lexicon & Grammar, also a Greek Lexicon and Websters English Lexicon.[159]

President Cowdery had a prosperous journey, according to the prayers of the Saints in Kirtland

21 November 1835 • Saturday

Saturday 21st at home, spent the day in examining my books and studying ⟨the⟩ ~~my~~ hebrew alphabet, at evening met with our hebrew Class to make some arrangments about a Teacher, it was decided by the voice of the School to send [p. 47] to N[ew] York for a Jew to teach us the language, if we could get released from the engagement we had made with Doct. Piexotto [Daniel Peixotto] to

---

157. Lorenzo Lewis was excommunicated almost two months earlier. (JS, Journal, 28 Sept. 1835.)

158. On JS's instructions to Cowdery regarding this trip, see JS, Journal, 2 Nov. 1835; see also Oliver Cowdery, Kirtland, OH, to Warren Cowdery, [Freedom, NY], 22 Nov. 1835, in Cowdery, Letterbook, 63.

159. The Hebrew Bible referred to here is probably Augustus Hahn, ed., *Biblia Hebraica,* 2nd ed. (Leipzig: Caroli Tauchnitz, 1833). The copy housed at the Community of Christ Library-Archives has an "FWC" endorsement inside the back cover, indicating that it was the property of F. G. Williams & Co. That repository also has evidence that this copy was previously in the possession of JS's descendants. The grammar is probably Moses Stuart, *A Grammar of the Hebrew Language,* 5th ed. (Andover, MA: Gould and Newman, 1835), as JS owned this manual. His copy is housed in the Community of Christ Library-Archives. The lexicon is probably Josiah M. Gibbs, *A Manual Hebrew and English Lexicon Including the Biblical Chaldee. Designed Particularly for Beginners,* 2nd ed. (New Haven, CT: Hezekiah Howe, 1832). The copy owned by the Community of Christ has a binding that matches the Stuart grammar and an "FWC" endorsement inside the back cover. "Websters English Lexicon" refers to a reprinting of Noah Webster's 1828 *American Dictionary of the English Language*—possibly one of the N. and J. White editions published in New York that year.

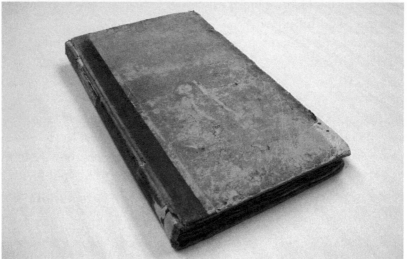

Hebrew Bible, lexicon, and grammar. On 20 November 1835, Oliver Cowdery presented Joseph Smith with a Hebrew Bible and several language books, purchased during Cowdery's visit to New York City. Handwritten notations in the volumes pictured here indicate they were purchased by the church at this time and may have been Smith's personal copies. Smith and other church members in Kirtland, Ohio, enthusiastically studied Hebrew throughout the winter of 1835–1836. Top: *A Manual Hebrew and English Lexicon,* by Josiah M. Gibbs, second edition, 1832 (smaller volume); *Biblia Hebraica,* edited by Augustus Hahn, second edition, 1833 (larger volume). Bottom: *A Grammar of the Hebrew Language,* by Moses Stuart, fifth edition, 1835. (Both photographs courtesy Community of Christ Library-Archives, Independence, MO. Photograph of Stuart volume by Lachlan Mackay.)

teach the language, having asertained that he was not qualified to give us the knowledge we wish to acquire[160]

22 November 1835 • Sunday

Sunday 22ᵈ went to meeting at the us[u]al hour,[161] Simeon Ca[r]ter preached from the 7ᵗʰ Chapt of Mathew; President [Sidney] Rigdon's brother in Law & Some other relatives were at meeting, in the after noon the meeting was held in the School-house also in the evening had a meeting, and Elder [Andrew] Squires who had withdrawn from the church made application, to return after giving him a severe chastisment, he was recieved, and his licence restored to him; when the case of Elder Squires was introduced, we organized into a regular council, Sylvester Smith was chosen Clerk and after conciderable altercation upon the subject & keen rebuke he was restored by the voice of the council & church & the clerk ordered to give him his licence as above stated.[162] On this night we had a snow storm

23 November 1835 • Monday

Monday 23ᵈ Several brethren called to converse with me, and see the records; recᵈ· a letter from Jared Carter, spent the day in conversing, and ⟨in⟩ studying, the hebrew, ⟨language⟩

This has been a stormy day [p. 48]

24 November 1835 • Tuesday

Tuesday 24ᵗʰ at home, spent the fore noon, instructing those that called to inquire concerning the things of God, in the last days: in the after-noon, we translated some of the Egyptian, records; I had an invitation, to attend a wedding at Br. Hiram [Hyrum] Smith's in the evening also to solemnize the matrimonial ceremony, ⟨between Newell Knights [Newel Knight] & Lydia Goldthwaite [Bailey]⟩ I and my wife, went, when we arrived a conciderable company, had collected, the bridegroom & bride came in, and took their seats, which gave me to understand that they were ready, I requesteded them to arise and join hands, I then remarked that marriage was an institution of h[e]aven institude [instituted]

---

160. Although Peixotto probably had some skill in Hebrew, JS and his associates now felt they had more promising options. While in New York, Cowdery had become "quite intimately acquainted with a learned Jew," with whom he may have discussed textbooks or potential instructors for the planned Hebrew School. (O. Cowdery to W. Cowdery, 22 Nov. 1835; see also C. [Oliver Cowdery], Kirtland, OH, 1 Feb. 1836, letter to the editor, *LDS Messenger and Advocate,* Feb. 1836, 2:268–271.)

161. Ten o'clock. (See JS, Journal, 13 Dec. 1835.)

162. Squires had joined the Methodists for a time. At this council, JS spoke on the "impropriety of turning away from the truth," and Sidney Rigdon spoke on the "folly of fellowshiping any doctrine or spirit aside from that of Christ." (Minute Book 1, 22 Nov. 1835.)

in the garden of Eden, that it was necessary that it should be Solemnized by the authority of the everlasting priesthood, before joining hands however, we attended prayers. I then made the remarks above stated;[163] The ceremony was original ⟨with me⟩ it was in substance as follows, You covenant to be each others companions through life, and discharge the duties of husband & wife in every respect to which they assented, I then pronounced them husband & Wife in the name of God and also ~~pronounced~~ the blessings that the Lord confered upon adam & Eve in the garden of Eden; that is to multiply and replenish the earth, with the addition of long life and prosperity; dismissed them and returned home.— The weather is freezing cold, some snow on the ground [p. 49]

25 November 1835 • Wednesday

Wednesday 25th spent the day in Translating.— To-day Harvey Redfield & Jesse Hitchcock arived here from Missourie; ⟨the latter says that he has no doubt, but that a dose of poison was administered to him in a boll of milk[164] but God delivered him⟩

26 November 1835 • Thursday

Thursday 26th at home, we spent the day in transcribing Egyptian characters

---

163. This marriage solemnized by JS for Newel Knight—a friend from JS's New York years—and Lydia Goldthwaite Bailey is the first known wedding performed by JS; ten more followed over the next two months.[a] Newel Knight recorded, "We received much Instruction from the Prophet concerning matrimony, & what the ancient order of God was, & what it must be again concerning marriage."[b] A statement on marriage published in August 1835 stated that weddings could be performed by either priesthood officers or "other authority,"[c] but on this occasion JS emphasized priesthood authority. After Geauga County authorities refused to issue Sidney Rigdon a license to perform marriages, apparently no other Latter-day Saint priesthood holders applied in that county.[d] Ohio state law allowed for regularly ordained ministers to solemnize marriages with or without a license if they fulfilled the statutory requirement for recording.[e] Thus JS probably believed—with some justification—that he acted within his statutory rights in performing marriages. However, the church was not legally incorporated in the state of Ohio at this time.[f] The arrest of Joseph Smith Sr., an ordained Latter-day Saint minister, in early 1838 on a charge of illegal performance of marriage suggests that the authority of Latter-day Saints to perform marriages in Ohio was still at least an open question at that time. The senior Smith was allowed to escape, and so the case did not come to trial.[g] (a. Bradshaw, "Joseph Smith's Performance of Marriages in Ohio," 24; see also Hartley, "Newel and Lydia Bailey Knight's Kirtland Love Story." b. Knight, Autobiography, [60]. c. "Marriage," ca. Aug. 1835, in Doctrine and Covenants 101, 1835 ed. d. Geauga Co., OH, Court of Common Pleas, Mar. 1835, final record bk. M, 380–381, microfilm, U.S. and Canada Record Collection, FHL. e. An Act Regulating Marriages [6 Jan. 1824], *Statutes of Ohio*, vol. 2, p. 1407, sec. 2. f. Vilate Kimball, Kirtland, OH, to Heber C. Kimball, Preston, England, 19, 21, and 24 Jan. 1838, Heber C. Kimball Collection, CHL. g. Historian's Office, "History of Luke Johnson," 6–7, Histories of the Twelve, ca. 1858–1880, CHL.)

164. JS History, 1834–1836, 136, adds: "by the hand of an enemy, with the intention to kill him. It sickened him & he vomited it up."

from the papyrus.—[165] I am severely afflicted with a cold.— to day Robert Rathbone [Rathbun Jr.] and George Morey arrived from Zion

27 November 1835 • Friday

Friday 27th much afflicted with my cold, yet able to be about and I am determined to overcom in the name of the Lord Jesus Christ,— spent the day in reading Hebrew at home.

The weather continues cold and unpleasant.— Br. [Warren] Parrish my scribe being afflicted with a cold, asked me to lay my hands on him in the name of the Lord I did so⟨, and in return I asked him to lay his hands on me & we were both relieved.—⟩

Prayer • 23 October 1835

Copy of a prayer offered up. on the 23[d] day of Oct 1835, by the following individuals, at 4 oclock P.M. viz. Joseph Smith jn, Oliver Cowdery; David Whitmer, Hirum [Hyrum] Smith John Whitmer, Sidn[e]y Rigdon, Samuel H. Smith, Frederick G. Williams, and W[m.] W. Phelps,[166] assembled and united in prayer, with one voice before the Lord, for the following blessings:[167]

> That the Lord will give us means sufficient to deliver us from all our afflictions and difficulties, wherein we are placed by means of our debts; that he will open the way and deliver Zion in the app[p. 50]ointed time[168] and that without the shedding of blood; that he will hold our lives precious, and grant that we may live to the common age of man, and never fall into the hands nor power of the mob in Missourie nor in any other place; that he will also preserve our posterity, that none of them fall even to the end of time; that he will give us the blessings of the earth sufficient to carry us to Zion, and that we may purchase inheritances in that land, even enough to carry on ⟨and accomplish⟩ the work unto which he has appointed us; and also that he will assist all others who desire, accordingly to his

---

165. The transcriptions made this day may have been the manuscripts now known as Kirtland Egyptian Papers, ca. 1835–1836, 8–9, CHL. (Gee, "Eyewitness, Hearsay, and Physical Evidence," 196.)

166. See also the earlier journal entry for 23 October 1835. The assembled group constituted the full membership of the church presidencies from both Ohio and Missouri, except for Joseph Smith Sr., for whom his son Samuel Smith may have been standing in.

167. TEXT: Residue from an adhesive wafer at the top of page 51 indicates that Warren Parrish probably copied the prayer into the journal from a loose manuscript that had been attached at that point.

168. In August 1834, JS declared to Missouri church leaders that 11 September 1836 was the "appointed time for the redemption of Zion." (JS, Kirtland, OH, to Lyman Wight et al., Missouri, 16 Aug. 1834, in JS Letterbook 1, p. 86.)

commandments, to go up and purchase inheritances; and all this easily and without perplexity, and trouble; and finally, that in the end he will save us in his Celestial Kingdom. Amen.

Oliver Cowdery   <u>Clerk</u>

28 November 1835 • Saturday

Saturday 28th at home, spent the morning in compareing, our journal.—[169]

~~This~~ Elder Josiah Clark called this morning to see me, he lives in Camel [Campbell] County K.Y about three miles above Cincinate [Cincinnati].

I am conciderably recovered from my cold, & I think I shall be able in a few days to translate again, with the blessing of God.— The weather is still cold and stormy, the snow is falling, & winter seems to be closing in ~~verry fast~~, all nature shrinks before the chilling blast('s) of rigid winter.—

Elder Clark above mentioned, has been biten by a mad Dog some three or four [p. 51] years since, has doctered, much, and received some benefit by so doing, but, is much afflicted notwithstanding, he came here that he might be benefited by the prayers of the church, accordingly we prayed for and layed our hands on him, in the name of the Lord Jesus Christ and anointed him with oil, and rebuked his affliction, praying our heavenly Father to hear and answer our prayers according to our faith

29 November 1835 • Sunday

Sunday morning 29th went to meeting at the us[u]al hour Elder [Isaac] morley preach^d and Bishop [Edward] Partridge in the afternoon;[170] their discourses were well adapted to the times in which we live, and the circumstances under which we are placed, their words were words of wisdom, like apples of gold in picture's of silver,[171] spoken in the simple accents of a child, yet sublime as the voice an angels, the saints, appeared to be much pleased with the beautiful discourses of these two fathers in Israel; after these servises closed, three of the Zion brethren[172] came forward and recieved their blessing

Solon Foster was ordained to the office of an Elder; the Lord's supper was then administered, and the meeting closed.

---

169. The entry for this date in JS's 1834–1836 history reads, "He spent the morning in comparing & correcting his journal." JS may have made the revisions near the end of the entry for 7 October 1835 at this time.

170. Morley served as one of Partridge's counselors in the Missouri bishopric. They had recently served a mission together in the eastern states. (See 85n91 herein.)

171. See Proverbs 25:11.

172. Veterans of the 1834 expedition to Missouri. (See "Zion brethren," in Glossary.)

returned home and spent the evening. The storm continues, the weather is verry cold [p. 52]

30 November 1835 • Monday

Monday morning 30th yet the snow is falling, and is sufficiently deep for sleighing,[173] this is an uncommon storm for this country, at this season of the year

spent the day in writing a letter for the Messenger & Advocate on the Subject of the Gathering;—[174] this afternoon, Henry Capron called to see me, he is an old acquaintance of mine, from Manchester New York, shewed him the Egyptian records

1 December 1835 • Tuesday

Tuesday December 1st 1835, at home spent the day in writing, for the M[essenger] & Advocate, the snow is falling and we have fine sleighing.[175]

2 December 1835 • Wednesday

Wednesday. 2nd a fine morning I made preparation, to ride to Painsvill [Painesville], with my wife and ~~children~~, family, also my Scribe,[176] we had our Sleigh and horses, prepared and set out, when we ~~arived~~ were passing through Mentor Street, we overtook a team with two men on the Sleigh. I politely asked them to let me pass, they granted my request, and as we passed them, they bawled out, do you get any revelation lately, with an adition of blackguard that I did not understand, this is a fair sample of the character of Mentor Street inhabitants,[177] who are ready to abuse and scandalize, men who never laid a

---

173. The snow and frozen rivers of winter often made travel easier than did the furrowed, muddy roads of other seasons. Wintertime in agrarian communities provided more leisure time for travel and visiting.

174. This was the third in a series of three letters written by JS and published in successive issues of the *LDS Messenger and Advocate* to provide instruction for traveling elders. The third letter contained an exegesis of Jesus's parables in Matthew 13, which JS applied to the establishment of the kingdom of God in the last days. (JS, "To the Elders of the Church of Latter Day Saints," *LDS Messenger and Advocate*, Dec. 1835, 2:225–230; see also Sept. 1835, 1:179–182; and Nov. 1835, 2:209–212.)

175. When Warren Cowdery copied JS's journal into the contemporaneous history, he omitted this entry for 1 December and instead copied in a revised version of the journal entry for 2 December. (JS History, 1834–1836, 138–139.)

176. JS History, 1834–1836, 138, states that he was joined by his family and by "some others of his house hold."

177. Mentor Street (now Mentor Avenue) ran northeast from Mentor to Painesville. Before joining with the Latter-day Saints, Sidney Rigdon led the Reformed Baptist congregation in Mentor, some of whom now deeply resented the new religion that had taken Rigdon and many from the neighboring Kirtland congregation. On Mentor-based opposition to the Mormons in 1835, see Adams, "Grandison Newell's Obsession," 170–173.

straw in their way, and infact those whos faces they never saw, and cannot, bring an acusation, against, either [p. 53] of a temporal or spirtual nature; except our firm belief in the fulness of the gospel and I was led to marvle ~~that~~ ~~God~~ at the long suffering and condescention of our heavenly Father, in permitting, these ungodly wretches, to possess, this goodly land, which is ~~the~~ indeed as beautifully situated, and its soil as fertile, as any in this region of country, and its inhabitance, ~~as~~ wealthy even blessed, above measure, in temporal things, and fain, would God bless, them with, ~~with~~ spiritual blessings, even eternal life, were it not for their evil hearts of unbelief, and we are led to ~~cry in~~ ~~our hearts~~ mingle our prayers with those saints that have suffered the like treatment before us, whose souls are under the altar crying to the Lord for vengance upon those that dwell upon the earth[178] and we rejoice that the time is at hand when, the wicked who will not repent will be swept ⟨from the earth⟩ with the besom of destruction[179] and the earth become an inheritance for the poor and the meek.—[180]

when we arived at Painsvill we called at Sister Harriet Hows [Howe's], and left my wife and family to visit her while we rode into Town to do some buisness,[181] ~~returned~~ called and visited H[orace] Kingsbury—

Returned and dined with Sister How, and returned home, had a fine ride the sleighing, is ~~fine~~ ⟨good⟩ and weather pleasant—[182] [p. 54]

3 December 1835 · Thursday

Thursday the 3ᵈ at home, wrote a letter to David Dort, ~~Michigan~~ Rochester Michigan, another to Almyra Scoby [Almira Mack Scobey] Liberty Clay co. Mo.[183] at, home all day,— at Evening, was invited with my wife, to attend, at Thomas Caricoes [Carrico Jr.'s], to join W[arren] Parrish & Martha H. Raymond in mattrimony, we found a verry pleasant and respectable company,

---

178. See Revelation 6:9–10.

179. See Isaiah 14:23. A besom is a broom, especially one made of twigs.

180. See Matthew 5:5; and Revelation, 27 and 28 Dec. 1832 and 3 Jan. 1833, in Doctrine and Covenants 7:4, 1835 ed. [D&C 88:17].

181. JS History, 1834–1836, 139, adds: "at the bank, and at various other places."

182. When Warren Cowdery copied JS's journal into the contemporaneous history that they were working on, he copied this journal entry for 2 December into the history entry for 1 December. For 2 December, Cowdery wrote, "Nothing of much importance transpired, suffice it to say that he of whom we write, spent the day in the society of his family, managing his domestic concerns, visiting, & receiving visitors, and instructing such, as desired a knowledge of the things of God." (JS History, 1834–1836, 138–139.)

183. JS's letters to his maternal cousin Almira Scobey and her sister's husband David Dort remain unlocated. He may have written to encourage them to move to Kirtland, where both apparently settled in 1836. (See Minutes, *LDS Messenger and Advocate*, Mar. 1837, 3:477; and Cumming and Cumming, *Pilgrimage of Temperance Mack*, 21.)

waiting when, we arived, we opened our interview with singing & prayer, after which, I delivered an address, upon the subject of matrimony, I then invited the, ⟨parties⟩ c̶o̶u̶p̶l̶e̶ to arise, who were to be joined in wedlock, I̶ and, solemnized the institution in a brief manner, and pronounced them husband and wife in the name of God according to the articles, and covenants of the ⟨church of the⟩ latter day Saints,[184] closed by singing and prayer, took some refreshment, and retired; having spent the evening, agreeably

4 December 1835 · Friday

Friday 4th to day, in company, with Vinson Knights [Knight], we drew, three hundred and fifty Dollars, out of Painsvill [Painesville] Bank,[185] on three months credit, for which we gave, the names of F G. Williams & Co N[ewel] K. Whitney John Johnson, & N̶e̶w̶e̶l̶ Vinson Knights, I also settled with Br. Hiram [Hyrum] Smith, and V. Knights, and paid said [K]nights $̶2̶0̶0̶4̶5̶ two hundred and f̶o̶r̶t̶i̶f̶y̶ forty five dollars,[186] I also paid, or have it in my power to pay, J[ob] Lewis[187] for which, blessing, I feel hartily, to thank my heavenly Father, and ask him, in the name of Jesus Christ, to enable us to extricate [p. 55] ourselves, from all t̶h̶e̶ embarasments whatever that we may not be brought into disrepute, in any respect, that our enemys may not have any power over us;— spent the day at home, devoted some time in studying ⟨the⟩ hebrew, language.— this has been a warm day with, some rain; our snow is melting verry fast,— This evening, a Mr. John Hol[l]ister of Portage County Ohio called to see me on S̶a̶t̶u̶r̶d̶a̶y̶ ⟨the subject⟩ of religion, he is a member of the close communion baptise Church,[188] he said he had come to enquire concerning the faith of our church having heard many reports, of the worst character about us, he seemed to be an honest enquirer after truth. I spent the evening in talking with him, I found him to be an honest candid man, and no particular peculiarities about him, only his simplisity, he tarried overnight with

---

184. The term "articles and covenants"—applied originally to the statement of principles and practices read and approved at the church's organization, 6 April 1830—refers here to the recently published Doctrine and Covenants, which compiled revelations and statements of belief such as the new article on marriage. ("Marriage," ca. Aug. 1835, in Doctrine and Covenants 101, 1835 ed.; see also Minute Book 1, 17 Aug. 1835.)

185. Apparently the Bank of Geauga, founded in 1831. (*History of Geauga and Lake Counties,* 216.)

186. JS History, 1834–1836, 140, revises this to two hundred fifty dollars.

187. In March 1834, Lewis evidently loaned JS or the church approximately one hundred dollars, which JS hoped to pay back at the end of 1835. JS's 1834–1836 history explains that Lewis was "much perplexed" concerning the debt. If JS paid Lewis, it must have been after May 1836. (JS History, 1834–1836, 140; Minute Book 1, 23 May 1836; see also JS, Journal, 1–2 Mar. 1834.)

188. Closed Communion Baptists took the sacrament of the Lord's Supper only with other Baptists. (Jeter, *Baptist Principles Reset,* chap. 13.)

me, and acknowledged in the ⟨morning⟩ that although he had thought he knew something about religion he was now sensible that he knew but little, which was the greatest, trait of wisdom that I could discover in him

5 December 1835 · Saturday

Saturday 5ᵗʰ the weather is cold and freezing, and the snow is falling moderately, and there is a prospect of sleighing again, spent the forenoon in studying, hebrew with Doct. [Frederick G.] Williams & President [Oliver] Cowdery, I am labouring under some indisposition of health laid down and slept a while, and [p. 56] and arose feeling tolerable well through the blessings of God,— I received a letter to day from Reuben M[c] Bride, Villanovia [Villanova] N. Y also another from, Parley [P.] Pratts mother in law[189] from Herkimer Co. N. Y of no consequence as to what it contained, but cost me 25, cents for postage, I mention this as it is a common occurence, and I am subjected to a great deal of expence in this way, by those who I know nothing about, only that they are destitute of good manners, for if people wish to be benefited with information from me, common respect and good breeding woud dictate, them to pay the postage on their letters.—[190]

6 December 1835 · Sunday

Sunday 6ᵗʰ 1835, went to meeting at the us[u]al hour, G[ideon][191] Carter preached a splendid discourse, in the after, ⟨noon⟩ we had an exortation, and communion.— Br. Draper insisted on leaving the meeting, some 2, or 3 weeks, since, before communion, and would not be prevailed upon to tarry a few moments although, we invited him to do so as we did not wish to have the house thrown into confusion, he observed that he would not if we excluded him from the church, to day, he attempted to make a confession, but it was not satisfactory to me, and I was constrained by the spirit to deliver him over to the bufetings of Satan. untill he should humble himself, and repent, of his sins, and make a satisfactory confession before the Church— [p. 57]

---

189. Thankful Cooper Halsey.

190. On this date, JS inserted a notice in the *LDS Messenger and Advocate* to inform the public "that whenever they wish to address me thro' the Post Office, they will be kind enough to pay the postage on the same. . . . [I] am unwilling to pay for insults and menaces,—consequently, must refuse *all*, unpaid." Until the introduction of postage stamps in the 1840s, the option of collecting postage from the addressee led to many abuses. Letters containing several pages or sent from afar could cost as much as a dollar. (JS, "To the Editor of the Messenger and Advocate," *LDS Messenger and Advocate*, Dec. 1835, 2:240; italics in original; Summerfield and Hurd, *U.S. Mail*, 45–46; Kelly, *United States Postal Policy*, 57–58.)

191. See JS History, 1834–1836, 141.

7 December 1835 • Monday

Monday 7th received a letter from Milton Holmes, and was much rejoiced to hear from, him, and of his prosperity in proclaiming the gospel,[192] wrote him a letter requesting, him to return to this place,

Spent the day in reading the hebrew. Mr. John Hollister called ~~and~~ to take the parting hand with me, and remarked that he had been in darkness all his days, but had now found the light and intended to obey it, also a number of brethren called this Evening to see the records, I exibited and explained them to their satisfaction. We have fine Sleighing

8 December 1835 • Tuesday

Tuesday morning the 8th at holm, spent the day in reading hebrew in company with, President [Oliver] Cowdery Doct. [Frederick G.] Williams Br. H[yrum] Smith & O. Pratte [Orson Pratt],

In the evening I preached, as us[u]al at the School House, had great liberty in speaking the congregation, were attentive, after the servises closed the brethren proposed to come and draw wood for me[193]

9 December 1835 • Wednesday

Wednesday 9th at home, the wind is strong and chilly, from the South, and their is a prospect of a storm Elder [Noah] Packard came in this morning and made me a present, of 12, dollars which he held in a note against me, may God bless him for his liberality, also James Aldrich, sent me my note by the hand of Jesse Hitchcock, on which [p. 58] there was 12, dollars, due, and may God bless him, for his kindness to me[194]

also the brethren whose names are written below opened the hearts in great liberality and payed ⟨me⟩ at the committee Store the sums set oposite their respective names

John Corrill.	5.00
Levi Jackman.	3.25
Elijah Fordham.	5.25

---

192. This journal entry may refer to Holmes's letter of 2 November 1835 reporting his preaching throughout 1835 in Tennessee and Illinois and his success in baptizing over forty people. (Milton Holmes, Hamilton Co., IL, 2 Nov. 1835, letter to the editor, *LDS Messenger and Advocate,* Jan. 1836, 2:255.)

193. This proposal to gather wood and the entries for the next two days suggest that JS's remarks included an expression of material and financial need.

194. In the largely barter economy, debts were often recorded on handwritten scraps of paper. These notes became a sort of scrip and circulated until retired by cash, labor, or barter. As in this case, the debt could be settled by the creditor's presenting his copy of the note as a gift to the debtor. (See McCabe, "Early Ledgers and Account Books," 5–12.)

James Em[m]ett.	5.00
Newel Knight.	2.00
Truman Angell	3.00
Wm. Felshaw	3.00
Emer Harris	1.00
Truman Jackson	1.00
Samuel Rolph [Rolfe]	1.25
Elias Higbee	1.00
Albert Brown	3.00
Wm F. Cahoon	1.00
Harlow Crosier	.50
Salmon Gee.	.75
Harvey Stanley	1.00
Zemira Draper	1.00
George Morey	1.00
John Rudd [Jr.]	.50
Alexander Badlam [Sr.]	1.00
	$40.50
with the adition of the 2, notes above	24.00

My heart swells with gratitude inexpressible when I realize the great condescention of my heavenly Fathers, in opening the hearts of these, my beloved
brethren [p. 59] to administer so liberally, to my wants and I ask God in the
name of Jesus Christ, to multiply, blessings, without number upon their heads,
and bless me with much wisdom and understanding, and dispose of me, to the
best advantage, for my brethren, and the advancement, of thy cause and
Kingdom, and whether my days are many or few whether in life or in death I
say in my heart, O Lord let me enjoy the society of such brethren

To day Elder Tanner[195] brought me the half of a fat[te]ned hog for the
be[ne]fit of my family.

And a few days since Elder S[hadrach] Roundy brought me a quarter of
beef and may all the blessings, that are named above, be poured upon their
heads, for their kindness toward me—

10 December 1835 • Thursday

of ⟨Wednesday ⟨Thursday⟩⟩ morning 10th a beautiful morning, indeed, and
fine sleighing, this day my brethren, meet according, to previous arangement,

---

195. Probably John Tanner.

to chop and haul wood for me,[196] and they have been verry industrious, and I think they have supplyed me, with my winters wood, for which I am sincerely grateful to each and every, one of them, for this expression of their, goodness towards me

And in the name of Jesus Christ I envoke the rich benediction of heavn to rest upon them, even all and their families, and I ask my heavenly Father [p. 60] to preserve their health's and those of their wives and children, that they may have strength. of body to perform, their, labours, in their several ocupations in life, and the use and activity of their limbs, also powers of intellect and understanding hearts, that they may treasure up, wisdom, and understanding, until and inteligence, above measure, and be preserved from plagues pestilence, and famine, and from the power of the adversary, and the hands of evil designing, men and have power over all their enemys; and the way be prepared before them, that they may journey to the land of Zion and be established, on their inheritances, to enjoy undisturbe[d], peace and happiness for ever, and ultimately, to be crowned with everlasting life in the celestial kingdom of God, which blessings I ask in the name of Jesus of Nazareth. Amen

I would remember Elder Leonard Rich who was the first one that proposed to the brethren, to assist me, in, obtaining wood for the use of my family, for which I pray my heavenly Father, to bless ⟨him⟩ with all the blessings, named above, and I shall ever remember him with much gratitude, for this testimony, of benevolence and respect, and thank the great I am,[197] for puting into his heart, to do me this kindness, and I say in my heart, I will trust in thy goodness, and mercy, forever, for thy wisdom and benevolence ⟨O Lord⟩ is unbounded and beyond the comprehension; of men and all of thy ways cannot be found out [p. 61]

This afternoon, I was called in company with President David Whitmer, to visit, Sister Angeline Works, who lives at Elder Booths[198] we found her verry sick, and so much deranged, that She did not, recognize her friends, and intimate acquaintences, we prayed for and layed hands on her her in the name of Jesus Christ, and commanded her in his name to receive he[r] senses, which was immediately restored to her we also asked a healing blessing

prayed that she might be restored to health; she said she was better.— On our return we found the brethren engaged, in putting out the board kiln which had taken fire, and after labouring for about one hour, against the ⟨this⟩

---

196. See JS, Journal, 8 Dec. 1835.

197. A biblical title for God, as in, for example, Exodus 3:14 and John 8:58.

198. Possibly Lorenzo Dow Booth, a member of the First Quorum of the Seventy. (Record of Seventies, bk. A, 4.)

distructive, element they succeded in conquering it, and, probably will save about one fourth part of the lumber, that was in it, how much loss the committee have sustained by this fire I do not know but it is conciderable as their was much lumber in the kiln[199]

There was about 200 brethren engaged on this occasion and displayed, much activity, and interest, for which they deserve much credit.

This evening I spent at hom[e], a number of brethren called. to see the records which I exibited to them, and they were much pleased with their interview [p. 62]

11 December 1835 · Friday

~~Thursday~~ Friday morning the 11th a fire broke out in a shoe-makers shop owned by Orson Johnson, but was soon, extinguished, by the active exertions of the brethren, but the family were much alarmed, the shop being connected with the⟨ir⟩ ~~house~~ ⟨dwelling⟩ house, they carryed their furniture into the street, but not much damage was sustained,— This is a pleasant morning, and their is a prospect of a thaw

Spent the day at home, in reading, and instructing, those who called for advise,— to day Elder Dayly & his wife[200] left for home.

12 December 1835 · Saturday

~~Friday~~ Saturday morning 11th ⟨12th⟩ at home, spent the fore noon in reading, at about 12 oclock a number of young person[s] called to see the ~~records~~ Egyptian records I requested my Scribe to exibit them, he did so, one of the young ladies, who had been examining them, was asked if they had the appearance of Antiquity, she observed with an air of contempt that they did not, on hearing this I was surprised at the ignorance she displayed, and I observed to her that she was an anomaly in creation for all the wise and learned that had ever examined them, without hesitation pronounced them antient, I further remarked that, it was downright ~~wickedness~~ ignorance bigotry and superstition that caused her to make the remark, and that I would put it on record, and I have done so because it is a fair sample of the prevailing spirit of the times [p. 63] showing that the victims of priestcraft and superstition, would not believe though one should rise from the dead.

At evening attended a debate, at Br. W[m.] Smiths, the question proposed to debate upon was, as follows.— was it necessary for God to reveal himself

---

199. The board kiln—an oven used for drying and seasoning wood—was preparing lumber for finishing the House of the Lord. The great loss of wood delayed completion of the House of the Lord. (JS History, 1834–1836, 144–145.)

200. Probably Moses and Almira Barber Daley.

to man, in order for their happiness,— I was on the affirmative and the last One to speak on that side of the question,— but while listning, with interest to the, ingenuity displayed, on both sides of the qu[e]stion, I was called, away to visit, Sister Angeline Work[s], who was suposed to be dangerously sick, Elder [John] Corrill & myself went and prayed for and layed hands on her in the name of Jesus Christ, She appeard to be better,— returned home

13 December 1835 • Sunday

Sunday morning ^the^ 13th at the us[u]al hour for meeting viz. at 10, oclk attended meeting, at the Schoolhouse on the flats, Elder J[esse] Hitchcock preach'd a verry feeling discourse indeed, in the afternoon Elder Peter Whitmer [Jr.], related his experiance, after which President F[rederick] G. Williams related his also, they both spoke of many things connected with the rise and progress of this church, which were interesting, and the Saints, listened, with much attention, after these serv[ic]es closed, the sacrament of the Lords Supper was administered, under the superintendance of President D[avid] Whitmer, who presided over the meeting during the day. I then made som remarks respecting [p. 64] prayer meetings, and our meeting was brought to a close, by invoking the blessings of heaven,

We then returned home, I ordered my horse saddled and myself and Scribe, rode to Mr. E Jennings, where I joined Ebenezer Robinson and Angeline Works, in matrimony, according to previous arangements, Miss ⟨Works⟩ had so far recoverd from her illness, that she was able to sit in her easy chair while I pronounced the mariage ceremony.—

We then rode to Mr. [Isaac] McWithy's a distance of about 3, miles from Town, where I had been Solicited, to attend, and solemnize, the matrimonial covenant betwe[e]n Mr. E[dwin] Webb & Miss E. A. McWithy [Eliza Ann McWethy], the parents and many of the connections of both parties were present, with a large and respectable company of friends, who were invited as guests; and after making the necessary arangements the company come to order, and the Groom & bride, with the attendants politely came forward, and took their seats, and having been requested, to make some preliminary remarks upon the subject of matrimony, touching the design of the All Mighty in this institution, also the duties, of husbands & wives towards eac[h]other, and after opening our interview, with singing and prayer, I delivered a lecture of about 40, minuits in length, during this time all seemed to be interested, excepting one or two individuals, who manifested, a spirit of grovling contempt, which I was constrained to reprove and rebuke sharply, after I had ~~been~~ closed my remarks, I sealed the matrim[p. 65]onial ceremony in the name of God, and pronounced the blessings of heaven. upon the heads of the young married couple we then closed by returning thanks.

A sumptuous feast was then spread and the company were invited to seat themselves, at the table by pairs, male & female commencing with the oldest, and I can only say that the interview was conducted with propriety and decorum, and our hearts were made to rejoice, while together, and all cheerfulness prevailed, and after spending the evening agreeably untill 9, oclock, we pronouncd a blessing, upon the company and withdrew, and returned hom[e]

To day the board kiln, took fire again[201]

14 December 1835 • Monday

Monday 14th this morning a number of brethren from, New York call[ed] to visit me, and see the Egyptian records, Elder [Martin] Harris also returned this morning, from Palmyra N[ew] York,[202] Br. Frazier Eaton, of the same place called and paid me a visit, a verry fine man also Sister Harriet How[e] called to pay us a visit

After dinner we went to attend the funeral of Sylvester Smiths youngest child.[203] in the evening meet according to notice previously given to make arangements to guard against fire, and organized a company for this purpose, counciled also on other affairs of temporal nature

To day Samuel Branum [Brannan] came to my house, much afflicted with a swelling on his left arm, which was occasioned by a bruise [p. 66] on his elbow, we had been called to pray for him and anoint him with oil, but his faith was not sufficient to effect, a cure, and my wife prepared a poultice of herbs and applyed to it and he tarryed with me over night[204]

Spent the day at home, reading hebrew, and visiting friends who called to see me,

To day I received a letter form Elder Orson Hyde from his own hand

15 December 1835 • Tuesday

Tuesday 15th spent the day at home, and as us[u]al was blessed with much company, some of which called to see the records Samuel Brannum [Brannan], is verry sick in consequence of his arm, it being much inflamed

---

201. JS History, 1834–1836, 147, adds: "in concequence of bad management."

202. Harris had been visiting family. (JS History, 1834–1836, 147.)

203. Sylvester M. Smith, no relation to JS, died of whooping cough at the age of two months. (Obituary for Sylvester M. Smith, *LDS Messenger and Advocate,* Dec. 1835, 2:240.)

204. A February 1831 revelation instructed that those without "faith to be healed, but [who] believe, shall be nourished with all tenderness with herbs and mild food." (Revelation, 9 Feb. 1831, in Doctrine and Covenants 13:12, 1835 ed. [D&C 42:43].)

This afternoon Elder Orson Hyde, handed me a Letter, the purport of which is that he is dissatisfyed with the committee,[205] in their dealings, with him in temporal affairs, that is that they do not deal as liberally ~~in~~ ⟨with⟩ him as they do with Elder William Smith, also requested me to reconcile the revelation, given to the 12, since their return from the East,[206]

That unless these things and others named in the letter, could be reconciled to his mind his honour would not stand united with them,— this I believe is the amount of the contents of the letter although much was written, my feelings on this occasion, were much laserated, knowing that I had dealt in righteousness with him in all things and endeavoured to promote his happiness and well being, as much as lay in my power, and I feel that these reflections are [p. 67] ungrateful and founded in jealousy and that the adversary is striving with all his subtle devises and influence to destroy him by causing a division amon[g] the twelve that God has chosen to open the gospel kingdom in all nations, but I pray my Heavenly Father in the name of Jesus of Nazeareth that he may be delivered from the power of the destroyer, ~~and~~ that his faith fail not in this hour of temptation, and prepare him and all the Elders to receive an endument, in thy house, even according to ~~thy~~ ⟨thine⟩ own order from time to time as thou seeest them worthy to be called into thy Solemn Assembly. [*20 lines blank*] [p. 68]

16 December 1835 • Wednesday

Wednesday morning the 16th the weather is extremely cold, this morning I went to the council room,[207] to lay before the presidency, the letter that I received yesterday from Elder O[rson] Hyde, but when I arived, I found that I had lost said letter, but I laid the substance of it as far as I could recollect before the council,— but they had not time to attend to it on the account of other buisness, accordingly we adjourned untill Monday Evening the 20th Inst. [208]

Returned home Elder McLellen [William E. McLellin] Elder B[righam] Young and Elder J[ared] Carter called and paid me a visit, with which I was much gratified, I exibited and explaind the Egyptian Records to them, and

---

205. The committee overseeing temple construction consisted of Hyrum Smith, Reynolds Cahoon, and Jared Carter. For the text of the Hyde letter, see JS, Journal, 17 Dec. 1835.

206. The revelation of 3 November 1835 named Hyde as having sinned against the Lord. (JS, Journal, 3 Nov. 1835.)

207. The council room was adjacent to the printing office on the second floor of the schoolhouse. (See JS, Journal, 31 Dec. 1835.)

208. Whether the council meeting was intended for Sunday, 20 December, or Monday, 21 December, is not clear; but there was apparently no need for further consultation after Hyde's 17 December visit with JS. (See JS, Journal, 17 Dec. 1835.)

explained many things to them concerning the dealings of God with the ancient⟨s⟩ and the formation of the planetary System,²⁰⁹ they seemed much pleased with the interview.

This evening according to adjournment I went to Br. Wᵐ Smiths, to take part in the debate that was commenced on saturday evening last,— after the debate was concluded, and a desision given in favour of the affirmative of the question,²¹⁰ some altercation took place, upon the impropiety of continue-ing the school fearing that it would not result in good.²¹¹

Br. Wᵐ oposed these measures and insisted on having another question proposed,²¹² and at length become much enraged particularly at me and used [p. 69] violence upon my person, and also upon Elder J. Carter and some oth-ers, for which I am grieved beyond expression, and can only pray God to for-give him inasmuch as he repents of his wickedness, and humbles himself before the Lord.

17 December 1835 • Thursday

Thursday morning 17ᵗʰ at home,— quite unwell,— This morning Elder Orson Hyde called to see me, and presented me with a copy of the letter that he handed me on Tuesday last, which I had lost

The following is a copy.

Dec 15ᵗʰ 1835
President Smith
Sir you may esteem it a novel circumstance to receive a written communication from me at this time.

My reasons for writing are the following. I have some things which I wish to communicate to you, and feeling a greater liberty to do it by writing alone by myself, I take this method; and it is generally the case that you are thronged with buisness and not convenient to spend much time in conversing upon subjects of the following nature. Therefore let

---

209. JS's 1834–1836 history adds that JS explained "many things concerning the dealings of God, with the ancients especially the system of astronomy as taught by Abraham, which is contained upon these manuscripts." (JS History, 1834–1836, 149; compare JS, Journal, 1 Oct. 1835.)

210. JS argued the affirmative side of the debate over whether it was "necessary for God to reveal himself to man, in order for their happiness." (JS, Journal, 12 Dec. 1835.)

211. A month earlier, JS expressed his misgivings about the debating school. (JS, Journal, 18 Nov. 1835.)

212. That is, a new topic was proposed for debate in the next session. Warren Parrish later wrote in JS's history that William "assert[ed] that he was in his own house and should insist on continuing the school regardless of consequences." (JS History, 1834–1836, 150.)

William Smith. Circa 1862. Joseph Smith's younger brother William attacked him during a dispute on the evening of 16 December 1835. Joseph Smith's journal discloses the strained relationship between the two over the next two weeks. The brothers were reconciled in a family meeting on New Year's Day 1836. (Courtesy L. Tom Perry Special Collections, Harold B. Lee Library, Brigham Young University, Provo, UT. Photograph of original by Alex D. Smith.)

these excuses paliate the novelty of the circumstance and patiently hear my recital.

After the committee had received their stock of fall and winter goods, I went to Elder [Reynolds] Cahoon and told him that I was destitute of a cloak and wanted him to trust me until Spring for materials to make one. He told me that [p. 70] he would trust me until January, but must then have his pay as the payments for the goods become due at that time. I told him that I know not from whence the money would come and I could not promise it so soon.

But in a few weeks after I unexpectedly obtained the money to buy a cloak and applyed immediately to Elder C for one and told him that I had the cash to pay for it, but he said that the materials for cloaks were all sold and that he could not accommodately me, and I will here venture a guess that he has not realized the cash for one cloak pattern.

A few weeks after this I called on Elder Cahoon again and told him that I wanted cloth for some shirts to the amount of 4 or 5 Dollars I told him that I would pay him in the spring and sooner if I could.

He told me let me have it not long after, my school was established and some of the hands who laboured on the house attended and wished to pay me at the Committee Store for their tuition.— I called at the Store to see if any nego[ti]ation could be made and they take me off where I owed them, but no such negotiation could be made. These with some other circumstances of like character called forth the following. reflections.

In the first place I gave the committee $275 in cash besides some more and during the last season have traveled thro the Middle and Eastern states to suport and uphold the store[213] and in so doing have reduced myself to nothing in a pecuniary point. Under [p. 71] these circumstances this establishment refused to render me that accomodation which a worldlings establishment would have gladly done, and one too, which never ⟨received⟩ a donation from my me nor in whose favour I never raised my voice or extended ⟨exerted⟩ my influence.

But after all this, thought I, it may be right and I will be still— Un[t]il not long since I asertained that Elder Wᵐ Smith could go to the store and get whatever he pleased, and no one to say why do ye so,

---

213. During their recent five-month mission, Hyde and his colleagues in the Quorum of the Twelve were assigned to solicit funds for the House of the Lord, for Zion, and for church publications. Hyde obviously considered the temple committee store an integral part of the financing of temple construction. (JS, Kirtland, OH, to the Quorum of the Twelve Apostles, 4 Aug. 1835, in JS Letterbook 1, pp. 90–93.)

until his account has amounted to seven Hundred Dollars or there abouts and that he was a silent partner in the conce[r]n[214] yet not acknowledged ⟨as⟩ such fearing that his creditors would make a hawl upon the Store.

While we were abroad this last season we straind every nerve to obtain a little something for our familys and regularly divided the monies equally for ought that I know, not knowing that William had such a fountain at hom[e] from whence he drew his support. I then called to mind the revelation in which myself, McLellen [William E. McLellin] and [David W.] Patten were chastened[215] and also the quotation in that revelation of the parable of the twelve sons; as if the original meaning referd directly to the twelve apostles of the church of the Latter day Saints, I would now ask if each one of the twelve has not an equal right to the same accomodations from that Store provided they are alike faithful. If not, with such a combination [p. 72] mine honor be not thou united.

If each one has the same right, take the baskets off from our noses or put one to Williams nose or if this cannot be done, reconcile the parable of the twelve sons with the superior priveleges that William has.

Pardon me if I speak in parables or parody.

A certain shepherd had twelve sons and he sent them out one day to go and gather his flock which were scattered upon the mountains and in the vallies afar off they were all obedient to their fathers mandate, and at Evening they returned with the flock, and one son received wool enough to make him warm and comfortable and also rec[d] of the flesh and milk of the flock, the other eleven received not so much as one kid to make merry with their freinds

These facts with some others have disqualified my mind for studying the Hebrew Language at present, and believing, as I do, that I must sink or swim, or in other words take care of myself, I have thought that I should take the most efficient means in my power to get out of debt, and to this end I proposed taking the school, but if I am not thought competent to take the charge of ~~the~~ it, or worthy to be placed in that station, I must devise some other means to help myself; altho having been ordained to that office under your own hand with a promise that it should not be taken from me.— [p. 73]

---

214. Ira Ames, the store clerk, later listed William Smith among the building committee members. (Ames, Autobiography, 1836.)
215. See JS, Journal, 3 Nov. 1835.

Conclusion of the whole matter is sutch I am willing to continue and do all I can provided we can share equal benefits one with the other, and upon no other principle whatever. If one has his suport from the "publick crib" let them all have it. But if one is pinched I am willing to be, provided we are all alike.

If the principle of impartiality and equality can be observed by all I think that I will not peep again—

If I am damned it will be for doing what I think is right.— There have been two applications made to me to go into business since I talked of taking the school, but it is in the world and I had rather remain in Kirtland if I can consistently

All I ask is Right

I Am Sir with
Respect Your ob^{t.} serv^{t.}
Orson Hyde

To President J. Smith jn

Kirtland Geauga C^{o.}
Ohio [p. 74]

Elder O. Hyde called and read the foregoing letter himself and, I explained upon the objections, he had set forth in it, and satisfyed his mind upon every point, perfectly and he observed after I had got through, that he was more than satisfyed, and would attend the hebrew school, and took the parting hand with me with every expression of friendship that a gentleman, and a Christian could manifest, which I felt to reciprocate, with the cheerfulness and entertain, the best of feeling for him, and most cheerfully forgive him the ingratude which was manifisted in his letter, knowing that it was for want of corect information, that his mind was disturbed as far as his reflections related to me.

But on the part of the committe, he was not treated, right in all thing, however all things, are settled amicably, and no hardness exists between. us or them[216]

My Father & Mother called this evening to see me upon the subject of the difficulty, that transpired at their house on wednesdy evening between me and my Br. William, they were sorely afflicted in mind on the account of that occurrence, I conversed with them, and showed convinced them that I was not

---

216. JS soon afterward spoke with Cahoon about extending credit at the temple committee store equally to the members of the Quorum of the Twelve. (JS History, vol. B-1, addenda, 2nG.)

to blame in taking the course I did, but had acted in righteousness, in all thing on that occasion I

I invited them to come and live with me, they concented to do so as soon as it ⟨is⟩ practicable [p. 75]

18 December 1835 • Friday

Friday morning 17ᵗʰ ⟨18ᵗʰ⟩ Insᵗ· at home Br. Hyrum Smith, called to see me and read a letter to me that he received from William [Smith], in which he asked, Hyrum ⟨his⟩ for ⟨for⟩givness for the abuse he offered to him, at the debate, he tarried, most of the fore noon, and conversed freely with me, upon the subject, of the difficulty, existing between me and Br. William, he said that he was, perfectly satisfied, with the course I had taken, with him, in rebuking, him in his wickedness,— but he is wounded to the verry soul, with the conduct of William, and altho he feels the tender feelings of a brother, toward him yet he can but look upon his conduct as an abomination in the sight of God

And I could pray in my heart that all my brethren were like unto my beloved brother Hyrum, who posseses the mildness of a lamb and the integrity of a Job, and in short the meekness and humility of Christ, and I love him with that love that is stronger than death; for I never had occasion to rebuke him, and nor he me which he declared when he left me to day [*7 lines blank*] [p. 76]

18ᵗʰ Insᵗ·

Copy of a letter from Br. William Smith[217]

Br. Joseph— Though I do not know but I have forfeited all right and title to the word brother, in concequence of what I have done, for I concider myself; that I am unworthy to be called one, after coming to myself and concidering upon what I have done I feel as though it was a duty, to make a humble confession to you for what I have done or what took place the other evening,— but leave this part of the subject at present,— I was called to an account by the 12, yesterday for my conduct; or they desired to know my mind or determination and what I was going to do I told them that on reflection upon the many difficulties that I had had with the church and the much disgrace I had brought upon myself in concequence of these things and also that my health would not permit me to go to school to ⟨make⟩ any preperations for the endument and that my health was such that I was not able to

---

217. TEXT: Residue from an adhesive wafer at the top of page 77 indicates that Warren Parrish probably copied the letter into the journal from a loose manuscript that had been attached at that point.

travel, I told them that it would be better for them to appoint one in the office that would be better able to fill it, and by doing this they would throw me into the hands of the church, and leave me where I was before I was chosen—

Then I would not be in a situation [p. 77] to bring so much disgrace upon the cause, when I fell into temptation, and perhaps by this I might obtain Salvation you know my passions and the danger of falling from so high a station, and thus by withdrawing from the office of the apostleship while their is salvation for me, and remaining a member in the church;

I feel a fraid if I do'nt do this it will be worse for me, some other day

And again my health is poor and I am not able to travel and it is necessary that the office, should not be idle— And again I say you know my passions and I am a fraid it will be worse for me, by and by

do so if the Lord will have mercy on me and let me remain as a member in the church, and then I can travel and preach, when I am able— do not think that I am your enemy for what I have done, perhaps you may say or ask why I have not remembered the good that you have done to me— When I reflect upon the ingury I have done you I must confess that I do not know what I have been ~~doing~~ about— I feel sorry for what I have done and humbly ask your forgiveness— I have not confidence as yet to come and see you for I feel ashamed of what I have done, and as I feel now I feel as thou[p. 78]gh all the confessions that I could make verbally or by writing would not be sufficient to atone for the transgression— be this as it may I am willing to make all the restitution you shall require, If I can stay in the church as a member— I will try to make all the satisfaction possible—

yours with respect
William Smith

do not cast me off for what I have done but strive to save me in the church as a member I do ~~repeat~~ repent of what I have done to you and ask your forgiveness— I concider the transgression the other evening of no small magnitude,— but it is done and I cannot help it now— I know brother Joseph you are always willing to forgive.

But I sometimes think when I reflect upon the many inguries I have done you I feel as though a confession was not hardly sufficient— but have mercy on me this once and I will try to do so no more—

The 12, called a council yesterday and sent over after me and I went over

This council rem[em]ber was called together by themselves and not by me

W^{m.} S [p. 79]

Letter to William Smith • 18 or 19 December 1835

Kirtland Friday Dec ~~17th~~ ⟨18th⟩ 1835

Answer to the foregoing Letter from Br. William Smith   a Copy

Br. William.

having received your letter I now procede to answer it, and shall first pro-cede, to give a brief naration of my feelings and motives, since the night I first came to the knowledge, of your having a debating school, which was at the time I happened, in with, Bishop [Newel K.] Whitney his Father and Mother[218] &c— which was the first that I knew any thing about it, and from that time I took an interest in them, and was delighted with it, and formed a determina-tion, to attend the school for the purpose of obtaining information, and with the idea of imparting the same, through the assistance of the spirit of the Lord, if by any means I should have faith to do so; and with this intent, I went to the school on ⟨last⟩ Wedensday night, not with the idea of braking up the school, neither did it enter into my heart, that there was any wrangling or jealousy's in your heart, against me;

Notwithstanding previous to my leaving home there were feelings of solemnity, rolling across my breast, which were unaccountable to me, and also these feelings continued by spells to depress my ~~feelings~~ ⟨spirit⟩ and seemed to manifest that all was not right, even after the ~~debate~~ school commenced, and during the debate, yet I strove to believe that all would work together for good; I was pleased with the power of the arguments, that were aduced, and did [p. 80] not feel to cast any reflections, upon any one that had spoken; but I felt that it was ~~my~~ ⟨the⟩ duty of old men that set as presidents to be as grave, at least as young men, and that it was our duty to smile at solid arguments, and sound reasoning, and be impreesed, with solemnity, which should be manifest in our countanance, when folly and that which militates against truth and righteous-ness, rears its head

Therefore in the spirit of my calling and in view of the authority of the priesthood that has been confered upon me, it would be my duty to reprove whatever I esteemed to be wrong fondly hoping in my heart that all parties, would concider it right, and therefore humble themselves, that satan might not take the advantage of us, and hinder the progress of our School.

---

218. Samuel and Susanna Kimball Whitney. Their visit to William Smith's debating school occurred one month earlier. (JS, Journal, 18 Nov. 1835.)

Now Br. William I want you should bear with me, notwithstanding my plainness—

I would say to you that my feelings, were grieved at the interuption you made upon Elder McLellen [William E. McLellin], I thought, you should have concidered your relation, with him, in your Apostle ship, and not manifest any division of sentiment, between you, and him, for a surrounding multitude to take the advantage of you:— Therefore by way of entreaty, on the account of the anxiety I had for your influence and wellfare, I said, unto you, do not have any feelings, or something to that amount, why I am thus particular, is that if You, have misconstrued, my feelings, toward you, you may be corrected.— [p. 81]

But to procede— after the school was closed Br. Hyrum [Smith], requested, the privilege, of speaking, you objected, however you said if he would not abuse the school, he might speak, and that you would not allow any man to abuse the school in your house,—

Now you had no reason to suspect that Hyrum, would abuse the school, therefore my feelings were mortifyed, at those unnecessa[r]y observations, I undertook to reason, with you but you manifisted, an inconciderate and stubourn spirit, I then dispared, of benefiting you, on the account of the spirit you manifested, which drew from, me the expression that you was as ugly as the Devil.

Father then commanded silence and I formed a determination, to obey his mandate, and was about to leave the house, with the impression, that You was under the influence of a wicked spirit, you replyed that you, would say what you pleased in your own house, Father replyed, say what you please, but let the rest hold their, toungs, then a reflection, rushed through my mind, of the, anxiety, and care I had ⟨hav⟩ had for you and your family, in doing what I did, in finishing your house and providin flour for your family &c and also father had possession in the house, as well, as your self; and when at any time have I transgressed, the commandments of my father? or sold my birthright, that I should not have the privilege of speaking in my fathers house, or in other words in my fathers family, or in your house, [p. 82] (for so we will call it, and so it shall be,) that I should not have the privilege, of reproving a younger brother, therefore I said I will speak, for I built the house, and it is as much mine as yours, or something, to that effect, (I should have said that. I helped finish the house,) I said it merely to show that it could not be, the right spirit, that would rise up for trifling matters, and undertake to put me to silence, I saw that your indignation was kindled against me, and you made towards me, I was not then to be moved, and I thought, to pull off my loose coat, least it should tangle me, and you be left to hurt me, but not with the intention, of hurting You, but you was to[o] soon for me, and having once fallen into the hands of a mob, and ~~now~~ been wounded in my side, and now into the hands of a brother, my side gave way, and after having been rescued, from your grasp, I left your house, with, feelings that were indiscribale, the scenery had changed, and all those expectations, that I had cherished, when going to your house, of brotherly kindness, charity forbearance and natural, affection, that in duty binds us not to make eachothers offenders for a word. ~~but~~

But alass! abuse, anger, malice, hatred, and rage ⟨with a lame side⟩ with marks, of violence ⟨heaped⟩ upon ~~my body~~ me by a brother, were the reflections of my disapointment, and with these I returned home, not able to sit down, or rise up, without help, but through the blessings of God I am now better.— [p. 83]

I have received your letter and purused it with care, I have not entertained a feeling of malice, against you, I am, older than you~~r~~ and have endured, more suffering, have been mar[r]ed by mobs, the labours of my calling, a series of persecution, and inguries, continually heaped upon me, all serve to debilitate, my body, and it may ⟨be⟩ that I cannot boast of being stronger, than you, if I could, or could not, would this be an honor, or dishonor to me,— if I could boast like David of slaying a Goliath, who defied the armies of the living God, or like Paul, of contending with Peter face to face, with sound arguments, it might be an honor, But to mangle the flesh or seek revenge upon one who never done you any wrong, can not be a source of sweet reflection, to you, nor to me, neither to an honorable father & mother, brothers, and sisters, and when we reflect, with what care ~~our parents~~ and with what unremiting diligence our parents, have strove to watch over us, and how many hours, of sorrow, and anxiety, they have spent over our cradles and bedsides, in times of sickness, how careful we ought to be of their feelings in their old age, it cannot be a source of sweet reflection to us to say or do any thing that will bring their grey hairs down with sorrow to the grave,

In your letter you asked my forgivness, which I readily grant, but it seems to me, that you still retain an idea, that I have given you reasons to be angry or disaffected with me,

Grant me the privelege of saying then, [p. 84] that however hasty, or harsh, I may have spoken, at any time to you, it has been done for the express purpose of endeavouring, to warn exhort, admonish, and rescue you, from falling into difficulties, and sorrows which I foresaw you plunging into, by giving way to that wicked spirit, which you call your passions, which you should curbe and break down, and put under your feet, which if you do not you, never can be saved, in my view, in the kingdom of God.

God requires the will of his creatures, to be swallowed up in his will.

You desire to remain in the church, but forsake your apostleship, this is a stratigem of the evil one, when he has gained one advantage, ~~your~~ he lays a plan for another, ~~by~~ ⟨but⟩ by maintaining your apostleship in rising up, and making one tremendeous effort, you may overcome your passions, and please God and by forsaking your apostleship, is not to be willing, to make that sacrafice that God requires at your hands and is to incur his displeasure, and without pleasing God do not think, that it will be any better for you, when a man falls one step he must regain that step again, or fall another, he has still more to gain, or eventually all is lost.

I desire brother William that you will humble yourself, I freely forgive you and you know, my unshaken and ~~unshaken~~ unchangable disposition I ~~think~~ know in whom I trust, I stand upon [p. 85] the rock, the floods cannot, no they shall not overthrow me, you know the doctrine I teach is true, and you know that God has blessed me, I brought salvation to my fathers house, as an instrument in the hand of God, when they were in a miserable situation, You know that it is my duty to admonish you when you do wrong this liberty I shall always take, and you shall have the same privelege, I take the privelege, to admonish you because of my birthright, and I grant you the privilege because it is my duty, to be humble and to receive rebuke, and instruction, from a brother or a friend.

As it regards, what course you shall persue hereafter, I do not pretend to say, I leave you in the hands of God and his church. Make your own desision, I will do you good altho you mar me, or slay me, by so doing my garments, shall be clear of your sins, and if at any time you should concider me to be an imposter, for heavens sake leave me in the hands of God, and not think to take vengance on me your self.

Tyrany ursurpation, and to take mens rights ever has and ever shall be banished from my heart.

David sought not to kill Saul, although he was guilty of crimes that never entered my heart.

And now may God have mercy upon my fathers house, may God take [p. 86] away enmity, from betwe[e]n me and thee, and may all blessings be restored, and the past be forgotten forever, may humble repentance bring us both to thee ⟨O God⟩ and to thy power and protection, and a crown, to enjoy the society of father mother Alvin Hyrum Sophron[i]a Samuel Catharine [Katharine] Carloss [Don Carlos] Lucy the Saints and all the sanctif[ie]d in peace forever⟨, is the prayer of⟩

~~This from~~ Your brother
Joseph Smith Jun

To William Smith

19 December 1835 • Saturday

Saturday morning the 19.̲ᵗʰ at home wrote the ⟨above⟩ letter to Br. W.̲ᵐ Smith **I have had many solemn feelings this day Concerning my Brothe[r] William and have prayed in my heart to fervently that the Lord will not ~~him~~ ⟨cast him⟩ off but ⟨he⟩ may return to the God of Jacob and magnify his apostleship and calling may this be his happy lot for the Lord of Glorys Sake Amen**

20 December 1835 • Sunday

Sunday the 20ᵗʰ At home all day and took solled [solid?] Comfort with my Family had many serious reflections also Brothers Palmer and Tailor [Jonathan Taylor] Came to see me I showed them the sacred record to their Joy and satifaction O may God have mercy upon these men and keep them in the way of Everlasting life in the name of Jesus Amen [p. 87]

21 December 1835 • Monday

Monday morni[n]g 21ˢᵗ· At home Spent this in indeavering to treasure up know[l]edge for the be[n]ifit of my Calling the ⟨day⟩²¹⁹ pas[s]ed of[f] very pleasantly for which I thank the Lord for his blessings to my soul his great mercy over my Family in sparingly our lives O Continue thy Care over me and mine for Christ sake

22 December 1835 • Tuesday

Tusday 22d At home ~~this~~ Continued my studys O may God give me learning even Language and indo [endue] me with qualifycations to magnify his name while I live I also deliv[er]ed an address to the Church this Evening the Lord blessed my Soul, my scribe also is unwell O my God heal him and for his kindness to me O my soul be thou greatful to him and bless him and he shall be blessed ~~of for ever~~ of God forever I believe him to be a faithful friend to me therefore my soul delighteth in him Amen

Joseph Smith Jr

23 December 1835 • Wednesday

/²²⁰Wednesday 23.̲ᵈ In the forenoon at home stud[y]ing the greek Language and aslo waited upon the brethren who came in and exhibiting to them the papirus, in the afternoon visited brother Leonard Rich with the relatives of bro Oliver Cowdery had not a very agreeable visit for I found them [p. 88] filled

---

219. TEXT: Insertion in the handwriting of Warren Parrish.
220. TEXT: Frederick G. Williams handwriting begins.

58

Monday Morning 21st At home Spent this in indeavering to treasure up knowledge for the beifit of my calling the day passed of very pleasantly for which I thank the Lord for his blessings to my soul his great mercy over my Family in sharing our lives O continue thy care over me and mine for Christ sake

Tuesday 22 At home this continued my studys O may God give me learning even Language and indow me with qhalifycations to magnify his name while I live I also delivered an address to the Church this Evening the Lord blessed my Soul, my scribe also is un= =well O my God heal him and for his kindness to me O my soul be thou greatful to him and bless him and he shall be blessed of for ever of God for =ever I believe him to be a faithful friend to me therefore my soul delighteth in him Amen

Joseph Smith Jr

Wednesday 23 In the forenoon at home Studing the greek Language and waited upon the brethren who came in and exhibiting to them the papyrus, in the afternoon visited brother Leonard Rich with the relation of bro Oliver Cowdery had not a very agreable visit for I found them

Inscribed prayer. Joseph Smith's narrative prose often broke into petitions for divine aid, as in the entry of 22 December 1835. Handwriting of Joseph Smith and Frederick G. Williams. JS, Journal, 1835–1836, p. 88, JS Collection, Church History Library, Salt Lake City. (Photograph by Welden C. Andersen.)

with prejudice against the work of the Lord and their minds blinded with superstition & ignorence &c[221]

24 December 1835 · Thursday

Thirsday 24th At home in the forenoon[222] in the afternoon assisted in running ⟨out⟩ a road across my farm by the commissionor who were appointd by the court for the same—[223]

25 December 1835 · Friday

Fryday 25[th.] At home all this day and enjoyed myself with my family it being Christmas day the only time I have had this privelige so satisfactorily for a long time

26 December 1835 · Saturday

Saturday 26 commenced studeing the Hebrew Language in company with bros Parish [Warren Parrish] & [Frederick G.] Williams[224] in the mean time bro Lyman Sherman came in and requested to have the word of the lord through me for said he I have been wrought upon to make known to you my feelings and desires and was promised ~~to have~~ that I should have a revelation ~~and~~ which should make known my duty

last evening a brother from the east called upon me for instruction whose name is Jonathan Crosby[225]

also in the course of the day ~~a~~ two gentlemen called upon me while I was cutting wood at the door and requestd an interview with the heads of the church which I agreed to grant to them on Sunday morning the 27 Ins[t] [p. 89] The following is a revelation[226] given to Lyman Sherman this day 26 Dec 1835

221. JS's 1834–1836 history states that JS and Rich visited Cowdery to meet with his relatives. These may have included his brother-in-law, Winslow Wilbur, whom Cowdery later described as "very stubborn, and ignorant, and withal far from God." Members of Cowdery's immediate family had recently joined the church. (JS History, 1834–1836, 163; Cowdery, Diary, 25 Feb. 1836; Revelation, 25 Nov. 1834, in Doctrine and Covenants 99, 1835 ed. [D&C 106]; Minute Book 1, 15 Jan. 1836; Backman, *Profile*, 19, 26, 80.)

222. JS History, 1834–1836, 163, adds: "in reading, meditation, & prayer."

223. The county board of commissioners had appointed a surveyor, Levi Edson, and a committee of three others to lay out the road. (Geauga Co., OH, Road Record, Mar. 1836, bk. C, 327–328, microfilm, U.S. and Canada Record Collection, FHL.)

224. JS's 1834–1836 history clarifies that on this day JS "commenced regularly, & systematically, to study the venerable Hebrew language; we had paid some little attention to it before." (JS History, 1834–1836, 163.)

225. Crosby later recounted arriving in Kirtland in the evening and going to see JS, who was entertaining several people at a Christmas supper but welcomed Crosby and put him up for the night. (Jonathan Crosby, Autobiography, 13–14.)

226. Now D&C 108.

Verily thus saith the Lord unto you my servant Lyman your sins are forgiven you because you have obeyed my voice in coming up hither this morning to receive councel of him whom I have appointed

Therefore let your soul be at rest concerning your spiritual stand-ing, and resist no more my voice, and arise up and be more careful henceforth in observing your vows which you have made and do make, and you shall be blessed with exceding great blessings. Wait patiently untill the time when the solemn assembly shall be called of my servants then you shall be numbered with the first of mine elders and receive right by ordination with the rest of mine elders whom I have chosen

Behold this is the promise of the father unto you if you continue faithful—

and it shall be fulfilled upon you in that day that you shall have right to preach my gospel wheresoever I shall send you from henceforth from that time, Therefore strengthen your brethren in all your conversation in all your prayers, and in all your exhortations, and in all your doings, and behold and lo I am with you to bless you and deliver you forever Amen

27 December 1835 • Sunday

/[227]Sunday morning 27[th] at the us[u]al hour, attended meeting at the School house, President [Oliver] Cowdery delivered a verry able and interesting dis-cource— in the after part of the day Br. [p. 90] Hyrum Smith & Bishop Partrige [Edward Partridge], delivered each a short and ⟨interesting⟩ lecture, after which, the sacrament of the Lords supper ⟨was administered⟩ and dis-missed, our meeting—

Those Gentlemen that proposed to have an interview with me on this morning,[228] did not come, and I conclude they were trifling characters

28 December 1835 • Monday

Monday morning the 28[th.] having prefered a charge against Elder Almon Babbit[t] for traducing my character, he was this morning called before the High Council, and I attended, with my witnesses, and substantiated my charge against him and he in part acknowledged his fault, but not satisfactory to the council, and after parleying with him a long time, and granting him every indulgence, that righeousness require the council adjourned, without obtain-ing a full confession from him—[229]

---

227. TEXT: Frederick G. Williams handwriting ends; Warren Parrish begins.
228. See JS, Journal, 26 Dec. 1835.
229. JS asked for an investigation "that my character and influence may be preserved as far as it can

on this day the council of the seventy meet to render an account of their travels and ministry, since they were ordained to that apostleship, the meeting was interesting indeed, and my heart was made glad while listning to the relations of those that had been labouring, in the vinyard of the Lord with such marvelous success, and I pray God to bleess them with an increas of faith, and power, and keep them [p. 91] all with the indurance of faith in the name of Jesus Christ, ⟨to⟩ ~~Amen~~ ⟨the end⟩

29 December 1835 • Tuesday

Tuesday morning the 29th at home untill about 10. oclock I then went to attend a blessing meeting[230] at Oliver Olneys, in company with my wife, & father and mother who had come to live with me,[231] also my scribe went with us a large company assembled and Father Smith arose and made some preliminary remarks, which were verry applicable, on occasions of this kind, after which ~~he opened the meeting by~~ a hymn was sung and he opened the meeting by prayer about 15 persons then received a patriarchal blessing under his hands—[232] the servises were then dismissed, as they commenced, viz. by singing and prayer.— a table was then spread and crowned with the bounties of nature, and after invoking the benediction of heaven upon the rich repast, we fared sumptuously, and suffice it to say that we had a glorious meeting, through out and I was much pleased with the harmony and decorum that existed among the brethren and sisters, we returned home and ~~spent the evening—~~ at early candlelight I went and preachd at the school house to a crowded congregation, who listened [p. 92] with attention, while I delivered a lecture of about 3, hours in length, I had liberty in speaking, some presbyterians were present, as I after learned, and I expect that some of my saying's set like a garment that was well fit[t]ed, as I exposed their abominations in the language of the scriptures, and I pray God that it may be like a nail in a sure place, driven by the master of assemblies,[233] Col. Chamberlains Son[234] called to day

---

in righteousness." Babbitt had been complaining that JS "got mad" after losing an argument at the debating school. Five days later, Babbitt gave a full confession and was restored to fellowship. (Minute Book 1, 28 Dec. 1835; JS, Journal, 2 Jan. 1836; Minute Book 1, 2 Jan. 1836.)

230. That is, a patriarchal blessing meeting. (Compare 84n85 herein.)

231. Twelve days earlier, JS invited his parents to move into his house from the home they shared with William Smith. (JS, Journal, 17 Dec. 1835.)

232. Among those who received blessings at this time were Lyman Wight, Ezra Hayes, and George Morey. (Patriarchal Blessings, 1:29–30, 37.)

233. See Ecclesiastes 12:11; and Isaiah 22:23–25.

234. Lee, Lorenzo, or Jacob Chamberlain, sons of Col. Jacob Chamberlain, who lived in Seneca Falls Township, Seneca County, New York. (Seneca Co., NY, Probate Records, Record of Wills,

30 December 1835 • Wednesday

Wednesday 30 spent the day in reading hebrew at the council room, in company with my Scribe which gave me much sattisfaction, on the account of his returning health, for I delight in his company

31 December 1835 • Thursday

~~Friday morning Jany. 1st, 1836~~ Thursday morning 31st. at home, after attending to the duties of my family, retired to the council room, to persue my studies, the council of the 12, convened in the ⟨upper⟩ room in the printing office directly over the room wher we were convened, in our ~~study~~ studies, they sent for me and the presidency, (or part of them,) to recieve council from us on the subject of the council, which is to be held on Saturday next

In the after noon I attended at the Chapel to give directions, concerning [p. 93] the upper rooms, and more especially the west room which I intend ocupying, for a translating room, which will be prepared this week

1 January 1836 • Friday

Friday morning Jany. 1st. 1836 this being the beginning of a new year, my heart is filled with gratitude to God, that he has preserved my life and the ~~life~~ ⟨lives⟩ of my family while another year has rolled away, we have been, sustained and upheld in the midst of a wicked and perverse generation, and exposed to all, the afflictions temptations and misery that are incident to human life, for which I feel to humble myself in dust and ashes, as it were before the Lord— but notwithstanding, the gratitude that fills my heart on retrospecting the past year, and the multiplyed blessings that have crowned our heads, my heart is pained within me because of the difficulty that ~~in~~ exists in my fathers family, the Devil has made a violent attack on Br. W^m [Smith] and Br Calvin [Stoddard][235] and the powers of darkness, seeme [to] lower over their minds and not only theirs but cast a gloomy shade over the minds of my ~~my parents and somee of my~~ brothers and sisters, which prevents them from seeing things as they realy are, and the powers of Earth & hell seem combined to overthrow us and the Church by [p. 94] causing a division in the family, and ~~is indeed~~ the adversary is bring[ing] into requisition all his subtlety to prevent the Saints

---

14 Nov. 1855, bk. E, 8–9, microfilm, U.S. and Canada Record Collection, FHL; Porter, "Study of the Origins," 272, 315–316.)

235. Tension surfaced between JS and William Smith in late October, was never fully resolved, and erupted again in a mid-December confrontation. Stoddard, the husband of JS's sister Sophronia, was censured sometime before 7 March 1836, when he made a confession in his elders quorum; on 26 October 1836, his church standing was restored. (JS, Journal, 29, 30, and 31 Oct. 1835; 16, 17, 18, and 19 Dec. 1835; Cook and Backman, *Kirtland Elders' Quorum Record,* 7 Mar. and 26 Oct. 1836.)

from being endowed, by causing devision among the 12, also among the 70, and bickerings and jealousies among the Elders and official members of the church, and so the leaven of iniquity foments and spreads among the members of the church,

But I am determined that nothing on my part shall be lacking to adjust and amicably dispose of and settle all family difficulties, on this day, that the ensuing year, and years, be they many or few may be spent in righteousneess before God, and I know that the cloud will burst and satans kingdom be laid in ~~ruin,~~ ⟨ruins⟩ with all his black designs, and the saints come forth like gold seven times tried in the fire, being made perfect throug[h] sufferings, and temptations,[236] and the blessings of heaven and earth multiplyed upon our heads which may God grant for Christ sake Amen—

Br. William came to my house and Br. Hyrum [Smith], also, Uncle John Smith, we went into a room in company with father and Elder Martin Harris,[237] ~~and~~ father, Smith then opened our interview by prayer after which, he expressed his feelings on the ocasion in a verry feeling and pathetic manner even with all the sympathy of a father whose feeling were wounded deeply on the [p. 95] account of the difficulty that was existing in the family, and while he addressed us the spirit of God rested down upon us in mighty power, and our hearts were melted Br. William made an humble confession and asked ~~our~~ my forgiveness for the abuse he had offered me and wherein I had been out of the way I asked his forgivness, and the spirit of confission and forgiveness, was mutual among us all, and we covenanted with each other in the Sight of God and the holy angels and the brethren, to strive from henceforward to build each other up in righteousness, in all things and not listen to evil reports concerning eachother, but like brethren, indeed go to eachother, with our grievances in the spirit of meekness, and be reconciled and thereby promote our own happiness and the happiness of the family and in short the happiness and well being of all.— my wife and Mother, ~~Uncle John~~ & my Scribe was then called in and we repeated the covenant to them that we had entered into, and while gratitude swelled our bosoms, tears flowed from our eys.— I was then requested to close our interview which I did with prayer, and it was truly a jubilee and time of rejoiceing [p. 96]

---

236. See Zechariah 13:9.

237. Harris, apparently brought in as a neutral third-party mediator, was a friend of the family from their New York days. JS's 1834–1836 history adds that the group retired to a "private room" in the morning. (Lucy Mack Smith, History, 1844–1845, bk. 5, [8]; bk. 6, [3]; JS History, 1834–1836, 167.)

2 January 1836 • Saturday

Saturday morning 2^(ond) acording to previous arangement, I went to council at 9 oclock,— this council was called, to set in judgment, on a complaint. prefered against Br. William [Smith], by Elder Orson Johnson[238] the council organized and opened by prayer and proceded to buisness, but before entering on the trial Br. William arose and humbly confessed the charges prefered against him and asked the forgivness of the council and the whole congregation a vote was then called to know whether his confession was satisfactory, and whether the brethren would extend the hand of fellowship to him again, with cheerfulness the whole congregation raised thier hands to receive him[239]

Elder Almon Babbit[t] also confessed ~~his~~ the charges which I prefered against him in a previous council,[240] and was received into fellowship, and some other buisness was transacted, in union and fellowship and the best of feelings seemed to prevail among the brethren, and our hearts were made glad on the occasion, and there was joy in heaven, and my soul doth magnify the Lord for his goodness and mercy endureth forever— council adjourned with prayer as us[u]al—

3 January 1836 • Sunday

Sunday morning 3^d went to meeting at the us[u]al hour President [Sidney] Rigdon, delivered a fine lecture upon the subject of revelation, in the afternoon I confirmed about 10 or 12 persons who [p. 97] had been baptised, among whom was M[arvel] C. Davis who was baptized at the intermission to day—[241] Br William Smith made his confession to the Church to their satisfaction, and was cordially received into fellowship again, the Lords supper was administered, and br. William gave out an appointment to preach in the evening, at early candlelight, and preachd a fine discourse, and this day ~~is~~ has been a day of rejoicing to me, the cloud that has been hanging over us has burst with blessings on our heads, and Satan has been foiled in his attempts to destroy me and the Church, by causing jealousies to arise in the hearts of some of the

---

238. Johnson brought charges against William Smith of "unchristian like conduct in speaking disrespectfully of President Joseph Smith J^unr. and the revelations & commandments given through him" and "for attempting to inflict personal violence" on him. These charges arose from William Smith's assault on JS two weeks earlier. Six of the seven most senior members of the Quorum of the Twelve sat on this high council to consider the charges against their fellow quorum member. (Minute Book 1, 29 Dec. 1835; JS, Journal, 16 Dec. 1835; Minute Book 1, 2 Jan. 1836.)

239. William Smith also promised to make the same confession before the church, which, as noted in the journal, occurred the following day. (Minute Book 1, 2 Jan. 1836.)

240. See Minute Book 1, 28 Dec. 1835 and 2 Jan. 1836.

241. Davis's rebaptism followed church discipline that occurred sometime after 17 August 1835, when he served as a substitute high council member. (Minute Book 1, 17 Aug. 1835.)

brethren, and I thank my heavenly father for, the union and harmony which now prevails in the Church[242]

4 January 1836 • Monday

Monday morning 4th meet and organized our hebrew School according to the arangements that were made on Saturday last, we had engaged Doct Piexotto [Daniel Peixotto] to teach us in the hebrew language, when we had our room prepared, we informed him that we were ready and our room prepared and he agreed to wait on us on this day and deliver his introductory lecture yesterday he sent us word that he [p. 98] could not come untill wedensday next a vote was called to know whether we would, submit to such treatment or not and carried in the negative,[243] and Elder Sylvester Smith appointed as clerk to write him on the subject and inform him that his servises, were not wanted,[244] and Elders Wm E MC,Lellen [McLellin] & Orson ⟨Hyde⟩ Johnson despached to Hudson Semenary, to hire a teacher, they were appointed by the voice of the School, to act for in their behalf— however we concluded to go on with our school and do the best we can untill we can obtain a teacher, and by the voice of the School I concented, to render them all the assistance I am able to, for the time being—[245] we are ocupying the translating room for the use of the School untill another room can be prepared, this is the first day that we have ocupied ⟨it⟩ this room which is the west room in the upper part of the Chappel,[246] which was concecrated this morning by prayer offered up by father Smith

This is a rainy time and the roads are extremely mud[d]y

meet this evening at the Chapel to make arangements for a Singing School after some altercation, a judicious arangement was made, a comittee of 6 was chosen, to take charge of the singing department, [p. 99]

---

242. This marks the end of a period of contention between JS and William Smith that began two months earlier. (See JS, Journal, 29, 30, and 31 Oct. 1835; 3 Nov. 1835; 16, 18, and 19 Dec. 1835; 1 and 2 Jan. 1836.)

243. After retaining Peixotto, the school sought to be released from its agreement with him. Peixotto apparently did not release the school from its agreement yet failed to appear as scheduled. (See JS, Journal, 21 Nov. 1835.)

244. The letter is not extant, but Peixotto's 5 January letter of reply and Warren Parrish's 11 January rejoinder were later transcribed into this journal. (JS, Journal, 18 Jan. 1836.)

245. As recorded in this journal, JS spent time on several days studying Hebrew after receiving books from Cowdery six weeks earlier. (See JS, Journal, 20 Nov. 1835.)

246. This was the westernmost of the five rooms on the third story of the House of the Lord, which JS intended to use as a translating room. (Robison, *First Mormon Temple,* 55, figs. 4–7; JS, Journal, 31 Dec. 1835.)

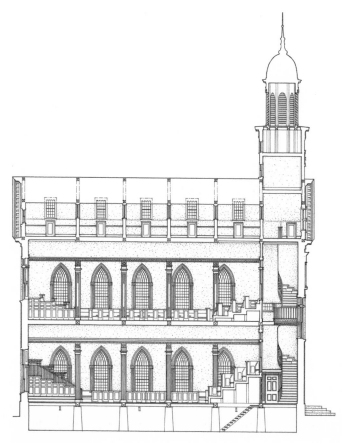

Interior of the House of the Lord. This longitudinal section shows the assembly rooms on the first and second stories of the building, with terraced pulpits on each end, and the five rooms of the third story. Joseph Smith used the westernmost (top left) room for an office. Drawing by Verdon W. Upham, Historic American Building Survey, 1934. (Courtesy Library of Congress, Washington DC.)

Joseph Smith's temple office. 1987. Smith established a personal office in the westernmost of the five rooms in the third story of the House of the Lord. The office was also used as a schoolroom for Hebrew study. (Courtesy Community of Christ Library-Archives, Independence, MO. Photograph by Elwin C. Robison.)

5 January 1836 • Tuesday

Tuesday 5ᵗʰ attended the Hebrew School, divided them into classes, had some debate with Elder Orson Pratt,²⁴⁷ he manifested a stubourn spirit, which I was much grieved at

6 January 1836 • Wednesday

Wedenesday 6ᵗʰ attended School again, and spent most of the fore noon in setling, the unplesant feelings that existed in the breast of Elder O[rson] Pratt and after much controversy, he confessed his fault and asked the forgivness of the whol school and was cheerfully forgiven by all

Elder Mc,Lellen [William E. McLellin] returned from Hudson, and reported to the school that he had hired a Teacher, to teach us the term of 7. weeks for $320, that is 40, Schollars for that amount, to commence in about 15, days hence,— he is highly celebrated as a hebrew schollar, and proposes to give us sufficient knowledge in the above term of time to read and translate the language²⁴⁸ [*6 lines blank*] [p. 100]

<u>Conference Minuits</u>

at a conference held at the School house on Saturday the 2ᵈ Jan 1836 the following individuals were appointed by the voice of the conference to be ordained to the office of Elders in the church of the latterday saints under the hands of President Joseph Smith jr

Sidney Rigdon Clerk—

> Vincent [Vinson] Knight
> Thomas Grover
> Elisha [Elijah] Fordham   <u>Eldrs</u>
> Hyram Dayton
> Samuel James
> John Herrott [Herritt]²⁴⁹

---

247. JS History, 1834–1836, 170, clarifies that the disagreement was over Hebrew pronunciation.

248. McLellin hired Joshua Seixas, a member of a prominent New York Jewish family, who had taught Hebrew in connection with several educational institutions. Seixas's Hebrew textbook was organized for a six-week curriculum. As noted in the journal, Seixas commenced classes 26 January. (Goldman, "Joshua/James Seixas," 73–77; Seixas, *Hebrew Grammar,* iv; see also F. C. Waite, Cleveland, OH, to Joseph L. Rubin, Washington DC, 19 Oct. 1933, in Milton V. Backman, Ohio Research Papers, ca. 1975, CHL; and Snow, "Who Was Professor Joshua Seixas?")

249. Only Knight, Grover, and Dayton are mentioned in the official minutes of the 2 January high council meeting. The conference to which the present minutes refer may have been an additional meeting held that day for which no original minutes are extant. (Minute Book 1, 2 Jan. 1836.)

7 January 1836 · Thursday

Thursday 7th attended a sumptuous feast at Bishop N[ewel] K. Whitneys this feast was after the order of the Son of God the lame the halt and blind wer invited according to the intruction of the Saviour[250]

our meeting was opened by singing and prayer offered up by father Smith, after which Bishop, Whitneys father & Mother[251] were bless[ed] and a number of others, with a patriarchal blessing, we then recieved a bountiful refreshment, furnished by the liberality of the Bishop the company was large,— before we parted we had some of the Songs of Zion sung, and our hearts were made glad while partaking of an antipast[252] of those [p. 101] Joys that will be poured upon the head of the Saints w[h]en they are gathered together on Mount Zion to enjoy eachothers society forever more even all the blessings of heaven and earth and where there will be none to molest nor make us afraid—[253]

returned home and spent the evening

8 January 1836 · Friday

Friday 8th Spent the day in the hebrew School, and made rapid progress in our studies

9 January 1836 · Saturday

Saturay 9th attended School in the fore noon— at about 11, oclock received the following note[254]

Thus saith the voice of the spirit to me, if thy Brother Joseph Smith jr will attend the feast at thy house this day (at 12 ocl) the poor & lame will rejoice at his presence & also think themselves honored—

Yours in friendship & Love

9th Jan.y 1836

N.K. W [Newel K. Whitney]

---

250. See Luke 14:12–14. As bishop in Ohio, Whitney had an ecclesiastical responsibility to administer to the poor. According to Elizabeth Ann Smith Whitney, this feast for the poor continued over the next three days, 7–9 January, with "Joseph and his two Counselors being present each day, talking, blessing, and comforting the poor." ([Elizabeth Ann Smith Whitney], "A Leaf from an Autobiography," *Woman's Exponent*, 1 Nov. 1878, 83; Orson Whitney, "Aaronic Priesthood," 129–130; see also JS, Journal, 9 Jan. 1836.)

251. Samuel and Susanna Kimball Whitney.

252. "A foretaste; something taken before the proper time." ("Antepast," in *American Dictionary*, 39.)

253. This phraseology appears throughout the Old Testament, as in, for example, Micah 4:2–4 and Zephaniah 3:13.

254. TEXT: Residue from an adhesive wafer at the top of page 103 indicates that Warren Parrish probably copied the note into the journal from a loose manuscript that had been attached at that point.

I dismissed the School in order to attend to this polite invitation, with my wife father & mother

We attended the feast, a large congregation assembled a number was blessed under the hands of father Smith, and we had a good [p. 102] time,[255] returned home and spent the evening

10 January 1836 · Sunday

Sunday 10[th] went to the meeting at the us[u]al hour Elder Wilber [Wilbur] Denton & Elder J. [Wilkins Jenkins] Salisbury, preached in the fore noon, in the after noon Br. Samuel [Smith] & Br. Carloss [Don Carlos] Smith, they all did well concidering their youth, and bid fair to make useful men in the vinyard of the Lord, administered the sacrament and dismissed

at the intermission to day 3, were baptised by Elder Martin Harris— returned home and spent the evening—

11 January 1836 · Monday

Monday morning 11th at home There being no school I spent the day at home, many brethren called to see me, among whom was Alva Beamon [Alvah Beman] from New York Jenesee [Genesee] Co. he has come to attend the Solemn Assembly,—[256] I delight in the society of my friends & brethren, and pray that the blessings of heaven and earth may be multiplyed upon their heads

12 January 1836 · Tuesday

Tuesday morning 12th at home,— this ⟨day⟩ I called on the presidency of the church, and made arangemants ~~for~~ to meet tomorrow at 10, oclock A.M [p. 103] to take into concideration the subject of the Solemn Assembly— This after noon, a young man called to see the Egyptian manuscripts, and I exibited them to him, he expressed great satisfaction, and appeared verry anxious to obtain a knowledge of the translation,— also a man was introduced to me by the name of Russel Wever [Russell Weaver] from Cambray Niagary [Cambria, Niagara] Co. N. Y this man is a preacher, in the church that is called Christian or Unitarian, ~~some~~ he remarked that he had but few minuits to spend with me, we entered into conversation, and had some little controversy upon the subject of prejudice, but soon come to ~~the~~ an understanding, he spoke of the gospel and said he believed it, adding that it was good tidings of great joy— I replyed that it was one thing, to proclaim good tidings and another to tell what those

---

255. This was the final day of a three-day feast. (JS, Journal, 7 Jan. 1836; 146n250 herein.)

256. Beman's arrival was presumably in response to advice from JS. (JS, Journal, 9–11 Nov. 1835, p. 95 herein.)

tidings are, he waived the conversation and withdrew— he was introduced by Joseph Rose—

13 January 1836 • Wednesday

Wednesday morning 13ᵗʰ at 10, oclock A. M meet in council with all the presidency of Kirtland and Zion ~~that~~ together ⟨all⟩ with ⟨all⟩ their councilors that could be found in this place however some of the councellors were absent, both of Kirtland and Zion

The presidency of the Seventy were also present, and ⟨many⟩ more [p. 104] of the Elders of the church of the latterday Saints—²⁵⁷ come to order, sung Adam-ondi-Ahman²⁵⁸ and opened by prayer offered up by Joseph Smith Sen—

⟨I⟩ ~~President John Smith~~ presided on the occasion

After the council was organized and opened ~~President Joseph Smith jn~~ ⟨I⟩ made some ~~verry pertinent~~ remarks in my introductory lecture before the authority of the church, this morning in general terms, laying before them the buisness of the day which was to suply some deficiencies in the ~~council~~ Bishop coun[c]il in this place after some altercation upon the most proper manner of proc[ee]ding Elder Vinson Knight was nominated by the Bishop and seconded by the presidency vote called of that body and caried vote was then called ~~for~~ from the high council of Zion and carried

vote was then called ~~for~~ from the twelve and carried—

vote then called ~~for~~ from the council of the Seventy and carried

vote then called ~~for~~ from the Bishop and his council from Zion and carried— Elder Knights was received by the universal voice and concent of all the authority of the Church as a councilor in the Bishops council ⟨in⟩ this place, to fill the place of Elder Hyrum Smith. who is ordained to the [p. 105] Presidency of the high council of Kirtland²⁵⁹

---

257. For this and other meetings during this period, formal minutes exist in addition to the journal entries. The minutes of this "grand council" held in the attic story of the printing office list in attendance the presidencies of Kirtland and Missouri, the Quorum of the Twelve, and the high councils and bishop-rics of Kirtland and Missouri. This was the first in a series of five days of meetings to better organize church leadership and to establish rules of conduct for the House of the Lord, which was nearing completion. Oliver Cowdery characterized the proceedings of the meeting held 15 January as "important business preparatory to the endowment." (Minute Book 1, 13 Jan. 1836, 200–203; Cowdery, Diary, 15 Jan. 1836.)

258. The text of this hymn was written by William W. Phelps, a member of the Missouri presidency in attendance at this council. (Hymn 23, *Collection of Sacred Hymns* [1835], 29–30; see also "Adam-ondi-Ahman," in Geographical Directory.)

259. Hyrum Smith was called as "assistant for the Bishop" in Kirtland, 10 February 1832. He was appointed an assistant president in the presidency of the high priesthood—and therefore in the presidency of the church—on 6 December 1834. In the period during which this journal entry was made, the presidency of the church were also the presidency of the Kirtland high council. Reference to them as the presidency of the high council at Kirtland, when specifying the presidency of the church might seem to

He was then ordained under the hands of Bishop N[ewel] K. Whitney to the office of a councillor also ~~of~~ to that of high priest

Council adjourned for one hour by singing the song, come let us rejoice in the day of salvation[260]

council assembled at one oclock P.M organized and proceded to buisness The first buisness this afternoon was to supply some deficiencies in the high council in Kirtland, the stake of Zion

John P. Greene was nominated and seconded by the presidency vote taken and carried in his favour by the unanimous voice of ~~the~~ all the authority of the church— he supplyes the place of President O[liver] Cowdery who is elected to the presidency of the high council in this place[261]

Elder Thomas Grover was nominated to supply the place of Luke Johnson who is chosen and ordained one of the twelve Apostles,—[262] the nomination was seconded and vote carried in his favour by all the authority present and he is received as a councilor in the high council in Kirtland

Elder Noah Packard was next nominated and seconded to supply the place of Sylvester Smith who is ordained to the presidency of the Seventy—[263] vote called and carried [p. 106] in his favour and Elder Packard was recived by the unanimous vote of all the authority present as a high councilor in Kirtland

Elder John Page was nominated, but was not present and his name droped

Elder Joseph Kingsbury was nominated and seconded, to fill the place of Orson Hyde, who is chosen and ordained one of the twelve,—[264] vote called and carried unanimously and Elder Kingsbury was recieved as a hi[g]h councilor in Kirtland

---

have been more appropriate, suggests that the terminology may have been in transition. See, for example, the reference to Oliver Cowdery later in this same entry and the 16 January 1836 reference to censure of the Twelve by "the presidency of the high council in Kirtland." (JS History, 1834–1836, 20; JS, Journal, 16 Jan. 1836; see also Ecclesiastical Organizational Charts, 452–454, 456 herein.)

260. The text of this hymn was written by William W. Phelps, a member of the Missouri presidency in attendance at this council. (Hymn 18, *Collection of Sacred Hymns* [1835], 24–25.)

261. JS ordained Oliver Cowdery "assistant President of the High and Holy Priesthood, . . . to assist in presiding over the whole church" a year earlier. (Entry for 5 Dec. 1834, in JS History, 1834–1836, 17.)

262. Johnson, an original member of the Quorum of the Twelve, was ordained an apostle eleven months earlier. (Minute Book 1, 14 Feb. 1835.)

263. Sylvester Smith was ordained a president of the Quorum of the Seventy more than ten months earlier. Minutes of the council clarify that Packard replaced not Sylvester Smith but Hyrum Smith, who was called to the Kirtland high council on 24 September 1834 to replace Sylvester Smith, who had been dropped from the council at that day's meeting. (JS History, vol. B-1, 578; Minute Book 1, 24 Sept. 1834 and 13 Jan. 1836.)

264. Hyde, an original member of the Quorum of the Twelve, was ordained an apostle eleven months earlier. (Minute Book 1, 15 Feb. 1835.)

Elder Samuel James, was nominated and seconded to fill the place of Joseph Smith Sen—[265] vote called and carried unanimously in his favour and Elder James was received as a high councilor in Kirtland

the new elected councilors were then called forward, in order as they were elected, and ordained under the hands of President's [Sidney] Rigdon P̶r̶e̶s̶ Joseph Smith Sen. and Hyrum Smith to the office of High Priests and councilors in this place, viz. Kirtland the Stake of Zion,— many great and glorious blessings were pronounced upon the heads of the⟨s[e]⟩ councilors by president S. Rigdon who was spokesman on the occasion[266]

Next proceded to supply the deficiencies in the Zion high council [p. 107] which were two viz. Elder's John Murdock and Solomon Hancock who were absent— Elder's Alva Bemon [Alvah Beman] and Isaac Mc Withy were nominated and seconded, to s[u]pply their place for the time being

vote taken of the whole assembly and carried in their favour, to serve as councilors in the high council of Zion, for the present[267]

Elder Nathaniel Miliken [Millikin] and Thomas Carrico [Jr.], were nominated and seconded to officiate as doorkeepers in the house of the Lord, vote called and carried, by the unamimous voice of the assembly

President's Joseph Smith jn S. Rigdon W[illiam] W. Phelps D[avid] Whitmer H[yrum] Smith, were nominated and seconded to draft rules and regulation to govern the house of the Lord vote called and carried by the unamimous voice of the whole assembly

The question was agitate[d] whether whispering, should be allowed in our councils and assemblys

a vote was called from the whole assembly and carried in the negative, that no whispering shall be allowed nor any one allowed, (except he is called upon or asks permission,) to speak [p. 108] loud in our councils or assemblies, upon any concideration whatever, and no man shall be interupted while speaking unless he is speaking out of place, and every man, shall be allowed to speak in his turn—[268] Elder Miliken objected to officiate in the house of the Lord as

---

265. Joseph Smith Sr. was appointed to the presidency a year earlier. Though he continued to serve as a council member, his advancement was recognized in council minutes by placing "President" after his name. (Entry for 6 Dec. 1834, in JS History, 1834–1836, 20; Minute Book 1, 18 Jan. 1835.)

266. For synopses of the blessings, see Minute Book 1, 13 Jan. 1836, 200–203.

267. A week earlier, a council at Kirtland permanently replaced five other members of the Missouri high council, four of whom had been called to the Quorum of the Twelve. (Minute Book 2, 6 Jan. 1836.)

268. This reaffirmed an earlier revelation: "Let not all be spokesmen at once; but let one speak at a time, and let all listen unto his sayings, that when all have spoken, that all may be edified of all, and that every man may have an equal privilege." (Revelation, 27 and 28 Dec. 1832 and 3 Jan. 1833, in Doctrine and Covenants 7:37, 1835 ed. [D&C 88:122]; see also Minute Book 1, 12 Feb. 1834.)

door keeper on account of his health, and ⟨was⟩ released by the voice of the assembly

The minuits of the council were then read,[269] and council adjourned untill Friday the 15th Inst. at 9, ocl A, M, at the ⟨west⟩ School room in the upper part of the Chapel

President S. Rigdon made a request to have some of the presidency lay their hands upon him and rebuke a severe affliction, in his face which troubles him most at night— Eldr's H. Smith and D. Whitmer by my request laid hands upon him and prayed for him and rebuked his disease in the name of the Lord Jesus Christ,— the whole assembly ~~said~~ responded — Amen

Elder D[avid] W. Patten also made a request in behalf of his wife for ⟨our⟩ prayers for her, ~~behalf~~ ⟨that⟩ she might be healed,— I offered up a pray for her recovery, the assembly responded Amen [p. 109]

President Rigdon then arose and made some verry appropriate remarks touching the enduement, and dismissed the assembly by prayer—

W[arren] Parrish   <u>Scribe</u>

This has been one of the best days that I ever spent, there has been an entire unison of feeling expressed in all our proceedings this day, and the Spirit of the God of Israel has rested upon us in mighty power, and it has ⟨been⟩ good for us to be here, in this heavenly place in Christ Jesus, and altho much fatiegued with the labours of the day, yet my spiritual reward has been verry great indeed

Returned home and spent the evening

14 January 1836 • Thursday

Thursday morning the 14th at 9, oclock, meet the hebrew class at the School room in the Chapel, and made some arangements, about our anticipated Teacher Mr J. Sexias [Joshua Seixas] of Hudson, Ohio—

I then retired to the council room in the printing office, to me[e]t, my colleagues who were appointed, with my self to draft rules and regulations to be observed in the house of the Lord in Kirtland built by the Church of the latter day saints, in the year of our Lord 1834,[270] which are as follows[271] [p. 110]

---

269. Minute Book 1, 13 Jan. 1836, 200–203.

270. The foundation and walls of the House of the Lord were built in 1834, completing the major structural stonework and masonry. Finishing work continued in 1835 and 1836. (Corrill, *Brief History of the Church*, 21; see also Robison, *First Mormon Temple*, 78–81, 149–157.)

271. The transcript of regulations that follows ends with the note "council adjourned sini di [sine die]." The committee that met on 14 January, however, was scheduled to present their draft regulations on the *following* day. This indicates that the transcript here was made from a copy of the rules as approved in

1st— It is according to the rules and regulations of all regular and legal organized bodies to have a president to keep order.—

2^ond— The body thus organized are under obligation to be in subjection to that authority—

3^d— When a congregation assembles in this house they shall submit to the following rules, that due respect may be paid to the order of worship—viz.

1st— no man shall be interupted who is appointed to speak by the presidency of the Church, by any disorderly person or persons in the congregation, by whispering by laughing by talking by menacing Jestures by getting up and running out in a disorderly manner or by offering indignity to the manner of worship or the religion or to any officer of said church while officiating in his office in any wise whatever by any display of ill manners or ill breeding from old or young rich or poor male or female bond or free black or white believer or unbeliever and if any of the above insults are offered such measures will be taken as are lawful to punish the aggressor or aggressors and eject them out of the house

2^ond— An insult offered to the ~~presidency~~ ⟨presiding⟩ Elder of said Church, shall be concidered an insult to the whole [p. 111] body, also an insult offered to any of the officers of said Church while officiating shall be considered an insult to the whole body—

3^d— All persons are prohibited from going up the stairs in times of worship

4th— all persons are prohibited from exploring the house except waited upon by a person appointed for that purpose—

5th— all persons are prohibited from going ⟨in⟩to the several pulpits except the officers who are appointed to officiate in the same

6th— All persons are prohibited from cutting marking or marring the inside or outside of the house with a knife pencil or any other instrument whatever, under pain of such penalty as the law shall inflict—

7th— All children are prohibited from assembling in the house above or below or any part of it to play or for recreation at any time, and all parents guardians or masters shall be ameneable for all damage that shall accrue in consequence of their children—

---

the meeting held on 15 January. (Minute Book 1, 13 Jan. 1836, 200–203, 231–233; 15 Jan. 1836, 203–205, 233–234.)

8th— All persons whether believers or unbelievers shall be treated with due respect by the ~~authority~~ ⟨authorities⟩ of the Church— [p. 112]

9[th]— no imposition shall be practiced upon any member of the church by depriving them of their ⟨rights⟩ in the house— council adjourned sini di [sine die]

returned home and spent the after no[o]n,— towards evening President [Oliver] Cowdery returned from Columbus, the capital of this State, I could not spend much time with him[272] being under obligation to attend at Mrs. Wilcoxs to join Mr. John Webb and Mrs Catharine [Catherine] Wilcox in matrimony also M[r.] Th[os] Carrico [Jr.] and Miss Elizabeth Baker at the same place, I found a large company assembled, the house was filled to overflowing, we opened our interview by singing and prayer suited to the occasion after which I made some remarks in relation to the duties that are incumbent on husbands and wives, in particular the great importance there is in cultivating the pure principles of the institution, in all it's bearings, and connexions with each other and society in general

I then invited them to arise and join hands, and pronounced the ceremony according to the rules and regulations of the Church of the latterday Saints[273]

~~Closed~~ after which I pronounced such blessings upon their heads as the Lord put into my heart ~~even~~ even the blessings of Abraham Isaac and Jacob, and dismissed by singing and prayer

we then took some refreshment [p. [113]] and our hearts were made glad with the fruit of the vine, this is according to pattern, set by our Saviour himself,[274] and we feel disposed to patronize all the institutions of heaven

I took leave of the congregation and retired

15 January 1836 • Friday

Friday the 15th at 9 oclock A.M meet in council agreeably to the adjournment, at the council room in the Chapel organized the authorities of the church agreeably to their respective offices in the same, I then made some observation respecting the order of the day, and the great responsibility we are under to transact all our buisness, in righteousness before God, inasmuch as our desisions will have a bearing upon all mankind and upon all generations to come

---

272. Oliver Cowdery had been in Columbus, Ohio, to serve as a delegate from Geauga County to the state Democratic Party convention. (Cowdery, Diary, 8–9 Jan. 1836.)

273. "Marriage," ca. Aug. 1835, in Doctrine and Covenants 101, 1835 ed.

274. Probably an allusion to John 2:1–11, which describes the wedding at Cana.

Sung the song Adam-Ondi-ahman and open[ed] by prayer — & proceeded to buisness, by reading the rules and regulations to govern the house of the Lord in Kirtland,— The vote of the presidency was called, upon these rules, and ~~carried~~ passed by the unanimous voice of this presidency ⟨viz.⟩ of the high council, some objections were raised by president [Oliver] Cowdery, but waived, on an explenation

The privilege of remarking upon the rules above named, was next granted [p. 114] to ⟨the⟩ high councillors of Kirtland, and after much altercation, their vote was called and unanimously passed, in favour of them

The investigation was then thrown before ~~the~~ the ⟨high⟩ counsel of Zion, some objections or inquiry, was made upon some particular items, which were soon settled, and their vote called ~~called~~ and passed unanimously in favour of them—

The twelve next investigated the subject of these rules, and their vote called and passed unanimously in favour of them— Counsel adjourned for one hour— 1, oclock P.M in counsil, come to order, and proceded to buisness

The subject of the rules to govern the house of the Lord, come next in order before the counsel of the Seventy, their vote called and carried unanimously

The vote of the Bishop ⟨of Zion⟩[275] and his counsellors was then called, and after, some debate was passed unanimously

The question was then thrown before the Bishop in Kirtland and his counsellors their vote called and carried in their favour— The above rules hav now passed through the several quorums, in their order, and passed by the unanimous vote of the whole, and are therefore received and established as a law to govern the house of the Lord in this place,— In the investigated of this subject, I found that many who had deliberated upon this subject [p. 115] were darkened in their minds, which drewforth, some remarks from me, respecting the privileges of the authorities of the church, that they should, each speak in his turn, and in his place, and in his time and season, that their may be perfect order in all things, and that every man, before he, makes an objection to any, item, that is thrown before them for their concideration, should be sure that they can throw light upon the subject rather than spread darkness, and that his objections be founded in righteousness which may be done by applying ourselves closely to study the, mind and will of the Lord, whose Spirit always makes manifest, and demonstrates to the understanding of all who are in possession, of his Spirit—

---

275. JS History, 1834–1836, 178, supplies "bishop in Kirtland" instead of Zion (Missouri).

Elder Carloss [Don Carlos] Smith was nominated and seconded, to be ordained to the high priesthood—[276] also to officiate as president to preside over that body in ~~this place~~ Kirtland— The vote was called of the respective quorums in their order and passed through the whole house by their unanimous voice—

Elder Alva Beemon [Alvah Beman], was nominated and seconded to officiate as President of the Elders in Kirtland Elder Beemon arose and asked permission to speak, and made the following remarks— Brethren you [p. 116] know that I am young and I am old and ignorant[277] and kneed much instructions, but I wish to do the will of the Lord— The vote of the several authorities was then called and carried unanimously—

William Cowdery [Jr.] was nominated and seconded to officiate as president over the priests of the Aaronic priesthood in Kirtland, the vote of the assembly was called, beginning at the Bishops council and passing through the several authorities untill it come to the presidency of the high counsel in Kirtland and receved their sanction having ⟨been⟩ carried, unanimously in all the departments, below

Oliver Olney was nominated and seconded to preside over the teachers in Kirtland ~~and~~ The vote of the assembly was called and passed unanimously

Ira Bond was nominated and seconded to preside ~~of~~ ⟨over⟩ the deacons in Kirtland— vote called and passed unanimously

Eldr. Carloss Smith was called forward to the seat of the presidency and ordained to the office's whereunto he was elected and many blessings pronounced [p. 117] upon his head, by Joseph Smith Sen S[idney] Rigdon and Hyrum Smith who were appointed to ordain him

⟨Also⟩ Eldr. Beemon recieved his ordination under the hands of the same, to the office whereunto he had been elected, and many blessings pronounced upon his head

Bishop [Newel K.] Whitney ⟨and his counselors⟩ then proceded to ordain Wᵐ· Cowdery to the office whereunto he had been called, viz. to preside over the priests of the Aaronic priesthood in Kirtland, many blessings were sealed upon his head—

⟨also⟩ Oliver Olney to preside over the teachers, in Kirtland with many blessings— also Ira Bond to preside over the deacons in Kirtland, with many blessings upon his head

---

276. That is, to be ordained a high priest.

277. Probably intended as "*you* are young and I am old and ignorant." At age sixty, Beman was considerably older than many of the men present.

next proceeded to nominated doorkeepers in the house of the Lord the officers of the several quorums were nominated seconded and carried that each should serve in their turn as doorkepers,— also ~~that~~ Nathaniel Mil[l]iken Thomas Carrico [Jr.] Samuel Rolph [Rolfe] and Amos R. Orton were elected to the office of doorkeepers[278] [p. 118]

nominated and seconded that the presidency of the high counsel hold the keys of the outer and inner courts of the Lords house in Kirtland, except one of the vestries ⟨keys⟩ which is to be held by the Bishopric of the Aaronic Priesthood

the vote of the assembly called and carried unanimously

nominated and seconded that John Carrill [Corrill] be appointed to take charge of the house of the Lord in Kirtland immediately The vote of the assembly called and passed unanimously[279]

President Rigdon then arose and delivered his charge to the assembly, his remarks were few and appropriate— adjourned by ~~singing and~~ prayer

W[arren] Parrish   <u>Scribe</u>

16 January 1836 • Saturday

Saturday morning the 16th by request I meet with the council of the 12 in company with my colleagues F[rederick] G Williams and S[idney] Rigdon

Council organized and opened by singing and prayer offered up by Thomas B. Marsh president of the 12

He arose and requested the privilege in behalf of his colleagues of speaking, each in his turn without being interupted; which was granted them— Elder Marsh proceeded [p. 119] to unbosom his feelings touching the mission of the 12, and more particularly respecting a certain letter which they recieved from the presidency of the high council in Kirtland, while attending a conference in the ~~East~~ State of Maine—[280] also spoke of being plased in our council, on Friday last below the council's of Kirtland and Zion having been previously placed next [to] the presidency, in our assemblies— also observed

---

278. Milliken had recently declined to serve as a doorkeeper and was released from this duty. (JS, Journal, 13 Jan. 1836.)

279. Corrill had been appointed to oversee "the finishing of the Lord's house." On this occasion, he was charged with enforcing the rules of conduct for the House of the Lord. (Corrill, *Brief History of the Church,* 22; Minute Book 1, 15 Jan. 1836.)

280. As reported in Quorum of the Twelve Apostles, Record, the quorum held conferences in Maine on 21 and 28 August 1835. The letter in question is JS, Kirtland, OH, to the Quorum of the Twelve Apostles, 4 Aug. 1835, in JS Letterbook 1, pp. 90–93. It conveyed reprimands and instructions to the Twelve from a high council consisting of the Kirtland and Missouri presidencies and others, and was signed by JS as moderator. Regarding the term "presidency of the high council in Kirtland," see 148n259 herein.

that they were hurt on account of some remarks made by President H[yrum] Smith on the trial of Gladden Bishop who had been previously tried before the council of the 12, while on their mission in the east, who had by their request thrown his case before the high council in Kirtland for investigation, and the 12 concidered that their proceedings with him were in some degree, discountenanced—[281]

~~The rest~~ ⟨remaining⟩ Elder Marsh then gave way to his brethren and they arose and spoke in turn untill they had all spoken acquiessing in the observations of Elder Marsh and mad[e] some additions to his remarks which are as follows— That the letter in question which they received from the presidency, in which two of their numbers were suspended,[282] and the rest severely chastened, and that too upon testimony which was unwarantable, and particu~~larly~~ stress was laid upon a certain letter which the presidency had received from Dr. [p. 120] W[arren] A. Cowdery of Freedom New York in which he prefered charges against them which were false, and upon which ~~they~~ ⟨we⟩ (the presiders[283]) had acted in chastning them and therefore, the 12, had concluded that the presidency had lost confidence in them,[284] and that whereas the church in this place, had carressed them, at the time of their appointment, to the appostleship they now treated them coolly and appear to have lost confidence in them also—

They spoke of their having been in this work from the beginning almost and had born the burden in the heat of the day and passed through many trials and that the presidency ought not to ~~have~~ suspect their fidelity nor loose confidence in them, neither have chastised them upon such testimony as was lying ~~before~~ before them— also urged the necessity of an explanition upon the letter which they received from the presidency, and the propriety of their having information as it respects their duties, authority &c— that they might come to ⟨an⟩ understanding in all things, that they migh[t] act in perfect unison and harmony before the Lord and be prepared for the endument— also that they had prefered a charge against Dr [Warren] Cowdery for his unchristian

---

281. From 4 May to 26 September 1835, the Quorum of the Twelve traveled through the eastern states and Upper Canada holding conferences and regulating the affairs of the church. In the East, the Twelve disciplined Bishop, whose case was reheard in Kirtland by the high council on 28 September 1835 with some apostles as witnesses. (See JS, Journal, 28 Sept. 1835.)

282. William E. McLellin and Orson Hyde.

283. TEXT: Possibly "presiden".

284. Warren Cowdery was president of the conference at Freedom, Cattaraugus County, New York, which the Quorum of the Twelve visited on their 1835 mission to the East. Cowdery had faulted the Twelve for not following JS's commission to raise money for building the House of the Lord. (JS, Kirtland, OH, to the Quorum of the Twelve Apostles, 4 Aug. 1835, in JS Letterbook 1, pp. 90–93.)

conduct which the presidency had disregarded—[285] also that President O[liver]
Cowdery on a certain occasion had made use of language to one of the [p. 121]
twelve that was unchristian and unbecoming any man, and that they would
not submit to such treatment

The remarks of all the 12 were made in a verry forcible and explicit manner
yet cool and deliberate; /[286]I arose

I observed that we had heard them patiently and in turn should expect to
be heard patiently also; and first I remarked that it was necessary that the 12
should state whether they were determined to persevere in the work of the
Lord, whether the presidency are able to satisfy them or not; vote called and
carried in the affirmative unaminously; I then said to them that I had not lost
confidence in them, and that they had no reason to suspect my confidence,
and that I would be willing to be weighed in the scale of truth today in this
matter, and risk it in the day of judgment; and as it respects the chastning contained in the letter in question which I acknowledge might have been expressed
in too harsh language; which was not intentional and I ask your forgiveness in
as much as I have hurt your feelings; but nevertheless, the letter that that Elder
Mc.lellen [William E. McLellin] wrote back to Kirtland while the twelve were
at the east was harsh also and I was willing to set the one against the other;[287]
I next proceeded to explain the subject of the duty of the twelve; and their
authority which is next to the present presidency, and that the arangement
of the assembly in this place on the 15 ᶦⁿˢᵗ /[288]in placing the high councils of
Kirtland and next [to] the presidency was because the buisness to be transacted
was buisness that related to that body in particular which was to [p. 122] fill
the several quorum's in Kirtland; not beca[u]se they were first in office, and
that the arangement was most Judicious that could be made on the occasion
also the 12, are not subject to any other than the first presidency; viz. myself
S. Rigdon and F G. Williams—[289] I also stated to the 12, that I do not continue
countinance the harsh language of President Cowdery to them neither in
myself nor any other man, although I have sometimes spoken to[o] harsh from
the impulse of the moment and inasmuch as I have wounded your feelings

---

285. See 159n291 herein.

286. TEXT: Warren Parrish handwriting ends; unidentified begins.

287. McLellin had criticized a coeducational school that Sidney Rigdon was conducting in Kirtland.
(JS, Kirtland, OH, to the Quorum of the Twelve Apostles, 4 Aug. 1835, in JS Letterbook 1, pp. 90–93; see
also 66n39 herein.)

288. TEXT: Unidentified handwriting ends; Warren Parrish begins.

289. Minutes of meetings over the next weeks consistently list the Quorum of the Twelve ahead of
the regular high council members, as the Twelve had requested, although after the council of presidents,
which included not only JS and his first two counselors but the full Kirtland and Missouri presidencies.
(Minute Book 1, 12 Feb. 1836; compare JS, Journal, 12 Feb. and 27 Mar. 1836.)

brethren I ask your forgivness, for I love you and will hold you up with all my heart in all righteousness before the Lord, and before all men, for be assured brethren I am willing to stem the torrent of all opposition; in storms in tempests in thunders and lightning by sea and by land in the wilderness or among fals brethren, or mobs or wherever God in his providence may call us and I am determined that neither hights nor depths principalities nor powers things present or to come nor any other creature shall separate me from you;[290] and I will now covenant with you before God that I will not listen too nor credit, any derogatory report against any of you nor condemn you upon any testimony beneath the heavens, short of that testimony which is infalible, untill I can see you face to face and know of a surity [p. 123] and I do place unlimited confidence in your word for I believe you to be men of truth, and I ask the same of you, when I tell you any thing that you place equal confidence in my word for I will not tell you I know anything which I do not know— but I have already consumed more time than I intended to when I commenced and I will now give way to my colleagues

President Rigdon arose next and acquiessed in what I had said and acknowledged to the 12, that he had not done as he ought, in not citing Dr. Cowdery to trial on the charges that were put into his hands by the 12, that he had neglected his duty in this thing, for which he asked their forgiveness, and would now attend to it if they desired him to do so,[291] and ~~Elder~~ ⟨Presdt⟩ Rigdon also observed to the 12 ~~that~~ ⟨if he⟩ ~~he might have~~ ⟨had⟩ spoken, or reproved too ~~harshe,~~ ⟨harshly,⟩ at any time and had injured their feelings by so doing he asked their forgivness.—

President Williams arose and acquiessed in the above sentiment's expressed by myself and President Rigdon, in full and said many good things

The President of the 12, then called a vote of that body to know whether they were perfectly satisfied with the [p. 124] explanation which we had given them and whether they would enter into the covenant we had proposed to them, which was most readily manifested in the affirmative by raising their hands to heaven, in testimony of their willingness and desire to enter into this

---

290. See Romans 8:38–39.

291. This did not occur until 5 March 1836, when JS met with Oliver Cowdery, Sidney Rigdon, the Quorum of the Twelve, and Warren Cowdery. As summarized by Oliver Cowdery, "The Twelve had prefered a charge against my brother [Warren Cowdery] for a letter he wrote last summer upon the subject of their teaching while at the Freedom conference. My brother confessed his mistake, upon the testimony of the Twelve, and said he was willing to publish that they were not in the fault, but that he was satisfied they delivered those instructions which he had supposed they had not." A statement of apology by Warren Cowdery followed. (Cowdery, Diary, 5 Mar. 1836; "Notice," *LDS Messenger and Advocate,* Feb. 1836, 2:263.)

covenant and their entire satisfaction with our explanation, upon all the difficulties that were on their minds, we then took each others by the hand in
confirmation of our covenant and their was a perfect unison of feeling on this
occasion, and our hearts overflowed with blessings, which we pronounced
upon eachothers heads as the Spirit gave us utterance my scribe is included in
this covenant ~~with~~ and blessings with us, for I love him, for ⟨the⟩ truth and
integrity that dwelleth in him and may God enable us all, to perform our vows
and covenants with each other in all fidelity and rightiousness before Him,
that our influence may be felt among the nations of the earth in mighty power,
even to rend the kingdom of darkness in sunder, and triumph over priestcraft
and spiritual wickedness in high places, and brake in pieces all ~~other~~ kingdoms
that are opposed to the Kingdom of Christ, and spread the light and truth of
the everlasting gospel from the rivers to the ends of the earth[292]

Elder Beemon [Alvah Beman] call[ed] for council upon the subject of his
returning home he wished to know whether it was best for him to return before
the Solemn Assembly [p. 125] or not, after taking it into concideration the
council advised him to tarry we dismissed by singing and prayer and retired[293]

W[arren] Parrish   scribe

17 January 1836 • Sunday

[294]Sunday morning the 17th Attended meeting at the schoolhouse at the
usual hour a large congregation assembled; I proceeded to organiize the several
quorums present; first, the presidency; then the twelve, and the seventy all who
were present also the counsellors of Kirtland and Zion.

President [Sidney] Rigdon then arose [295]and observed that instead of
preaching the time would be occupied, by the presidency and twelve in
speaking each in their turn untill they had all spoken, the Lord poured out his
spirit upon us, and the brethren began to confess their faults one to the other
and the congregation were soon overwhelmed in tears and some of our hearts
were too big for utterance, the gift of toungs, come upon us also like the rushing of a mighty wind, and my soul was filled with the glory of God,[296]

---

292. See Daniel 2:45; and Zechariah 9:10.

293. Following this day of reconciliation, JS retired to his home, where he was joined by Oliver
Cowdery, John Corrill, and later Martin Harris. They performed ritual washings "that we might be clean
before the Lord for the Sabbath, confessing our sins and covenanting to be faithful to God." (Cowdery,
Diary, 16 Jan. 1836.)

294. TEXT: Warren Parrish handwriting ends; unidentified begins.

295. TEXT: Unidentified handwriting ends; Warren Parrish begins.

296. William W. Phelps wrote that "the presidents commenced the meeting by confessing their sins
and forgiving their brethren." Oliver Cowdery added that the presidents "ask[ed] forgiveness" in order to
be "prepared for the endowment,—being sanctified and cleansed from all sin." Phelps also recorded that

In the after noon I joined three couple in matrimony, in the publick congregation, whose names are as follows— Wm F. Cahoon and Maranda [Miranda] Gibbs ~~Larona~~ Harvy Stanly [Harvey Stanley] and Larona [Lerona] Cahoon— also Tunis Rap[p]leye and Louisa Cutler,— We then administered the Lord supper and dismissed; the congregation; ⟨which⟩ was so dense that it was [p. 126] verry unpleasant for all—[297] we were then invited to Elder Cahoons to a feast which was prepared on the occasion, and had a good time while partaking of the rich repast that was spread before us, and I virely [verily] realized that it was good for brethren to dwell together in unity, ~~even~~ like the dew upon the mountains of Israel, where the Lord command[e]d blessings, even life for ever more,[298]

Spent the evening at home

18 January 1836 · Monday

Monday the 18th attended the hebrew school,— This day the Elders School was removed into the Chapel in the room adjoining ours—[299] nothing very special transpired

copy of a Letter
Willoughby January 5th 1836

To Elder W[arren] Parrish
    Sir

    I have received an <u>open</u> note[300] from M^r. Sylvester Smith informing me that your School concidered itself dissolved from all ingagements with me, for this I was not unprepared. But he adds that I must excuse

---

there was "speaking and singing in tongues, and prophecying, as on the day of Pentacost." (William W. Phelps, [Kirtland, OH], to Sally Phelps, [Liberty, MO], [18 Jan. 1836], William W. Phelps, Papers, BYU; Cowdery, Diary, 17 Jan. 1836; see also Acts 2:2–4.)

297. Cahoon later recalled, "I should suppose what with the people in the Church & outside as well there was 3000 people assembled." According to Ohio law, a couple could become eligible for marriage either by obtaining a marriage license or by publishment—giving sufficient public notice of intent. Cahoon noted that JS used the occasion to use publishment, "instead of taking out a licence from the County Court the marriage notice being published several times previously in the church which custom was allowed by the laws of the state." (Cahoon, Autobiography, 44–45; An Act Regulating Marriages [6 Jan. 1824], *Statutes of Ohio*, vol. 2, p. 1407, sec. 6.)

298. See Psalm 133:1–3.

299. The Elders School moved from the schoolroom below the printing office to the third floor of the House of the Lord, in the room adjoining the westernmost room where the Hebrew School met. (See JS, Journal, 4 Jan. 1836; compare JS History, vol. B-1, 693.)

300. The seal on the letter was apparently opened prior to Peixotto's receipt. See the postscript to Parrish's rejoinder, which follows.

him for saying that I appear to be willing to trifle with you in regard to appointments time, &c—

This insinuation is unworthy of me beneath my sence of honour, and I [p. 127] could hope unwaranted by any mean suspicion of your whole body— I wrote for books to New York by Mʳ· [Oliver] Cowdery— not but ~~I could~~ I could not have taught the rudiments without them— but because I wished to make my instruction philosophically availing as well as mere elementary. In this object I thought myself confirmed by you, my books have not come as yet & are probably lost— of the pecuniary value I seek not.— I borowed a book of Elder [John F.] Boynton, & told him, believing, him to be responsible that Wednesday would be best for me to deliver a publick lecture owing to my engagements here. I here was officially informed when the School was to be opened by me.—

The addition of insult to wrong may be gratifying to small minds— mine is above it, scorns and repud[i]ates it.—

I am verry respectfully
Your verry ob. Servt.
Daniel L M. Piexotto [Peixotto]

/³⁰¹The Answer³⁰²

Kirtland Jan 11ᵗʰ 1836

Dr. Piexotto [Daniel Peixotto],
   Sir,

I received yours of the 5ᵗʰ Inst in which you manifested much indignation and considered your hounour highly insulted by us as a body, if not by me as an individual, and deprecated our conduct because we informed you that you appeard willing to trifle with us, as it [p. 128] respects our engagement with you to teach our Hebrew class I have acted in this matter as agent for the School; the time agreed upon for you to commence, was not to be protracted, at farthest later than Dec 15ᵗʰ and the class have ever till now, considered themselves bound by the engagement I made with you.— When Elder [Oliver] Cowdery and myself called, you set a time that you would come over to Kirtland and have our agreement committed to writing, but did not come, some were displeased, I excused you; some days passed without

---

301. TEXT: Warren Parrish handwriting ends; unidentified begins.

302. TEXT: Residue from an adhesive wafer at the top of page 129—as well as some paper residue still stuck to the wafer residue—indicates that the unidentified scribe probably copied Parrish's letter into the journal from a loose manuscript that had been attached at that point.

our hearing from you; at length Dr [Frederick G.] Williams called and you specified another time that you would come, (which is some 2 or 3 weeks since) the class were again disappointed, I again plead an excuse for you; on last saturday week, or in other words on the 2 Inst our class met and agreed to organize ~~the~~ on Monday morning the 4 Inst, at 9 oclock A,M, and by the voice of the school I was appointed to wait on you, and advertize your honour that we were ready, and should expect you to attend at that ~~hour~~ hour; presuming that you would be ready at this late period to fulfill your engagement if you ever intended to; and accordingly I called, and informed you of the arangements we had made, but on account of your arangements at the <u>Medical University</u> I was willing to exceed my instructions, and let you name the hour that you would wait on us on that day, which was at 4 o clock P,M,

Sunday the 3 inst, I learned from Elder Boyanton [John F. Boynton] that it would be most convenient for you to call on Wedensday, the school knew nothing of this as a body, on Monday morning we met, and I was called upon to report which I did; I also stated what I had [p. 129] heard from Elder Boyanton, the voice of the class was called to know, whether they considered themselves any longer under obligation to you, and whether they would wait any longer for you, and carried in the negative.

Now sir, what could I say in your behalf? I answer, nothing; I should have considered it an insult to have asked 40 men who had laid by every other consideration to attend this school, to lay upon their oars 3 days longer with the impression on their minds, (and justly too) that it would be altogether uncertain whether you would come then or not.

With these things lying before us, we are told by your <u>honour</u> that it may be gratifying to small minds to add <u>insult</u> to <u>wrong</u>; and you also informed me in your note, that you was not unprepared for the inteligence it contained, which is virtually saying that you intended the abuse you have heaped upon us.

I assure you sir that I have ever entertained the best of feelings towards you, and have recognized you as a friend in whom I could repose unlimited confidence and whith whom I have acted in good faith, and I am not a little surprized on this occasion, that you should treat us with such marked contempt. and then upbraid us with adding insult to wrong; small as you may consider our minds, we have

sufficient discernment to discover this insult, although offered by your
<u>honour</u>, and sufficient good manners not to insult or wrong any man.
Respectfully your most obedient humble servant

<u>Warren</u> <u>Parrish</u>

P.S. The note that we sent you, was well sealed when it was put into
the hands of the messenger; which you informed me you recieved open,

Yours

<u>W. P.</u> [p. 130]

/[303]~~Monday morning the 18th at 9 oclock, attended the hebrew school, noth-~~
~~ing special transpird on this day— spent the evening at home with my family—~~

19 January 1836 • Tuesday

Tuesday the 19th spent the day at school, the Lord blessed us in our studies,— this day we commenced reading in our hebrew bibles with much success,
it seems as if the Lord opens our minds, in a marvelous manner to understand
this word in the original language, and my prayer is that God will speedily
indue us with a knowledge of all languages and toungs, that his servants may
go forth for the last time, to bind up the law and seal up the testimony[304]

Form of

Marriage Certificate—[305]

I hereby certify that agreeably to the rules and regulations of the
church of christ of Latter-Day Saints,[306] on matrimony, were joined in
marriage M^r. William F. Cahoon and Miss Nancy M. Gibbs, both of
this place, on Sabbath the 17th instant.

Joseph Smith Jun

Kirtland Ohio Jan. 18th 1836   Presiding Elder of said church [p. 131]

[5 *lines blank*]

---

303. TEXT: Unidentified handwriting ends; Warren Parrish begins.

304. See Isaiah 8:16; and Revelation, 27 and 28 Dec. 1832 and 3 Jan. 1833, in Doctrine and Covenants
7:23, 1835 ed. [D&C 88:84]. An 1833 revelation charged the church presidency to "become acquainted with
all good books, and with languages, tongues and people." (Revelation, 8 Mar. 1833, in Doctrine and
Covenants 84:5, 1835 ed. [D&C 90:15].)

305. JS was required to file such certificates with the county clerk within three months of a wedding.
(An Act Regulating Marriages [6 Jan. 1824], *Statutes of Ohio*, vol. 2, p. 1407, sec. 8.)

306. When organized in New York, the church was denominated the "Church of Christ." In 1834,
presumably to avoid confusion with other Ohio congregations using the same name, the name was
changed to the "Church of the Latter Day Saints." In this and other instances, a combined form is used.
Later, a 26 April 1838 revelation incorporated both previous official names: "For thus shall my Church be
called in the Last days even the Church of Jesus Christ of Latter Day Saints." (Anderson, "I Have a
Question"; Revelation, 26 Apr. 1838, in JS, Journal, 26 Apr. 1838, p. 258 herein [D&C 115:4].)

20 January 1836 • Wednesday

Wednesday morning 20ᵗʰ attended school at the us[u]al hour,³⁰⁷ and spent the day in reading and lecturing, and made some advancement in our studies,—

At evening I attended at John Johnsons with my family, on a matrimonial occasion, having been invited to do so, ~~and~~ to join President John F. Boynton and Miss Susan Lowell in marriage, a large and respectable company assembled, and were seated by Eldr's O. Hyded [Orson Hyde] & W[arren] Parrish in the following order— The presidency and their companions in ~~their~~ first seats the twelve apostles in the second the 70, in the third, and the remainder of the congregation seated with their companions

after the above arangments were made Eldʳ· Boynton & his Lady with their attendants, came in and were seated in front of the presidency,— a hymn was sung, after which I adressed a throne of grace,— I then arose and read aloud ~~the~~ ⟨a⟩ licence granting any minister of the gospel the priviledge of solemnizing the rights of matrimony,³⁰⁸ and after calling for objection if any there were, against the anticipated alliance between Eldr. Boynton & Miss Lowell ~~to~~ and waiting sufficient time, I observed that all forever after this must hold their peace—

I then envited them to join hands and I pronounced the ceremony according to the rules and regulations of the church of the Latter-day-Saints,³⁰⁹ ~~and~~ ⟨in⟩ the name of [p. 132] God, and in the name of Jesus Christ, I pronounced upon them the blessings of Abraham Isaac and Jacob and such other blessings as the Lord put into my heart, and being much under the influence of a cold I then gave way and President S[idney] Rigdon arose and delivered a verry forcible address, suited to the occasion, and closed the servises of the evening by prayer— Eldr. O. Hyde Eldʳ· L[uke] Johnson³¹⁰ & Eldr. W. Parrish who served on the occasion, then presented the presidency with three servers filled with glasses of wine, to bless, and it fell to my lot to attend to this duty, which I cheerfully discharged, it was then passed round in order, then the

---

307. The Hebrew School met at nine o'clock in the morning, Monday through Saturday. (See JS, Journal, 14 Jan. 1836; and stricken material at end of JS, Journal, 18 Jan. 1836.)

308. The wording of the standard marriage license issued in Geauga County at this time did not suggest that a minister could perform a marriage without a license from a court of common pleas. Most likely, JS, who did not have such a license, was reading instead from section 2 of the 1824 Ohio "Act Regulating Marriages," which, in part, authorized "the several religious societies, agreeably to the rules and regulations of their respective churches, to join together as husband and wife, all persons not prohibited by this act." (An Act Regulating Marriages [6 Jan. 1824], *Statutes of Ohio*, vol. 2, p. 1407, sec. 2; Bradshaw, "Joseph Smith's Performance of Marriages in Ohio," 28, 34–37, 57.)

309. A reference to the church article on marriage. ("Marriage," ca. Aug. 1835, in Doctrine and Covenants 101, 1835 ed.)

310. Luke Johnson and Orson Hyde were the son and son-in-law of John Johnson, the host of the wedding.

cake, in the same order, and suffise it to say our hearts were made ~~cheerful and~~ glad, while partaking of the bounty of the earth, which was presented, untill we had taken our fill, and Joy filled every bosom, and the countenances of old, and young, alike, seemed to bloom with the cheerfulness and smiles of youth and an entire unison of feeling seemed to pervade the congregation, and indeed I doubt whether the pages of history can boast of a more splendid and inocent wedding and feast than this for it was conducted after the order of heaven, who has a time for all thing and this being a time of rejoicing, we hartily embraced it, and conducted ourselves accordingly— Took leave of the [p. 133] company and returned home—

21 January 1836 • Thursday

Thursday morning the 21ˢᵗ This morning a minister from conneticut by the name of John W. Olived called at my house and enquired of my father if ~~Smith~~ the pro[p]het live's here he replied that he did not understand him. Mr. Olived asked the same question again and again and recieved the same answer, he finally asked if Mr. Smith lives here, father replyed O yes Sir I understand you now,— father then stept into my room, and informed me that a gentleman had called to see me, I went into the room where he was, and the first question he asked me, after passing a compliment, was to know how many members we have in our church, I replyed to him, that we hav ~~about~~ between 15 hundred and 2,000 in this branch,—[311] He then asked me wherin we differ from other christian denomination I replyed that we believe the bible, and they do not,—[312] however he affirmed that he believed the bible, I told him then to be baptised,— he replied that he did not realize it to be his duty— But ~~after~~ ⟨when⟩ ~~laying~~ ⟨laid⟩ ~~him~~ before him the principles of the gospel, viz. faith and repentance and baptism for the remission ⟨of sins⟩ and the laying on of hands for the reseption of the Holy Ghost[313] ⟨he manifested much surprise⟩— I then observed that the [p. 134] hour for school had arived, and I must attend The man seemed astonished at our doctrine but by no means hostile

At about 3, oclock P.M I dismissed the School and the presidency; retired to the loft of the printing office, where we attended to the ordinance of washing our bodies in pure water, we also perfumed our bodies and our heads, in

---

311. Compare JS's estimate given three months earlier. (JS, Journal, 30 Oct. 1835.)

312. JS gave the same answer to this question two years later. ([JS], editorial, *Elders' Journal,* July 1838, 42.)

313. These principles, as emphasized in Acts 2:38, were practiced in the church from its founding and first articulated as fundamental doctrines in an 1831 revelation. (Revelation, 7 May 1831, in Doctrine and Covenants 65:2, 1835 ed. [D&C 49:11–14].)

the name of the Lord[314] at early candlelight, I meet with the presidency, at the west school room in the Chapel to attend to the ordinance of annointing our heads with holy oil— also the councils of ~~Zion~~ Kirtland and Zion, meet in the two adjoining rooms,[315] who waited in prayer while we attended to the ordinance,— I took the oil in my ⟨left⟩ ~~right~~ hand, father Smith being seated before me and the rest of the presidency encircled him round about,— we then streched our right hands to heaven and blessed the oil and concecrated it in the name of Jesus Christ— we then laid our hands on, our aged fath[er] Smith, and invoked, the blessings of heaven,— I then annointed his head with the concecrated oil, and sealed many blessings upon ~~his~~ ⟨him,⟩ ~~head,~~ the presidency then in turn, laid their hands upon his head, begenning at the eldest, untill they had all laid their hands on him, and pronounced such blessings, upon his head as the Lord put into their hearts— all blessing him to be our patraark [patriarch], ~~and~~ ⟨to⟩ annoint our [p. 135] heads, and attend to all duties that pertain to ~~this~~ ⟨that⟩ office.—[316] I then took the seat, and father annoint[ed] my head, and sealed upon me, the blessings, of Moses, to lead Israel in the latter days, even as moses led ~~them~~ ⟨him⟩ in days of old,— also the blessings of Abraham Isaac and Jacob,— all of the presidency laid their hands upon me and pronounced upon my head many prophesies, and blessings, many of which I shall not notice at this time, but as Paul said, so say I, let us come to vissions and revelations, ~~the—~~[317] The heavens were opened upon us and I beheld the celestial kingdom of God,[318] and the glory thereof, whether in the body or out I cannot tell,— I saw the transcendant beauty of the gate ~~that enters~~, through which the heirs of that kingdom will enter, which was like unto circling flames of fire, also the blasing throne of God, whereon was seated the Father and the Son,— I saw the beautiful streets of that kingdom, which had the appearance of being paved with gold— I saw father Adam, and Abraham and Michael[319]

---

314. Washing and anointing, and the connected blessings and sealings of blessings, were sanctifying prerequisites to endowment with power in the House of the Lord. In the coming days, these ordinances were given to all priesthood officers, passing along lines of hierarchy and seniority, culminating in the solemn assembly on 30 March 1836.

315. Oliver Cowdery recorded, "At evening the presidents of the Church, with the two bishop[s] and their counsellors, and elder Warren Parrish, met in the presidents' room, the high councils of Kirtland and Zion in their rooms." (Cowdery, Diary, 21 Jan. 1836.)

316. Joseph Smith Sr. was ordained patriarch on 6 December 1834. (Entry for 6 Dec. 1834, in JS History, 1834–1836, 20; Patriarchal Blessings, 1:1, 9.)

317. See 2 Corinthians 12:1–3. Part of the following vision was later canonized (D&C 137).

318. Four years earlier, JS and Sidney Rigdon reported seeing a vision of three different kingdoms in heaven—denominated celestial, terrestrial, and telestial—with a revelation that attaining the highest kingdom, the celestial, requires strict adherence to all the principles and ordinances of the gospel. (Vision, 16 Feb. 1832, in Doctrine and Covenants 91:5, 7, 1835 ed. [D&C 76:50–70, 92–96].)

319. Parrish's transcription of JS's vision seems to differentiate Adam and the archangel Michael as

and my father and mother, my brother Alvin [Smith] that has long since slept,[320] and marvled how it was that he had obtained ~~this~~ an inheritance ⟨in⟩ ~~this~~ ⟨that⟩ kingdom, seeing that he had departed this life, before the Lord ⟨had⟩ set his hand to gather Israel ⟨the second time⟩ and had not been baptized for the remission of sins— Thus ~~said~~ came the voice ⟨of the Lord un⟩to me saying all who have [p. 136] died with[out] a knowledge of this gospel, who would have received it, if they had been permited to tarry, shall be heirs of the celestial kingdom of God— also all that shall die henseforth, with⟨out⟩ a knowledge of it, who would have received it, with all their hearts, shall be heirs of that kingdom, for I the Lord ⟨will⟩ judge all men according to their works according to the desires of their hearts— and ~~again I also beheld the Terrestial kingdom~~ I also beheld that all children who die before they arive to the years of accountability, are saved in the celestial kingdom of heaven—[321] I saw the 12, apostles of the Lamb, who are now upon the earth who hold the keys of this last ministry, in foreign lands, standing together in a circle much fatiegued, with their clothes tattered and feet swolen, with their eyes cast downward, and Jesus ⟨standing⟩ in their midst, and they did not behold him, ~~he~~ the Saviour looked upon them and wept— I also beheld Elder McLellen [William E. McLellin] in the south, standing upon a hill surrounded with a vast multitude, preaching to them, and a lame man standing before him, supported by his crutches, he threw them down at his word, and leaped as an heart [hart] by the mighty power of God

Also Eldr Brigham Young standing in a strange land, in the far southwest, in a desert place, upon a rock in the midst of about a dozen men of colour, who, appeared hostile [p. 137] He was preaching to them in their own toung, and the angel of God standing above his head with a drawn sword in his hand protecting him, but he did not see it,— and I finally saw the 12, in the celestial kingdom of God,— I also beheld the redemption of Zion, and many things which the toung of man, cannot discribe in full,— Many of my brethren who

two separate individuals. Yet JS identified Michael as Adam at least a year earlier and made the same identification four years later. (Oliver Cowdery, Kirtland, OH, to John Whitmer, [Liberty, MO], 1 Jan. 1834, in Cowdery, Letterbook, 15; Revelation, ca. Aug. 1830, in Doctrine and Covenants 50:2, 1835 ed. [D&C 27:11]; Richards, "Pocket Companion," 74–75; Robert B. Thompson, Sermon notes, 5 Oct. 1840, JS Collection, CHL.)

320. The death in 1823 of beloved eldest son Alvin at age twenty-five deeply affected the Smith family. (Porter, "Alvin Smith"; Anderson, "Alvin Smith Story.")

321. A passage from the book of Moses taught that "Christ hath atoned for original guilt wherein the sins of the Parents cannot be answered upon the heads of the Children for they are whole from the foundation of the world." JS later expanded on this doctrine. (Old Testament Revision 1, p. 14 [Moses 6:54]; Matthew L. Davis, Washington DC, to Mary Davis, New York City, NY, 6 Feb. 1840, CHL; Woodruff, Journal, 20 Mar. 1842.)

Vision of a glorious afterlife. Joseph Smith reported that on 21 January 1836 he beheld a vision of the "celestial kingdom," or highest level of heaven. The 1835–1836 journal manifests the epistemological challenge of capturing the content of this and other visions. The stricken passage "again I also beheld the Terrestial kingdom," followed by further description of the celestial kingdom, indicates that Smith also beheld the middle of three levels of heaven—a part of the vision to which this account never returned. Handwriting of Warren Parrish. JS, Journal, 1835–1836, p. 137, JS Collection, Church History Library, Salt Lake City. (Photograph by Welden C. Andersen.)

received this ordinance with me, saw glorious visions also,— angels ministered unto them, as well as my self, and the power of the highest rested upon, us the house was filled with the glory of God, and we shouted Hosanah to ~~the~~ God and the Lamb

I am mistaken, concerning my receiving the holy anointing first after father Smith, we received ⟨it⟩ in turn according to our age, (that is the presidency,)[322]

My Scribe also recieved his anointing ⟨with us⟩[323] and saw in a vision the armies of heaven protecting the Saints in their return to Zion— ⟨& many things that I saw⟩[324]

The Bishop of Kirtland with his counsellors and the Bishop of Zion with his counsellors, were present with us, and received their, annointing under the hands of father Smith and confirmed by the presidency and the glories of heaven was unfolded to them also—

We then invited the counsellors of Kirtland and Zion[325] ~~and Kirtland~~ into our room, and President Hyrum [p. 138] Smith annointed the head of the president of the counsellors in Kirtland and President D[avid] Whitmer the head of the president, of the counsellors of Zion—[326]

The president of each quorum then annointed the heads of his colleagues, each in his turn beginning, at the eldest

The vision of heaven ~~were~~ ⟨was⟩ opened to these also, some of them saw the face of the Saviour, and others were ministered unto by holy angels, and the spirit of propesey and revelation was poured out in mighty power, and loud hosanahs and glory to God in the highest, saluted the heavens for we all communed with the h[e]avenly host's,— and I saw in my vision all of the presidency in the Celistial Kingdom of God, and, many others who were present[327]

---

322. The presidents each received an anointing from Joseph Smith Sr., and then each president's anointing was confirmed by the other presidents. (Partridge, Journal, 21 Jan. 1836.)

323. According to Missouri bishop Edward Partridge, Parrish was anointed after the bishoprics. (Partridge, Journal, 21 Jan. 1836.)

324. Parrish may have made this insertion the following day, when he and others "spent the time in rehearsing to each other the glorious scenes that transpired on the preceding evening, while attending to the ordinance of holy anointing." (JS, Journal, 22 Jan. 1836.)

325. That is, members of the Kirtland and Missouri high councils.

326. Hyrum Smith anointed John Smith president of the Kirtland high council, and David Whitmer anointed Simeon Carter president of the Missouri high council. Thus, while the presidency of the church and the Missouri presidency, respectively, constituted the presidencies of the Kirtland and the Missouri high councils, each high council could now also function with its own senior or presiding officer from among the members of the council. (Partridge, Journal, 21 Jan. 1836; see also Minute Book 1, 17 Aug. 1835.)

327. Oliver Cowdery and Edward Partridge also recorded that many of those present saw visions. (Cowdery, Diary, 21 Jan. 1836; Partridge, Journal, 21 Jan. 1836.)

Our meeting was opened by singing and prayer offered up by the head of each quorum, and closed by singing and invoking the benediction of heaven with uplifted hands,[328] and retired between one and 2, oclock in the morning [*9 lines blank*] [p. 139]

22 January 1836 • Friday

Friday morning the 22^(ond) attended at the school room at the us[u]al hour,— But insted of persuing our studies /[329]we ~~commenced~~ spent the time in rehearsing to each other the glorious scenes that transpired on the preceding evening, while attending to the ordinance of holy anointing.— At evening we met at the same place, with the council of the 12 and the presidency of the 70 who were to receive this ordinance; the high councils of Kirtland and Zion were present also:[330] we called to order and organized; the Presidency then proceeded to consecrate the oil; we then laid our hands upon Elder Thomas B. Marsh who is the president of the 12 and ordained him to the authority of anointing his brethren, I then poured the concecrated oil upon his head in the name of Jesus Christ and sealed such blessings upon him as the Lord put into my heart; the rest of the presidency then laid their hands upon him and blessed him each in their turn beginning at the eldest; he then anointed ⟨and blessed⟩ his brethren from the oldest to the youngest, I also laid my hands upon them and prounounced many great and glorious upon their heads; the heavens were opened and angels ministered unto us.[331]

Then 12 then proceeded to anoint and bless the presidency of the 70 and seal upon their heads power and authority to anoint their brethren; the heavens were opened upon Elder Sylvester Smith and he leaping up exclaimed, The horsemen of Israel and the chariots thereof. ~~President Rigdon arose~~ /[332]Br. Carloss [Don Carlos] Smith was also, annointed and ~~ordained~~ blessed to preside over the high preisthood.—[333] President [Sidney] Rigdon, arose to conclude the servises of the evening [p. 140] by invoking the benediction of heaven

---

328. JS delivered this closing prayer. (Partridge, Journal, 21 Jan. 1836.)

329. TEXT: Warren Parrish handwriting ends; unidentified begins.

330. The Kirtland and Missouri bishoprics were also present. (Cowdery, Diary, 22 Jan. 1836.)

331. Apostle Heber C. Kimball, who was present, recounted many years later that "when the Twelve in a circle were anointed, [the apostle] John stood in their midst." (School of the Prophets Provo Records, 18 May 1868, 39; see also Cowdery, Diary, 22 Jan. 1836.)

332. TEXT: Unidentified handwriting ends; Warren Parrish begins.

333. Oliver Cowdery similarly recorded that "Don Carlos Smith was ordained and annointed president of the high priesthood of the Melchisedek priesthood, by the presidents of the Church," while Edward Partridge recorded that the various members of the Kirtland and Missouri church presidencies anointed Don Carlos Smith "president of the high priests in Kirtland." (Cowdery, Diary, 22 Jan. 1836; Partridge, Journal, 22 Jan. 1836.)

~~of heaven~~ upon the Lords anointed ⟨which he did⟩ in an eloquent manner the congregation shouted a loud hosannah the gift of toungs, fell upon us in mighty power, angels mingled ~~themselves~~ their voices with ours, while their presence was in our midst, and unseasing prasis [praises] swelled our bosoms for the space of half an hour,——[334] I then observed to the brethren that it was time to retire, we accordingly ⟨closed⟩ our interview and returned home at about 2. oclock in the morning /[335]& the spirit & visions of God attended me through the night

23 January 1836 · Saturday

Saturday 23.ʳᵈ. attended at the school room as usual & we came together filled with the spirit as on the past evening & did not feel like stud◊ying but commenced conversing upon heavenly things & the day was spent agreably & profitably— ~~Father~~ ⟨Elder⟩ Alvah Beaman [Beman] had been tempted to doubt the things which we recd. on saturday evening & he made an humble confession & asked forgiveness of the school whi[c]h was joyfully given— & ~~the old man~~ said he would try to resist Satan in future

24 January 1836 · Sunday

Sunday Jany 24. Met the several quorems in the room under the printing office & after organizing & op[e]ning by prayer called upon the High council of Kirtland to proceede and confess their sins as th[e]y might be directed by the spirit— & they occupied the first part of the day and confessed & exhorted as the spirit led.— P.M. attended again & saw ⟨the⟩ Bread & wine administered to the quorems & brethren who were present——

In the evening met the Presidency in ~~high~~ ⟨the⟩ room over the printing room & counseled on the subject of endowment & the preperation necessary for [p. 141] the solemn Assembly which is to be called when the House of the Lord is finished[336]

---

334. Edward Partridge recorded that Sidney Rigdon instructed the group "to shout hosannah blessed be the name of the most high God" and that "the shout & speaking in unknown tongues lasted 10 or 15 minutes." Oliver Cowdery recorded that "almost all present broke out in tongues and songs of Zion." Partridge added that during this evening, "more especially at the time of shouting, a number saw visions as they declared unto us." (Partridge, Journal, 22 Jan. 1836; Cowdery, Diary, 22 Jan. 1836.)

335. TEXT: Warren Parrish handwriting ends; Sylvester Smith begins.

336. Oliver Cowdery recorded that the presidency "conversed upon the time of, and preperation and sanctification for the endowment." (Cowdery, Diary, 24 Jan. 1836.)

25 January 1836 • Monday

Jany. 25. Monday. Recd. a line from my scribe informing me of his ill health as follows—

> Brother Joseph,
>
> My great desire to be in your company & in the Assembly of the Saints where God opnes [opens] the heavens & exhibits the treasures of eternity is the only thing that has stimulated me for a number of days past to leave my house; for be assured, dear brother, my bodily afflic-tion is severe; I have a violent ⟨cough⟩ more especially nights, which deprives me of my appetite, & my strength fails, & writing has a par-ticular tendency to injure my lungs while I am under the influence of such a cough I therefore, with reluctance send your journal to you untill my health improves
>
> Yours in heart
Warren Parrish
>
> P.S.
> Brother Joseph,
> pray for me, & ask the prayers of the class on my account also.

———

Appointed Elder Sylvester Smith acting Scribe for the time being or till Eld. Parrish shall recover his health— spent the day at home receiving visiters &c

26 January 1836 • Tuesday

Tuesday 26— M^r [Joshua] Seixas arived from Hudson to teach the hebrew Languge & I attended upon the organizing of the class for the purpos of receiving his lectures in hebrew grammar— his hours of instruction are from ten to Eleven A.M. & from two to three P.M. his introduction pleased me much. I think he will be a help to the class in learning the Hebrew[337]———

27 January 1836 • Wednesday

Wednesday. attended school as usual & other matters which came before me to attend to [p. 142]

———

337. After three weeks of study under the temporary instruction of JS, the Hebrew School finally secured the services of a professional teacher. On Seixas and his qualifications, see 145n248 herein. For eight of the next nine weeks, JS and about eighty other students attended Seixas's courses, which generally met every day except for Sundays. (Hyrum Smith, Kirtland, OH, to Elias Smith, East Stockholm, NY, 27 Feb. 1836, CHL; see also Ogden, "Kirtland Hebrew School.")

28 January 1836 • Thursday

Thursday ⟨28⟩ attended school at the usual hours In the evening met the quorems of High Priests in the west room of the upper loft of the ~~Lord,~~ Lord⟨'s⟩ house & in company with my council of the presidency— consecrated & anointed the cousellors of the President of the High priesthood[338] & having instructed them & set the quorem in order I left them to perform the holy anointing— & went to the quorem of Elders in the other end of the room. I assisted in anointing the counsellors of the President of the Elders[339] & gave them the instruction necessary for the occasion & left the President & his council to anoint the Elders[340] while I should go to the adjoining room & attend to organizing & instructing of the quorem of the Seventy—

I found the Twelve Apostles assembled with this quorem & I proceeded with the quorem of the presedincy[341] to instruct them & also the seven presidents of the seventy Elders to call upon God with uplifted hands to seal the blessings which had been promised to them by the holy anoint[in]g As I organized this quorem with the presedincy in this room, Pres. Sylvester Smith saw a piller of fire rest down & abide upon the heads of the quorem as we stood in the midst of the Twelve.

When the Twelve & the seven were through with their sealing prayers I called upon Pres. S[idney] Rigdon to seal them with uplifted hands & when he he had done this & cried hossannah that all congregation should join him & shout hosannah to God & the Lamb & glory to God in the highest— It was done so & Eld. Roger [p. 143] Orton saw a ~~flaming~~ ⟨mighty⟩ Angel riding upon a horse of fire with a flaming sword in his hand followed by five others— encircle the house & protect the saints even the Lords anointed from the power of Satan & a host of evil spirits which were striving to disturb the saints—

Pres. Wm Smith[342] one of the Twelve saw the h[e]avens op[e]ned & the Lords host protecting the Lords anointed, Pres. Z. Coltrine [Zebedee Coltrin]

---

338. Don Carlos Smith was appointed president of the Kirtland high priests two weeks earlier. His initial counselors have not been identified. (See JS, Journal, 15 Jan. 1836.)

339. JS performed the anointings with the other members of the council of presidents. (Cook and Backman, *Kirtland Elders' Quorum Record*, 28 Jan. 1836.)

340. President Alvah Beman anointed twenty-four elders, and "some spake with tongues and prophecied." (Cook and Backman, *Kirtland Elders' Quorum Record*, 28 Jan. 1836.)

341. This "quorem of the presedincy" is apparently identical to the "council of the presidency" mentioned earlier in this entry and was composed of the church presidencies from Kirtland and Missouri.

342. The designation of apostle William Smith as a president, also repeated 6 February, is evidently a mistake by scribe Sylvester Smith. William Smith was not seated among the church presidents at the dedication of the House of the Lord, and there is no known reference to him as an assistant president. (JS, Journal, 27 Mar. 1836, p. 201 herein.)

one of the seven saw the saviour extended before him as upon the cross & little after crowned with a glory upon his head above the brightness of the sun after these things were over & I a glorious vision which I saw had passed[343] I instructed the seven presidents to proceede & anoint the seventy & returned to the room of the High Priests & Elders & attended to the sealing of what they had done with uplifted hands, the Lord had assisted my bro. Carloss [Don Carlos Smith] the Pres. of the High Priests to go forward with the anointing of the High priests so that he had performed it to the acceptance of the Lord, notwithstanding he was verry young & inexperienced in such duties & I felt to praise God with a loud hossannah for his goodness to me & my Fathers family & to all the children of men— praise the Lord all ye his saints— praise his holy name— after these quorems were dismissed I retired to my home filled with the spirit & my soul cried hossannah to God & the Lamb through ⟨the⟩ silent watches of the night & while my eyes were closed in sleep the visions of the Lord were sweet unto me & his glory was round about me

praise the Lord— [p. 144]

29 January 1836 • Friday

Friday 29. attended school & read hebrew— recd. the following line from the Presidency of the Elders—

> Kirtland Jany. 29. AD. 1836
>
> To the Presidents of the church of Latter day Saints. Beloved Bret[hren] feeling ourselves amenable to you for our proceedings as the presidency of the first quorem of Elders in Kirtland, & believing that we are to be govorned by you; we desire to know if we are to receive all those who are recommended to us by Elders for ordination, or shall we receive none only those who have written recommendations from you. please answer our request

Alvah Beman	Pres.
Reuben Hadlock [Hedlock]	Counsel
John Morton	

E. M. Green [Evan M. Greene]   Ck

---

343. Harrison Burgess later recounted that "Joseph Exclaimed aloud, 'I behold the Saviour, the Son of God,'" evidently at this meeting. (Burgess, Autobiography, 4.)

Answered the above verbally[344] & attended to various duties. P.M. I called in all my Father's family & made a feast— ⟨& related my feeling towards them⟩ My Father pronounced the following Patriarchial blessings[345]

Henry Garrett,
        born in Deerfield. Onieda Co. N. y. Sept 5. AD. 1814
        Bro. I bless thee by the authority of the Priesthood Lord had eye upon thee, Satan seek destruction relativs also I seal thee unto lif. power to tread the adversa[r]y under thy feet & be useful reclaim friends, be a son of God, an heir jointly with Jesus Christ,[346] stand on the earth if faithful till thou hast recd. all the desires of thy heart which are in righteousness, the Lord shall bless thy chil[dren] after thee with the blessings of Abraham Isaac & Jacob, shall walk with companion to the [p. 145] House of God & see his glory fill the house & thou shalt receive all the blessings which thy heart can desire— I seal these blessings upon thee in the name of Jesus Amen

Charles H. Smith
        born in Potsdam St. Lawrence Co Ny. April 16. 1817
        Thou art in thy youth— satan will lay many snares for thee but I secure thee by the power of the holy priesthod from his grasp, thou hast no Father— an orphan, The Lord shall watch over thee & keep thee & thou shalt receive the priesthood & be mighty in word, save Fathers house receive all the blessings of the Earth even of A[braham] I[saac] & Jacob— stand on earth till Redeamer come & do all that the power of the holy priesthood can qualify thee for, I seal these blessings upon thee in the name of Jesus Amen

Marietta Carter
        born in Benson, Rutland Co. V.t. April 1. AD. 1818
        Thou art an orphan & the Lord shall bless thee more than thy own Father could do if he had not been taken from thee— thy name is

---

344. The next day "the Presidency of the Church" met and determined "that no one be ordained to an office in the Church in Kirtland without the voice of the several quorums when assembled for church business." (Minute Book 1, 30 Jan. 1836.)

345. It was the practice of the church patriarch at this time to bless the fatherless or church members whose fathers did not belong to the church. Of the six persons whose blessings are listed in this entry, five—Charles Smith, son of Samuel Smith (an uncle of JS); and the four Carter sisters, daughters of John S. Carter—are known to have been fatherless at this time. (Patriarchal Blessings, vol. 1, especially p. 8; Burial marker, Potsdam, NY, transcribed by Larry C. Porter, in Berrett, *Sacred Places,* 2:113; "Afflicting," *The Evening and the Morning Star,* July 1834, 176.)

346. See Romans 8:17.

written in the Book of life— become a companion & a mother— Lord
bless thy children & some of them shall prophecy— thy Father laid
down his life for the redemption of Zion— his spirit watches over
thee— thy heart shall be filled with light not sleep in the dust— see
thy Redeamer come in the clouds of heaven. & be caught up to meet
him & be ever with him—[347] these blessings I seal upon thee in the
name of Jesus Amen [p. 146]

Angeline Carter
 born in Benson Rutland Co. V.t. Augst 26 1823
 Thou art a child— thy heart is pure & Satan shall have no power
over thee because of thy blessing God shall be thy Father, an heir with
Jesus— observe the words of thy friends who care for thee & seek to
please them, The Lord will give thee children & wisdom to teach them
righteousness, & they shall be blest of the Lord & call thee blessed, a
daughter of Abraham live till satisfied with life. I seal the[e] up unto
eternal life in the name of Jesus Amen

Jo[h]anna Carter
 born in Putnam [blank] Ny—
 Nov. 26. AD. 1824
 I seal the blessings of a Father, thy Father is no more, blessings of
Abraham Isaac & Jacob, strength health healed of all infirmites—
Satan have no power to afflict— Lord guard thee by his holy Angels—
name written in heaven— eyes op[e]ned to see visions Angels minister
unto thee— a companion— lead thee to the house of God— see the
glory of God fill the house see the end of this generation— have power
to stand against all the power of Satan & overcome through the faith
which is in Jesus. I seal thee up unto eternal life in the name of the
Lord Jesus Amen

Nancy Carter
 born in Benson Rutland Co. V.t—
 Feby. 26 AD. 1827
 Thou art a child— the Lord loves thee Satan shall seek in vain to
destroy thee— Lord raise friends for thee which shall guard thee from
the destroyer, thy name is written in heaven live to see the winding up
of this generation [p. 147] Angels shall watch over thee in thy youth

---

347. See, for example, Matthew 24:30; 26:64; 1 Thessalonians 4:16–17; and Vision, 16 Feb. 1832, in
Doctrine and Covenants 91:7, 1835 ed. [D&C 76:102].

eyes op[e]ned— see thy God— raise children in righteousness & they shall be blest & call thee blessed because of thy diligence in teaching them the doctrine of the kingdom, I seal all these blessings upon thee in the name of Jesus Am[en]

Written & recorded by
<u>Sylvester Smith</u>   scribe

This was a good time to me & all the family rejoiced together— we continued the meeting till about eight o clock in the evening & related the goodness of God to us in op[e]ning our eyes to see the visions of heaven & in sending his holy Angels to minister unto us the word of life— we sang the praise of God in animated strains & the power of love & union was felt & enjoyed—

30 January 1836 • Saturday

Saturday 30. Attended school as usual. & waited upon several visiters & showed them the record of Abraham— Mʳ [Joshua] Seixas our hebrew teacher examined them with deep interest & pronouncd them to be original beyound all doubt, he is a man of excellent understanding— & has a knowledge of many languages which were spoken by the Antints [ancients]— he is an honorabl man so far as I can judge as yet— in the evening went to the upper rooms of the Lord's house & set the different quorems in order—[348] instructed the Presidents of the seventy concerning the order of their anointing & requested them to proceed & anoint the seventy[349] having set all the quorems in order I re[p. 148]turned to my house being weary with continual anxiety & labour in puting all the Authorities in [order?] & in striving to purify them for the solemn assembly according to the commandment of the Lord

31 January 1836 • Sunday

Sunday 31. 1836 Attended divine service in the schoolhouse organized the several quorems of the Authoraties of the church— appointed door keepers to

---

348. Oliver Cowdery's minutes call this a "conference of the Presidency." The minutes record resolutions that Harvey Whitlock be "restored" to "full fellowship," that all Kirtland ordinations be preapproved by assembled quorums, and that elders quorum president Alvah Beman give the church presidents a list of all elders living in Kirtland. Several weeks earlier, JS wrote Whitlock that if he would repent and return to Kirtland, he would be received into church fellowship. The resolution for approving ordinations was clarified 12 February 1836. From the list of elders, the church presidency selected men for a Second Quorum of the Seventy in early February 1836. (Minute Book 1, 30 Jan. 1836; JS, Journal, 16 Nov. 1835; 3 and 7 Feb. 1836; Minutes, 12 Feb. 1836, pp. 184–185 herein.)

349. Oliver Cowdery recorded meeting "with the 70, elders & priests, who were anointing." (Cowdery, Diary, 30 Jan. 1836; compare Cook and Backman, *Kirtland Elders' Quorum Record*, 30 Jan. 1836; and Post, Journal, 30 Jan. 1836.)

keep order about the door because of the crowd & to prevent the house from being excessively crowded— The high council of Zion occupied the first part of the day in speaking as they were led & relating experincies trials &.c.— P.M. house came to order as usual & Pres. Sidney Rigdon delivered a short discours & we attended to the breaking of bread the season was as interesting as usual— In the evening my Father attended to the blessing of three Brethren[350] at Pres. O. Cowderies [Oliver Cowdery's]— spent the evening at home

1 February 1836 • Monday

Monday Febuary 1. attended scholl as usual— & in company with the other committe[351] organized another class of 30 to receive Mʳ [Joshua] Seixas Lectures on the hebrew— in the evening attended to ⟨the⟩ organizing the of the quorems of High priests— Elders— Seventy & Bishops in the uper rooms of the house of the Lord & after blessing each quorem in the name of the Lord I left them & returned home

had an other interview with Mʳ Seixas our hebrew teacher & related to him some of the dealings of God to me— & gave him some of the evidences of the work of the latter days— he list[e]ned candidly & did not oppose [p. 149]

2 February 1836 • Tuesday

Tuesday Febuary 2. AD. 1836 Attended school as usual[352] & various duties went to the schoolhouse in the evening & heard an animated discourse delivered by Pres. S[idney] Rigdon he touched the outlines of our faith— showed the scattering & gathering of Israel from the scriptures & the stick of Joseph in the hands of Eaphraim & The law of Eaphraim aside from that of Moses[353] It was an interesting meeting— the spirit bore record that the Lord was well pleased!—

---

350. One of these was Ebenezer Robinson, who had previously boarded with JS and been baptized by him. (Patriarchal Blessings, 1:108; JS, Journal, 16 and 17 Oct. 1835.)

351. The "other committe" refers to the other members of a committee responsible for the Hebrew School. In addition to JS, its members included Sidney Rigdon, Frederick G. Williams, and Oliver Cowdery. (JS et al., Kirtland, OH, to Henrietta Seixas, 13 Feb. 1836, in Cowdery, Letterbook, 77–78; Cowdery, Diary, 1, 6, and 7 Feb. 1836.)

352. Oliver Cowdery, who attended the school, recorded that "the new class of 31 members took their first lesson." (Cowdery, Diary, 2 Feb. 1836.)

353. See Ezekiel 37:15–20. A JS revelation identified the "stick of Ephraim" as the Book of Mormon. The laws of Ephraim and Moses refer to the Book of Mormon and the Bible respectively. (Revelation, ca. Aug. 1830, in Doctrine and Covenants 50:2, 1835 ed. [D&C 27:5]; see "Mrs. Laura Owen's Defense against the Various Charges that Have Gone Abroad," *Times and Seasons*, 1 Feb. 1841, 2:301; and Thompson, *Evidences in Proof of the Book of Mormon*, 23–34.)

3 February 1836 • Wednesday

Wednesday 3. attended our hebrew lecture P̶. ⟨A.⟩ M. & studied with O[liver] Cowdery & Sylvester Smith P. M.—

received many visiters— & showed the records of Abraham— my Father blest three with a patriarchial blessing— Eld. A[lvah] Beman handed in the names of seventy of his quorem— designed for another seventy if God will—[354]

4 February 1836 • Thursday

Thursday 4. attended school & assisted in forming a class of 22 to read at 3.0 clock P.M the other 23 reads at 11-0.clock the first class recit[e]s at a quarter before 10 ⟨Am⟩ & the second at a quarter before 2-p.m.[355] we have a great want of books but are determined to do the best we can— may the Lord help us to obtain this language that we may read the scriptures in the language in which they were givn

5 February 1836 • Friday

Friday 5. Attended school & assisted the committe to make arangements for supplying the third & Fourth classes with books—[356] concluded to divide a bible into several parts for the benefit of said classes

continued my studies in the hebrew— recd. several visiters & attended various duties [p. 150]

6 February 1836 • Saturday

Saturday 6. called the anointed together to receive the seal of all their blessings,[357] The High Priests & Elders in the council room as usual— The

---

354. Beman was president of the elders quorum. A list of ten elders chosen by the church presidency to be in a Second Quorum of the Seventy was read in the elders quorum two days earlier. On the following day, 4 February, the names of seventy elders were presented to the presidents of the Seventy and accepted. The church presidency met for final approval of the ordinations on Sunday, 7 February. (Post, Journal, 1 and 4 Feb. 1836; JS, Journal, 7 Feb. 1836.)

355. The Hebrew School by this time consisted of about eighty students organized into four classes. (Cowdery, Diary, 1, 2, and 4 Feb. 1836; Hyrum Smith, Kirtland, OH, to Elias Smith, East Stockholm, NY, 27 Feb. 1836, CHL.)

356. Students attending the Hebrew School were now double the number Joshua Seixas had contracted to teach. Church leaders cooperated with Seixas to publish an abridged version of the already compact textbook that he had created for his unique short courses. The following day, JS and the other members of the school committee wrote to Seixas's wife, Henrietta, asking to purchase her Hebrew lexicon. (JS, Journal, 6 Jan. 1836; H. Smith to E. Smith, 27 Feb. 1836; *Supplement to J. Seixas' Manual Hebrew Grammar, for the Kirtland, Ohio, Theological Institution* [New York: West and Trow, 1836]; JS et al., Kirtland, OH, to Henrietta Seixas, 13 Feb. 1836, in Cowdery, Letterbook, 77–78; Cowdery, Diary, 6 Feb. 1836.)

357. JS held this meeting in the evening. (Cowdery, Diary, 6 Feb. 1836.)

Seventy with the Twelve in the second room & the Bishop in the 3— I laboured with each of these quorems for some time to bring to the order which God had shown to me which is as follows— first part to be spent in solemn prayer before god without any talking or confusion & the conclusion with a sealing prayer by Pres. Sidney Rigdon when all the quorems are to shout with one accord a solemn hosannah to God & the Lamb with an Amen— amen & amen—[358] & then all take seats & lift up their hearts in silent prayer to God & if any obtain a prophecy or vision not to rise & speak that all may be edefied & rejoice together I had considerable trouble to get all the quorems united in this order— I went from room to room repeatedly & charged each separately— assuring them that it was according to the mind of God yet notwithstanding all my labour— while I was in the east room with the Bishops quorems I f[e]lt by the spirit that something was wrong in the quorem of Elders in the west room— & I immediately requested Pres. O[liver] Cowdery & H[yrum] Smith to go in & see what was the matter— The quorem of Elders had not observed the order which I had given them & were reminded of it by Pres. Carloss [Don Carlos] Smith & mildly requested to observe order & continue in prayer & requested— some of them replied that they had a teacher of their own & did not wish to be troubled by others[359] this caused the spirit of the Lord to withdraw [p. 151] This interrupted the meeting & this quorem lost th[e]ir blessing in a great measurs—[360] the other quorems were more careful & the quorem of the Seventy enjoyed a great flow of the holy spirit many arose & spok[e] testifying that they were filled with the holy spirit which was like fire in their bones so that they could not hold their peace but were constrained

---

358. Cowdery recorded that the anointings "were sealed by uplifted hands and praises to God." (Cowdery, Diary, 6 Feb. 1836; see also Cook and Backman, *Kirtland Elders' Quorum Record*, 6 Feb. 1836; and "Hosanna," in Glossary.)

359. Don Carlos Smith was the recently appointed president of the high priests, who were meeting in the same room with the elders. The "teacher of their own" was possibly elders quorum president Alvah Beman, who instructed in their meetings. (Cook and Backman, *Kirtland Elders' Quorum Record*, 15 Jan.–11 Feb. 1836.)

360. The elders quorum minutes record that JS and his counselors in the presidency "came and sealed our anointing by prayer and shout of Hosanna" and then "gave us some instructions and left us." Alvah Beman then addressed those present, and "several spoke and there seemed to be a cloud of darkness in the room." After Oliver Cowdery and Hyrum Smith came into the room to resolve the problem, "the cloud was broken and some shouted, Hosanna and others spake with tongues." JS reprimanded the elders and instructed them concerning the proselytizing work they would commence after being endowed. JS stated, "This night the key is turned to the nations; and the angel John is about commencing his mission to prophesy before kings, and rulers, nations tongues and people."[a] This prophesying was part of John the Revelator's mission to "gather the tribes of Israel" in the last days.[b] (a. Cook and Backman, *Kirtland Elders' Quorum Record*, 6 Feb. 1836; see also Revelation 10:11. b. Answers to questions, ca. Mar. 1832, in Revelation Book I, p. 143 [D&C 77:14]; compare JS, Journal, 3 Apr. 1836.)

to cry hosannah to God & the Lamb & glory in the highest. Pres. W<u>m</u> Smith one of the twelve saw a vision of the Twelve & Seven in council together in old England & prophecied that a great work would be done by them in the old ~~con-~~ ~~try~~ contries & God was already beginning to work in the hearts of the p[e]ople— Prs. Z. Coltrine [Zebedee Coltrin] one of the seven saw a vision of the Lords Host— & others were filled with the spirit & spake in tongues & prophecied— This was a time of rejoicing long to be rememberd! praise the Lord—[361]

7 February 1836 • Sunday

Sunday Feby 7. 1836 /[362]attended ~~the~~ meeting at the us[u]al hour the quorums, were seated according to their official standing in the church,— The Bishop of Zion and his counsellors ocupied the fore noon in confession and exortation— The Bishop of Kirtland and his counsellors, occupied, the stand in the afternoon,— the discourses of these two quorums were verry interesting, a number of letters of commendation were presented and read, a vote called and all received into the church in Kirtland,—[363] bread was broken and blessed, and while, it was passing President [Sidney] Rigdon, commenced speaking from Acts 2<u>d</u> and continued about 15, minuits. his [p. 151][364] reasoning was cogent,— the wine was then blessed and passed after which meeting, dismissed— at evening meet with the presidency in the loft of the Printing-office, in company with the presidency of the 70, to chose other 70. also—[365] Blessed one of the Zion brethren,—[366] dismissed and retired—

8 February 1836 • Monday

Monday morning the 8<u>th</u> [367] attended School at the us[u]al hour,— nothing worthy of note transpired— in the afternoon lectured in upper room of the printing office with some of the brethren,— at evening ~~Mr~~ visited Mr [Joshua]

---

361. Oliver Cowdery also recorded that "many saw visions, many prophesied, and many spake in tongues." (Cowdery, Diary, 6 Feb. 1836.)

362. TEXT: Sylvester Smith handwriting ends; Warren Parrish begins.

363. The founding articles of the church required that church members moving from one congregation to another take with them "a letter certifying that they are regular members and in good standing." (Revelation, 10 Apr. 1830, in Doctrine and Covenants 2:27, 1835 ed. [D&C 20:84].)

364. TEXT: The second of two pages numbered "151".

365. The church presidency gave final approval to the list of elders who earlier in the week had been approved as prospective members of a Second Quorum of the Seventy by the elders quorum and by the presidents of the Seventy. The new members of the Seventy were formally called and ordained during the following week. (Cowdery, Diary, 7 Feb. 1836; JS, Journal, 3 Feb. 1836; Cook and Backman, *Kirtland Elders' Quorum Record,* 8 and 11 Feb. 1836; Post, Journal, 13 Feb. 1836.)

366. Alvin Winegar, a member of the 1834 expedition to Missouri. (Blessing of Alvin Winegar, 7 Feb. 1836, private possession, copy in CHL; see also "Zion brethren," in Glossary.)

367. Minutes of a high council for this date appear following the entry of 10 February 1836.

Seixas, in company with President's [Sidney] Rigdon & [Oliver] Cowdery, he converses freely, is an interesting man— This day Elder [Warren] Parrish my scribe, received my journal again, his health is so much improved that he thinks he will be able, with the blessing of God to perform this duty

9 February 1836 · Tuesday

Tuesday the 9th spent the day in studying the hebrew language,— we have pleasant weather and fine sleighing—

Spent the evening at home

10 February 1836 · Wednesday

Wednesday morning the 10th at home at 10. oclock ~~meet~~ ⟨met⟩ at School room to read hebrew

In the afternoon, read in the upper room of the printing-office— at 4. oclock called at the School room in the chapel, to make some arrangments, concerning the classes— on my return home I was informed that Br. Hyrum Smith had cut himself [p. 152] I immediately repaired to his house and found him badly wounded in his ⟨left⟩ arm, he had fallen on his axe, which caused a wound about, 4 or 5 inches in length Dr. [Frederick G.] Williams was sent for immediately ~~and~~ who when he came in sewed it up and dressed it, and I feel to thank God that it is no worse, and I ask my heavenly Father in the name of Jesus christ to heal my brother hyrum ~~Smith~~ of his wound, and bless my fathers family one and all, with peace and plenty, and ultimately eternal life—

Minutes · 8 February 1836

/[368]Feb 8th 1836. Met in council,[369] meeting opened with prayer by President Hyrum Smith; Levi Jackman supplied the place ~~of~~ of Joseph Coe.

Sister [blank] entered a complaint against Joseph Keeler, after hearing the testimony the councillors proceeded to give their council after which Pres. Hyrum Smith arose and made some remarks, the same was agreed to by President David Whitmer after which the Presidency gave room for the parties to speak both of which made a few remarks, the Pres then decided that Joseph Keeler be acquited a vote of the council was called, the council agreed to the decision of the Presidincy.

Jesse Hitchcock   Clerk.[370]

---

368. TEXT: Warren Parrish handwriting ends; unidentified begins.

369. TEXT: Residue from an adhesive wafer at the top of page 154—as well as a small scrap of paper still attached to the wafer residue—indicates that the unidentified scribe probably copied the minutes into the journal from a loose manuscript that had been attached at that point.

370. These minutes may have been intended for transcription in Minute Book 1. It is unclear whether

11 February 1836 · Thursday

/³⁷¹Thursday mornin 11ᵗʰ Feby 1836 at home— attended the School and read hebrew with the morning Class— spent the afternoon in reading, and exibiting the Egytian records to those who called to see me and heavens blessings have attended me.— [p. 153]

12 February 1836 · Friday

Friday 12ᵗʰ spent the day in reading hebrew, and attending to the duties of my family, and the duties of the church, nothing very special transpired meet this evening to make arangements concerning ordinations³⁷²

13 February 1836 · Saturday

Saturday 13ᵗʰ spent the fore noon in reading Hebrew.— at noon I prepared a horse and sleigh, for Professer [Joshua] Seixas, to go to Hudson to visit his family³⁷³

14 February 1836 · Sunday

Sunday 14ᵗʰ attended to the ordinance of baptism, before meeting— at the us[u]al hour attended meeting, the presidents of the 70, expressed their ~~feeling,~~ feelings, on the occasion, and their faith in the book of Mormon, and the revelations,— also their entire confidence in ⟨all⟩ the quorums that are organized in the church of Latter day Saints— had a good time, the spirit of God rested upon the congregation;— administered the sacrament and confirmed, a number who had been baptised, and dismissed

Minutes · 12 February 1836

Kirtland Feb 12ᵗʰ 1836,³⁷⁴ I ~~meet~~ ⟨met⟩ in the School room in the chapel in company with the several quorums to take into concideration the subject of ordinations, as mentioned at the top of this page

opened by singing and prayer I then arose and made some remarks upon the object of our meeting, which were as follows— first that many are desiring

---

JS was present for this meeting of the high council.

371. TEXT: Unidentified handwriting ends; Warren Parrish begins.

372. Minutes of this meeting to standardize ordinations appear following the entry of 14 February 1836.

373. Seixas's family remained in Hudson, some thirty road miles to the south. His wife, Henrietta Raphael, had by then given birth to eight children, seven of whom, ranging in age from infant to thirteen years old, are known to have been living in early 1836. (Stern, *First American Jewish Families*, 264.)

374. The first entry for this date appears above in chronological order. For the official minutes, see Minute Book 1.

to be ordained to the ministry, who are [p. 154] not called and consequntly the Lord is displeased— secondly, many already have been ordained who ought [not] to hold official stations in the church because they dishonour themselves and the church and bring persecution swiftly upon us, in consequence of their zeal without k[n]owledge—[375] I requested the quorum's to take some measures to regulate the same, I proposed some resolutions and remarked to the brethren that the subject was now before them and open for discussion

The subject was taken up and discussed by President's S[idney] Rigdon O[liver] Cowdery Eldr. M[artin] Harris and some others, and resolutions drafted, by my scribe who served as clerk on the occasion— read and rejected— it was then proposed that I should indite resolutions which I did as follows[376]

1st— Resolved. that no one be ordained to any office in the church in this stake of Zion at Kirtland without the unanimous voice of the several ~~quorums~~ bodies that constitute this quorum who are appointed to do church buisness in the name of said church— viz the presidency of the church & council the 12, apostles of the Lamb the 12 high counsellors of Kirtland the 12, high counsellors of Zion, the Bishop of Kirtland & his counsellors the Bishop of Zion and his counsellors— the 7. presidents of the Seventies; untill otherwise ordered by the said quorums.—[377] [p. 155]

2ond— and further resolved that no one be ordained in the branches of said church abroad unless they are recommended by the ~~church~~ voice of ~~that~~ ⟨the⟩ respective branches of the church to which they belong, to a general conference appointed by the heads of the church, and from that conference receive their ordination.—[378] [8 lines blank]

---

375. JS gave similar instruction two years earlier. (Orson Hyde, "The Elders in Kirtland, to Their Brethren Abroad," *The Evening and the Morning Star*, Dec. 1833, 120.)

376. Warren Parrish was both the clerk for the council meeting and the scribe for this journal entry. The resolutions recorded in both the council minute book and this entry appear to have been copied from an original document that is no longer extant. (Compare Minute Book 1, 12 Feb. 1836.)

377. This restated and clarified a resolution passed by a conference of the presidency of the church on 30 January 1836. After the Missouri leaders returned home, Kirtland leaders returned to the earlier practice of nominating and ordaining local leaders without first seeking such comprehensive approval. (Minute Book 1, 30 Jan. 1836; 3 and 9 Sept. 1837.)

378. The following day, the Quorum of the Twelve accepted the first resolution as stated and proposed an amendment to the second to specify that the Twelve—rather than "the heads of the church"— were to appoint the conferences that would ratify all ordinations recommended by branches outside the Kirtland stake. This followed from their understanding of instructions that JS had given them almost a year earlier and that had been published in the Doctrine and Covenants.[a] The Twelve's amendment was not accepted, and the resolution passed.[b] The new policy outlined in the second resolution was apparently followed for a time.[c] However, requiring such approval for every ordination probably became impractical and was soon abandoned.[d] (a. Minute Book 1, 13 Feb. 1836; Revelation, ca. Apr. 1835, in Doctrine and

15 February 1836 · Monday

Monday the 15th attended the Hebrew School at the usual hour,—[379] Spent the afternoon in reading hebrew, and receiving and waiting upon visitors—[380] on this day we commenced translating the Hebrew-language, under the instruction of professor [Joshua] Seixas, and he acknowledg's that we are the most forward of any class he ever taught, the same length of time

16 February 1836 · Tuesday

Tuesday the 16th atten[d]ed School at the usual hour and resumed our translating and made rapid progress many, called to day to see the House of the Lord, and to visit me and see the Egytian manuscripts— we have [p. 156] extremely cold weather and fine sleighing

17 February 1836 · Wednesday

Wednesday the 17th attend[ed] the school and read and translated with my class as usual, and my soul delights in reading the word of the Lord in the original, and I am determined to persue the study of languages untill I shall become master of them, if I am permitted to live long enough, at any rate so long as I do live I am determined to make this my object, and with the blessing of God I shall succe[e]d to my sattisfaction,— this evening Elder Joseph Coe called to make some arangements about the Egyptian records and the mummies, he proposes to hire a room at J[ohn] Johnsons Inn and exibit them there from day to day at certain hours, that some benefit may be derived from them— I complied with his request, and only observed that they must be managed with prudence and care especially the manuscripts[381]

Covenants 3:12, 30, 1835 ed. [D&C 107:33, 58]. *b.* JS, Journal, 3 Mar. 1836; see also Minute Book 1, 17, 18, and 22 Feb. 1836; 3 and 19 Mar. 1836. *c.* See, for example, Minute Book 1, 24 Feb. and 17 Mar. 1836. *d.* Minute Book 1, 10 June 1836; see also 2 Oct. 1837.)

379. Because Seixas—who had gone home to Hudson for the weekend—had not yet arrived to give instruction, JS and Oliver Cowdery oversaw the eleven o'clock class. Seixas apparently returned later in the day. (JS, Journal, 13 Feb. 1836; Cowdery, Diary, 15 Feb. 1836.)

380. JS also met this afternoon with several associates, with whom he prayed for Seixas and his family. Oliver Cowdery recorded that JS prayed that Seixas might "embrace the gospel and believe the book of Mormon" and "that we may be benefitted with the knowledge he has of languages." (Cowdery, Diary, 15 Feb. 1836.)

381. Seven months earlier, Coe loaned eight hundred dollars to help purchase the mummies and papyri, expecting to be quickly repaid from the sales of JS's translation of the papyri. With the translation still unpublished, Coe desired to recoup his losses by exhibiting the mummies and papyri. (Joseph Coe, Kirtland, OH, to JS, Nauvoo, IL, 1 Jan. 1844, JS Collection, CHL; see also Todd, *Saga of the Book of Abraham*, 196–200.)

18 February 1836 • Thursday

Thursday the 18th spent the day as usual in attending to my family concerns, ~~and~~ receiving and waiting upon those who called for instruction and attending to my studies,

19 February 1836 • Friday

Friday the 19th attended with the morning class and translated— professor [Joshua] Seixas [p. 157] handed me the names of a few whom he had selected from the first class, and requested us to meet together this afternoon and lecture, which we did in the upper room of the printing-office— The names are as follows: President's S[idney] Rigdon O[liver] Cowdery W[illiam] W. Phelps— Bishop E. Partrige [Edward Partridge] Eldr's E. McLellen [William E. McLellin] O[rson] Hyde O[rson] Pratt Sylvester Smith Myself and Scribe— these professor Seixas requested to meet one hour earlyer on the following morning— I conversed with Mr. Seixas upon the subject of religion, at my house this afternoon, he listened with attention and appeared interested with my remarks, and I believe the Lord is striving with him, by his holy spirit, and that he will eventually embrace the new and everlasting covenant, for he is a chosen vessel unto the Lord to do his people good,—[382] but I forbear lest I get to prophesying upon his head— this evening President Rigdon and myself called at Mr. Seixas lodgings and conversed with him upon the subject of the School, had a pleasant interview

20 February 1836 • Saturday

Saturday morning the 20th at home attending to my domestick concerns, at 9 oclock attended the school and translated with the morning class— spent the after-noon with my class in the printing-office— spent the evening at home [p. 158]

21 February 1836 • Sunday

Sunday the 21st Feb 1836 Spent the day at home, in reading meditation and prayer— I reviewed my lessons in Hebrew— On this day some 3 or 4 persons were baptised and the powers of darkness seem to be giving way on all sides,

---

382. In his classes and friendships, Seixas had long been exposed to Christian ministers and divinity students and had possibly experienced some form of Christian conversion. Four days earlier, JS prayed with others "that we may become his teachers in the things of salvation." (Joshua Seixas, Charlestown, MA, to Elizabeth, 22 Feb. 1834, Papers of the Seixas Family, American Jewish Historical Society, New York City; Joshua Seixas, Utica, NY, to John J. Shipherd, Oberlin, OH, 29 May 1835, Office of the Treasurer Records, Oberlin College Archives; Goldman, "Joshua/James Seixas"; Cowdery, Diary, 15 Feb. 1836.)

many who have been enemies to the work of the Lord are beginning to enquire in to the faith of the Latter day Saints and are friendly

22 February 1836 • Monday

Monday the 22ⁿᵈ translated Hebrew with the 1ˢᵗ class in the morning at— returned home and, made out my returns to the county clerk on 11. marriages which I have solemnized within 3. months past 8, by license from the clerk of the court of common pleas in Geauga county Ohio, and 3, by publishment,[383] sent them to chardon by Elijah Fuller— I baptised John O. Waterman. I spent the afternoon translating at with my scribe Elder W[arren] Parrish at his house at 4. oclock meet, Professor [Joshua] Seixas and the school committee[384] at printing office to make some arangements for the advancement of the several classes

The lower room of the chapel is now prepared for painting—[385]

This afternoon the sisters meet met to make the veil of the Temple[386] Father Smith presided over them and gave them much good instruction, closed by singing & prayer [p. 159]

23 February 1836 • Tuesday

Tuesday the 23ᵈ read and translated Hebrew— This afternoon the sisters

---

383. Ohio state law required a marriage certificate signed by the officiator to be submitted to the county clerk within three months of the wedding.ᵃ JS therefore had only two days left to file the certificate for Newel and Lydia Goldthwaite Bailey Knight, the first of the eleven he sent to the county seat on this day. JS's scribe Warren Parrish helped him make out the returns, including the one for Parrish's own marriage.ᵇ The reverse of each license bears a 22 February 1836 notation of JS's return in the handwriting of Parrish. On marriages for which the couples had obtained licenses, see JS, Journal, 24 Nov. 1835; 3 and 13 Dec. 1835; 14 and 20 Jan. 1836; and Cowdery, Diary, 3 Feb. 1836. On marriages legitimized by publishment, see JS, Journal, 17 Jan. 1836; and 161n297 herein. (a. An Act Regulating Marriages [6 Jan. 1824], *Statutes of Ohio*, vol. 2, p. 1407, sec. 8. b. State of Ohio, Marriage Licenses, John H. Boynton and Susan Lowell, 17 Nov. 1835; Warren Parrish and Martha H. Raymond, 17 Nov. 1835; Edwin Webb and Eliza Ann McWethy, 17 Nov. 1835; Newell Knight and Lydia Goldthwaite, 25 Nov. 1835; Ebenezer Robinson and Angeline Eliza Works, 12 Dec. 1835; Thomas Carrico and Betsey Baker, 4 Jan. 1836; Joseph C. Kingsbury and Caroline Whitney, 26 Jan. 1836, CHL.)

384. The committee that oversaw the Kirtland Hebrew School: JS, Sidney Rigdon, Frederick G. Williams, and Oliver Cowdery. (JS et al., Kirtland, OH, to Henrietta Seixas, 13 Feb. 1836, in Cowdery, Letterbook, 77–78; Cowdery, Diary, 1, 6, and 7 Feb. 1836.)

385. On this day, JS appointed Brigham Young to oversee the painting and finishing of the House of the Lord. (Historian's Office, "History of Brigham Young," 14.)

386. The "veil of the Temple" consisted of heavy white canvas curtains that could be raised or lowered to isolate the pulpits on either the east or the west end of the main assembly room or to divide the room into sections. This allowed for more than one meeting at a time and provided privacy for prayers and ceremonies. These curtains were also "veils" as described in biblical accounts of temples. Painting the interior of the House of the Lord and preparing the veils marked the finishing stages of construction, which had begun in June 1833. (Robison, *First Mormon Temple*, 85–96.)

met again at the chapel to work on the v[e]il toward the close of the day I met with the presidency & many of the brethren in the house of the Lord— I made some remarks from the pulpit upon the rise and progress of the church of Christ of Latter day Saints and pronounced a blessing upon the Sisters for the liberality in giving their servises so cheerfully to make the veil for the Lord's house also upon the congregation and dismissed

24 February 1836 · Wednesday

Wednesday the 24th attended to my studies as usual— at evening met the quorums at the school-room in the chapel to take into concideration the propriety or impropriety of ordaining a large number of individuals who wish to be ordained to official stations in the church— each individual's nam[e] was presented and the voice of the assembly called and all of them except 7. were rejected—[387] Their ordinations defered untill another time— O[rson] Hyde O[liver] Cowdery and Sylvester Smith were nominated and seconded to draft and ⟨make⟩ regulations concerning licenses— vote of the assembly called and unanimously passed[388]

Thomas Burdick nominated and seconded to officiate as clerk to record licenses, and receive pay for his servises accordingly [p. 160]

vote called and passed unanimously also nominated and seconded that the 12, and presidents of the 70, be see that the calls for preaching in the regions round about Kirtland be attended to, and filled by judicious Elders of this church—[389]

adjourned, and closed by singing and prayer—

25 February 1836 · Thursday

Thursday the 25th of Feb 1836 attended to my studies as usual, and made some proficiency,— in the afternoon I was called upon by President [Sidney]

---

387. William Wightman, Charles Wightman, David Cluff, Truman Jackson, Reuben Barton, and Daniel Miles were approved for ordination as elders and Moses Daley as a high priest. Nineteen others were rejected. (Minute Book 1, 24 Feb. 1836.)

388. Imperfect record keeping in the various conferences and branches of the church, which would be compounded with the extensive ministry of traveling elders that was expected to follow the anticipated "endowment of power from on high," made it necessary to centralize licensing. The proposed regulations were presented to church leaders the following week. (JS, Journal, 3 Mar. 1836.)

389. While waiting for the endowment, a number of elders served short-term proselytizing missions in the vicinity. (Benjamin Brown, Kirtland, OH, to Sarah M. Brown, Mar. 1836, Benjamin Brown Family Collection, CHL; see also, for example, Historian's Office, "History of Brigham Young," 14; Orson Hyde, Kirtland, OH, 4 May 1836, letter to the editor, *LDS Messenger and Advocate,* Apr. 1836, 2:296; George M. Hinkle, Kirtland, OH, 26 Mar. 1836, letter to the editor, *LDS Messenger and Advocate,* Apr. 1836, 2:304; and "From Our Elders Abroad," *LDS Messenger and Advocate,* Apr. 1836, 2:303–304.)

Rigdon to go and visit his wife[390] who was verry sick,— I did so in company with my scribe, we prayed for ~~her~~ and annointed her in the name of the Lord and she began to recover from that verry hour— Returned home and spent the evening

26 February 1836 • Friday

Friday the 26th attended and read hebrew with the first class in the morning— spent the afternoon in the printing office— settled som misunderstanding between Br. Wm Smith and professor [Joshua] Seixas—

27 February 1836 • Saturday

Saturday morning the 27th I prepared ~~a~~ my horse and sleigh for Mr [Joshua] Seixas to ride to Hudson to visit his family, he is to return on monday next— attended with my class at the printing office [p. 161] both in the fore and afternoon, and lectured on, and translated Hebrew— we have cold weather and fine sleighing

28 February 1836 • Sunday

Sunday the 28th This morning two gentlemen late from Scotland called to see me, to make inquiry about the work of the Lord in these last days, they treated me with respect, and the interview was pleasing to me, and I presume interesting to them, they attended our meeting, with me, and expressed a satisfaction in what they heard

They spoke of Irvin [Edward Irving] the oriental reformer and his prop[h]esies—[391] after meeting,— I returned home and spent the after part of the day and evening in reading and translating the Hebrew

29 February 1836 • Monday

Monday the 29th spent the day in studying as usual.— a man called to see

---

390. Phoebe Brook Rigdon.

391. Irving, formerly a Scottish Presbyterian minister, had recently helped to found the Catholic Apostolic Church. Like JS, Irving anticipated an imminent advent and emphasized both the ecclesiastical offices and the spiritual gifts of the primitive church.[a] The Catholic Apostolic Church had sent an envoy to Latter-day Saint church leaders in Kirtland several months earlier, but he had never returned to Great Britain.[b] Later, an editorial in the church newspaper in Nauvoo under JS's editorship stated that Irving and his followers "counterfeited the truth perhaps the nearest of any of our modern sectarians."[c] Irving authored a number of eschatological works, such as *The Last Days* (London: R. B. Seeley and W. Burnside, 1828) and *The Signs of the Times* (London: Ellerton and Henderson, [1829]).[d] (a. "Irving, Edward" and "Catholic Apostolic Church," in *Oxford Dictionary of the Christian Church,* 847–848, 306. b. Whitmer, History, 74–76; JS History, vol. B-1, 594. c. [JS], "Try the Spirits," *Times and Seasons,* 1 Apr. 1842, 3:746; see also Lively, "Comparative Study of Two Minority Millenarian Groups," 53–63; and Underwood, *Millenarian World of Early Mormonism,* 134–138. d. See Carlyle, *Prophetical Works of Edward Irving.*)

the house of the Lord in company with another gentleman, on entering the door they were politely invited by the gent[l]eman who has charge of the house to take of[f] their hats one of them complyed with the request unhesitatingly while the other obsereved that he would not take of[f] his hat nor bow to Jo Smith but that he had made Jo bow to him at a certain time— he was immediately informed by Eldr [George] Morey the keeper of the house that his first buisness was to leave ⟨it⟩ ~~the house~~ for when [p. 162] a man imposed upon me he was imposed upon himself, the man manifested much anger, but left the house.— for this independence and resolution of Eldr Morey I respect him and for the love he manifests toward me, and may Israels God bless him and give him an ascendency over all his enemies—

This afternoon Professor [Joshua] Seixas returned from Hudson, and brought a few more bibles and one grammar of his 2ᵈ edition.—[392] the weather is warm & our sleighing is failing fast

1 March 1836 · Tuesday

Tuesday March the 1ˢᵗ 1836 attended School, in the fore noon in the afternoon at the printing office and read and translated with my class untill 4. oclock— returned home and attended to my domestic concerns

We have fine sleighing which is uncommon in this country at this season of the Year

2 March 1836 · Wednesday

Wednesday the 2ᵒⁿᵈ persued my studies as usual— at 7 oclock in the evening, the first class met, agreeably to the request of Mʳ· [Joshua] Seixas at Eldr O[rson] Hydes to spend one hour in translating,— dismissed and returned home

3 March 1836 · Thursday

Thursday the 3ᵈ attended to my studies in the hebrew.— some misunderstanding, took place between [p. 163] Professor [Joshua] Seixas and some of the schollars respecting, the sale of some Bibles,— his feelings were much hurt appearantly, he made some remarks concerning it to each class at noon he called on the School committee with his feelings much depressed, we gave him all the satisfaction we could in righteousness, and his feelings were measurbly allayed

---

392. Seixas, *Hebrew Grammar*.

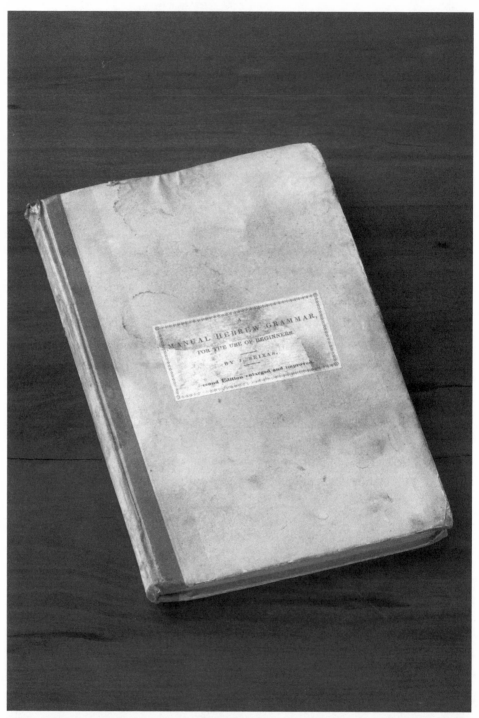

Hebrew School textbook. *Manual Hebrew Grammar for the Use of Beginners,* by Joshua Seixas, second edition, 1834. Seixas used this 1834 edition of his textbook when he began teaching Hebrew in Kirtland, Ohio, in January 1836. A reduced edition was soon published to accommodate the swelling ranks of his Mormon students. (Church History Library, Salt Lake City. Photograph by Welden C. Andersen.)

/³⁹³This evening the several quorums met agreeably to adjourment and were organized according to their official standing in the church.³⁹⁴

I then arose and made some remarks on the object of our meeting which are as follows.

1ˢᵗ To receive or reject certain resolutions that were drafted by a commitee chosen for that purpose at a preceeding meeting respecting licenses for elders and other official members.³⁹⁵

2ⁿᵈ To sanction by the united voice of the quorum certain resolutions respecting ordaining members; that had passed through each quorum seperately for without any alteration or amendment except⟨ing⟩ in the quorum of the twelve.³⁹⁶

The council opened by singing and prayer. President O[liver] Cowdery then arose and read the resolutions respecting licenses three times, the third time he read the article ⟨resolutions⟩ he gave time and oppertunity after reading each article for objections to be made if any there were; no objections were made—³⁹⁷ I then observed that these resolutions must needs pass through each quorum seperately begining at the presidency /³⁹⁸and concequently it must first be thrown into the hands of the president of the Deacon⟨s⟩ & his council as equal rights & privileges are my motto, and one [p. 164] man is as good as another, if he behaves as well, and that all men should be esteemed alike, without regard to distinction's of an official nature,— the resolutions passed through the quorums of the Deacons by their unanimous voice

It was then thrown before the presidnt of the Teachers and his council and passed unanimously—

---

393. TEXT: Warren Parrish handwriting ends; unidentified begins.

394. This council, held in the House of the Lord, included all the quorums and councils. For the official minutes, see Minute Book 1, 3 Mar. 1836.

395. See JS, Journal, 24 Feb. 1836.

396. See JS, Journal, 12 Feb. 1836.

397. Cowdery served as chairman of the committee chosen to draft the resolutions for centralizing priesthood licensing. The first resolution decreed that all church licenses would be issued from church headquarters in Kirtland and recorded in a single record book kept there. Other resolutions mandated establishing a chairman and clerk and procedures to issue licenses to new officers, issuing new licenses to current license holders, and publicizing newly issued licenses in the church newspaper. The final resolution provided for a pro tempore chairman and clerk. Although there were no objections to the resolutions, a proposed addition empowered the pro tempore officers to act in the absence of the chairman or clerk.ᵃ The church-endorsed licenses assured conferences and branches that the elders bearing them were legitimate officers. The new regulations were published in the February issue of the church newspaper, which had not yet been issued.ᵇ (a. Minute Book 1, 3 Mar. 1836; see also Cowdery, Diary, 3 Mar. 1836. b. Minutes, *LDS Messenger and Advocate*, Feb. 1836, 2:266–268.)

398. TEXT: Unidentified handwriting ends; Warren Parrish begins.

Next into the hands of the Presedents of the preists & his council and passed unanimously

then into the hands of the Bishop's council of Kirtland & passed unanimously

from them to the Bishop of Zion & his council & passed unanimously—

Next into the hands of the president of the ~~high preists & his~~ Elders & his council & passed unanimously

From them into the hands of the president of the High-Preists & his council and passed unanimously

Next into the hands of the presidents of the 70. & passed unanimously

from them to the high council of ⟨Zion⟩ ~~Kirtland~~ & passed unanimously—

from them to the high council of Kirtland & passed unanimously—

~~& Lastly in~~ and then into the hands of the 12. & passed unanimously

& lastly into the hands of the presidency of the Church & all the quorums and recd their sanction,— having now passed through all the quorums, the resolutions are received as as Law to govern the Church [p. 165]

I was nominated & seconded for a standing chairman & F[rederick] G. Williams for clerk to is[s]ue licenses to the official members of the church S[idney] Rigdon for chairman protem & O. Cowdery clerk— vote called from the several quorums in their order & passed unanimously[399]

I then made some remarks on the amendment of the 12. upon the resolutions recorded on pages 155 & 156.[400] President T[homas] B. Marsh made some observations after me, & then called a vote of his quorum, to asertain whether they would repeal their amendment or not 9. of the 12. vote in the affirmative & 3. in the negative,[401] and the original bill was passed, which is recorded on the pages above named— dismissed by prayer & retired 1/2 past 9. oclock

4 March 1836 · Friday

Friday the 4th ~~Feby~~ ⟨March⟩ 1836 attended school as usual— The sleighing is ~~falling~~ failing fast, the icy chains of winter seem to be giving way under the influence of the returning Sun, & spring will soon open to us with all his charms

5 March 1836 · Saturday

Saturday the 5th Attended school— in the afternoon the board kilns to fire

---

399. As chairman, JS signed nearly three hundred of the new licenses before the end of May. (Kirtland Elders' Certificates, 1–157.)

400. See Minutes, 12 Feb. 1836, p. 185 herein.

401. John F. Boynton, Orson Pratt, and Lyman Johnson. Two weeks later, these three met with the presidency of the church and withdrew their objections. (Minute Book 1, 3 and 19 Mar. 1836.)

& the lumber principally consumed— this is the 5 or 6 time it has burnt this winter if my memory serves me, corectly.—

6 March 1836 • Sunday

Sunday the 6ᵗʰ Spent the day at home, in the enjoyment ⟨of the society⟩ of my family, around the social fireside[402] [p. 166]

7 March 1836 • Monday

~~March the 7ᵗʰ Monday~~ Monday March 7ᵗʰ 1836 spent the day in attending to my studies

At Evening met with my class at Professor [Joshua] Seixas Room, & translated the 17ᵗʰ chapter of Genesis,— after the class was dismissed I was requested, to tarry with the rest of the School committee, to mak[e] some arangements about paying Mᵣ Seixas for his ~~tuition~~ instruction, & to engage him for another qr., we did not arive at any thing definite upon this point,— however ~~he~~ Mr Seixas has agreed to ~~stay~~ ⟨teach us⟩ 3. weeks longer, after having a vacation of 2. weeks at the expiration of this course, & perhaps a qr.[403]

8 March 1836 • Tuesday

Tuesday the 8ᵗʰ attended school & translated most of the 22. chapter of Gen[esis] after my class were dismissed, retired to the printing office and translated 10. verses of Ex[odus] 3ᵈ which with the 1ˢᵗ & 2ⁿᵈ Psalms are our next lesson

9 March 1836 • Wednesday

Wednesday the 9ᵗʰ Attended School as usual— ~~This day the snow is falling~~

10 March 1836 • Thursday

Thursday 10ᵗʰ Attended School, in the morning, in the afternoon, read Hebrew in the office at evening went down to Professor [Joshua Seixas's] room

---

402. JS's apparent absence from Sunday's worship services may be attributed to limitations of meeting space. Oliver Cowdery recorded that he did not attend the meeting this day "in consequence of there not being sufficient room for so many in the small houses occupied for meetings." Caroline Barnes Crosby later observed that the seating in the schoolhouse during these months was so limited that church members "decided on taking their turns in staying away, as the weather was cold, and it was unpleasant for those who stood outside." (Cowdery, Diary, 6 Mar. 1836; Caroline Barnes Crosby, Autobiography.)

403. This marked the end of the sixth week of the originally contracted seven-week instruction period. Seixas resumed instruction from 14 to 29 March. The class this term was held for a total of eight weeks and two days.ᵃ Seixas also taught for an additional term in Kirtland that summer.ᵇ (a. See JS, Journal, 6 Jan. and 29 Mar. 1836. b. Truman Coe, "Mormonism," Ohio Observer, 11 Aug. 1836, 31–32; Jonathan Crosby, Autobiography, 14.)

to be instructed by him, in the language on the account of the storm the class did not meet. [p. 167]

11 March 1836 • Friday

Friday the 11ᵗʰ meet with the morning class, at 9. oclock,— at 10. went into the office and made a divission of our class for private studies for our better accommodation, & advancement in the language we are persuing

President's [Sidney] Rigdon [William W.] Phelps & [Oliver] Cowdery and myself meet at the printing office Eldr's O[rson] Pratt Sylvester Smith & Bishop Partrige [Edward Partridge], at L[uke] Johnson's

Eldr's McLellen [William E. McLellin] O[rson] Hyde & W[arren] Parrish on the flats— this evening our class ~~meet~~ met at Mr [Joshua] Seixas room & spent an hour in our studies,— class dismissed & retired except the school committee, who tarried and made some arangements with Mr Seixas about continuing longer with us & bringing his family to this place

This has been a very stormy day and the snow is, still falling fast, & the prospect is fair for another run of sleighing which is uncommon for this country at this season of the Year

12 March 1836 • Saturday

Saturday the 12ᵗʰ engaged a team to go to Hudson after Mr [Joshua] Seixas family ⟨& goods⟩ also a Horse and cutter for himself & wife,— we have cold weather & fine sleighing— I was informed to day that a man by the name of Clark froze to death, last night near this place, who was under the influenc of ardent spirits; O my God how long will this monster intemperance [p. 168] find it's victims on the earth, me thinks until the earth is swept with the wrath ~~of~~ and indignation of God, and christ's kingdom becomes universal.[404] O come Lord Jesus and cut short thy work in rightieousness.[405]

---

404. An 1833 revelation warned against drinking wine and "strong drinks," but the language of this entry reflects the national temperance movement, which lamented the physical, social, and spiritual suffering caused by drunkenness and alcoholism. The temperance movement derived much of its strength from evangelical Protestants who, like JS, commonly viewed the issue from a millenarian perspective. (Revelation, 27 Feb. 1833, in Doctrine and Covenants 80:1, 1835 ed. [D&C 89:5–7]; *Eighth Report of the American Temperance Society,* 6; Blocker, *American Temperance Movements,* 11–17; Abzug, *Cosmos Crumbling,* 81–104.)

405. See Revelation 22:20; Romans 9:28; and Revelation, 22 and 23 Sept. 1832, in Doctrine and Covenants 4:16, 1835 ed. [D&C 84:97]; see also the same plea in JS's prayer to dedicate the House of the Lord, in JS, Journal, 27 Mar. 1836, p. 209 herein.

Eldr Solomon Hancock received a letter to day, from Missouri bearing the painful inteligence, of the death of his wife.[406] May the Lord bless him and comfort him in this hour of affliction

13 March 1836 • Sunday

Sunday the 13th of March 1836 met with the presidency & some of the 12. and counseled with them upon the subject of removing to Zion this spring, we conversed freely upon the importance of her redemption, and the necessity of the presidency removing to that place, that their influence, might be more effectually, used in in gathering the saints to that country, and we finally come to the resolution to emigrate on or before the 15th of May next, if kind providence smiles, upon us and openes the way before us[407]

14 March 1836 • Monday

Monday the 14th Attended School as usual Professor [Joshua] Seixas returned from Hudson with his family

15 March 1836 • Tuesday

Tuesday the 15 At School in the forenoon in the afternoon, met in the printing office, recd, and waited upon those who called to see me, and attended to my domestick concerns— at evening met in the printing office & recd a lecture, on grammar [p. 169]

16 March 1836 • Wednesday

Wednesday the 16th persued my studies in the Hebrew language,— at evening met the quorum of singers in the chapel, they performed admirably, concidering the advantages they have had[408]

---

406. Alta Adams Hancock died in January in Clay County, Missouri. (Obituary for Alta Hancock, *LDS Messenger and Advocate,* Feb. 1836, 2:272.)

407. Two days earlier, Missouri church leaders Edward Partridge, Isaac Morley, John Corrill, and William W. Phelps were appointed to purchase new land in Missouri for Latter-day Saint immigration.*a* They departed Kirtland shortly after the solemn assembly and purchased the land in northern Missouri where the Latter-day Saints later founded Far West.*b* JS did not move to Missouri until early 1838, when conditions in Kirtland deteriorated to the point that a revelation directed the presidency to move west without delay.*c* (a. Whitmer, History, 83; Partridge, Journal, May–July 1836. b. Johnson and Romig, *Index to Early Caldwell County. c.* Revelation, 12 Jan. 1838–C, in Revelations Collection, CHL; see also JS, Journal, 8 July 1838, pp. 283–284 herein.)

408. The singers were likely preparing to perform at the dedication of the House of the Lord that took place eleven days later. (See JS, Journal, 27 Mar. 1836.)

17 March 1836 · Thursday

Thursday the 17ᵗʰ At school in the morning, in the afternoon in the office at evening, met with the quorums in the west school-room of the Lord's House to receive or reject certain individuals whose names were presented for ordination's a number were received, by the united voice of the assembly[409]

18 March 1836 · Friday

Friday the 18ᵗʰ attended School with the morning class,— at 10. oclock, went to the school-house to attend a the funeral of Susan Johnson, daughter of Esekiel [Ezekiel] Johnson, she is a member of the church of Latter day Saints & remained strong in the faith, untill, her spirit, took it's exit from time to eternity[410]

May God bless and comfort her afflicted parents, family connexions, and friends— President [Sidney] Rigdon delivered a fine discourse on the occasion, and much solemnity prevailed

19 March 1836 · Saturday

Saturday the 19ᵗʰ Read Hebrew with the morning class.— Spent the day in, attending [p. 170] to my domestick concerns, and the affairs of the church[411]

20 March 1836 · Sunday

Sunday the 20ᵗʰ March 1836 attended the house of worship, as usual the quorum of high preists, delivered short addresses to the congregation, in a very feeling, and impressive manner,— at the intermission at noon one individual was baptised— in the afternoon, administered the Lords Supper, as we are wont to do on every Sabath, and the Lord blessed our souls with the out pouring of his spirit, and we were made to rejoice in his goodness,

21 March 1836 · Monday

Monday the 21ˢᵗ at school in the morning— at after school went to the printing office and prepared, a number of Elders licinses, to send by Elder [Ambrose] Palmer to the court [in] Medina County in order to obtain licenses

---

409. John Gaylord, Erastus Wightman, Osmon Duel, Chapman Duncan, Joshua Bosley, and Heman Hyde were sustained for ordination; four others were rejected. (Minute Book 1, 17 Mar. 1836.)

410. Susan Johnson died two days earlier in Kirtland at age twenty-one. (Benjamin F. Johnson, "A Life Review," 16–17, Benjamin Franklin Johnson, Papers, CHL.)

411. These church affairs included an evening meeting of the various quorums in the House of the Lord, where JS gave instruction on the "sealing power" and the solemn assembly to be held at the end of the month. (Cook and Backman, *Kirtland Elders' Quorum Record,* 19 Mar. 1836.)

to marry, as the court in this county will not grant us this privelege.—[412] To day 10 persons were baptized, in this place

22 March 1836 • Tuesday

Tuesday the 22[ond] read Hebrew with the morning class,— to day 5. young-men were received into the church by baptism, in this place— This is a stormy day, the snow is nearly a foot deep, an uncommon storm, for this season of the year [p. 171]

23 March 1836 • Wednesday

Wednesday the 23[d.] ⟨M[ar]ch⟩ 1836 Attended School— this is a pleasant day and fine sleighing— 2. more were received into the church by baptism

24 March 1836 • Thursday

Thursday the 24th Attended School as usual in the evening, met with my class at the printing-office, and rec[d] a lecture from professor [Joshua] Seixas upon the Hebrew language

After we were dismissed, we called at the School-room to hear the ⟨choir⟩ ~~quire~~ of Singers, perform, which they did admirably

On this day 5. more were rec[d] into the Church by baptism

25 March 1836 • Friday

Friday the 25th Attend[ed] School with the morning class— also at 5 oclock P.M and rec[d] a lecture upon the Hebrew Grammar— We have pleasant weather and good sleighing—

26 March 1836 • Saturday

Saturday the 26th At home attending to my domestick concerns in the morning.— after brekfast met with the presidency to make arangements for the solemn assembly which occupied the remainder of the day[413]

---

412. These were probably fresh prints of licenses designed following the priesthood licensing regulations passed earlier in the month.[a] The new licenses would be used to demonstrate that their holders were "regularly ordained minister[s] of the gospel" eligible for licenses to perform marriages.[b] On a previous attempt to obtain such a license, see 110n163 herein. Two Mormon applications to Medina County were granted in June 1836.[c] (a. See JS, Journal, 3 Mar. 1836. b. Geauga Co., OH, Court of Common Pleas, Mar. 1835, final record bk. M, 380–381, microfilm, U.S. and Canada Record Collection, FHL. c. Bradshaw, "Joseph Smith's Performance of Marriages in Ohio," 23, 40.)

413. Oliver Cowdery recorded, "Met in the president's room pres. J Smith, jr S[idney] Rigdon, my brother W[arren] A. Cowdery & Elder W[arren] Parrish, and assisted in writing a prayer for the dedication of the house." (Cowdery, Diary, 26 Mar. 1836.)

27 March 1836 · Sunday

Sunday morning the 27th The congregation began to ~~assembly~~ ⟨assimble⟩ ⟨at the chapel⟩ at about 7 oclock one hour ~~early~~ ⟨earlier⟩ than the doors were to be opened many brethren had come in from the region's [p. 172] round about to witness the dedication of the Lord's House and share in his blessings and such was the anxiety on this occasion that some hundreds, (probably five or six,) assembled ~~collected~~ before the doors were opened—

The presidency entered with the door kepers and aranged them at the inner and outer doors also placed our stewards to receiv donations from those who should feel disposed to contribute something to defray the expenses of building the House of the Lord—⁴¹⁴ ⟨we also dedicated the pulpits & consecrated them to the Lord⟩⁴¹⁵ The doors were then opened President [Sidney] Rigdon President [Oliver] Cowdery and myself seated the congregation as they came in, ~~we received about~~ and according to the best calculation we could make we received between 9 and 10,00 ⟨hundred⟩⁴¹⁶ which ~~was~~ is as many as can be comfortably situated we then informed the door keepers that we could receive no more, and a multitude were deprived of the benefits of the meeting on account of the house not being sufficiently capacious to receive them, and I felt to regret that any of my brethren and sisters should be deprived of the Meeting, and I recommended them to repair to the School-house and hold a meeting which they did and filled that house ⟨also⟩⁴¹⁷ and yet many were left out—⁴¹⁸

The assembly were then organized in the following manner,— viz.

~~President F G. Williams~~ Presdt. Joseph Smith⟨, Sen.⟩⁴¹⁹ ~~and Presdt W. W. Phelps occupied the first pulpit ⟨in the west end of the house⟩ for the Melchisedec priesthood, Presdt. S. Rigdon, Myself, and Prest. Hyrum Smith the 2ond— Presdt D. Whitmer Presdt O. Cowdery and Presdt John. Whitmer the 3d— The 4th was~~ [p. 173] ~~occupied by the president of the high priests and~~

---

414. Three years later, John Corrill, who helped supervise finishing work, wrote that at this time the church still owed about thirteen thousand dollars of the forty thousand dollars in building expenses. As is mentioned later in this journal entry, nine hundred sixty dollars was collected on this occasion. (Corrill, *Brief History of the Church,* 21; Post, Journal, 27 and 28 Mar. 1836; see also Ames, Autobiography, 1836.)

415. When enclosed by the hanging "veils," the pulpits functioned as an inner sanctum analogous to the veiled "most holy place" in Solomon's temple. (2 Chronicles 3:8–14; 4:22; 5:7; Robison, *First Mormon Temple,* 94; see also JS, Journal, 29 Mar. and 3 Apr. 1836; 188n386 herein.)

416. TEXT: Insertion in unidentified handwriting.

417. TEXT: Insertion in unidentified handwriting.

418. Stephen Post recorded, "The doors were opened at 8 & to be closed at 9 A.M. however they were closed before 9 on account of the house being full many retired to, & filled the school room, under the printing office which holds 400 or 450 & many went home." The dedication service was held again four days later for those who could not be seated on this day. (Post, Journal, 27 Mar. 1836; JS, Journal, 31 Mar. 1836.)

419. TEXT: ", Sen." written over "(my Father),".

his counsellors, and 2 choirister's— The 12. apostles on the right, the high council of Kirtland on the left, The pulpits (in the east end of the house) for the Aaronic priesthood were occupied in the following manner— The Bishop of Kirtland and his counsellors in the first pulpit— (the) Bishop of Zion and his counsellors in the 2^ond— the presdt. of the priest and his counsellors in the 3^d— the presdt. of the Teachers and his counsellors in the 4th—420 the high council of Zion on the right, the 7. presdt of the Seventies on the left

West end of the. house

Presdt. F[rederick] G. Williams Presdt. Joseph Smith, Sen and Presdt. W[illiam] W. Phelps occupied the 1st pulpit for the Melchisedic priesthood— Presdt. S. Rigdon myself and Presdt Hyrum Smith in the 2^ond—421

Presdt. D[avid] Whitmer Presdt. O. Cowdery and Presdt. J[ohn] Whitmer in the 3^d.— The 4th was occupied by the president of the high-preists and his counsellors, and 2 choiristers— The 12. Apostles on the right in the 3. highest seats—

The presdt of the Eldrs his clerk & counsellors in the seat immediatly below the 12— The high council of Kirtland consisting of 12, on the left in the 3, first seats— the 4th seat below them was occupied by the presidency's Eldr's W[arren] A. Cowdery & W[arren] Parrish who served as scribes.—

The pulpits in the east end of the house for the Aaronic priesthood were occupied as follows.— The Bishop of Kirtland and his counsellors in the 1st pulpit,— The Bishop of Zion and his counsellors in the 2^ond— The presdt. of the priests and his counsellors in the 3^d.— The presdt. of the Teachers in and his counsellors (& one choirister) in the 4th— The high council of Zion consisting of [p. 174] 12. counsellors on the right— The presdt of the Deacons and his counsillors in the seat below them.— The 7. presdts of the Seventies on the left— The choir of singers were seated in the 4 corners of the room in seats prepared for that purpose— (rec^d by contribution $960.00)

---

420. TEXT: Warren Parrish canceled the phrase "the 7. Presdt of the seventies" at this point and made other less substantive emendations prior to crossing out the entire revised passage.

421. The members of the church presidency were seated by age. Joseph Smith Sr., the oldest, was flanked by Williams and Phelps, the next two oldest. JS was flanked by the next two oldest in the second tier of pulpits. The remaining presidents occupied the third tier. The center pulpit of the highest stand, or "1st pulpit," was reserved for the president of the church, but on this and other occasions JS deferred that pulpit to his father. (Corrill, *Brief History of the Church*, 21–22; Plan of the House of the Lord for the Presidency, 1833, CHL; Woodruff, Journal, 27 Nov. 1836.)

West end of lower court, House of the Lord. 1912. Presiding officers of the Melchizedek, or higher, priesthood sat in the west pulpits of the lower court during the dedication of the House of the Lord in Kirtland, Ohio, 27 March 1836. The center pulpit of the highest stand was reserved for the president of the church, but on this and other occasions, Joseph Smith yielded the seat to his father. (Church History Library, Salt Lake City. Photograph by C. Edward Miller.)

9 oclock A. M the servises of the day were opened by Presdt S. Rigdon by reading 1ˢᵗ the 96 Psalm[422] secondly the 24ᵗʰ Psalm—[423] the choir then sung hymn on the 29ᵗʰ page of Latter day Saints collection of hymn's—[424] prayer by Presdt Rigdon choir then sung hymn on 14ᵗʰ page[425] Presdt Rigdon then ⟨read⟩[426] the 18, 19, & 20, verses of the 8ᵗʰ chapter of Mathew and preached more particularly from the 20ᵗʰ verse.— his prayer and address were very forcibly ⟨forcible⟩ and sublime, and well adapted to the occasion.—[427] after he closed his services ⟨sermon⟩, he called upon the several quorums commenceing with the presidency, to manifest by rising up, their willingness to acknowledge me as a prophet and seer and uphold me as such by their p[r]ayers of faith, all the quorums in their turn, cheerfully complyed with this request he then called upon all the congregation of Saints, also to give their assent by rising on their feet which they did unanimously

After an intermission of 20, minutes[428] the servises of the day were resumed, by singing Adam ondi ahman.[429] /[430]I then made a short address and called upon the several quorums, and all the congregation of saints to acknowledge the Presidency as Prophets and Seers, and uphold them by their prayers, they

---

422. Psalm 96 admonishes its hearers to praise the Lord, for "strength and beauty are in his sanctuary," and to "come into his courts" (vv. 4–8). Latter-day Saints called the main floors of the House of the Lord "courts," as with the courts of Solomon's temple. (Revelation, 1 June 1833, in Doctrine and Covenants 95:3, 1835 ed. [D&C 95:15–17]; Minute Book 1, 3 June 1833; compare 2 Chronicles 4:9.)

423. Psalm 24 states that only those with "clean hands, and a pure heart" should enter the Lord's "holy place," where "the King of glory shall come in" (vv. 3–7).

424. Page 29 contains the beginning of Hymn 23, "Adam-ondi-Ahman," which actually opened the second session of the services. According to Oliver Cowdery's minutes, the choir first sang the millenarian Hymn 19, written by apostle Parley P. Pratt, which begins with the line "Ere long the vail will rend in twain." (Minutes, *LDS Messenger and Advocate*, Mar. 1836, 2:274; Hymn 19, *Collection of Sacred Hymns* [1835], 25–26.)

425. Hymn 8, by William W. Phelps. The hymn begins with the lines "O happy souls who pray / Where God appoints to hear! / O happy saints who pay / Their constant service there!" (*Collection of Sacred Hymns* [1835], 14–15.)

426. TEXT: Insertion in unidentified handwriting.

427. Matthew 8:20 contains Jesus's ironic comment that "the foxes have holes, and the birds of the air have nests; but the Son of man hath not where to lay his head." Rigdon preached for two and a half hours, comparing the Jewish sects described in the New Testament to the Protestant sects of early nineteenth-century America. Rigdon argued that in both cases, the rejection of revelation brought sectarian differences. (Minutes, *LDS Messenger and Advocate*, Mar. 1836, 2:275–276.)

428. With the exception of some women who left the building to check on their children, the congregation remained seated during the intermission, which took place in late morning. The day had been appointed for fasting. (Minutes, *LDS Messenger and Advocate*, Mar. 1836, 2:276; Post, Journal, 27 Mar. 1836; Benjamin Brown to Sarah M. Brown, Mar. 1836, Benjamin Brown Family Collection, CHL.)

429. Hymn 23, by William W. Phelps. (*Collection of Sacred Hymns* [1835], 29–30; see also "Adam-ondi-Ahman," in Geographical Directory.)

430. TEXT: Warren Parrish handwriting ends; unidentified begins.

all covenanted to do so by rising; I then called upon the quorums and congregation of saints to acknowledge the 12 [p. 175] Apostles who were present as Prophets and Seers and special witnesses to all the nations of the earth, holding the keys of the kingdom, to unlock it or cause it to be done among all nations them; and uphold them by their prayers, which they assented to by rising,[431]

I then called upon the quorums and congregation of saints to acknowledge the high council of Kirtland in all the authorities [authority] of the Melchisedec priesthood and uphold them by their prayers which they assented to by rising. I then called upon the quorums and congregation of saints to acknowledge and uphold by their prayer's the Bishops of Kirtland and Zion and their counsellors, the Presidents of the Priests in all the authority of the Aaronic priesthood, which they did by rising. I then called upon the quorums and congregation of saints to acknowledge the high-council of Zion, and uphold them by their prayers in all the authority of the high priesthood which they did by rising. I next called upon the quorums and congregation of saints to acknowledge the Presidents of the seventy's who act as their representives as ⟨Apostles and⟩ special witnesses to the nations to assist the 12 in opening the gospel kingdom, among all people and to uphold them by their prayer's which they did by rising— I then called upon the quorums and all the saints to acknowledge president of the Elders and his counsellors and uphold them by their prayers which they did by rising—. The quorums and congregation of saints were then called upon to acknowledge and uphold by their prayer's the Presidents of the Priests, Teachers, and Deacons and their counsellors, which they did by rising.

N. B. The Presidents were of the seventy's were acknowledged first after the 12 Apostles [p. 176]

The hymn on the hundred and 14 page was then sung,[432] after which I offered to God the following dedication prayer.

Prayer,
At the dedication of the Lord's House in Kirtland Ohio March 27, 1836.— by Joseph Smith, jr. President of the Church of the Latter Day Saints.[433]

---

431. TEXT: A pound sign inserted here is keyed to a corresponding pound sign inserted immediately before the note at the foot of page 176. Both insertions appear to be later redactions.

432. Hymn 84, by Isaac Watts, which begins, "How pleased and blest was I." The closing stanza reads, "My tongue repeats her vows, / 'Peace to this sacred house! / For here my friends and kindred dwell:' / And since my glorious God / Makes thee his blest abode, / My soul shall ever love thee well." (*Collection of Sacred Hymns* [1835], 114–115.)

433. The prayer was previously composed to be read at the dedication. (Cowdery, Diary, 26 Mar. 1836;

Thanks be to thy name, O Lord God of Israel, who keepest covenant and shewest mercy unto thy servants, who walk uprightly before
thee with all their hearts; thou who hast commanded thy servants to
build an house to thy name in this plase. (Kirtland.) And now thou
beholdest, O Lord, that so thy servants have done, according to thy
commandment. And now we ask the[e], holy Father, in the name of
Jesus Christ, the Son of thy bosom, in in whose name alone salvation
can be administered to the children of men: we ask the[e], O Lord, to
accept of this house, the workmanship of the hands of us, thy servants,
which thou didst command us to build; for thou knowest that we have
done this work through great tribulation: and out of our poverty we
have given of our substance to build a house to thy name, that the Son
of Man might have a place to manifest himself to his people.

And as thou hast said, in a revelation given unto us, calling us thy
friends, saying— "Call your solemn assembly, as I have commanded
you; and as all have not faith, seek ye diligently and teach one another
words of wisdom; yea, seek ye out of the best books words of wisdom:
Seek learning, even by study, and also by faith.

"Organize yourselves; prepare every ~~thing~~ needful thing, and
establish a house, even a house of prayer, a house [of] fasting, a house
of faith, a house of learning [p. 177] a house of glory, a house of order,
a house of God: that your incomings may be in the name of the Lord,
that your out goings may be in the name of the Lord: that all your
salutations may be in the name of the Lord, with uplifted hands to the
Most High."[434]

And now, Holy Father, we ask thee to assist us, thy people with thy
grace in calling our solemn assembly, that it may be done to thy honor,
and to thy divine acceptance, and in a manner that we may be found
worthy in thy sight, to secure a fulfilment of the promises which thou
hast made unto us thy people, in the revelatio[n]s given unto us: that thy
glory may rest down upon thy people, and upon this thy house, which
we now dedicate to thee, that it may be sanctified and consecrated to be
holy, and that thy holy presence may be continually in this house; and
that all people who shall enter upon the threshold of the Lord's house
may feel thy power and be constrained to acknowledge that thou hast
sanctified it, and that it is thy house, a place of thy holiness.

---

see also Prayer, 27 Mar. 1836, in *Prayer, at the Dedication of the Lord's House,* 1–2 [D&C 109].)
434. Quotation of Revelation, 27 and 28 Dec. 1832 and 3 Jan. 1833, in Doctrine and Covenants 7:36,
1835 ed. [D&C 88:117–120]. The same language is reiterated two paragraphs later in this prayer.

And do thou grant, holy Father, that all those who shall worship in this house, may be taught words of wisdom out of the best books, and that they may seek learning, even by study, and also by faith; as thou hast said; and that they may grow up in thee and receive a fulness of the Holy Ghost, and be organized according to thy laws, and be prepared to obtain every needful thing, and that this house may be a house of prayer, a house of fasting, a house of faith, a house of glory, and of God, even thy house: that all the incomings of thy people, into this house, may be in the name of the Lord; that all their outgoings, from this house, may be in the name of the Lord; that all their salutations may be in the name of [p. 178] Lord, with holy hands uplifted to the Most High; and that no unclean thing shall be permitted to come into thy house to pollute it.

And when thy people transgress, any of them, they may speedily repent and return unto thee, and find favour in thy sight, and be restored to the blessings which thou hast ordained, to be poured out upon those who shall reverence thee in this thy house.

And we ask, holy Father, that thy servants may go forth from this house, armed with thy power, and that thy name may be upon them and thy glory be round about them, and thine angels have charge over them; and from this place they may bear exceeding great and glorious tidings, in truth, unto the ends of the earth, that they may know that this is thy work, and that thou hast put forth thy hand, to fulfil that which thou hast spoken by the mouths of thy prophets concerning the last days.

We ask the[e]; holy Father; to establish the people that shall worship and honorably hold a name and standing in this thy house, to all generations, and for eternity that no weapon formed against them shall prosper; that he who diggeth a pit for them shall fall into the same himself; that no combination of wickedness shall have power to rise up and prevail over thy people, upon whom thy name shall be put in this house: and if any people shall rise against this people, that thine anger be kindled against them: and if they shall smite this people, thou wilt smite them— thou wilt fight for thy people as thou didst in the day of battle, that they may be delivered from the hands of all their enimies.

We ask thee, holy Father, to confound, and astonish, and bring to shame, and confusion, all those who have [p. 178][435] spread lying reports abroad over the world against thy servant or servants, if they will not

---

435. TEXT: The second of two pages numbered "178".

repent when the everlasting gospel shall be proclaimed in their ears, and that all their works may be brought to nought, and be swept away by the hail, and by the judgments, which thou wilt send upon them in thine anger, that their may be an end to lyings and slanders against thy people: for thou knowest, O Lord, that thy servants have been innocent before thee in bearing record of thy name for which they have suffered these things; therefore we plead before thee for a full and complete deliverence from under this yoke. Break it off O Lord: break it off from the necks of thy servants, by thy power, that we may rise up in the midst of this generation and do thy work!

O Jehovah, have mercy upon this people, and as all men sin, forgive the transgressions of thy people, and let them be blotted out forever. Let the anointing of thy ministers be sealed upon them with power from on high: let it be fulfilled upon them as upon those on the day of Pentacost: let the gift of tongues be poured out upon thy people, even cloven tongues as of fire, and the interpretation thereof. And let thy house be filled, as with a rushing mighty wind, with thy glory.

Put upon thy servants the testimony of the covenant that where they go out and proclaim thy word, they may seal up the law, and prepare the hearts of thy saints for all those judgements thou art about to send, in thy wrath, upon the inhabitants of the earth because of their transgressions, that thy people may not faint in the day of trouble. [p. 179]

And whatever city thy servants shall enter, and the people of that city receive their testimony, let thy peace and thy salvation be upon that city, that they may gather out from that city the righteous, that they may come forth to Zion, or to her stakes, the places of thine appointment, with songs of everlasting joy,— and until this be accomplished let not thy judgements fall upon that city.

And whatever city thy servants shall enter, and the people of that city receive not their testimony of thy servants, and thy servants warn them to save themselves from this untoward generation let it be upon that city according to that which thou hast spoken, by the mouths of thy prophets; but deliver thou, O Jehovah, we beseech thee, thy servants from their hands, and cleanse them from their blood. O Lord, we delight not in the destruction of our fellow men: their souls are precious before thee; but thy word must be fulfilled:— help thy servants to say, with thy grace assisting them, thy will be done, O Lord, and not our⟨s⟩.

We know that thou hast spoken by the mouth of thy prophets, terrible things concerning the wicked in the last days, that thou wilt pour out thy judgements; without measure; therefore, O Lord, deliver thy people from the calamity of the wicked; enable thy servants to seal up the law and bind up the testimony, that they may be prepared against the day of burning.

We ask thee, holy Father, to remember those who have been driven by the inhabitants of Jackson county Missouri, from the lands of their inheritance, and break off, O Lord, this yoke of affliction [p. 180] that has been put upon them. Thou knowest, O Lord, that they have been greatly oppressed and afflicted, by wicked men, and our hearts flow out in sorrow because of their grevious burdens. O Lord, how long wilt thou suffer this people to bear this affliction, and the cries of the innocent ones to ascend up in thine ears, and their blood to come up in testimony before thee and not make a display of thy power in their behalf?

Have mercy, O Lord, upon that wicked mob, who have driven thy people, that they may cease to spoil, that they may repent of their sins, if repentance is to be found; but if they will not, make bare thine arm, O Lord, and redeem that which thou didst appoint a Zion unto thy people.

And if it cannot be otherwise, that the cause of thy people may not fail before thee, may thine anger be kindled and thine indignation fall upon them that they may be wasted away, both root and branch from under heaven; but inasmuch as they will repent, thou art gracious and merciful, and will turn away thy wrath, when thou lookest upon the face of thine anointed.

Have mercy, O Lord, upon all the nations of the earth: have mercy upon the rulers of our land may those principles which were so honorably and nobly defended: viz, the constitution of our land, by our fathers, be established forever.

Remember the kings, the princes, the nobles, and the great ones of the earth, and all people; and the churches: all the poor, the needy and the afflicted ones of the earth, that their hearts may be softened when thy servants shall go out from thy house, O [p. 181] Jehovah, to bear testimony of thy name, ⟨that⟩ their prejudices may give way before the truth, and thy people may obtain favour in the sight of all, that all the ends of the earth may know that we thy servants have heard thy voice, and that thou hast sent us, that from among all these thy servants, the sons of Jacob, may gather out the righteous to build a holy city to thy name, as thou hast commanded them.

We ask thee to appoint unto Zion other stakes besides this one, which thou hast appointed, that the gathering of thy people may roll on in great power and majesty, that thy work may be cut short in righteousness.

Now these words, O Lord, we have spoken before thee, concerning the revelations and commandments which thou hast given unto us, who are i[de]ntified with the Gentiles;— But thou knowest that we have a great love for the children of Jacob who have been scattered upon the mountains; for a long time in a cloudy and dark day.

We therefore ask thee to have mercy upon the children of Jacob, that Jerusalem, from this hour, may begin to be redeemed; and the yoke of bondage may begin to be broken off from the house of David, and the children of Judah may begin to return to the lands which thou didst give to Abraham, their father, and cause that the remnants of Jacob, who have been cursed and smitten, because of their transgression, to be converted from their wild and savage condition, to the fulness of the everlasting gospel, that they may lay down their weapons of bloodshed and cease their rebellions. And may [p. 182] all the scattered remnants of Israel, who have been driven to the ends of the earth, come to a knowledge of the truth, believe in the Messiah, and be redeemed from oppression, and rejoice before thee.

O Lord, remember thy servant Joseph Smith jr. and all his afflictions and persecutions, how he has covenanted with Jehovah and vowed to thee O mighty God of Jacob, and the commandments which thou hast given unto him, and that he hath sincerely strove to do thy will.— Have mercy, O Lord, upon his wife and children, that they may be exalted in thy presence, and preserved by thy fostering hand,— Have mercy upon all their immediate connexions, that their prejudices may be broken up, and swept away as with a flood, that they may be converted and redeemed with Israel and know that thou art God.

Remember, O Lord, the presidents, even all the presidents of thy church, that thy right hand may exalt them with all their families, and their immediate connexions, that their names may be perpetuated and had in everlasting remembrance from generation to generation.

Remember all thy church, O Lord, with all their families, and all their immediate connexions, with all their sick and afflicted ones, with all the poor and meek of the earth; that the kingdom which thou hast set up without hands, may become a great mountain and fill the whole earth, that thy church may come forth out of the wilderness of darkness, and shine forth fair as the moon, clear as the sun, and terrible as an army with banners, and be adorned as a bride for that day when [p. 183] thou shalt unveil the heavens, and cause the mountains to flow down at thy presence, and the valley's to be exalted, the rough places made smooth; that thy glory may fill the earth.

That when the trump shall sound for the dead, we shall be caught up in the cloud to meet thee, that we may ever be with the Lord, that our garments may be pure, that we may be clothed upon with robes of righteousness, with palms in our hands, and crowns of glory upon our heads, and reap eternal joy for all our sufferings.

O Lord, God Almighty, hear us in these our petitions, and answer us from heaven, thy holy habitation, where thou sittest enthroned, with glory, honour, power majesty, might, dominion, truth, justice judgement, mercy and an infinity of fulness, from everlasting to everlasting.

O hear, O hear, O hear us, O Lord, and answer these petitions, and accept the dedication of this house, unto thee, the work of our hands, which we have built unto thy name; and also this church to put upon it thy name. And help us by the power of thy spirit, that we may mingle our voices with those bright shining seraphs, around thy throne with acclamations of praise, singing hosanna to God and the Lamb: and let these thine anointed ones be clothed with salvation, and thy saints shout aloud for joy.

Amen and Amen.

/[436]Sung Hosanah to God and the Lamb[437] after which the Lords supper was administered

I then bore testimony of the administering of angels.—[438] Presdt Williams also arose and testified that while Presdt Rigdon was making [p. 184] his first

---

436. TEXT: Unidentified handwriting ends; Warren Parrish begins.

437. Hymn 90, by William W. Phelps, which begins with the line "The Spirit of God like a fire is burning." The chorus emphasized the idea of angels joining the Latter-day Saints as they shouted hosannas and amens in the temple. The six stanzas of the hymn addressed every major aspect of the rituals, ceremonies, and eschatology that were featured in the House of the Lord: an endowment of power from on high, solemn assemblies, washing and anointing, washing of feet, proselytizing, the gathering of Israel, the second coming of Jesus Christ, and the millennial reign of peace. Following the hymn, JS asked whether the quorums and congregation approved of the dedicatory prayer. The voting was unanimously affirmative. (*Collection of Sacred Hymns* [1835], 120–121; Minutes, *LDS Messenger and Advocate,* Mar. 1836, 2:280–281.)

438. Oliver Cowdery's minutes report that JS "arose and bore record of his mission." Stephen Post recorded that JS "testified of the Angel of the Lord's appearing unto him to call him to the work of the Lord, & also of being ordained under the hands of the Angel of the covenant." (Minutes, *LDS Messenger and Advocate,* Mar. 1836, 2:281; Post, Journal, 27 Mar. 1836.)

prayer an angel entered the window and ⟨took his⟩ seated ~~himself~~ between father Smith, and himself, and remained their during his prayer[439] Presdt David Whitmer also saw angels in the house[440]

We then sealed the proceedings of the day by a shouting hosanah to God and the Lamb 3 times sealing it each time with Amen, Amen, and Amen[441] and after requesting all the official members to meet again in the evening we retired—[442]

met in the evening and instructed the quorums respecting the ordinance of washing of feet which we were to attend to on wednesday following[443]

28 March 1836 • Monday

Monday the 28. M[ar]ch 1836 Attended school— nothing worthy of note transpired

29 March 1836 • Tuesday

Tuesday the 29th Attended school, which was the last day of our course of lectures in Hebrew by Professor [Joshua] Seixas,—[444] ~~After we dismissed made~~

---

439. Stephen Post recorded Williams stating that the angel came through the window behind the pulpit. Edward Partridge recorded that "Williams saw an angel" but interlinearly inserted "or rather the Savior"—possibly conflating Williams's vision of an angel with the vision of Jesus Christ shared by JS and Oliver Cowdery a week later. Years later, Truman Angell recalled that JS identified this angel as the apostle Peter. (Post, Journal, 27 Mar. 1836; Minutes, *LDS Messenger and Advocate,* Mar. 1836, 2:281; Partridge, Journal, 27 Mar. 1836; Angell, Autobiography, 16.)

440. Years later, George A. Smith recalled that David Whitmer said he saw three angels during the meeting that was held on the evening of this day. (George A. Smith, in *Journal of Discourses,* 15 Nov. 1864, 11:10.)

441. See "Hosanna," in Glossary. Following the Hosanna Shout, Brigham Young and David W. Patten spoke and sang in tongues, after which JS "blessed the congregation in the name of the Lord." (Minutes, *LDS Messenger and Advocate,* Mar. 1836, 2:281; Post, Journal, 28 Mar. 1836.)

442. Oliver Cowdery's minutes record that the meeting ended "a little past four P. M.," seven hours after it began. (Minutes, *LDS Messenger and Advocate,* Mar. 1836, 2:281.)

443. Benjamin Brown wrote that when JS opened this meeting, he declared that "the day of Penticost was continued." Stephen Post recorded that JS expounded on "the order of dedicating a house to God" from the account of Solomon's temple dedication in 2 Chronicles 6 and gave instruction "relative to our preaching & to our endowment." Post also recorded that "Angels of God came into the room, cloven tongues rested upon some of the Servants of the Lord like unto fire, & they spake with tongues & prophesied." Oliver Cowdery recorded, "The Spirit was poured out—I saw the glory of God, like a great cloud, come down and rest upon the house, and fill the same like a mighty rushing wind. I also saw cloven tongues, like as of fire rest upon many, (for there were 316 present,) while they spake with other tongues and prophesied." (Benjamin Brown to Sarah M. Brown, Mar. 1836, Benjamin Brown Family Collection, CHL; Post, Journal, 27 and 28 Mar. 1836; Cowdery, Diary, 27 Mar. 1836; see also Partridge, Journal, 27 Mar. 1836.)

444. This concluded the eight weeks and two days of instruction received by JS and other Latter-day Saints. The following day Seixas signed a certificate that recorded JS's completion of the course and encouraged him to continue his studies. In the years to come, JS occasionally studied Hebrew and used

~~some arangements for our meeting on the morrow; attended to my domestick concirns, nothing very special transpired~~

~~At evening I met with the presidency in the Temple of the Lord and the Lord commanded us to tarry and santify ourselves by washing our feet~~

At 11 oclock A. M. Presidents Joseph Smith jun Frederick G. Williams, Sidney Rigdon, Hyrum Smith, and Oliver Cowdery met in the most holy place in the Lords house[445] and sought for a revelation from Him, to teach us concerning our going to Zion, and other im[p. 185]portant matter after uniting in prayer, the voice of the Spirit was that we should come into this place three times, and also call the other presidents, the two Bishops and their councils (each to stand in his place) and fast through the day and also the night and that during this, if we would humble ourselves, we should receive further communication from Him.

After this word was received, we immediately sent for the other brethren who came. The presidency proceeded to ordain George Boosinger to the high priesthood and annoint him.

This was in consequence of his having administered unto us in temporal things in our distress. And also because he left the place just previous to the dedication of the Lords house to bring us the temporal means previously named.

Soon after this, the word of the Lord came to us through Presdt. J. Smith jun that those who had entered the holy place[446] must not leave the house untill morning but send for such things as were necessary, and also, that during our stay we must cleans ourt feet and partake of the sacrament that we might be made holy before Him, and thereby be qualified to officiate in our calling upon the morrow in washing the feet of the Elders.

Accordingly we proceeded and cleansed our faces and our feet, and then proceeded to wash each others feet.— president S. Rigdon first washed presdt J. Smith jun and then in [p. 186] turn was washed by him— after which president Rigdon washed presdt J. Smith Se͟n. and Hyrum Smith ⟨prsdt⟩ J. Smith jun washed presdt F. G Williams, and then pres. Hyrum Smith washed president David Whitmer's feet and president Oliver Cowdery's, then pres

his knowledge of the language in sermons and writings. (Certificate, J. Seixas to JS, Kirtland, OH, 30 Mar. 1836, JS Collection, CHL; Ogden, "Kirtland Hebrew School," 163–166; see also Zucker, "Joseph Smith as a Student of Hebrew"; and Walton, "Professor Seixas.")

445. Probably the veil-enclosed pulpits on the west side of the lower court, which were separately consecrated before the general dedication two days earlier. (See JS, Journal, 27 Mar. 1836, p. 200 herein.)

446. Probably the lower court, or ground level, of the House of the Lord, where foot washing occurred the following day as well. (Partridge, Journal, 30 Mar. 1836.)

D. Whitmer washed pres. W[illiam] W. Phelps feet and in turn pres Phelps washed pres John Whitmers feet.

The Bishops and their councils were then washed:[447] After which we partook of the bread and wine.[448] The Holy S[p]irit rested down upon us and we continued in the Lords house all night prophesying and giving glory to God[449]

30 March 1836 • Wednesday

/[450]Wedensday morning 8 o clock March 30th 1836 According to appointment the presidency, the 12, the seventies, the high ~~councils~~ councils, the Bishops and their entire quorums, the Elders, and all the official members in this stake of Zion amounting to about 300 met in the temple of the Lord to attend to the ordinance of washing of feet,[451] I ascended the pulpit and remarked to the congregation that we had passed through many trials and afflictions since the organization of this church and that this is a year of Jubilee to us and a time of rejoicing,[452] and that it was expedient for us to prepare bread and wine sufficient to make our hearts glad, as we should not probably leave this house until morning; to this end we should call on the brethren to make a contrubution, the stewards passed round and took up a liberal contribution and messengers were dispatched for bread and wine; tubs water and towels were prepared ⟨and⟩ I called the house to order, and the presidency proceeded to wash the feet of the 12 pronouncing many prophecy's and blessings upon them in the name of the Lord Jesus, the brethren began to

---

447. The washing of feet constituted the last of the rituals that also included washing, anointing, and blessing. The officers who received the ordinance this day administered it to others at the solemn assembly the next day.

448. Missouri bishop Edward Partridge recorded that the washing of feet lasted "till about dusk," after which those present "partook of bread and wine a feast." Missouri president William W. Phelps wrote that "they partook of the sacrament, as the Passover." (Partridge, Journal, 29 Mar. 1836; William W. Phelps, Kirtland, OH, to Sally Phelps, Liberty, MO, Apr. 1836, William W. Phelps, Papers, BYU.)

449. Missouri bishop Edward Partridge recorded that those present "prophesied and spake in tongues & shouted hosannas. the meeting lasted till day light." (Partridge, Journal, 29 Mar. 1836; see also W. Phelps to S. Phelps, Apr. 1836.)

450. TEXT: Warren Parrish handwriting ends; unidentified begins.

451. Though women participated in the dedication, only men with priesthood ordination attended this session. George A. Smith later remarked that some Mormon women were upset that the solemn assembly was exclusively for men. (George A. Smith, in *Journal of Discourses*, 18 Mar. 1855, 2:215.)

452. An allusion to the Israelite year of Jubilee, a special sabbatical year occurring every fifty years. The sabbatical year followed the seventh cycle of seven years. The Mormon jubilee paralleled in some respects the Israelite Jubilee, which was begun at the temple on the Day of Atonement—a day of fasting on which the high priest of Israel performed ritual purifications in the temple for the redemption of Israel and its priests. The church celebrated the jubilee for the seven days preceding the beginning of the church's seventh year since organization. (Leviticus 16; 25:8–10; W. Phelps to S. Phelps, Apr. 1836.)

prophesy [p. 187] upon each others heads, and cursings upon the enimies of Christ who inhabit Jackson county Missouri continued prophesying and blessing and sealing them with Hosanna and Amen until nearly 7 o clock P.M.[453] the bread ⟨& wine⟩ was then brought in, and I observed that we had fasted all the day; and lest we faint; as the Saviour did so shall we do on this occasion, we shall bless the bread and give it to the 12 and they to the multitude, after which we shall bless the wine and do likewise;[454] while waiting ~~for the wine~~ I made the following remarks, that the time that we were required to tarry in Kirtland to be endued would be fulfilled in a few days,[455] and then the Elders would go forth and each must stand for himself, that it was not necessary for them to be sent out two by two as in former times;[456] but to go in all meekness in sobriety and preach Jesus Christ & him crucified not to contend with others on the account

---

453. Edward Partridge recorded that "the priests teachers & deacons [were] in one corner the vails having been let down, and the other officers occupied the rest of the lower room." Stephen Post reported that "the washing was commenced by the presidents who first washed the 12 & the 7 presidents of the seventies the 12 & 7 then commenced washing until the whole were washed." According to Partridge, "The washing of feet was performed by noon, then they began to prophecy and speak in tongues adding shouts of hosanna, to God and the Lamb with amen and amen this continued till dark." Similarly, Post recorded that the men "prophesied, spake and sang in tongues" in the four parts of the curtained lower court. (Partridge, Journal, 30 Mar. 1836; Post, Journal, 30 Mar. 1836.)

454. An allusion not only to Matthew 15:32–38—when Jesus fed the multitude bread and fish "lest they faint"—but also to the Book of Mormon, 1830 ed., 490–491, 496 [3 Nephi 18:1–11; 20:1–9]—when Jesus administered bread and wine as the sacrament of the Lord's Supper. William W. Phelps wrote that "the sacrament was administered, as the feast of the Passover for the first time in more than 1800 years."[a] Most Jews began their weeklong Passover celebrations two days later on the evening of 1 April.[b] Stephen Post recorded that the men "partook of bread & wine in commemoration of the marriage supper of the Lamb," a phrase mentioned in Revelation 19:9 as a symbolic representation of the second coming of Jesus Christ.[c] In November 1835, JS taught that after the completion of the temple, Latter-day Saints would "stand in holy places ready to meet the bride groom when he comes."[d] (a. W. Phelps to S. Phelps, Apr. 1836; compare Snow, Journal, [24]. b. Ricks, "Appearance of Elijah and Moses," 484–485. c. Post, Journal, 30 Mar. 1836. d. JS, Journal, 12 Nov. 1835.)

455. William W. Phelps wrote that the jubilee and Passover that began at the solemn assembly ended a week later on 6 April, which date was "set apart as a day of prayer, to end The feast of the passover. and in honor of the Jubilee of the church: it being Six years to this day." However, Phelps also wrote that elders began leaving Kirtland on 1 April. (W. Phelps to S. Phelps, Apr. 1836; see also Partridge, Journal, 6 Apr. 1836.)

456. John Corrill later explained that now "every man was accountable to God for his own doings."[a] Previous revelations instructed Latter-day Saint elders to travel "two by two" according to New Testament pattern,[b] although some elders, such as Peter Dustin, traveled alone.[c] In the months following the endowment, William E. McLellin, Erastus Snow, and perhaps others proselytized alone, but this change in practice apparently became neither widespread nor long standing.[d] (a. Corrill, Brief History of the Church, 26. b. Revelation, 9 Feb. 1831, in Doctrine and Covenants 13:2, 1835 ed. [D&C 42:6]; Revelation, 6 June 1831, in Doctrine and Covenants 66:3, 1835 ed. [D&C 52:10]; Mark 6:7; Luke 10:1. c. William W. Phelps, Kirtland Mills, OH, to Sally Phelps, Liberty, MO, 16 Sept. 1835, CHL. d. Erastus Snow, Kirtland, OH, 30 Dec. 1836, letter to the editor, LDS Messenger and Advocate, Jan. 1837, 3:440; McLellin, Journal, Apr.–June 1836.)

of their faith or systems of religion but pursue a steady course, this I delivered by way of commandment, and all that observe them not will pull down persecution upon ~~your~~ ⟨thier⟩ heads, while those who do shall always be filled with the Holy Ghost, this I pronounced as a prophesy, sealed with a Hosanna & amen. Also that the seventies are not called to serve tables[457] or preside over churches to settle difficulties, but to preach the gospel and build them up, and set others who do not belong to these quorums to preside over them who are high priests— the twelve also are not to serve tables, but to bear the keys of the kingdom to all nations, and unlock them and call upon the seventies to follow after them and assist them. The 12 are at liberty to go wheresoever they will [p. 188] and if one shall say, I wish to go to such a place let all the rest say Amen.

The seventies are at liberty to go to Zion if they please or go wheresoever they will and preach the gospel and let the redemtion of Zion be our object, and strive to affect it by sending up all the strength of the Lords house whereever we find them,[458] and I want to enter into the following covenant, that if any more of our brethren are slain or driven from their lands in Missouri by the mob that we will give ourselves no rest until we are avenged of our enimies to the uttermost, this covenant was sealed unaminously by a hosanna and Amen.— I then observed to the ~~quorums~~— quorum⟨s⟩ that I had now completed ~~their~~ organization of the church and we had passed through all the necessary ceremonies, that I had given them all the instruction they needed and that they now were at liberty after obtaining their lisences to go forth and build up the kingdom of God,[459] and that it was expedient for me and the presidency to retire, having spent the night previous in waiting upon the Lord in his temple, and having to attend another dedication on the morrow, or conclude the one commenced on the last sabbath for the benifit of those of my brethren and sisters who could not get into the house on the former occasion but that it was expedient for the brethren to tarry all night and worship before the Lord in his house I left the meeting in the charge of the 12 and retired at about 9 o clock in the evening; the brethren continued exhorting, prophesying and speaking in tongues until 5 o clock in the morning— the Saviour made

---

457. That is, to involve themselves in local ministry—see Acts 6:1–4.

458. This reflects the language in several JS revelations. (Revelation, 16 and 17 Dec. 1833, in Doctrine and Covenants 97:7, 1835 ed. [D&C 101:55–58]; Revelation, 24 Feb. 1834, in Doctrine and Covenants 101:5, 1844 ed. [D&C 103:22]; Revelation, 22 June 1834, in Doctrine and Covenants 102:5, 1844 ed. [D&C 105:16].)

459. Several church leaders had their licenses renewed on this day. By the end of May, JS issued almost three hundred of the new licenses mandated by the licensing reforms of 3 March 1836. (JS, Journal, 3 Mar. 1836; Kirtland Elders' Certificates, 1–157, CHL.)

his appearance to some,[460] while angels minestered unto others, and it was a penticost and enduement indeed, long to be remembered for the sound shall go forth from this place into all the [p. 189] world, and the occurrences of this day shall be handed down upon the pages of sacred history to all generations, as the day of Pentecost, so shall this day be numbered and celebrated as a year of Jubilee and time of rejoicing to the saints of the most high God.

31 March 1836 • Thursday

Thursday morning 8 o clock March 31st This day being set apart to perform again the ceremonies of the dedication for the benifit of those who could not get into the house on the preceeding sabbath I repaired to the temple at 8 o clock A.M. in company with the presidency, and arranged our door-keepers and stewards as on the former occasion, we then opened the doors and a large congregation entered the house and were comfortably seated, the authorities of the church were seated, in their respective order and the services of the day were commenced prosecuted and terminated in the same manner as at the former dedication and the spirit of God rested upon the congregation and great solemnity prevailed.[461]

1 April 1836 • Friday

/[462]Friday th[e] 1st day of April 1836 At home most of the day, many brethren called to see me. some on temporal & some on Spiritual buisiness, among the number was Leeman [Leman] Copley, who testified against me in a suit I brought against Doctor P. Hulburt [Philastus Hurlbut] for threatning my life, he confessed that he bore a fals testimony against me, in that suit but verily thought at the time that he was right but on calling to mind all all the circumstances connected the with the things that transpired at that time he was [p. 190] convinced that he was wrong, and humbly confessed it and asked my forgivness, which was readily granted, he also wished to be received into the church again by baptism, and was received according to his desire, he gave me his confession in writing/[463]

---

460. Four months earlier, JS taught the twelve apostles that "all who are prepared and are sufficiently pure to abide the presence of the Saviour will see him in the solem assembly." (JS, Journal, 12 Nov. 1835.)

461. At the second dedication, attendees almost filled the meeting room on the ground floor. The meeting generally followed the order of the initial dedication but lasted until about nine o'clock that night, five hours longer than the first dedication. William W. Phelps wrote that the second dedication surpassed the first "in sublimity and solemnity as well as in order." (Partridge, Journal, 31 Mar. 1836; Post, Journal, 31 Mar. 1836; William W. Phelps, Kirtland, OH, to Sally Phelps, Liberty, MO, Apr. 1836, William W. Phelps, Papers, BYU.)

462. TEXT: Unidentified handwriting ends; Warren Parrish begins.

463. TEXT: Warren Parrish handwriting ends.

———— ∾ ————

Editorial Note

The journal ends with two entries penned by Warren Cowdery, a scribe who had been writing history for JS. Unlike Warren Parrish and other scribes in this journal, who referred to themselves in the third person and JS in the first, Warren Cowdery referred to JS in the third person. Cowdery's work on JS's 1834–1836 history also produced third-person accounts. In that endeavor, he had before him a first-person text (the earlier entries of this journal), which he changed to third person as he copied them into the history.

The first of Cowdery's entries and the opening of the second read as if Cowdery were an observer of what he described. The account of the 3 April vision of Jesus Christ, however, reports details and a long direct quotation that only the two participants—JS and Warren's younger brother Oliver Cowdery—could have known. For this material, Warren Cowdery must have relied on another original text—no longer extant—or on oral reports from either or both of the participants. If Warren Cowdery was working from a prior text, that would directly parallel the method that produced the third-person 1834–1836 history. This account of the vision was later recast in first person as part of the history JS began in 1838, and in that form it was incorporated into the published Latter-day Saint canon (D&C 110) in 1876.[464]

———— ∾ ————

2 April 1836 • Saturday

/[465]Saturday April 2ᵈ Transacted business, (although of a temporal nature) in company with S[idney] Rigdon, O[liver] Cowdery, J[ohn] Whitmer F[rederick] G. Williams, D. Whimer [David Whitmer] & W[illiam] W. Phelps, which was to have a bearing upon the redemption of Zion.[466] The positive manner in which he expressed himself on this, ⟨his⟩ favorite theme, was directly calculated to produce conviction in the minds of those who heard him, that his whole soul was engaged in it. notwithstanding on a superficial view of the same subject they might differ from him in judgement. It was determined in council, after mature deliberation, that he and O. Cowdery should act in concert in raising funds for the accomplishment of the aforesaid object.[467] As soon as the above plan was settled, he and O. Cowdery set out together, and their success was such in one half day, as to give them pleasing

---

464. JS History, vol. B-1, 727–728.

465. TEXT: Warren Cowdery handwriting begins.

466. This meeting, composed of the members of F. G. Williams & Co., took place in the upper room of the printing office and was convened to find ways to settle debts of the firm and raise money for purchasing land in Missouri. This meeting may also have initiated the dissolution of the firm, which occurred two months later. (Minute Book 1, 2 Apr. 1836; "Notice," *LDS Messenger and Advocate,* June 1836, 2:329; see also 197n407 herein.)

467. Williams and Rigdon were appointed to settle debts of the firm, while JS and Cowdery were appointed to raise money for purchasing land in Missouri. (Minute Book 1, 2 Apr. 1836.)

West pulpits, lower court, House of the Lord. 1934. During a Sunday meeting on 3 April 1836, Joseph Smith and Oliver Cowdery secluded themselves behind the hanging temple curtains at the west pulpits of the lower court. Warren Cowdery, brother to Oliver Cowdery and scribe to Joseph Smith, recorded in Smith's journal that they there experienced visions of Jesus Christ and ancient prophets. (Courtesy Library of Congress, Washington DC. Photograph by Carl F. Waite.)

anticipations, ~~and~~ assure them that they were doing the will of God and that his work prospered in their hands

3 April 1836 · Sunday

Sabbath April 3ᵈ He attended meeting in the Lord's House, assisted the other Presidents of the Church in seating the congregation and then became an attentive listener to the preaching from the Stand. T[homas] B. Marsh & D[avid] W. Patten[468] spoke in the A. M. to an attentive audience of about 1000 persons. In the P. M. he assisted the other Presidents in distributing the elements of the Lords Supper to the church, receiving them from the ~~Hands~~ "Twelve" whose privilige it was to officiate in the sacred desk this day.[469] After having performed this service to his brethren, he retired to the pulpit, the vails being dropped,[470] [p. 191] and bowed himself with O. Cowdery, in solemn, but silent prayer to the Most High. After rising from prayer the following vision[471] was opened to both of them.

The vail was taken from their minds and the eyes of their understandings were opened. They saw the Lord standing upon the breast work of the pulpit before them. and under his feet was a paved work of pure gold, in color like amber: his eyes were as a flame of fire; the hair of his head was like the pure snow, his countenance shone above the brightness of the sun,[472] and his voice was as the sound of the rushing of great waters, even the Voice of Jehovah, saying, I am the first and the last. I am he who liveth. I am he who was slain.[473] I am your Advocate with the Father. Behold your sins are forgiven you.[474] You are clean before me, therefore, lift up your heads and rejoice, let the hearts of your brethren rejoice and let the hearts of all my ~~brethren~~ ⟨people⟩ rejoice, who have with their might, built this house to my name. For behold I have accepted this house and my name shall be here; and I will manifest myself to my people, in mercy, in this House, Yea I will appear unto my servants and speak unto

---

468. The two most senior members of the Quorum of the Twelve.

469. The administration of the sacrament of the Lord's Supper, as well as confirmations and blessings of children, took place simultaneously in the four sections of the lower court, which was divided by curtains at this time. (Post, Journal, 3 Apr. 1836.)

470. According to Stephen Post, "The presidency took the pulpit during the confirmation & blessing of the children." The veils not only enclosed the pulpits but subdivided them into their four levels. JS and Cowdery apparently secluded themselves within the top tier, which was reserved for the presidency. (Post, Journal, 3 Apr. 1836; Robison, *First Mormon Temple,* 19, 85; see also William W. Phelps, Kirtland, OH, to Sally Phelps, Liberty, MO, Apr. 1836, William W. Phelps, Papers, BYU.)

471. Now D&C 110.

472. See Acts 26:13.

473. See Revelation 1:13–18.

474. See 1 John 2:1, 12; and Revelation, Sept. 1830–A, in Doctrine and Covenants 10:1–2, 1835 ed. [D&C 29:3, 5].

and bowed himself with O. Cowdery, in solemn but silent prayer to the Most High. After rising from prayer the following vision was opened to both of them.

The vail was taken from their minds and the eyes of their understandings were opened. They saw the Lord standing upon the breast work of the pulpit before them, and under his feet was a paved work of pure gold, in color like amber; his eyes were as a flame of fire, the hair of his head was like the pure snow, his countenance shone above the brightness of the sun, and his voice was as the sound of the rushing of great waters, even the voice of Jehovah, saying I am the first and the last, I am he who liveth, I am he who was slain, I am your Advocate with the Father, Behold your sins are forgiven you, you are clean before me, therefore, lift up your heads and rejoice, let the hearts of your brethren rejoice and let the hearts of all my people rejoice, who have with their might, built this house to my name. For behold I have accepted this house and my name shall be here; and I will manifest myself to my people in mercy in this House. Yea I will appear unto my servants and speak unto them with mine own voice, if my people will keep my commandments and do not pollute this Holy House. Yea the hearts of thousands and tens of thousands shall greatly rejoice in consequence of the blessings which shall be poured out, and the endowment with which my servants have already been endowed and shall hereafter be endowed in this House. And the fame of this House shall spread to foreign lands, and this is the beginning of the blessing which shall

them with mine own voice, if my people will keep my commandments and do not pollute this Holy House. Yea the hearts of thousands and tens of thousands shall greatly rejoice in consequence of the blessings which shall be poured out, and the endowment with which my servants have already been endowed and shall hereafter be endowed in this House. and the fame of this House shall spread to foreign lands, and this is the beginning of the blessing, which shall [p. 192] be poured out upon the heads of my people. even so amen. After this vision closed, the Heavens were again opened unto them and Moses appeared before them and committed unto them the Keys of the gathering of Israel from the four parts of the Eearth and the leading of the ten tribes from the Land of the North.[475] After this Elias appeared and committed the dispensation of the gospel of Abraham, saying, that in them and their seed all generations after them should be blessed.[476] After this vision had closed, another great and glorious vision burts [burst] upon them, for Elijah, the Prophet, who was taken to Heaven without tasting death,[477] also stood before them, and said, behold the time has fully come which was spoken of by the mouth of Malachi, testifying, that he should be sent before the great and dreadful day of the Lord come, to turn the hearts of the Fathers to the children, and the children to the fathers, lest the whole earth be smitten with a curse.[478] Therefore, the Keys of this dispensation are committed into your hands, and by this ye may know that the great and the dreadful day of the Lord is near, even at the doors[479] [*12 lines blank*] [p. 193]

---

475. JS's translation of the Book of Mormon, as well as subsequent prophecies, stated that in the last days the lost ten tribes would return from the "north countries." (Book of Mormon, 1830 ed., 488, 567 [3 Nephi 17:4; Ether 13:11]; Revelation, 3 Nov. 1831, in Doctrine and Covenants 100:3, 1835 ed. [D&C 133:26]; JS, Kirtland, OH, to N. C. Saxton, Rochester, NY, 4 Jan. 1833, in JS Letterbook 1, pp. 14–18.)

476. JS used the generic name "Elias" to refer to various messengers who appeared as "forerunners" to the first or second comings of Jesus Christ. (See, for example, New Testament Revision 2, part 2, p. 106 [Joseph Smith Translation, John 1:26]; New Testament Revision 1, p. 42 [Joseph Smith Translation, Matthew 17:14]; Revelation, ca. Aug. 1830, in Doctrine and Covenants 50:2, 1835 ed. [D&C 27:6–7]; and Woodruff, Journal, 10 Mar. 1844.)

477. See 2 Kings 2:11.

478. See Malachi 4:5–6; and Revelation, ca. Aug. 1830, in Doctrine and Covenants 50:2, 1835 ed. [D&C 27:9]. JS later recounted that the visit of Elijah was foretold by the angel Moroni in 1823. He also taught that Elijah restored the keys "of the fulness of the Melchezedek Priesthood," including the authority to perform ceremonies that would "seal" for eternal duration marriages and parent-child relationships for both the living and the dead. (JS History, vol. A-1, 5–6; Robert B. Thompson, Sermon notes, 5 Oct. 1840, JS Collection, CHL; Coray, Notebook, 13 Aug. 1843; JS, Journal, 27 Aug. 1843, JS Collection, CHL; Woodruff, Journal, 10 Mar. 1844.)

479. See Malachi 4:5; Matthew 24:33; and Mark 13:29.

———— ∞ ————

Editorial Note

This account of visitations closes the journal. After more than six months of almost daily recording of developments in Kirtland, entries ceased. For nearly two years, there were no more entries written in this or in any other JS journal.

Religious gatherings in the newly completed temple continued. According to an account Heber C. Kimball dictated about three years later, the following Wednesday, 6 April 1836—the sixth anniversary of the organization of the church—was especially significant. Church officers fasted and gathered in the temple. After the men had observed the Lord's Supper and the ritual of washing of feet, "the meeting continued on through the night, the spirit of prophecy was poured out upon the Assembly. . . . also Angels administered to many, for they were seen by many." Kimball remembered "a marvellous spirit of prophecy" that continued for several days. The men who had shared these experiences in the House of the Lord visited "from house to house, administering bread and wine, and pronouncing blessings upon each other."[480] Others later remembered an intensity of spirit associated with the temple for weeks, even months. Eliza R. Snow wrote of "an abiding holy heavenly influence" following the dedication and declared that "many extraordinary manifestations" of God's power were experienced after the events recorded in this journal.[481]

Revelation had declared that being "endowed with power from on high" was a prerequisite for the redemption of Zion in Missouri,[482] and once that prerequisite was met, JS and his associates immediately turned their attention to fund raising and other preparations for the redemption of Zion. By the time JS's diary entries resumed in March 1838, conditions for JS in Ohio had deteriorated to the point that he had moved to Missouri and to a new set of challenges and opportunities.

———— ∞ ————

480. Kimball, "History," 43; see also William W. Phelps, Kirtland, OH, to Sally Phelps, Liberty, MO, Apr. 1836, William W. Phelps, Papers, BYU; Corrill, *Brief History of the Church*, 23.

481. Tullidge, *Women of Mormondom*, 99.

482. Revelation, 22 June 1834, in Doctrine and Covenants 102:3, 10, 1844 ed. [D&C 105:9–13, 33].

Record book containing first Missouri journal. This church record book, entitled "General," contains an 1838 list of church members, Joseph Smith's journal for March–September 1838, a copy of a letter Smith wrote from the jail in Liberty, Missouri, and the aborted beginning of another record. In 1845, the volume was turned over and used for recording patriarchal blessings. JS, Journal, Mar.–Sept. 1838, Church History Library, Salt Lake City. (Photograph by Welden C. Andersen.)

JOURNAL,
MARCH–SEPTEMBER 1838

Source Note

JS, "The Scriptory Book—of Joseph Smith Jr—President of The Church of Jesus Christ, of Latterday Saints In all the World," Journal, Mar.–Sept. 1838; handwriting of George W. Robinson and James Mulholland; 69 pages; in "General," Record Book, 1838, verso of Patriarchal Blessings, vol. 5, CHL. Includes redactions and archival marking.

JS's "Scriptory Book" is recorded on pages 15 to 83 of a large record book entitled "General" that also includes a list of church members in Caldwell County, Missouri (pages 2–14), a copy of JS's 16 December 1838 letter from the jail in Liberty, Missouri (pages 101–108), and an aborted record partially entitled "Recor" in unidentified handwriting (page 110). The book, which measures 13 x 8¼ x 1¾ inches (33 x 21 x 4 cm), has 182 leaves of ledger paper sized 12½ x 7¾ inches (32 x 20 cm) with thirty-seven lines in blue ink per page. There are eighteen gatherings of various sizes, each of about a dozen leaves. The text block is sewn all along over three vellum tapes. The heavy pink endpapers each consist of a pastedown and two flyleaves pasted together. The text block edges are stained green. The volume has a hardbound ledger-style binding with a hollow-back spine and glued-on blue-striped cloth head-bands. It is bound in brown split-calfskin leather with blind-tooled decoration around the outside border and along the turned-in edges of the leather on the inside covers. At some point the letter "G" was hand printed in ink on the front cover. The original leather cover over the spine—which appears to have been intentionally removed—may have borne a title or filing notation.

The journal is inscribed in black ink that later turned brown and is almost entirely in the hand-writing of George W. Robinson. James Mulholland's handwriting appears in a copy of the 23 July 1837 revelation for Thomas B. Marsh (D&C 112) on pages 72–74. Running heads added by Robinson throughout the journal indicate the months of the entries on the page. The volume was later used in Nauvoo, Illinois, as a source for JS's multivolume manuscript history of the church. During the preparation of the history, redactions and use marks were made in graphite pencil. Redactions in graphite and ink may have been made at other times as well. In 1845, the book was turned over so that the back cover became the front and the last page became the first. This side of the book was used to record patriarchal blessings. The original spine may have been removed at this time. The spine is now labeled with a number "5", designating its volume number in a series of books of patriarchal blessings.

The volume is listed in Nauvoo and early Utah inventories of church records, indicating continu-ous custody.[1] At some point, the leaf containing pages 54 and 55 was torn from the journal. This removed leaf—which is transcribed herein and contains, among other writings, the earliest extant text

---

1. Historian's Office, "Schedule of Church Records"; "Historian's Office Catalogue," [2]; "Index of Records and Journals," [12], Catalogs and Inventories, 1846–1904, CHL; JS, Journal, Mar.–Sept. 1838, microfilm, JS Collection, CHL.

of an 8 July 1838 revelation for the Quorum of the Twelve (D&C 118)—was for a time kept in Revelation Book 2.[2] It is now part of the Revelations Collection at the Church History Library.

Historical Introduction

Following the climactic events they experienced in the House of the Lord in spring 1836, JS and church members renewed their efforts on three fronts: proselytizing, raising funds to purchase land in Missouri on which to settle increasing numbers of Latter-day Saints, and building a larger and stronger Latter-day Saint community in Kirtland, Ohio. But in neither Missouri nor Ohio did events unfold as expected. Success in gathering converts to Missouri provoked renewed external opposition, again forcing church members in that state to relocate. Meanwhile, conflicts engulfed JS in Kirtland.

Revelations directed Latter-day Saint elders to proselytize throughout the world after being empowered in the House of the Lord. A modest beginning during the remainder of 1836 crescendoed the following year with missionary service throughout the United States and Canada and the successful launching of a ministry in England. Their mission was not only to preach and make converts but also to gather the descendants of the biblical house of Israel, now scattered throughout the world. Converts were encouraged to move to designated locations in Missouri and Ohio. The Mormon quest to establish Zion in Missouri, temporarily abandoned after the Saints' expulsion from Jackson County, was thereby reinvigorated.

Beginning in April 1836, JS and his associates engaged in an aggressive fund-raising campaign for land purchases in Missouri.[3] Meanwhile, converts flocked to Clay County, Missouri, to join the Latter-day Saints who had been expelled from Jackson County in 1833. The rapid growth of the Mormon population eroded the tolerance of other Clay County residents, who concluded in late June 1836 that the Saints must leave. By then threats of violence and the intimidation of incoming Mormons made the once welcoming community much less so.[4] Returning to Jackson County was also an unrealistic option.

Attempting to prevent future hostilities—and probably to divert Mormon immigration away from more coveted lands—on 29 December 1836, the Missouri legislature created Caldwell County, northeast of Clay County, exclusively for Mormon settlement.[5] That act gave rise to conflicting expectations. Many Missourians believed the Latter-day Saints were thereafter to confine their settlement to Caldwell County.[6] The Saints willingly left Clay County and established headquarters at Far West in Caldwell County, but they made no formal commitment to limit their settlement to one county. Indeed, they anticipated

---

2. Best, "Register of the Revelations Collection," 19.

3. Minute Book 1, 2 Apr. 1836; JS, Journal, 2 Apr. 1836.

4. "Public Meeting," *LDS Messenger and Advocate,* Aug. 1836, 2:353–355; Stokes, "Wilson Letters," 504–509.

5. An Act to Organize the Counties of Caldwell and Daviess [29 Dec. 1836], *Laws of the State of Missouri* [1836], 46–47; *History of Caldwell and Livingston Counties,* 103–105; Riggs, "Economic Impact of Fort Leavenworth," 129.

6. "The Mormons in Carroll County," *Missouri Republican,* 18 Aug. 1838, [2], daily edition; "Mormonism," *Kansas City Daily Journal,* 12 June 1881, 1; Willard Snow, Petition for redress, no date, Library of Congress Collection, National Archives, Washington DC.

establishing numerous additional stakes of Zion elsewhere in northwestern Missouri. Tension over future Mormon expansion was inherent in the arrangement.

Conflict also increased at church headquarters in Kirtland. In seeking to establish a sacral society directed by prophetic leadership, JS crossed conventional boundaries between religious and secular affairs. For him, God's commandments made no distinction between the spiritual and the temporal.[7] Subjecting oneself to a religious leader's direction in temporal matters clashed with American ideals of unfettered individual freedom. As the Mormon population of Kirtland continued to grow, JS and his associates conceived expansive plans for that community. A pivotal element was a bank, which could help provide capital for development. Though they were unable to obtain a state charter—an ultimately fatal flaw—they nevertheless established a financial institution in January 1837. The "Kirtland Safety Society" faltered early, due in part to negative publicity, the refusal of many area banks to accept Safety Society notes, and the predatory actions of outsiders who systematically acquired its notes and quickly demanded payment in specie, thus depleting its reserves. The Safety Society suspended such payments in late January, then failed several months later during the recession that gripped the United States.[8] Stresses related to the bank failure, mounting personal debt of Kirtland Mormons, and church indebtedness due to construction of the House of the Lord caused some to question the scope and legitimacy of JS's prophetic leadership. Some of JS's closest associates became disaffected. Prominent among the dissenters were JS's former secretary Warren Parrish, several apostles, a number of the members of the Quorum of the Seventy, and the Three Witnesses to the Book of Mormon plates. Their discontent escalated from dismay with JS's financial leadership to rejection of his religious leadership.[9]

Such views eventually spread to nearly one-third of the church's general leadership and over ten percent of the local church membership in Ohio. Declaring JS a fallen prophet, Parrish and others attempted to establish a church of their own and to take control of the House of the Lord.[10] Oliver Cowdery, saddled with crushing personal financial losses, privately disparaged JS.[11] Some dissidents sought to replace JS with David Whitmer as church president.[12] Frederick G. Williams clashed with JS over the Safety Society.[13] Compounding JS's problems was the antipathy of numerous non-Mormon residents of Kirtland and vicinity, some of whom used both the legal system and threats of violence to harass him and other Latter-day Saints.[14]

In fall 1837, JS moved vigorously to reassert his authority as church president. At a conference in September, he and church leaders loyal to him disciplined dissidents in

---

7. Revelation, Sept. 1830–A, in Doctrine and Covenants 10:9, 1835 ed. [D&C 29:34–35].

8. Adams, "Chartering the Kirtland Bank," 467–482; Backman, *Heavens Resound,* 314–321; "James Thompson's Statement," in *Naked Truths about Mormonism,* Apr. 1888, 3.

9. Esplin, "Emergence of Brigham Young," chaps. 5–6.

10. Backman, *Heavens Resound,* 323–329, 437n68.

11. Minute Book 2, 12 Apr. 1838; Oliver Cowdery, Far West, MO, to Warren Cowdery, [Kirtland, OH], 21 Jan. 1838, in Cowdery, Letterbook, 80–83.

12. Historian's Office, "History of Brigham Young," 15.

13. Williams, "Frederick Granger Williams," 254–256.

14. Adams, "Grandison Newell's Obsession," 168–188.

Ohio—including three apostles and a number of members of the Kirtland high council. Meanwhile, problems developed among church leaders in Missouri, where the high council, the bishopric, and apostles Thomas B. Marsh and David W. Patten decried unilateral actions by the Missouri presidency. Concern focused particularly on the management by counselors John Whitmer and William W. Phelps of the proceeds from the sale of property in Far West.[15] When Marsh traveled to Kirtland in summer 1837, he probably informed JS of these Missouri leadership issues. To underscore the importance of unity and to prepare the way for changes in Missouri leadership if they should be required, JS sent minutes of the September Kirtland conference to Missouri, along with a revelation, additional written counsel, and verbal instructions conveyed by Marsh and JS's brother Hyrum Smith, an assistant counselor in the presidency. Soon after, JS and his loyal first counselor, Sidney Rigdon, traveled to Caldwell County, Missouri, where with Hyrum Smith they met with local church leaders in early November and reached what seemed to be a satisfactory resolution of most of the outstanding issues. At a conference the following day, the local presidency were retained after they made confessions in response to objections raised against them. However, the First Presidency underwent major changes. Frederick G. Williams, JS's second counselor, was removed from office after considerable discussion and replaced with Hyrum Smith. The name of Oliver Cowdery, who earlier was placed next to JS in the presidency, was not even presented for approval on this occasion; thus he was silently displaced.[16] After JS's return to Kirtland, it became evident that unresolved issues in Missouri required further attention.

An 1831 revelation had signaled that Kirtland would eventually yield to Missouri as the major gathering center for the Latter-day Saints.[17] When arrangements were completed in late 1836 for Mormon settlement in Caldwell County, renewed large-scale migration of Mormons to Missouri became feasible. JS and the presidency had anticipated moving there earlier in 1836 to direct the resettlement of incoming converts, but the delay in establishing a permanent Missouri location and the entanglements of Kirtland kept them in Ohio. By late 1837, JS was planning to move as soon as possible.[18] Threatened by dissidents and pursued by creditors, he learned in January 1838 of his impending arrest on a charge of illegal banking—quite likely a ruse devised by his opponents to drive him from Ohio.[19] JS and Rigdon had already been found guilty of such a charge in October 1837, had been fined $1,000 each, and had an appeal pending.[20] On 12 January, a new revelation directed that JS and the presidency were to terminate their work in Kirtland "as soon as it is practicable"

15. Minute Book 2, 3 and 5–7 Apr. 1837; Thomas B. Marsh, [Far West, MO], to Wilford Woodruff, [Vinalhaven, ME], 1838, *Elders' Journal,* July 1838, 37–38. Missouri church president David Whitmer spent most of 1836 and 1837 in Kirtland.

16. Minute Book 2, 6 and 7 Nov. 1837.

17. Revelation, 11 Sept. 1831, in Doctrine and Covenants 21:4, 1835 ed. [D&C 64:21–22].

18. [JS], editorial, *Elders' Journal,* Nov. 1837, 28.

19. Adams, "Grandison Newell's Obsession"; Historian's Office, "History of Luke Johnson," 6, Histories of the Twelve, ca. 1858–1880, CHL.

20. Firmage and Mangrum, *Zion in the Courts,* 56–57.

and move to Missouri.[21] JS and Rigdon left within a few hours and were joined soon afterward by their families.

While JS was en route to Far West, his supporters there were working to root out dissent among local church leadership. Senior apostle Thomas B. Marsh and members of the Missouri high council conducted, in each of five settlements, meetings of church members in which the conduct of the Missouri presidency was reviewed. Marsh indicated that the meetings were conducted according to instructions from JS. The outcome of each meeting was that the leadership of the presidency—consisting of David Whitmer, William W. Phelps, and John Whitmer—was rejected. The Missouri high council and bishopric replaced the presidency with an interim presidency of Marsh and apostle David W. Patten, and soon afterward the high council excommunicated Phelps and John Whitmer.[22] The reassertion of authority in Missouri under JS and those loyal to him was well under way when JS reached Far West on 14 March 1838.

George W. Robinson, who was appointed the church's general clerk and recorder in Ohio in September 1837, arrived in Far West on 28 March 1838, two weeks after JS, and was immediately pressed into service. Within a day or two of arriving, he began writing what would become the present journal. Robinson made his initial inscriptions in a general church record book that already included a roster of Latter-day Saints living in Caldwell County. He began writing on the first blank page following the previously inscribed roster, the final page of which was later washed clean of ink in order to provide space to prefix a title page to the "Scriptory Book." The journal Robinson kept for JS documents critical developments in the struggle of JS and the presidency to maintain leadership of the church and to fulfill ambitious plans for Zion in Missouri. It records their efforts to found settlements outside their headquarters and gathering center in Caldwell County during spring and summer 1838, as well as the first signs of the deterioration of that effort. The journal is primarily a documentary record. Several key developments are depicted only by documents copied into the record without narrative ligatures.

The journal entries only occasionally provide insights into intentions, perceptions, evaluations, and feelings. When they do so, Robinson's perspective is usually represented. In the journal entries, Robinson refers to JS in the third person and to himself in the first. Thus references to "I" or "myself" in the journal entries usually indicate Robinson rather than JS.

The journal opens with a brief retrospective account, apparently dictated by JS, of his arrival in Far West on 14 March 1838. Then follows a copy of a motto recently composed by JS and signed by JS, Robinson, and a half-dozen prominent Latter-day Saints. The motto reflected JS's experiences with dissent and persecution in Kirtland and signaled his determination to vigorously assert the Latter-day Saints' right to establish themselves in Missouri and to pursue their goals without harassment. JS's letter of 29 March 1838, copied on pages 23–26 of the journal, indicates that the motto was already inscribed in the journal by that date.

Following the motto are two sets of questions and answers about the book of Isaiah. A series of transcripts or summaries of eight documents follows. These materials relate to a

---

21. Revelation, 12 Jan. 1838–C, in Revelations Collection, CHL; see also JS, Journal, 8 July 1838, pp. 283–284 herein.

22. Minute Book 2, 5–10 Feb. and 10 Mar. 1838.

seven-month series of events that culminated in the 12–13 April 1838 excommunications of
Oliver Cowdery and David Whitmer. As indicated by the date on the title page of the journal, 12 April 1838, Robinson apparently began transcribing these documents and entries on
the same day that Cowdery was excommunicated. Cowdery's trial seems to have been the
motivating factor for transcribing this set of documents and creating an ongoing record
with its own identity. These documents include minutes, instructions, and revelations originally written in Ohio as early as 3 September 1837; minutes of a conference in which
Brigham Young joined Thomas B. Marsh and David W. Patten as "Presidents Pro. Tem" of
the church in Missouri; and terse synopses of the excommunication proceedings. In stark
contrast to the frank evaluations of key leaders that JS dictated for his earliest journal, the
present journal's businesslike documentary treatment yields little insight into the inter-
personal dynamics of their estrangement or the impact that severing ties to former close
associates had on JS. Robinson also copied a letter from a Missouri landholder offering
property at De Witt, Carroll County, to JS as a strategic site for control of commerce in the
region. A purchase was eventually consummated, and Latter-day Saints settled there, anger-
ing those Missourians who objected to Mormon settlement outside Caldwell County.

Following copies of brief personal revelations that JS dictated for apostles David W.
Patten and Brigham Young in mid-April 1838, Robinson recorded JS's 26 April 1838 revelation mandating the continued growth of Far West, the construction of a temple there,
and the establishment of Latter-day Saint settlements in that vicinity. The revelation sanc-
tioned the name for the church that JS and others had recently begun to use: the Church of
Jesus Christ of Latter Day Saints.

After inscribing this substantial body of recapitulations and copied documents,
Robinson recorded daily journal entries, beginning with an entry for 27 April 1838. By this
point, Robinson was serving as a scribe to the First Presidency, and the journal focused not
only on JS but also on Sidney Rigdon (Robinson's father-in-law) and Hyrum Smith, both
counselors in the church presidency. Frequently, but not consistently, the scribe accompanied JS and the presidency on trips away from Far West. However, since the record book
was large, Robinson likely did not carry it with him on every occasion, and a number of
entries may not have been recorded until several days later.

The first day of Robinson's regular journal entries, 27 April, was the same day JS,
Rigdon, and Robinson started JS's history. Thus a promising record-keeping routine began
to be established, which lasted for six weeks. Entries for the first three weeks document a
brief interlude of settled existence in Far West, with JS and his counselors collaborating on
the history, studying grammar, and attending meetings, and JS working his garden.
However, the presidency was soon on the move again. After receiving word of a sizable
migration of Latter-day Saints to Missouri, they left Far West for Daviess County in mid-
May to select and survey lands for future arrivals. JS's labors in the north were punctuated
by brief visits home, during one of which Emma Smith gave birth to their son Alexander.

Settling in sparsely settled Daviess County offered incoming Latter-day Saints, many
of whom were poor, a place to live while neither buying nor renting. As squatters on United
States government land, heads of households could apply for preemption rights (first right
of purchase) on up to 160 acres of land that they occupied, pending completion of official
government land surveys. Applicants were not required—or even allowed—to pay the

government for the land until after the surveys were completed. Then, to acquire title to the property, they were to pay the relatively low price of $1.25 per acre prior to an announced date, after which their property would otherwise be offered for sale to the general public, along with the unclaimed land in the surveyed area. The selection and private surveying of Daviess County land by JS and his colleagues provided the basis for orderly and relatively compact settlement coordinated by church officials.[23] Settling in Caldwell County, by contrast, involved more conventional purchases. Government surveys were already completed for that county, and government land was already being sold.

The pattern of record keeping became more varied after the presidency and their scribe traveled to Daviess County in early June. Robinson's daily entries lapsed as the Mormons laid out a city plot for a Latter-day Saint settlement at Adam-ondi-Ahman, began building homes, and organized a stake. They persisted in creating the new settlement despite their Missouri neighbors' earlier attempt to frighten the area's first Mormon settlers into leaving Daviess County.[24]

Meanwhile, tensions continued between JS and the majority who supported him on the one hand and prominent excommunicants who remained in Caldwell County after being expelled from the church on the other. JS and Rigdon came to feel that peace and harmony among the Latter-day Saints—essential if they were to succeed in establishing Zion in Missouri—was impossible as long as these individuals remained among them. After Rigdon denounced these former leaders in a sermon in mid-June,[25] they were threatened with violence, and several of them left the county. Active in compelling their departure was a new volunteer paramilitary organization of Mormon men called the Danites, of which Robinson was an officer. The Danites sought to rid the church of dissent, to ensure the fulfillment of church leaders' directives, and later to help combat external threats against the Saints.

Although Robinson's journal keeping for JS lapsed for most of June and July, he did note significant developments in three early July entries consisting primarily of copied correspondence and revelations. He wrote an entry for 4 July, when Sidney Rigdon's oration at the Mormons' celebration of Independence Day at Far West signaled their intentions to expand beyond the confines of Caldwell County and warned that they would not countenance persecution.[26] The entry for 6 July is a copy of a letter received that day from Heber C. Kimball and Orson Hyde, en route to Far West after completion of their mission to the British Isles. It is followed by Robinson's transcription of a letter from JS's brother Don Carlos Smith reporting the circumstances of members of the extended Smith family moving together from Kirtland to Far West. At least six of the eight revelations recorded at that point in the journal were read to a church congregation at Far West on 8 July. Three dated 12 January 1838, the day that JS left Kirtland for Far West, focused on the church presidency, reinforcing their authority, establishing stringent requirements for any attempts to discipline them, and directing them to leave Kirtland and move to Missouri as soon as possible. Five more revelations, all

---

23. Walker, "Mormon Land Rights."

24. Gentry, "Latter-day Saints in Northern Missouri," 153–156; Baugh, "Call to Arms," 106.

25. Reed Peck, Quincy, IL, to "Dear Friends," 18 Sept. 1839, pp. 23–25, Henry E. Huntington Library, San Marino, CA; Corrill, *Brief History of the Church,* 30.

26. *Oration Delivered by Mr. S. Rigdon,* 12.

dated 8 July, provided directions for the reorganization of the Quorum of Twelve and a pros-elytizing mission that they were to undertake in Europe, called for tithing to be instituted in the church, and gave instructions for several church leaders and former leaders. Between the January revelations and the July revelations, Robinson recorded a brief synopsis, from a mil-lenarian perspective, of contemporary developments affecting the church in Missouri, includ-ing consequences of the expulsion of dissidents in June and the influx of numerous Latter-day Saint settlers to northwestern Missouri.

Robinson did not resume regular journal entries until 26 July. From that point, his journal keeping was relatively consistent through 10 September, when the journal ends. These entries show that expansion beyond Caldwell County—an integral part of Mormon plans—came at a price. Mormon immigrants from Canada were assigned to settle in Daviess County during summer 1838, and on 6 July, "Kirtland Camp," the largest single group of Saints to leave Kirtland for Missouri, began their laborious trek.[27] Their arrival made it evident to the Mormons' neighbors in Daviess County that within a few months the Mormons would outnumber other citizens. Meanwhile, in late July, Carroll County residents pressed the Saints to leave De Witt. Further growth of Mormon numbers and influence was unthinkable for many residents of northwestern Missouri.

On election day, 6 August, William Peniston, a candidate for the state legislature, mounted a whiskey barrel at the village square at Gallatin, Daviess County, to persuade a crowd of men to prevent the Latter-day Saints from voting. A brawl ensued, and at Far West, JS heard from an otherwise credible non-Mormon source that the corpses of Latter-day Saint casualties were being withheld from church members in Daviess County, a report later proved false.[28] JS accompanied a body of armed men to Daviess County to recover the bodies for burial but learned at Adam-ondi-Ahman that, despite multiple injuries, there were no fatalities on either side. There they also heard a rumor that local justice of the peace Adam Black was raising a mob to avenge blows the Mormons had landed in the Gallatin fracas. JS and his associates, now including prominent Adam-ondi-Ahman resident Lyman Wight, visited the home of Black, who a year earlier had warned Latter-day Saints to leave the county. The Mormons found no mob but obtained a signed commitment from Black that the rights of Latter-day Saints would be protected. The following day, a delegation of prominent Daviess County citizens met with JS, Wight, and other Latter-day Saints at Adam-ondi-Ahman, where both sides exchanged pledges to avoid injuring the other and to settle any disputes through legal channels.[29]

In violation of these commitments, Black and Peniston used an embellished account of the encounter at Black's home to mobilize both legal and vigilante action against the Mormons. Peniston traveled with others to Richmond, Ray County, to recruit volunteers to help protect the old settlers of Daviess County. While there, Peniston showed local citi-zens an affidavit from Black claiming that the Mormon party that visited his house had threatened him with immediate death if he refused to sign their agreement.[30] Peniston filed

---

27. Tyler, "Daily Journal," 6 July 1838.
28. Hartley, *My Best for the Kingdom,* chap. 6.
29. Baugh, "Call to Arms," 103–111.
30. "Public Meeting," *Missouri Republican,* 8 Sept. 1838, [1], "for the country" edition.

a complaint with Austin A. King, judge of the Fifth Judicial Circuit Court of Missouri. King's jurisdiction included both Caldwell and Daviess counties, as well as Ray, Clay, Carroll, Clinton, and Livingston counties. King issued a warrant for the arrest of JS and Lyman Wight.[31] Then Black, Peniston, and their allies fanned out to recruit volunteers from additional counties. After Black's visit to Livingston County, Missouri newspapers spread claims that Mormons had threatened additional Daviess County settlers, destroyed crops, and perhaps even murdered Peniston and other prominent residents.[32] Some counties, such as Ray and Chariton, responded by sending investigative committees.[33] When JS and Wight were not arrested as anticipated, Peniston and other members of a Daviess County "Committee of Vigilance" again agitated throughout northwestern Missouri for volunteers to gather to Daviess County—this time to drive the Latter-day Saints out of the county.[34]

Black's assertion that JS and other Latter-day Saints had threatened his life, coupled with a new claim that JS and Wight were resisting arrest, confirmed Missourians' fears that the Latter-day Saints considered themselves above the law. Many Missourians concluded that they should take the law into their own hands.[35] The vigilantes called for men from other counties to come armed to Daviess County on 7 September in preparation for an 8 September offensive against the Mormons.

In hopes of heading off confrontation and to counter the notion that they would not be subject to the law, JS and Wight submitted to arrest and attended a preliminary hearing on a charge of riot. On 7 September 1838, when JS appeared at the hearing, he was greeted by the anti-Mormons who had gathered in Daviess County. Judge King heard testimony and bound JS and Wight over for trial, but the anti-Mormon vigilantes were not pacified.[36] The assault originally scheduled to begin on 8 September was merely postponed for two days while the vigilantes arranged with sympathizers in Ray County to deliver a stockpile of rifles on 9 September. As the present journal was coming to a close, Mormon companies of Caldwell County militia headed for Daviess County to protect the Latter-day Saints residing there. Another Mormon militia unit intercepted the shipment of weapons from Ray County, foiling plans for the offensive. After the vigilantes' plan was thwarted, they confined their efforts for a time to terrorizing outlying Mormon homes; in response, Latter-day Saint militia from Far West entered Daviess County. In mid-September, state militia intervened. Mormon and non-Mormon groups from outside Daviess County were sent home, and crisis, for the moment, was averted.[37]

——————— ✧ ———————

31. William Peniston, Affidavit, Ray Co., MO, 10 Aug. 1838, private possession, copy in CHL; State of Missouri, Warrant for JS and Lyman Wight, Ray Co., MO, 10 Aug. 1838, private possession, copy in CHL.

32. See, for example, "The Mormons," *Missouri Argus,* 6 Sept. 1838, [1].

33. JS, Journal, 11 Aug. 1838; "The Mormon Difficulties," *Niles' National Register,* 13 Oct. 1838, 103.

34. "Mormons Once More," *Hannibal Commercial Advertiser,* 25 Sept. 1838, [1].

35. LeSueur, *1838 Mormon War in Missouri,* 70.

36. LeSueur, *1838 Mormon War in Missouri,* 77–83.

37. David R. Atchison, Grand River, MO, to Lilburn W. Boggs, Jefferson City, MO, 17 Sept. 1838, Mormon War Papers, Missouri State Archives, Jefferson City; LeSueur, *1838 Mormon War in Missouri,* 87–89, 96–97.

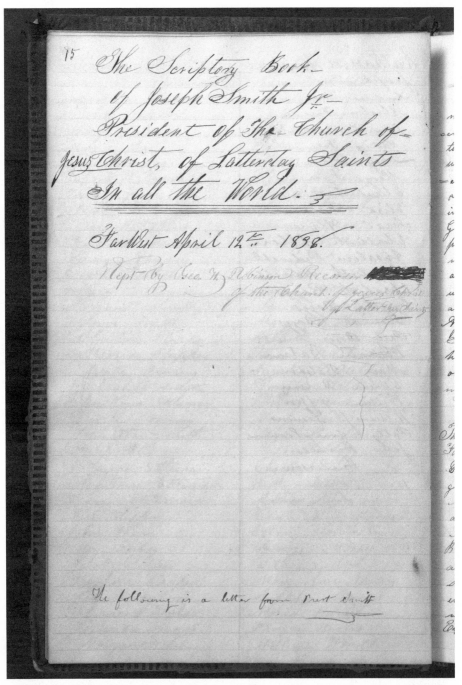

Beginning of first Missouri journal. Scribe George W. Robinson began this "Scriptory Book" as a repository for copying various scripts—letters, revelations, and meeting minutes—constituting documentary journal entries. Even after it took on the function of a regular journal, it continued to be the repository for copies of additional documents. Robinson began the text in a general church record book on the first blank page following a previously inscribed document, a roster of Latter-day Saints living in Caldwell County, Missouri. Later, the final page of the roster was washed in

The Scriptory Book of Joseph Smith Jr. President of the Church of Jesus Christ, of Latter day Saints In all the World.

Far West April 12th 1838.

order to provide space to prefix a title page to the Scriptory Book. The image on the right demonstrates the recovery of the original text made possible by multispectral imaging. Handwriting of George W. Robinson. JS, Journal, Mar.–Sept. 1838, p. 15, Church History Library, Salt Lake City. (Photograph on left by Welden C. Andersen. Multispectral image on right by Gene A. Ware.)

/³⁸⟨The Scriptory Book——³⁹

of Joseph Smith Jʳ·——

President of The Church of

<u>Jesus Christ</u>, of Latterday Saints⁴⁰

<u>   In all the World.   </u>

Far West April 12ᵗʰ· 1838.

⟨Kept by Geo. W. Robinson⁴¹ Recorder
of the Church of Jesus Christ
of Latter Day Saints⟩
[*17 lines blank*]
⟨The following is a letter from Prest Smith☞⁴²⟩ [p. 15]

———— ∽ ————

Editorial Note

On the night of 12 January 1838, JS and Sidney Rigdon left Kirtland, Ohio, on horse-back to escape the threat of arrest and violence. They stayed with friends in Norton, Ohio, until their families arrived. Enemies in pursuit, inclement weather, and lack of provisions complicated the journey. The families sometimes traveled together and sometimes apart until, in eastern Illinois, they separated because of sickness in the larger and more unwieldy Rigdon group, which included scribe George W. Robinson.⁴³

---

38. TEXT: George W. Robinson handwriting begins.

39. Naming this record the "Scriptory Book" apparently indicated that it was intended to be a reposi-tory for various "scripts," or written texts, and not revelatory scripture in particular. Webster defined *scriptory* as "written; expressed in writing; not verbal." ("Scriptory," in *American Dictionary*, 731.)

40. This name for the church became official following a revelation of 26 April 1838. (See Revelation, 26 Apr. 1838, in JS, Journal, 26 Apr. 1838, p. 258 herein [D&C 115:4].)

41. Robinson was appointed general church recorder and clerk in September 1837 in Kirtland and was sustained in that office on 6 April 1838 in Missouri. (Minute Book 1, 17 Sept. 1837; Minutes, 6 Apr. 1838, p. 250 herein.)

42. In the journal the drawn "digit" or "fist" points to the "Motto of the Church of Christ of Latterday Saints," which is transcribed into the journal on the facing page. The digit apparently refers to the tran-script of the motto rather than the retrospective material that precedes it. However, two letters "from Prest Smith" are among the documents copied into the pages that immediately follow, and so it is possible that the digit was meant to refer to one of them instead.

43. Letter to the Presidency in Kirtland, 29 Mar. 1838, p. 247 herein; JS History, vol. B-1, 780; Van Wagoner, *Sidney Rigdon*, 203–204, 211–212.

At the beginning of their journey, JS and Rigdon wrote to William W. Phelps in Missouri requesting assistance.[44] In response, the Missouri high council organized wagon teams to meet the families and help them finish their journey.[45] John Barnard met JS and his family at Huntsville, Randolph County, Missouri—about one hundred miles from Far West, Missouri—and brought them to Far West in his carriage.[46] The retrospective opening entry, penned by scribe Robinson after his arrival in late March, was apparently dictated by JS.

———— ❦ ————

On the 13th. day of March I[47] with my family and some others arrived within 8 milds [miles] of Far West and put up at brother Barnerds [John Barnard's] to tarry for the night. Here we ware meet by an escort of bretheren from the town who came to make us welcome to their little Zion.[48] On the next day as we ware about entering the town Many of the bretheren came out to meet us who also withe open armes welcomed us to their boosoms. We were immediately received under the hospitable roof of George W. Harris who treated us with all kindness possible. here we refreshed ourselves withe much sattisfaction after our long and tedious Journey and the bretheren braught in such necessaries as we stood in need of for our presant comfort and necessities.[49]

After being here two or three day's my Brother Samuel [Smith] arrived with his family an[d] shortly after his arrival while walking with him & cirtain other bretheren the following sentements occured to my mind.—

Motto of the Church of Christ of <u>Latterday</u> <u>Saints</u>.[50]
The Constitution of our country formed by the Fathers of Liberty.
Peace and good order in society Love to God and good will to man.

---

44. See Oliver Cowdery, Far West, MO, to Warren Cowdery and Lyman Cowdery, Kirtland, OH, 24 Feb. 1838, in Cowdery, Letterbook, 87–90.

45. Minute Book 2, 24 Feb. 1838.

46. Historian's Office, "History of Brigham Young," 21.

47. JS. However, after this retrospective entry, first-person pronouns in this journal generally refer to scribe George W. Robinson.

48. These men were Thomas B. Marsh, John Corrill, and Elias Higbee, among others. (Letter to the Presidency in Kirtland, 29 Mar. 1838, p. 245 herein.)

49. This in contrast to being refused lodging during severe weather on the journey. (JS, Journal, 29 Dec. 1842, JS Collection, CHL.)

50. JS's 29 March 1838 letter to the Kirtland stake presidency expressly mentions that the motto was already copied into the present journal and also that George W. Robinson arrived in Far West the previous day. As Robinson was a signatory to the motto, and as all of the motto's signatures appear in the journal in Robinson's handwriting, the motto was apparently both originally committed to writing and copied into the Scriptory Book on 28 or 29 March 1838. (See p. 247 herein.)

All good and wholesome Law's; And virtue and truth above all things

And Aristarchy[51] live forever!!!

But Wo to tyrants, Mobs, Aristocracy, Anarchy and Toryism:[52] And all those who invent or seek out unrighteous and vexatious lawsuits under the pretext or color of law or office, either religious or political.[53]

Exalt the standard of Democracy! Down [p. 16] with that of Priestcraft, and let all the people say Amen! that the blood of our Fathers may not cry from the ground against us.

Sacred is the Memory of that Blood which baught for us our liberty.

Signed   Joseph Smith J[r.]
          Geo. W. Robinson   Thomas B. Marsh
                                             D[avid] W. Patten
                                             Brigham Youngs [Young]
                                             Samuel H. Smith
                                             George M. Hinkle
                                             John Corrill.—[54]

---

51. "A body of good men in power, or government by excellent men." ("Aristarchy," in *American Dictionary*, 51.)

52. JS's sentiments are best understood in light of the brutal expulsion of the Latter-day Saints from Jackson County in 1833 and internal and external conflicts at Kirtland. After JS and Sidney Rigdon were attacked by a mob in Hiram, Ohio, in 1832, JS and other Saints in northeastern Ohio were confronted with numerous threats and some actual instances of mobbing and other violence.[a] Wording in the motto was also echoed in JS's letter of 29 March 1838 identifying JS's former scribe Warren Parrish and associated Kirtland dissenters as "Aristocrats or Anarchys."[b] Parrish's group had held meetings to renounce what they considered JS's superstitious doctrine, and for months they had attempted to control meetings in the House of the Lord, even resorting to violence.[c] Usage of *Tory* or *Toryism* in this context refers to what might be called "resident enemy sympathizers."[d] Sampson Avard later testified that in October 1838, during the Mormon conflict in Missouri, JS stated that Saints in Caldwell County who "did not take arms in defence of the Mormons of Davi[es]s should be considered as tories, and should take their exit from the county."[e] (a. Parkin, "Conflict at Kirtland," 248–263; Adams, "Grandison Newell's Obsession," 170–172, 177–180. b. See Letter to the Presidency in Kirtland, 29 Mar. 1838, p. 246 herein. c. Parkin, "Conflict at Kirtland," 246–265. d. "Tory," also "Toryism," in *American Dictionary*, 846. e. Sampson Avard, Testimony, Richmond, MO, Nov. 1838, in State of Missouri, "Evidence.")

53. Eber Howe, editor of the *Painesville Telegraph*, later recounted, "Many of our citizens thought it advisable to take all the legal means within their reach to counteract the progress of so dangerous an enemy in their midst, and many law suits ensued."[a] A campaign of legal harassment against JS had been waged under the direction of Mentor, Ohio, businessman Grandison Newell.[b] (a. Howe, *Autobiography and Recollections*, 45. b. Adams, "Grandison Newell's Obsession"; Backman, *Heavens Resound*, 321–323; for impact of this on JS, see Letter to the Presidency in Kirtland, 29 Mar. 1838, p. 246 herein.)

54. Marsh, Patten, and Young were the three most senior members of the Quorum of the Twelve. After the Missouri presidency was deposed in February 1838, Marsh and Patten constituted a temporary

Questions regarding the Book of Isaiah

Quest. on Scripture.[55]

1ˢᵗ· Who is the stem of Jessee spoken of in the 1ˢᵗ· 2ᵈ· 3ᵈ· 4ᵗʰ· and 5ᵗʰ· verses of the 11ᵗʰ· Chap. of Isiah.

Ans. Verely thus saith the Lord   It is Christ

Q. 2ᵈ· What is the Rod spoken of in the 1ˢᵗ· verse of the 11ᵗʰ· ~~verse~~ Chap. that shoud come of the stem of Jessee.

Ans. Behold thus saith ⟨the Lord⟩ it is a servant in the hands of Christ who is partly a decendant of Jessee as well as of Ephraim or of the house of Joseph, on whome thare is Laid much power.

Qest 3ᵈ· What is the Root of Jessee spoken of in the 10ᵗʰ· verse of the 11ᵗʰ· Chap.

Ans. Behold thus saith the Lord; it is a decendant of Jessee as well as of Joseph unto whom rightly belongs the Priesthood and the kees of the Kingdom for an ensign and for the geathering of my people in the Last day.—[56] [p. 17]

Questions from Elias Higbee regarding the Book of Isaiah

Questions by Elias Higby [Higbee]

1ˢᵗ· Q. What is ment by the command in Isiah 52ᵈ· chap 1ˢᵗ· verse which saith Put on thy strength O Zion and what people had I[sa]iah referance to

A. He had reference to those whome God should call in the last day's who should hold the power of Priesthood to bring again zion and the redemption of Israel.

And to put on her strength is to put on the authority of the priesthood which she (zion) has a right to by lineage: Also to return to that power which she had lost

Ques. 2ᵈ· What are we to understand by zions loosing herself from the bands of her neck 2ᵈ· verse.

A. We are to understand that the scattered remnants are exorted to to return to the Lord from whence they have fal[l]en which if they do the promise

---

presidency, to which Young was added on 6 April 1838 after his arrival in Missouri. Samuel Smith, JS's brother, was present when JS conceived the motto, according to the text that precedes the motto herein. Hinkle and Corrill were Missouri church officials. (Minute Book 2, 10 Feb. and 6 Apr. 1838.)

55. The five questions and answers were later canonized as D&C 113.

56. JS's revelations and teachings repeatedly described JS in similar terms, as a servant of God who held "keys" of authority and would gather Israel in the last days.ᵃ JS's revelations also stated that descendants of the biblical Abraham, Isaac, Jacob, and Joseph had a hereditary right to the priesthood.ᵇ (a. See, for example, Revelation, ca. Aug. 1830, in Doctrine and Covenants 50:3, 1835 ed. [D&C 27:13]; and JS, Journal, 3 Apr. 1836; compare Isaiah 11:12. b. See, for example, Revelation, 6 Dec. 1832, in Doctrine and Covenants 6:3, 1835 ed. [D&C 86:8–10]; and Revelation, 6 Aug. 1833, in Doctrine and Covenants 85:6, 1835 ed. [D&C 98:32]; see also Brigham Young, in *Journal of Discourses*, 8 Apr. 1855, 2:268–269.)

of the Lord is that he will speak to them or give them revelation See 6^(th.) 7^(th.) and 8^(th.) verses The bands of her neck are the curses of God upon her or the remnants of Israel in their scattered condition among the Gentiles.

—————— ❦ ——————

Editorial Note

George W. Robinson here copied into the journal a series of transcripts or summaries, all but one of which pertain to JS's reinforcement of his leadership of the church and the removal and replacement of several leaders. The first documents were from late summer 1837, when after months of determined opposition, JS finally moved against dissidents.[57] On 3 September 1837 JS convened a conference in Kirtland, Ohio, that sustained him as president and "rejected" dissenting apostles and some others. The following day JS wrote a letter, here copied into this journal, to the Latter-day Saints in Missouri informing them of the stabilization of authority in Kirtland and including a copy of the conference minutes. The letter also warned them of Oliver Cowdery, David Whitmer, and others who were or soon would be in Missouri and whose support JS questioned. A revelation dated 4 September, the same date as the letter, also declared that Missouri leaders John Whitmer and William W. Phelps must repent of certain unnamed offenses or be removed from office. Together, these documents raised questions about Cowdery and the entire Missouri presidency, all of whom were in Missouri by the time JS arrived there in early November 1837 to hold a conference with the same purpose as the September conference in Ohio. JS and church leaders aired and presumably resolved concerns about the Missouri leaders in a meeting the day before the conference and in the conference itself, but they did not reach agreement with Oliver Cowdery. After JS returned to Ohio, tensions and problems involving the Missouri presidency also resurfaced.[58]

—————— ❦ ——————

Letter to John Corrill and the Church in Missouri • 4 September 1837

The following letter I wrote previous to my leaving Kirtland and sent by the hand of T[homas] B. Marsh[59]

Sept 4^(th) A.D. 1837
Kirtland Geauga Co. Ohio

---

57. Esplin, "Emergence of Brigham Young," 295–299.

58. Minute Book 2, 6, 7, and 10 Nov. 1837; JS History, vol. B-1, 775–779; Esplin, "Emergence of Brigham Young," chaps. 6–7.

59. Soon after this letter was written, Marsh, president of the Quorum of the Twelve, left Kirtland for his home in Far West, accompanied by Hyrum Smith, JS's brother and assistant counselor in the presidency, with instructions to deliver the letter to Missouri. They arrived in October. (Thomas B. Marsh, [Far West, MO], to Wilford Woodruff, [Vinalhaven, ME], 1838, *Elders' Journal*, July 1838, 36; Historian's Office, "T B Marsh," [2], Histories of the Twelve, ca. 1858–1880, CHL.)

Joseph Smith J^r. Pres^t of the Church ⟨of Christ⟩ of Latter Day Saints in all the world[60]

To John Corroll [Corrill] & the whole Church in Zion [p. 18] Sendeth greeting,[61] Blessed be the God of and father of our Lord Jesus Christ Who has blessed you with many blessings in Christ, And who has delivered you many times from the hands of your enimies And planted you many times in an heavenly or holy place, My respects & love to you all, and my blessings upon all the faithfull & true harted in the new & everlasting covenant & for as much as I have desired for a long time to see your faces, & converse with you & instruct you in those things which have been revealed to Me partaining to the Kingdom of God in the last days, I now write unto you offering an appolegy, My being bound with bonds of affliction by the workers of iniquity and by the labours of the Church endeaveroung in all things to do the will of God, for the salvation of the Church both in temporal as well as spiritual things. Bretheren we have waided through a scene of affliction and sorrow thus far for the will of God, that language is inadequate to describe pray yea therefore with more earnestness for our redemption, You have undoubtedly been informed by letter & otherwise of our difficulties in Kirtland which are now about being settled and that you may have a knowlege of the same I subscribe to you the following minuits of the comitte, of the whole Church of Kirtland the authorities &.c. refering you to my brother Hyrum [Smith] & br T. B. Marsh for further particulars also that you [p. 19] may know how to proceed to set in order & regulate the affairs of the Church in zion whenever they become disorganized[62] The minuits are as follows;

Minuits of a Conference assembled in committee of the whole Church on the 3rd. of Sept. 1837 9 o clock A.M. G[eorge] W. Robinson was called upon to take the minuits of the conference, S[idney] Rigdon then presented Joseph Smith Jr to the Church to know if they still

---

60. George W. Robinson also utilized the phrase "in all the world" to designate JS's presidential jurisdiction on the title page of this journal. By appending "in all the world" to his title, JS emphasized his authority over the church in Missouri and its presidency. The 7 November 1837 conference held in Missouri repeated the action of the 4 September Kirtland conference, reported in the minutes below, sustaining JS as "the first President of the whole Church, to preside over the same." (Minute Book 2, 7 Nov. 1837.)

61. In directing his letter to Corrill and Missouri church members generally, JS bypassed the Missouri presidency and bishopric. Corrill was serving as "agent to the Church and Keeper of the Lord's store House." (Minute Book 2, 22 May 1837.)

62. On 17 September, two weeks after this letter was written, a conference authorized JS and Rigdon "to go & appoint other Stakes or places of gathering." On 27 September, they and others left for Missouri, where in a November conference they set the church in order and made arrangements to enlarge Far West. (Minute Book 1, 17 Sept. 1837, 243; [JS], editorial, *Elders' Journal*, Nov. 1837, 27.)

looked upon & would still receive & uphold him as the Pres^t· of the whole Church And the vote was unanimous in the affirmative: Prs^t· Smith then presented S. Rigdon & F[rederick] G. Williams for his councilors and to constitute with himself the three first Pres^t· of the Church. Vote unanimous in the affirmative, Pres^t· Smith then intro- dused O[liver] Cowdery, J[oseph] Smith Sen. Hiram Smith & John Smith for assistant Councilors.[63] These last four together with the three first are to be concidred the heads of the Church, Carried unanimously. Voted that N. K. Whitny [Newel K. Whitney] hold his office as Bishop & continue to act as such in Kirtland & that R[eynolds] Cahoon & V[inson] Knight continue to act as councilors to the Bishop The Twelve Apostles were then presented one by one When T. B. Marsh D[avid] W. Patten B[righam] Young H. C. Kimble [Heber C. Kimball] O[rson] Hyde P[arley] P. Pratt O. Prat [Orson Pratt] Wm Smith W^m E McLellin, were received unanimously in their Apostleship Luke & Lyman Johnson & J[ohn] F. Boynton were rejected & cut off though privi- leged with conffesing and making sattisfaction, Elder Boynton (which was the only one present at the time) arose and endeavoured to confess, Justifying himself ~~in~~ ⟨on⟩ ⟨in⟩ his former conduct by reason of the fail- ure of the Bank &c his conduct was strongly protested by Elder [p. 20] Brigham Young in a plain and energetic manner, Stating verious rea- sons why he would or could not receive him into fellowship until a hearty conffession and repentance was manifested, He was followed by Elder Marsh who acquiesed in testimo[n]y & resolutions[64] Elder Boynton again arose & still attributed his difficulties to the failure of the Bank, stating that he had understood the Bank was instituted by the will of God, and he had been told that it never should fail let men do what they would Pres^t· Smith then arose and stated that if this had

---

63. Previously, the church presidency consisted of JS as president and five assistant presidents. After December 1834, Cowdery ranked first among the assistants. Their separation here into counselors and assistant counselors with Cowdery among the latter clearly constituted a demotion for Cowdery, if not for Joseph Smith Sr. and Hyrum Smith, who were already ranked behind Rigdon and Williams. John Smith, formerly the president of the Kirtland high council, was a new addition to the presidency. (Entries for 5 and 6 Dec. 1834, in JS History, 1834–1836, 17–20.)

64. Minute Book 1 includes at this point a summary of remarks by Sidney Rigdon regarding apostles John F. Boynton and Lyman Johnson, who operated a store in Kirtland: "President Rigdon then arose, & made an address of conciderable length, showing the starting point or cause of all the difficuly of Elders Boyngton & Johnson, he allso cautioned all the Elders, concrning leaving their calling to persue any ocupation derogatory to that calling, assuring them that if persued, God would let them run themselves into difficulties, that he may stop them in their career, that salvation may come unto them." (Minute Book 1, 3 Sept. 1837.)

been declared, no one had authority from him for so doing, For he had allways said unless the institution was conducted on richeous [righteous] principals it would not stand, A Vote was then taken to know if the congregation was sattisfied with Boyntons confession Voted in the negative[65] Conf— Adjourened for one hour——

Conferance assembled at 2 o clock P M. Op[e]ned by reading singing & prayer, The Pres[t.] then arose & said he would call upon the church to know if they were sattisfied with their High Council and should proceed to name them individualy John Johnson Joseph Coe Joseph Kingsbury & Martin⟨*⟩[66] Harris wire [were] objected to, also John P Green[e] but this case put over untill he should be present, Noah Packard Jared Carter Samuel H Smith, These were voted to retain their office Oliver Granger Henry G. Sherwood W[m] Marks Mahue [Mayhew] Hillman Harlow Readfield [Redfield] Asa[h]el Smith Phinehas [Phineas] Richards & David Dort were chosen to fill the place of those objected to,[67] The Pres[t.] then called upon the congregation to know if the recent appointed presidents of the seventies should stand in their calling Voted that John Gaylord James Foster Salmon Gee Daniel S Miles Joseph Youngs [Young] Josiah Butterfield [p. 21] & Levi Handcock [Hancock] should retain his ⟨their⟩ office as Pres[ts] of the Seventies John Gould was objected. The Pres then arose and made some remarks concerning the formers Pres[ts] of the Seventies, the callings and authorities of their Priesthood &c. &c. Voted that the old Presidents of the seventies be refered to the quorum of High Priests, And also that of if any of the members of the quorum of the seventies should be dissattisfied & would not submit to the Present order, and receive these last Presidents that they Should have power to demand their Lisence & they should no longer be concidered members of the church[68]

---

65. Luke and Lyman Johnson and John F. Boynton soon made acceptable confessions and regained church fellowship and their place in the Quorum of the Twelve. (Minute Book 1, 10 Sept. 1837.)

66. TEXT: The asterisk, inscribed in the margin next to Harris's name, references a note reading "over *" that appears at the foot of manuscript page 22. This "over" footnote refers the reader to the top of manuscript page 23, which adds part of a mistakenly passed-over section of minutes.

67. This copy omits information in the original minutes about four vacancies in the Kirtland high council, in addition to the four listed above, that these eight men were to fill. Samuel James was absent on a mission; the asterisk inserted earlier in this entry keys to a copy of this single omission that was added later in this entry. Also, Thomas Grover had "moved to the west," John Smith had been chosen to be "one of the Presidents of the church," and Orson Johnson had been excommunicated. (Minute Book 1, 3 Sept. 1837.)

68. The original minutes do not record a decision about disciplinary action for seventies unwilling to accept the arrangements. (Compare Minute Book 1, 3 Sept. 1837.)

Conferance Closed by Prayer by the President
~~Joseph Smith Jr   Pres~~ᵗ   ~~George W. Robinson   Clerk~~
G[eorge] W Robinson   Clk   Joseph Smith Jr   Presᵗ

Dear Brotheren

Oliver Cowdery has been in transgression,[69] but as he is now chosen as one
of the Presidents or councilors I trust that he will yet humble himself & magnify his calling but if he should not, the church will soon be under the neces-
saty of raising their hands against him Therefore pray for him, David Whitmer
Leonard Rich & others have been in transgression but we hope that they may
be humble & ere long make sattisfaction to the Church otherwise they cannot
retain their standing, Therefore we say unto you beware of all disaffected
Characters for they come not to build up but to destroy & scatter abroad,[70]
Though we or an Angel from Heaven preach any other Gospel or introduce
[any other?] order of things ⟨than⟩ those things which ye have received and are
authorized to received from the first Presidency let him be accursed,[71] May
God Almighty Bless you all & keep you unto the coming & kingdom of our
Lord and Savior Jesus Christ; Yours in the Bonds of the new ⟨covenent⟩—
J. Smith, Jr.

over * [p. 22]

Samu[e]l James was objected to by reason of his absence on a
mission and circumstances such that it is impossible for him to attend
to the duties of this office[72]

~~J. Smith J~~ᵗ~~ Pres~~ᵗ   ~~George W Robinson   (Clerk~~

---

69. Following the completion of the House of the Lord in Kirtland, Cowdery participated with JS and
other members of the First Presidency in major business initiatives.ᵃ As church leaders had no corporate
protection, the failure of these ventures during the national depression in 1837 plunged Cowdery into
debt.ᵇ Cowdery and others blamed these financial reverses on JS.ᶜ (a. Adams, "Chartering the Kirtland
Bank." b. See John Whitmer, Far West, MO, to Oliver Cowdery and David Whitmer, Kirtland Mills,
OH, 29 Aug. 1837, Western Americana Collection, Beinecke Rare Book and Manuscript Library, Yale
University. c. See Oliver Cowdery, Far West, MO, to Warren Cowdery, [Kirtland, OH], 21 Jan. 1838, in
Cowdery, Letterbook, 80–83; Oliver Cowdery, Far West, MO, to Warren Cowdery and Lyman Cowdery,
[Kirtland, OH], 4 Feb. 1838, in Cowdery, Letterbook, 83–86; Fullmer, Autobiography, [1]; see also
Synopsis of Oliver Cowdery Trial, 12 Apr. 1838, pp. 251–254 herein.)

70. Soon after the 3 September 1837 conference, Cowdery and Whitmer left Kirtland. Both arrived in
Missouri weeks before JS and Sidney Rigdon, and both were in attendance at the 7 November 1837 conference in Missouri. (Minute Book 1, 17 Sept. 1837; Minute Book 2, 7 Nov. 1837.)

71. See Galatians 1:8.

72. When copying the minutes into the letter, Robinson accidentally overlooked this passage concerning James's inability to serve on the high council. He therefore recorded the passage at the top of page 23.
(Compare Minute Book 1, 3 Sept. 1837.)

Revelation regarding John Whitmer and William W. Phelps • 4 Sept. 1837
Revelation to Joseph Smith Jr Given
in Kirtland Geauga Co. Ohio Sept 4ᵗʰ 1837
Making known the transgression of John Whitmer W[illiam] W. Phelps[73]
Verily thus saith the Lord unto you my Servent Joseph. My Servents John Whitmer & William W Phelps have done those things which are not pleasing in my sight Therefore if they repent not they shall be removed out of their places Amen—[74]

J Smith Jr

The above letter & revelation relative to the transgression and removal from office [of] D[avid] Whitmer O[liver] Cowdery J. Whitmer ⟨&.⟩ W. W. Phelps has been fulfiled as will be seen in the following Sequence

Letter to the Presidency in Kirtland • 29 March 1838
Far West March 29ᵗʰ A.D. 1838
To the ~~first~~ Presidency of the Church of Jesus Christ of Latter Day Saints in Kirtland
Dear & well beloved brotheren. Through the grace & mercy of our God, after a long & tedious journey of two months & one day, I and my family arrived in th[e] city of Far West Having been met at Huntsville 120 miles from this by brotheren with teams & money to forward us on our Journey When within eight miles of the City of Far West We were met by an [p. 23] escort of bretheren from the city Who were T[homas] B. Marsh John Corril[l] Elias Higby [Higbee] & severel others of the faithfull of the West Who received us with open armes and warm hearts and welcomed us to the bosom of their sosciety On our arrival in the city we wire [were] greeted on every hand by the saints who bid us welcom; Welcome; to the land of their inheritance Dear bretheren you may be assured that so friendly a meeting & reception paid us Will [well] for our long seven years of servictude persecution & affliction in the midst of our enimies in the land Kirtland yea verily our hearts were full and we feel greatfull to Almighty God for his kindness unto us. The

---

73. It appears that JS sent a copy of this revelation with his 4 September 1837 letter to John Corrill and the church in Missouri. (See pp. 240–244 herein.)

74. Thomas B. Marsh, one of the temporary presidents who replaced the Missouri presidency in 1838, later accused Whitmer and Phelps of using the land for personal interests and for making transactions independent of the high council and bishopric. During his visit to Missouri in November 1837, JS attempted to resolve problems regarding the "disposition of the Town plot and the purchase of land" originally purchased by Whitmer and Phelps using donations of church members. (Minute Book 2, 6 Nov. 1837 and 10 Mar. 1838; Thomas B. Marsh, [Far West, MO], to Wilford Woodruff, [Vinalhaven, ME], 1838, *Elders' Journal*, July 1838, 37.)

particulars of our Journey brotheren cannot weell be writen but we trust that the same God who has protected us will protect you also, and will sooner or later grant us the privilege of seeing each other face ⟨to⟩ face & of rehersing ~~of~~ all our sufferings We have herd of the destruction of the printing office which we presume to believe must have been occasioned by the Parrishites or more properly the Aristocrats or Anarchys as we believe, The saints here have provided a room for us and daily necessary's which is brought in from all parts of the co. to make us comfortable, so that I have nothing to do but to attend to my spiritual concerns or the spiritual affairs of the Church The difficulties of the Church had been ajusted before arrival here by a Judicious High Council With T. B. Marsh & D[avid] W Patten who acted as Pres. Pro. Tem. of the Church of zion being appointed by the voice of the Council & Church Wm. W. Phelps & John Whitmer having been cut off from the Church,[75] D[avid] Whitmer remains as yit The saints at this time are in union & peace & love prevails throughout, in a word Heaven smiles upon the saints in Caldwell. Various & many have been the falshoods writen from thence [p. 24] to this place, but have prevailed nothing, We have no uneaseness about the power of our enimies in this place to do us harm B<u>r</u> Samuel H Smith & family arrived here soon after we did in go[o]d health. Br B[righam] Young Br D[aniel] S. Miles & Br L[evi] Richards arrivd here when we did, They were with us on the last of our journey which ad[d]ed much to our sattisfaction, They also are well They have provided places for their families & are now about to break the ground for seed, Being under the hand of wicked vexatious Lawsuits for seven years past my buisness was so dangerous that I was not able to leave it, in as good a situation as I had antisipated, but if there are any wrongs, They shall all be noticed so far as the Lord gives me ability & power to do so,[76] say to all the brotheren that I have not forgotton them, but remember them in my prayers, Say to Mother [Sarah] Beaman that I remembr her, Also Br Daniel Carter Br Stong [Ezra Strong] & family Br [Oliver] Granger & family, Finally I cannot innumerate them all for the want of room I will just name Br Knights [Vinson Knight] the Bishop &c. My best respects to them all ~~for the want of room~~ & I

---

75. Under the direction of Marsh and Patten of the Quorum of the Twelve, who were serving as presidents pro tempore of the church in Missouri, the Missouri high council excommunicated Phelps and Whitmer a few days before JS's arrival. The principal charge was that they had unjustifiably obligated Bishop Edward Partridge to pay them $2,000 after they transferred to him responsibility for the sale of property in Far West. (Minute Book 2, 10 Mar. 1838; see also Minute Book 2, 3 and 5–7 Apr. 1837; and Thomas B. Marsh, [Far West, MO], to Wilford Woodruff, [Vinalhaven, ME], 1838, *Elders' Journal*, July 1838, 37–38.)

76. JS later assigned Oliver Granger to settle JS's remaining debts in Kirtland. (Certificate, JS et al. to Oliver Granger, Commerce, IL, 13 May 1839, in JS Letterbook 2, pp. 45–46; JS, Nauvoo, IL, to Oliver Granger, New York, [23] July 1840, in JS Letterbook 2, pp. 159–161.)

commend them and the Church of God in Kirtland to our Heavenly Father & the word of his grace, which is able to make you wise unto Salvation I would just say to Br. [William] Marks, that I saw in a vision while on the road that whereas he was closely persued by an innumerable concource of enimies and as they pressed upon him hard as if they were about to devour him, It ⟨&⟩ had seemingly attained some degre[e] of advantage over him But about this time a chariot of fire came and near the place and the Angel of the Lord put forth his hand unto Br. Marks & said [p. 25] unto him thou art my son come <u>here,</u> and immediately he was caught up in the Chariot and rode away triumphantly out of their midst and again the Lord said I will raise th[ee] up for a blessing unto many people Now the particulars of this whole matter cannot be writen at this time but the vision was evidently given to me that I might know that the hand of the Lord would be on his behalf   J Smith Jr

I transmit to you the folowing motto of the Church of Jesus Christ of Latter day Saints Recorded on Pages 16 & 17 of J Smith Jr Scriptory Record Book A. We left Pres. [Sidney] Rigdon 30 miles this side of Parris [Paris] Illinois in consequence of the sickness of Br. G[eorge] W. Robinsons wife,[77] on yesterday br Robinson arrived here who informed us that his father in Law (S. Rigdon) was at Huntsville detained there on account of the ill health of his wife, They will probaly be here soon,[78] Choice seeds of all kinds of fruit also Choice breed of Cattle would be in much demand also, best blood of horses garden seeds of every description also hay seed of all sorts, all of these are much needed in this place

Verry respetfully I subscribe myself your servent in Christ our Lord & Savior

> Joseph Smith Jr
> Pres^t· of the Church of
> Jesus Christ of
> Latterday Saints

————— ⁊ —————

Editorial Note

The following letter, which concerns a potential land purchase, interrupts the series of documents dealing with dissenting church leaders. After transcribing this letter, George W. Robinson copied in four more documents in that series. Despite the Caldwell County

---

77. JS's later history recounted that he left Rigdon and the Rigdon family at Terre Haute, Indiana, about twenty miles east, not west, of Paris. Rigdon's son also recounted his family parting with JS in Indiana and then traveling to Paris. (JS History, vol. B-1, 780; Rigdon, "Life Story of Sidney Rigdon," 62.)

78. Rigdon arrived at Far West six days later, 4 April 1838. (JS History, vol. B-1, 786.)

"solution" to the "Mormon problem" in Missouri—namely, Caldwell County, and only Caldwell County, for the Mormons—by early 1838 shrewd observers of northwest Missouri saw the potential for competition between the Latter-day Saints and their neighbors beyond Caldwell County. In this letter David Thomas, an owner of land in Carroll County, suggested that the Latter-day Saints purchase land in that area as a strategic site for settlement and commerce. Thomas's letter introduced JS to Henry Root, who visited JS on 1 April 1838. Church leaders later met with Thomas and Root and eventually agreed to purchase land from Root at De Witt, where Saints proceeded to settle.[79]

—————— ☙ ——————

Letter from David Thomas • 31 March 1838
Pleasent [Pleasant] Park Mo. March 31ˢᵗ 1838
Respected Sir

Permit me to introduce to your acquaintance Mr Henry Root of Dewit [De Witt] near this place on Missouri river His buisness I am unacquainted with, Though any thing he may say to you, you may put the most implisit confidence in, as I have allways found him to be a man of truth & honor, neither have I ever [p. 26] known him to give a misrepresentation of any part, He is a merchant and I suppose doing a moderate buisness[.] his place is now, onley laid out about a year since a beautifull sight to the river, and a first rate landing And Sir permit me to say to you, if you could make it convenient or for your advantage to settle in this County, I would let you have part of my land[.] There is yet to enter adjoining my land, as good land is in the world, I have no doubt you can do as weell here in forming a settlement and probaly better than any place in the state The facilities of the river will be of great servise ~~to~~ in settling this uper country besid[e]s some of the knowing ones have aimed to uproot you, but here you can break them down in turn,[80] I will join you in the speculation if necessary and if possible the church[.] I will have after paying for 1600 acres of land $4,000, If they pay me in Far West, enough give my respects to Mrs Smith & accept for yourself

a friends respect

David Thomas

Elder Joseph Smith Jr

---

79. Baugh, "Call to Arms," 144–145.

80. Located at the confluence of the Grand and Missouri rivers, De Witt was a strategic site for facilitating Mormon participation in regional commerce. The Saints were able to haul agricultural products from Far West by wagon to Adam-ondi-Ahman and then ship them on the Grand River to De Witt landing, and from there on the Missouri River to other markets. (Riggs, "Economic Impact of Fort Leavenworth," 130.)

N.B. P.S. Further I own a section of land in Monroe [County] near the forks of Salt river, and if necessary sell or make a settlement there I know of no man in the world I would rather entertain than yourself I would be glad if you would find whether my debt is secure in that place, and let me know Please to help me if you can do so without being oppressive to your feelings or interest these I do not wish you [to?] violate for me Mr Root is my confidential friend anything [you?] may say to him is safe, if you cannot come [p. 27] a line from you at any time will be thankfully Received through the mail or otherwise D.T.

I expect Mr Root is on the buisness which I have named to you in this, We have consulted on this buisness by others——   David Thomas

Letter to John Whitmer • 9 April 1838

Letter Sent to John Whitmer in consequence of witholding the records of the church in the city of Far West when called for by the Clerk[81] &c

Far West April 9th 1838

Mr J. Whitmer

Sir. We were desireous of honouring you by giving publicity to your notes on the history of the Church of Latter day Saints, after such corrections as we thaught would be necessary; knowing your incompetency as a historian, and that your writings coming from your pen, could not be put to the press, without our correcting them, or elce the Church must suffer reproach; Indeed Sir, we never supposed you capable of writing a history; but were willing to let it come out under your name notwithstanding it would realy not be yours but ours. We are still willing to honour you, if you can be made to know your own interest and give up your notes, so that they can be corrected, and made fit for the press. But if not, we have all the materials for another, which we shall commence this week to write[82]

                                        your humble Servents
Attest   Joseph Smith Jr
    E[benezer] Robinson   Sidney Rigdon
    Clerk   Presidents of the whole
                                     Church of Latterday Saints

---

81. John Whitmer was excommunicated a month earlier. Appointed church historian in 1831, he commenced working on—or more likely keeping records for—a history of the church that year. He also had copies of other church records. (Minute Book 2, 10 Mar. 1838; Revelation, ca. 8 Mar. 1831–B, in Doctrine and Covenants 63, 1835 ed. [D&C 47]; Whitmer, History, 1.)

82. The church presidency never received Whitmer's history or historical notes and began writing a new history of the church about three weeks later. In 1903, the Reorganized Church of Jesus Christ of Latter Day Saints purchased Whitmer's history from George Schweich, David Whitmer's grandson. (JS, Journal, 27 Apr. 1838; *History of the Reorganized Church,* 62–63.)

N.B. * over— [p. 28]

*The preceding letter to John Whitmer was entered through a mistake occupying a space not belonging to it. not standing in its place[83]

Minutes • 6 April 1838

Minuits of a Conf. of the authorities of the Church of Latter day Saints Assembled at their first quarterly Conference in the City of Far West April 6th 1838 for the aniversary of the organization of the church, Also to transact Church buisness,

Presidents Joseph Smith Jr & Sidney Rigdon Presided Presidency 2nd George Morey & Demick [Dimick] Huntington, were appointed Sexton and door keepers John Corril[l] & Elias Higby Higbee ⟨Historians⟩ 3 T[homas] B. Marsh, D[avid] W. Patten, & B[righam] Young of the twelve were appointed Presidents Pro. Tem of the city of Far West ⟨Church of Christ of L.D. Saints in Missouri.⟩, as the former Pres. D[avid] Whitmer W. W. Phelps [William W. Phelps] John Whitmer had been put out of their office[84] 4th George W. Robinson was elected as general Church Clerk & Recorder to keep a record of the whole Church also as Scribe for the first Presidency

5th Ebinezer [Ebenezer] Robinson was Chosen Clerk & Recorder for the city Far West ⟨High Council & Church in Mo.⟩ also for the High Council

The remainder of the proceedings will be seen in the record kept by E Robinson Also the trial of the expresidents as will be seen by the following abridgement[85]

----------- ∾ -----------

Editorial Note

In late January and early February 1838, Thomas B. Marsh and David W. Patten, senior members of the Quorum of the Twelve, and the Missouri high council investigated the actions and attitudes of the Missouri presidency—David Whitmer, William W. Phelps, and John Whitmer—and conducted a series of meetings of the general membership of the church in Caldwell County that resulted in the removal of the presidency from office. Marsh indicated that the proceedings were carried out according to instructions from JS.[86] Phelps and John Whitmer were excommunicated on 10 March 1838, just days before the

---

83. George W. Robinson apparently intended that this letter be copied into the journal in chronological order, which would have placed it after the minutes of the 6 April conference rather than before them.

84. Young now joined Marsh and Patten as presidents pro tempore. The three most senior members of the Quorum of the Twelve now presided over the church in Missouri.

85. In the local church record book, Ebenezer Robinson, the clerk and recorder for the church in Missouri, kept more complete minutes of the three-day conference and of the trials. (Minute Book 2, 6–8 and 12–13 Apr. 1838.)

86. Minute Book 2, 20 and 26 Jan. 1838; 5–10 Feb. 1838.

arrival of JS in Far West.[87] A month later, with JS present, Oliver Cowdery, David Whitmer, and apostle Lyman Johnson were tried and excommunicated in separate proceedings. George W. Robinson recorded a summary of those proceedings in this journal.

The extent to which the church and its leaders should be involved in its members' temporal affairs was a central issue in 1837 and 1838. Dissenters were critical of JS's decisions and even of his very involvement in nonecclesiastical matters. The financial decisions of Oliver Cowdery and other leaders in Missouri, which were not in keeping with JS's views of how church leaders should operate, were the basis for some of the charges against the Missouri presidency in January and February of 1838, charges that resulted in their removal from office.[88] These decisions were also central in the April excommunication trial of Oliver Cowdery.

Cowdery faced nine charges relating to financial management and loyalty to JS and the church. The trial proceeded according to official instructions for trying "a president of the high priesthood" before a "common council of the church," which consisted of a bishop acting as a "common judge" assisted by twelve high priests.[89] In a letter written to the high council, Cowdery underscored his refusal to be "influenced, governed, or controlled, in my temporal interests by any ecclesiastical authority or pretended revelation what ever." Denouncing JS's ecclesiastical interventions in his personal financial affairs as a violation of "Constitutional privileges and inherent rights," Cowdery announced his withdrawal from church membership.[90]

———— ✿ ————

Synopsis of Oliver Cowdery Trial • 12 April 1838

Charge prefered against O[liver] Cowdery before the high Council in Far West Mo.— by Elder Seymour Brounson [Brunson],

To the Bishop and Council of the Church of Jesus Christ of Latter Day Saints, [p. 29]

I do hereby prefer the following Charges against Oliver Cowdery, which consists of nine in number. 1ˢᵗ For persecuting the bretheren, by urging on vexatious lawsuits against the Bretheren and thus distressing the inocent.[91] 2ⁿᵈ For seeking to destroy the Character of Pres.

87. Minute Book 2, 10 Mar. 1838.

88. See Minute Book 2, 20 and 26 Jan. 1838; 5–10 Feb. 1838.

89. Revelation, 11 Nov. 1831–B, in Doctrine and Covenants 3:33, 37, 1835 ed. [D&C 107:74, 82–84].

90. Oliver Cowdery, Far West, MO, to Edward Partridge, 12 Apr. 1837, in Minute Book 2, 12 Apr. 1838. For a more complete record of the trial, kept by Ebenezer Robinson, see Minute Book 2, 12 Apr. 1838.

91. In the minutes of the trial, this charge reads, "For stirring up the enemy to persecute the brethren by urging on vexatious Lawsuits and thus distressing the innocent."ᵃ Cowdery was evidently developing a debt-collection practice, probably advising and preparing paperwork on small debts in relationship with established attorneys. The council heard testimony that Cowdery was connected with recent demands and writs served to collect notes from other Latter-day Saints, including JS.ᵇ A foundational revelation regarding church conduct directed Saints to resolve problems within church courts and not "before the

Prominent church excommunicants. In 1837–1838, conflicts over church authority and financial management led to the excommunication of several prominent church leaders. These included Oliver Cowdery, assistant counselor in the church presidency (top left); David Whitmer, president of the church in Missouri (top right); and Whitmer's counselors in the presidency, William W. Phelps (bottom left) and John Whitmer (bottom right). (David Whitmer image courtesy Community of Christ Library-Archives, Independence, MO. All others: Church History Library, Salt Lake City.)

Joseph Smith Jr by falsly insinuating that he was guilty of adultery &c.[92] 3ʳᵈ· By treating the Church with contempt by not attending meeting.[93] 4ᵗʰ· For virtually denying the faith by declaring that he would not be governed by any eclesiasticle authority nor revelation whatever in his temporal affairs. 5ᵗʰ For selling his lands in Jackson Co. Contrary to the revelations.[94] 6ᵗʰ For writing and sending an insulting letter to Pres. T[homas] B. Marsh while on the high Council attending to the duties of his office as president of the Council and ⟨by⟩ insulting the high Council with the contents of said letter:[95] 7ᵗʰ For

world."ᶜ Especially following the financial reverses of 1837, Saints considered bringing "brethren before the magistrates for debt" a serious breach of fellowship.ᵈ In June, JS's brother Hyrum Smith and several other Saints signed a document accusing Cowdery of supporting "vexatious lawsuits" against the Saints in Kirtland to "cheat and defraud" them.ᵉ (a. Minute Book 2, 12 Apr. 1838. b. Oliver Cowdery, Far West, MO, to Warren Cowdery and Lyman Cowdery, Kirtland, OH, [10] Mar. 1838, in Cowdery, Letterbook, 90–93; see also Minute Book 2, 12 Apr. 1838. c. Revelation, 23 Feb. 1831, in Doctrine and Covenants 13:23, 1835 ed. [D&C 42:89]. d. Record of Seventies, bk. A, 30 July 1837, 31–32; 5 Dec. 1837, 37. e. Sampson Avard et al., Far West, MO, to Oliver Cowdery et al., Far West, MO, June 1838, in State of Missouri, "Copies of Part of the Evidence," [21].)

92. Testimony from George W. Harris, David W. Patten, and Thomas B. Marsh confirmed that Cowdery had made such insinuations about JS's relationship in Kirtland with a young woman named Fanny Alger. At the trial, JS stated that as Cowdery "had been his bosom friend, therefore he intrusted him with many things"—apparently confirming the reality of a confidential relationship with Alger. JS then "gave a history respecting the girl business."ᵃ This history may have regarded the origins of the Mormon practice of polygamy. Revelation claimed by JS sanctioning the polygyny practiced by Old Testament patriarchs was evidently related to JS's 1831 work on revision of the Bible.ᵇ Kirtland Mormons, including Alger's family, viewed the relationship as an early plural marriage. Nevertheless, an estranged Cowdery insisted on characterizing the relationship as "a dirty, nasty, filthy affair of his and Fanny Alger's."ᶜ (a. Minute Book 2, 12 Apr. 1838. b. Bachman, "Ohio Origins of the Revelation on Eternal Marriage"; Compton, In Sacred Loneliness, 27. c. Oliver Cowdery, Far West, MO, to Warren Cowdery, [Kirtland, OH], 21 Jan. 1838, in Cowdery, Letterbook, 80–83; see also Parkin, "Conflict at Kirtland," 128–135.)

93. Cowdery joined with David and John Whitmer in defending their absences from regular Far West church services. (See Oliver Cowdery, Far West, MO, to Warren Cowdery and Lyman Cowdery, [Kirtland, OH], 4 Feb. 1838, in Cowdery, Letterbook, 83–86.)

94. After receiving news that a mob had forced church leaders in Missouri to sign an agreement to leave Jackson County—the site designated by revelation for the city of Zion—JS wrote to the leaders, "It is the will of the Lord . . . that not one foot of land perchased should be given to the enemies."ᵃ After an earlier sheriff's sale for court costs, Cowdery with William W. Phelps and John Whitmer held residual title to three lots and full title to another. They sold their interest in the four lots on 11 January 1838.ᵇ (a. JS, Kirtland, OH, to William W. Phelps et al., [Missouri], 18 Aug. 1833, JS Collection, CHL; see also JS, Kirtland Mills, OH, to Edward Partridge et al., Liberty, MO, 10 Dec. 1833, in JS Letterbook 1, pp. 70–75. b. Jackson Co., MO, Deed Records, 11 Jan. 1838, bk. F, 54–56, microfilm, U.S. and Canada Record Collection, FHL; Oliver Cowdery, Far West, MO, to Warren Cowdery and Lyman Cowdery, [Kirtland, OH], 4 Feb. 1838, in Cowdery, Letterbook, 83–86; Minute Book 2, 12 Apr. 1838.)

95. As temporary president of the church in Missouri, Marsh presided over the March high council trial of William W. Phelps and John Whitmer. During the trial, Marsh received a letter from David Whitmer, Phelps, and John Whitmer declaring that the council was "an illegal tribunal" and

leaving his Calling in which God had appointed him by revelation for
the sake of filthy lucre & turning to the practice of Law. 8th For dis-
grasing the Church by being Connected in the Bogus buisness as common report says.[96] 9th For dishonestly retaining Notes after they had
been Paid,[97] and finally for leaving or forsaking the cause of God and
returning to the begerly elements of the world, neglecting his high
and holy Calling Contrary to his profession
    April 11th 1838[98]———

The Bishop and high Council assembled at the Bishops office, in trial of
the above Charges April 12th 1838 After the organization of the Council the
above Charges were read. Also a letter from O. Cowdery, as will be found
recorded in the Church record of the city of Far West Book A.[99] The 1st 2nd 3rd
7th 8th & 9th Charges were Sustained [p. 30] The 4th & 5th Charges were

---

that members of the council were prejudiced against them. Moreover, they signed the letter as church presidents—thereby rejecting the earlier decisions by the high council and the church in Missouri that removed them from office. The letter was written and attested by Cowdery and delivered by his nephew Marcellus. Cowdery certified the delivered copy as "Clerk of High Council"—an implicit assertion of the authority of the former presidency and the illegitimacy of Marsh and the proceedings of his council. These sentiments were made explicit in a letter to his brothers. (Minute Book 2, 10 Mar. 1838; Oliver Cowdery, Far West, MO, to Warren Cowdery and Lyman Cowdery, Kirtland, OH, [10] Mar. 1838, in Cowdery, Letterbook, 90–93.)

96. *Bogus* at this time was associated with counterfeit coin.*a* The council found the charge "sustained satisfactoryly by circumstantial evidence." JS testified that he had warned Cowdery of an arrest warrant that would be served against Cowdery in Kirtland for purchasing "Bogus money & dies" and that when JS and Rigdon confronted Cowdery, he denied the charge. JS and Rigdon then warned Cowdery to leave Kirtland if guilty, and JS recounted that "that night or the next he left the country."*b* Eight years later, in a letter to his brother-in-law, Cowdery vigorously denied having committed "crimes of theft, forgery, &c. Those which all my former associates knew to be false."*c* (*a.* "Bogus," in *Oxford English Dictionary,* 1:242; [JS], editorial, *Elders' Journal,* Aug. 1838, 58. *b.* Minute Book 2, 12 Apr. 1838. *c.* Oliver Cowdery, Tiffin, OH, to Phineas Young, Nauvoo, IL, 23 Mar. 1846, CHL.)

97. Sidney Rigdon explained in the trial that in January 1837, he and JS bought out Cowdery's interest in the Kirtland printing office by making out notes to him. Cowdery, however, then wanted to purchase from them a press and some of the type. They agreed, "on conditions that he should give up the notes above refered to." Rigdon stated that Cowdery took the press and more than his share of the type, "but the notes he did not give up." There is no evidence, however, that Cowdery attempted to collect on the notes or sell them to a third party. (Minute Book 2, 12 Apr. 1838; regarding how notes functioned as scrip, see 117n194 herein.)

98. Cowdery wrote that he received notice of the complaint on 9 April 1838, which indicates the possibility that the version of Seymour Brunson's complaint copied into the hearing record is misdated or is a revised version of the charges. (See Minute Book 2, 12 Apr. 1838.)

99. Cowdery responded specifically to and acknowledged the validity of only the fourth and fifth charges. Denouncing JS's ecclesiastical interventions in his personal financial affairs as a violation of "Constitutional privileges and inherent rights," Cowdery announced his withdrawal from church membership. (Minute Book 2, 12 Apr. 1838.)

rejected[100] & the 6th withdrawn Consequently he (O. Cowdery) was concidered no longer a member of the Church of Jesus Christ of Latterday Saints Voted by the high Council that Oliver Cowdery be no longer a Committee to select locations for the gathering of the Saints[101]——

——— ❧ ———

Editorial Note

The day following Oliver Cowdery's trial, the Missouri high council tried former Missouri president David Whitmer for his membership in the church. At this high council hearing, Whitmer was to be tried as a high priest, which Whitmer rejected because he still considered himself president and refused to recognize as legitimate the earlier proceedings that removed him from office.[102] Although the 7 November 1837 conference clarified that he presided only over the church in Missouri, Whitmer still believed that he should instead be tried not only as president in Missouri but as a president of the high priesthood and therefore not subject to the decision of a regular council of high priests—and that attending the council and "a[n]swering to charges as a High Priest, should be acknowledgeing the correctness and legality of those former assumed Councils." Nonetheless, believing that the high council was determined to remove him at all costs—even, he charged, if it required violating the church order outlined in revelations—Whitmer announced by letter his withdrawal from the church's "fellowship and communion." After reading Whitmer's letter, the council concluded that "it was not considered necessary to investigate the case, as he had offered contempt to the Council by writing the above letter" and that Whitmer was therefore "not worthy a membership in the Church," whereupon he was excommunicated.[103]

This same day the high council also heard the case of Lyman Johnson, a member of the Quorum of the Twelve. The letter of charges against Johnson included specific instructions regarding an earlier judicial matter, instructions that Johnson rejected as a violation of his constitutional rights. He therefore responded to the letter by refusing to cooperate and by announcing his withdrawal from fellowship with the Saints until that matter was removed

---

100. The minutes show no discussion of charges 4 through 6, noting only the rejection of charges 4 and 5 and the withdrawal of charge 6. The council may have rejected the very charges that Cowdery acknowledged in order to avoid addressing the problematic issues highlighted in Cowdery's protest: ecclesiastical control of individuals' temporal affairs and the sale of Jackson County property. After Cowdery sold his property, the prospects for returning to Jackson County continued to dwindle, and within months Bishop Newel K. Whitney sold the central church lots. (Minute Book 2, 12 Apr. 1838; Jackson Co., MO, Deed Records, 3 July 1838, bk. F, 52, microfilm, U.S. and Canada Record Collection, FHL.)

101. According to the Missouri council minutes, the decision to remove Cowdery from the committee was made the following day in connection with the trial for David Whitmer. This committee—which originally consisted of Cowdery, David W. Patten, John Corrill, and Lyman Wight—was appointed at a church council on 6 November 1837 to search for possible sites for Latter-day Saint settlements in northern Missouri. (Minute Book 2, 13 Apr. 1838; 6 Nov. and 7 Dec. 1837; [JS], editorial, *Elders' Journal*, Nov. 1837, 27–28; Oliver Cowdery, Far West, MO, to Warren Cowdery, [Kirtland, OH], 21 Jan. 1838, in Cowdery, Letterbook, 80–83.)

102. See 253n95 herein.

103. Minute Book 2, 13 Apr. 1838.

from the charges. Johnson's hearing, which included testimony of a number of witnesses, resulted in his excommunication.[104]

———————— ✌ ————————

Synopsis of David Whitmer and Lyman Johnson Trials • 13 April 1838

The following Charges were prefered against David Whi[t]mer before the high Council which assembled on the 13[th] of April 1838 for the purpose of attending to such Charges.[105] Which Charges are as follows

> 1[st] For not observing the words of wisdom,[106] 2[nd] For unchristian-like conduct in neglecting to attend to meeting*s* in uniting with and possesing the same spirit of the desenters 3rd In writing letters to the desenters in Kirtland unfaivorable to the Cause, and to the Character of Joseph Smith Jr.[107] 4th In neglecting the duties of his calling and seperating himself from the Church while he has a name among us. 5th For Signing himself Pres. of the Church of Christ after he had been cut off, in an insulting, letter to the High Council,

After reading the above Charges together with a letter sent to the Pres. of said Council, (a copy of which may be found recorded in Far West record Book A.)[108] The Council considered the charges sustained and Consequently Considred him no longer a member of the Church of Jesus Christ of Latterday Saints.—

Also the same day and date a Charge was prefered against Lyman E Johnson consisting of 3 charges[109] ~~which~~ which were read together with a letter from him

––––––––––––––––––––––

104. For a more detailed record of the hearings involving Whitmer and Johnson, see Minute Book 2, 13 Apr. 1838.

105. Apostle Thomas B. Marsh presided over this Missouri high council meeting in his capacity as temporary president of the church in Missouri, assisted by apostles David W. Patten and Brigham Young, acting in their capacities as Marsh's assistants. JS also attended the trial. (Minute Book 2, 13 Apr. 1838.)

106. An 1833 revelation that referred to itself as "a word of wisdom" proscribed tobacco, wine, "strong drinks," and "hot drinks"—commonly understood to include tea and coffee.[a] However, individuals were generally disciplined for nonobservance only in instances of flagrant intoxication or in combination with more serious charges of other kinds.[b] Whitmer used tobacco, coffee, and tea and reportedly stated that he did not consider coffee and tea to be hot drinks.[c] (*a.* Revelation, 27 Feb. 1833, in Doctrine and Covenants 80, 1835 ed. [D&C 89]; Peterson, "Word of Wisdom," 20, 22–23. *b.* Backman, *Heavens Resound,* 257–261. *c.* Minute Book 2, 26 Jan. and 5 Feb. 1838; compare "Letters from David and John C. Whitmer," *Saints' Herald,* 5 Feb. 1887, 89.)

107. No Whitmer letters of this nature are known to be extant.

108. Minute Book 2 includes a copy of Whitmer's 13 April letter in connection with the minutes of the 13 April disciplinary proceedings against Whitmer.

109. According to the official record, seven charges were preferred against apostle Johnson, not three: first, for "persecuting brethren" by encouraging and supporting "vexatious lawsuits"; second, for

in answer to them Which will be ⟨found⟩ recorded in Far West record [p. 31] Book A.[110] The charges were sustained and he was consequently cut off from the Church.——

Editorial Note

The previous entry concludes the series of copied items regarding discipline of church leaders. At this point George W. Robinson copied in three nearly contemporaneous revelations.

Revelation for David W. Patten • 11 April 1838

Revelation to D[avid] W. Patten. given April 11th. 1838 Verily thus Saith the Lord, it is wisdom in my Servant D. W. Patten, that he settle up all his buisness, as soon as he possibly, can, and make a disposition of his merchandise, that he may perform a mission unto me next spring, in company with ~~with~~ others even twelve including himself, to testify of my name and bear glad tidings unto all the world,[111] for verrily thus Saith the Lord that inasmuch as there are those among you who deny my name, others shall be planted in their stead and receive their bishoprick Amen.——

Revelation for Brigham Young • 17 April 1838

Revelation given to Brigham Young at Far West April 17th 1838. Verrily

---

"virtually denying the faith" by supporting dissenters and "treating the Church with contempt" by failure to attend church meetings and observe church practices; third, for "seeking to injure the character" of JS; fourth, for physically attacking Phineas Young; fifth, for "speaking reproachfully of the authority of Caldwell County" by saying that he could not obtain justice in a lawsuit before the county court and that he would appeal the decision; sixth, for lying; and seventh, for cheating a man out of property. (Minute Book 2, 13 Apr. 1838.)

110. Minute Book 2 includes a copy of Johnson's 12 April letter in connection with the minutes of the 13 April disciplinary proceedings against Johnson.

111. Beginning in 1835, Patten and other members of the Quorum of the Twelve anticipated preaching overseas, but they were hampered by disunity and then dissension within their quorum.[a] By assignment from JS, apostles Heber C. Kimball and Orson Hyde had already led an initial mission to England, and they were preparing to return to the United States.[b] An 8 July 1838 revelation called the Twelve to proselytize "over the great waters" beginning in April 1839.[c] Mortally wounded in the battle at Crooked River on 25 October 1838, Patten did not journey to the British Isles with the Twelve.[d] (a. Revelation, ca. Apr. 1835, in Doctrine and Covenants 3:11, 1835 ed. [D&C 107:23]; Thomas B. Marsh and David W. Patten, Far West, MO, to Parley P. Pratt, Toronto, Upper Canada, 10 May 1837, in JS Letterbook 2, pp. 62–63; Esplin, "Emergence of Brigham Young," chap. 6. b. Kimball, "History," 54–56; Historian's Office, "History of Orson Hyde," 16, Histories of the Twelve, ca. 1858–1880, CHL; Allen et al., Men with a Mission, chap. 2. c. Revelation, 8 July 1838–A, in JS, Journal, 8 July 1838, p. 285 herein [D&C 118:4]. d. Kimball, "History," 86.)

thus Saith the Lord, Let my Servant Brigham Young go unto the place which he has baught on Mill Creek and there provide for his family until an effectual door is op[e]ned for the suport of his family untill I shall command [him] to go hence, and not to leave his family untill they are amply provided for Amen.[112]——

Revelation • 26 April 1838

Revelation[113] given in Far West, April 26⟨th⟩, 1838, Making known the will of God, concerning the building up of this place and of the Lord's house &c.

Verrily thus Saith the Lord unto you my Servant Joseph Smith Jr. and also my Servant Sidney Rigdon, and also my Servant Hyrum Smith, and your counselors who are and who shall be hereafter appointed,[114] and also unto my Servant Edward Partridge and his Counsilors, and also unto my faithfull Servants, who are of the High Council of my Church in zion (for thus it shall be called) and unto all the Elders and people of my Church of Jesus Christ of Latter Day Saints, Scattered abroad [p. 32] in all the world, For thus shall my Church be called in the Last days even the Church of Jesus Christ of Latter Day Saints,[115] Verrily I say unto you all; arise and shine forth ~~forth~~ that thy light may be a standard for the nations and that thy gathering to-gether upon the land of zion and upon her stakes may be for a defence and for a reffuge from the storm and from wrath when it shall be poured out without mixture upon the whole Earth, Let the City Far West, be a holy and consecrated land unto me, and ⟨it shall⟩ be called ⟨most⟩ holy for the ground upon which thou standest is holy Therefore I command you to build an house unto me for the gathering togeth~~er~~ing of my Saints that they may worship me, and let there be a begining of this work; and a foundation and a preparatory work, this following Summer; and let the begining be made on the 4ᵗʰ day of July next; and from that time forth let my people labour diligently to build an house, unto my name, and in one year from this day, let them recommence laying the foundation of my house; thus let them from that time forth laibour diligently untill it shall be finished, from

---

112. Almost three months later, JS dictated a revelation with similar content to the Twelve. (Revelation, 8 July 1838–A, in JS, Journal, 8 July 1838, p. 285 herein [D&C 118].)

113. Now D&C 115.

114. Hyrum Smith was appointed second counselor to JS on 7 November 1837, replacing Frederick G. Williams. (Minute Book 2, 7 Nov. 1837.)

115. The church organized in 1830 as the "Church of Christ" but later adopted the more distinctive name "The Church of the Latter Day Saints."ᵃ The revelation recorded here made official the name that had recently emerged as a combination of the two earlier forms.ᵇ (a. "Communicated," *The Evening and the Morning Star*, May 1834, 160. b. See, for example, Minute Book 2, 9 Apr. 1831; JS, Journal, 5 Dec. 1834; Letter to John Corrill and the Church in Missouri, 4 Sept. 1837, p. 241 herein; and Letter to the Presidency in Kirtland, 29 Mar. 1838, p. 245 herein.)

Book A. He charge were Sustained and he was consequently cut off from the Church.

Revelation to D. W. Patten. given April 11th 1838
Verily thus saith the Lord, it is wisdom in my Servant D. W. Patten, that he settle up all his buisness, as soon as he possibly can, and make a disposition of his merchandise, that he may perform a mission unto me next spring, in company with others Even twelve including himself, to testify of my name and bear glad tidings unto all the world, for Verily thus Saith the Lord that inasmuch as there are those among you who deny my name, others shall be planted in their Stead and receive their Bishoprick Amen.

Revelation given to Brigham Young at Far West April 17th 1838. Verily thus Saith the Lord; Let my servant Brigham Young go unto the place which he has bought on Mill Creek and there provide for his family until an effectual door is opened for the suport of his family untill I Shall command to go hence, and not to leave his family untill they are amply provided for Amen

Revelation given in Far West, April 26. 1838. Making Known the will of God, concerning the building up of this place and of the Lords house &c Verily thus saith the Lord unto you my Servant Joseph Smith jr. and also my Servant Sidney Rigdon and also my Servant Hyrum Smith, and your cou-nsilors who are and who Shall be hereafter appointed. and also unto my Servant Edward Partridge and his Counsilors, and also unto my faithfull Servants who are of the High Council of my Church in Zion (for thus it Shall be called) and unto all the Elders and people of my Church of Jesus Christ of Latter Day Saints, Scattered abroad

Revelations copied into journal. Page 32 contains all or part of four of the documents copied into the beginning of Joseph Smith's first Missouri journal: a synopsis of the trials of David Whitmer and Lyman Johnson, a revelation for David W. Patten, a revelation for Brigham Young, and a revelation regarding the gathering of the Saints and an intended temple at Far West, Missouri. Handwriting of George W. Robinson. JS, Journal, Mar.–Sept. 1838, p. 32, Church History Library, Salt Lake City. (Photograph by Welden C. Andersen.)

the Corner Stone thereof unto the top thereof, untill there shall not any thing remain that is not finished.[116]

Verrily I say unto you let not my servant Joseph neither my Servant Sidney, neither my Servant Hyrum, get in debt any more for the building of an house unto my name. But let my house be built unto my name according to the pattern which I will shew unto them, and if my people build it not according to the pattern which I Shall shew unto their presidency, I will not accept it at their hands, But if my people do build it according to the pattern which I shall shew unto their presidency, even my servant Joseph and his Councilors; then I will accept it at [p. 33] the hands of my people, And again; Verrily I say unto you it is my will, that the City Far West should be built up spedily, by the gathering of my Saints, and also that other places should be appointed for stakes in the regions round about as they shall be manifested unto my Servant Joseph from time to time. For behold I will be with him and I will Sanctify him before the people for unto him have I given the Keys of this Kingdom and ministry even so— Amen.

---------- ∽ ----------

Editorial Note

Up to this point in the journal, George W. Robinson apparently copied documents to catch up on recent events. From this point forward, the journal generally consists of regular entries, especially during the next six weeks. However, given the large size of the record book containing this journal, it is unlikely that Robinson carried it as he accompanied JS on various activities. A number of entries may have been written several days after the events.

---------- ∽ ----------

27 April 1838 • Friday

Friday April the 27th 1838. This day was chiefly spent in writing a history of this Church from the earliest perion [period] of its existance up to this date, By Presidents, Joseph Smith Jr & Sidney Rigdon, myself also ~~was~~ engaged in keeping this record[117]

---

116. The Saints in Caldwell County previously made preparations for the construction of a temple at Far West and in July 1837 commenced excavating for a foundation.ᵃ In November 1837, however, while visiting the Saints in Far West, JS gave instructions to postpone work on the temple until "the Lord shall reveal it to be his will to be commenced."ᵇ (a. Minute Book 2, 5 Aug. 1837; William W. Phelps, Far West, MO, 7 [July] 1837, letter to the editor, *LDS Messenger and Advocate,* July 1837, 3:529. b. Minute Book 2, 6 Nov. 1837; see also Thomas B. Marsh, [Far West, MO], to Wilford Woodruff, [Vinalhaven, ME], 1838, *Elders' Journal,* July 1838, 38.)

117. Having failed to obtain John Whitmer's earlier work on a history of the church, JS and his associates here began the work anew. Work on this history continued under JS's direction until his

28 April 1838 • Saturday

Saturday 28ᵗʰ This morning Presᵗˢ Smith & [Sidney] Rigdon & myself, were invited ~~into~~ attend the High Council; and accordingly attended, the buisness before the high council, was the trial of ~~an~~ case appealed, from the branch of the Church, near gymans [Guymon's] horse mill; Whereas [*blank*] [Henry] Jackson was plantiff, and Aaron Lyon defendant.[118] Council called to order. T[homas] B. Marsh &. D[avid] W. Patten, Presiding, It appeared in calling the council to order, that some of the seats were vacated; the council then proceeded to fill those seats: &c. And as there appeared to be no persons to fill Said Seats, Eligible to that office; Presidents Smith & Rigdon, were strongly solisited to act as councilors, or to Preside, and let the then presiding officers sit on the council; &c. They accepted of the former proposal, and accordingly Presᵗ· Smith was choosen to act on the part of the defence, and to speak upon the case, togeth[er] with Geo. W. Harris. ~~and~~ Presᵗ· Rigdon, was chosen to act on the part of the prossecution, and to speak upon the case together with Geo. M. Hinkle, after the council was organized, and op[e]ned by prayer; the notorious case of Aaron Lyon, was called in question; after some arbitrarious[119] speeches, to know whether witnesses should be admitted, to testify against A. Lyon, or whether he should have the privilege of confessing his own Sins, It was desided; that witnesses Should be admited, and also the writen testimo[p. 34]ny of the ~~said~~ wife of Said Jackson.[120] Naw as to this man Lyon, it is a well known ⟨fact,⟩ and without contradiction, that he has been in transgression ⟨ever⟩ Since he first came into Kirtland, which is some four, or five years since, as appeared this day, by different witnesses, which are unimpeacible [unimpeachable]. Witnesses against ~~the~~ ⟨this⟩ man Lyon, were these 1,ˢᵗ Sarah Jackson, wife of said plaintiff, Jackson. ~~one~~ ⟨an⟩[121] Br. Best:[122] also Br. [Shadrach] Roundy. Br John P. ~~Pound~~ Barnand [Barnard]: also Br. Thomas

---

death. The work was then carried on under the direction of Willard Richards and later by George A. Smith, who completed the six massive manuscript volumes in Utah. (249n81 herein; Jessee, "Writing of Joseph Smith's History.")

118. Aaron Lyon was charged with improperly using priesthood authority to attempt to coerce Sarah Jackson, Henry Jackson's wife, to marry Lyon. (Minute Book 2, 28 Apr. 1838, 137–140, 157–159.)

119. "Not governed by any fixed rules." ("Arbitrary," in *American Dictionary,* 48.)

120. According to Sarah Jackson's written testimony, Lyon claimed to have received revelation that her husband Henry, in Illinois at the time, had died, that she should marry Lyon, and that if she refused him she would be "forever miserable." Lyon led her to believe that she would suffer "the vengeance of God" if she did not marry him. (Minute Book 2, 28 Apr. 1838, 157–159.)

121. TEXT: Possibly "and".

122. Possibly Henry Best. (Henry Best, Petition for redress, 12 Jan. 1840, Library of Congress Collection, National Archives, Washington DC.)

Girmon [Guymon]; also Br Benjamin, and the plantiff;[123] Which testimony says, Whereas, the plantiff, had some time last season, sent his wife from Alton, Illinois, to this country as he himself could not come, at that time, accordingly his wife Mrs Jackson, came and settled in the branch first above mentioned, Now the ⟨this⟩ man Lyon had settled in this branch also, and was their presiding high priest, and had gained to himself great influence in and on over that branch, and it also appears that the this man had great possessions, and (if we may judge from testimony given this day) calculates to keep them let the saints of God's necessity necessities be what they may, and it also appears that this man was in want of a wife (if actions bespeak the desires of any man) consequently set his wits to work to get one, he commences by getting (as he said,) revelations from God, that he must marry Mrs Jackson, or that she was the woman for to make his wife, and it appeared that these revilations were frequently received by him, and shortly introdused them to Mrs. Jackson, It also was manifested that the old man had sagasity enough to know; that unless he used his priestly office, he to assist him in accomplishing his designs, ⟨he would fail in the attempt;⟩ he therefore told Mrs. Jackson that he had a had a revelation from god that her husband was dead &c. and that She must concent to marry him, or she would be forever miserable; for he had seen her future state of existance, and that she must remember, that whoom soever he blessed, would be blessed, and whom soever he cursed, would be cursed, [p. 35] influencing her mind if possible, to believe his power was sufficient, to make her forever miserable; provided she complied not with his request. &c.[124] Accordingly, they came to an agreement, and were soon to be married, but fortunately or unfortunately for both parties previous to the nuptial arrival of the nuptial day, Behold!! to the asstonishment of our defendant, the husband of Mrs. Jackson arrived at home, and consequently, disanuled the proceedings of the above alluded parties,[125] the old gentleman Lyon, at this time (if not before,) knew verry well, that his god who gave his these revelations, (if any revelations he had,) must of course be no less than the devil, and in order to paliate the justice of his crime, sadled the whole burden upon the devil, that in

---

123. Best had housed Sarah Jackson while living at Guymon's mill. Roundy, a member of the Second Quorum of Seventy; Barnard, a large landholder; and Guymon, the owner of the local mill, were all prominent members of the community. Benjamin testified that a Calvin Reed had also related a vision that Henry Jackson was dead. (Minute Book 2, 28 Apr. 1838, 138–139; Record of Seventies, bk. A, 6; Foote, Autobiography, 15 Sept. and 7 Oct. 1838.)

124. According to Sarah Jackson's written testimony, Lyon told her that JS "told him to be cautious who he cursed in the name of the Lord, for who he cursed was cursed, and who he blessed was blessed." (Minute Book 2, 28 Apr. 1838, 159.)

125. Henry Jackson arrived in the area sometime in November, about five months after his wife settled there. (Minute Book 2, 28 Apr. 1838, 138.)

scourging the person, who had previously befriended him, and counseled him in his former days; peradventure he might extricate himself from the Snare, of his own setting, and dictation. But, alass!! to[o] late for the old man, the testimony, being closed, and the Sword of Justice, began to be unsheathed, which fell upon the old man like a scourge of ten thousand lashes, wielded by the hand of President S. Rigdon & George M. Hinkle, inspired by the spirit of justice, accompanied with a flow of elequence, which searched for the feelings, like the sting of so many scorpions, which served to atone for past iniquity. there were no feelings that were not felt after, there were no sores that were not probed, there were no excuses rend[e]red that were not exceptionable. After Justice had ceased to weild ~~his~~ ⟨its⟩ sword, Mercy then advanced to rescue its victom, which inspired the heart of President J. Smith Jr, & Geo W. Harris who, with profound elequence ⟨&⟩ with ⟨a⟩ deep & sublime thought, with clemency of feeling, spoke in faivour of ~~mercy~~ the defendant, but in length of time, while mercy appeared to be doing her utmost, in contending against justice, the latter at last gained the ascendency, and took full ~~power over~~ ⟨possession of⟩ the mind of [p. 36] the speaker,[126] who leveled a voley of darts, which came upon the old man, like ⟨a⟩ huricanes upon the mountain tops, which seemingly, was about to sweep the victom entirely out of the reach of mercy, but amidst the clashing of the sword of Justice, mercy still claimed the victom, and saved him still in the church of Jesus Christ of Latter Day Saints, and in this last kingdom Happy is it for those whose sins (like this mans) goes before them to Judgement, that they may yet repent and be saved in the Kingdom of our God. Council desided, that inasmuch as this man, had confessed his sins, and asked for, forgiveness, and promised to mark well the path of his feet, and do, (inasmuch as lay in his power.) what God, Should ~~required~~ at his hand⟨s⟩. accordingly, it was decided, that he give up his license as High Priest, and stand as a member in the Church, this in consequence of his being concidered not capable of dignifying that office, &c Council Adjourned

Geo. W. Robinson, <u>Scribe</u>

29 April 1838 • Sunday

Sunday the 29th. This day was spent chiefly in meeting with the saints. in this place, and in administering unto them, the word of Life.

30 April 1838 • Monday

Monday, the 30.th This day was spent by the first Presidency, in writing the

---

126. The council minutes do not clarify which speaker.

history of the Church; and in resitation of grammer lessions, which ressitations is attended to, ~~in the~~ ⟨each⟩ morning previous to writing.

1 May 1838 · Tuesday

⟨May⟩

Tuesday 1ˢᵗ May 1838, This day was also spent in writing Church History, by the first Presidency

2 May 1838 · Wednesday

Wednersday 2ⁿᵈ This day was also spent in writing history, and ⟨receiving⟩ lectures on grammer. by President [Sidney] Rigdon. [p. 37]

3 May 1838 · Thursday

Thursday the 3.ʳᵈ. This day also was spent in Writing & parsing and in administering to the Sick.

4 May 1838 · Friday

Friday 4.ᵗʰ. This day also was spent in studying, & writing history, by the presidency. also ⟨a⟩ letter from J[ohn] E. Page.[127]

5 May 1838 · Saturday

Saturday 5.ᵗʰ This day was spent, by the Presidency, in writing for the Elders Journal.[128] Also received intelligence from Cannada, by one br— Bailey. who called upon Pres. Smith, and stated that two hundred Wagons, with families; would probably be here in three weeks.[129] The presidency also attended an address, dilivered by Gen. Willson [John Wilson]. upon ~~Politics.~~ ⟨Political matters⟩ General Willson. is a candidate for Congress. (~~he is~~ a Federalist.)[130]

---

127. The letter from Page, who was proselytizing in Canada, may have concerned the immigration of Canadian converts to Missouri. (See JS, Journal, 5 May 1838.)

128. JS and his associates were preparing materials for the first Missouri issue of the *Elders' Journal* (July 1838).

129. Many Mormon converts from Canada made their way to Missouri during 1838, including a group led by Almon Babbitt that arrived at Far West in late July and a group of about thirty families accompanied by missionary John E. Page that arrived in De Witt during the last week of September 1838. However, no known group of Canadian immigrants was as large as or arrived as soon as the group described in Bailey's report. (JS, Journal, 28 July 1838; Gentry, "Latter-day Saints in Northern Missouri," 199; see also Baugh, "Call to Arms," 158.)

130. Wilson, from Randolph County, belonged to the Whig Party. The Federalist Party died out in the second decade of the nineteenth century, but Democrat rhetoric commonly attacked the new Whig Party by casting its members as reconstituted aristocratic Federalists. The *Northern Times*—the political newspaper published by the Mormons in Kirtland—had portrayed the Whigs in this manner. (*Encyclopedia of the History of Missouri*, 6:484; Holt, *Rise and Fall of the American Whig Party*, 2–3; "The

(April & May 1838)

—the Speaker, who leveled a voley of darts, which came upon the old man like a huricane upon the mountain tops, which seemingly was about to sweep the victim entirely out of the reach of mercy, but amidst the clashing of the sword of justice, mercy still claimed the victory, and saved him still in the Church of Jesus Christ of Latter Day Saints, and in this last kingdom. Happy is it for those whose sins (like this mans) goes before them to judgement, that they may yet repent and be saved in the kingdom of our God. Council decided, that inasmuch as this man, had confessed his sins, and asked for forgiveness, and promised to mark well the path of his feet, and do, (inasmuch as lay in his power) what God, Should require at his hands. Accordingly it was decided, that he give up his license as High Priest, and stand as a member in the Church, this in consequence of his being considered not capable of dignifying that office, &c Council Adjourned

                    Geo. W. Robinson, Scribe

Sunday the 29th. this day was spent chiefly in meeting with the Saints in this place, and in administering unto them, the word of Life.

Monday the 30th. this day was Spent by the first Presidency, in writing the history of the Church, and in resitation of Grammer Lessons, which resitation is attended to, each morning previous to writing.

May

Tuesday 1st May 1838. This day was also Spent in writing Church History, by the first Presidency

Wednesday 2nd This day was also Spent in writing history, and receiving letters on Grammer, by President Rigdon.

Entries recorded in first Missouri journal. Entries in this journal often focused on the activities of the church's First Presidency, as in this conclusion to the entry for 28 April and in the complete entries for 29 April–2 May 1838. Handwriting of George W. Robinson. JS, Journal, Mar.–Sept. 1838, p. 37, Church History Library, Salt Lake City. (Photograph by Welden C. Andersen.)

6 May 1838 • Sunday

Sunday 6ᵗʰ This day, President Smith. delivered a discourse. to the people. Showing, or setting forth the evils that existed, and would exist, by reason of hasty Judgement or dessisions upon any subject, given by any people. or in judgeing before they hear both sides of the question,[131] He also cautioned them against men men, who should come here whining and grouling about their money, because they had helpt the saints and bore some of the burden with others. and thus thinking that others, (who are still poorer and who have still bore greater burden than themselves) aught to make up their loss &c.[132] And thus he cautioned them to beware of them for here and there they through [throw?] out foul insinuations, to level as it were a dart to ⟨the⟩ best interests of the Church, & if possible to destroy the Characters of its Presidency He also instructed the Church, in the mistories of the Kingdom of God; giving them a history of the Plannets &c. and of Abrahams writings upon the Plannettary System &c.[133] In the after part of the day Presᵗ Smith spoke upon different subjects he dwelt some upon the Subject of Wisdom, & upon the word of Wisdom. &c.[134]—— [p. 38]

7 May 1838 • Monday

Monday 7ᵗʰ This day was spent in company with Judge Morain [Josiah Morin] one of our neighbouring County Judges, also the Demecratic candidate for the State Senate.[135] & in company with Elder Cohoon [Reynolds Cahoon] & P[arley] P. Pratt, who this day arrived in this place, the former.

Election," *Northern Times,* 2 Oct. 1835, [2]; see also "Extract of a Letter to the Editor of the Telegraph," *Painesville Telegraph,* 17 Apr. 1835, [3].)

131. Among other things, JS may have been cautioning the Saints against reacting hastily to the electioneering speech delivered by John Wilson the day before. In his discourse the following Thursday, Rigdon discussed "both sides"—the policies of both Wilson's Whig party and the opposing Democratic party. (JS, Journal, 10 May 1838.)

132. Following the depression of 1837 and the collapse of the Kirtland Safety Society, some Latter-day Saints aggressively sought the repayment of debts, including those owed by fellow church members, through legal means. Prominent among these creditors were excommunicants Lyman Johnson and Oliver Cowdery. (See Minute Book 2, 12 and 13 Apr. 1838; and Synopsis of Oliver Cowdery Trial, 12 Apr. 1838, p. 251 herein.)

133. This understanding grew out of JS's work on the Egyptian papyri that he acquired while living in Kirtland. (See JS, Journal, 1 Oct. and 16 Dec. 1835.)

134. A reference to either or both the general gift of the spirit and the particular "word of wisdom" dictated by JS as a revealed health code, which was an issue in the 13 April trial of David Whitmer. (1 Corinthians 12:8; Book of Mormon, 1830 ed., 586 [Moroni 10:9]; Revelation, ca. 8 Mar. 1831–A, in Doctrine and Covenants 16:7, 1835 ed. [D&C 46:17]; Revelation, 27 Feb. 1833, in Doctrine and Covenants 80, 1835 ed. [D&C 89].)

135. Daviess County judge Josiah Morin was campaigning for state senator on the Democratic ticket in the August 1838 election. (LeSueur, *1838 Mormon War in Missouri,* 59–60.)

from Kirtland. and the latter from the City of New York; where he had been preaching for some time past; And our hearts were made glad with the pleasing inteligence⟨s⟩ of ⟨the⟩ gathering of the Saints flocking from all parts of the world to this land; to avoid the destructions which are coming upon this generation, as spoken by all the holy Prophets since the world began

8 May 1838 · Tuesday

Tuesday 8ᵗʰ This day Presidents, J. Smith Jr. & S[idney] Rigdon spent the day with Elder Cohoon [Reynolds Cahoon] in visiting the place he had selected, to live, also in some private buisness of their own, also in the after part of the day, in answering the questions proposed in the Elders Journal. Vol. 1ˢᵗ No. 2ⁿᵈ Pages 28⟨th⟩, & 29⟨th⟩[136] On yesterday our beloved Brother Thomas B, Marsh, lost his Son James who died near the close of the day, This lad, brother though young, adorned his profession as a saint of God, and died in the faith of the everlasting Gospel;

9 May 1838 · Wednesday

Wednersday 9ᵗʰ· This day, the Presidency, attended the funeral of James Marsh, And Presᵗ· Smith was requested to preach the funeral discourse, and accordingly complied, and we were greatly edified upon the occasion,

10 May 1838 · Thursday

Thursday 10ᵗʰ This day, President S[idney] Rigdon, delivered an address in the Schoolhouse in the south west quarter of the City, upon the Subjects of the Political policy of our Nation, to a large concourse of People from all quarters of the county and even from other counties [p. 39]

Allthough, he being verry hoarse, with a ~~bad~~ ⟨Severe⟩ cold, yet being assisted, by the spirit, and power, of Allmighty God, was enabled to elucidated the policy, to the understanding of all present, Both of the Federal party, and also of the Democratic party, from the time of ~~this~~ ⟨their⟩ first appearance in our country; endeavering to give an impartial hearing on both Sides of the question, In consequence of One Gen Willsons [John Wilson's] speech, delivered

---

136. In the November 1837 issue of the *Elders' Journal*, JS stated that questions relating to the church's basic tenets had been "daily and hourly asked by all classes of people" while he was traveling to and from Missouri with Rigdon in fall 1837. The questions were published in the second (and last Kirtland) issue, with the promise of being answered in the next issue. Because both the editor, JS, and the publisher, Thomas B. Marsh, had moved to Missouri, the next issue did not appear until July 1838, as the first Missouri issue of the resuscitated paper. ([JS], editorial, *Elders' Journal*, Nov. 1837, 28–29; [JS], editorial, *Elders' Journal*, July 1838, 42–44; see also JS History, vol. B-1, 794–796.)

upon Politics in the same place, a short time previous to this:[137] Who touched upon one side of the matter only; He being a Federalist, and knowing that for the good of his cause, and for the safety of his electionereing campaign: it would be policy for him to dwell on one side of the question onley; But the Politics of this Church (with but few exceptions onley,) are that of ~~the~~ Democracy; which is ~~the~~ ⟨Allso⟩ the feelings of the speaker ⟨who spoke⟩ this day, and ⟨all⟩ of ⟨all⟩ the first presidency, It ⟨is⟩ my principles also.[138] Pres^t Smith, and myself attended the Delivery of said speech and were highly edified

11 May 1838 • Friday

~~Thursday~~ Friday 11th This day, the presidency attend[ed] the Council of the Bishop, in case of the trial of Wm E. Mc.Lellen [McLellin] & Doctor McCord,[139] Who were found in transgression. M^r. Mc.Cord, arose, and said, he was sorry to troubl the council on his account, for he had intended to withdraw from the church, before he left the place. he also stated, he had no confidence in the work of God, neither in his Prophet, which he ⟨has⟩ raised up in these last days, and consequently should go his own way, he accordingly gave up his License, and departed W^m. E. Mc.Lellin, also said the same. He further said he had no confidence in the heads of the Church, beleiving they had transgressed, and got out of the way, and consequently ⟨he⟩ left of[f] praying and keeping the commandments of God, and went his own way, and indulged himself in his lustfull desires. But when he heard, that [p. 40] the first presidency, had made a general settlement and acknowleged their sins,[140] he then began to pray again, and to keep the commandments of God. Though when interogated by Pres^t smith he said he had seen nothing out of the way himself but it was heresay, and thus he judged from heresay. But we are constrained to say, O!! foolish Man! what excuse is that thou renderest, for thy sins, that because thou hast heard of some mans transgression, that thou shouldest leave thy God, and forsake thy prayers, and turn to those things that thou knowest to be contrary to the will of God, we say unto thee, and to all such, beware! beware! for God will bring the[e] into Judgement for thy sins.[141]

---

137. Wilson spoke five days earlier, as noted in this journal.

138. In Ohio, JS and the Latter-day Saints faithfully supported the Democratic Party—a pattern that continued in Missouri. Political editorials in Mormon newspapers generally agreed with Jacksonian Democrats on prohibiting nullification, restricting the national bank, and protecting the common man from aristocratic oppression. (Hill, *Quest for Refuge,* 64–66; Parkin, "Mormon Political Involvement in Ohio," 484–502.)

139. A "Dr. McCord" served as a member of the high council at Far West, 23 December 1837. (Minute Book 2, 23 Dec. 1837.)

140. No such "general settlement" or acknowledgment has been identified.

141. Neither this journal nor the Missouri council minutes indicate what action was taken regarding

12 May 1838 · Saturday

Saturday 12<u>th</u>. This day Pres<u>ts</u> Smith & [Sidney] Rigdon together with myself, attended the High Council to Lay before ~~them~~ it, some buisness pertaining to themselves directly, and individually.

The presidency laid before ~~them~~ high Council, their situation, as to maintaining their families in the situation & relation they stood to the Church. spending, as they have, for eight years, their time ~~and~~ tallents & property in the service of the Church, and are now reduced as it were, to absolute begery, and still were detained in service of the Church, and it now become necessary that something should be done for their support, ~~or~~ either by the Church, or else they must do it themselves, of their own ~~labour,~~ labours, and if the Church said help yourselves, they would thank them, and immediately do so, but if the Church said serve us, then some provisions must be made for them.[142] The subject was taken into concideration, by the Council (who acts for the Church), and thouroughly investigated. Whereupon [p. 41] the Council voted to authorize the Bishop, to give or to make over to Pres<u>ts.</u> Joseph Smith J<u>r</u> & Sidney Rigdon each an eighty of land,[143] situate adjacent to the city Corporation which land is the property of the Church. Also voted that a committee of three, be appointed, of the council, to contract with said presidency to their sattisfaction, for their sevices, this present year, not for preaching or for receiving the word of God by revelation, neither for instructing the saints in richteousness, but for services rendered in the Printing establishment, in translating the ~~words~~ ancient records &c. &c. The Committee, which consisted of Geo. W. Harris, Elias Higbee & Simeon Carter, who agreed that Pres<u>ts.</u> Smith & Rigdon should be entitled to, & receive for this year [*blank*] as a just remuneration for their Services.[144]

McLellin at this time, although a biographical sketch of McLellin that appeared in a later church periodical asserted that he was excommunicated during this period for "unbelief and apostacy." By autumn 1838 and into the 1840s, McLellin was actively associated with dissenters from the church in Missouri, Iowa, and Illinois. (Historian's Office, "History of William E. Mc. Lellin," 3, Histories of the Twelve, ca. 1858–1880, CHL, published in *Deseret News,* 12 May 1858, 49; Porter, "Odyssey of William Earl McLellin," 323–332.)

142. Revelations dated shortly after the organization of the church emphasized the duty of the church to provide for such material needs, but general church poverty had precluded such support. (Revelation, July 1830–A, in Doctrine and Covenants 9:2, 4, 1835 ed. [D&C 24:3, 9]; Revelation, 4 Feb. 1831, in Doctrine and Covenants 61:3, 1835 ed. [D&C 41:7]; Revelation, Feb. 1831–A, in Doctrine and Covenants 14:3, 1835 ed. [D&C 43:13–14].)

143. Eighty acres of land.

144. JS and the church faced not only limited economic resources but also the dilemma of financially supporting church officers while avoiding scriptural proscriptions against priestcraft. Prior to JS's and Rigdon's arrivals in Far West, the Missouri high council decided to financially support other church officers, including high counselors, the clerk of the high council, the patriarch, and the church agent.^a The

13 May 1838 · Sunday

Sunday 13ᵗʰ. Today Presᵗ R[eynolds] Cahoon (late Presᵗ of Kirtland) delivered a discourse to the saints, in the former part of the day, and Presᵗ [Sidney] Rigdon, preached the funeral sermon of [Joseph] Swain Williams, son of F[rederick] G. Williams in the after part of the day.

14 May 1838 · Monday

Monday 14ᵗʰ Presᵗ· Smith spent this day in ploughing for, himself in his garden. Presᵗ [Sidney] Rigdon spent the day in correcting and prepareing matter for the press,¹⁴⁵ and also ⟨spent a short time⟩ in Company with Elder Harlow Readfield [Redfield], who arrived this day from Kirtland Ohio. And I have spent this day in helping Presᵗ smith, and also in writing,

18 May–1 June 1838 · Friday–Friday

Friday 18ᵗʰ To day Presidents J Smith Jr & S[idney] Rigdon and T[homas] B. Marsh D[avid] W. Patten Bishop E Partridg [Edward Partridge] E[lias] Higbee, S[imeon] Carter, A[lanson] Ripley, myself and many others, left Far West to visit the north countries for the purpose of Laying off stakes of Zion, making Locations & laying claims for the gathering of the saints for the benefit of the poor, and for the upbuilding of the Church of God,¹⁴⁶ We traveled this day to the mouth of Honey Creek, which [p. 42] is a tribuitary to Grand River, where

---

council minutes, like the present journal entry, do not record an agreed-upon amount of remuneration.ᵇ However, Ebenezer Robinson, the council clerk, recounted years later that the committee made a later recommendation to the high council of an annual stipend of $1,100 for each of the presidency. Robinson further recounted that when word of the action became known, "the members of the church, almost to a man, lifted their voices against it" and the resolution was revoked.ᶜ (*a.* Minute Book 2, 6 Dec. 1837. *b.* Minute Book 2, 13 May 1838. *c.* Ebenezer Robinson, "Items of Personal History of the Editor," *The Return,* Sept. 1889, 136–137.)

145. The day before, the high council appointed Rigdon to correct the spelling and language of letters for publication in the *Elders' Journal.* (Minute Book 2, 12 May 1838.)

146. JS and Sidney Rigdon were assigned on 17 September 1837 to identify new locations for Latter-day Saint settlements.ᵃ They left Kirtland ten days later, and in November, after their arrival in Far West, a committee was assigned to explore the "north country" and help fulfill the mandate originally given to JS and Rigdon. Committee member Oliver Cowdery subsequently devoted about three weeks in November to exploring and surveying; the identity and participation of other committee members is not clearly documented.ᵇ A revelation of 26 April 1838 directed that the Latter-day Saints were to begin new stakes of Zion in the vicinity of Far West.ᶜ As recorded earlier in this journal, on 5 May JS received a report of hundreds of converts immigrating from Canada, which may have increased the urgency to plan new settlements. The persons named were church officials except for Ripley, who was the surveyor.ᵈ (*a.* Minute Book 1, 17 Sept. 1837. *b.* [JS], editorial, *Elders' Journal,* Nov. 1837, 27–28; Minute Book 2, 6 Nov. and 7 Dec. 1837; 13 Apr. 1838; Oliver Cowdery, Far West, MO, to Warren Cowdery, [Kirtland, OH], 21 Jan. 1838, in Cowdery, Letterbook, 80–83. *c.* Revelation, 26 Apr. 1838, in JS, Journal, 26 Apr. 1838, p. 260 herein [D&C 115:18]. *d.* Swartzell, *Mormonism Exposed,* 9–10.)

we camped for the night, we passed this day a beautifull country of land, a majority of which is Prarie which signifies untimbered land and thickly covered with grass and weeds, there is a plenty of wild game in this land, such as Deer, Turkey, Hens, Elk, &.c. we saw a large black wolf, Prest smith put on his dog after the wolf and ⟨we⟩ followed on after, but the wolf out run us and we lost, ~~the~~ ⟨Him⟩ ~~wolf~~ we have nothing to fear in camping out except Rattle sknakes which are ~~peculiar~~ ⟨natural⟩ to this country, though not verry numerous, we turn our horses loose and let them feed in the prairie,

⟨19 sat⟩ The next morning we struck our tents, and marched crossed Grand river at the mouth of Honey Creek at a place called Nelsons ferry, Grand River is as large beautifull deep and rapid stream and will undoubtedly admit of steam Boat and other water craft navigation, and at the mouth of honey creek is a splendid harbour for the safety of such crafts, and also for landing freight We next kept up the river mostly in the timber for ten miles, untill we came to Col. Lyman Wight's[147] who lives at the foot of Tower Hill, a name appropriated by Pres^t smith, in consequence of the remains of an old Nephitish Alter an Tower, ~~In the after~~ where we camped for the sabath, In the after part of the day, Prest⟨^s⟩ smith and Rigdon and myself, went to Wights. Ferry about a half mile from this place up the river, for the purpose of selecting and laying claims to city plott near said Ferry, in Davis [Daviess] County Township 60, Range 27 & 28, and Sections 25, 36, 31, 30, which was called Spring Hill a name appropriated by the bretheren present, But after wards named by the mouth of [the] Lord and was called Adam Ondi Awmen [Adam-ondi-Ahman], because said he it [p. 43] is the place where Adam shall come to visit his people, or the Ancient of days shall sit as spoken of by Daniel the Prophet,[148]

⟨20⟩ Sunday was spent principally at Adam Ondi Awmen, but at the close of the day we struck our tents and traveled about six miles north and camped for the knight, we had in company at this place Judge Morain [Josiah Morin] and company traveling also to the north, ⟨21 M[onday]⟩ in the morning after making some Locations in this place which is in Township 61 Range 27, & 28, we next returned to Robinsons Grove about two miles in order to secure some land near grand river which we passed the day previous, and finding a mistake in the ⟨former⟩ survey concluded to send the surveyor south 5 or 6 miles to obtain correct survey, we did so, and some of us taried to obtain water for the camp

---

147. Wight had participated in the November–December 1837 exploration of Daviess County and the country north of Far West to find new sites for Latter-day Saint settlement, purchased preemption rights to land and a cabin from Adam Black, and moved to the Spring Hill area. Wight had a strategic role in promoting settlement in the area. (Berrett, *Sacred Places*, 4:377; [JS], editorial, *Elders' Journal*, Nov. 1837, 28.)

148. A reference to Daniel 7:13–14. Part of the last sentence of this entry is now D&C 116.

Lyman Wight. Circa 1850s. Wight, a colonel in the Caldwell County, Missouri, militia, moved to neighboring Daviess County, circa February 1838, residing in the area that became the Mormon community of Adam-ondi-Ahman. Wight was appointed a counselor in the presidency of the Adam-ondi-Ahman stake and the local leader of the Danites, a private Mormon militia. (Courtesy Community of Christ Library-Archives, Independence, MO.)

Adam-ondi-Ahman. 2000. In May 1838, Joseph Smith and his surveying party selected a site for a Mormon community overlooking this bend of the Grand River, east of Lyman Wight's ferry. The ferry was probably located at the large sandbar that is visible at the bottom of this southeast-facing photograph. Adam-ondi-Ahman became the principal Mormon settlement in Daviess County, Missouri. (© Intellectual Reserve, Inc. Photograph by Matthew Reier.)

In the evening we held a council, to consult the bretheren upon the subject of our journey to know whether it is wisdom to go immediately into the north country or to tarry here and about here to secure the land on grand river &.c. The Bretherin spoke their minds ~~verrily~~ ⟨verry⟩ freely upon the subject, Prest Smith said he felt impressed to tarry and secure the land near by, all that is not secured between this and Far West especially on grand river, Prest Rigdon said if they should go to north in this expedition he thought it best to go immediately to that place, but thought it best by all means, to secure the land near by on the river &c, The question was put by Pres^t Smith and carried unanymously in favour of having the land secured on the river and between this place and Far West,[149] ⟨22⟩ The next day Pres^t Rigdon with a company went to the east of the camp and selected some of the best locations in the country, and returned with news of good locations in that vicinity yet [p. 44] to be secured, ~~in that vicinity~~ Pres^t Smith and myself followed on in their course, but could not find them and consequently returned to the camp in Robinsons Grove, we next scouted west in order to obtain some game to suply our necessities but found or killed none, we [saw?] some ancient antiquities about one mile West of the camp, which conscisted of stone mounds, appearently laid up in squire [square] piles, though somewhat decayed and obliterated, by the almost continual rains undoubtedly these were made to seclude some valuable treasures deposited by the aborigionees of this land[150]

⟨20 3⟩ The next day we all traveled and located lands East, on Grove Creek and near the city of Adam Ondi Awman, towards knight Pres^t⟨s⟩ smith & S, Rigdon went to Col. Wights and the remainder returned to the tents,

⟨24⟩ The next morning the company returned to Grove Creek to finish the survey, Prest. Rigdon and Col. Wight also returned to the surveying, and Prs^t smith returned to Far West

---

149. This was preemption land that would not become available for purchase from the federal government until November 1838. The Preemption Act of 1830 allowed settlers to obtain first right of purchase to such federal land that had not yet been made available for sale by occupying a parcel of land and applying for preemption rights. Paying $1.25 per acre after an official survey was completed and copies of the plats were deposited at the local branch of the General Land Office, but before the land was offered for sale to the general public, completed the process and "secured" the land. Identifying and conducting their own survey of lands that they wished to purchase—the task JS's party was undertaking—was a key part of the process, but only the beginning. (LeSueur, *1838 Mormon War in Missouri,* 110; An Act to Grant Pre-emption Rights to Settlers on the Public Lands [29 May 1830], *Public Statutes at Large,* 21 Cong., 1 Sess., chap. 208, pp. 420–421; *General Public Acts of Congress* 2:548; Walker, "Mormon Land Rights.")

150. The Grand River ran west of the Robinson's grove campsite. The thousands of American Indian mounds concentrated along the rivers of the greater Mississippi River watershed provoked continual speculation among white Americans. Regarding the origins of the mounds, see Silverberg, *Mound Builders of Ancient America.*

⟨25⟩ Friday this day our company went up the river and made some locations,[151] in the after part of the day we struck our tents, and mooved to Col. Wights

⟨26⟩ The next day we surveyed land across the river opposite <u>Adam-Ondi-Awmen</u> ⟨27⟩ sunday was spent principally at Co[l.] Wights. ⟨28⟩ The next morning we started for home <u>Far West</u>. about noon we met ⟨Prs[t(s.)]⟩ J Smith J and Hyram [Hyrum] Smith, and Some 15 or 20 others, who were going to seek locations in the <u>north</u>, we continued our way home where we arived Monday evening and found our families well &c, ⟨30⟩ th[e] 30 Prest Hyram Smith returned ⟨to⟩ Far West. Friday 1st of June Prest J Smith Jr returned on account of his wifes sickness who was delivered of a son[152]

———— ⁊ ————

Editorial Note

Though George W. Robinson's journal keeping lapsed for most of June and July, he did summarize a pivotal month from 4 June through 4 July 1838 in two journal entries. JS spent much of June north of Far West in Daviess County, Missouri, at the newly designated Mormon settlement of Adam-ondi-Ahman, where he organized a stake on 28 June 1838[153]— one year after some of the first Mormon settlers in Daviess County had been warned by local residents that they must leave.[154] However, on 17 June JS was present at Far West when his counselor Sidney Rigdon preached a provocative sermon. In response to ongoing activities of prominent excommunicated dissenters in Caldwell County that threatened to disrupt the community and undercut church leadership, Rigdon used as his text Matthew 5:13, likening the excommunicants to salt that had lost its savor and was "henceforth good for nothing but to be cast out, and trodden under foot of men." According to one observer, JS seconded the thrust of Rigdon's remarks.[155] Following the "Salt Sermon," George W. Robinson—the scribe for this journal—and eighty-two other Mormon men signed a letter warning Oliver Cowdery, David Whitmer, John Whitmer, William W. Phelps, and Lyman Johnson to leave Caldwell County within three days or be expelled by force. Later accounts claimed that the letter accused the excommunicants of counterfeiting and other crimes of deceit, stealing, and persecuting the Latter-day Saints through lawsuits.[156] John Whitmer

---

151. Possibly including the future Mormon settlement of Grindstone Fork. (See Berrett, *Sacred Places*, 4:462.)

152. Alexander Hale Smith, born 2 June 1838.

153. "Conference Minutes," *Elders' Journal*, Aug. 1838, 60–61.

154. William W. Phelps, Far West, MO, 7 [July] 1837, letter to the editor, *LDS Messenger and Advocate*, July 1837, 3:529.

155. Reed Peck, Testimony, Richmond, MO, Nov. 1838, in State of Missouri, "Evidence"; Reed Peck, Quincy, IL, to "Dear Friends," 18 Sept. 1839, pp. 23–27, Henry E. Huntington Library, San Marino, CA; see also Corrill, *Brief History of the Church*, 29–30; and [JS], editorial, *Elders' Journal*, Aug. 1838, 54.

156. Sampson Avard et al., Far West, MO, to Oliver Cowdery et al., Far West, MO, June 1838, in State of Missouri, "Copies of Part of the Evidence," [17–24]; Ebenezer Robinson, "Items of Personal History of the Editor," *The Return*, Oct. 1889, 145–147.

later recounted that Robinson, at the presidency's instigation, began suing the named men, as well as Frederick G. Williams, "by attachment for debts" and soon seized most of their belongings.[157] All but Phelps, who wrote to the church presidency of his good intentions and willingness to rectify any wrong he had committed, soon left Far West under threats of physical violence.[158] Though driving the men from Far West may have eased tensions within the community, the subsequent agitations of the outcasts increased tension between the Latter-day Saints and Missourians in neighboring counties.[159]

In a 4 July oration at Far West, two and a half weeks after the Salt Sermon, Rigdon evoked the spirit of the United States Declaration of Independence by insisting that the Latter-day Saints must be free to act unhampered by persecution and specifically stated that they would not countenance vexatious lawsuits. After reviewing previous outrages suffered by the Latter-day Saints in Missouri, Rigdon concluded his speech by declaring that should opponents again use violence against the Latter-day Saints, the Saints would not only defend themselves but also wage "between us and them a war of extermination," a threat that came back to haunt the Latter-day Saints in coming months.[160] Rigdon's defiant remarks were understood by adversaries as a declaration of independence from Missouri law.[161]

———— ∞ ————

4–5 June 1838 • Monday–Tuesday • With June–July 1838 Postscript

Monday 4th Pres[ts.] J Smith Jr S[idney] Rigdon [p. 45] Hyram [Hyrum] Smith & myself and others left this place for Adam Ondi Awman [Adam-ondi-Ahman], we stayed this knight at br. Moses Daileys [Daley's], the next morning we went to Col. [Lyman] Wights. it rained and was somewhat wet We continued surveying and building houses &c for some time day after day, the Surveyors run out the city plott and we returned to Farr West This day was spent in diverse labors for the Church together with a greater share of this month and the ensuing one[162]

4 July 1838 • Wednesday

July 4th 1838 This day was spent in cellebrating the 4 of July in commemo-ration of the decleration of ⟨the⟩ Independance of the United States of America,

---

157. Whitmer, History, 86–87; see also Corrill, *Brief History of the Church,* 30.

158. Reed Peck, Testimony, Richmond, MO, Nov. 1838, in State of Missouri, "Evidence"; William W. Phelps, Testimony, Richmond, MO, Nov. 1838, in State of Missouri, "Evidence"; Whitmer, Daybook, 19 June 1838; Reed Peck to "Dear Friends," 18 Sept. 1839, pp. 25–27; compare Corrill, *Brief History of the Church,* 30.

159. See JS, Journal, 8 July 1838, p. 284 herein.

160. *Oration Delivered by Mr. S. Rigdon,* 12; compare covenants described in JS, Journal, 24 Sept. 1835 and 30 Mar. 1836.

161. See Gentry, "Latter-day Saints in Northern Missouri," 75–77; LeSueur, *1838 Mormon War in Missouri,* 47–53; and Hill, *Quest for Refuge,* 77–81.

162. TEXT: The ink of the final sentence of this entry does not match that of the previous part of the entry. It does match that of the following entry, for 4 July, which was inscribed a month later.

and also to make our decleration of Independance from all mobs and persecutions which have been inflicted upon us time after time ⟨un⟩till we could bear it no longer. being driven by ruthless mobs and enimies of the truth. from our homes our property confiscated our lives exposed and our all jeopardized by such conduct, We therefore met on this day in Far West M<u>o</u>.[163] to make our decleration of independance, and to Lay the cornerstones of the house of the Lord agreeably to the commandment of the Lord unto us given April 26ᵗʰ 1838, as recorded on Page⟨ˢ·⟩ 32, 33, & 34 Book A.—[164] An address was deliverd by Presᵗ S[idney] Rigdon,[.] Prest J Smith Jr Prest of the day, Prest H[yrum] Smith Vice Presᵗ· & Prest. S. Rigdon Orator, R[eynolds] Cahoon Chief Marshial G[eorge] M. Hinkle, & J[efferson] Hunt, assᵗ· Marshaul, and myself commanded the Regiment,[165] The order of the day was most splendid and beautifull Several thousands of spectators were present to witness the sene, The address a was delivred on the public squire [square] under the hoisted flagg representing the Liberty and independence [p. 46] of these United States of America.

Shortly after Presᵗˢ· J, Smith Jr S, Rigdon H. Smith and myself, left this place for Adam Ondi Awman [Adam-ondi-Ahman] we saw a deer or two on the way. Prest Smith set his dogs after them one of which was a gray hound which caut the deer but could not hold him, although he threw him down, yet he injoured the dog so badly that he let him go, and we lost him, The race was quite amusing indeed.

I would mention or notice something about O[liver] Cowdery David Whitmer Lyman E Johnson and Johnson Whitmer who b[e]ing guilty of bace iniquities and that to[o] manifest in all the eyes of all men, and being often entreated would continue in their course seeking the Lives of the First Presidency and to overthrow the Kingdom of God which they once testified off [of]. Prest Rigdon preached one sabbath upon the salt that had lost its savour, that it is henceforth good for nothing but to be cast out, and troden

---

163. The event began at ten in the morning with a procession of infantry and cavalry composed of militia and Danite officers, a martial band, various church authorities, the temple architects, and other prominent Latter-day Saints. After the procession, the four cornerstones for the temple were laid by priesthood leaders. Missourian Joseph McGee estimated that five thousand Latter-day Saints were in attendance. ("Celebration of the 4ᵗʰ of July," *Elders' Journal,* Aug. 1838, 60; Baugh, "Call to Arms," 86–87, 87n50.)

164. That is, in this journal. (See pp. 258–260 herein.)

165. Cahoon was a member of the recently organized stake presidency in Adam-ondi-Ahman. Hinkle and George W. Robinson were colonels in the Caldwell County regiment of the state militia; Hunt was a major. (*History of Caldwell and Livingston Counties,* 139; Dibble, "Philo Dibble's Narrative," 88–89.)

Temple lot in Far West. 1907. An April 1838 revelation commanded the Latter-day Saints to build a house of the Lord in Far West, Missouri. The Saints laid the cornerstones for the temple on 4 July 1838 as part of their commemoration of American independence. Expulsion of the Saints from the state precluded the temple's construction. (Church History Library, Salt Lake City. Photograph by George Edward Anderson.)

under foot of men,[166] And the wicked flee when no man pursueth,[167] These men took warning, and soon they were seen bounding over the prairie like the scape Goat to carry of[f] their own sins[168] we have not seen them since, their influence is gone, and they are in a miserable condition, so also it [is] with all who turn from the truth to Lying cheating defrauding & swindeling[169]

Some time past was spent in trying to obtain pay from these men who are named above, who have absconded, and endeavered to defraud their creditors [p. 47]

Editorial Note

At this point, George W. Robinson copied into the journal a number of documents. Regular journal entries do not resume until 26 July 1838. Robinson first copied a letter JS received on 6 July from returning missionaries Orson Hyde and Heber C. Kimball and one from JS's brother Don Carlos en route from Kirtland, Ohio, to Far West with family and friends. Then in an entry for 8 July, Robinson recorded three Ohio revelations dated six months earlier—the day that JS left Kirtland for Far West—and five additional revelations dated 8 July. The revelations related to the leadership crisis and persecution in Kirtland and to the challenges of reordering church leadership and resources in Missouri. Sandwiched between the 12 January revelations and the 8 July revelations is Robinson's brief summary of further developments he observed in June and early July as Latter-day Saint settlers poured into Caldwell and Daviess counties and residents from surrounding areas tried to assess the complaints of the dissenters who had recently been expelled from Caldwell County.

---

6 July 1838 • Friday

July 6th This day received a letter from Orson Hyde & Heber C Kimball Two of the Twelve Apostles of the Lamb in these last Days, who having been

---

166. The "Salt Sermon" was preached 17 June 1838.

167. See Proverbs 28:1.

168. See Leviticus 16:8, 21–22.

169. The June 1838 letter warning dissenters to leave Caldwell County accused them of counterfeiting, theft, persecution through legal action, and numerous other offenses.[a] Several of the accusations were overdrawn and unsubstantiated. Cowdery and Johnson initiated or threatened lawsuits to compel debt collections, which violated the communitarian ethics of the Saints. John Whitmer with William W. Phelps purchased the Far West town site with church money and then personally profited on sale of lots, as indicated in the minutes of their excommunication.[b] Scribe George W. Robinson, personally and as a son-in-law to Rigdon and clerk to the First Presidency, viewed the dissenters as traitors and enemies. (a. See Sampson Avard et al., Far West, MO, to Oliver Cowdery et al., Far West, MO, June 1838, in State of Missouri, "Copies of Part of the Evidence," [17–24]. b. Minute Book 2, 10 Mar. 1838.)

on a mission to England Just returned to Kirtland Ohio and dated same place,[170] Directed to Pres.ᵗ J. Smith Jr.

Dear Brother Joseph

In health peace & saf[e]ty we arrived in this place on monday last,[171] from the scene of our labor during the past year after a passage of 31 days. We cannot give a full account of our labors now, but suffise it to say the standard of truth is reared on the other side of the great waters, and hundreds are now fi[gh]ting the good fight of faith, beneath the shade of its glorious banner. We have fought in the name of the Lord Jesus, and under the shadow of the cross we have conquered, Not an enimy has risen up against us, but that has fallen for our sakes, Every thing we have done has prospered, and the God of the Holy Prophets has been with us, and to him belongs the praise Our bretheren in the East are poor yet rich in faith and the peace of our God abides upon them, we have not interfeered with the priests at all except when we have been assalted by them, We have preached repentance & baptism & baptism & repentance, We have strictly attended to our own buisness and have let others alone We have experienced the truth of solomons words which are as follows When a mans ways please the Lord he maketh his enimies that they are at peace with him[172] our enimies have seen their entire insufficincy to stand against the power of truth manifest through us, and have gone away and left us in peacefull possession of [p. 48] the field, Concerning the Nicholatine Band of which you warned us against we would say God is not there, and we are not there, they deal in sand stone & bogus,[173] but we in faith hope & Charity We have not means to situate our families in Far West at present and as we have not been chargable to the Church hitherto, we

---

170. Kimball and Hyde, with others, left from New York City on a proselytizing mission to England on 1 July 1837 and arrived back in Kirtland in May 1838. Their mission, which resulted in more than fifteen hundred converts, marked the introduction of Mormonism in Europe. (Allen et al., *Men with a Mission,* chap. 2.)

171. 21 May 1838. (Historian's Office, "History of Orson Hyde," 16, Histories of the Twelve, ca. 1858–1880, CHL; Fielding, Journal, 75–76.)

172. See Proverbs 16:7.

173. Many of those estranged from the church still resided in Kirtland when Hyde and Kimball returned there in May 1838. "Sand stone & bogus" may be an allusion to a story about dissenter Warren Parrish, who allegedly traveled to Tinker's Creek, Ohio, to buy a box of bogus, or counterfeit coin, and discovered upon his return that the box contained only "sand and stones."ᵃ JS had apparently equated at least some of the estranged church members at Kirtland with the heretical Nicolaitan sect mentioned in the New Testament.ᵇ (a. [JS], editorial, *Elders' Journal,* Aug. 1838, 58. b. See Revelation 2:6, 15; and Revelation, 8 July 1838–E, in JS, Journal, 8 July 1838, p. 290 herein [D&C 117:11].)

do not like to become a burthen to them in the extreme state of poverty to which they are reduced, We can preach the gospel when the Lord is with us, and by it we can live, and the time will come when we shall have means to settle with the saints. Kirtland is not our home, it looks dolefull here, We shall go westward as soon as we can, the folks here tell many dark and pittifull tales about yourself & others. but the faults of our bretheren is poor entertainment for us, We have no accusation to bring for the Lord has shown us that he has taken the matter into his own hands, and every secret shall be braught to light and every man chastened for his sins, untill he confess and forsake them and then he shall fined mercy Therefore we can say we are at peace with God and with all mankind, and if any creature has aught against us, we have naught against him, and we say forgive us for Christ sake, We should be glad to see all our bretheren of the Twelve, and we s[h]all as we can consistantly, our good wishes and best respects to them To yourself Bro. Sidney [Rigdon] and families, and to all the faithfull bretheren and sisters in Christ Jesus our Lord, Will you or some other of the bretheren write us soon and let us know the true state of things in Far West, We have been gone allmost a year and have heard but very little, but we now hear much, We would like to know if a spirit of union prevails &c. &c. We are as ever your bretheren in the bonds of the everlasting covenant,

H.C. Kimball

To Pres^t J, Smith Jr.

Orson Hyde

We are one [p. 49]

The following is letter from Don C[arlos] Smith

Nine Miles from Terre Haute Ind.

Bro. Joseph

I sit down to inform you of our situation at the present time. I started from Norton Ohio the 7th of May, in company with Father, W^m. [Smith], Jenkins salsbury [Wilkins Jenkins Salisbury], W^m. McClerry [McCleary] & Lewis Rob[b]ins, and families, also sister singly [Margaret Leasure Singley] is one of our number, we started with 15 horses seven wagons, & two cows, we have left two horses by the way sick one with a swelling ~~in~~ ⟨on⟩ his shoulder, a 3rd horse (as it were our dependance) was taken lame, last evening and is not able to travel, and we have stop[p]ed to docter him We were disappointed on every hand before we started, in getting money, we got no assistance whatever only as we have taken in sister singly and she has assisted us as far as her means extends, we had when we started $75 dollars in money, we sold the 2 cows for $13.50 per cow we have sold of your goods to the amt of $45.74 and now we have only $25 dollars to carry 28 souls & 13 horses, 500 miles, we have lived very close and camped out knight, notwithstanding the rain & cold, & my babe[174] only 2 weeks old when we started, Agness [Agnes Coolbrith Smith] is very feeble Father & Mother are not well but very much fatigued, Mother has a severe cold, and it is nothing in fact but the prayer of faith and the power of God, that will sustain them and bring them through, our carriage is good and I think we shall be braught through, I leave it with you and Hyram [Hyrum Smith] to devise some way to assist us to some more expence money, we have had unaccountable ~~road~~ ⟨bad⟩ roads, had our horses down in the mud, and broke of[f] one wagon tongue [p. 50] and fills,[175] and broke down the carriage twice and yet we are all alive and camped on a dry place for allmost the first time, Poverty is a heavy load but we are all obliged to welter under it, it is now dark and I close, may the Lord bless you all and bring us together is my prayer Amen

All the arrangements that bro. Hyram left for getting money failed, they did not gain us one cent

To J. Smith Jr.   Don C. Smith

8 July 1838 · Sunday

The following Revelation⟨ˢ⟩ ~~was~~ ⟨were⟩ read in the congregation this day, which was given in Ohio——

Revelation Given at the French Farm in Kirtland Geauga Co. Ohio.[176] In the presence of J. Smith Jr., S[idney] Rigdon V[inson] Knight & Geo. W. Robinson January 12th 1838.——

---

174. Sophronia, daughter of Don Carlos and Agnes Coolbrith Smith. (Lucy Mack Smith, History, 1845, 36.)

175. Probably "thills," the shafts between which a single animal is harnessed. ("Thill," in *American Dictionary*, 835.)

176. JS and his parents lived in the area of Kirtland known as the French farm. Although the Peter French farm was purchased by the church several years earlier and subdivided into lots, including the temple lot, Kirtland residents continued to refer to that part of the community as the French farm. (Historian's Office, "History of Luke Johnson," 6, Histories of the Twelve, ca. 1858–1880, CHL; Geauga Co., OH, Deed Records, 10 Apr. 1833, 17:359–361; 23 Sept. 1836, 22:497–498; 18 Apr. 1837, 24:424–425; Lake Co., OH, Duplicate Tax Records, 1841, "No. 6 Kirtland," 200, microfilm, U.S. and Canada Record Collection, FHL.)

When inquiry was made of the Lord relative to the trial of the first Presidency of the Church of Christ of Latter Day Saints, For transgressions according to the item of law, found in the Book of Covenants 3rd. Section 37 Verse

Whether the descision of such an Council of one stake, shall be conclusive for Zion and all her stakes[177]

> Thus saith the Lord, Let the first Presidency of my Church, be held in full fellowship in Zion and all her stakes, untill they shall be found transgressors, by such an high Council as is named in the above alluded section, in Zion, by three witnesses standing against each member of said Presidency, and these witnesses shall be of long and faithfull standing, and such also as cannot [p. 51] be impeached by other witnesses before such Council, and when a descision is had by such and Council in Zion, it shall only be for Zion, it shall not answer for her stakes, but if such descision be acknowledged by the Council of her stakes, then it shall answer for her stakes, But if it is not acknowledged by the stakes, then such stake may have the privilege of hearing for themselves or if such descision shall be acknowlededged by a majority of the stakes, then it shall answer for all her stakes And again,

The Presidency of my Church, may be tried by the voice of the whole body of the Church in Zion, and the voice of a majority of all her stakes[178] And again

Except a majority is had by the voice of the Church of Zion and a majority of all her stakes, The Charges will be concidered not sustained and in order to sustain such Charge or Charges, before such Church of Zion or her stakes, such witnesses must be had as is named above, that is the witnesses to each President, who are of long and faithfull standing, that cannot be immpeached by other witnesses before the Church of Zion, or her stakes, And all this saith the Lord because of wicked

---

177. See Revelation, 11 Nov. 1831–B, in Doctrine and Covenants 3:37, 1835 ed. [D&C 107:82–84]. This indicated that a president of the high priesthood could be tried before a "common council" and that the decision of such council should be final.

178. Authorizing consideration of charges against the church presidency by the general membership of the church in Zion and in the stakes, as an alternative to a trial before high councils in Zion and the stakes, was a novel approach. Thomas B. Marsh and the Missouri high council followed a similar procedure in bringing charges against the Missouri presidency before the general membership of the church in Caldwell County, Missouri, in early February 1838. Marsh indicated that he was acting in accordance with instructions from JS, which Marsh may have received during JS's visit to Missouri in November 1837. (See Historical Introduction to this journal, 228–229 herein.)

and asspiring men, Let all your doings be in meekness and in humility before me even so Amen—[179]

Revelation Given the same day January 12th 1838, upon an inquiry being made of the Lord, whether any branch of the Church of Christ of Latter Day Saints can be concidered a stake of Zion, untill they have acknowledged the authority of the first Presidency by a vote of such Church

Thus saith the Lord, Verrily I say unto nay. [p. 52] you Nay

No stake shall be appointed, except by the first Presidency, and this Presidency be acknowledged, by the voice of the same, otherwise it shall not be counted as a stake of Zion and again except it be dedicated by this presidency it cannot be acknowledged as a stake of Zion, For unto this end have I appointed them in Laying the foundation of and establishing my Kingdom Even so Amen.[180]

Revelation Given the same day January 12th 1838.

Thus saith the Lord, let the Presidency of my Church, take their families as soon as it is practicable, and a door is open for them, and moove to the west, as fast as the way is made plain before their faces, and let their hearts be comforted for I will be with them, Verrily I say unto you, the time has come, that your labor' are finished in this place for a season. Therefore arise— and get yourselves, into a land which I shall show unto you, even a land flowing with milk & honey,[181] You are clean from the blood of this Generation people, And wo, unto those

179. In May 1837, JS was the target of a complaint from Lyman Johnson and Orson Pratt to the bishop and his council in Kirtland, charging him with "lying & misrepresentenation—also for extortion—and for speaking disrespectfully, against his brethren behind their backs." While the charges produced no documented result, they illustrated a potential problem. In order to protect the presidency against removal by special interests or localized opposition, the revelation of 12 January 1838 stipulated qualifications for witnesses and required the concurrence of a majority of the stakes with any adverse decision made in Zion. (Complaint, Lyman Johnson and Orson Pratt, Kirtland, OH, to Bishop and council, Kirtland, OH, 29 May 1837, Newel K. Whitney, Papers, BYU.)

180. A priesthood conference in Kirtland in autumn 1837 commissioned JS and Sidney Rigdon to designate locations for additional stakes. By clarifying that this was exclusively the prerogative of the presidency of the church, and by requiring that the membership of prospective stakes accept the leadership of the presidency, this revelation foreclosed the possibility that ad hoc "stakes" might be created for the purpose of removing the presidency. (Minute Book 1, 17 Sept. 1837.)

181. Echoing Exodus 3:8 and other passages of the Old Testament, this language was used in earlier revelations to describe Zion in Missouri. (Revelation, 2 Jan. 1831, in Doctrine and Covenants 12:4, 1835 ed. [D&C 38:18–20]; compare Revelation, 20 July 1831, in Doctrine and Covenants 27:1, 1835 ed. [D&C 57:1–5].)

who have become your enimies, who have professed my name saith the
Lord, for their Judgement lingereth not, and their damnation slum-
bereth not, Let all your faithfull friends arise with their families also,
and get out of this place, and gather themselves together unto Zion and
be at peace among yourselves, O ye inhabitants of Zion, or their shall be
no saf[e]ty for you; <u>Even so Amen</u>.[182] [p. 53]

It hap[pe]ned about these times that some excitement was raised in the
adjoining Counties, that is Ray & Clay, against us, in consequence of
the sud[d]en departure of these wicked character[s], of the apostates from this
Church, into that vicinity, reporting false stories, and statements,[183] but when
they come to hear the other side of the question their feeling were all allayed
upon that subject especially, The emigration to this land is verry extensive, and
numerous, some few are troubled with the <u>ague and fever</u>, The first Presidency
are chiefly engaged in counciling and settling the emigrants to this land,[184] The
prophets [prophecies] are ~~fulling~~ fulfilling very fast upon our heads, and in our
day and generation, They are gathering from the North & from the South
from the East & from West, unto Zion, for safety against the day of wrath,
which Is to be poured out with out mixture upon this generation according to
the prophets,—[185]

The following Revelation was given in Far West M<u>o</u>. July 8<u>th.</u> 1838. And
read this day in the congregation of the saints,
    Revelation[186] Given to the Twelve Apostles July 8th 1838 in Far West Mo in
the presence of J smith Jr. S[idney] Rigdon, H[yrum] smith, E[dward] Partridge
I, Morly [Isaac Morley] J[ared] Carter, S[ampson] Avard T[homas] B, Marsh &
G[eorge] W, Robinson

---

182. Both JS and Sidney Rigdon left Kirtland the night of the same day this revelation was received,
12 January 1838. Oliver Cowdery left Kirtland in September 1837; the revelation therefore did not apply to
him. Hyrum Smith left Kirtland in early March. (JS History, vol. B-1, 780, 784, 786; JS, Journal, Mar.–
Sept. 1838 [undated entry], p. 237 herein; Letter to the Presidency in Kirtland, 29 Mar. 1838, p. 245 herein;
Minute Book 1, 17 Sept. 1837; Oliver Cowdery, Far West, MO, to Warren Cowdery and Lyman Cowdery,
[Kirtland, OH], 4 Feb. 1838, in Cowdery, Letterbook, 83–86; Hyrum Smith, Commerce, IL, to "the
Saints Scattered Abroad," Dec. 1839, *Times and Seasons,* Dec. 1839, 1:21; Hyrum Smith, "Book of
Reckords," [28–29].)
    183. See pp. 274–275 herein on events in July 1838 resulting in the departure of leading dissenters
from Far West.
    184. The presidency spent much of June 1838 planning and directing settlement in Adam-ondi-
Ahman and De Witt. (Gentry, "Latter-day Saints in Northern Missouri," chap. 7.)
    185. See Revelation, 26 Apr. 1838, in JS, Journal, 26 Apr. 1838, p. 258 herein [D&C 115:6]; see also
Revelation 14:10.
    186. Now D&C 118.

Making known the will of the Lord concerning the Twelve Show unto us
thy will O, Lord concerning the Twelve.

Verily thus saith the Lord, Let a conference be held immediately,
Let the Twelve be organized, Let men be appointed to supply the
place(s) of those who [are?] fallen,[187] Let my servent Thomas remain for
a season in the land of Zion, to publish my word let the residue continue to preach from that hour, and if they will do this in all Lowliness
of heart in meekness in and pureness and long suffering I the Lord
God give unto them a promise, that [p. 54]— I will provide for their
families, and an effectual door shall be op[e]ned for them, from henceforth, And next spring let them depart to go over the great waters, and
there promulge my gospel in the fullness thereof, and to bear record
of my name, Let them take leave of my Saints in the city Far West,
on the Twenty sixth day of April next, on the building spot of mine
house saith the Lord, Let my servent <u>John Taylor</u>, and also my servant
<u>John E Page</u>, and also my servent <u>Willford [Wilford] Woodruff</u> and
also my servent <u>Willard Richard</u>s be appointed to fill the places of
those who have fallen, and be officially Notified of their appointment
<u>even so Amen</u>[188]

Revelation Given the same day, and at the same place, and read the same
day in the congregations of the saints
Making known the duty of <u>F[rederick] G. Williams & Wm W. Phelps</u>

Verrily thus saith the Lord in consequence of their transgressions,
their former standing has been taken away from them And now if they
will be saved, Let them be ordained as Elders, in my Church, to preach
my gospel and travel abroad from land to land and from place to place,

---

187. Members of the Quorum of the Twelve who had been removed were John F. Boynton, Luke
and Lyman Johnson, and William E. McLellin. (Minute Book 2, 7 Apr. 1838; Letter to John Corrill and
the Church in Missouri, 4 Sept. 1837, p. 242 herein; Historian's Office, "History of William E.
Mc. Lellin," 3, Histories of the Twelve, ca. 1858–1880, CHL.)

188. Marsh, president of the Quorum of the Twelve, responded to the revelation by calling a meeting the next day with Rigdon and the available members of the Twelve (five including Marsh). They
agreed to inform absent and newly appointed members of the quorum to come to Far West to prepare for
their expected mission abroad.[a] With the exception of Willard Richards, who was proselytizing in
England, the newly appointed apostles formally joined the quorum by April 1839.[b] (a. Minutes, *Elders'
Journal,* Aug. 1838, 61. b. Minute Book 2, 19 Dec. 1838; Woodruff, Journal, 26 Apr. 1839; Historian's
Office, "History of Brigham Young," 25.)

(July 1838)

It happened about these times that some excitement was raised in the adjoining Counties, that is Ray & Clay, against us, in consequence, of the sudden departure of these wicked character, of the apostates from this Church, into that vicinity, report -ing false stories, and statements, but when they come to hear the other side of the question their feeling were all allayed upon that subject especially, The Emegration to this land is very extensive, and numerous, Some few are troubled with the ague and fever, The first Presidency are chiefly engaged in counciling and settling the emegrants to this land, The Prophets are fulfilling very fast upon our heads, and in our day and generation, They are gathering from the North & from the South, from the East & from West, unto Zion, for safety against the day of wrath, which is to be found out without mixture upon this generation according to the prophets,

Sec 118

The following Revelation was given in Far West Mo July 8th 1838, And read this day in the congregation of the Saints,

Revelation Given to the Twelve Apostles July 8th 1838 in Far West Mo in the presence of J Smith jr S Rigdon, H. Smith, E Partridge I Morley J Corrill S. Avard I. B. Monck & G. W. Robinson

Making known the will of the Lord concerning the Twelve Show unto us thy will O Lord, concerning the Twelve.

Verily thus Saith the Lord, Let a conference be held immediately, Let the Twelve be organiz -ed, Let men be appointed to supply the place of those who fallen, Let my servant Thomas remain for a season in the land of Zion, to publish my word let the residue continue to preach from that hour, and if they will do this in all Lowliness of heart in meekness and pureness and long Suffering I the Lord God give unto them a promise, that

---

Leaf removed from journal. This leaf, containing pages 54 and 55 of the March–September 1838 journal, records 8 July 1838 revelations directed to the Twelve Apostles and to Frederick G. Williams and William W. Phelps. The leaf was torn out of the journal and is currently part of the Revelations

(July 1[8]38)

— I will provide for their families, And an effectual door shall be opened for them, from henceforth, And next spring let them depart to go over the great waters, and there promulge my Gospel in the fullness thereof, and to bear record of my name Let them take leave of my Saints in the City Far West, on the twenty sixth day of April next, on the building spot of mine house Saith the Lord Let My servent John Taylor and also my servent John E Page, And also my servent Wilford Woodruff And also my servent Willard Richards be appointed to fill the places of those who have fallen, and be officially Notified of their appointment— Even so Amen——

~~~~~~~~

Revelation Given the same day, and at th same place, and read th same day in th Congreya tions of the Saints

Making Known the duty of F— G. Williams & Wm W. Phelps.

Verily thus Saith the Lord in Consequence of their transgressions, their former Standing has been taken away from them And now if they will be saved Let them be ordained as Elders in my Church, to preach my gospel and travel abroad from land to land And from place to place, to gather mine Elect unto me Saith the Lord And let this be their labors from hence forth Even so Amen ~~~

~~~~~~~~

Collection at the Church History Library. Handwriting of George W. Robinson. (Photographs by Welden C. Andersen.)

to gather mine Elect unto me saith the Lord, and let this be their labors from hence forth <u>Even so Amen</u>[189] [*6 lines blank*] [p. 55]

Revelation.[190] Given the same day, and read at the same time, of the pre-ceeding ones J̶u̶n̶. ⟨July⟩ 8⟨th⟩ 1838

O! Lord, show unto thy servents how much thou requirest of the properties of thy people for a Tithing?

Answer.

Verrily thus saith the Lord I require all their surpluss, property to be put into the hands of the Bishop of my Church of Zion, for the building of mine house and for the Laying the foundation of Zion, and for the priesthood, and for the debts of the presidency of my Church, and this shall be the begining of the tithing of my people, and after that, those, who have thus been tithed, shall pay one tenth of all their interest anually, And this shall be a standing Law unto them forever, for my holy priesthood saith the Lord, Verrily I say unto you, it shall come to pass, that all those who gather unto the land of Zion, shall be tithed of their surpluss properties, and shall observe this Law, or they shall not be found worthy to abide among you. and I say unto you, If my people observe not this Law, to keep it holy, and by this law sanctify the Land of Zion unto me, that my Statutes and my Judgements, may be kept thereon that it may be most holy, behold verrily I say unto you, it shall not be a land of Zion un<u>to</u> you, and this shall be an ensample unto all the stakes of Zion, <u>even so Amen</u>.[191] [*5 lines blank*] [p. 56]

---

189. Williams had been a counselor to JS in the general church presidency, and Phelps had been a counselor in the Missouri church presidency. Williams was perceived as sympathizing with the dissenters and was replaced in the general church presidency during the November 1837 conference in Missouri. He may have been subsequently excommunicated, as he was rebaptized and reconfirmed in August 1838. Williams was excommunicated 17 March 1839 at Quincy, Illinois, and restored to fellowship at Commerce, Illinois, 8 April 1840. Phelps was removed from office in February 1838 for violating church policy by sell-ing property in Jackson County and for his conduct of financial affairs in connection with the disposition of property in Far West. He was excommunicated 10 March 1838 for "persisting in unchristian-like con-duct" in connection with those property transactions. In June, Phelps wrote a conciliatory letter to the church presidency. (Minute Book 2, 7 Nov. 1837 and 5–9 Feb. 1838; [JS], editorial, *Elders' Journal,* Aug. 1838, 57; Williams, "Frederick Granger Williams," 254–256; JS, Journal, 5 Aug. 1838; "Extracts of the Minutes of Conferences," *Times and Seasons,* Nov. 1839, 1:15; "Conference Minutes," *Times and Seasons,* Apr. 1840, 1:95; Minute Book 2, 10 Mar. 1838; Letter to the Presidency in Kirtland, 29 Mar. 1838, p. 246 herein; William W. Phelps, Testimony, Richmond, MO, Nov. 1838, in State of Missouri, "Evidence.")

190. Now D&C 119.

191. A February 1831 revelation established a church law to provide for the economic needs of the Latter-day Saints through consecration of property. However, any property and reserves accrued in Missouri under that system were lost as a result of the expulsion from Jackson County. By autumn 1837,

Revelation[192] Given the same day July 8th 1838

Making known the desposition of the properties tithed, as named in the preceeding revelation—

Verrily thus saith the Lord, the time has now come that it shall be disposed of, by a council composed of the first Presidency of my Church and of the Bishop and his council and by ⟨my⟩ high Council, and ⟨by⟩ mine own voice unto them saith the Lord, even so Amen.

Revelation[193] Given to Wm. Marks, N[ewel] K, Whitney Oliver Granger & others. ⟨Given⟩ in Zion. July 8th 1838[194]

Verrily thus saith the Lord unto my servent Wm. Marks, and also unto my servent N, K, Whitney, Let them settle up their buisness spedily, and Journey from the land of Kirtland before I the Lord sendeth the snows again upon the ground, Let them awake and arise and come forth and not tarry for I the Lord command it, therefore if they tarry, it shall not be well with them, let them repent of all their sins and of all their covetous desires, before me saith the Lord. For what is property unto me saith the Lord. Let the properties of Kirtland be turned out for debts saith the Lord, ~~the Lord~~ Let them go; saith the Lord, and whatsoever ~~remaines~~ remaineth let it remain in your hands saith the Lord, for have I not the fowls of heaven and also the fish of the sea, and the bea[s]ts of the Mountains, have I not made the earth, do I not hold the destinies of all the armies of the Nations of the earth, therefore will I not make the solitary places to bud, and to bloss[p. 57]om, and to bring forth in abundence saith the Lord, Is there not room enough upon the mountains of Adam Ondi Awmen [Adam-ondi-Ahman], and upon the plains of Olaha Shinehah, or in the land where Adam dwelt; that you should not covet that which is but the drop, and neglect the more weighty matters, Therefore come up hither unto the Land of my people, even Zion, let my servent Wm. Marks. be

---

temple building, publication costs, caring for the poor, and legal fees and fines had financially exhausted the church. (Revelation, 9 Feb. 1831, in Doctrine and Covenants 13, 1835 ed. [D&C 42]; Newel K. Whitney et al., Kirtland, OH, to "the Saints scattered abroad," 18 Sept. 1837, *LDS Messenger and Advocate,* Sept. 1837, 3:561–564.)

192. Now D&C 120.

193. Now D&C 117.

194. Granger carried this revelation from Far West to Marks and Whitney, the president and bishop of the church in Kirtland. The First Presidency added a postscript encouraging all Kirtland Latter-day Saints to migrate to Far West. (Sidney Rigdon et al., Far West, MO, to William Marks and Newel K. Whitney, Kirtland, OH, 8 July 1838, JS Collection, CHL.)

faithfull over a few things, and he shall be a ruler over many. Let him preside in the midst of my people in the City Far West and let him be blessed with the blessings of my people. Let my servant N. K. Whitney be ashamed of the Nicholatine band,[195] and of all their secret abominations, and of all his littleness of soul before me saith the Lord and come up unto the land of Adam Ondi Awman, and be a bishop[196] unto my people Saith the Lord, not in name but in deed saith the Lord. And again verrily I say unto you I remember my servant Oliver Granger, behold verrily I say unto him, that his name shall be had in sacred rememberance from Generation to Generation <u>for ever and ever,</u> saith the Lord. Therefore let him contend ernestly for the redemption of the first presidency of my Church saith the Lord, and when he falls he shall rise again for his sacrafice shall be more sacred unto me, than his increase saith the Lord,[197] Therefore, let him come up hither spedily unto the land of Zion, and in due time he shall be made a merchent unto my name Saith the Lord, for the benefit of my people,[198] Therefore let no man despise my servant Oliver [p. 58] Granger, but let the blessings of my people be upon him forever and ever, and again verrily I say unto you, let all my servents in the Land of Kirtland rem[em]ber the Lord their God, and mine house also, to keep and preser[v]e it holy, and to overthrow the money Changers[199] in mine own due time Saith the Lord, even so Amen—

---

195. See Revelation 2:6, 15; and JS, Journal, 6 July 1838.

196. Whitney, appointed bishop of Kirtland in 1831, still resided there. After settling some financial affairs in Kirtland, he departed for Missouri, but he did not reach Adam-ondi-Ahman before conflict broke out between the Latter-day Saints and other Missourians. (Whitney, "Newel K. Whitney," 130.)

197. Granger was placed in charge of the church's financial affairs in Kirtland despite near blindness. His efforts to settle the debts of the First Presidency earned praise from Kirtland area creditors. (Certificate, JS et al. to Oliver Granger, Commerce, IL, 13 May 1839, in JS Letterbook 2, pp. 45–46; JS History, vol. C-2, 361; "Recommendatory Letters &c.," Painesville, OH, 19, 26, and 27 Oct. 1838, in JS Letterbook 2, pp. 40–41.)

198. On 8 July, Granger was already en route from Kirtland to Far West, but he had not yet arranged to relocate himself and his family to Missouri. After reaching Far West, he obtained a copy of the revelation and then returned to Kirtland, where he delivered it to the remaining Latter-day Saints. After settling some business matters, he began the return trip to Missouri with his family. JS's history recounts that Granger "went 70 miles into Missouri, and was driven back by the mob." (JS History, vol. C-2, 361.)

199. An allusion to John 2:13–16 and to attempts by creditors or by dissenters to take over the House of the Lord in Kirtland. (Hepzibah Richards, Kirtland, OH, to Willard Richards, Bedford, England, 18–19 Jan. 1838, Willard Richards, Papers, 1821–1854, CHL.)

———— ✑ ————

Editorial Note

JS, his counselors in the presidency, and clerk George W. Robinson reportedly visited Adam-ondi-Ahman about two days after the 8 July 1838 meeting held in Far West.[200] Journal keeping resumed about two weeks later, with regular entries through 10 September, when the journal ends.

———— ✑ ————

26 July 1838 • Thursday

July 26ᵗʰ 1838 This day the first presidency, High Council, & Bishops Court, to met to take into concideration, the disposing of the publick properties in the hands of the Bishop, in Zion, for the people of Zion have commenced liberally to consecrate agreeably to the revelations, and commandments of the Great I am of their surpluss properties &c.[201]

It was agreed that the first presidency keep all their properties, that they can dispose of to their advantage and support, and the remainder be put into the hands of the Bishop or Bishops, agreeably to the commandments, and revelations,

1ˢᵗ· Mooved seconded & carried unanimously, That the first presidency shall have their expences defrayed in going to Adam Ondi Awman [Adam-ondi-Ahman], and also returning therefrom That the Bishop of Zion pay one half, and the Bishop of Adam Ondi Awman the other half[202]

2ⁿᵈ· Mooved seconded & carried unanimously— that all the traveling expences of the first presidency, shall be defrayed in traveling at any time or place [p. 59]

3ʳᵈ· Mooved seconded & carried unanimously That the Bishop be authorized to pay orders coming from the east inasmuch as they will consecrate liberally, but this to be done under the inspection of the first presidency[203]

---

200. JS History, vol. B-1, 804.

201. An 8 July 1838 revelation stated that all the Saints' surplus property should be consecrated, or donated, to the church. (Revelation, 8 July 1838–C, in JS, Journal, 8 July 1838, p. 288 herein [D&C 119].)

202. That is, Missouri bishop Edward Partridge and Adam-ondi-Ahman's acting bishop, Vinson Knight. Bishop Newel K. Whitney was directed in an 8 July 1838 revelation to move from Kirtland to Adam-ondi-Ahman but was prevented from doing so by escalating conflict in Missouri that autumn. (Revelation, 8 July 1838–E, in JS, Journal, 8 July 1838, pp. 289–290 herein [D&C 117].)

203. Latter-day Saints emigrating from Kirtland, who had entrusted the church there with proceeds from the sale of their Kirtland properties, were presenting "orders" from the church to the bishop that noted their donations and recommended they receive land in Missouri. (Corrill, *Brief History of the Church,* 27; Reed Peck, Quincy, IL, to "Dear Friends," 18 Sept. 1839, pp. 14–15, Henry E. Huntington Library, San Marino, CA; 1838 receipts, Kirtland financial papers, ca. 1838, CHL.)

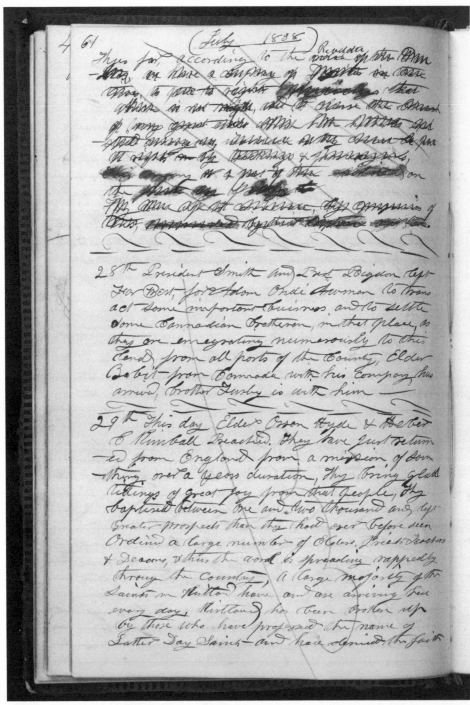

Journal entry regarding Danites. When Joseph Smith's first Missouri journal was used for drafting Smith's multivolume manuscript history, the description of the Danites, a Mormon paramilitary organization, in the entry for 27 July 1838 was scribbled through. The passage was further obscured on one or more subsequent occasions. Some restorative work has been done in order to recover the original inscription. Handwriting of George W. Robinson. JS, Journal, Mar.–Sept. 1838, p. 61, Church History Library, Salt Lake City. (Photograph by Welden C. Andersen.)

4ᵗʰ That the first presidency shall have the prerogative to say to the Bishop whose orders, shall or may be paid by him in this place or in his Jurisdiction. <u>carried unanymously</u>

5ᵗʰ· Mooved seconded and carried That the Bishop of Zion receive all consecrations, east, west, & south, who are not in the Jurisdiction of a Bishop of any other stake.

6ᵗʰ Mooved & carried, that we use our influence to put a stop to the selling of Liquior in the City Far West or in our midst, That our streets may not be filled with drunkeness and that we use our influence to bring down the price of provisions.—

7ᵗʰ· Mooved, seconded & carried unanymously that <u>br. Wᵐ W. Phelps,</u> be requested to draw up a petition to remove the county seat to Far West²⁰⁴

27 July 1838 • Friday

July 27ᵗʰ some time past the bretheren or saints have come up day after day to consecrate, and to bring their offerings into the store house of the lord, to prove him now herewith and se[e] if he will not pour us out a blessings that there will not be room enough to contain it,²⁰⁵ They have come up hither [p. 60] Thus far, according to the ord[e]r of the Dan-Ites, we have a company of Danites in these times, to put to rights physically that which is not righ[t], and to clense the Church of verry great evils which hath hitherto existed among us, inasmuch as they cannot be put to rights by teachings & persuaysons,²⁰⁶ This company or a part of them exibited on the fourth day of July

They come up to consecrate, by companies of tens, commanded by their Captain over ten.²⁰⁷

---

204. Apparently no county seat had yet been designated for Caldwell County, although commissioners were authorized in 1836 to choose one. The petition should therefore have called not for its removal to Far West but for its official establishment there. There is no direct contemporary evidence that a county seat in Caldwell County was determined before 1842, when new commissioners were assigned that responsibility. (An Act to Organize the Counties of Caldwell and Daviess [29 Dec. 1836], *Laws of the State of Missouri* [1836], 46–47; An Act to Establish Permanently the Seat of Justice for Caldwell County [16 Dec. 1842], *Laws of the State of Missouri* [1842–1843], 375–376.)

205. See Malachi 3:10. In late 1837, both JS and the Kirtland bishopric drew on this passage of the Bible to encourage the Saints to be liberal in their financial donations to the church. ([JS], editorial, *Elders' Journal*, Nov. 1837, 28; Newel K. Whitney et al., Kirtland, OH, to "the Saints scattered abroad," 18 Sept. 1837, *LDS Messenger and Advocate*, Sept. 1837, 3:562.)

206. The Danites, a Mormon paramilitary organization, were organized in conjunction with Sidney Rigdon's "Salt Sermon" and the warning out of dissenters in mid-June. (JS, Journal, 4 July 1838; Baugh, "Call to Arms," 79–80.)

207. The Danite organization incorporated some features of the ancient Israelite organization outlined in the Bible.ᵃ Dissenters later claimed that the Danites applied implicit coercion to fellow Saints to consecrate, or donate, their surplus property to the church as directed in an 8 July 1838

28 July 1838 • Saturday

28ᵗʰ President Smith and Presᵗ· [Sidney] Rigdon left Far West, for Adam Ondi Awman [Adam-ondi-Ahman] to transact some important buisness and to settle some Cannadian bretheren, in that place, as they are emegrating numerously to this land from all parts of the Count[r]y, Elder Babit [Almon Babbitt] from Cannada with his company, has arrived, brother [Theodore] Turley is with him—

29 July 1838 • Sunday

29ᵗʰ This day Elder Orson Hyde & Heber C Kimball Preached. They have just returned from England from a mission of somthing over a years duration,[208] They bring glad tidings of great joy from that people, They baptised between one and two thousand and left Greater prospects than they had ever before seen Ord[a]ined a large number of Elders, Priests Teachers & Deacons, & thus the ~~word~~ work is spreading rappedly throug[h] the country, A large majority of the saints in Kirtland have and are arriving here every day, Kirtland has been broken up by those who have professed the name of Latter Day Saints and have denied the faith [p. 61] which they once preached and by their preaching gathered many saints into this land, and now have betrayed them, O Justice! where hast thou fled, And thou administrationis whither hast thou concealed thyself,

30 July 1838 • Monday

30ᵗʰ Monday. This day the circuit court of our circuit sits in this place commencing today, Judge [Austin A.] King presiding Judge,[209] quite a number of Lawyers were here, from Liberty & Richmond &c., They have Just returned from Davi[es]s County session, Prst. Hyram [Hyrum] Smith & myself attended court,

---

revelation.ᵇ (a. Rockwood, Journal, 22 Oct. 1838; John Corrill, Testimony, Richmond, MO, Nov. 1838, in State of Missouri, "Evidence"; compare Exodus 18:25; and Deuteronomy 1:15. b. See Corrill, *Brief History of the Church*, 45–46; Reed Peck, Quincy, IL, to "Dear Friends," 18 Sept. 1839, pp. 34–51, Henry E. Huntington Library, San Marino, CA; JS, Journal, 8 July 1838, p. 288 herein [D&C 119].)

208. Hyde and Kimball left Kirtland for Great Britain in June 1837. After returning to Kirtland on 21 May 1838, they relocated their families to Far West. Kimball arrived in Far West on 25 July 1838, and Hyde, who had stopped in Richmond, Missouri, arrived within the next four days. (Kimball, "History," 56, 83–84.)

209. Austin A. King was a judge of the Fifth Judicial Circuit Court of Missouri. That court's jurisdiction included both Caldwell and Daviess counties as well as Ray, Clay, Carroll, Clinton, and Livingston counties. (An Act to Establish Judicial Circuits, and to Prescribe the Times and Places of Holding Courts [21 Jan. 1837], *Laws of the State of Missouri* [1836], p. 56, sec. 12.)

Austin A. King. Circa 1855–1865. King served as a judge of Missouri's Fifth Judicial Circuit, which included Caldwell and Daviess counties, from 1837 to 1848. (Courtesy Library of Congress, Washington DC.)

31 July 1838 • Tuesday

Tuesday 31ˢᵗ· This day was spent principaly in Court by most of the Presidency. Judge [Austin A.] King. waited upon President J. Smith Jr and spent a short time with him, Counselor [Thomas] Burch, who is also the Circuit Attorney called upon Prest. [Sidney] Rigdon this day, and had a short interview with him, solesiting him verry hard, to preach, this evening as he said those gentlemen of his profession wished to hear him, as also did Judge King, but being quite fatigued in consequence of his absence and labors, returning last evening with Presᵗ· Smith, from Adam Ondi Awman [Adam-ondi-Ahman], Court adjourned for its regular sessions.

1–3 August 1838 • Wednesday–Friday

Wendnersday August 1ˢᵗ· 2ⁿᵈ· 3ʳᵈ· were all spent by the first Presidensy at home, being somewhat fatigued, in consequence of insesant labors, therefore nothing of importance tra[n]spired during this time, we saw the publication of the Oration deliverered by [p. 62] Presᵗ· [Sidney] Rigdon on the 4ᵗʰ day July 1838 it was published in the Far West, a paper published in Liberty Clay County Mo.²¹⁰

5 August 1838 • Sunday

Sunday the 5ᵗʰ The first presidency attended meeting this day, at the usual place of worship²¹¹ Erastus Snow preached a discourse, Prest Smith made some observations immediately after, by way of instructions to the Elders in particular relative wisdom &c. Presᵗ [Sidney] Rigdon deliverered a short discourse in the after part of the day and at the Close thereof Elder Simeon Carter and myself were called upon to administer unto several by the laying on of hands for their confermation and the giving of the Holy Ghost, Br. F[rederick] G, Williams was among the number, who being rebaptized a few days since was this day confermed,²¹²

---

210. Ebenezer Robinson also published Rigdon's oration as a pamphlet. As editor of the *Elders' Journal*, JS recommended that all Mormon families own a copy, "as it contains an outline of the suffering and persecutions of the Church from its rise. As also the fixed determinations of the saints . . . for to be mobed any more without taking vengeance, we will not." (*Oration Delivered by Mr. S. Rigdon*; [JS], editorial, *Elders' Journal*, Aug. 1838, 54.)

211. Probably the schoolhouse. (Minute Book 2, 24 Feb. 1838; Rigdon, "Life Story of Sidney Rigdon," [68].)

212. Williams was removed from the First Presidency in the November 1837 conference held in Far West, but an 8 July 1838 revelation stated that Williams could redeem himself by serving a proselytizing mission as an elder. (See JS, Journal, 8 July 1838, pp. 285–288 herein.)

6 August 1838 • Monday

Monday 6th This day is the day for General Election throughout the state for officers, office seekers from without the Church who depend verry much on our help, begin to flatter us with smooth stories but we understand them verry well through the wisdom of God given unto us they cannot deceive us for God is with us and very near us, for he speaks often unto us, through the means he has appointed

met in the morning in Council with the first presidency at Pres[t.] Smiths house, to take into concideration the conduct of certain Cannada bretheren, who had gone contrary to council and settled at the forks of Grand River[213] whereupon it was agreed that they must return to Adam Ondi Awman [Adam-ondi-Ahman] according to the Council of God, or they would not be concidered one among us [p. 63] Just as the Lord has said in a revelation to us Given July 8th 1838,[214]

In the after part of the day a meeting was held in the school house as follows

> At meeting of the Citizens of Caldwell County assembled in the City Far West, The meeting was called to order, by Calling Judge Elias Higbee to the Chair and appointing Geo. W. Robinson Secretary
>
> After some remarks made by the Chairman relative to the object of this meeting, the resignation of the present Post Master W[m.] W. Phelps, and in appointing his successor[215]
>
> Mr. S[idney] Rigdon was nominated seconded and Carried unanymously to succeed W[m] W. Phelps in the post office department, and that he be recommended to the Post Master Gen. as the person of our choice, as citizens of this City, and also worthy of our suffrage

---

213. The company of Canadian immigrants whom JS directed to settle at Adam-ondi-Ahman a week earlier. (JS, Journal, 28 July 1838; Berrett, *Sacred Places*, 4:464–467.)

214. Five revelations were dated 8 July 1838. One stated, "Is there not room enough upon the mountains of Adam Ondi Awmen . . . Therefore come up hither unto the Land of my people." (Revelation, 8 July 1838–E, in JS, Journal, 8 July 1838, p. 289 herein [D&C 117:8–9].)

215. Phelps was removed from the Missouri presidency in February 1838, excommunicated in March, and warned to leave town in June. However, as Phelps later recounted, he remained in Far West, having promised that if he had "wronged any man," he "would make him satisfaction." Phelps also recounted that "efforts were made to get the post office from me, (being postmaster) by a demand for it." He was able to delay his removal by explaining the law concerning his appointment, but he agreed that if publicly recalled, he would resign after receiving notification from the postmaster general. (Minute Book 2, 5–9 Feb. and 10 Mar. 1838; Sampson Avard et al., Far West, MO, to Oliver Cowdery et al., Far West, MO, June 1838, in State of Missouri, "Copies of Part of the Evidence," [17–24]; William W. Phelps, Testimony, Richmond, MO, Nov. 1838, in State of Missouri, "Evidence.")

Dated Far West M<u>o</u>. August 6th 1838—
Geo. W. Robinson. <u>Secretary.</u>

Elias Higbee
<u>Cha[i]r.</u>

Minutes • 6 August 1838

August 6th. 1838. This afternoon the citizens of Far West assembled in the school house in the S. W. qr. of the Town,

The meeting was opened by Calling Judge Elias Higbee to the Chair, and appointing Geo W Robinson Secretary

⟨1st.⟩ Whereupon it was unanimously agreed that the Citizens of the Counties of Caldwell & Davi[es]s [p. 64] aught and should have a weekly News paper published for their information upon the news of the day. Pres<u>t</u>. Smith said the time had come when it was necessary that we should have somthing of this nature to unite the people and aid in giving us the news of the day &c.

Whereupon it was unanimously agreed that Prest. S[idney] Rigdon should Edit the same[216]

⟨2nd⟩ That a petition be drawn up to remove the County seat to this place

Some remarks were made by Pres^{t.} Rigdon upon the subject, showing the great necess⟨3rd.⟩ity[217] of so doing. ⟨3rd.⟩ And that it is the duty of the bretheren to come into Cities to build and live and Carry on their farms out, of the City

Pres^{t.} Smith spoke upon the same subject of mooving into Cities to live, according to the order of God, he spoke quite lengthy and then Pr^{est.} H[yrum] Smith spoke and endeavoured to impress it upon the ~~same~~ minds of the Saints,[218]

7–9 August 1838 • Tuesday–Thursday

Tuesday the 7th This morning an alarm come from Galliton [Gallatin] the County seat of Davi[es]s County. that during the Election on yesterday at that place some two or three of our bretheren were killed in consequence of

---

216. The church earlier published such a paper, the *Northern Times,* in Kirtland, Ohio, and later published another, *The Wasp,* in Nauvoo, Illinois. Events precluded publication of the prospective Missouri weekly. (Crawley, *Descriptive Bibliography,* 51–53, 192–193.)

217. TEXT: "necess[*end of line*]⟨3rd.⟩ity". George W. Robinson initially misplaced the insertion "3rd." in the left margin where the word "necessity" ran across the line break.

218. In 1833, JS sent a plat for the city of Zion to the Latter-day Saints in Jackson County, Missouri, with an explanation of his conception of an ideal city. The platted city, laid out in square blocks, was intended and reserved for public buildings and private residences, whereas farmlands were located outside the plat. The city plan was a model for future Mormon settlements. (Plat of City of Zion, 1833, CHL.)

the Malignity of the Missourians,[219] it was reported that the citizens of Daviess County who were opposed to our religion, did endeavor to prohibit the bretheren from voting at the election in that place, and that, the men who were killed were left upon the ground and not suffered to be intered, and that the majority of that county were determined to drive the [p. 65] bretheren from the county, under these conciderations quite a number of us volunteered to go to the assistance of our bretheren in that place accordingly some 15 or 20 men started from this place armed and equipt for our defence[220] the bretheren from all parts of the County, followed after and continued to come and join us,[221] and before we arrived at Col. [Lyman] Wights we had quite a large company Prest.(s.) Smith and [Sidney] Rigdon and H[yrum] Smith, alll the first presidency, General [Elias] Higbee Gen. [Sampson] Avard myself[222] and many others to[o] tedious to mention at this time or in this record, were in the company, it was put upon me to take the command in consequence of my holding the office of Colonel. whose duty it is to command one regiment, we marched without much intermision untill we reached Col. Wights, however some of our small parties were attacked, I think on twice in going over, but, no serious injury done, we reached Col. Wights that same evening found some of the bretheren assembled for to receive council upon what to do ac. [&c] as a number of thes[e] men who were at the battle the day before, were there and I believe all of them, and were threatened with vengence by some of their enimies, some of the bretheren were wounded badly but none killed, quite a number of the Missourians were badly wounded some with their sculs cracked as reported, about 150 Missourians faut against from 6 to 12 of our bretheren,[223]

219. Despite serious injuries, no Mormons are known to have been killed. Such exaggerated rumor and fears on both sides intensified an already violent and dangerous confrontation.

220. Danite general Sampson Avard led this initial group of men, whose immediate purpose was to recover the corpses of the rumored victims for burial. (Sampson Avard, Testimony, Richmond, MO, Nov. 1838, in State of Missouri, "Evidence"; JS, Affidavit, Caldwell Co., MO, 5 Sept. 1838, JS Collection, CHL.)

221. JS later recounted that recruits traveled in small groups, "two, three, and four in companys, as we got ready." (JS, Affidavit, Caldwell Co., MO, 5 Sept. 1838, JS Collection, CHL.)

222. Higbee was "Captain General" of the Danites—the ranking officer in the organization. Avard was a subordinate general and George W. Robinson a colonel in the same organization. Robinson was also a colonel in the Caldwell County regiment of the state militia. (Dibble, "Philo Dibble's Narrative," 88; Reed Peck, Quincy, IL, to "Dear Friends," 18 Sept. 1839, p. 48, Henry E. Huntington Library, San Marino, CA; Sampson Avard, Testimony, Richmond, MO, Nov. 1838, in State of Missouri, "Evidence"; Reed Peck, Testimony, Richmond, MO, Nov. 1838, in State of Missouri, "Evidence.")

223. William Peniston, a Whig candidate for the Missouri House of Representatives, earlier approached Lyman Wight, a loyal Daviess County Mormon Democrat, hoping to gain votes from the Latter-day Saints. When Wight queried Peniston about his involvement in an earlier threat to expel the Saints from Daviess County, Peniston tried but failed to persuade Wight that his attitude had changed. Having concluded that he would not get the Mormon vote, on election day Peniston mounted

our bretheren faut like tigers they cleared the ground at that time, in knocking down and drag[g]ing out, the principal men who faught so bravely were John L Butler, Hyram [Hiram] Nelson, [p. 66] whose names aught to be immortalized, from the courage the⟨y⟩ possessed and their determination in this thing and for the victory they gained

We tarried all knight at that place and in the morning we called to se[e] squire Adam Black who was mainfestly an enimy of ours, for the evidences were before us that he did last summer unite himself to a band of mobers to drive our brethern from the County and to prohibit them from settleing in the County and that personally warned many of said bretheren to leave in a certain given time or they should be further delt with,[224] he was obliged to confess this when interrogated upon the subject and in consequences of the violation of his oath as a magistrate in the County of Daviess, we required him to give us some sattisfaction so that we might know whether he was our friend or enimy, and whether he would administer the laws of our country or not in justice for people, we presented him with a paper to sign which was an article of peace, but he being jealous of us would not sign it but said he would draw one himself and sign it to our sattisfaction, he did so, and we left him in peace,[225] The same evening some of our the citizens of the County came to visit

a barrel at Gallatin and denounced the Saints and their right to vote. According to Mormon accounts, Missourian Richard Weldon attacked Samuel Brown, a Mormon, who had come to vote. A brawl ensued, in which initially about eight Saints fought against about thirty or more Missourians. (Rigdon, *Appeal to the American People,* 15–18; Butler, Autobiography, 18–20; Sidney Rigdon, Far West, MO, to Sterling Price, 8 Sept. 1838, draft, CHL; John D. Lee and Levi Stewart, Statement, ca. 1844–1845, Historian's Office, JS History Documents, ca. 1839–1856, CHL; for a well-documented retelling and analysis of the election day fracas, see Hartley, *My Best for the Kingdom,* chap. 6.)

224. In July 1837, after Latter-day Saints began settling in southern and western Daviess County, William W. Phelps wrote, "Public notice has been given by the *mob* in Davis county, north of us, for the Mormons to leave that county by the first of August, and go into Caldwell."[a] Black, a local justice of the peace, was involved in the effort that season to press the Mormons to evacuate the county.[b] In addition, JS and others with him on this August 1838 expedition had heard a rumor that Black planned to lead a mob attack on Adam-ondi-Ahman the following day.[c] (a. William W. Phelps, Far West, MO, 7 [July] 1837, letter to the editor, *LDS Messenger and Advocate,* July 1837, 3:529; "A History, of the Persecution, of the Church of Jesus Christ, of Latter Day Saints in Missouri," *Times and Seasons,* Mar. 1840, 1:65. b. Adam Black, Statement, 27 July 1838, Library of Congress Collection, National Archives, Washington DC. c. JS, Affidavit, Caldwell Co., MO, 5 Sept. 1838, JS Collection, CHL; see also Adam Black, Testimony, Daviess Co., MO, 18 Sept. 1838, in *Document Containing the Correspondence,* 161.)

225. It appears that the first Mormons to contact Black on this occasion were a group of about seventeen Mormon men, including Lyman Wight and Cornelius Lott, who confronted Black that morning about the rumor that he would lead a mob against them. The group intended to get Black to sign a written statement that he as a justice of the peace would do the Saints justice. The delegation returned with the news that Black "insulted them, and gave them no satisfaction," after which over one hundred Mormons, including JS, then traveled to Black's. Sampson Avard, a leading Danite, led a group of two or three men into Black's house, presented him with a written statement promising to uphold the law, and,

us to sue for peace,[226] we told them we would [meet?] their principal men in a committee on the next day at that place at twelve o,clock, accordingly we did so, and entered into a covenant of peace with their principal men of said County for inst[ance] Judge [Josiah] Morin Mr. [John] Williams Mr. [James] Turner Mr. [Jacob] Rogers and many others[227] [p. 67] The covenant of peace was to preserve each others rights, and stand in their defence, that if men should do wrong they, neither party should uphold them or endeavour to secret them from Justice but they shall be delivered up even all all offendrs to be delt with according to law and Justice Upon these terms we parted in peace, and soon every man left the ground and returned to his habitation,[228] we came home the same knight arrived at home about 12 Oclock at knight, and found all well in Far West

10 August 1838 • Friday

Friday 10th Nothing of importance transpired this day the presidency were at home, being somwhat fatigued did not leave their houses to transact much buisness,

---

Black reported later, threatened to kill him if he did not sign. It appears that only after Black refused to sign the statement was JS brought in to break the impasse. A compromise was reached in which Black drew up his own statement. JS later stated that "no violence was offered to any individual, in his [JS's] presence or within his knowlege, and that no insulting language was given by either party."[a] Later that day, Black signed another statement, an affidavit accusing the Latter-day Saints of surrounding his home, attacking him, and threatening him with instant death if he did not sign their document. The affidavit said that JS and Lyman Wight led an armed group of over one hundred men.[b] In the following months, Black and Peniston made this confrontation a cause célèbre and used it to stir up animosity against the Mormons.[c] (a. Adam Black, Affidavit, Daviess Co., MO, 28 Aug. 1838, Mormon War Papers, Missouri State Archives, Jefferson City; JS, Affidavit, Caldwell Co., MO, 5 Sept. 1838, JS Collection, CHL; Robert Wilson, Gallatin, MO, to James Minor, Jefferson City, MO, 18 Mar. 1841, in *Document Containing the Correspondence,* 161–162. b. "Public Meeting," *Missouri Republican,* 8 Sept. 1838, [1], "for the country" edition. c. See, for example, JS, Journal, 11 Aug. 1838.)

226. This Daviess County contingent came from Millport and included John Williams, William Slade, and Sheriff William Morgan. ("Public Meeting," *Missouri Republican,* 8 Sept. 1838, [1], "for the country" edition; Sidney Rigdon, Far West, MO, to Sterling Price, draft, 8 Sept. 1838, CHL.)

227. Morin had just been elected to the state senate, and Williams, a Democrat, had just defeated William Peniston for a seat in the Missouri House of Representatives. Turner was a clerk of the circuit court. Acting as a committee on behalf of the Mormons were John Smith, Reynolds Cahoon, Lyman Wight, and Vinson Knight—the presidency and temporary bishop of the Adam-ondi-Ahman stake—and others. (Rigdon, *Appeal to the American People,* 22, 24–25; Leopard et al., *History of Daviess and Gentry Counties,* 95; "Conference Minutes," *Elders' Journal,* Aug. 1838, 61; Baugh, "Call to Arms," 85.)

228. Wight later recounted: "But while some of their leading men were entering into this contract, others were raising mobs." (Lyman Wight, Testimony, 1 July 1843, Nauvoo Municipal Court Docket Book, 125.)

11 August 1838 • Saturday

Saturday 11th This morning the first presidency left this place for the forks of Grand river, in company with Elder Almon Babbit[t], to visit Elder Babbits company who came on with him from Cannada, and settled contrary to council on the forks of grand river, to give such council as is needed,[229] This afternoon a committe from Ray County came into this place to inquire into the procedings of our sosciety in going armed into the County of Daviess, as complaint had been entered by Adam Black and others in said county of Ray And said committee desired to confer with a committee that might be appointed by our Citizens,[230] Accordingly a meeting was called of the Citisens of Caldwell County to meet in the City Hall in the City Far West At 6 O clock P.M. The following is are the minuits of a meeting held in Far West in the City Hall [p. 68]

At a meeting of the citisens of Caldwell County, met in the city Hall, in Far West August 13th ⟨11th⟩ 1838, To take into concideration certain movements on the part ⟨of the citisens⟩ of the County Ray, wherein they have accused the people of our sosciety of breaking the peace, even in defending our rights and those of our bretheren in of late in the County of Daviess

Meeting called to order by calling Bishop E[dward] Partridge to the <u>Chair</u>, and appointing Geo. W. Robinson <u>Secretary</u>

1[st] Resolved   That a committee of seven be appointed on the part of the Citisens of Caldwell to confer with and wait on the Committee on the part of the Citisens of the County of Ray

2[nd.] Resolved   That this committe with th[e]ir secretary, have power to answer such questions and interrogatories as shall be put by the committee of the County of Ray, and as are named in the document

---

229. Babbitt's company of Canadian immigrants had been directed to settle at Adam-ondi-Ahman. (JS, Journal, 6 Aug. 1838.)

230. On 9–10 August, William Peniston and others from Daviess County went to Ray County, where they presented a citizens' committee with an affidavit from Black charging that the Mormons had threatened Adam Black's life. They requested that Ray County provide militia to defend the original Daviess settlers from the Latter-day Saints. The committee recommended that Peniston present his evidence to circuit judge Austin A. King for King's use in investigating alleged lawbreaking by the Mormons and that King should immediately initiate criminal proceedings against JS and Wight. Peniston made an affidavit with Judge King, accusing JS and Lyman Wight of leading a group of armed Mormons in a "highly insurrectionary and unlawful" manner in Daviess County, attacking Black, and threatening to kill Peniston and others. The meeting of Ray County citizens also appointed William Hudgens, Thomas Hamilton, and Israel Hendley as an investigative committee to visit Caldwell and Daviess counties. ("Public Meeting," *Missouri Republican,* 8 Sept. 1838, [1], "for the country" edition; William Peniston, Affidavit, Ray Co., MO, 10 Aug. 1838, private possession, copy in CHL; see also Corrill, *Brief History of the Church,* 34; and JS, Journal, 7–9 Aug. 1838.)

presented to this meeting purporting to be the preamble and resolutions and resolves, of said meeting of said citisens of Ray[231]

3rd. Resolved—That whereas the document presented as above named had no date or signiture either as <u>Chairman</u> or secretary That this committee shall sattisfy themselves of the fact or reasons given, and act accordingly

4th Resolved   That this Committee report again to this meeting as soon as may be together with all information received

  Geo. W. Robinson <u>Secretary.</u> Edward Partridge <u>Chair.</u>[232]

[p. 69]

12 August 1838 • Sunday

Sunday 12th This day the first presidency were in the north country, not having returned from the forks of Grand river, to which place they went with Elder Babbit [Almon Babbitt], I remained in Far West during this Journey taken by them.[233]

13 August 1838 • Monday

Monday 13th This day was spent as usual, the first Presidency returned at evening all sound and well, though some what fatigued with the Journey, they were chased some 10 or 12 miles by some evil designing persons but escaped out of their hands, men were sent to notify them, that a writ had been ishued by Judge [Austin A.] King the circuit Judge to aprehend Prest. Joseph Smith Jr & Lyman Wight for defending their rights &c.[234] They met ~~them~~ the presidency about 8 miles from this place and all returned ⟨safe⟩ to this place,

---

231. The Ray County committee's resolutions expressed disapproval of "all improper and unlawful collection of people for any purpose whatever" and charted measures for investigating Black and Peniston's claims and supporting the legal process. ("Public Meeting," *Missouri Republican,* 8 Sept. 1838, [1], "for the country" edition.)

232. The proposed Caldwell County committee may have organized and met with the Ray County delegates before the latter left Far West on 12 August for Adam-ondi-Ahman to confer with JS (who was visiting there), Lyman Wight, and other Daviess County Latter-day Saints. (Swartzell, *Mormonism Exposed,* 32; compare "Public Meeting," *Missouri Republican,* 8 Sept. 1838, [1], "for the country" edition.)

233. Anson Call, who had begun farming a large tract of land at the "Forks of Grande River" before the Canadian immigrants reached that vicinity, wrote that the presidency visited there on a Sunday in September and instructed the Saints to leave for either Adam-ondi-Ahman or Far West. The context Call provided and the information available concerning the presidency's whereabouts in September suggest the visit took place on 12 August rather than in September. (Call, Autobiography and Journal, 10; Call, Statement, 30 Dec. 1885, 10–12.)

234. Based on William Peniston's affidavit, King on 10 August issued an arrest warrant for JS and Wight. The warrant may have been based on Missouri's statutes for riot, under which they were later formally charged. Daviess County sheriff William Morgan came to Far West to serve the warrant on JS three days later. (State of Missouri, Warrant for JS and Lyman Wight, Ray Co., MO, 10 Aug. 1838, private

14 August 1838 · Tuesday

Tuesday 14ᵗʰ This day was spent by the presidency in secular buisness of their own

15 August 1838 · Wednesday

The 15ᵗʰ was also spent in the same manner

16–18 August 1838 · Thursday–Saturday

The 16ᵗʰ was spent principally at home,²³⁵ the sherriff of Daivess County²³⁶ acompanied by Judge [Josiah] Morin: called on Presᵗ· Smith and notified him that he had a writ for take him into Daviess County and try him, for visiting that County as before stated, Presᵗ· Smith did not refuse to be taken, as some people had reported that he would not be taken nor submit to the Law, ²³⁷ but he said he would or calculated always to submit to the Laws of our Country. But he told the Sheriff that he wished to be tried in his own County as the Citisens of Daviess County were [p. 70] highly exasperated toward him, he further stated that the Laws of our Country gave him this privilege, the sheriff did not serve his writ upon hearing this, and said he would go to Richmond and see Judge [Austin A.] King upon the subject,²³⁸ Presᵗ· Smith told him he

---

possession, copy in CHL; William Peniston, Affidavit, Ray Co., MO, 10 Aug. 1838, private possession, copy in CHL; An Act Concerning Crimes and Their Punishments [20 Mar. 1835], *Revised Statutes of the State of Missouri* [1835], pp. 202–203, art. 7, secs. 6–8; State of Missouri, Recognizance of JS and Lyman Wight, Daviess Co., MO, 7 Sept. 1838, private possession, copy in CHL; State of Missouri, Indictment of JS and Others for Riot, Daviess Co., MO, Apr. 1839, copy, Boone Co., MO, Circuit Court Records, Western Historical Manuscript Collection, Ellis Library, University of Missouri, Columbia.)

235. TEXT: The remainder of this entry was inscribed with a sharper instrument and matches the entries for 20–23 August, indicating that it was recorded at a later time.

236. William Morgan. (*History of Daviess County*, 243.)

237. These rumors were not without foundation. JS arrived in Missouri indignant about the "vexatious lawsuits" he had experienced in Ohio.ᵃ Sidney Rigdon's public declaration at the Mormon Fourth of July celebration that such suits would not be tolerated soon spread throughout northern Missouri.ᵇ Also in early July, JS instructed that John Cleminson, clerk of the Caldwell County court, should not issue any warrants stemming from "vexatious" claims. William W. Phelps, a judge of the Caldwell County court, reported these instructions to circuit court judge Austin A. King during the next term of the court in Caldwell.ᶜ As Mormon dissenter John Corrill later recounted, when Black and others reported the confrontation at Black's home, "it was said that L. Wight and J. Smith would not be taken, but would die first."ᵈ (*a.* JS, Journal, Mar.–Sept. 1838 [undated entry], p. 238 herein; Letter to the Presidency in Kirtland, 29 Mar. 1838, p. 246 herein. *b.* "Mormon Difficulties," *Missouri Republican,* 22 Sept. 1838, [2], daily edition. *c.* John Cleminson, Testimony, Richmond, MO, Nov. 1838, in State of Missouri, "Evidence"; William W. Phelps, Testimony, Richmond, MO, Nov. 1838, in State of Missouri, "Evidence"; Reed Peck, Quincy, IL, to "Dear Friends," 18 Sept. 1839, p. 37, Henry E. Huntington Library, San Marino, CA. *d.* Corrill, *Brief History of the Church,* 34.)

238. Missouri law allowed change of venue for cases in which "the minds of the inhabitants of the county in which the cause is pending are so prejudiced against the defendant that a fair trial cannot be

would remain at home untill he should return. etc. The sheriff accordingly returned and found Pres^t· Smith at home where he had been during his absence The sheriff informed him very gravely that he (Pres^t Smith) was out of his jurisdiction and that he (Said Sheriff) could not act in this county he therefore returned as tight [light?] as he came[239]

20–21 August 1838 · Monday–Tuesday

20th This day the inhabitants of the different parts of the Town or County met to organize themselves into companies called agricultural Companies, the presidency were there and took a part in the same, one Company was established called the western agricultural com-[pan]y who voted to take in one field for grain containing twelve sections which is seven thousands Six hundred & eighty acres of land Another Company was organised Called the eastern agricultural Company the number of acres is not yet asertained, the next day another Company was organised Called the southern Agri. Comp-y field to be as large as the first one,[240]

---

had therein." Newly appointed to his office, Sheriff Morgan was apparently unaware that this provision had no bearing on the place of arrest and could be applied only after an indictment. According to Sidney Rigdon, Morgan said he intended to ask King if the warrant could be "so altered as to have his trial in this county." Months later, after being indicted in April 1839, JS successfully sought a change of venue. (An Act to Regulate Proceedings in Criminal Cases [21 Mar. 1835], *Revised Statutes of the State of Missouri* [1835], pp. 486–487, art. 5, sec. 16; *History of Daviess County*, 243; Sidney Rigdon, Far West, MO, to Sterling Price, 8 Sept. 1838, draft, CHL; Daviess Co., MO, Circuit Court Record, Apr. 1839, bk. A, 67–68, Daviess Co. Circuit Court, Gallatin, MO.)

239. A sheriff's jurisdiction extended only to the borders of his own county. However, Morgan could have worked through a local magistrate to serve JS's warrant. While King reportedly informed Sheriff Morgan of these facts, Morgan chose not to involve Caldwell County authorities when he returned to Far West, but rather informed JS—in effect—that he (Morgan) would not pursue the matter further at that time. (Practice and Proceedings in Criminal Cases [21 Mar. 1835], *Revised Statutes of the State of Missouri* [1835], p. 475, art. 2, secs. 4–5; S. Rigdon to S. Price, 8 Sept. 1838.)

240. Reed Peck later recounted that four firms were organized and that a new revelation was presented requiring all church members to join one of the firms, to which they would consecrate all of their land and property. John Corrill's more evenhanded account held that the new plan was an opportunity whereby "every male member of the Church could become a member of the firm," that the land was to be leased "for a term of years," and that in the distribution of profit, "more regard was to be paid towards the needs and wants of the members, than to the amount of the stock put in." Corrill also recounted that "Smith said every man must act his own feelings, whether to join or not," though Sampson Avard vigorously promoted recruitment. (Reed Peck, Quincy, IL, to "Dear Friends," 18 Sept. 1839, pp. 51–53, Henry E. Huntington Library, San Marino, CA; Corrill, *Brief History of the Church*, 46.)

22 August 1838 • Wednesday

22nd. This day was spent part of the time in counciling with several bretheren upon different subjects,[241] Bretheren continue to gather into Zion daily[242]

23 August 1838 • Thursday

23rd. This day was spent in such municipal labors as they saw was necessary, in this place

24–30 August 1838 • Friday–Thursday

Friday the 24th [243] This day was spent at home by the first Presidency as also was the 25, 26, 27, 28, 29 & 30,th[244] [p. 71]

Revelation for Thomas B. Marsh • 23 July 1837

/[245]A Revelation[246] given Kirtland July 23rd. 1837.

The word of the Lord unto Thomas, B. Marsh concerning the twelve Apostles of the Lamb.[247]

---

241. Latter-day Saint Warren Foote recorded, "Today the report is that the troops have been called out against the Mormons, and having a permit from the Governor they were going to take 'Joe Smith,' and Sidney Rigdon, but they had run away." (Foote, Autobiography, 22 Aug. 1838.)

242. Less than a month later, JS and Sidney Rigdon wrote, "There are thousands gathering this season The road is full companies of frequently 10, 20 & 30 wagons arrives, some almost daily . . . the road is litterly lined with wagons between here and Ohio." (JS and Sidney Rigdon, Far West, MO, to Stephen Post, Bloomfield, PA, 17 Sept. 1838, Stephen Post, Papers, CHL.)

243. TEXT: This dateline was written in the same ink as the previous entry. The following line is in a different ink and matches the 31 August entry that George W. Robinson penned after James Mulholland's interlude as scribe for this journal. It appears then that Robinson wrote this line on or shortly after 31 August.

244. George W. Robinson may have been unable to record more detailed information from these dates because the journal was likely in the possession of James Mulholland, who inscribed the revelation to Marsh that follows. During these days, rumors about the Latter-day Saints' actions in Daviess County were quickly spreading into neighboring counties. (LeSueur, *1838 Mormon War in Missouri*, 67–71; Baugh, "Call to Arms," 114–117.)

245. TEXT: George W. Robinson handwriting ends; James Mulholland begins.

246. Now D&C 112.

247. As president of the Quorum of the Twelve, Marsh had expected to lead that body in a proselytizing mission to Europe. In May 1837, he and fellow apostle David W. Patten sent notice from Far West that they would convene a meeting of the Twelve in Kirtland on 24 July 1837 to restore unity among the quorum in preparation for that mission. Before Marsh arrived in Kirtland, however, JS dispatched apostles Heber C. Kimball and Orson Hyde to begin proselytizing in England. Several others of the Twelve were dissatisfied with JS's leadership. Concerned about his divided quorum and distressed about his own role as president, Marsh asked for divine direction. This revelation for Marsh is dated the day prior to the conference that was planned for the Twelve but that was not held because of disaffection or absence of several of its members. (Esplin, "Emergence of Brigham Young," 273–281; Esplin, "Exalt Not Yourselves," 117–119.)

Verily thus saith the Lord unto you my servant Thomas, I have heard thy prayers and thine alms have come up as a memorial before me in behalf of those thy brethren who were chosen to bear testimony of my name and to send it abroad among all nations, kindreds, tongues and people and ordained through the instrumentality of my servants.

Verily I say unto you there have been some few things in thine heart and with thee, with which I the Lord was not well pleased; nevertheless inasmuch as thou hast abased thyself thou shalt be exalted: therefore all thy sins are forgiven thee. Let thy heart be of good cheer before my face, and thou shalt bear record of my name, not only unto the Gentiles, but also unto the Jews; and thou shalt send forth my word unto the ends of the earth.

Contend thou therefore morning by morning, and day after day let thy warning voice go forth; and when the night cometh let not the inhabitants of the earth slumber because of thy speech. Let thy habitation be known in Zion, and remove not thy house, for I the Lord have a great work for ~~you~~ ⟨thee⟩ to do, in publishing my name among the children of men, therefore gird up your loins for the work. Let your feet be shod also for thou art chosen, and thy path lyeth among the mountains and among many nations, and by thy word many high ones shall be brought low; and by thy word many low ones shall be exalted, thy voice shall be a rebuke unto the transgressor, and at thy rebuke let the tongue of the slanderer cease its perverseness. Be thou humble and the Lord thy God shall lead thee by the hand and give thee an answer to thy prayers, I know thy heart and have heard thy prayers concerning thy brethren. Be not partial towards them in love above many others, but let your love be for them as for yourself, and let your love abound unto all men and unto all who love my name. And pray for your brethren of the twelve. Admonish them sharply for my name's sake, and let them be admonished for all their sins, and be ye faithful before me unto my name; and after their temptations and much tribulation behold I the Lord will feel after them, and if they harden not their hearts and stiffen not their necks against me they shall be converted and I will heal them.

Now I say unto you, and what I say [p. 72] unto you, I say unto all the twelve. Arise and gird up your loins, take up your cross, follow me, and feed my sheep. Exalt not yourselves; rebel not against my servant Joseph for Verily I say unto you I am with him and my hand shall be over him; and the keys which I have given him, and also to youward shall not be taken from him untill I come.

Verily I say unto you my servant Thomas, thou art the man whom I have chosen to hold the keys of my kingdom (as pertaining to the twelve) abroad among all nations, that thou mayest be ~~thy~~ my servant to unlock the door of the kingdom in all places where my servant Joseph, and my servant Sidney [Rigdon], and my servant Hyrum [Smith], cannot come, for on them have I laid the burden of all the Churches for a little season: wherefore whithersoever they shall send you, go ye, and I will be with you and in whatsoever place ye shall proclaim my name an effectual door shall be opened unto you that they may receive my word. Whosoever receiveth my word receiveth me, and whosoever receiveth me receiveth those (the first presidency) whom I have sent, whom I have made counsellors for my name's sake unto you. And again I say unto you, that whosoever ye shall send in my name, by the voice of your brethren the twelve, duly recommended and authorized by you, shall have power to open the door of my kingdom unto any nation whithersoever ye shall send them, inasmuch as they shall humble themselves before me and abide in my word, and hearken to the voice of my spirit.

Verily verily! I say unto you, darkness covereth the earth and gross darkness the ~~people~~ minds of the people, and all flesh has become corrupt before my face! Behold vengeance cometh speedily upon the inhabitants of the earth. A day of wrath! A day of burning! A day of desolation! Of weeping! Of mourning and of lamentation! And as a whirlwind it shall come upon all the face of the earth saith the Lord. And upon my house shall it begin and from my house shall it go forth saith the Lord. First among those among you saith the Lord; who have professed to know my name and have not known me and have blasphemed against me in the midst of my house saith the Lord

Therefore see to it that you trouble not yourselves concerning the affairs of my Church in this place saith the Lord, but purify your hearts before me, and then go ye into all the world and preach my gospel unto every creature who have not received it and he that believeth and is baptized shall be saved, and he that believeth not, and is not baptized [p. 73] shall be damned. For unto you (the twelve) and those (the first presidency) who are appointed with you to be your counsellors and your leaders, is the power of this priesthood given for the last days and for the last time, in the which is the dispensation of the fulness of times: which power you hold in connection with all those who have received a dispensation at any time from the beginning of the creation, for verily I say unto you the keys of the dispensation which ye have received have came down from the fathers; and last of all being sent down from heaven unto you. Verily I say unto you, Behold how great is your calling.

Cleanse your hearts and your garments, lest the blood of this generation be required at your hands. Be faithful untill I come for I come quickly and my reward is with me to recompense every man according as his work shall be! I am Alpha and Omega. Amen.

/²⁴⁸The above revelation was given in Kirtland, and was not here in time to insert in its proper sequence²⁴⁹

G[eorge] W. R[obinson] Recorder.

31 August 1838 • Friday

Friday the 31ˢᵗ· Presᵗ· Joseph spent some considerable time this day in conversation with br. John Corril[l], in consequence of some expressions made by him in pressence of some considerable number of bretheren present, who might perhaps be weak in the faith, as they had not been long in the place, therefore consequently were made verry unwisely,²⁵⁰ Br. Corrilˢ· conduct for some time past, has been verry unbecoming indeed especially a man in whoom so much confidence has been placed, He has been difficulted to keep track and walk step, by step, with the great wheal which is propelled by the arm of the great Jehovah, he says he will not yeald his Judgement, to any thing proposed by the Church, or any individuals of the Church, or even the voice of the great (I am,) given through the appointed organ, as revelation, but will always act upon his Judgement [p. 74] let him believe in whatever religion he may, he says he will always say what he pleases, for he says he is a republican, and as such he will do, say, act, and believe, what he pleases,²⁵¹

Let the reader mark such republicanism as this, That a man should oppose his own Judgement to the Judgement of God, and at the same time profess to believe in the same God, when that God has said, "the wisdom of God, is foolishness with men, and the wisdom or Judgment of men is foolishness with

---

248. TEXT: James Mulholland handwriting ends; George W. Robinson begins.

249. Marsh reportedly recorded this revelation into his own book as JS dictated it in July 1837. It is possible that JS had not retained a copy and that therefore his clerk could not copy the revelation in its "proper sequence" when copying other Kirtland documents into the beginning of the present journal. Vilate Murray Kimball, wife of apostle Heber C. Kimball, had made a transcript of the revelation from Marsh's copy and sent it to her husband in England. Kimball had recently returned from England and may have provided his copy as the basis for this version, as the two closely resemble each other with the exception of distinctive punctuation and occasional wording variants. (JS, Journal, 29 July 1838; Vilate Murray Kimball, Kirtland Mills, OH, to Heber C. Kimball, Preston, England, 12 Sept. 1837, Heber C. Kimball Collection, 1837–1898, CHL.)

250. Reed Peck later recounted that JS reproved Corrill for expressing doubt regarding a revelation directing all Latter-day Saints to join the recently organized cooperatives. (Reed Peck, Quincy, IL, to "Dear Friends," 18 Sept. 1839, pp. 53–54, Henry E. Huntington Library, San Marino, CA; see also JS, Journal, 20–21 Aug. 1838.)

251. Corrill's statement embodied a central point of dispute for recent dissenters: that they would not submit to "popery and religious tyrany." The early American ideology of republicanism focused on the concepts of a commonwealth of a virtuous and independent citizenry of white males with equal rights and opportunities under the law. It was conventionally contrasted with tyrannies of political and religious absolutism. ([Warren Cowdery], editorial, *LDS Messenger and Advocate*, July 1837, 3:538; Watson, *Liberty and Power*, chap. 2.)

God.[252] Prest. [Sidney] Rigdon also made some observations to br. Corril, which he afterwards acknowleged were correct, and that he understood things different after the interview, from what he did before,

——————— ∽ ———————

Editorial Note

As September began, rumors of Mormon violence, fanned by Adam Black, William Peniston, and others, put northwestern Missouri on a war footing. Sheriff William Morgan had intended to arrest JS on 16 August but was ultimately dissuaded because of a jurisdictional issue.[253] Within his own jurisdiction of Daviess County, Morgan apparently intended to arrest Lyman Wight as well but was intimidated by Wight's defiant posture. Missouri newspapers reported that the sheriff went to Wight's home with the intent of arresting him but found the home surrounded by armed Latter-day Saints. Wight was reported to have threatened "that he would not be taken alive—that the law had never protected him, and he owed them no obedience."[254] On 29 August 1838, Peniston and other members of a Daviess County "Committee of Vigilance" wrote that JS and Wight "say they will not be taken, nor submit to the law of the land" and that "two or three" attempts had been made to arrest them.[255] By 2 September 1838, Peniston, Black, and other Daviess County residents had solicited aid from Ray, Livingston, Clay, Lafayette, Jackson, Carroll, Howard, Chariton, and possibly other Missouri counties.[256]

On 4 September, in consultation with General David Atchison, JS and Wight agreed to be tried on charges stemming from Adam Black's affidavit, with Atchison and Alexander Doniphan to serve as their legal counsel. They requested that circuit court judge Austin A. King of Richmond, Clay County, conduct a preliminary hearing on the matter in Daviess County. King agreed to do so "for the sake of giving quiet to the country" and instructed Sheriff William Morgan of Daviess County to "go to Mr. Wight who will submit to your process . . . when you go to execute your process on Wight you need take no one with you."[257] The hearing took place on 7 September, but it failed to bring peace to Daviess County as outsiders continued to mobilize—now not merely to bring JS and Wight to justice but to drive the Mormons from the county.

——————— ∽ ———————

252. See 1 Corinthians 3:19.

253. JS, Journal, 16–18 Aug. 1838.

254. "Mormon War," *Missouri Republican,* 8 Sept. 1838, [1], "for the country" edition; see also Austin A. King, Ray Co., MO, to William Morgan, Daviess Co., MO, 4 Sept. 1838, William Morgan, Papers, CHL.

255. "Mormons Once More," *Hannibal Commercial Advertiser,* 25 Sept. 1838, [1].

256. Hiram Cumstock, Livingston Co., MO, to "the Citizens of Carroll County," 12 Aug. 1838, *Missouri Argus,* 6 Sept. 1838, [1]; "The Mormon Difficulties," *Niles' National Register,* 13 Oct. 1838, 103; "The Mormons," *Missouri Argus,* 13 Sept. 1838, [3].

257. A. A. King to W. Morgan, 4 Sept. 1838.

1 September 1838 • Saturday

Saturday 1ˢᵗ· Sept. 1838 —— —— —— —— —— —— —— The first Presidency ~~their Scribe, &~~ Judge [Elias] Higbee (as surveyor,) Started this morning for the half-way house[258] (as it is called) Kept [by] br. [Waldo] Littlefield, some 14 or 15 miles from Far West directly north, For the purpose of appointing a city of Zion, for the gathering of the saints in that place, for safety and from the storm which will soon come upon this genneration,[259] and that the bretheren may be together in the hour of the coming of the son of man and that they may receive instruction⟨s⟩ to prepare them for that great day which will come upon this generation as a thief in the knight,[260]

There is great exitement at present among the misourians seeking if possible an accasion against us they are continually chafing us, and provoking us to anger if possible, one sene of ~~threats~~ threatning after an=other.[261] but we do not fear them [p. 75] For the Lord God the eternal Father is our God and Jesus the mediator is our saviour, and in the great I am, is our strength and confidence we have been driven time after time and that without cause and smitten again and again, and that without provocation, untill we have prooved the ~~world~~ ⟨wordd⟩ with kindness, and the ~~world~~ ⟨wordd⟩ proved us, that we have no designs against any man or set of men That we injure no man. That we are peasibl with all men, minding our own buisness, and our buisness only, we have Suffered our rights and our liberties to be taken, from us, we have not avenged ourselves of those wrongs, we have appealed to magistrates, to Sheriffs, to Judges, to govonour⟨s⟩ and to the President of the United States, all in vain,[262] yet we have yealded, peacibly to all these things, we have not complained at the great God, we murmur⟨ed⟩ not, but peacibly left all, and retired into the back Country in the broad and wild Prairie, in the barren & desolate

---

258. The Littlefield "halfway house" was located in southern Daviess County approximately halfway between Far West and Adam-ondi-Ahman—a strategic location for Mormon settlement. George W. Robinson and others may have believed at this time that the halfway house was located just inside Mormon-controlled Caldwell County. (See JS, Journal, 4 Sept. 1838; compare 6 Sept. 1838.)

259. See Revelation, 26 Apr. 1838, in JS, Journal, 26 Apr. 1838, p. 258 herein [D&C 115:6].

260. See Revelation, ca. 7 Mar. 1831, in Doctrine and Covenants 15:3, 1835 ed. [D&C 45:19].

261. Fueled by the accusations of Black and Peniston, rumors of Mormon lawlessness and mobilization helped to rally anti-Mormon vigilantes in neighboring counties. Hyrum Smith later testified that the vigilantes who were gathering in Daviess County began stealing Mormon livestock, threatening physical violence, and even taking prisoners. (Hiram Cumstock, Livingston Co., MO, to "the Citizens in Carroll County," 12 Aug. 1838, *Missouri Argus*, 6 Sept. 1838, [1]; Hyrum Smith, Testimony, 1 July 1843, Nauvoo Municipal Court Docket Book, 61–63; George A. Smith, Autobiography, 108; Swartzell, *Mormonism Exposed,* 31.)

262. Following their expulsion from Jackson County, the Latter-day Saints sought redress through political and legal channels including writing to United States president Andrew Jackson. (Parkin, "History of the Latter-day Saints in Clay County," chap. 4.)

plains, and there commenced anew, we made the desolate places to bud and blosom as the rose, and now the fiend like rase are disposed to give us no rest, Their Father (the Devil) is hourly calling upon them to be up and doing, and they like willing and obedient children need not the second admonition, But in the name of Jesus Christ the Son of the Living God we will ~~do it~~ endure it no longer, if the Great God will arm us with courage, with strength and with power, to resist them in their persecutions. We will not act on the offensive but always on the defensive, our rights and [p. 76] our rights and our liberties shall not be taken from us, and we peacibly submit to it, as we have done heretofore, but we will avenge ourselves of our enimies, inasmuch as they will not let us alone,[263] But to return again to our subject We found the place for the city, and the bretheren were instructed to gather immediately into it, and soon they should be organised according to the Laws of God,* ⟨*A more particular history of this city will be given hereafter, perhaps ~~at the~~ ⟨at its⟩ organization and dedication,—⟩[264]

We found a new route home saving I should think 3 or 4 miles, we arrived at Far West about Day light down

2 September 1838 • Sunday

Sunday 2ⁿᵈ· The first Presidency attended worship as usual the fore part of the Day, Presᵗ· ~~& myself~~ ⟨Smith⟩ did not attend in the after part of the day, but retired to Presᵗ· Smithˢ· to examine the church recordˢ· Br. Joseph spent some considerable part of the afternoon in company with a gentlemen from Livingston County, who had become considerable ex[c]ited, on account of a large collection of people saying to take Joseph Smith Jr. & Lyman Wight, for going to one Adam Blackˢ· as has been previously stated, and recorded in this record,[265] and as they said Presᵗ· Smith and Col. Wight, had resisted the officer, who had endeavoured to take them etc. and accordingly these men were assembling to take them (as they said) They are collecting from every part of the Country to Daviess County. report says they are collecting from Eleven Counties,[266] to help take two men [p. 77] who had never resisted the Law or

263. George W. Robinson's sentiments reflect those recently expressed by his father-in-law, Sidney Rigdon, at the Fourth of July celebration and those in the covenant concerning Missouri administered by JS at the solemn assembly in 1836. An 1833 revelation allowed such actions after patiently suffering persecution more than three times. (*Oration Delivered by Mr. S. Rigdon,* 12; JS, Journal, 30 Mar. 1836; Revelation, 6 Aug. 1833, in Doctrine and Covenants 85:5, 1835 ed. [D&C 98:23–31].)

264. George W. Robinson inscribed this insertion, keyed by asterisks, at the foot of the page. Events precluded the development of the community, which was planned to be named Seth. (Berrett, *Sacred Places,* 4:371–372.)

265. See JS, Journal, 7–9 Aug. 1838.

266. In response to Daviess County's solicitations for aid, Howard County responded by sending an

officer, neither thought of doing so, and this they knew at the same time, or many of them at least,[267] This looks a leettle to[o] much like mobocracy, it foretells some evil intentions, the whole uper Missouri is all in an uproar and confusion,[268] This evening we sent for General [David R.] Atchison of Liberty Clay County, who is the major General of this division, we sent for him to come and counsil with us, and to se[e] if he could not put a stop to this collecion of people, and to put to a stop to hostilities in Daviess County,[269] we also sent a letter to Judge [Austin A.] King containing a petition, for him to assist in putting down and scattering the mob, which are collecting at Daviess,[270]

---

investigative committee, as did Chariton County. Both committees returned to report that the alarmist reports were exaggerated.[a] Livingston County, on the other hand, had already decided to send volunteers, as did Jackson County two days later.[b] By 13 September 1838, between two hundred and three hundred volunteers—principally from Livingston, Carroll, and Saline counties—had gathered near Millport. John Corrill later recounted that JS received news of four thousand armed men assembling.[c] (a. "The Mormons," *Missouri Argus*, 13 Sept. 1838, [3]; "The Mormon Difficulties," *Niles' National Register*, 13 Oct. 1838, 103. b. Hiram Cumstock, Livingston Co., MO, to "the Citizens of Carroll County," 12 Aug. 1838, *Missouri Argus*, 6 Sept. 1838, [1]; "The Mormons—Public Meeting," *Jeffersonian Republican*, 22 Sept. 1838, [2]. c. Alexander Doniphan, Grand River, MO, to David R. Atchison, Richmond, MO, 15 Sept. 1838, Mormon War Papers, Missouri State Archives, Jefferson City; David R. Atchison, Grand River, MO, to Lilburn W. Boggs, Jefferson City, MO, 17 Sept. 1838, Mormon War Papers; Corrill, *Brief History of the Church*, 34.)

267. An investigative committee sent from Chariton County later reported that JS and Wight said they had "at all times been willing to give themselves up to an officer, to administer law, but not willing to be taken by a mob who were threatening their lives daily, and who were endeavoring to drive them from the county." Circuit court judge Austin A. King later wrote to Daviess County sheriff William Morgan that Wight "considers the excitement so great against him in your county that he is unwilling to be tried before a justice of the peace of the county." ("The Mormon Difficulties," *Niles' National Register*, 13 Oct. 1838, 103; Austin A. King, Ray Co., MO, to William Morgan, Daviess Co., MO, 4 Sept. 1838, William Morgan, Papers, CHL.)

268. The petition of the Daviess County Committee of Vigilance to the residents of Clay County explicitly called for help in bringing Wight and JS to justice but implicitly called for driving the Latterday Saints from the county and was widely understood in this light. The petitions called for residents of other counties to assemble in Daviess County on 7 September 1838. (See "Mormons Once More," *Hannibal Commercial Advertiser*, 25 Sept. 1838, [1]; and JS, Journal, 7 Sept. 1838.)

269. Years later, Latter-day Saint Philo Dibble—a lieutenant colonel in the Caldwell County regiment of the state militia—claimed that he suggested that JS send for Atchison, as he was "a lawyer and a friend to law." Atchison was in fact already commissioned to handle the situation and arrived at Far West the following day. Three days earlier, he had been ordered by Governor Lilburn W. Boggs through Adjutant General B. M. Lisle to raise a force of four hundred men able to travel for the purpose of keeping the peace in Caldwell, Daviess, and Carroll counties. (Dibble, "Philo Dibble's Narrative," 88; B. M. Lisle, Jefferson City, MO, to David R. Atchison, Richmond, MO, 30 Aug. 1838, Mormon War Papers, Missouri State Archives, Jefferson City.)

270. King responded on 10 September to this 2 September letter and to another message from JS and Sidney Rigdon regarding the capture of three gunrunners and weapons by the Mormons. King indicated that he had sent a message to General David R. Atchison, "who I presume will do his duty. in reference to dispensing the armed force on grand river," and that he hoped direct conflict would be avoided until

3 September 1838 • Monday

Monday Sep^t. 3rd. Nothing of importance transpired this day, onley reports concerning the collection of the mob. in Daviess County Which in part has been collecting and collected ever since the election in Daviess which was on the sixth of August last as has been heretofore mentioned.

This evening General [David R.] Atchison arrived in Town

4 September 1838 • Tuesday

Tuesday 4th This day was spent in council with the Gen. [David R. Atchison] He says he will do all in his power to disperce the mob. &c. We employed him and [Alexander] Doniphan (his partner)²⁷¹ as our Lawyer and counselor in Law, They are concidered the first Lawyers in the Uper Missouri, Prest. [Sidney] Rigdon & myself commenced this day the study of Law under General⟨ˢ⟩ Atchison & Doniphon [p. 78] They think by dilligent application we can be admitted to the bar. in twelve month⟨ˢ⟩.²⁷² The result of the council was, that, Prest. Smith & Col. [Lyman] Wight volunteer and be tried by Judge [Austin A.] King in Daviess County (Col Wight.) being present being previously notified to attend the council. Accordingly Thursday next was appointed for the trial,²⁷³ and word to that amount, was sent to Judge King (who had priviously agreed to volunteer and try the case) to meet all at br. [Waldo] Littlefield^s. near the county line south of Daviess,²⁷⁴

~~We all return~~

Atchison accomplished that task. (Austin A. King, Richmond, MO, to JS and Sidney Rigdon, Far West, MO, 10 Sept. 1838, CHL.)

271. Scribe George W. Robinson apparently misunderstood the relationship. In a biographical sketch of Atchison, Doniphan wrote, "We kept our offices together, although never partners, and were very warm personal friends." (*History of Clinton County,* 441.)

272. Rigdon eventually became an attorney. There is no evidence that George W. Robinson ever did. (Nauvoo City Council Minute Book, 1 Nov. 1841, 28.)

273. Setting the preliminary hearing for 6 September preempted the plans of the Daviess County Committee of Vigilance to join with citizens of other counties to take Wight on 7 September. While Atchison and the Latter-day Saints agreed to request that the preliminary hearing be held on 6 September at Littlefield's, King instructed Daviess County sheriff William Morgan to arrange for a suitable location in south Daviess County without specifying a date. ("Mormons Once More," *Hannibal Commercial Advertiser,* 25 Sept. 1838, [1]; Austin A. King, Ray Co., MO, to William Morgan, Daviess Co., MO, 4 Sept. 1838, William Morgan, Papers, CHL.)

274. The decision to hold a preliminary hearing near the Caldwell-Daviess border was apparently a compromise decision both to hear the complaint in the county where the event took place and to assuage the fear JS and Wight had of being lured into a trap in an area controlled by enemies. (See JS, Journal, 16–18 Aug. and 2 Sept. 1838.)

Legal counsel to Joseph Smith. David R. Atchison (top) and Alexander Doniphan (bottom) were retained as Joseph Smith's legal counsel on 4 September 1838. Atchison, here shown circa 1844–1860, was a major general in the Missouri state militia. As the commanding officer over the division covering the northwestern Missouri counties, he was assigned by Governor Lilburn W. Boggs in August 1838 to maintain the peace in that vicinity. Doniphan, here shown circa 1860s, was a brigadier general in the state militia and served under Atchison's command. (Atchison image courtesy Library of Congress, Washington DC. Doniphan image courtesy Community of Christ Library-Archives, Independence, MO.)

5 September 1838 · Wednesday

Wendnersday 5th Judge [Austin A.] King came to town, on his way to Daviess, to meet the above named engagement Gen. [David R.] Atchison had gone before Judge King arrived, the Judge stayed all knight,[275]

6 September 1838 · Thursday

Thursday the 6th Prest. Smith repaired to br. [Waldo] Littlefields to stand trial, he was accompanied by several of the bretheren among whoom was Prest. Hyram [Hyrum] Smith Judge E[lias] Higbee & myself &c. &c. Prest Smith thought it not wisdom to make his appearance before the public in conse-quence of the many threats made against him and the high state of exitement in that place, The trial could not go on in consequence of the absence of the Plaintiff[276] and lack of testimony, consequently the court adjourned till tomor-row at 10 Oclock at A Mr. [John] Raglins some 6 or 8 miles farther south, and also he is a real mob character, he lives within [p. 79] one half mile of Caldwell County line,[277] We all returned this evening to Far West,

7 September 1838 · Friday

Friday the 7th We all met at [John] Raglins agreeable to adjournment,

We did not know but there would be a distirbance among the mob charac-ters, today,[278] we accordingly had an army of men placed at the county line so as to be ready at a minuits warning if there should be any difficulty at the trial,[279] the trial commenced Mr. Penningston [William Peniston] who was the prossecutor had no witnesses but Adam Black who contrived to swear a great may things that never had an existace [existence] untill he swore them

275. On this date, in preparation for the upcoming preliminary hearing, JS swore an affidavit before Caldwell County judge Elias Higbee giving his account of the 8 August confrontation at the home of Adam Black. (JS, Affidavit, Caldwell Co., MO, 5 Sept. 1838, JS Collection, CHL; Rigdon, *Appeal to the American People,* 26–28.)

276. Adam Black.

277. The Raglin property near the Caldwell-Daviess county line was approximately seven miles southeast of Waldo Littlefield's "halfway house." JS's cousin George A. Smith later recounted that the preliminary hearing was actually held near Raglin's property "in a grove about a quarter of a mile from the Caldwell county line." (Berrett, *Sacred Places,* 4:497; George A. Smith, Autobiography, 110.)

278. This was the appointed day on which the Daviess County Committee of Vigilance had requested citizens of other counties to arrive to take Wight. Years later, Philo Dibble recounted that on JS's arrival at Raglin's, a number of people began cursing and threatening him but were warned by General David R. Atchison to behave peacefully. ("Mormons Once More," *Hannibal Commercial Advertiser,* 25 Sept. 1838, [1]; Dibble, "Philo Dibble's Narrative," 89.)

279. A company of Latter-day Saints in the Caldwell County militia hid themselves in the woods at the border during the night before the hearing. (Allred, Reminiscences and Diary, 5; George A. Smith, Autobiography, 110; Foote, Autobiography, 6 and 7 Sept. 1838.)

and I presume, never entered the heart of any man[280] And in fine I think he swore by the Job. (as he was employed so to do by Penningston.)

The witnesses on the part of the defence was Dimick B. Huntington, Gideon Carter Adam Lightner & myself,[281] The Judge bound Pres^t Smith & Col. [Lyman] Wight over to court in a five hundred dollar bond,[282] there was no proof against them criminal, but it is suposed he did it to pasify as much as possible the feelings of the mobers. he (the Judge) stating after in my presence that there was nothing proven against them worthy of bonds,[283] but they submitted without murmering a word, gave the bonds with sufficient securities, and all returned home the same evening, We found two persons in Daviess at the trial, from, which Gentlemen were sent from Charriton [Chariton] County as a committe to enquire into all this matter. as the mobers had sent [p. 80] to that place for assestance, they said to take Smith & Wight, but their object was to drive the brethren from the County of Daviess as was done in Jackson County, They said the people in Charriton did not se[e] proper to send help without knowing for what purpose they were doing it, and this they said was their errand, They came home with us, to hold a council with us, in order to

280. Black's testimony was probably similar to his affidavit, in which he stated that the Latter-day Saint men who surrounded his home threatened him with instant death if he would not sign their written agreement for him to uphold the law. ("Public Meeting," *Missouri Republican*, 8 Sept. 1838, [1], "for the country" edition; Adam Black, Affidavit, Daviess Co., MO, 28 Aug. 1838, Mormon War Papers, Missouri State Archives, Jefferson City.)

281. Huntington, Carter, and George W. Robinson—all Danites—may have supplied eyewitness testimony along the lines of JS's 5 September 1838 affidavit arguing that Black was not threatened in JS's presence or to his knowledge. Lightner, married to Latter-day Saint Mary Elizabeth Rollins Lightner, lived in Caldwell County but was not a church member. (Quinn, *Origins of Power*, 481–483; JS, Affidavit, Caldwell Co., MO, 5 Sept. 1838, JS Collection, CHL; Mary Elizabeth Rollins Lightner, autobiography, *Utah Genealogical and Historical Magazine* 17 [July 1926]: 198.)

282. JS and Wight were bound over to appear at the next term of the Daviess circuit court on 29 November 1838 to answer a misdemeanor charge.^a By that date, the two were in custody on a charge of treason among other charges in connection with the Mormon conflict of October 1838.^b In April 1839, a grand jury for the Daviess County circuit court indicted them for riot, a misdemeanor, in connection with the Adam Black confrontation.^c The trials on these charges, however, never occurred.^d (a. State of Missouri, Recognizance of JS and Lyman Wight, Daviess Co., Missouri, 7 Sept. 1838, private possession, copy in CHL. *b. Document Containing the Correspondence,* 158. *c.* State of Missouri, Indictment of JS and Others for Riot, Daviess Co., MO, Apr. 1839, copy, Boone Co., MO, Circuit Court Records, Western Historical Manuscript Collection, Ellis Library, University of Missouri, Columbia; An Act Concerning Crimes and Their Punishments [20 Mar. 1835], *Revised Statutes of the State of Missouri* [1835], p. 202, art. 7, sec. 6. *d.* 336n12 herein.)

283. Some newspaper reports concluded that Black's testimony was shown to be either questionable or false. Sterling Price and Edgar Flory, from Chariton County, reported that at the trial Black conceded that JS "may have said that he [Black] would not be forced to sign any [statement]" and that "Smith proves that he assured Mr. Black that he should not be forced to sign any instrument of writing but that he requested it as a favor." ("Mormon Difficulties," *Missouri Republican*, 22 Sept. 1838, [2], daily edition; "The Mormon Difficulties," *Niles' National Register*, 13 Oct. 1838, 103.)

learn the facts of this great exitement, which is as it were turning the world up side down,[284]

8 September 1838 • Saturday

Saturday the 8th. Sept. The Presidency met in council with the committe above named, from Charriton [Chariton] County, together with General [David R.] Atchison, where a relation was given of this whole matter, the present state of exitement and the cause of all this confusion,[285] These Gentlemen expressed their fullest sattisfaction upon this matter considering they had been outrageously imposed upon, in this matter, They left this afternoon appearntly perfectly sattisfied with the interview,[286] News came this evening that the mob were to attack Adam Ondi Awman [Adam-ondi-Ahman],

9 September 1838 • Sunday

Sunday the 9th This morning a company in addition to what went last evening went to Adam Ondi Awman [Adam-ondi-Ahman] to assist the bretheren there in their defence against the mob.[287] Capt. Wm Al[l]red took a company of ten men, all mounted, and went to entrsect a team with guns and amunition from Richmond for the mob in Daviess,[288] they found the wagon broke down

---

284. Like Ray County, Chariton County had not immediately sent volunteers at the call of Adam Black. Instead they first appointed Sterling Price and Edgar Flory an investigative committee on 3 September 1838. Price, at that time serving in the Missouri House of Representatives, later served as United States congressman, Missouri governor, and Confederate general in the Civil War. (JS, Journal, 11 Aug. and 2 Sept. 1838; "The Mormon Difficulties," *Niles' National Register,* 13 Oct. 1838, 103; Eiserman, "Sterling Price," 117–118, 124–125, 129.)

285. The recent charge by Missourian Nathan Marsh that the Latter-day Saints were plotting a revolt with American Indians may have been a concern expressed in the meeting. JS and Rigdon made a sworn statement on this day before Caldwell County court justice Elias Higbee denouncing the charge and affirming their commitment to the laws of Missouri and of the United States. ("The Mormons," *Hannibal Commercial Advertiser,* 18 Sept. 1838, [3]; "The Mormon Difficulties," *Niles' National Register,* 13 Oct. 1838, 103.)

286. The committee returned to Chariton and reported that JS and Wight were "willing to give themselves up to an officer, to administer law, but not willing to be taken by a mob." The committee further reported that the old settlers of Daviess County "insist that the Mormons are disagreeable neighbors, and that they are not willing to live in the county with them." ("The Mormon Difficulties," *Niles' National Register,* 13 Oct. 1838, 103.)

287. Warren Foote reported that the Caldwell County regiment of the state militia was mustered. Having moved their target date in order to avoid the Sabbath, gathered vigilantes planned to drive the Latter-day Saints from the county on Monday, 10 September. (Foote, Autobiography, 9 Sept. 1838; "The Mormons," *Hannibal Commercial Advertiser,* 18 Sept. 1838, [3].)

288. When the Latter-day Saints in Far West learned that stolen arms and ammunition were being shipped from Ray County to reinforce anti-Mormon vigilantes gathered in Daviess County, Caldwell County militia captain William Allred was authorized to take volunteers and intercept the arms shipment. (JS History, vol. B-1, 822; Baugh, "Call to Arms," 125.)

and the boxes of guns drawn into the high grass near by the wagon [p. 81] no one present that could be discovered, in a short time two men [on] horse back came from towards the camp of the mob and immediately behind them was a man with a wagon, they all came up and were taken by virtue of a writ supposing them to be the men who were abetting the mob. in carying the guns and amunition to those murderers, Yea and murderers to[o]! in cool blood,

The men were taken together with the guns to Far West the guns were destributed among the bretheren for their defence, and the prisoners were held in custorday,

This was a glorious day indeed the plans of the mob were fruustrated in loosing their guns, and all th[e]ir efforts appeared to be blasted, or blast[ed] before carried into effect, The mob continue to take prisioners at their pleasure some th[e]y keep and some they let go,[289] they try all in their power to make us commit the first act of violence they freeqently send in word that they are tortureing the prisioners to death, in the most agravvating manner, but we understand all their ways, and their cunning and wisdom is not past finding out

10 September 1838 · Monday

Monday 10ᵗʰ Today we proceeded to trial of those prisioners they said they wished for an opportunity of getting bail so as to obtain counsil; they were given to understand that no bail could be taken, for this purpose, but that he could have a sufficient time to send for counsil if he wished, the court accordingly adjourned untill Wendnessday [p. 82] following,

The Prisioners names were John B Comer Alem [Allen] Miller Wᵐ· L McHaney, They were braught before Albert Petty a Justice of the Peace in Far West[290]

---

289. Latter-day Saints named Umpstead and Owens were being held captive by this time. Latter-day Saint Jonathan Hoopes was accosted, plundered, threatened, and held captive on 10 September. Missouri vigilantes in and around Daviess County also accosted and threatened Latter-day Saints George Teeples, Asahel Lathrop, John Murdock, and Rufus Allen around this time. (Austin A. King, Richmond, MO, to JS and Sidney Rigdon, Far West, MO, 10 Sept. 1838, JS Collection, CHL; Baugh, "Call to Arms," 129–132.)

290. Comer was a resident of Ray County, where the Jäger rifles which the men were transporting had been stolen. Miller and McHaney were from Daviess County, where they planned to distribute the rifles to gathered vigilantes. Petty allowed the prisoners two days to arrange for counsel. (George Pitkin, Testimony, 1 July 1843, Nauvoo Municipal Court Docket Book, 116; Alexander Doniphan, Grand River, MO, to David R. Atchison, Richmond, MO, 15 Sept. 1838, Mormon War Papers, Missouri State Archives, Jefferson City; JS History, vol. B-1, 823; Rigdon, *Appeal to the American People,* 25–26.)

———— ৫১ ————

Editorial Note

Following his entry for 10 September, George W. Robinson inscribed a dateline, indicating an unfulfilled intention to continue record keeping. The abrupt end of Robinson's record probably related to his responsibilities as an officer in the Mormons' Caldwell County militia. At the time this journal was set aside, brief entries were already being made in another journal by clerk James Mulholland.

JS and Sidney Rigdon wrote to Judge Austin A. King asking what should be done with prisoners Comer, Miller, and McHaney and the stolen rifles. King directed that they should release the prisoners.[291] On 12 September, Petty convened a preliminary hearing at which evidence was presented and the prisoners were held to bail to appear at the next session of the circuit court.[292] Brigadier General Alexander Doniphan arrived at Far West later that day with orders from Major General David R. Atchison to resolve the matter. Doniphan ordered the rifles along with the principal suspect, John Comer, to be returned to Ray County. Considering the detention of McHaney and Miller illegal, Doniphan released them on their promise of good behavior.[293]

———— ৫১ ————

11 September 1838 · Tuesday
    Tuesday 11th. Sept. [*28 lines blank*] [p. 83]

291. Austin A. King, Richmond, MO, to JS and Sidney Rigdon, Far West, MO, 10 Sept. 1838, JS Collection, CHL.
292. JS History, vol. B-1, 823.
293. Alexander Doniphan, Grand River, MO, to David R. Atchison, Richmond, MO, 15 Sept. 1838, Mormon War Papers, Missouri State Archives, Jefferson City.

JOURNAL,
SEPTEMBER–OCTOBER 1838

Source Note

JS, "Memorandum &c &c," Journal, Sept.–Oct. 1838; handwriting of James Mulholland; 3 pages; JS Collection, CHL. Includes redactions and archival marking.

Makeshift notebook, 10 x 4 inches (25 x 10 cm). Six 10 x 8 inch (25 x 20 cm) sheets of canary-yellow endpapers folded lengthwise to make this notebook of twelve leaves (twenty-four pages). On pages 1 and 2, James Mulholland wrote notes and indexlike references to the 1835 edition of the Doctrine and Covenants—probably for personal use. On pages 3 through 5, Mulholland kept JS's journal in black ink that later turned brown. Upside down at the bottom of page 5 is a personal notation by Mulholland: "An acct of my labors last fall [autumn 1838] I have received pay for 2 month at $20 pr— $40". The back cover of the manuscript bears two inscriptions in black ink, now turned brown. Near the top, the following is written in large characters in Mulholland's handwriting: "James Mulholland | M —— | Joseph Smith | S — | Joural". The characters symbolically transcribed here as dashes are Mulholland's ditto marks, with "M ——" standing for Mulholland and "S —" for Smith. Above this, in much smaller characters, is written "Sept.ʳ 3. 1838". Written sideways in the middle of the page near the outside edge is the notation "James Mulholland | vs | Joseph Smith | 1838". These two inscriptions may also be in Mulholland's handwriting. Creases in the document show that it has been evenly folded in two places to reduce it to pocket size. Having the document on his person would have facilitated Mulholland's ability to track JS's whereabouts to within the hour.

The first page of the notebook bore a small, round seal of orange wax (now removed). When folded, the inscriptions noted above were evidently the outside cover titles. Needle holes along the spine indicate that at some point the document was sewn. Perhaps this journal, like the second JS journal kept by Mulholland (see next journal in this volume), was not sewn at the time of its original use. On pages 6 to 11, Mulholland later recorded his own activities in 1839. Textual redactions and use marks made in graphite pencil were added by later scribes who used the journal to produce the multivolume manuscript history of the church. The notebook also bears archival marking on page 18: "Mulholland, James | Journal kept for | Joseph Smith jun. | 1839" in ink and "A. J"—late nineteenth- and early twentieth-century assistant church historian Andrew Jenson—in graphite pencil.

This thin, unbound journal was probably among the miscellaneous documents collectively listed in Nauvoo and early Utah inventories of church records.[1] Early inventories, Jenson's archival notation, and recent archival records indicate that this journal—like the other JS journals—has remained in continuous church custody.[2]

---

1. Historian's Office, "Schedule of Church Records," [2]; "Inventory," [2]; "Historian's Office Inventory," [3], Catalogs and Inventories, 1846–1904, CHL.

2. See Johnson, *Register of the Joseph Smith Collection*, 7.

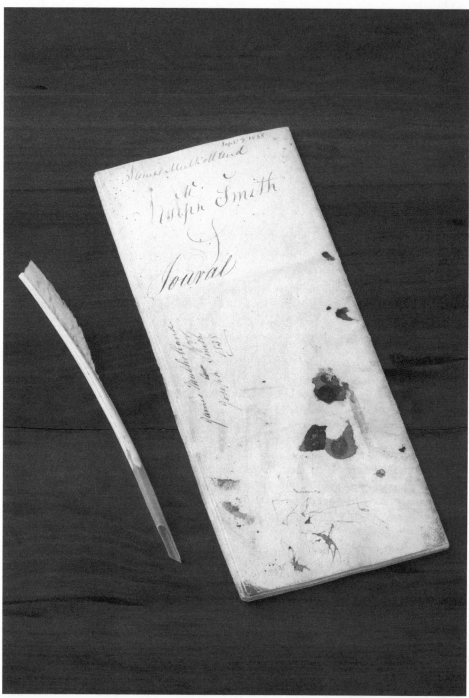

Back cover of second Missouri journal. By assignment, Joseph Smith's scribe James Mulholland used this makeshift notebook to record daily notes for Smith from early September to early October 1838. Mulholland also used the notebook to record personal notes and his own journal for 1839. Handwriting of James Mulholland. JS, Journal, Sept.–Oct. 1838, JS Collection, Church History Library, Salt Lake City. (Photograph by Welden C. Andersen.)

Historical Introduction

This enigmatic document covers the period from early September to early October 1838, a month of mounting difficulties for JS and the Latter-day Saints living in north-western Missouri. JS apparently hired James Mulholland as a clerk in late August or early September, at which time Mulholland copied a revelation[3] into the preceding journal, which covers March to September 1838. At the beginning of the present journal Mulholland noted that he "Commenced to write" for JS on 3 September 1838, which may refer to the date he began various clerking responsibilities or to the date of his first journal entry. Because the datelines of the first two entries, 3 and 4 September, appear to have been inscribed at the same time, Mulholland evidently began keeping the journal on the evening of 4 September or sometime on 5 September. Meanwhile, George W. Robinson was making the final week of entries for the preceding journal.

On 4 September, JS received legal counsel from Missouri attorney and militia general David R. Atchison regarding efforts then under way to prosecute JS and Lyman Wight for allegedly threatening Daviess County justice of the peace Adam Black. After Latter-day Saints who had come to vote in Gallatin on 6 August were attacked, JS had led more than one hundred men to Black's home, demanding that he sign a statement promising to uphold the law and protect the Mormons in their civil rights. An affidavit made by Daviess County citizen William Peniston—which accused JS and Wight of unlawfully leading a group of armed Mormons in Daviess County and threatening Black's life—resulted in the issuance of arrest warrants against the two Mormon leaders. Moreover, Black and Peniston ignited a wildfire of rumors about what JS and his vigilantes had done and intended to do in Daviess County. The rumors spread throughout northwestern Missouri, portending further legal trouble and retribution.[4]

At the 4 September meeting, Atchison, in addition to urging JS and Wight to submit to a preliminary hearing, may have counseled JS to keep a daily record that could be used in a court of law to document his whereabouts. Whether or not JS was so counseled, this or something similar appears to be the purpose of the present "Memorandum." Except for a five-day gap spanning 9 to 13 September, Mulholland recorded an entry for each day of this monthlong journal. The terse entries document little more than JS's comings and goings from his home, noting the time of day when Mulholland saw him. Mulholland enjoyed a vantage point from within JS's home, where Mulholland lived, apparently as one of the many boarders that JS kept over the years.[5] This journal may be the result of an assignment to Mulholland to document JS's presence in Caldwell County and witness JS's time at home. For the period of overlap with JS's preceding journal, it complements George W. Robinson's record of JS's activity when not at home.

The preceding journal recorded by Robinson demonstrates that even after the 6 August skirmish at Gallatin, JS continued to vigorously and openly prepare to settle additional Latter-day Saints in Daviess County despite mounting opposition to the growing Mormon

---

3. Revelation, 23 July 1837, in JS, Journal, 23 July 1837, pp. 306–308 herein [D&C 112].

4. LeSueur, *1838 Mormon War in Missouri,* 65–80; Baugh, "Call to Arms," 103, 107–119.

5. Emma Smith, Sally Hinkle, Caroline Clarke, and James Mulholland, Statement, ca. Mar. 1839, in JS History, vol. C-1, 906.

presence there. Meanwhile, the failure to arrest JS and Wight based on Black's and Peniston's accusations led to the marshaling of volunteers from surrounding counties to take the pair by force if necessary. JS and Wight signaled their willingness to submit to the legal process by appearing soon afterward before Judge Austin A. King, but their appearance failed to quell the anti-Mormon vigilantism already in motion.

The present journal reports on four additional weeks of JS's activities in Far West, but this journal's skeletal entries give little hint of the gathering storm that soon engulfed the Mormons and their neighbors. With northwestern Missouri in an uproar, General Atchison called out militia, who successfully averted armed conflict in Daviess County in September. But by mid-October an extensive network of vigilantes in northwestern Missouri began to eliminate substantial Mormon settlement outside Caldwell County.[6] Some of the anti-Mormon forces that had been disbanded in Daviess County through militia intervention regrouped in Carroll County, where, after issuing an ultimatum to the De Witt Mormons to evacuate by 1 October, they and local anti-Mormons laid siege to the village. A militia force sent there to preserve peace proved unreliable for that purpose because many of its members sympathized with anti-Mormons. Learning of the plight of the De Witt Saints, JS mobilized two small companies of men that left Far West on 5 October to offer relief. JS led the second group, consisting of about twenty men, which arrived in De Witt the following day.[7]

Mulholland's entry for 5 October reported: "did not see him [JS] all the afternoon, understood that he went from home." Mulholland then added a dateline under which to write an entry for the following day—suggesting that he expected JS to return by then. However, a round-trip journey from Far West to De Witt and back would inevitably have taken more than one day, suggesting that Mulholland was not privy to JS's thoughts and plans. The journal entry for 6 October remained blank, concluding Mulholland's record.

After Governor Lilburn W. Boggs rejected an appeal for aid, JS assisted in evacuating the De Witt settlers to Far West, arriving there by 14 October.[8] Any attempt by Mulholland to observe and record JS's movements in the following weeks would have been largely futile, given JS's extended absences from home as events spiraled out of control.

———— ☙ ————

Commenced to write for President
Joseph Smith Jun[r]
on Monday the 3rd September 1838
Memorandum &c &c

---

6. Anderson, "Clarifications of Boggs's Order," 37–41.

7. Baugh, "Call to Arms," 154–155, 163–173.

8. JS, "Bill of Damages against the State of Missouri on Account of the Sufferings and Losses Sustained Therein," Quincy, IL, 4 June 1839, JS Collection, CHL; see also Perkins, "Prelude to Expulsion," 276; and Baugh, "Call to Arms," 163–181.

3 September 1838 • Monday

Monday Septr 3rd At home all or greater part of day

4 September 1838 • Tuesday

Tuesday 4th— Breakfast with him 1/2 past 7 oclock, ~~dined~~ at home for dinner a little before noon, & again in the even[in]g between 5 & 6 oclock.

5 September 1838 • Wednesday

Wednesday 5th— At home for breakfast at 1/2 past 7 also for dinner from 1 to 2 oclock at home in the evening about 6 oclock.

6 September 1838 • Thursday

Thursday 6th— ~~He rode out on Horseback~~ He left home a horseback 1/2 past 7. morn[in]g

At home again the even[in]g before dark.[9]

7 September 1838 • Friday

Friday 7th— Saw him leave home about sun rising and heard, and saw him at home between 10 and 11 oclock same night.[10]

8 September 1838 • Saturday

Saturday 8th--- At home about 8 oclock morn at home between 2 & 3 oclock Afternoon.

9–13 September 1838 • Sunday–Thursday

No memorandum from 8th to 14[11]

---

9. JS traveled to Daviess County, Missouri, with others to appear at a preliminary hearing to assess accusations of Adam Black and William Peniston relative to the incident at the Black residence. Because Black, the complainant, did not appear, the hearing was rescheduled for the following day. (JS, Journal, 6 Sept. 1838, p. 316 herein.)

10. As on the previous day, JS traveled to Daviess County with others to appear at a preliminary hearing. (JS, Journal, 7 Sept. 1838, pp. 316–318 herein.)

11. This week marked an escalation of tensions in northwestern Missouri. On the evening of 8 September, the Latter-day Saints received news that enemies in Daviess County were preparing to attack Adam-ondi-Ahman. A group of Mormon men left for Daviess County that night and the next day to aid the Latter-day Saints there. Also on 9 September, Latter-day Saints from Caldwell County intercepted and detained three men carrying a shipment of rifles from Ray County to Daviess County to reinforce vigilantes there. General David R. Atchison ordered eight companies of Missouri militia from Clay and Ray counties to ride to Caldwell and Daviess counties to intervene between the armed antagonists and enforce the law. (JS, Journal, 8 and 9 Sept. 1838, pp. 318–319 herein; Baugh, "Call to Arms," 125–127, 132–135.)

Ideas &c &c &c
When [Judah] is gathered, the Lord will also bring
again the assyrian captivity viz: Israel—
The Spirit poured out upon all flesh[?] that your
Sons & daughters shall prophesy. Joel—
promise, book of Mormon page 541 & 34th
no imposter would attempt to make such—
for instance the promise of the Holy Ghost—

Another angel—a falling away came
Saviour did not come until his time came
so also the book of Morm—
Proof that Gentiles were not the other sheep
that is. The Saviour Said. I am not sent
Save to the lost Sheep of the house of Israel—
Jealousy of the Chinese, hid up 6 million
children of Israel——
In England 1000 souls in 9 months
unbelief Close the way to knowledge
Ephraimites to be the hunters & fishers—
Testimony of the Spirit will seal to
destiny of them——
The difference between Saints & world is
that Saints know, the world do not.—

Commenced to write, for President

Joseph Smith Jun

on Monday the 3rd September 1838

——— Memorandum &c &c [of day]
Monday Septt 3rd} At home all or greater part
Tuesday 4th— Breakfast with him ½ past 7
oclock, dined at home for dinner a little
before noon, & again in the evening between
5 & 6 oclock.
Wednesday 5th— At home for breakfast at ½ past 7
Also for dinner from 1 to 2 oclock
in the evening about 6 oclock.
Thursday 6th— Breakfast
At home on horseback in [...]
At home again in the evening before dark.
Friday 7th— Saw him leave home about sunrising
and heard, and Saw him at home between
10 and 11 oclock Same night.—
Saturday 8th— At home about 8 oclock
at home between 2 & 3 oclock Afternoon.—

[...] 15—

[...] 16th— At home all day

[...] 17th— Saw him early morning
also afternoon again at 3 oclock
Tuesday 18— At home all day & unwell.
in better health towards evening.

Mulholland memoranda. James Mulholland's record covering Joseph Smith's life from 3 September to 5 October 1838 is fully contained in three pages of a hand-stitched notebook in which he also kept personal notes and later a journal of his own. Some of Mulholland's personal notes and the entire Smith

Wednesday 19th At home in the morning for break fast, about 8 oclock. --- also for dinner about 1 oclock and in the evening before bed time

Thursday 20th — At home from morning untill about 10 oclock went out on horseback & returned at about sunset or rather before it at home all evening

Friday 21st — Saw him at home at breakfast

Saturday 22nd — At home early in the morning & at breakfast about ½ past 7 oclock Saw him ride out a horseback about 9 oclock.

Sunday 23rd — At home & at meeting all day also in evening about 9 oclock

Monday 24 — At home at breakfast and before, Saw him ride out a horseback about ½ past 8 oclock morning. Returned home about 5 oclock evening

Tuesday 25th At home for breakfast about 8 oclock saw him go out a horseback & saw him again between 11 & 12 oclock at which he was untill about ½ past 5 evening Saw him at home in evening about ½ past 6.

Wednesday 26th — At home morning early also at breakfast between 7 & 8 oclock Saw him ride out between 10 & eleven oclock And saw him at home again 9 oclock evening

Thursday 27th At home before & at breakfast 8 oclock saw him again at 9 oclock in the evening & between 5 and 6 oclock in the City.

Friday 28th — At home for breakfast about 8 oclock. Saw him walk out about nine, Saw him again between one and two at home all afternoon. saw him ride out about sunset.

Saturday 29th — Did not see him untill about 3 oclock afternoon, Saw him then come home a horseback. at home all evening.

Sunday 30th — At home for breakfast untill ten oclock, went from home at that time.

Monday 1st October — Not at home untill about 5 oclock afternoon, at home all the evening.

Tuesday 2nd — At home for breakfast & out ½ past 7 oclock Saw him again in the evening about ½ past four oclock, again at supper about ½ past 6 oclock.

Wednesday 3rd — At home before and at breakfast also about one oclock afternoon.

Thursday 4th — Saw him at home about morning all the forenoon, ... at noon. In the evening again about 8 oclock.

Friday 5th — Saw him early in the morning say 7 oclock, again about 10 oclock, did not see him in the afternoon, understand that he went from home.

Saturday 6th —

journal are shown here. Handwriting of James Mulholland. JS, Journal, Sept.–Oct. 1838, pp. 2–5, JS Collection, Church History Library, Salt Lake City. (Photographs by Welden C. Andersen.)

14 September 1838 · Friday

Friday 14th— At home about 3 P.M & all the evening.

15 September 1838 · Saturday

Saturday 15th— At home early in morning for breakfast & dinener say 9 & 2 oclock

16 September 1838 · Sunday

Sunday 16th— At home all day

17 September 1838 · Monday

Monday 17th Saw him early morning
again at 9 oclock forenoon
also afternoon

18 September 1838 · Tuesday

Tuesday 18— At home all day & unwell. in better health towards evening.
[p. [3]]

19 September 1838 · Wednesday

Wednesday 19th— At home in the morning for breakfast, about 8 oclock.—
also in for dinner about 1 oclock and in the evening before bed time.

20 September 1838 · Thursday

Thursday 20th— At home from morning untill about 10 oclock went out on horseback & returned at about sunset or rather before it— at home all evening

21 September 1838 · Friday

Friday 21^{rst}— Saw him at home at breakfast

22 September 1838 · Saturday

Saturday 22nd— At home early in the morn[in]g & at breakifast about 1/2 past 7 oclock saw him ride out a horseback about 9 oclock.

23 September 1838 · Sunday

Sunday 23rd— At home & at meeting all the day also saw him ⟨at home⟩ evening about 9 oclock.

24 September 1838 • Monday

Monday 24[th]— At home at breakfast and before, Saw him ride out on horseback about 1/2 past 8 oclock morn[in]g.

Returned home about 5 oclock ev[en]ing

25 September 1838 • Tuesday

Tuesday 25[th]— At home for breakfast about 8 oclock saw him go out a horseback saw him again between 11 & 12 oclock at which he was untill about 1/2 past 5 even[in]g Saw him at home in evening about 1/2 past 6.

26 September 1838 • Wednesday

Wednesday 26[th]— At home morning early also at breakfast between 7 & 8 oclock. Saw him ride out ~~on~~ between 10 & eleven oclock and saw him at home again 9 oclock evening

27 September 1838 • Thursday

Thursday 27[th]— At home before & at breakfast 8 oclk saw him again at 4 oclock in the even[i]ng & between 5 and 6 oclock in the City.[12] [p. [4]]

28 September 1838 • Friday

Friday 28[th]— At home for breakfast about 8 oclock. Saw him walk out about nine, saw him again between one and two at home all afternoon, saw him ride out about sunset.

29 September 1838 • Saturday

Saturday 29[th]— Did not see him untill about 3 oclock afternoon, saw him then come home a horseback—. at home all evening.

30 September 1838 • Sunday

Sunday 30th— At home for breakfast and utill [until] ten oclock, went from home at that time.

1 October 1838 • Monday

Monday 1[rst] October Not at home untill about 5 oclock afternoon, at home all the evening.

---

12. As JS resided within the boundaries platted for Far West, James Mulholland apparently meant that he had seen JS in or around the public square in the center of town.

2 October 1838 • Tuesday

Tuesday 2^(nd.)— At home for breakfast about 1/2 past 7 oclock saw him again in the ev[en]ing about 1/2 past four oclock, again at supper about 1/2 past 6 oclock[13]

3 October 1838 • Wednesday

Wednesday 3^(rd)— At home before and at breakfast also about one oclock afternoon.[14]

4 October 1838 • Thursday

Thursday 4^(th)— Saw him at home about sunrise, all the forenoon, and at noon. In the evening again about 8 oclock.

5 October 1838 • Friday

Friday 5^(th)— Saw him early in the morning say 7 oclock, again about 10 oclock, did not see him all the afternoon, understood that he went from home.

6 October 1838 • Saturday

Saturday 6^(th)— [*blank lines*] [p. [5]][15]

---

13. The Kirtland Camp, a group of over five hundred Latter-day Saints that left Kirtland, Ohio, in July 1838, traveled through Far West on this day en route to Adam-ondi-Ahman. JS's history later recounted that he "went in company with Sidney Rigdon, Hyrum Smith, Isaac Morley, and George W. Robinson and met them some miles out and escorted them into the city." They arrived in Far West about five o'clock that evening. (JS History, vol. B-1, 800–801, 831; see also Kirtland Camp, Journal, 2 Oct. 1838; and Tyler, "Daily Journal," 2 and 4 Oct. 1838.)

14. The Kirtland Camp resumed its journey to Adam-ondi-Ahman this morning. JS's history later recounted that he and others "went with them, a mile or two" and then "returned from thence to the city, where [he] spent the remainder of the day." (JS History, vol. B-1, 831; compare Tyler, "Daily Journal," 3 Oct. 1838.)

15. JS left Far West on 5 October to aid in the evacuation of Mormons from De Witt, Carroll County, arriving there the following day. He returned to Far West by 14 October. (JS, "Bill of Damages against the State of Missouri on Account of the Sufferings and Losses Sustained Therein," Quincy, IL, 4 June 1839, JS Collection, CHL; see also Perkins, "Prelude to Expulsion," 273–274; and Baugh, "Call to Arms," 163–181.)

JOURNAL, 1839

Source Note

JS, "Minute Book. 1839 J. Smiths Journal Escape from Prison," Journal, Apr.–Oct. 1839; handwriting of James Mulholland; 15 pages; JS Collection, CHL. Includes redactions and archival marking.

Makeshift notebook, 10 x 4 inches (25 x 10 cm). The journal was fashioned by folding eight 10 x 8 inch (25 x 20 cm) sheets of paper in half lengthwise to form the notebook of sixteen leaves (thirty-two pages). Inscriptions that reach the end of a line and cross the gutter onto another leaf indicate that the folded pages were not sewn during their original use. Wear on the first and last pages indicates that the pages were not bound for some time. The text of the journal is inscribed on the first fifteen pages in black ink that later turned brown. The remaining seventeen pages are blank. At some point a cover for the notebook was made with a 10 x 16 inch (25 x 41 cm) sheet of blue-colored cover stock folded in half twice to create a 10 x 4 inch cover, which was then pamphlet bound with hand stitching. On the front cover, James Mulholland wrote "Minute Book. | 1839 | J. Smiths Journal | Escape from Prison" with seven decorative underlines in black ink. On the back cover, the lines "Joseph Smith's Journal | Escape from Prison 1839" are written sideways near the top in black ink. This notation, in unidentified handwriting, appears to be early archival marking. Textual redactions and use marks made in graphite pencil were added by later scribes who used the journal to produce the multivolume manuscript history of the church.

This thin journal was probably among the miscellaneous documents collectively listed in Nauvoo and early Utah inventories of church records.[1] The use of the journal in connection with the manuscript history, early inventories, and recent archival records indicate that this journal—like the other JS journals—has remained in continuous church custody.[2]

Historical Introduction

Following their success in forcing the Mormons to evacuate the village of De Witt in Carroll County, Missouri, in October 1838, anti-Mormon vigilantes applied similar pressure in Daviess County, beginning with raids on isolated Mormon homes. State militia commander Alexander Doniphan acknowledged that his troops could not be relied upon to maintain order or to protect the Latter-day Saints' property rights. The Mormons mounted a preemptive strike in Daviess County beginning in mid-October, targeting the property of vigilantes.

---

1. Historian's Office, "Schedule of Church Records," [1]; "Inventory," [2]; "Historian's Office Inventory," [3], Catalogs and Inventories, 1846–1904, CHL.

2. See Johnson, *Register of the Joseph Smith Collection,* 7.

First Illinois journal. Following Joseph Smith's escape from incarceration in Missouri and his arrival in Illinois, he immediately contracted his former scribe James Mulholland to begin keeping this journal and to help with other record-keeping endeavors. Handwriting of James Mulholland. JS, Journal, 1839, JS Collection, Church History Library, Salt Lake City. (Photograph by Welden C. Andersen.)

Burning and plundering by both sides and the evacuation of most of Daviess County's non-Mormon residents led to outright warfare. After a company of Ray County volunteers captured three Latter-day Saints in an area lying between Caldwell and Ray counties, JS helped mobilize a company of Mormons from Caldwell County as a rescue party. The ensuing battle at Crooked River on 25 October, at which two Mormons, their guide, and one Missourian were killed, gave rise to exaggerated reports that the Mormons had killed or captured the entire Ray County contingent and were about to attack Richmond, the seat of Ray County. In the wake of this news and word of Mormon depredations in Daviess County, in late October 1838 Missouri governor Lilburn W. Boggs decried Mormon "outrages" and ordered a large militia force to "exterminate" the Mormons or drive them from the state. JS and other leaders were arrested and incarcerated, and most Mormons left Missouri in early 1839, trudging eastward for more than 150 miles and crossing the Mississippi River into Illinois.[3]

After a grueling confinement through the winter in the jail at Liberty, Missouri, JS and his fellow Mormon prisoners were transported to Daviess County for a grand jury investigation. There they were indicted for treason, riot, arson, burglary, and receiving stolen goods but were granted a change of venue to Columbia, Missouri, for their contemplated trial. During the journey to the new location, the guards allowed their prisoners to escape.[4]

On 22 April 1839, six days after their escape, JS and his companions crossed the Mississippi River into Illinois. There they reunited with thousands of other Latter-day Saint refugees from Missouri, many of whom had received a sympathetic, hospitable reception from the citizens of Quincy, Illinois. That same day, JS rehired James Mulholland, who had performed clerical work for him the previous autumn. Mulholland began his record in this small journal by noting JS's escape in Missouri and then, beginning with JS's arrival in Quincy, kept a contemporaneous record for six months.

During the period covered by this journal, Mulholland worked closely with JS, recording JS's history and occasionally accompanying him in his travels. Unlike the September–October 1838 journal, which Mulholland kept for JS in Missouri, the present journal benefits from JS reporting to his scribe some of the activities that took place in Mulholland's absence. A few of the entries in these instances may have been dictated by JS, although most entries were based on Mulholland's observation.

While keeping this journal for JS, Mulholland was also keeping his own journal, which he wrote in the back of the record he had kept for JS during autumn 1838. Mulholland's personal journal entries, where illuminating, are used to annotate the parallel entries he wrote for JS in the present journal. When he was separated from JS, Mulholland also focused entries in JS's journal on Mulholland's own activities. Mulholland's use of first-person narration to refer sometimes to himself and sometimes to JS requires careful reading to determine whose activities are being described.

---

3. LeSueur, *1838 Mormon War in Missouri,* chaps. 7–14; Baugh, "Call to Arms," chaps. 7–12; Hartley, "Almost Too Intolerable a Burthen," 9–10, 36–37.

4. Hyrum Smith, Testimony, 1 July 1843, Nauvoo Municipal Court Docket Book, 78; Lyman Wight, Testimony, 1 July 1843, Nauvoo Municipal Court Docket Book, 131–132; Promissory Note, JS to John Brassfield, 16 Apr. 1839, JS Collection, CHL.

The Illinois resumption of JS's record keeping reflected the reestablishment of characteristically Mormon procedures that were suspended during the upheaval in Missouri. Record keeping lapsed during the Mormon War, the imprisonment of JS, and the expulsion of the Latter-day Saints from the state. The principle of gathering—at least in an official sense—also lapsed during the aftermath of that expulsion. Latter-day Saints realized that their practice of gathering to create religious communities, though mandated by revelation, aroused antagonism of nearby citizenry wherever they settled. In the interest of survival, should they now intersperse with others, coming together for worship but not living in tight-knit, exclusive communities? Writing from jail in Liberty in January 1839, JS acknowledged that for the present "the gathering of necessity [is] stopt."[5]

Yet the gathering did not stop. Even without JS's direction, many of the Mormons fleeing Missouri sought collective refuge in western Illinois and thereby kept the question of gathering alive. In March, before JS's escape, a church conference at Quincy conducted by Brigham Young confronted the question of whether to "gather" or "scatter." Young advised settling "in companies," or at least in sufficiently close proximity to establish congregations.[6]

Within days of his arrival in Quincy, JS decisively arranged for a new gathering place. In the months to come, he taught that a gathered community of believers was essential for building a house of the Lord. As was true for Kirtland, Ohio, and as JS had intended for Far West, Missouri, this new gathering place was to become a city with a temple.[7]

After purchasing some land about fifty miles upriver, at Commerce in Hancock County, Illinois, JS moved his family and his people there. The riverfront site had poor harbors and swampy lowlands plagued with malaria-bearing mosquitoes. This journal offers glimpses of JS's involvement in land purchases and community planning that provided a basis for a cluster of Mormon settlements on both sides of the Mississippi. The journal also records JS's trips to Quincy, Plymouth, and Macomb, Illinois, and other nearby places to visit family, groups of Latter-day Saints, and regional political and commercial centers.

Meanwhile, JS and members of the Quorum of the Twelve clung tenaciously to another facet of the Mormon mission: widespread proselytizing. An 1838 revelation commanded the Twelve to depart from Far West, Missouri, on 26 April 1839 for a mission to Europe.[8] From jail in Liberty, JS reminded the apostles of that obligation.[9] Enemies declared it in advance a false revelation, as they now had the power to prevent it from being fulfilled. Nonetheless, as diary entries began in mid-April 1839, members of the Quorum of the Twelve under acting president Brigham Young had just left Quincy to return to Missouri to fulfill the injunction. Their predawn meeting on 26 April 1839 at Far West marked the symbolic beginning of their mission abroad. But with much preparation remaining, they returned to Illinois and did not actually depart for the East until late summer. In the intervening

---

5. JS et al., Liberty, MO, to Heber C. Kimball and Brigham Young, Far West, MO, 16 Jan. 1839, JS Collection, CHL.

6. "Extracts of the Minutes of Conferences," *Times and Seasons,* Nov. 1839, 1:15.

7. Leonard, *Nauvoo,* 235–237.

8. See Revelation, 8 July 1838–A, in JS, Journal, 8 July 1838, p. 285 herein [D&C 118].

9. JS et al., Liberty, MO, to Heber C. Kimball and Brigham Young, Far West, MO, 16 Jan. 1839, JS Collection, CHL.

months, JS met frequently with the eight or nine available apostles to teach them and help them prepare. JS also attempted to strengthen and unify the quorum by helping to resolve the status of two apostles—Orson Hyde and William Smith—who had abandoned the Latter-day Saints during the Missouri crisis. The departure of the Twelve was marked by lengthier-than-usual journal entries reporting sermons and admonitions, indicative of the significance attached to the mission.

The resettlement of the Mormons in Commerce and vicinity and the resumption of church affairs—including the departure of the Twelve to Britain—were hampered by a malaria epidemic that ravaged the area from late June to November. When JS was pre-occupied with aiding the victims of the scourge for eleven weeks in July, August, and September, journal entries were scaled back to weekly summaries. While the entries suggest the duration and centrality of JS's focus on relieving the sick, they characteristically only skim the surface. For months, the Smith home and environs served as a hospital of sorts, with JS and Emma nursing malaria victims. The couple moved their own family into a tent to provide better care in their house for the sick. JS himself contracted the disease but soon recovered and continued to minister to the afflicted. Mulholland spent three weeks in late August and early September caring for his own wife, who was ill.[10]

Despite the epidemic, the Latter-day Saints remained at their new headquarters. When the disease abated somewhat, JS became increasingly involved in arrangements for a new, larger town that would soon eclipse and absorb Commerce. At a general conference of the church convened at Commerce in early October 1839, JS advocated—and the membership of the church affirmed—that this was a suitable location to be designated a stake of Zion and a gathering place for the Saints.

Even while JS built a new stake, Missouri still occupied much of his attention. In the months and years following the expulsion of his people from that state, JS sought persistently to call attention to the losses and injustices the Latter-day Saints had suffered and, if possible, to obtain government compensation. He left Commerce on 29 October 1839, two weeks after the conclusion of this journal, to visit Washington DC to seek relief and redress from the federal government. The next day, a gravely ill James Mulholland was taken to Emma Smith's makeshift hospital, where he died on 3 November, possibly a victim of the malaria epidemic.[11] It is not clear to what extent the cessation of journal entries after 15 October resulted from Mulholland's illness or from a lack of access to JS. Daily entries did not resume until December 1841, more than two years later, when Willard Richards took up the pen a few months after his return from missionary service in England.

———— ๑ ————

10. Tullidge, *Women of Mormondom,* 213–214; Historian's Office, "History of Brigham Young," 34–35; Woodruff, Journal, 12, 19, 22, and 25 July 1839; Mulholland, Journal, 19 Aug.–8 Sept. 1839.

11. Emma Smith, Nauvoo, IL, to JS, Washington DC, 6 Dec. 1839, Charles Aldrich Autograph Collection, State Historical Society of Iowa, Des Moines.

⟨Minute Book.
1839
J. Smiths Journal
Escape from Prison⟩
[*front cover*]

1839.

16 April 1839 • Tuesday

Escaped Aprile 16ᵗʰ ¹²

22–23 April 1839 • Monday–Tuesday

President Smith and his fellow prisoners, arrived safe at Quincy Ill. on ~~Tuesday~~ ⟨Monday⟩ the 22ⁿᵈ of April and spent all next day greeting and receiving visits from his brethren and friends¹³———

24 April–3 May 1839 • Wednesday–Friday

In the evening of the 24ᵗʰ met in council with the Church— when a committee was appointed to go to Ioway [Iowa] &c. of which he was one. Went to Ioway made purchases & returned on friday the 3ʳᵈ May—¹⁴

---

12. While being taken from Gallatin, Daviess County, Missouri, to Columbia, Boone County, Missouri, in compliance with a change of venue in their legal case, JS and fellow prisoners escaped with the cooperation of their guards near Yellow Creek. Some sources point to the possibility that the prisoners were intended to be held without bail—as hostages—until their people evacuated Missouri. If that was the case, the purpose of their incarceration was now largely fulfilled. (Promissory Note, JS to John Brassfield, 16 Apr. 1839, JS Collection, CHL; compare JS, Journal, 28 Feb. 1843, JS Collection, CHL; see also Madsen, "Missouri Court of Inquiry"; Hyrum Smith, Testimony, 1 July 1843, Nauvoo Municipal Court Docket Book, 78; and Lyman Wight, Testimony, 1 July 1843, Nauvoo Municipal Court Docket Book, 131–132.)

13. In his own journal, James Mulholland noted that on this day he began again to "write for the Church." (Mulholland, Journal, 22 Apr. 1839.)

14. In addition to JS, this committee, which was assigned to visit Iowa "for the purpose of making locations for the church," also included Vinson Knight and Alanson Ripley. The council determined that church members should "move on to the north as soon as they possibly can."ᵃ The committee left Quincy the following day, 25 April 1839, to assess possibilities on both the Iowa and Illinois sides of the Mississippi River. The initial acquisitions of land in the area of Commerce, Illinois, occurred on 30 April. They consisted of 47.17 acres located south of Commerce from Isaac Galland, two additional parcels totaling 12.2 acres from Galland, and about 130 acres from Hugh White.ᵇ The church purchased additional land from Galland in Lee County, Iowa, in May and June. Deeds list a total of 18,920 acres in Iowa purchased from Galland by the church.ᶜ (a. General Church Minutes, 24 Apr. 1839; compare JS History, vol. C-1, 929. b. Hancock Co., IL, Deed Records, 30 Apr. 1839, bk. 12G, 247, microfilm, U.S. and Canada Record Collection, FHL; Hancock Co., IL, Bonds and Mortgages, 30 Apr. 1839, 1:31–32, microfilm, U.S. and Canada Record Collection, FHL. c. Lee Co., IA, Deed Records (Keokuk), 29 May 1839, 1:507–510; 26 June 1839, 2:3–6, 13–16, microfilm, U.S. and Canada Record Collection, FHL; JS History, vol. C-1,

First page of first Illinois journal. James Mulholland, who kept Joseph Smith's journal after Smith's arrival in Quincy, Illinois, on 22 April 1839, began retrospectively with Smith's 16 April escape from incarceration in Missouri. A hole is burned in part of the page. Handwriting of James Mulholland. JS, Journal, 1839, p. 1, JS Collection, Church History Library, Salt Lake City. (Photograph by Welden C. Andersen.)

4 May 1839 • Saturday

Saturday 4th May presided at general Conference near Quincy Ill.[15]

5 May 1839 • Sunday

Sunday Do [ditto] continued.[16]

6 May 1839 • Monday

Monday ⟨6th⟩ met in council with the twelve [an]d[17] others Quincy Ill—[18]

7 May 1839 • Tuesday

Tuesday Do [ditto]——— Do Do[19]

10 May 1839 • Friday

May 10, Moved with his family To Commerce Hancock Co. Ill.[20]

931–932; Alanson Ripley, statements, ca. Jan. 1845, in Historian's Office, JS History Documents, ca. 1839–1856, CHL.)

15. The church held the three-day conference, 4–6 May 1839, at the Presbyterian campground two miles north of Quincy.[a] The conference minutes, in James Mulholland's handwriting, report that JS "addressed a few observations on the state of his own peculiar feelings, after having been so long separated from his brethren." The conference temporarily suspended apostles Orson Hyde and William Smith from acting in their office; they regained standing by the end of June. The conference also ratified the actions of other members of the Quorum of the Twelve on 26 April 1839 at the temple site at Far West, Missouri, where they ordained new apostles to fill vacancies in their quorum and officially commenced their mission to Europe.[b] (a. Woodruff, Journal, 4, 5, and 6 May 1839. b. General Church Minutes, 4 May 1839; JS, Journal, 25 May and 27 June 1839.)

16. The conference this day focused on plans for obtaining legal redress for the depredations committed against the Latter-day Saints in Missouri as well as for securing their rights in Illinois. Sidney Rigdon was assigned to present the church's case before the national government in Washington DC. Almon Babbitt was authorized to represent the church to the state government in Springfield, Illinois. Lyman Wight was appointed to gather affidavits regarding individual losses in Missouri to be forwarded to Washington. (General Church Minutes, 5 May 1839.)

17. TEXT: "[*hole burned in paper*]d". The top of the "n" is visible at the edge of the hole.

18. Two sessions of the conference were held this day. At the first session, a general gathering, sixty men were ordained as elders or as members of the Quorum of the Seventy and eighteen men were assigned to accompany the Quorum of the Twelve to Europe. William Marks was appointed to preside over the church in Commerce, with the church's bishops to assist him in leadership, which effectively established a new gathering center for the church in Illinois. Later in the day, a second session of the conference involving JS, the Twelve, and the bishops was held at the home of Bishop Edward Partridge. (Woodruff, Journal, 6 May 1839; General Church Minutes, 6 May 1839.)

19. Although the three-day general conference ended on Monday, JS spent Tuesday in council and conversation with church leaders and members. (Kimball, "History," 104.)

20. JS and family left Quincy on 9 May, accompanied by James Mulholland, and arrived in Commerce on 10 May. (Mulholland, Journal, 9 May 1839; Foote, Autobiography, 9 May 1839.)

13–14 May 1839 • Monday–Tuesday

Monday 13ᵗʰ Transacted various business with Bʳ [Oliver] Granger &c²¹ at home attending to general business—

Tuesday Do [ditto] ~~wednesday~~, Do

14–19 May 1839 • Tuesday–Sunday

On the 14 I returned to Quincy so kept no ~~record~~ ⟨Minute⟩ of course, I got back here Sunday ev[en]ing the 19ᵗʰ May.²² [p. [1]]

20–24 May 1839 • Monday–Friday

Monday 20ᵗʰ this week at home and employed dictating letters²³ and attending to the various business of the Church²⁴

25 May 1839 • Saturday

On Saturday 25, met in conference with the twelve, and others of the church Wᵐ Smith. case disposed of—²⁵

---

21. At the conference held in Quincy, Illinois, a week earlier, Granger was appointed an agent for the church with a commission to oversee remaining church business in Kirtland, Ohio. (Certificate, JS et al. to Oliver Granger, Commerce, IL, 13 May 1839, in JS Letterbook 2, pp. 45–46; JS, Nauvoo, IL, to Oliver Granger, New York, [23] July 1840, in JS Letterbook 2, pp. 159–161.)

22. James Mulholland recorded in his personal journal that his wife accompanied him on the return to Commerce, suggesting that one purpose for his visit in Quincy was to effect a permanent move to Commerce. While his scribe was away, JS remained in Commerce, busy with various matters of church business, including directing the survey of the city plot. (Mulholland, Journal, 14–19 May 1839; JS History, vol. C-1, 940; Woodruff, Journal, 18 May 1839; Historian's Office, "History of Brigham Young," 28.)

23. JS wrote to William W. Phelps declining his offer to sell property in Missouri for Joseph Smith Sr. JS also wrote letters to Newel K. Whitney and others, urging them to move to Commerce. (William W. Phelps, Far West, MO, to John P. Greene, Quincy, IL, 23 Apr. 1839, in JS Letterbook 2, p. 7; JS, Commerce, IL, to William W. Phelps, Far West, MO, 22 May 1839, in JS Letterbook 2, p. 7; JS, Commerce, IL, to Newel K. Whitney, 24 May 1839, in JS Letterbook 2, p. 13; JS, Commerce, IL, to G. W. Harris, Quincy, IL, 24 May 1839, in JS Letterbook 2, pp. 11–12; JS and Emma Smith, Commerce, IL, to "Judge Cleveland and Lady," Quincy, IL, 24 May 1839, in JS Letterbook 2, p. 12.)

24. On 21 May, JS and other church leaders surveyed several square miles of land in Iowa across the river from Commerce. (Woodruff, Journal, 21 May 1839.)

25. William Smith was suspended from the Quorum of the Twelve at the 4–6 May 1839 conference.ᵃ Wilford Woodruff, also a member of the quorum, recorded that the Twelve "spent the day in council with Joseph" at his home and that "Brother Wᵐ· Smith was restored to his quorum."ᵇ The council also discussed Lyman Wight's letters—recently published in the *Quincy Whig*—regarding depredations committed against the Latter-day Saints in Missouri.ᶜ (*a.* General Church Minutes, 4 May 1839. *b.* Woodruff, Journal, 25 May 1839; see also Kimball, "History," 104. *c.* JS, Commerce, IL, to Lyman Wight, Quincy, IL, 27 May 1839, in JS Letterbook 2, pp. 13–14; "Difference of Opinion," *Quincy Whig*, 25 May 1839, [1]; JS et al., Commerce, IL, to Robert B. Thompson, Quincy, IL, 25 May 1839, in JS Letterbook 2, p. 11.)

26 May 1839 • Sunday

Sunday at home, Elder O. Pratte [Orson Pratt] & John Taylor preached[26]

27 May–8 June 1839 • Monday–Saturday

Monday 27th and beginning of the week at home, latter part of week he, (President Smith) went to Quincy with others of the Presidency and returned on Wednesday 5[th] June[27] ~~Spent greater part of latter part study and~~ Latter part at home

9 June 1839 • Sunday

Sunday ~~11[th]~~ ⟨9[th]⟩ at meeting with wife and family at Brother Bosiers [Squire Bozarth's]— ⟨Elder [John E.] Page pre[ach]ed[28]— Elder Page baptised one woman⟩

10 June 1839 • Monday

Monday ~~12[th]~~ ⟨10[th]⟩ began to study & prepare to dictate history—[29]

11 June 1839 • Tuesday

Tuesday commenced to dictate and I to write history—[30]

12–14 June 1839 • Wednesday–Friday

wednesday Thursday & Friday Generally so employed

15 June 1839 • Saturday

Saturday 15th June left home with his family on a visit [p. [2]]

---

26. Wilford Woodruff's journal clarifies that Pratt and Taylor preached in JS's home. (Woodruff, Journal, 26 May 1839.)

27. At Quincy, JS met with Latter-day Saints, instructed members of the Quorum of the Seventy, and prepared licenses for missionaries. On 4 June, JS dictated a lengthy list of Missouri losses. (Woodruff, Journal, following 17 June 1839; Richards, "Pocket Companion," 63–73; Missionary certificates for Brigham Young, George A. Smith, and Wilford Woodruff, Quincy, IL, 3 June 1839, signed by Sidney Rigdon, Hyrum Smith, and JS, JS Collection, CHL; JS, "Bill of Damages against the State of Missouri on Account of the Sufferings and Losses Sustained Therein," Quincy, IL, 4 June 1839, JS Collection, CHL; compare JS, "Extract, from the Private Journal of Joseph Smith Jr.," *Times and Seasons,* Nov. 1839, 1:7.)

28. TEXT: "pre[*hole burned in paper*]ed".

29. JS began work on a new history the year before. JS and Mulholland evidently resumed work on the history at this time. (See JS, Journal, 30 Apr. 1838; 1, 2, 3, and 4 May 1838; and Mulholland, Journal, 10–13 June 1839.)

30. James Mulholland's handwriting appears in the surviving pages of a draft of the beginning of JS's 1838–1856 history and in the first fifty-nine pages of the complete manuscript. Mulholland's personal journal also records their work on the history. (JS History, 1839 [draft]; Jessee, "Writing of Joseph Smith's History," 441, 450, 464; JS History, vol. A-1, 1–59; Mulholland, Journal, 10–13 June 1839.)

——— ⁊ ———

Editorial Note

JS's departure on 15 June began an eleven-day visit to his brother William, at Plymouth, Hancock County, and brother Don Carlos, near Macomb, McDonough County, Illinois. He also met with his brother Samuel while in McDonough County. The following three journal entries record Mulholland's observations in the Commerce area during JS's absence.

——— ⁊ ———

16 June 1839 · Sunday

Sunday 16th Meeting held br Bosiers [Squire Bozarth's] Brs Rose[31] and [Theodore] Turley presiding I was present and considered that Br Rose ⟨spoke⟩ not ⟨in⟩ acco[r]dance with the doctrines of the Church, nor with the Spirit of God Others thought so too———

President [Sidney] Rigdon preached at Montrose———

Bishop [Newel K.] Whitney arrived here—

17 June 1839 · Monday

Monday 17th Bishop [Vinson] Knight, arrived returned to Quincy on [blank][32]

18 June 1839 · Tuesday

Tuesday evening, Br Rose baptised one man named [blank] at Pst. [Sidney] Rigdon's place

——— ⁊ ———

Editorial Note

When JS returned to Commerce, he reported his activities to James Mulholland. The scribe recorded another journal entry for 15 June and continued with retrospective entries of JS's travel and activities while away from Commerce visiting his brothers.

——— ⁊ ———

15–17 June 1839 · Saturday–Monday

15th June Started on Saturday morning ⟨15th June⟩ with my family— on a visit to Br Carlos [Don Carlos Smith] met Br Wm [Smith] on the prairie, found him in good spirits— went with him to his house ⟨in Plymouth— C.⟩, found his family all well staid over night, and had a very satisfactory visit. Next

---

31. Possibly Joseph Rose. (1840 U.S. Census, Adams Co., IL, 78.)

32. JS's history has Knight returning to Quincy the same day, 17 June. (JS History, vol. C-1, 956.)

day went on to B⟨r⟩ Don C Smiths, M⟨c⟩Donough Co. near ⟨the village of⟩ M⟨c⟩Comb [Macomb]. Staid there untill monday, and there met with br Saml. Smith, who I had not before seen since our deliverance from prison.

18 June 1839 • Tuesday

Tuesday 18ᵗʰ went to a the house of a man by the name of Mathews,³³ during the [p. [3]] evening the neighbors came in, and I gave them a short discourse,

20 June 1839 • Thursday

Thursday following went to Elder Zebedee Coulters [Coltrin's],³⁴ from there were invited to visit a brother br Vance's³⁵ which wee did and there gave to the brethren and friends of the Neigborhood,³⁶ a brief history or account of the coming forth of the Book of Mormon,

22–23 June 1839 • Saturday–Sunday

Saturday 22ⁿᵈ we returned to Don C's [Don Carlos Smith's] place, and on Sunday went to Br Wilcox's³⁷ and there preached to a very crowded congregation and so eager were they to hear that a part of them stood out in the rain during the sermon, & ⟨in⟩ general they all expressed good satisfaction as to what they had heard.

24–25 June 1839 • Monday–Tuesday

Monday 24ᵗʰ started for home and got as far as Br Parkins [Ute Perkins Sr.], near Fountain green, Hancock Co— when they insisted that we should tarry, and on Tuesday we held meeting, and spoke with considerable liberty to a large congregation,

---

33. Possibly Anson Mathews. (1840 U.S. Census, Hancock Co., IL, 169; "A Record of the Names of the Members of the Church," Nauvoo, IL, 1842, [21], in Record of Members, 1841–1845, microfilm, U.S. and Canada Record Collection, FHL.)

34. Coltrin, president of the local congregation, apparently lived in or near Macomb, McDonough County, Illinois. (Notice, *Times and Seasons,* Dec. 1839, 1:31.)

35. Probably John Vance, who lived in or near Macomb, McDonough County, Illinois. (Notice, *Times and Seasons,* Dec. 1839, 1:31; Woodruff, Journal, 11–12 Aug. 1839; "Agents for the Times and Seasons," *Times and Seasons,* Feb. 1840, 1:64.)

36. The local Latter-day Saint congregation consisted of about seventy members. (Notice, *Times and Seasons,* Dec. 1839, 1:31.)

37. Probably Benjamin Wilcox, who lived in or near Macomb, McDonough County, Illinois. (Notice, *Times and Seasons,* Dec. 1839, 1:31.)

26 June 1839 · Wednesday

Wednesday 26th arrived all safe & sound, at home,— Commerce Ill.,

———— ⁊ ————

Editorial Note

Contemporaneous journal keeping resumed at about this point in the journal.

———— ⁊ ————

27 June 1839 · Thursday

Thursday, attended a conference [p. 4] of the Twelve— at which time B[r] Orson Hyde, made his confession and was restored to the Priesthood again,[38]

28 June 1839 · Friday

Friday transacting business of various kinds, Counseling the brethren &c &c

29 June 1839 · Saturday

Saturday at home principally

30 June 1839 · Sunday

Sunday at Meeting at B[r] Bosiers [Squire Bozarth's] Bore testimony to a crowded audience concerning the truth of this work & also of the truth of the Book of Mormon &c. &c.

1 July 1839 · Monday

Monday 1[rst] July, Spent the day principally counseling with the Brethren—

---

38. This was the third day of a three-day conference held by the Twelve, which commenced before JS's return to Commerce. Hyde was disaffected from the church in Missouri, where he and Thomas B. Marsh made a statement that apostle Wilford Woodruff characterized as "fals testimony against the presidency & the Church before the authorities of the State of Missouri which was a leading cause of the Governour's calling out thirty thousand of the Militia against the Church of Jesus Christ of Latter Day Saints." Woodruff's journal also clarifies that Hyde was restored this day to full fellowship in the Quorum of the Twelve, from which he and William Smith had been suspended in May 1839.[a] At the conference, JS gave instructions on faith, repentance, baptism, the gift of tongues, the resurrection, and the doctrine of election. Woodruff recorded that JS presented one of a "vast number of the Keys of the Kingdom of God" to the Twelve "for there benefit in there experience & travels."[b] The conference inaugurated a series of meetings in which JS instructed the Twelve in preparation for their mission to Europe.[c] (*a.* Esplin, "Emergence of Brigham Young," chap. 7, esp. pp. 339–343; chap. 9, esp. p. 399; Woodruff, Journal, 25 June 1839; 338n15 herein. *b.* Richards, "Pocket Companion," 15–22; Woodruff, Journal, 27 June 1839. *c.* See Woodruff, Journal, 2 and 7 July 1839.)

2 July 1839 · Tuesday

Tuesday, Spent this day— on the Iowa side of the [Mississippi] river
Forenoon went in company with Elders [Sidney] Rigdon & H[yrum] Smith,
Bishops [Newel K.] Whitney & Knights [Vinson Knight] and others to visit a
purchase lately made by bro^(ther) Knights as a location for a town,

Advised that a town be built there,[39]

Afternoon, met with the twelve & Some of the Seventies who are about to
proceed on their mission to Europe. the nations of the earth, and the Islands of
the sea,[40] The meeting was [p. 5] opened by singing and prayer after which The
Presidency proceeded to bless two of the Twelve, who had lately been ordained
into that quorum viz: Wilford Woodruff & George ⟨a⟩ Smith[41] & one of the
Seventies viz Theodore Turley after which a blessing⟨s⟩ was ⟨were⟩ also pronounced by them on the heads of the wives of ⟨some of⟩ those about to ⟨go⟩
abroad.[42] The meeting was then addressed by President Hyrum Smith, by way
of advice to the Twelve &c &c chiefly concerning the nature of their mission,
their practicing prudence & ~~charity~~ humility in their plans ⟨or subjects⟩ ~~of~~ for
preaching, the necessity of their not trifling with their office, and of holding
on strictly to the importance of their mission & the authority of the priesthood. —— I—— (President Joseph Smith Jr) then addresst them, and gave
much instruction calculated to ~~if~~ guard them against selfsufficiency, selfrigh-
teousness & selfimportance, touching upon many subjects of importance &
value to all who wish to walk humbly before the Lord, but especialy teaching

---

39. On 26 June, Knight, acting as a church agent, purchased land in the "Half-Breed Tract," Lee
County, Iowa, that totaled 16,281.78 acres according to the property deeds, at a cost of approximately
$41,200.[a] Wilford Woodruff recorded that the group "rode four miles down the river to see the place
called Blefens point whare the Saints expected to build a town, Joseph pronounced it good & we
returned."[b] "Blefens point" apparently was named after a previous landowner, "J. P. Blevins." This land
later became the Latter-day Saint settlement of Nashville, Iowa.[c] (a. See Lee Co., IA, Deed Records,
26 June 1839, 2:3–6, 13–16, microfilm, U.S. and Canada Record Collection, FHL. b. Woodruff, Journal,
2 July 1839; see also 27 June 1839. c. Woodruff, Journal, 28 June 1839; Lee Co., IA, Deed Records, 26 June
1839, 2:5–6; 22 Jan. 1841, 2:547, microfilm, U.S. and Canada Record Collection, FHL; Elias Smith,
Journal, 24 and 29 June 1839; *History of Lee County,* 679.)

40. This meeting was held at Brigham Young's Montrose lodgings on the Iowa side of the river.
(Woodruff, Journal, 2 July 1839.)

41. Woodruff and Smith were ordained apostles 26 April 1839 at the temple lot in Far West, Missouri,
when the Twelve symbolically commenced their mission to Europe, in accordance with revelation.
(Woodruff, Journal, 26 Apr. 1839; Minutes, Far West, MO, 26 Apr. 1839, JS Letterbook 2, pp. 138–139;
Revelation, 8 July 1838–A, in JS, Journal, 8 July 1838, p. 285 herein [D&C 118].)

42. The presidency laid hands on Brigham Young's wife, Mary Ann Angell Young; John Taylor's wife,
Leonora Cannon Taylor; and Wilford Woodruff's wife, Phoebe Carter Woodruff. (Woodruff, Journal,
2 July 1839.)

them [p. 6] to observe charity & wisdom, & fellow feeling with Love, one towards another in all things & under all circumstances.[43]

3 July 1839 • Wednesday

Wednesday July 3rd, Baptized Dr Isaac Galland & confirmed him by the water edge— about two hours afterwards, ordained him to the office of an elder.[44]

Aftrenoon dictating History—

4–5 July 1839 • Thursday–Friday

Thursday & Friday (assisted by Br Newel Knight) dictating History[45]

6 July 1839 • Saturday

Saturday also at home Studying Church records &c &c

7 July 1839 • Sunday

Sunday July 7th Meeting held in the open air as a large assemblage was expected to ~~witness~~ ⟨Lis[ten] to⟩ the farewell addresses of the 12 who were then about to take their departure on this most important mission. ⟨viz⟩ to the nations of the earth, and the Islands of the sea Elder John E. Page, being the first of the 12 present, opened the meeting by addressing a few words ⟨of an⟩ introductory nature after which singing and prayer were observed, when Elder Page, delivered a very interesting discourse on the subject of the Book of Mormon recapitulating in short terms the subjects of a former discourse on the same subject— [p. 6][46] and afterwards proceeded to read portions from the ~~the~~ Bible and Book of Mormon concerning the best criterions whereby to judge of its authenticity. And then went on to show that no impostor would ever

---

43. JS explicitly directed his comments toward the Twelve, encouraging them to cooperate and support each other while on their mission in Europe. Heber C. Kimball later reported that around this time JS also spoke of "unfolding keys of knowledge to detect Satan, and preserve us in the favor of God." (Woodruff, Journal, 2 July 1839; Richards, "Pocket Companion," 11; Kimball, "History," 106.)

44. In April 1839, the church purchased land in the Commerce area and on the Iowa side of the Mississippi River from Galland, an early settler of the area. (Leonard, *Nauvoo,* 165; Cook, "Isaac Galland," 270; Hancock Co., IL, Deed Records, 30 Apr. 1839, bk. 12G, 247, microfilm, U.S. and Canada Record Collection, FHL; see also 336n14 herein.)

45. The Knight family was prominent in the Colesville, New York, branch of the church during the first year of the church's organization. Knight presumably assisted with the history by providing information about his experiences with JS and the church in the period between April and August 1830. (See JS History, vol. A-1, 37–53.)

46. TEXT: The second of two pages numbered "6"; page numbers remain one off through the rest of the journal.

Isaac Galland. Latter-day Saints purchased nearly nineteen thousand acres in Iowa from Galland, as well as land in the vicinity of Commerce, Illinois. Galland was baptized and ordained to the priesthood by Joseph Smith on 3 July 1839. (Church History Library, Salt Lake City.)

attempt to make such promises as are contained [in] pages 541 and 34th—⁴⁷ which he did in a very satisfactory manner. ⟨& then bore testimony⟩ ~~after which the meeting adjourned for~~ one hour,——— Afternoon——— The meeting was again opened by prayer &c Elder John Taylor spoke on the subject of this dispensation— The other angel which John saw.— having the everlasting gospel to preach &c &⁴⁸——— ⟨hee then bore testimony of the truth of the Book of Mormon &c &c⟩

Elder [Wilford] Woodruffs address went chiefly to exhortation to the Saints to perseverance after which he bore his testimony also.

Eder Orson Hyde next came forward and having alluded to his own late fall, exhorted all to perseverance in the things of God, expressed himself one with his brethren, and bore testimony to his knowledge of the truth and the misery of falling from it.

Elder Brigham Young made some very appropriate remarks, and also bore testimony to the truth of these [p. 7] things, and gave an invitation to come forward and be baptized when three manifested their determination to renounce the world. and take upon themselves the name of Jesus Christ.

One brother was then confirmed after which President S[idney] Rigdon addressed the meeting in a very feeling manner, showing that it must be no small matter which ⟨could⟩ induce men to leave their families and their homes to travel over all the earth, amidst persecutions and trials such as always followed the preaching of this gospel; he then addressed himself to the twelve and gave them some cou[n]sel and consolation— as far as in his power. after which I (JS—) requested their prayers & promised to pray for them &c &c⁴⁹

The meeting was large & respectable a large number were present who did not belong to our Church The most perfect order prevailed throughout, The meeting dismissed about 1/2 past five oclock. when we repaired to the waters and the three candidates were baptized & confirmed. [p. 8]

---

47. The promises to which Page referred were apparently on pages 541 and 534 of the original 1830 edition of the Book of Mormon, not the 1837 edition. Those pages of the original edition correspond to Ether 2:4–13 and Mormon 8:26–36 in the modern edition of the Book of Mormon. Promises found on page 541 concern freedom for the "land which is choice above all other lands," contingent on the inhabitants serving Jesus Christ. The content of page 534 focuses on conditions that would prevail when the Book of Mormon would be brought forth "out of the earth."

48. Taylor, like other Latter-day Saints, believed that the "everlasting gospel" had been restored to the earth by an angel, as prophesied by John the Revelator. (See Revelation 14:6–7; and Revelation, 3 Nov. 1831, in Doctrine and Covenants 100:4, 1835 ed. [D&C 133:36–40].)

49. Wilford Woodruff recorded that JS encouraged the Twelve with an allusion to his own recent imprisonment: "If you are placed whare you can ownly see your Brethren through the grates of a window while in Irons because of the gospel of Jesus Christ remember Brother Joseph has been in like circumstances also." (Woodruff, Journal, 7 July 1839.)

———— ❧ ————

Editorial Note

Beginning in late June, malaria borne by the mosquitoes that infested the area's swamplands spread among the Latter-day Saints. Parley P. Pratt later recounted that "a majority of the people were prostrated with malignant fevers, agues, etc."[50] JS spent most of this week and much of the following month ministering to the sick. Having been recently driven from Missouri, many still lived in crowded, ramshackle accommodations. Zina Huntington, whose mother died of the sickness 8 July, later recounted that JS "saw to our being taken care of, as well as circumstances would permit—for there were hundreds, lying in tents and wagons, who needed care as much as we. Once Joseph came himself and made us tea with his own hands, and comforted the sick and dying."[51] Among the sick were JS's father and apparently his son Joseph Smith III.[52] Brigham Young later recounted that JS "had taken the sick into his house and dooryard until his house was like an hospital, and he had attended upon them until he was taken sick himself and confined to his bed several days."[53]

———— ❧ ————

8–20 July 1839 • Monday–Saturday

Monday Tuesday & Wednesday selecting Hymns, with the 12[54]

About this time sickiness began to manifest itself much amongst the brethren as well as among the inhabitants of the place, so that this week and next was generally spent in visiting the sick, and ministering unto them, some had faith enough and were healed, others had not,

21 July 1839 • Sunday

Sunday the 21ʳˢᵗ no meeting on account of much rain, and much sickness, however, many of the sick were ⟨on⟩ this day, raised up by the power of God, through the instrumentality of the Elders of Israel ministering to them in the name of Jesus Christ[55]

---

50. Pratt, *Autobiography*, 324.

51. Tullidge, *Women of Mormondom*, 213–214; see also Huntington, Diary, 1.

52. Woodruff, Journal, 12 and 19 July 1839; "The Memoirs of President Joseph Smith," *Saints' Herald*, 20 Nov. 1934, 1479.

53. Historian's Office, "History of Brigham Young," 34; see also Mace, Autobiography, 31.

54. Brigham Young and others of the Twelve later took this selection of hymns on their mission to the British Isles, and it provided a basis for the new collection of hymns they published there in 1840. (*A Collection of Sacred Hymns, for the Church of Jesus Christ of Latter-day Saints, in Europe,* ed. Brigham Young, Parley P. Pratt, and John Taylor [Manchester, England: W. R. Thomas, 1840]; Crawley, *Descriptive Bibliography,* 121–124; Hicks, *Mormonism and Music,* chap. 2.)

55. JS called on a number of men to bless the sick—among them his brother Don Carlos Smith, his cousin George A. Smith, and apostles John Taylor and Wilford Woodruff. (Woodruff, Journal, 12 July

22–23 July 1839 • Monday–Tuesday

Monday & Tuesday ⟨also⟩ the sick were ministered unto, with great success but many still remain sick & new cases occurring daily.[56]

28 July–3 August 1839 • Sunday–Saturday

Sunday 28 meeting held as usual. B[rother] P[arley] P, Pratt, preached,[57] on the gathering of Israel, and in the ~~evening~~ afternoon Orson Pratt addressed the church, on the necessity of keeping the commandments of God. [p. 9] After which I spoke & admonished the church individually to set his house in order, to make clean the insid[e of] the platter,[58] and to meet on the next sabbath to partake of sacrament in order that by our obedieence to the ordinances, we might be enabled to prevail with God against the destroyer, and that the sick may be healed.

All this week chiefly spent among the sick, who in general are gaining strength, and recovering health

4 August 1839 • Sunday

Sunday 5ᵗʰ ⟨4ᵗʰ⟩ August, Church came together for prayer meeting and sacrament,[59] Exhorted the Church at length, concerning the necessity of being righteous and clean at heart before the Lord, many others also spoke, especially some of the twelve who were present, professed their willingness to proceed on their mission to Europe, without either purse or Scrip &c &c &c[60]

1839; Benjamin F. Johnson to George F. Gibbs, Salt Lake City, UT, 1903, 8–9, Benjamin Franklin Johnson, Papers, CHL.)

56. In a personal history, Brigham Young later wrote that on 22 July, "Joseph arose from his bed of sickness and the power of God rested upon him he commenced in his own house and dooryard, commanding the sick in the name of Jesus Christ to arise and be made whole, and they were healed according to his word; he then continued to travel from house to house, and from tent to tent upon the bank of the river, healing the sick as he went." Young further reported that JS crossed the Mississippi and healed a number of Iowa Saints, including Young himself. (Historian's Office, "History of Brigham Young," 34–35.)

57. Pratt, one of the last two to escape from prison in Missouri, had just recently rejoined the Latter-day Saints in Commerce. (Parley P. Pratt, Commerce, IL, to Aaron Frost, Bethel, ME, 21 July 1839, Parley P. Pratt, Letters, 1838–1839, CHL; Pratt, *Autobiography*, chaps. 22–23, 32–33, 36.)

58. To purify oneself from within. (See Matthew 23:25–26; and Luke 11:39.)

59. Wilford Woodruff characterized this as a "meeting of Prayer & fasting." (Woodruff, Journal, 4 Aug. 1839.)

60. Heber C. Kimball reported JS's instruction to travel without purse or scrip "according to the revelations of Jesus Christ." Latter-day Saint missionaries commonly followed the pattern established by the ministry of Jesus's disciples to "carry neither purse, nor scrip"—money bag or traveling bag—meaning to depend on the hospitality and assistance of others. (Kimball, "History," 111; Mark 6:8; Luke 10:4; Revelation, July 1830–A, in Doctrine and Covenants 9:7, 1835 ed. [D&C 24:18]; Revelation, 22 and 23 Sept. 1832, in Doctrine and Covenants 4:13, 1835 ed. [D&C 84:77–78].)

the sacrament was administered a spirit of humility and harmony prevailed, and the church passed a resolution that the 12 proceed as soon as possible[61] and that they would provide for their families[62]——— [p. 10]

11–17 August 1839 • Sunday–Saturday

Sunday 11th At meeting

forenoon

a Sermon by P[arley] P, Pratt

afternoon 1 baptized and 4 confirmed viz Br Hibbard his wife & little son & daughter.[63] ⟨& sacrament administered⟩

This week chiefly spent visiting the sick, sickness much decreased———

News from Kirtland By D[imick] Huntington[64] [blank lines]

18–24 August 1839 • Sunday–Saturday

Sunday 18th not at meeting

Self and wife ro◊de out———

forenoon

Sermon by Orson Pratt

on the order & plan of creation

3 baptized

Afternoon three confirmed and one ordained an Elder

---

61. Sickness and poverty delayed and staggered the departure of the Twelve. Wilford Woodruff and John Taylor departed during the week following this Sunday gathering, but others did not leave until later in the fall. (Woodruff, Journal, 25 July 1839; 7 and 8 Aug. 1839; Historian's Office, "History of Brigham Young," 35; Allen et al., *Men with a Mission,* chap. 4.)

62. In the wake of the recent expulsion from Missouri, the impoverished church had difficulty keeping the agreement to provide for the families of the traveling apostles. A few months after the departure of the Twelve, Hyrum Smith wrote to Parley P. Pratt with considerable understatement, "The families of the Twelve are generally well, but not altogether so comfortably situated as I could wish owing to the poverty of the Church." (Hyrum Smith, Nauvoo, IL, to Parley P. Pratt, New York City, NY, 22 Dec. 1839, in JS Letterbook 2, pp. 80–81; see also Allen et al., *Men with a Mission,* chap. 11.)

63. Probably Davidson and Sarah Tilton Hibbard with their children William and Melvina. (Gregg, *History of Hancock County,* 221, 964; JS History, vol. C-1, 972; "The Memoirs of President Joseph Smith," *Saints' Herald,* 13 Nov. 1934, 1454; 1830 U.S. Census, Hancock Co., IL, 286; 1840 U.S. Census, Hancock Co., IL, 185; 1850 U.S. Census, Hancock Co., IL, 291; 1880 U.S. Census, Nauvoo, Hancock Co., IL, 197A; Hancock Co., IL, Marriage Register, 1829–1915, bk. A-1, 100, 10 May 1847, microfilm, U.S. and Canada Record Collection, FHL.)

64. A number of Latter-day Saints still resided in Kirtland. The conference held 4–6 May 1839 at Quincy, Illinois, resolved to advise Latter-day Saints living in the eastern states to gather to Kirtland if they did not want to travel as far as Commerce. (Turley, Journal, 11–14; General Church Minutes, 4 May 1839.)

This week chiefly spent among the sick also,
New purchase made[65]

25–31 August 1839 • Sunday–Saturday

Sunday 25th at meeting
⟨Sickness decreasing⟩

1–7 September 1839 • Sunday–Saturday

Sunday 1[rst] Septr, at meeting also, Spoke concerning some errors [p. [11]] in
br P[arley] P. Pratt's works[66] &c &c &c
This week sickness much decreased

8–14 September 1839 • Sunday–Saturday

Sunday 8th Septe— — — —
[*blank line*][67]
Monday & greater part of week visiting the sick and attending to business
of the new town[68] &c &c
Friday at noon left home for Brother W[m] Smiths place[69] ⟨returned home
Saturday evening.⟩

15 September 1839 • Sunday

Sunday 15th visiting the sick

16–21 September 1839 • Monday–Saturday

Monday 16th ~~and greater part of the went to Burlington and returned~~ and
greater part of the week arranging business of town lots &c[70]

---

65. On 12 August 1839, the previous week, William White sold the church eighty acres adjoining
Commerce, north of the land obtained from Hugh White that May. (Leonard, *Nauvoo*, 54–59.)

66. These "errors" probably included some of the doctrinal positions in Parley P. Pratt, *A Voice of
Warning and Instruction to All People, Containing a Declaration of the Faith and Doctrine of the Church
of the Latter Day Saints, Commonly Called Mormons* (New York: W. Sandford, 1837), of which the second
edition (1839) contains several substantial revisions. (See Crawley, *Descriptive Bibliography*, 97–98.)

67. TEXT: The remainder of the entry is written in lighter ink.

68. The land purchased by the church the prior month for Latter-day Saint settlement. The newly
platted land, adjoined to but distinct from Commerce, was soon named Nauvoo and was eventually
reorganized to subsume Commerce. (JS, Journal, 18–24 Aug. 1839; 351n65 herein; Leonard, *Nauvoo*,
54–59.)

69. At Plymouth, Illinois. (JS, Journal, 15–17 June 1839, p. 341 herein.)

70. JS and his counselors in the presidency sold lots this week from the land the church had earlier purchased for Latter-day Saint settlement. (See, for example, Deed, JS et al. to Randolph Alexander, Nauvoo,
IL, 18 Sept. 1839, Newel K. Whitney, Papers, BYU; and Deed, JS et al. to Moses Nickerson, Nauvoo, IL,
18 Sept. 1839, JS Collection, CHL.)

Wednesday went to Burling, I T [Burlington, Iowa Territory] and returned on Thursday evening[71]

Friday and Saturday at home

22–28 September 1839 • Sunday–Saturday

Sunday 22nd attended & presided at meeting— Spoke concerning the ⟨other⟩ comforter[72] &c &c &c

This week transacting various business at home greater part of time except when visiting the sick, all in general ~~except~~ recovering but some very slowly——

29 September–6 October 1839 • Sunday–Sunday

Sunday 29th Meeting at own house After others had spoken, Spoke and explained concerning uselessness of preaching [p. 12] to the world about great judgements but rather to preach the simple gospel— Explained concerning the coming of the son of Man &c that all will be raised to meet him[73] but the righteous will remain with him in the cloud whilst all the proud and all that do wickedly will have to return to the earth, and suffer his vengeance which he will take upon them this is the second death &c &c

Also that it is a false idea that the saints will escape all the judgements whilst the wicked suffer— for all flesh is subject to suffer— and "the righteous shall hardly escape"[74] still many of the saints will escape— for the just shall live by faith—[75] yet many of the righteous shall fall a prey to disease to pestilence ~~&c and yet~~ &c by reason of the weakness of the flesh and yet be saved in

---

71. JS's later history has him traveling to Burlington, but the history may mistakenly assume he is the referent of the statement in this journal that James Mulholland was keeping for him. Mulholland's personal journal of the same period indicates that Mulholland, at least, did travel to Burlington, whether JS did or not. (JS History, vol. C-1, 967; Mulholland, Journal, 19 Sept. 1839.)

72. Expounding John 14:16–17, 26. JS's history for this date, prepared under the direction of Willard Richards, adds the phrase "as I had previously taught the Twelve"—apparently referring to JS's 27 June 1839 instructions to the Twelve regarding the doctrine of election.[a] Whereas the New Testament identifies the Comforter as the Holy Ghost, JS equated the "other" Comforter with having one's "calling & Election made sure." Willard Richards recorded that JS clarified that the "other Comforter" is Jesus Christ and that "when any man obtains this last Comforter he will have the personage of Jesus Christ to attend him or appear unto him from time to time. & even he will manifest the Father unto him & they will take up their abode with him, & the visions of the heavens will be opened unto him & the Lord will teach him face to face & he may have a perfect knowledge of the mysteries of the kingdom of God." JS explained that a person was worthy to receive the other Comforter "when the Lord has thoroughly proved him & finds that the man is determined to serve him at all hazard."[b] (a. JS History, vol. C-1, 967; see also 343n38 herein. b. Richards, "Pocket Companion," 19–21.)

73. See 1 Thessalonians 4:16–17.

74. An August 1831 apocalyptic revelation stated that "the saints also shall hardly escape." (Revelation, 30 Aug. 1831, in Doctrine and Covenants 20:9, 1835 ed. [D&C 63:34].)

75. See Romans 1:17; Galatians 3:11; and Hebrews 10:38.

the kingdom of God[76] So that it is an unhallowed principle to say that such and such have transgressed because they have been preyed upon by disease or death for all flesh is subject to death and the Saviour has said, "Judge not "lest ye be judged".[77]

All the fore part of this week at home and preparing for conference Thursday met in council and on

Saturday 5ᵗʰ October 1839 met in general conference which continued Saturday and Sunday—[78] the assemb[p. [13]]lage was very large— a great deal of business was transacted, and great instruction given

See Conference Minutes—[79]

6–12 October 1839 • Sunday–Saturday

Week beginning Sunday 6ᵗʰ october

after conference busied in attending to general affairs of the Church— principally about home

13 October 1839 • Sunday

Sunday 13ᵗʰ at meeting in the Grove meeting small on account of cold weather

15 October 1839 • Tuesday

Tuesday 15ᵗʰ octᵗ afternoon went to Quincy in company with Br Hiram [Hyrum Smith] J. S. Fulmer [John S. Fullmer] and Bishop [Vinson] Knight— Quite a number of families moving in— [1/2 page blank] [p. [14]]

---

76. Over a dozen Latter-day Saints living in and along the Mississippi River valley had died over the summer, including infants and children, JS's uncle Silas Smith, and family members of close friends. (Obituary for Silas Smith, *Times and Seasons,* Dec. 1839, 1:32; see various obituaries in *Times and Seasons,* Dec. 1839–Oct. 1840; see also Tullidge, *Women of Mormondom,* 213–214.)

77. See Matthew 7:1; and Luke 6:37.

78. The conference continued into Monday, 7 October 1839. (Minutes, *Times and Seasons,* Dec. 1839, 1:30–31.)

79. The church newspaper reported that JS "spoke at some length upon the situation of the Church, the difficulties they had had to contend with, and the manner in which they had been led to this place; and wished to know the views of the brethren whether they wished to appoint this a stake or not, stating that he believed it to be a good place and suited for the saints."ᵃ The conference organized a stake in Commerce and a branch of the church across the river in Iowa Territory. JS had decided to join Sidney Rigdon on a previously announced mission to Washington DC to attempt to obtain redress for the injustices suffered by the Latter-day Saints in Missouri, and the conference appointed Judge Elias Higbee to accompany them. JS delivered several addresses, including an admonition to elders to preach with the Holy Ghost and avoid speculative teaching.ᵇ (a. Minutes, *Times and Seasons,* Dec. 1839, 1:30–31. b. Minutes, Commerce, IL, 5 Oct. 1839, JS Letterbook 2, pp. 164–167.)

———— ❧ ————

Editorial Note

Two weeks after the final entry in the present journal, JS and his traveling companions departed on their appointed mission to Washington DC. There they met with members of Congress and with United States president Martin Van Buren, who declined to support their request for redress of losses suffered in Missouri. By late February 1840, JS returned home, leaving Elias Higbee to pursue congressional action that ultimately failed to materialize as the Saints were advised to direct their appeals to the state of Missouri—a hopeless task under prevailing circumstances.[80]

JS's next journal entry was not written until 13 December 1841, some twenty-two months after his return from Washington. By then a struggling Commerce had become a dynamic Nauvoo, reinforced by immigrants from Great Britain and focused by a new revelation proclaiming Nauvoo a temple city. From December 1841 until JS's death in June 1844, scribe Willard Richards—and in his absence British convert William Clayton— would write a connected narrative in JS's journals.

———— ❧ ————

---

80. Leonard, *Nauvoo,* 275–276.

REFERENCE
MATERIAL

Chronology for the Years 1832–1839

This brief chronology is designed as a reference tool for situating any particular journal entry or range of entries among the principal events of JS's life. It includes major journeys and migrations, births and deaths of children, selected revelations, essential developments in ecclesiastical organization, and other significant incidents. Readers wishing to conduct further research may consult the documented chronology posted on the Joseph Smith Papers website.

1832

January	25	Sustained as "President of the High Priesthood," Amherst, Ohio.
February	16	Vision of nearly universal salvation in three levels of heaven, Hiram, Ohio.
March	8	Selected Sidney Rigdon and Jesse Gause as counselors in presidency of the high priesthood, Hiram.
	29/30	Adopted son Joseph died, Hiram.
April	2	Departed Hiram on journey to Independence, Jackson County, Missouri, to meet with Latter-day Saints and conduct church business.
June		Returned to Kirtland, Ohio, from journey to Independence.
September	22–23	Revelation on priesthood and proselytizing, Kirtland.
Fall		Departed Kirtland on journey with Newel K. Whitney to New York and other cities in eastern United States to buy merchandise and proselytize.
November	6	Son Joseph Smith III born, Kirtland.
		Returned to Kirtland from journey to eastern United States. Living above Newel K. Whitney store, Kirtland.
December	27–28	Revelation mandating establishment of "house of God" in Kirtland and instruction and purification for those called to ministry, Kirtland. Additional revelation on same subject, 3 January 1833.

1833

January	23	Conducted first session of School of the Prophets, Kirtland.
February	27	Revelation on dietary code that became known as "Word of Wisdom," Kirtland.
March	18	Retained Sidney Rigdon and selected Frederick G. Williams as counselors in presidency of the high priesthood, Kirtland.
May	6	Revelation on nature of Christ and truth, Kirtland.
June	1	Revelation chastising Latter-day Saints for failure to build God's "house" as earlier mandated, Kirtland.

	6	Latter-day Saints began construction on temple, Kirtland.
	25	Sent plat for city of Zion with temple plan to Missouri Latter-day Saints, Kirtland.
July	2	Concluded work on "New Translation," or inspired revision, of Bible, Kirtland.
	20	Vigilantes, demanding removal of Latter-day Saints from Jackson County, destroyed printing press and tarred and feathered Edward Partridge and Charles Allen, Independence.
	23	Under duress, Latter-day Saints in Jackson County agreed with demands of vigilantes to leave the county.
August	9	Oliver Cowdery arrived in Kirtland with news of Jackson County citizens' demands for expulsion of Latter-day Saints.
October	5	Departed Kirtland on journey to Mount Pleasant, Upper Canada, to proselytize.
November		Latter-day Saints fled Jackson County, migrating primarily to Clay County, Missouri.
	4	Returned to Kirtland from journey to Mount Pleasant.
	25	In Kirtland, notified by Orson Hyde and John Gould that Latter-day Saints had been expelled from Jackson County earlier in month.

1834

February	by 12	Moved from upper story of Whitney store to his own house north of temple lot, Kirtland.
	17	Organized first high council, Kirtland.
	22	Notified of condition of exiled Latter-day Saints in Clay County by Parley P. Pratt and Lyman Wight, Kirtland.
	24	Revelation in Kirtland commanding organization of expedition (later known as Zion's Camp) to relieve Saints driven from Jackson County and to help them return to their properties.
	26	Departed Kirtland on journey to Pennsylvania and New York to raise funds and recruit volunteers for Zion's Camp.
March	28	Returned to Kirtland from journey to New York and Pennsylvania.
April	2–4, 7–9	Attended court as complainant in state lawsuit against Doctor Philastus Hurlbut, who was put under bond to keep the peace and not harm JS, Chardon, Ohio.
	21	Attended church conference in Norton, Ohio, to raise funds and recruit volunteers for Zion's Camp.
May	5	Departed Kirtland on journey to Missouri at head of Zion's Camp.
June	19	Vigilantes assembled to attack Zion's Camp but abandoned venture because of severe rainstorm, Fishing River Township, Clay County.

22   Revelation in Washington Township, Clay County, indicating that redemption of Zion must "wait for a little season" until elders were "endowed with power from on high" in Kirtland temple.

late   With other members of Zion's Camp, suffered outbreak of cholera, Liberty Township, Clay County.

July   7   Organized high council for church in Missouri and ordained David Whitmer president of the church in Missouri and potential successor to JS, Liberty Township.

late   Returned to Kirtland from expedition to Missouri.

October   16   Departed Kirtland on journey to Pontiac, Michigan, to meet with Latter-day Saints and proselytize in area.

late   Returned to Kirtland from journey to Pontiac.

December   5   Appointed Oliver Cowdery an assistant president of the church, Kirtland.

6   Appointed brother Hyrum Smith and father, Joseph Smith Sr., as additional assistant presidents of the church, Kirtland.

9   Received patriarchal blessing from father, Kirtland.

1835

February   14   Three Witnesses to the Book of Mormon selected Quorum of the Twelve Apostles, Kirtland.

28   Organized Quorum of the Seventy, Kirtland.

May   4   Twelve Apostles departed Kirtland on journey to northeastern states and Upper Canada to supervise outlying branches of church.

July   early   Purchased Egyptian mummies and papyri associated with later book of Abraham translation, Kirtland.

August ca. 10–23   Traveled from Kirtland to Michigan to visit Latter-day Saints.

17   Church conference approved publication of Doctrine and Covenants, Kirtland.

Fall   Worked periodically on book of Abraham translation, Kirtland.

October   7–11   Attended father during serious illness, Kirtland.

November   24   Solemnized his first recorded wedding, marrying Newel Knight and Lydia Goldthwaite Bailey, Kirtland.

December   16   Injured by brother William Smith, Kirtland.

ca. 17–29   Parents moved into his home, Kirtland.

1836

January   1   Reconciled with brother William, Kirtland.

21   Administered and received ritual washings and anointings with priesthood leaders; vision of celestial kingdom, Kirtland.

26   Began receiving formal instruction in Hebrew, Kirtland.

March	27	Dedicated temple, Kirtland.
	29	Administered and received ritual washing of feet with priesthood leaders in temple, Kirtland.
	30	Held solemn assembly in temple, Kirtland.
	31	Repeated temple dedication ceremonies for those who could not be seated on 27 March, Kirtland.
April	3	Vision of Jesus Christ, Moses, Elias, and Elijah in temple, Kirtland.
May	17	Escorted grandmother Mary Duty Smith from Fairport Harbor, Ohio, to Kirtland.
June	20	Son Frederick Granger Williams Smith born, Kirtland.
	29	Clay County, Missouri, citizen committee demanded that Latter-day Saints leave county.
July	25	Departed Kirtland on journey to conduct business in New York City and to search for rumored cache of money in a house in Salem, Massachusetts.
September		Returned to Kirtland from journey to New York and Massachusetts.
December	29	Missouri legislature approved bill creating Caldwell County for Mormon settlement, Jefferson City, Missouri.

1837

January	9	Kirtland Safety Society Anti-Banking Company opened doors to public without state banking charter, Kirtland.
February		Traveled to Monroe, Michigan, in connection with recent purchase of Bank of Monroe.
	19	Spoke in temple denouncing dissenters, Kirtland.
April	6	Held solemn assembly in temple on anniversary of church's organization, Kirtland.
	13	Charged with hiring men to kill Grandison Newell, Painesville, Ohio.
May	28	Defended himself in worship service against accusations of dissenters, Kirtland.
June	5	Discharged in Grandison Newell case, Chardon, Ohio.
	8	Completed his withdrawal from Kirtland Safety Society, apparently recognizing likelihood of failure, having made arrangements for resolution of outstanding debts.
	11	Instructed and set apart as missionaries to England apostles Heber C. Kimball and Orson Hyde and priest Joseph Fielding, Kirtland; two days later, with Willard Richards, they departed Kirtland to fulfill their mission.
	12	Onset of severe personal illness, Kirtland.

July	23	Revelation on duties of Twelve Apostles and their president, Thomas B. Marsh, Kirtland.
	28	Departed Kirtland on journey to Toronto, Upper Canada, to visit Latter-day Saints.
	late	Church newspaper acknowledged failure of Kirtland Safety Society, Kirtland.
August	27	Returned to Kirtland from journey to Toronto.
September	3	Presided over conference at which apostles Luke Johnson, Lyman Johnson, and John F. Boynton were "disfellowshipped," Kirtland.
	10	Presided over conference at which apostles Luke Johnson, Lyman Johnson, and John F. Boynton confessed errors and were received back into church fellowship, Kirtland.
	17	Appointed 109 missionaries, Kirtland.
	27	Departed Kirtland on journey to northwest Missouri to identify places for Latter-day Saints to settle.
November	7	Held church conference, Far West, Caldwell County, Missouri, at which Frederick G. Williams was removed from the presidency and Hyrum Smith appointed in his place.
December	10	Returned to Kirtland from journey to Missouri. Faced dissenters forming rival church, Kirtland.
	late	High council excommunicated twenty-eight dissenters, including Martin Harris, Warren Parrish, and apostles Luke Johnson and John F. Boynton, Kirtland.

1838

January	12	Departed Kirtland for move to Far West.
March	14	Arrived at Far West.
April	12	Church council excommunicated Oliver Cowdery, Far West.
	13	Church council excommunicated David Whitmer and Lyman Johnson, Far West.
	26	Revelation clarifying name of church and commanding Latter-day Saints to build a house of the Lord, Far West.
	27	Commenced writing detailed history of the church, Far West.
May	18	Departed Far West on journey to Daviess County, Missouri, to select sites for new Mormon settlements.
	19	Planned Mormon settlement at Spring Hill (soon renamed Adam-ondi-Ahman), Daviess County.
June	1	Returned to Far West from journey to Daviess County.
	2	Son Alexander Hale Smith born, Far West.
	28	Organized stake at Adam-ondi-Ahman, Daviess County.

July	4	Presided over Independence Day celebration that included ceremonial laying of temple cornerstones and public address by Sidney Rigdon declaring Saints' intent to defend themselves from persecution, Far West.
	6	About five hundred Latter-day Saints constituting "Kirtland Camp" departed Kirtland, migrating to Missouri.
	8	Revelations on tithing and other subjects, Far West.
August	6	Fight broke out at Gallatin, Daviess County, during attempt to prevent Latter-day Saints from voting in election; injuries and rumor of deaths resulted.
	8	With large company of men, called upon Daviess County justice of the peace Adam Black, asking that he uphold the law, Grand River Township, Daviess County.
	11	Departed Far West on journey to "forks of Grand River," northwest of Daviess County, Missouri, to warn company of Canadian Latter-day Saints who had settled outside of Adam-ondi-Ahman area contrary to his directions.
September	7	Appeared for preliminary hearing with Lyman Wight before Judge Austin A. King on charges arising from confrontation with Adam Black; gave bonds for later court appearance, Honey Creek Township, Daviess County.
October	2	Members of Kirtland Camp arrived, Far West.
	5–14	Led rescue company to defend besieged Latter-day Saints at De Witt, Carroll County, Missouri; assisted with evacuation and migration to Far West.
	18–21	Mormon forces plundered and burned residences and businesses of perceived opponents and communities supportive of anti-Mormon vigilantes, Daviess County.
	25	Mormon militia attacked volunteers from Ray County, Missouri, who had kidnapped Latter-day Saints. Two Latter-day Saints, their guide, and one citizen of Ray County were killed at Crooked River, unorganized territory attached to Ray County.
	27	Missouri governor Lilburn W. Boggs issued order to treat the Latter-day Saints as enemies and exterminate them or drive them from state if necessary, Jefferson City.
	30	Vigilantes attacked outlying community of Latter-day Saints, killing seventeen and wounding fourteen, Haun's Mill settlement, Grand River Township, Caldwell County.
	31	Taken prisoner by state militia, Far West.
November	1	Sentenced to death by military court. Execution prevented by opposition of Brigadier General Alexander Doniphan, Goose Creek camp, Rockford Township, Caldwell County.
	9	Confined at Richmond, Ray County, pending outcome of court of inquiry.

| | 29 | Ordered bound over for trial in Daviess County for treason and other charges. |
| December | 1 | Incarcerated, Liberty, Clay County. |

1839

February		Large-scale evacuation of Latter-day Saints from Missouri migrating to Illinois.
March	20	Commenced writing epistle from jail to exiled Latter-day Saints, Liberty.
April	ca. 6–8	Traveled from Liberty to Gallatin, Daviess County, to attend grand jury hearing on crimes allegedly committed in Daviess County.
	11	In Gallatin, indicted by grand jury for treason and other charges but granted change of venue.
	12	Departed Gallatin on journey to Columbia, Boone County, Missouri, to stand trial.
	16	Allowed to escape while en route to Columbia for trial, Chariton County, Missouri.
	22	Reunited with family, who were residing in home of John and Sarah Cleveland, Quincy, Illinois.
	ca. 25	Began investigating land for Mormon settlement, Illinois and Iowa.
	30	Church agents made initial purchases of land for Mormon settlement in Commerce, Illinois.
May	9–10	Moved from Quincy to log home in Commerce.
June	11	Resumed recording history with scribe James Mulholland, Commerce.
July	21–23	Performed faith healing of sick Latter-day Saints, Commerce, Illinois, and Montrose, Iowa.
August	8	John Taylor and Wilford Woodruff departed Commerce for British Isles, initiating overseas proselytizing mission of Twelve Apostles.
October	5–7	Presided over general church conference, which organized stakes in Commerce and Iowa for newly settled Mormon migrants, Commerce.
	29	Departed Commerce for Washington DC to seek redress for Mormon property losses in Missouri.

Geographical Directory

This directory provides geographical descriptions of most of the places mentioned in this volume of *The Joseph Smith Papers*. It includes towns and villages, counties and states, and landforms and waterways, except for nonspecific or unidentifiable references such as "prairie." It includes many specific structures mentioned in the journals, such as schoolhouses and inns. It also includes some institutions that moved from place to place, such as the printing office and the Elders School.

Each place is listed with a complete political location and, in most cases, with grid coordinates for one or more reference maps (pages 381–395 herein) on which the place appears. Many entries also include information such as municipal history, population, and distinctive natural environments, as well as details more particular to the significance of the place within JS's journals for the years 1832 to 1839. Unless otherwise noted, all places were within the United States of America in the 1830s. Spellings of the time period have been used for proper nouns. "LDS church" refers to the church established by JS in 1830 and later known as the Church of Jesus Christ of Latter-day Saints.

In many instances, it is not clear whether municipal places mentioned in the journals refer to proper towns or villages or to a general community area and outlying residences within a township of the same name. When the journal is ambiguous, the directory references the township but notes formal municipal units that bear the same name and are within the township. Readers wishing to conduct further research may consult the documented geographical directory posted on the Joseph Smith Papers website.

Adam-ondi-Ahman, Grand River Township, Daviess County, Missouri. MAP 8: B-4; MAP 9: C-3. Originally unspecified area in Missouri that JS revelations designated as place where Adam blessed his posterity after leaving Garden of Eden. While seeking new areas in Daviess Co. for settlement, JS and others surveyed town site on east bluffs of Grand River near home and ferry of Latter-day Saint Lyman Wight, May 1838. JS announced area as gathering place for Saints, May 1838. First called Spring Hill; renamed after JS identified area as Adam-ondi-Ahman, May 1838. Latter-day Saint nickname "Diahman." Large groups of Saints, many from Kirtland, began settling, June 1838. Connected to Far West by way of county seat, Gallatin, on road built by Saints. Soon became principal Mormon settlement in Daviess Co. Stake organized 28 June 1838. Under pressure from vigilantes, Mormon settlers from outlying areas of Daviess Co. took refuge here. As population of 400 grew to over 1,000, houses filled to overflowing, and many lived in tents and wagons. Responding to threats against Far West, able-bodied men in Adam-ondi-Ahman served in Caldwell Co. militia, late Oct. 1838. After surrender of Far West, state militia arrived at Adam-ondi-Ahman, 8 Nov. 1838, and gave Mormons ultimatum: evacuate county within ten days or remain, unarmed and unprotected, subject to vigilante retaliation. Town almost completely abandoned by 20 Nov. 1838. Offered at public sale and purchased by local residents, 24 Nov. 1838.

Allegany County, New York. Map 3: D-5.

Alton, Madison County, Illinois. Map 9: D-6. Incorporated as town, 1833. Incorporated as city, 1837. 1838 population about 2,500.

Ashtabula Township, Ashtabula County, Ohio. Map 3: E-3; Map 4: C-6. Settled by New Englanders about 1801. Organized 1808. Important transportation hub in Western Reserve with Ashtabula Harbor on Lake Erie and Cleveland-Buffalo road two miles from lake. 1830 population about 1,600. Economic center of township, at intersection of Ashtabula River and Cleveland-Buffalo road, settled early 1800s. Incorporated as Ashtabula borough, 1828. Incorporated as village, 1831.

Bainbridge Township, Chenango County, New York. Map 3: D-8. Organized as Jericho, 1791, as part of land given by New York to "Vermont sufferers" who lost land titles after land dispute between New York and Vermont. Name changed to Bainbridge, 1814. Hilly land cut by Susquehanna River. 1835 population about 3,000. Included Bainbridge and South Bainbridge villages. Bainbridge village, on Susquehanna River, incorporated 1829. Township contained Episcopal, Methodist, Congregationalist, Baptist, and Universalist churches.

Barnstable County, Massachusetts. Not mapped.

Benson Township, Rutland County, Vermont. Map 3: C-10. Settled 1783. 1830 population about 1,500. Location of first branch of LDS church in Vermont, established 1831, mostly of former members of local Freewill Baptist congregation. Branch eventually had about 100 members, many of whom migrated to Ohio and Missouri by 1833.

Bishop's office, Far West, Rockford (now in Mirabile) Township, Caldwell County, Missouri. Not located. Not mapped. Joseph Holbrook wrote, "I built an office for Bishop Edward Pa[r]tridge in Far West. and finished it for him I also built a dwelling house for him." Used for several purposes, including council meetings.

Board kiln, Kirtland, Kirtland Township, Geauga (now in Lake) County, Ohio. Not located. Not mapped. Used to dry wood for building projects, principally for House of the Lord in Kirtland. JS's scribe Warren Parrish wrote that kiln was near temple. Caught fire several times, 1835–1836.

Brantford Township, Wentworth County, Gore District, Upper Canada (now in Brant County, Ontario, Canada). Map 3: C-3. In 1784, area designated by British government for Mohawk Indians to compensate for their losses in American Revolution as well as their faithfulness to Britain. Known as Brant's ford. White settlers began arriving, 1805, and Mohawks eventually surrendered land to Crown, 1830. Included Brantford town, commercial point on Grand River established 1830 and soon principal settlement. Described in 1832 as having about a dozen mercantile stores, two taverns, and many homes. 1846 population about 2,000.

Buffalo, Erie County, New York. Map 1: B-6; Map 3: D-5. Settlement surveyed around 1800. Incorporated as village, 1813, but mostly destroyed later that year during War of 1812. Became major center of trade with completion of Erie Canal, 1825. Incorporated as city, 1832. 1830 population about 8,600. 1835 population about 20,000.

Burlington, Burlington Township, Des Moines County, Iowa Territory (now state). Map 9: B-5. Settled around 1833. Capital of Wisconsin Territory, 1837; capital of Iowa Territory, 1838–1841. 1836 population about 500. 1855 population about 11,000.

Caldwell County, Missouri. MAP 8: B-3; MAP 9: C-2. Described in 1886 as "one-third timber and two-thirds prairie." Much of terrain cut deeply by creeks. Missouri state legislature created county for Latter-day Saints, 29 Dec. 1836, in attempt to solve "Mormon problem." Major Mormon immigration followed. Summer 1838 population around 5,000 with at least nineteen Mormon settlements. Expansion of Mormon settlements beyond county brought conflict between Saints and other Missourians that escalated into violence. Governor Lilburn W. Boggs ordered that Saints be exterminated or driven from state, Oct. 1838. State militia took JS and other Mormon leaders as prisoners and forced remaining Saints to leave. Almost all Caldwell Co. Saints evacuated by spring 1839. 1840 population less than 1,500.

Cambria Township, Niagara County, New York. MAP 3: C-5.

Cambridge Township, Washington County, New York. MAP 3: C-10. Settled by New England squatters, 1760s. Included Cambridge village. More heavily settled by Scottish Presbyterian immigrants who clustered in settlement named Coila, where Robert Matthews grew up.

Campbell County, Kentucky. MAP 4: F-2.

Canada. MAP 1: A-6; MAP 2: A-11; MAP 3: B-6. In late eighteenth and early nineteenth centuries, Americans and British subjects used term *Canada* in reference to British colonies of Upper Canada and Lower Canada in North America. Former territory of Canada divided into Upper Canada and Lower Canada, 1791; reunited, 1841. 1830 populations for Lower Canada and Upper Canada about 500,000 and 230,000, respectively. JS proselytized in Upper Canada, Oct. 1833. Many Saints who were baptized into LDS church in Canada emigrated to Mormon communities in U.S. Boundaries corresponded roughly to present-day Ontario (Upper Canada) and Quebec (Lower Canada), with exception of unclear western boundary.

Catlin Township, Tioga (now in Chemung) County, New York. MAP 3: D-7.

Cattaraugus County, New York. MAP 3: D-5.

Centreville (now Centerville) Township, Allegany County, New York. MAP 3: D-5. Included Centreville post office and settlement.

Chardon Township, Geauga County, Ohio. MAP 4: C-5. 1830 population about 900. Included Chardon town, platted in 1808 and selected as Geauga Co. seat because of central location though only sparsely inhabited through 1810s. JS and other Latter-day Saints occasionally traveled to Chardon for legal business or to visit local church members. JS's sisters Katharine Smith Salisbury and Sophronia Smith Stoddard resided in or near Chardon Township.

Chariton County, Missouri. MAP 8: B-5; MAP 9: C-3.

Chautauque (now Chautauqua) County, New York. MAP 3: D-4.

Chenango County, New York. MAP 3: D-8. Created 1798. 1830 population about 37,000.

China (now Arcade) Township, Genesee (now in Wyoming) County, New York. MAP 3: D-5.

Cincinnati, Hamilton County, Ohio. MAP 1: C-5; MAP 4: E-2.

City hall, Far West, Rockford (now in Mirabile) Township, Caldwell County, Missouri. NOT LOCATED. NOT MAPPED. Far West schoolhouse apparently also functioned as city hall and courthouse as well as church meetinghouse. Probably a schoolhouse located in town's southwest quarter school lot. See also "Schoolhouse, Far West."

Clay County, Missouri. MAP 8: C-3; MAP 9: C-2. County organized from Ray Co., 1822. Originally included land now part of several surrounding counties. 1830 population about 5,300. 1836 population about 8,500. 1840 population about 8,300. Refuge for Latter-day Saints driven out of Jackson Co., 1833. 1834 Mormon population about 1,200. Citizens demanded Saints leave, summer 1836. Most Saints migrated to newly formed Caldwell Co. by 1838. During Mormon-Missourian conflict, militia from Clay Co. assembled to combat Mormons but did not fight. JS spent winter 1838–1839 in jail at county seat, Liberty.

Clermont County, Ohio. MAP 4: E-2.

Cleveland, Cleveland Township, Cuyahoga County, Ohio. MAP 1: B-5; MAP 3: E-2; MAP 4: C-5. Described in 1833 as occupying "an elevated point below the entrance of Cuyahoga r[iver] into lake Erie." First settled 1797. Incorporated as village, 1815. Incorporated as city, 1836. Transformed into center of business and trade at opening of Ohio and Erie Canal in 1827. 1830 population about 1,100. 1835 population about 5,100. Often visited by JS and Latter-day Saints residing in and around Kirtland for commercial purposes or en route to other locations.

Cobourg, Hamilton Township, Northumberland County, Newcastle District, Upper Canada (now in Ontario, Canada). MAP 3: C-5. First settled 1790s. Located on York-Kingston stagecoach road. 1832 population over 1,000. Incorporated as village, 1837.

Colborne (now in Simcoe), Townsend Township, Norfolk County, London District, Upper Canada (now in Norfolk County, Ontario, Canada). MAP 3: D-3. First settled 1798.

Collins Township, Erie County, New York. MAP 3: D-5.

Columbus, Franklin County, Ohio. MAP 1: C-5; MAP 4: E-3. Incorporated as borough, 1816. Incorporated as city, Feb. 1834. Franklin Co. seat. Capital of Ohio.

Commerce (now Nauvoo), Hancock County, Illinois. MAP 1: B-3; MAP 9: B-5; MAP 10: C-5; MAP 11. Located just upstream from first chain of rapids on Mississippi River. From bank of river, several feet above high-water mark, ground described as nearly level for six or seven blocks then gradually sloping sixty to seventy feet up to what later became temple block. After ascent, ground was level and continued into prairie. European Americans settled, 1820s. Laid out 1834. Known as town, 1837. Adjacent town, Commerce City, laid out 1837; both square with shore of river, as opposed to later east-west orientation of Nauvoo plat. Described in 1837 as having two stores, one grocery, and twelve or fifteen families. Panic of 1837 created buyers' market for land at Commerce and Commerce City. Latter-day Saints who resided at Quincy, Illinois, after expulsion from Missouri planned settlement in area and began purchasing large tracts of land including Commerce City and part of Commerce, 1839. JS moved with family to Commerce, May 1839, into log house on bank of river. When post office changed from Commerce to Nauvoo in Apr. 1840, entire area became known as Nauvoo.

Committee store, Kirtland, Kirtland Township, Geauga (now in Lake) County, Ohio. NOT LOCATED. NOT MAPPED. Established by temple building committee to support those working on House of the Lord in Kirtland.

Connecticut. Map 1: B-7; Map 2: B-12; Map 3: E-11.

Copley Township, Medina (now in Summit) County, Ohio. Map 4: C-5. Formed 1819. 1830 population about 410.

Daviess County, Missouri. Map 8: B-3; Map 9: C-2. Created from Ray Co., Dec. 1836. Described in 1874 as "equally divided between gently rolling prairie and fine timber lands." European Americans settled, 1830. Sparsely inhabited until 1838. Small number of Mormons settled by 1837. JS led expedition into county to survey possible future settlements for Latter-day Saints, May 1838. Significant Mormon settlements in county were Adam-ondi-Ahman, Marrowbone, Honey Creek, and Lick Fork. As Mormon population of county grew, so did antagonism of neighboring Missourians who feared Saints would soon dominate county. On election day, candidate William Peniston denounced right of Saints to vote and violence erupted, 6 Aug. 1838. JS and others traveled to county to help Saints. Vigilantes from neighboring counties joined Daviess residents to harass and intimidate Saints in county. Anticipating attack, Saints made preemptive strike, plundering and burning property in Millport, Gallatin, and Grindstone Fork, settlements known to harbor vigilantes. Responding to reports of Mormon depredations, Missouri governor Lilburn W. Boggs ordered state militia to area; issued new order to exterminate Saints or drive them from state, Oct. 1838. Ultimatum given essentially compelling all Saints to leave county, early Nov. 1838. Many moved to Caldwell Co., where they stayed until moving to Illinois and Iowa, winter–spring 1839. 1840 population about 2,800.

Deerfield Township, Oneida County, New York. Map 3: C-8.

De Witt, Grand River (now in De Witt) Township, Carroll County, Missouri. Map 8: C-5; Map 9: C-3. Located on bluffs north of Missouri River, about eight miles above mouth of Grand River. First settled 1821. Laid out with name Elderport, 1836. Name changed to De Witt when acquired by land speculator Henry Root, 1837, who later interested church leaders in its strategic location. Though seventy miles from Far West, provided port at confluence of Grand and Missouri rivers for importing goods needed by Latter-day Saints in northern Missouri and for exporting their farm products. Latter-day Saints from Ohio began moving into area, July 1838. Saints faced sustained opposition on arrival. Vigilantes besieged Saints in De Witt in attempt to expel them from area, 1 Oct. 1838. Saints surrendered residency, 11 Oct. 1838. About 400 Saints abandoned homes and property. Missouri River, which flowed near De Witt in 1830s, now flows more than a mile east of town.

Elders School, Kirtland, Kirtland Township, Geauga (now in Lake) County, Ohio. Not mapped. Initially held in lower floor of schoolhouse. Moved to third floor of House of the Lord, in room adjoining westernmost room where Hebrew School met, 18 Jan. 1836. See also "Schoolhouse, Kirtland" and "House of the Lord, Kirtland," in this directory; and "School of the Prophets," in Glossary.

Elk Creek Township, Erie County, Pennsylvania. Map 3: E-3. Incorporated 1800. 1830 population about 560. Situated on Elk Creek. Included Elk Creek post office. JS traveled through during missions, 1833, 1834.

Ellicottville Township, Cattaraugus County, New York. Map 3: D-5. Formed 1820. 1830 population about 630. Included Ellicottville village, Cattaraugus Co. seat, incorporated 1837. Three taverns reported in village, 1836.

Erie County, New York. MAP 3: D-5.

Erie County, Pennsylvania. MAP 3: D-3.

Fairview post office, Fairview, Farmersville (now in Freedom) Township, Cattaraugus County, New York. NOT MAPPED.

Farmersville Township, Cattaraugus County, New York. MAP 3: D-5. Formed 1812. 1830 population about 1,000. Included Farmersville village, with post office, and Fairview post office. JS traveled through on mission, Mar. 1834.

Far West, Rockford (now in Mirabile) Township, Caldwell County, Missouri. MAP 1: C-3; MAP 8: B-3; MAP 9: C-2. Town site purchased 1836, before Caldwell Co. was organized for Latter-day Saints in Missouri. Originally Missouri church presidency counselors William W. Phelps and John Whitmer held land in trust for church. Warren Foote described town site as "high rolling prairie" between Shoal and Goose creeks. Had 150 houses by 1838. During Mormon period, population as high as about 3,000 to 5,000. Foote described homes as "very scattering, and small, being chiefly built of hewed logs." Had four dry goods stores, three family groceries, six blacksmith shops, two hotels, printing office (where *Elders' Journal* was printed), and at least two schoolhouses. Temple planned; cornerstones laid 4 July 1838. Although Latter-day Saints wanted Far West designated as Caldwell Co. seat, it never became such. JS's home from 14 Mar. 1838 until 31 Oct. 1838. As church headquarters, was center of Mormon activity in Missouri. Site where Saints surrendered and Missouri militia took JS and other leaders prisoner, late Oct. and early Nov. 1838, after Missouri governor Lilburn W. Boggs issued order to exterminate Saints or drive them from state. Leaders were sent to jail, and remaining Saints were forced to leave state.

"The flats," Kirtland, Kirtland Township, Geauga (now in Lake) County, Ohio. NOT MAPPED. Lowlands on north end of Kirtland, where John Johnson inn, Newel K. Whitney store, and old schoolhouse were located. Location of intersection of the two main roads through Kirtland.

"Forks of Grand River," unorganized area attached to Clinton County (now in Gentry County), Missouri. MAP 8: A-3; MAP 9: B-2. Also known as Three Forks for convergence of west fork, middle fork, and east fork of Grand River. About thirty miles northwest of Adam-ondi-Ahman. Area settled 1834. First Mormon settlers, among whom were many Canadian Saints, arrived 1838. First Presidency visited Canadian Saints, 11 Aug. 1838; JS counseled them to leave for Adam-ondi-Ahman or Far West. Within three months, Missourians forced Saints to leave area.

Fountain Green, Hancock County, Illinois. MAP 9: B-6. Latter-day Saints settled among earlier inhabitants, 1839.

Freedom Township, Cattaraugus County, New York. MAP 3: D-5. Settled 1811. Township created 1820. 1835 population about 1,800. Warren Cowdery appointed to preside over Latter-day Saints in area. JS preached at Freedom, 1834. Freedom branch had 70 members, 1835. Included Freedom village.

"French Farm," Kirtland, Kirtland Township, Geauga (now in Lake) County, Ohio. NOT MAPPED. 103 acres formerly owned by Peter French. Purchased for LDS church for $5,000, 1833. Area used to build houses, including JS's, and community buildings, such as new schoolhouse and House of the Lord. Kirtland residents called area "French Farm" as late as 1838. Much of land later deeded to John Johnson Jr.

Gallatin, Honey Creek (now in Union) Township, Daviess County, Missouri. MAP 8: B-4; MAP 9: C-3. Laid out and planned as county seat, 1837, and considered as such, but designation not official until 1841. Incorporated as town, 1851. Incorporated as city, 1857. 1860 population about 450. Several Latter-day Saints attempted to vote at Gallatin but were attacked by local Missourians, 6 Aug. 1838. After Mormon-Missouri conflict broke out, Saints launched preemptive strike against anti-Mormon vigilantes in Gallatin, Oct. 1838.

Geauga County, Ohio. MAP 3: E-2; MAP 4: C-5. First settled 1798. Created from Trumbull Co., 1805. Soil described in 1833 as "tolerably well watered, but heavily timbered." Settled largely by New Englanders. 1830 population about 16,000. County seat Chardon. Latter-day Saints operated under Geauga Co. jurisdiction during stay in Kirtland, often traveling to Chardon for legal and other business. Lake Co. formed from Geauga's seven northern townships, including Kirtland, 1840.

Genesee County, New York. MAP 3: D-5.

Geneseo, Geneseo Township, Livingston County, New York. MAP 3: D-6. Incorporated as village, 1832. 1842 population about 900. 1835 population of township about 2,700. Geneseo branch of LDS church had twenty-four members, 1835.

Grand River. MAP 8: A-3; MAP 9: B-2. Grand River valley described in 1837 as "fertile, well-timbered country, that is beginning to attract emigrants, and is now settling very fast." Lyman Wight built cabin near river at future site of Adam-ondi-Ahman, Feb. 1838. JS and others surveyed land near river for future Mormon settlement, May 1838. Described in 1839 as "navigable for small vessels." Farming along river caused heavy silting, making navigation increasingly difficult, and by 1870 navigation in Daviess Co., Missouri, entirely ceased.

"Grove," Commerce (now Nauvoo), Hancock County, Illinois. NOT LOCATED. NOT MAPPED. Before completion of Nauvoo temple, all large meetings were held outdoors. Several groves located near temple, on west and east apparently, had stands for speakers.

Grove Creek, Daviess County, Missouri. MAP 8: A-4. Probably present-day Pilot Grove Creek, which runs through Grand River Township northeast of Adam-ondi-Ahman.

Guymon's horse mill, Blythe Township, Caldwell County, Missouri. MAP 8: B-3. Near small Mormon settlement. Probably within current Kingston Township.

"Halfway house." See "Littlefield's halfway house."

Hancock County, Illinois. MAP 9: B-5; MAP 10: E-5. Formed from Pike Co., 1825. Described in 1837 as predominantly prairie and "deficient in timber." 1830 population about 480. 1835 population about 3,200. 1840 population about 9,900. Early settlers mainly from middle and southern states. Included Commerce (later Nauvoo), where Latter-day Saints eventually reestablished themselves, 1839–1846, following expulsion from Missouri, 1838. Saints also settled in several other communities throughout Hancock Co. JS shot and killed at jail in county seat, Carthage, 1844.

Hebrew School, Kirtland, Kirtland Township, Geauga (now in Lake) County, Ohio. NOT MAPPED. Usually held in westernmost of five rooms in third, or attic, story of House of the Lord in Kirtland. Room also used by JS as ecclesiastical office space and intended as translating room. See also "Hebrew School," in Glossary.

Herkimer County, New York. NOT MAPPED.

Honey Creek, Honey Creek and Grindstone (now in Liberty, Sheridan, Union, and Monroe) townships, Daviess County, Missouri. MAP 8: B-4. Large navigable branch of Grand River named for "bee trees" along banks. Settled by Latter-day Saints by Nov. 1837.

House of the Lord (planned site), Far West, Rockford (now in Mirabile) Township, Caldwell County, Missouri. NOT MAPPED. Plans for Far West included house of the Lord, or temple, on central block. Latter-day Saints in Caldwell Co. made preparations for construction and commenced excavating foundation, 3 July 1837. However, while JS was visiting Latter-day Saints in Far West, decision was made to postpone work on temple until "the Lord shall reveal it to be his will to be commenced." JS revelation directed that temple be built, 26 Apr. 1838. According to John W. Rigdon, son of Sidney Rigdon, Far West temple was to have been similar to Kirtland temple in function, including lower floor or auditorium and upper floor to be used for school. A Caldwell Co. history states that excavation for foundation was 120 x 80 feet and 5 feet deep. Cornerstones of temple laid at northeast corner of public square, 4 July 1838. Foundation not completed when Saints expelled from state, Nov. 1838–Apr. 1839. Quorum of the Twelve commanded in July 1838 revelation to depart on European mission from temple site on 26 Apr. 1839. The Twelve, at risk of their lives, returned to Far West on that date to officially commence mission.

House of the Lord, Kirtland, Kirtland Township, Geauga (now in Lake) County, Ohio. MAP 5: E-3 (ITEM P); MAP 6: E-3 (ITEM T); MAP 7: E-3 (ITEM BB). Jan. 1831 revelation commanded Latter-day Saints to migrate to Ohio, where they were to "be endowed with power from on high." Revelation of Dec. 1832 directed Saints to "establish . . . a house of God." Revelation of 1 June 1833 chastened Saints for not building house. Cornerstones laid 23 July 1833; temple completed Mar. 1836. Had three stories: on first two floors, large rooms for assemblies; on attic level, five rooms or offices. Included variety of pulpits in tiers at either end of assembly rooms for various priesthood offices. Used for variety of purposes, both before and after dedication, including confirmations, ordinations, quorum organizations, anointings, Elders School, and Hebrew School. Temple dedicated 27 Mar. 1836 and again 31 Mar. 1836. Long-anticipated solemn assembly held 30 Mar. 1836. JS's journal records that in temple on 3 Apr. 1836, JS and Oliver Cowdery received priesthood "keys," or authority, from ancient prophets Moses, Elias, and Elijah and saw Jesus Christ. See also "Hebrew School" and "School of the Prophets," in Glossary.

"Hudson Seminary." Western Reserve College, Hudson Township, Portage (now in Summit) County, Ohio. NOT MAPPED. Charter obtained for college at Hudson, 1826. 1830s curriculum consisted of theology, languages, philosophy, and mathematics. 1830 faculty consisted of president and three known permanent teachers, one of whom was assigned languages, likely Latin and Greek. Joshua Seixas taught Hebrew there, Dec. 1835–Jan. 1836, not as part of curriculum but apparently in cooperation with college. College moved to Cleveland, 1882.

Hudson Township, Portage (now in Summit) County, Ohio. MAP 4: C-5. Settled about 1800. Organized by 1802. 1830 population about 780. Included Hudson village, incorporated 1837. Western Reserve College chartered 1826.

Huntsville, Salt Spring Township, Randolph County, Missouri. MAP 9: C-4. Settled 1829. Randolph Co. seat. Described in 1837 as having brick courthouse and seven stores but no church buildings. Latter-day Saints traveling to and from Missouri often passed through Huntsville, which was on established road.

Iowa Territory (now state). MAP 1: B-2; MAP 2: C-8. Organized as territory containing all present-day Iowa, much of present-day Minnesota, and parts of North and South Dakota, 1838. 1840 population about 43,000. Several Mormon communities established in Iowa across Mississippi River from Commerce (later Nauvoo), Illinois, especially communities within Zarahemla stake, centered at Montrose, 1839 and early 1840s. 1841 population of Zarahemla stake about 750, but stake then reduced to branch as most Latter-day Saints moved to Commerce. JS visited Iowa, Apr.–May and July 1839.

Jackson County, Missouri. MAP 8: C-3; MAP 9: D-2. Described as originally containing half timber and half prairie. Settled 1808 at Fort Osage, a defensive military base and Indian trading post. Organized 1826. Named after U.S. president Andrew Jackson. Contained fertile lands along Missouri River as well as Santa Fe Trail entrepôt, attracting immigration from other parts of state. 1830 population about 2,800. Size reduced considerably in 1833 by creation of Van Buren and Bates counties from southern portion. 1836 population about 4,500. 1840 population about 7,600. JS appointed missionaries to proselytize among Indians living west of Missouri, autumn 1830. Latter-day Saints first entered Jackson Co., Jan. 1831. JS revelation of July 1831 designated Independence as "the center place" of Zion, where Saints were to gather and build temple, and instructed Saints to buy up land in Independence and westward to border of county/state. Saints purchased land and settled in Independence and four additional communities to the west. 1832 Mormon population about 810. Summer 1833 Mormon population about 1,200. Mob violence erupted as increasing numbers of Saints entered Missouri, July 1833. Earlier settlers forcibly expelled Saints from county by November. Most displaced Saints settled across Missouri River in Clay Co. JS led group of Saints on Zion's Camp expedition in failed effort to redeem Mormon lands in Jackson Co., summer 1834. See also "Zion."

Jefferson County, New York. MAP 3: B-8. Latter-day Saint proselytizing in county very successful, 1830s.

John Johnson inn, Kirtland, Kirtland Township, Geauga (now in Lake) County, Ohio. MAP 6: C-4 (ITEM J); MAP 7: C-4 (ITEM J). Two-story building built by Peter French, 1827. First brick building in Kirtland. Common room had capacity for fifty people. Purchased by LDS church, 1833, and managed by Newel K. Whitney. John Johnson Sr. granted license to keep tavern or inn there, 5 Apr. 1834. Office for church and first printing establishment in Kirtland. Egyptian mummies and papyri displayed at inn. See also "Printing office, Kirtland."

Kirtland, Kirtland Township, Geauga (now in Lake) County, Ohio. MAP 1: B-5; MAP 3: E-2; MAP 4: C-5; MAP 5; MAP 6; MAP 7. Settled 1810. Township organized 1817. Kirtland community not incorporated until twentieth century. Governance during Mormon period at township level. 1831 population in Kirtland Township about 70 Latter-day Saints and 1,100 others. 1838 population about 2,000 Saints and 1,200 others. 1839 population about 100 Saints and 1,500 others. Sidney Rigdon, then Reformed Baptist preacher, had following there, beginning 1826. Many of his followers joined LDS church, 1830. Church membership grew quickly, and Kirtland community became headquarters of church as well as JS's home, 1831. Kirtland organized as "stake of Zion," with presidency,

bishopric, and high council. House of the Lord built 1833–1836. JS and other Saints participated in School of the Prophets as well as other schools devoted to wide variety of subjects,
including Hebrew. Mormon press in Kirtland published newspapers, hymnal, second
edition of Book of Mormon, and Doctrine and Covenants. Rapid immigration of Saints
posed difficulty for both Saints and others. With increased demand for land in Kirtland,
prices rose. Need for capital led to establishment of Kirtland Safety Society, but failure to
obtain state charter, negative publicity, and other problems led to failure of bank. Under
threats from dissidents and outside antagonists, JS and other church leaders fled Kirtland,
early 1838. Other loyal Saints followed.

Lamb's tavern, Ashtabula Township, Ashtabula County, Ohio. Not mapped. An
1833 Ohio gazetteer lists two taverns in Ashtabula Township: one in Ashtabula borough,
one in Ashtabula East village. Both likely located on main road through Ashtabula
Township.

Laona, Pomfret Township, Chautauque (now Chautauqua) County, New York.
Map 3: D-4. Village with about forty domiciles, 1836. 1842 population about 400.

Le Ray Township, Jefferson County, New York. Map 3: B-8.

Liberty, Liberty Township, Clay County, Missouri. Map 8: C-3; Map 9: C-2.
Settled mainly by Kentuckians, 1820s. Incorporated as town, 1829. Clay Co. seat. Described
in 1837 as having fourteen stores and four groceries. After expulsion from Jackson Co.,
many Latter-day Saints found refuge in Clay Co., 1833. During expulsion of Mormons from
Missouri, 1838, JS spent winter 1838–1839 in jail at Liberty.

Littlefield's "halfway house," Honey Creek Township, Daviess County, Missouri.
Map 8: B-3. Residence on Dog Creek about halfway between Far West and Adam-ondi-
Ahman owned by Latter-day Saint Waldo Littlefield. Described as "log building perhaps
twenty feet square."

Livingston County, Missouri. Map 8: B-4; Map 9: C-3. Organized 1837. 1840 population about 4,300.

Livingston County, New York. Map 3: D-6.

Livonia Township, Livingston County, New York. Map 3: D-6. Created 1808. 1830
population about 2,700. Included Livonia village.

**Lodi (now Gowanda), Perrysburg and Collins townships, Cattaraugus and Erie
counties, New York.** Map 3: D-5. Settled 1816. Called Lodi, 1826. Incorporated as Gowanda
village, 1848. Straddled Cattaraugus River and thus was in two different townships and two
different counties. 1842 population about 700. Cattaraugus Co. portion of Lodi transferred
from Perrysburg to Persia Township when that township was created, 1835.

Macomb, McDonough County, Illinois. Map 9: B-6. Incorporated as city, 1841.
McDonough Co. seat. JS's brother Don Carlos Smith lived nearby, 1839.

Manchester Township, Ontario County, New York. Map 3: D-6. Settled 1793.
Formed 1821. 1830 population about 2,800. Smith family farm in northwest corner of township, 1819–1829. JS reported that his first vision of Deity occurred in woodland on or near
family's township property, 1820. JS also reported that angel appeared to him in 1823 and
told him about gold plates buried in hill in Manchester Township, about three miles from
Smith home. JS visited hill, now known as Hill Cumorah, annually 1823–1827, until he

obtained plates and began translation of Book of Mormon. Family left area, late 1830. See also "Palmyra Township."

McDonough County, Illinois. MAP 9: B-6. Formed from Pike Co., 1825, but not organized until 1829. 1835 population about 2,900. 1840 population about 5,300.

"Medical University." Willoughby Medical College, Willoughby, Willoughby Township, Cuyahoga (now in Lake) County, Ohio. NOT MAPPED. Also known as "medical school" or "Willoughby University." First phase in what was hoped to be four colleges as part of Willoughby University of Lake Erie. Established 1834. Dissolved by 1847. Daniel Peixotto was teaching at medical college when Latter-day Saint leaders asked him to come to Kirtland to teach Hebrew.

Medina County, Ohio. MAP 4: C-5. Organized 1818. 1830 population about 7,600. Summit Co. formed from Portage, Medina, and Stark counties, 1840.

"Mentor Street." Mentor Road (now Mentor Avenue or U.S. 20), Geauga County, Ohio. NOT MAPPED. Road running southwest from Painesville to Mentor. Intersected with road leading south into Kirtland.

Michigan Territory (now state). MAP 1: A-4; MAP 2: B-9. Organized as territory, 1805. De facto state government organized within territory, 1836, although not formally recognized as state by federal government until 1837.

Mill Creek (settlement), Blythe Township (now in Hamilton and Kingston townships), Caldwell County, Missouri. MAP 8: B-3. Brigham Young purchased eighty acres on Mill Creek, 1837. JS revelation in 1838 directed Young to settle family on this land.

Missouri. MAP 1: C-3; MAP 2: C-8. Area acquired by U.S. in Louisiana Purchase, 1803. Established as territory, 1812. Thousands immigrated, mainly from South. Missouri Compromise, 1820, allowed Missouri into Union as slave state, 1821. 1830 population about 140,000. 1836 population about 240,000. 1840 population about 380,000. JS revelation designated vicinity of Independence, Jackson Co., as "center place" of Zion, 1831, and Latter-day Saints began immigrating. Whereas most Missouri immigrants came from western frontier of American South, most Saints immigrated from Northeast. Regional and cultural differences caused tension and eventually violence. Saints driven from Jackson Co. to Clay and other counties in state, 1833. Clay Co. citizens demanded Saints leave county, 1836, and Missouri state legislature created Caldwell Co. specifically for Saints. JS moved to Far West in Caldwell Co., which became new church headquarters, 1838. Saints expanded northward into Daviess Co. and eastward into Carroll Co. Conflict in Daviess and Carroll counties escalated to point that Missouri governor Lilburn W. Boggs issued order to exterminate Saints or drive them from state. JS taken prisoner by Missouri militia, late 1838, and incarcerated through winter in jail at Liberty, Clay Co., while Saints driven from state. See also "Zion."

Missouri River. MAP 9: C-1. Described in 1839 as having currents of about five to six miles per hour above confluence with Mississippi River, with flooding season March–July. Major westward travel route, with landing three miles from Independence courthouse, Jackson Co., Missouri.

Monroe County, Missouri. MAP 9: C-4. Organized 1831.

Montrose Township, Lee County, Iowa Territory (now state). MAP 9: B-5. Fort Des Moines military barracks established near Mississippi River, 1834; abandoned, 1837.

Settlement in vicinity named Montrose, 1837. Township created 1841. Included Montrose town. Several Latter-day Saints settled in township after being driven from Missouri, 1838–1839. Center of Zarahemla stake, formed while Saints headquartered at Nauvoo, Illinois.

Mount Pleasant, Brantford Township, Wentworth County, Gore District, Upper Canada (now in Brant County, Ontario, Canada). Map 3: C-3. 1846 population about 130. JS preached at Mount Pleasant and baptized several people during mission to Upper Canada, Oct. 1833.

Nelson's ferry, Honey Creek and Grand River townships (now in Union Township), Daviess County, Missouri. Map 8: B-4. Various owners operated ferry at confluence of Grand River and Honey Creek beginning in 1831.

Newburgh Township, Cuyahoga County, Ohio. Map 4: C-5. Also spelled "Newburg." Formed 1814. 1830 population about 870. Included Newburgh village. Now part of metropolitan Cleveland.

Newbury, Miami Township, Clermont County, Ohio. Map 4: E-2. Also spelled "Newberry." Probably now Mulberry.

New Portage, Norton Township, Medina (now in Summit) County, Ohio. Map 4: C-5. Settled by 1815. Almost annihilated by epidemic in late 1820s, possibly typhus. Home of one of largest branches of LDS church, early 1830s. JS attended several church conferences in New Portage. Participants in march of Zion's Camp expedition traveling with JS gathered initially at New Portage, first week of May 1834.

New York. Map 1: B-6; Map 2: B-11; Map 3. Admitted as state, 1788. 1805 population about 770,000. 1830 population about 1,900,000. 1835 population about 2,200,000. 1840 population about 2,400,000. Heavy European immigration to U.S. through harbor of New York City. Canals, particularly Erie Canal completed in 1825, escalated inland commercial activity. Western New York known as "burned-over district" during JS's early life because of numerous religious revivals of Second Great Awakening. Smith family lived in New York, 1816–1831. JS married in South Bainbridge (now Afton), 1827. Book of Mormon published in Palmyra, 1830. LDS church organized, 1830. Three main branches of church in 1830 at Fayette, Manchester, and Colesville. Latter-day Saints emigrated, 1831. JS traveled through New York in 1832, 1833, 1834, 1836, and 1837.

New York City, New York County, New York. Map 1: B-7; Map 3: F-10. Incorporated 1665. Before 1898, covered only Manhattan Island. Harbor contributed to dramatic economic and population growth. By 1790, largest city in U.S. 1830 population of New York city and county about 200,000. 1840 population about 310,000.

Niagara County, New York. Map 3: C-5.

Norton Township, Medina (now in Summit) County, Ohio. Map 4: C-5. Settled 1810. Formed 1818 from Wolf Creek Township. Location of reported "great Mormon excitement," 1832–1838. 1830 population about 650. Until 1830, primarily populated by immigrants from New England; heavy German Pennsylvanian immigration began, 1830s. Included New Portage town, where Mormon missionaries proselytized and organized large branch of church.

Ohio. Map 1: B-5; Map 2: B-10; Map 4. French exploration, 1669. British possession following French and Indian War, 1763. Ceded to U.S., 1783. Permanent white settlement, 1788. Admitted as state, 1803. 1830 population about 940,000. 1840 population about

1,500,000. Mormon missionaries preached in Western Reserve of northeastern Ohio, Oct. 1830. After Reformed Baptist preacher Sidney Rigdon and many of his congregants joined LDS church, JS revelation declared "the Ohio" was to be first formal gathering place of newly organized church. JS's home and church headquarters, 1831–1838.

Olah Shinehah. NOT MAPPED. Associated with Adam-ondi-Ahman. Shinehah defined as "sun" and Olea as "moon" in JS's translated book of Abraham. See also "Adam-ondi-Ahman."

Onondaga County, New York. MAP 3: D-7.

"Painesville Bank." Bank of Geauga, Painesville, Painesville Township, Geauga **(now in Lake) County, Ohio.** NOT MAPPED. Organized 1831, with capital stock of $100,000. Originally located on first floor of building at corner of Main and State streets in Painesville village. New building completed 1836. Made loan to JS, 1835.

Painesville Township, Geauga (now in Lake) County, Ohio. MAP 4: C-5. Created and settled 1800. 1830 population about 1,500. Flourished economically because of location at harbor on Lake Erie and on major route of overland travel for western migration. Included Painesville village, laid out about 1805. Incorporated as town, 1832. Disputed with smaller Chardon over location of county seat. County seat of newly formed Lake Co., 1840. Early center of anti-Mormon activities. JS arrested and tried in Painesville several times.

Palmyra Township, Wayne County, New York. MAP 1: B-6; MAP 3: C-6. First permanent white settlement, ca. 1789. 1810 population about 2,100. 1830 population about 3,400. Joseph Smith Sr. family lived in or near Palmyra, 1816–1830. JS had 5,000 copies of Book of Mormon printed at E. B. Grandin printing office on Main Street in Palmyra village, 1829–1830. Printing financed by Palmyran Martin Harris, who pledged his 300-acre farm located just north of village as collateral and later sold 151 acres to pay for it. Smith family left Palmyra Township, late 1830. See also "Manchester Township."

Paris, Edgar County, Illinois. NOT MAPPED. Land for village donated 1823. 1837 population about 280. 1843 population about 350. Not officially organized and incorporated until 1849.

Perrysburg Township, Cattaraugus County, New York. MAP 3: D-4. Also spelled "Perrysburgh." Created 1814. Known as "Perry" until 1818. 1830 population about 2,400. 1835 population about 1,600. Dayton Township formed from Perrysburg, 1835. Branch of LDS church organized in Perrysburg, 1833; within new Dayton Township, 1835.

Perry Township, Geauga (now in Lake) County, Ohio. MAP 4: C-5. Settled 1808. Township formed 1815. 1830 population about 1,100. Included Perry village.

Pittsburgh, Allegheny County, Pennsylvania. MAP 1: B-6. Also spelled "Pittsburg." 1830 population about 13,000. 1830 greater metropolitan population about 20,000.

Pleasant Park, Grand River (now in De Witt) Township, Carroll County, Missouri. MAP 8: C-5. Located about four miles west of De Witt.

Plymouth, Hancock County, Illinois. MAP 9: B-6. Village where members of JS's family lived. His sister Katharine Smith Salisbury lived with her husband in Plymouth, 1838. His brother William Smith moved to farm there, 1839. William Smith owned tavern in Plymouth that his brother Samuel Smith came to manage in 1842.

Portage County, Ohio. MAP 4: C-5. Included Hiram, where JS lived 1831–1832. Also included Hudson, location of Western Reserve College, where Joshua Seixas was teaching when church representatives arranged with him to provide Hebrew instruction to Latter-day Saints in Kirtland.

Potsdam Township, St. Lawrence County, New York. MAP 3: B-8. Included Potsdam village, incorporated 1831. Joseph Smith Sr. visited township with son Don Carlos Smith, 1830, and with brother John Smith, 1836, to proselytize members of extended Smith family.

Printing office, Kirtland, Kirtland Township, Geauga (now in Lake) County, Ohio. MAP 6: E-3 (ITEM S); MAP 7: E-3 (ITEM AA). After printing office in Independence, Missouri, was destroyed, JS and other church leaders determined to set up print shop in Kirtland under firm name F. G. Williams & Co. Oliver Cowdery purchased press in New York, Oct. 1833. Press dedicated Dec. 1833. Printing office located in John Johnson inn until late 1834, when it was moved to second story of schoolhouse immediately west of House of the Lord. Resumed publication of Missouri newspaper *The Evening and the Morning Star* and later launched new paper, *LDS Messenger and Advocate,* which was then followed by *Elders' Journal.* Published local political paper *Northern Times,* first LDS church hymnal, first edition of Doctrine and Covenants, and second edition of Book of Mormon. Destroyed by fire, 15 Jan. 1838. See also "John Johnson inn" and "Schoolhouse, Kirtland," in this directory; and entries on the various newspapers in Works Cited.

Public square, Far West, Rockford (now in Mirabile) Township, Caldwell County, Missouri. NOT MAPPED. Three acres, including site of anticipated temple.

Putnam Township, Washington County, New York. MAP 3: C-10.

Quincy, Adams County, Illinois. MAP 9: C-5. Located on bluffs of Mississippi River. Settled 1822. Incorporated 1839. Adams Co. seat. 1837 population about 600. 1840 population about 2,300. Manufacturing and shipping center west of Chicago important because of river port. Mormon exiles from Missouri, including JS's family, found refuge in Quincy, winter 1838–1839. JS arrived in Quincy after escape from imprisonment, late Apr. 1839, and soon planned for settlement upriver in area of Commerce, Illinois. JS and family moved to Commerce (later Nauvoo), May 1839.

Ray County, Missouri. MAP 8: C-3; MAP 9: C-2. Created from Howard Co., 1820. Initially included all Missouri land north of Missouri River and west of Grand River. Seat of Fifth Judicial Circuit Court. County seat Richmond. 1830 population about 2,600. 1836 population about 6,600. 1840 population about 6,600. Latter-day Saints forcibly driven from homes in Jackson Co. crossed Missouri River and took refuge in Clay, Ray, and other counties, 1833. Caldwell Co. militia clashed with Ray Co. militia at Crooked River in unorganized territory attached to Ray Co., in attempt to rescue Mormon prisoners, 25 Oct. 1838.

Richmond, Richmond Township, Ray County, Missouri. MAP 8: C-4; MAP 9: C-3. Settled 1827. Ray Co. seat. Described in 1837 as having seven stores. 1843 population about 500. As seat of Fifth Judicial Circuit Court of Missouri, Richmond also had courthouse and jail. JS and other Latter-day Saints were incarcerated and attended preliminary hearing in Richmond to answer charges connected with Mormon-Missourian conflict, Nov. 1838.

Robinson's grove, Grindstone or Grand River Township, Daviess County, Missouri. MAP 8: A-3. Natural grove. Site of base camp for JS and others while surveying land in Daviess Co. for Mormon settlement. Possibly within sixty acres of land later allocated to survey party member George W. Robinson.

Rochester, Avon Township, Oakland County, Michigan Territory (now state). Map 4: B-3.

Rushford Township, Allegany County, New York. Map 3: D-5. Included Rushford village with 1842 population about 700.

Rutland County, Vermont. Map 3: C-10.

Salt River, Missouri. Map 9: C-5.

Schoolhouse, Far West, Rockford (now in Mirabile) Township, Caldwell County, Missouri. Not located. Not mapped. Building functioned as church meetinghouse and probably used as city hall and courthouse. Contemporary sources mention schoolhouse in 1837 and new schoolhouse in Feb. 1838 but give no specific location for either. Later sources mention schoolhouse in southwest part of town and one on central public square. Questionable whether there was schoolhouse on central public square during Mormon period. See also "City hall, Far West."

Schoolhouse, Kirtland, Kirtland Township, Geauga (now in Lake) County, Ohio. Map 6: E-3 (item S); Map 7: E-3 (item AA). Structure measuring 30 x 38 feet built autumn–winter 1834. Located immediately west of House of the Lord in Kirtland. Elders School met there until 1836. Ground floor used as schoolroom and also used as meetinghouse prior to completion of temple. Second floor housed printing office and office for presidency. Third-floor attic or loft also used for meetings. Destroyed by fire, 15 Jan. 1838. See also "Printing office, Kirtland" and "Schoolhouse on the flats, Kirtland."

"Schoolhouse on the flats," Kirtland, Kirtland Township, Geauga (now in Lake) County, Ohio. Map 5: C-4 (item N); Map 6: C-4 (item N); Map 7: C-4 (item N). First frame schoolhouse in Kirtland, built on Kirtland "flats," the lowlands on northern side of community, 1819. Latter-day Saints occasionally used for church meetings. See also "Schoolhouse, Kirtland."

Silver Creek (settlement), Hanover Township, Chautauque (now Chautauqua) County, New York. Map 3: D-4. Located at mouth of Silver Creek (or Steer Creek) on Lake Erie, in northwest corner of Hanover Township. Incorporated as village, 1848.

South Dennis, Dennis Township, Barnstable County, Massachusetts. Not mapped.

Spafford Township, Onondaga County, New York. Map 3: D-7. Included Spafford village.

Springfield Township, Erie County, Pennsylvania. Map 3: E-3. Settled 1796. Incorporated 1800. 1830 population about 1,500. 1840 population about 2,300. Mormon missionaries frequently passed through this area in travels between Ohio and New York. JS traveled through Springfield on missions, 1833, 1834. Branch of LDS church organized in Springfield, 1832.

Spring Hill. See "Adam-ondi-Ahman."

Springville, Concord Township, Erie County, New York. Map 3: D-5. Incorporated as village, Apr. 1834.

St. Catharines, Grantham Township, Lincoln County, Niagara District, Upper Canada (now in Ontario, Canada). Map 3: C-4. Founded 1790. Incorporated as town, 1845.

St. Lawrence County, New York. Map 3: B-8.

Terre Haute, Harrison Township, Vigo County, Indiana. Not mapped. Laid out and incorporated 1816. Vigo Co. seat. 1837 population about 1,100. 1843 population about 2,000.

Thompson Township, Geauga County, Ohio. Map 4: C-5. Settled 1800. Incorporated 1801. Surveyed 1809. 1830 population about 740. 1840 population about 1,000. Group of Latter-day Saints who immigrated to Ohio from Colesville, New York, were directed to settle on extensive Thompson landholdings of new convert Leman Copley, who had offered land for that purpose, May 1831. By end of June 1831, Copley revoked his invitation, and Colesville group of Saints moved to Missouri.

Tioga County, New York. Map 3: D-7.

Tower Hill, Grand River Township, Daviess County, Missouri. Not mapped. Hill adjoining Spring Hill along bluffs of Grand River in platted Spring Hill town (later Adam-ondi-Ahman).

United States of America. Map 1; Map 2. 1805 population about 6,000,000. 1830 population almost 13,000,000. 1844 population about 20,000,000.

Upper Canada. Map 1: A-5; Map 2: A-11; Map 3: B-4. British colony of Canada divided into Upper Canada and Lower Canada, 1791; reunited, 1841. Upper Canada's boundaries corresponded roughly to portion of present-day Ontario south of Hudson Bay watershed. 1840 population about 230,000. Immigrants mainly from England, Scotland, and U.S. largely displaced indigenous peoples in most fertile areas by 1830s. Principally Protestant. JS proselytized in Upper Canada, Oct. 1833.

Villanova Township, Chautauque (now Chautauqua) County, New York. Map 3: D-4. Also spelled "Villenova." Created from Hanover Township, 1823. 1830 population about 1,100. 1835 population about 1,500. 1840 population about 1,700.

Warsaw Township, Genesee (now in Wyoming) County, New York. Map 3: D-5. Included Warsaw village.

Washington County, New York. Map 3: C-10.

Waterford, Townsend Township, Norfolk County, London District, Upper Canada (now in Ontario, Canada). Map 3: D-3. Located on road between Colborne and Brantford. 1846 population about 150. Had Baptist church, two taverns, and three stores. Now part of Nanticoke city.

Wesleyville, Mill Creek Township, Erie County, Pennsylvania. Map 3: D-3. Laid out 1828. Small village of about fifteen or twenty domiciles, 1843. Named after Methodism founder John Wesley.

Westfield Township, Chautauque (now Chautauqua) County, New York. Map 3: D-4. Formed 1829. 1830 population about 2,500. 1835 population about 3,000. Included Westfield village, settled 1800 and incorporated Apr. 1833 with three churches, ten stores, four taverns, and about a hundred domiciles in 1836. Westfield branch of LDS church had about 75 members, 1835. Latter-day Saint Job Lewis hosted conferences of local church and likely housed traveling elders. JS likely stayed with Lewis when traveling through on mission to Upper Canada, Oct. 1833, and again on recruiting mission for Zion's Camp expedition, Mar. 1834. Center for fund raising and recruiting for Zion's Camp expedition, Mar. 1834.

West Lodi (post office), Lodi (now Gowanda), Perrysburg Township, Cattaraugus County, New York. NOT LOCATED. NOT MAPPED. Established ca. 1830 in Lodi village on west side of creek that divided village into two townships in two different counties.

Wight's ferry, Grand River and Grindstone (now in Grand River and Marion) townships, Daviess County, Missouri. MAP 8: B-4. Latter-day Saint Lyman Wight settled on Grand River early 1838 and established ferry half mile upstream. JS and others surveyed land at and near ferry for town named Spring Hill (later Adam-ondi-Ahman), May 1838.

Willoughby, Willoughby Township, Cuyahoga (now in Lake) County, Ohio. MAP 4: C-5. Formerly Chagrin in Chagrin Township. Home of Willoughby Medical College, after which village and township were renamed, 1834. Incorporated as village, 1853. 1839 population about 750. JS purchased goods in Willoughby, early Oct. 1835.

Zion. NOT MAPPED. Term used by early Latter-day Saints both as name for God's people generally and for a particular place where God's people dwell. JS revelation of July 1831 designated Missouri as primary area where Saints were to gather and "the place for the city of Zion." Mormon settlements elsewhere not considered Zion itself, but "stakes" of Zion. About 1,200 Mormons lived in Independence, Jackson Co., Missouri, and vicinity by summer 1833 but were driven from county by year's end. After expulsion, JS and church members continued to refer to exiled Saints residing in nearby Clay Co. and vicinity as Zion but considered their location there temporary pending return to Jackson Co. Several revelations concerned the "redemption" of Zion—reinstatement of Saints to their lands in Jackson Co. Beginning in 1837, after return to Jackson Co. in near future proved impossible, JS and Saints began also to refer to Far West, the Mormon center in Caldwell Co., Missouri, as Zion. In 1840, after Saints were driven from Missouri and established headquarters in Illinois, JS declared Zion was entire American continent and any place Saints gathered. See also "Zion" and "Stake," in Glossary.

Maps

The following eleven maps, made by professional cartographic methods, show almost every town and city mentioned in this volume of *The Joseph Smith Papers,* along with other features and boundaries, as they existed in the period indicated in the title of each map.

The three maps of Kirtland, Ohio, show all plots of land that existed within the area shown as of the date indicated in the title of each map. They list ownership of properties mentioned in the journals or otherwise relevant to this volume. All three maps show structures significant for the community or relevant to this volume for which locations have been established.

During Kirtland's economic turmoil in 1837, some property owners temporarily transferred ownership to others. Such temporary arrangements captured here include William Marks receiving title from JS and from Sidney Rigdon; Orson Hyde from Newel K. Whitney; and a number of individuals from their close relatives (see Map 7 and its corresponding key).

To locate a particular place on these maps, consult the Geographical Directory in this volume. The directory provides grid coordinates and other information for each place.

1. Volume Overview, 1832–1839
2. States, Territories, and Provinces, 1832–1839
3. New York and Vicinity, 1832–1835
4. Ohio, 1832–1839
5. Portion of Kirtland Township, Ohio, 31 December 1833
6. Portion of Kirtland Township, Ohio, 31 December 1835
7. Portion of Kirtland Township, Ohio, 12 January 1838
8. Northwest Missouri, 1832–1838
9. Northern Missouri, Western Illinois, and Southern Iowa, 1839
10. Church Land Purchases, April–August 1839
11. Church Land Purchases, Commerce, Illinois, and Vicinity, 1839

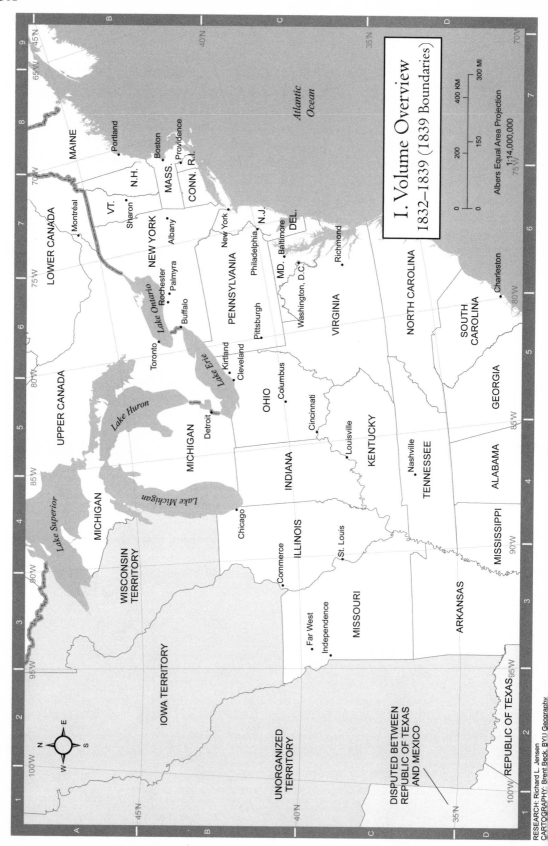

I. Volume Overview
1832–1839 (1839 Boundaries)

Albers Equal Area Projection
1:14,000,000

Atlantic
Ocean

LOWER CANADA

UPPER CANADA

MAINE

Portland

Montréal

VT.

N.H.

Boston
Providence
MASS.
CONN. R.I.

Sharon

NEW YORK

Albany

New York
N.J.
DEL.
Philadelphia
MD.
Baltimore
Washington, D.C.

PENNSYLVANIA

Pittsburgh

Lake Ontario
Rochester
Palmyra
Buffalo

Toronto

Lake Erie
Kirtland
Cleveland

Lake Huron

OHIO
Columbus

Cincinnati

VIRGINIA

Richmond

NORTH CAROLINA

SOUTH
CAROLINA

Charleston

MICHIGAN

Detroit

Lake Superior

MICHIGAN

Lake Michigan

INDIANA

KENTUCKY

Louisville

Nashville

TENNESSEE

GEORGIA

ALABAMA

WISCONSIN
TERRITORY

Chicago

ILLINOIS

St. Louis

Commerce

MISSISSIPPI

IOWA TERRITORY

Far West
Independence

MISSOURI

ARKANSAS

UNORGANIZED
TERRITORY

DISPUTED BETWEEN
REPUBLIC OF TEXAS
AND MEXICO

REPUBLIC OF TEXAS

N
W E
S

300 MI
400 KM
200
150

45°N
40°N
35°N

65°W
70°W
75°W
80°W
85°W
90°W
95°W
100°W

RESEARCH: Richard L. Jensen
CARTOGRAPHY: Brent Beck, BYU Geography

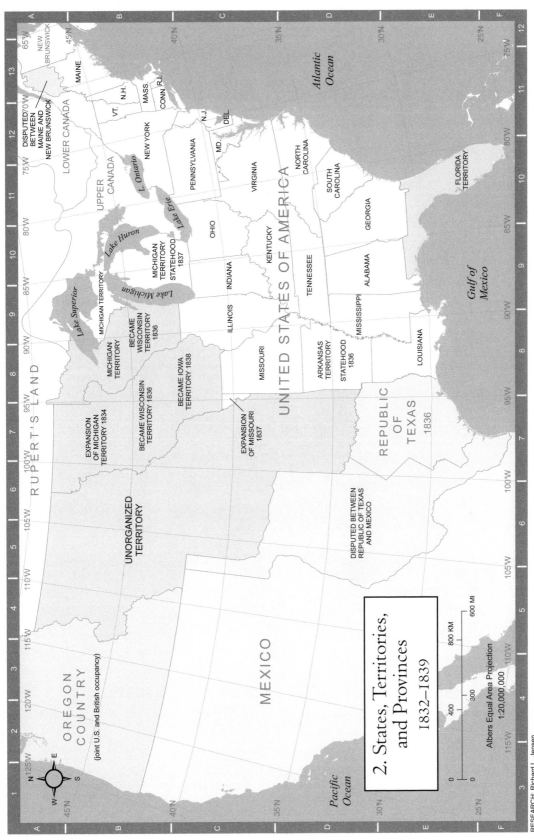

2. States, Territories, and Provinces 1832–1839

Albers Equal Area Projection
1:20,000,000

0 — 300 — 400 — 600 MI
0 — 400 — 800 KM

RESEARCH: Richard L. Jensen
CARTOGRAPHY: Brent Beck, BYU Geography

384

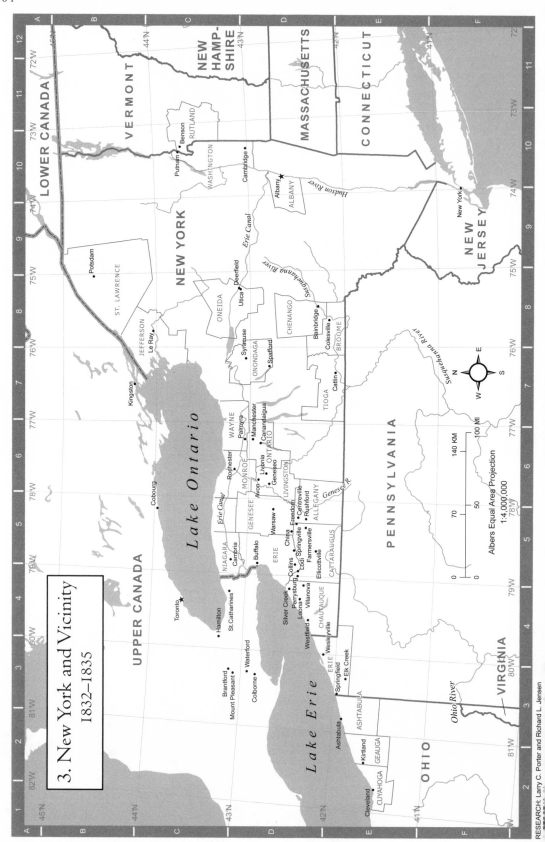

3. New York and Vicinity
1832–1835

Albers Equal Area Projection
1:4,000,000

RESEARCH: Larry C. Porter and Richard L. Jensen

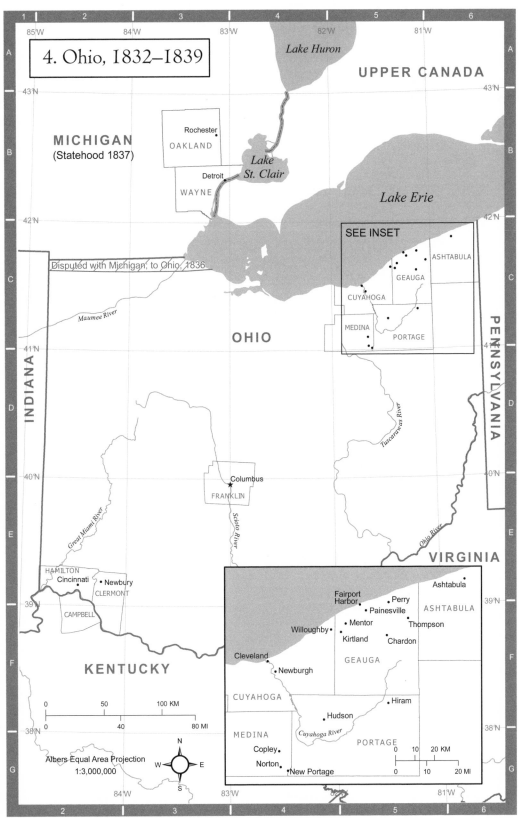

4. Ohio, 1832–1839

Lake Huron

UPPER CANADA

MICHIGAN
(Statehood 1837)

OAKLAND

Rochester

Lake
St. Clair

Detroit

WAYNE

Lake Erie

SEE INSET

ASHTABULA

GEAUGA

CUYAHOGA

Disputed with Michigan; to Ohio, 1836

Maumee River

OHIO

MEDINA

PORTAGE

PENNSYLVANIA

INDIANA

Tuscarawas River

Columbus

FRANKLIN

Scioto River

Great Miami River

Ohio River

VIRGINIA

HAMILTON

Cincinnati

Newbury

CLERMONT

CAMPBELL

KENTUCKY

Ashtabula

Fairport
Harbor

Perry

Painesville

ASHTABULA

Willoughby

Mentor

Thompson

Kirtland

Chardon

Cleveland

GEAUGA

Newburgh

CUYAHOGA

Hiram

Hudson

MEDINA

Cuyahoga River

PORTAGE

Copley

Norton

New Portage

0   50   100 KM

0   40   80 MI

Albers Equal Area Projection
1:3,000,000

N
W   E
S

0   10   20 KM

0   10   20 MI

RESEARCH: Larry C. Porter and Robin Scott Jensen
CARTOGRAPHY: Isaac Montague and Brent Beck, BYU Geography

Portion of Kirtland Township, Ohio
31 December 1833

Selected Structures
- A. Loud-Lyman gristmill
- B. Loud-Lyman sawmill
- C. Milldam
- D. Newel K. and Elizabeth Ann Whitney house
- E. N. K. Whitney & Co. red store
- F. N. K. Whitney & Co. white store
- G. Tannery
- H. Bark mill
- I. Tannery vats
- J. Newel K. Whitney brick house
- K. Distillery
- L. Sawmill
- M. Ashery
- N. Schoolhouse on the flats
- O. Methodist Episcopal church
- P. House of the Lord (temple)

Selected Properties and Owners
1. N. K. Whitney & Co.
2. N. K. Whitney & Co.
3. N. K. Whitney & Co.
4. Austin Loud
5. Newel K. Whitney
6. Newel K. Whitney
7. Elijah Smith
8. N. K. Whitney & Co.
9. N. K. Whitney & Co.
10. Elijah Smith
11. N. K. Whitney & Co.
12. N. K. Whitney & Co.
13. N. K. Whitney & Co.
14. Leonard Rich
15. Newel K. Whitney
16. Newel K. Whitney
17. Andrew Bardsley
18. Frederick G. Williams

Index of Selected Owners
Bardsley, Andrew, 17
Loud, Austin, A, B, 4
Lyman, Azariah, A, B
N. K. Whitney & Co., E, F, 1–3, 8–9, 11–13
Rich, Leonard, 14
Smith, Elijah, 7, 10
Whitney, Newel K., D, J, 5–6, 15–16
Williams, Frederick G., 18

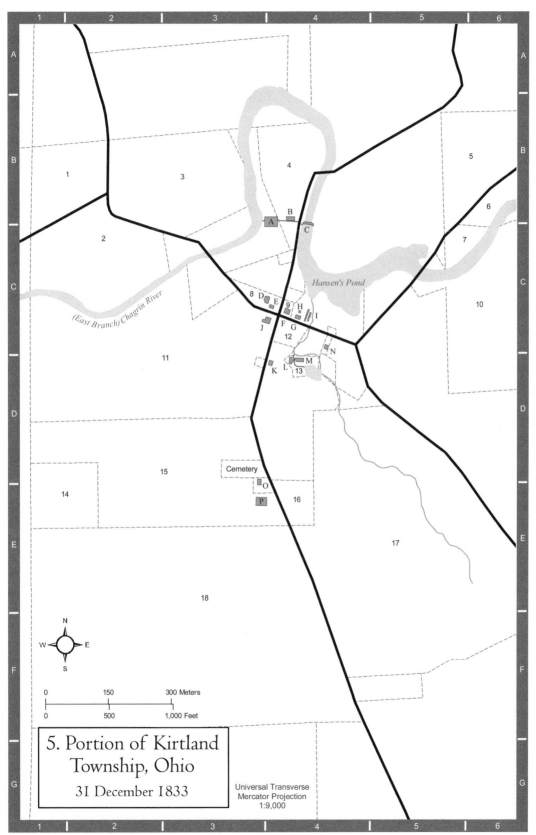

5. Portion of Kirtland
Township, Ohio

31 December 1833

Universal Transverse
Mercator Projection
1:9,000

(East Branch) Chagrin River

Hansen's Pond

Cemetery

N
W — E
S

0   150   300 Meters
0   500   1,000 Feet

RESEARCH: Mark Staker, Lyle Briggs, Lissa Thompson, Richard L. Jensen, Jared Tamez, Richard Bennett
CARTOGRAPHY: Brent Beck, Derek Farnes, Kent Simons, BYU Geography

Portion of Kirtland Township, Ohio
31 December 1835

Selected Structures

A. Loud-Lyman gristmill
B. Loud-Lyman sawmill
C. Milldam
D. Newel K. and Elizabeth Ann Whitney house
E. N. K. Whitney & Co. red store
F. N. K. Whitney & Co. white store
G. Tannery
H. Bark mill
I. Tannery vats
J. John Johnson inn
K. Distillery
L. Sawmill
M. Ashery
N. Schoolhouse on the flats
O. Joseph Smith Jr. and Emma Smith house
P. Joseph Smith Sr. and Lucy Mack Smith house
Q. Methodist Episcopal church
R. John Johnson Sr. and Elsa Johnson house
S. Schoolhouse/printing office
T. House of the Lord (temple)
U. Sidney and Phoebe Rigdon house

Selected Properties and Owners

1. N. K. Whitney & Co.
2. N. K. Whitney & Co.
3. N. K. Whitney & Co.
4. Austin Loud and Azariah Lyman
5. Austin Loud and Azariah Lyman
6. Austin Loud
7. Frederick G. Williams
8. Frederick G. Williams
9. Elijah Smith
10. Ira Bond
11. Azariah Lyman
12. Newel K. Whitney
13. Martha Raymond
14. Newel K. Whitney
15. Sidney Rigdon
16. Samuel Smith
17. Elijah Smith
18. N. K. Whitney & Co.
19. N. K. Whitney & Co.
20. Newel K. Whitney
21. Ira Bond
22. Leonard Rich
23. Joseph Smith Jr.
24. Newel K. Whitney
25. Oliver Cowdery
26. Newel K. Whitney
27. Oliver Cowdery
28. Joseph Smith Jr.
29. Sidney Rigdon
30. Joseph Smith Jr.
31. Edmund Bosley
32. Joseph Smith Jr.
33. Jacob Bump

Index of Selected Owners

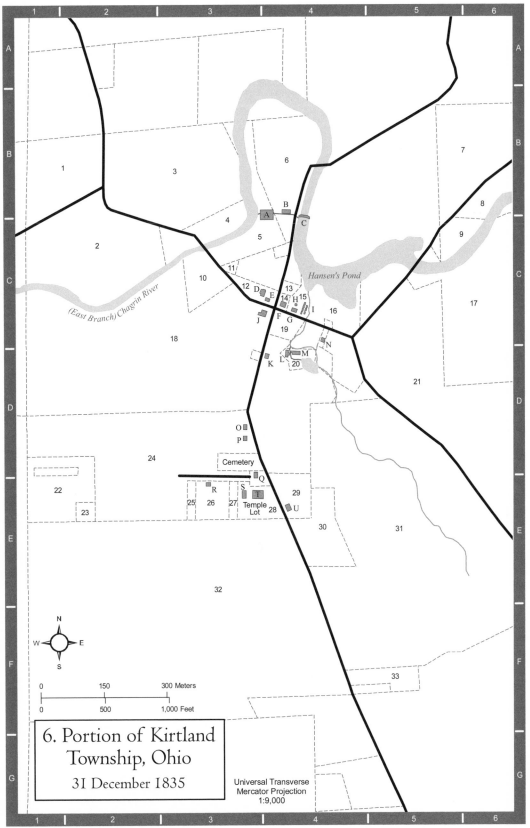

Hansen's Pond

(East Branch) Chagrin River

Cemetery

Temple Lot

N
W   E
S

0   150   300 Meters

0   500   1,000 Feet

6. Portion of Kirtland Township, Ohio
31 December 1835

Universal Transverse Mercator Projection
1:9,000

RESEARCH: Mark Staker, Lyle Briggs, Lissa Thompson, Richard L. Jensen, Jared Tamez, Richard Bennett
CARTOGRAPHY: Brent Beck, Derek Farnes, Kent Simons, BYU Geography

Portion of Kirtland Township, Ohio
12 January 1838

Selected Structures

A. Loud-Lyman gristmill
B. Loud-Lyman sawmill
C. Milldam
D. Newel K. and Elizabeth Ann Whitney house
E. N. K. Whitney & Co. red store
F. N. K. Whitney & Co. white store
G. Tannery
H. Bark mill
I. Tannery vats
J. John Johnson inn
K. Distillery
L. Sawmill
M. Ashery
N. Schoolhouse on the flats
O. Orson and Marinda Hyde house
P. Sylvester and Elizabeth Smith house
Q. Joseph Smith Jr. and Emma Smith house
R. Joseph Smith Jr. store
S. Joseph Smith Sr. and Lucy Mack Smith house
T. Boynton and Johnson store (John F. Boynton and Lyman Johnson)
U. Methodist Episcopal church
V. John F. and Susannah Boynton house
W. John Johnson Sr. and Elsa Johnson house
X. Lyman and Sarah Johnson house
Y. Luke and Susan Johnson house
Z. Oliver and Lydia Granger house
AA. Schoolhouse/printing office
BB. House of the Lord (temple)
CC. Sidney and Phoebe Rigdon house
DD. Bank and administrative headquarters
EE. Jacob and Abigail Bump house/ Kirtland Hotel
FF. George W. and Athalia Robinson house

Selected Properties and Owners

1. Jacob Bump
2. Oliver Granger
3. Eliphalet Boynton
4. John Johnson Jr.
5. John Johnson Jr.
6. John Johnson Jr.
7. Austin Loud and Azariah Lyman
8. Austin Loud and Azariah Lyman
9. Austin Loud
10. Eliphalet Boynton
11. Austin Loud
12. Eliphalet Boynton
13. Heber C. Kimball
14. Heber C. Kimball
15. Elijah Smith
16. Azariah Lyman and Quartus Clark
17. Azariah Lyman and Quartus Clark
18. Azariah Lyman
19. Thomas Burdick
20. Orson Hyde
21. Eliphalet Boynton
22. Martha Raymond Parrish
23. Orson Hyde
24. Nancy Rigdon
25. Samuel Smith
26. Elijah Smith
27. John Johnson Jr.
28. N. K. Whitney & Co.
29. Jacob Bump
30. William Marks
31. Ira Bond
32. Marinda Hyde
33. Marinda Hyde
34. John Johnson Jr.
35. Sylvester Smith
36. Parley P. Pratt
37. Oliver Granger
38. Joseph Smith Sr.
39. William Marks
40. John Johnson Jr.
41. John F. Boynton and Lyman Johnson
42. Newel K. Whitney
43. Joseph Smith Sr.
44. Vinson Knight
45. Ira Bond
46. William Marks
47. Leonard Rich
48. Samuel Smith
49. Vinson Knight
50. Oliver Olney
51. Susannah Boynton
52. John Johnson Sr.
53. Sarah Johnson
54. Susan Johnson
55. Oliver Granger
56. William Marks
57. William Marks
58. Jared Carter, Reynolds Cahoon, Hyrum Smith, Joseph Smith Jr., and Sidney Rigdon
59. Jonathan Crosby
60. William Marks
61. George W. Robinson
62. Susannah Boynton
63. William Marks
64. William Marks
65. William Smith
66. John F. Boynton
67. Jacob Bump
68. Jared Carter
69. William Smith
70. Oliver Granger
71. William Marks
72. Edmund Bosley
73. William Marks
74. William Marks
75. Eliphalet Boynton
76. Martha Raymond Parrish
77. Hyrum Smith
78. William Marks
79. William Marks
80. Jacob Bump
81. Jacob Bump

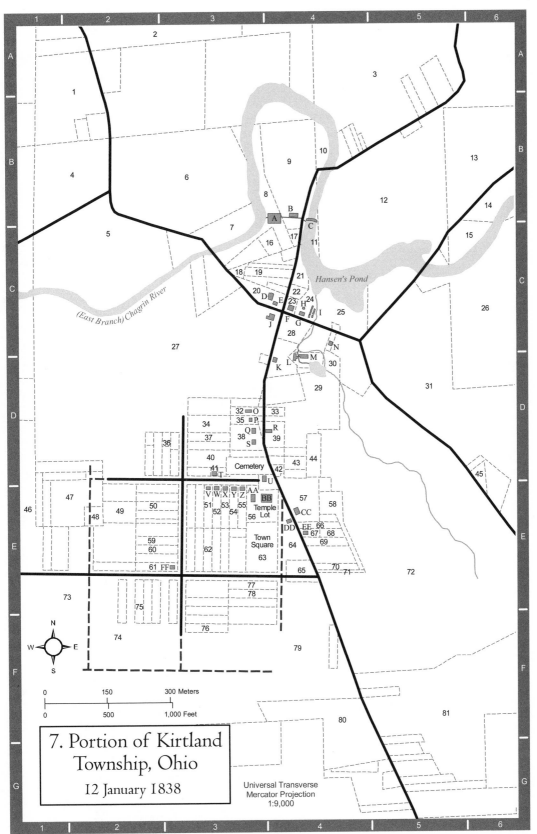

7. Portion of Kirtland Township, Ohio

12 January 1838

Universal Transverse
Mercator Projection
1:9,000

RESEARCH: Mark Staker, Lyle Briggs, Lissa Thompson, Richard L. Jensen, Jared Tamez, Richard Bennett
CARTOGRAPHY: Brent Beck, Derek Farnes, Kent Simons, BYU Geography

392

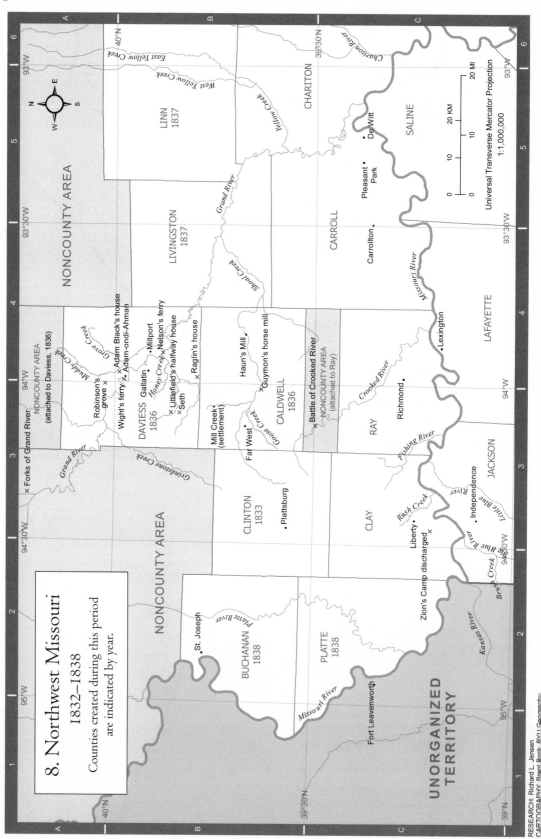

8. Northwest Missouri
1832–1838

Counts created during this period are indicated by year.

RESEARCH: Richard L. Jensen
CARTOGRAPHY: Brandon Plewe, BYU Geography

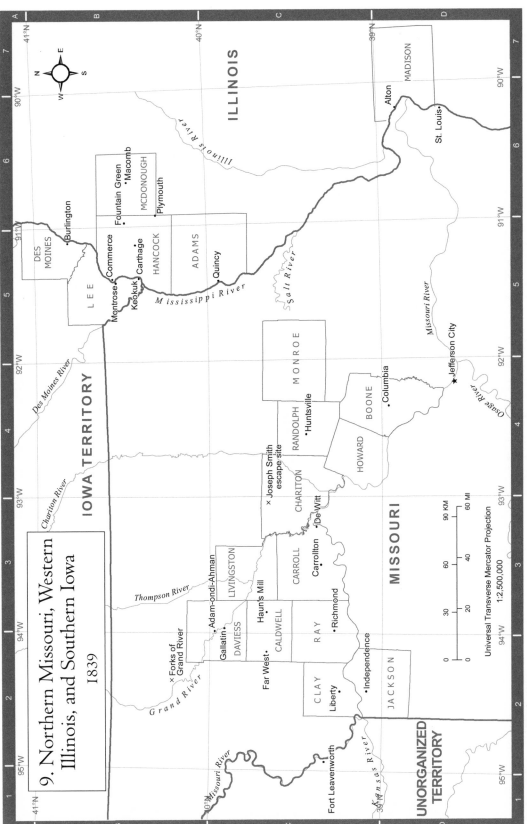

9. Northern Missouri, Western Illinois, and Southern Iowa 1839

RESEARCH: Larry C. Porter and Robin Scott Jensen.
CARTOGRAPHY: Isaac Montague and Brent Beck, BYU Geography

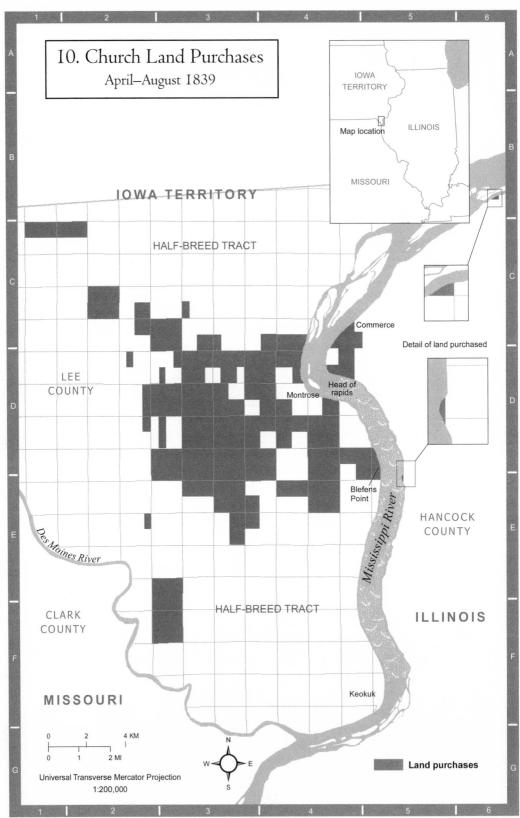

10. Church Land Purchases
April–August 1839

IOWA TERRITORY

ILLINOIS

MISSOURI

Map location

IOWA TERRITORY

HALF-BREED TRACT

Commerce

Detail of land purchased

LEE COUNTY

Montrose

Head of rapids

Blefens Point

HANCOCK COUNTY

Des Moines River

Mississippi River

ILLINOIS

CLARK COUNTY

HALF-BREED TRACT

Keokuk

MISSOURI

0   2   4 KM
0   1   2 MI

N
W   E
S

Universal Transverse Mercator Projection
1:200,000

Land purchases

RESEARCH: Robin Scott Jensen
CARTOGRAPHY: Brent Beck, BYU Geography

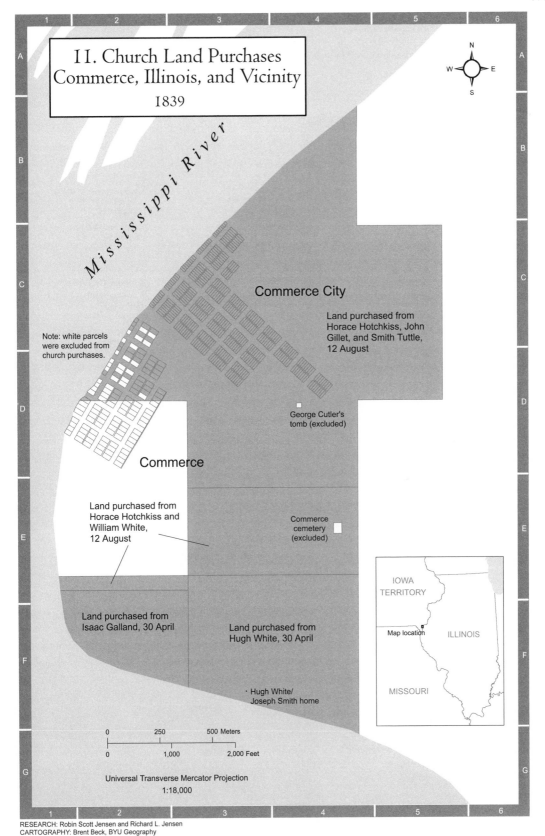

II. Church Land Purchases
Commerce, Illinois, and Vicinity
1839

Commerce City

Land purchased from
Horace Hotchkiss, John
Gillet, and Smith Tuttle,
12 August

Note: white parcels
were excluded from
church purchases.

George Cutler's
tomb (excluded)

Commerce

Land purchased from
Horace Hotchkiss and
William White,
12 August

Commerce
cemetery
(excluded)

Land purchased from
Isaac Galland, 30 April

Land purchased from
Hugh White, 30 April

· Hugh White/
Joseph Smith home

IOWA
TERRITORY

Map location

ILLINOIS

MISSOURI

0   250   500 Meters
0   1,000   2,000 Feet

Universal Transverse Mercator Projection
1:18,000

Mississippi River

RESEARCH: Robin Scott Jensen and Richard L. Jensen
CARTOGRAPHY: Brent Beck, BYU Geography

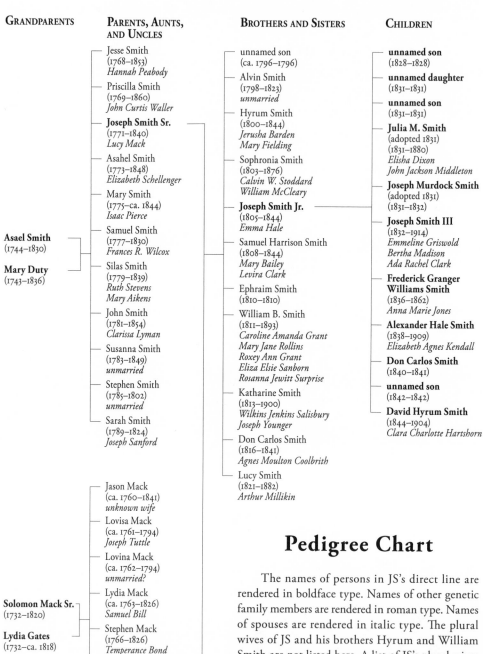

| GRANDPARENTS | PARENTS, AUNTS, AND UNCLES | BROTHERS AND SISTERS | CHILDREN |

GRANDPARENTS · **PARENTS, AUNTS, AND UNCLES** · **BROTHERS AND SISTERS** · **CHILDREN**

PARENTS, AUNTS, AND UNCLES

Jesse Smith
(1768–1853)
Hannah Peabody

Priscilla Smith
(1769–1860)
John Curtis Waller

Joseph Smith Sr.
(1771–1840)
Lucy Mack

Asahel Smith
(1773–1848)
Elizabeth Schellenger

Mary Smith
(1775–ca. 1844)
Isaac Pierce

Samuel Smith
(1777–1830)
Frances R. Wilcox

Silas Smith
(1779–1839)
Ruth Stevens
Mary Aikens

John Smith
(1781–1854)
Clarissa Lyman

Susanna Smith
(1783–1849)
unmarried

Stephen Smith
(1785–1802)
unmarried

Sarah Smith
(1789–1824)
Joseph Sanford

GRANDPARENTS

Asael Smith
(1744–1830)

Mary Duty
(1743–1836)

Jason Mack
(ca. 1760–1841)
unknown wife

Lovisa Mack
(ca. 1761–1794)
Joseph Tuttle

Lovina Mack
(ca. 1762–1794)
unmarried?

Lydia Mack
(ca. 1763–1826)
Samuel Bill

Stephen Mack
(1766–1826)
Temperance Bond

Daniel Gates Mack
(ca. 1770–by 1841)
Sally Ball

Solomon Mack Jr.
(1773–1851)
Esther Hayward
Hulda Hayward Whipple
Betsy Way Alexander

Lucy Mack
(1775–1856)
Joseph Smith Sr.

Solomon Mack Sr.
(1732–1820)

Lydia Gates
(1732–ca. 1818)

BROTHERS AND SISTERS

unnamed son
(ca. 1796–1796)

Alvin Smith
(1798–1823)
unmarried

Hyrum Smith
(1800–1844)
Jerusha Barden
Mary Fielding

Sophronia Smith
(1803–1876)
Calvin W. Stoddard
William McCleary

Joseph Smith Jr.
(1805–1844)
Emma Hale

Samuel Harrison Smith
(1808–1844)
Mary Bailey
Levira Clark

Ephraim Smith
(1810–1810)

William B. Smith
(1811–1893)
Caroline Amanda Grant
Mary Jane Rollins
Roxey Ann Grant
Eliza Elsie Sanborn
Rosanna Jewitt Surprise

Katharine Smith
(1813–1900)
Wilkins Jenkins Salisbury
Joseph Younger

Don Carlos Smith
(1816–1841)
Agnes Moulton Coolbrith

Lucy Smith
(1821–1882)
Arthur Millikin

CHILDREN

unnamed son
(1828–1828)

unnamed daughter
(1831–1831)

unnamed son
(1831–1831)

Julia M. Smith
(adopted 1831)
(1831–1880)
Elisha Dixon
John Jackson Middleton

Joseph Murdock Smith
(adopted 1831)
(1831–1832)

Joseph Smith III
(1832–1914)
Emmeline Griswold
Bertha Madison
Ada Rachel Clark

Frederick Granger Williams Smith
(1836–1862)
Anna Marie Jones

Alexander Hale Smith
(1838–1909)
Elizabeth Agnes Kendall

Don Carlos Smith
(1840–1841)

unnamed son
(1842–1842)

David Hyrum Smith
(1844–1904)
Clara Charlotte Hartshorn

Pedigree Chart

The names of persons in JS's direct line are rendered in boldface type. Names of other genetic family members are rendered in roman type. Names of spouses are rendered in italic type. The plural wives of JS and his brothers Hyrum and William Smith are not listed here. A list of JS's plural wives will appear in a forthcoming volume. Further information about many of the people listed here can be found in the Biographical Directory. Readers wishing to conduct further research may consult the documented pedigree chart posted on the Joseph Smith Papers website.

Biographical Directory

This register contains brief biographical sketches for most of the persons mentioned in this volume. These persons include church leaders, members of JS's family, people JS encountered on his travels, and acquaintances. The directory also includes information about the scribes of documents in this volume, as well as a few influential individuals named only in footnotes or other annotation. Plural wives of JS, his brothers Hyrum and William Smith, and others are not listed here. A list of JS's plural wives will appear in a forthcoming volume.

The biographical entries identify persons by complete name (correctly spelled), birth and death dates, and additional information, such as parentage and birthplace, migrations and places of residence, dates of marriage and names of spouses, occupation and denominational affiliation, religious and civic positions, and place of death. Key figures with major significance to JS's activities in the volume receive the fullest biographical sketches. People who pass through only briefly with little impact on events of the volume receive much briefer descriptions, often with less data than is available. Because unverified and sometimes incorrect data has been recirculated for decades, professional genealogists on the staff of the Joseph Smith Papers Project have utilized original sources to ensure accuracy.

Entries for women are generally listed under their final married names, with appropriate cross-references under maiden names or earlier married names. Partial names in the text, such as "Mr. Bradley," are not included in this directory when research could not determine the full name. In some cases, a footnote in the text provides possible identifications. The online index to this volume can often lead the reader to helpful information.

Locations that are noted include city or town, county, and state, when identified, for the first mention of a locale in each sketch. The following locales are given without county and state: Kirtland (Geauga Co., Ohio); Far West (Caldwell Co., Missouri); Commerce (later Nauvoo, Hancock Co., Illinois); Nauvoo (Hancock Co., Illinois); Winter Quarters (unorganized U.S. territory, now in Omaha, Douglas Co., Nebraska); and Salt Lake City (Salt Lake Co., Utah Territory). The counties and states of a handful of well-known cities have been omitted. "LDS church" refers to the church established by JS in 1830 and later known as the Church of Jesus Christ of Latter-day Saints. "RLDS church" refers to the church known originally as the New Organization and subsequently as the Reorganized Church of Jesus Christ of Latter Day Saints (1860–2001) and the Community of Christ (2001 to the present). Unless otherwise noted, "baptized" (or "rebaptized") refers to baptism (or rebaptism) in connection with the religious movement founded by JS during his lifetime.

Even the fullest entries in this directory provide, of necessity, only a bare skeleton of a person's life. Readers wishing to conduct further research may consult the documented biographical directory posted on the Joseph Smith Papers website.

Andrus, Hazard (ca. 1790–3/6 Mar. 1861/1862), farmer; born in New York. Lived in Cayuga Co., New York, by 1812. Served in War of 1812. Married Fanny Bishop, 19 June 1824, in Chautauque Co., New York. Lived in Portage Township, Allegany Co., New York,

1830. Lived in vicinity of Fairview, Cattaraugus Co., New York, 1834. Moved to Cass Co., Michigan Territory, by 1836. Died at Edwardsburg, Cass Co., Michigan.

Angell, Truman Osborn (5 June 1810–16 Oct. 1887), carpenter, joiner, architect; born at North Providence, Providence Co., Rhode Island. Son of James W. Angell and Phebe Morton. Baptized, Jan. 1832. Married Polly Johnson of Genesee Co., New York, 7 Oct. 1832. Labored on Kirtland temple. Moved to Missouri. Moved to Nauvoo, 1841. Directed joiner work on Nauvoo temple under architect William Weeks. Migrated to Salt Lake Valley, 1847. Served mission to Europe, to study architecture and preach, 1856. Served as church architect on two occasions. Died at Salt Lake City.

Atchison, David Rice (11 Aug. 1807–26 Jan. 1886), lawyer, judge, agriculturist, politician; born at Frogtown, near Lexington, Fayette Co., Kentucky. Son of William Atchison and Catherine Allen. In 1830, moved to Liberty, Clay Co., Missouri, where he became prominent lawyer. Retained as lawyer for Mormon redress petitions during Jackson Co., Missouri, expulsion, 1833. Elected to lower house of Missouri legislature, 1834 and 1838. Assisted Alexander W. Doniphan in working with state legislature to create Caldwell Co., Missouri, as haven for Mormons, 1836. Commanding officer of third division of state militia, which included both Caldwell and Daviess counties as well as several surrounding counties in northwestern Missouri at commencement of Mormon conflict, 1838. Appointed judge of Twelfth Judicial Circuit, which included Platt and Clinton counties, 1841. Served in U.S. Senate, 1843–1855. President pro tempore of Senate for several sessions. Vice president of U.S. under Franklin Pierce, 18 Apr. 1853–4 Dec. 1854. Died at Gower, Clinton Co., Missouri.

Avard, Sampson (23 Oct. 1800–15 Apr. 1869); born at St. Peter, Isle of Guernsey, Channel Islands, Great Britain. Migrated to U.S. prior to 1835. Married Eliza, a native of Virginia. Baptized and ordained an elder by Orson Pratt, 1835, at Freedom, Beaver Co., Pennsylvania. Served mission near his home with Erastus Snow, 1836. Moved to Kirtland, 1836. Ordained a high priest before Oct. 1837. Migrated to Far West, by 1838. Served on Far West high council. Prominent in Missouri Danite activities, 1838. Moved to Illinois, by 1850. Died at Edwardsville, Madison Co., Illinois.

Babbitt, Almon Whiting (1 Oct. 1812–Sept. 1856), attorney; born at Cheshire, Berkshire Co., Massachusetts. Son of Ira Babbitt and Nancy Crosier. Baptized and settled at Kirtland, 1833. Married Julia Ann Johnson, 23 Nov. 1833. Participant in Zion's Camp expedition to Missouri, 1834. Appointed member of First Quorum of the Seventy, Feb. 1835. Served mission to Upper Canada, 1837–1838. Led company of Canadian Latter-day Saints to Missouri, 1838. Appointed president of Kirtland stake, 1841. Presiding elder over Macedonia, Hancock Co., Illinois, branch, 1843. Member of Council of Fifty. Appointed one of five special trustees responsible for financial and temporal affairs in Nauvoo, 1846. Appointed postmaster of Nauvoo, 1846. Migrated to Salt Lake Valley, 1849. Appointed secretary of Utah Territory. Was killed about 120 miles northwest of Fort Kearney, Nebraska Territory.

Badlam, Alexander, Sr. (28 Nov. 1808–1 Dec. 1894); born at Dorchester, Suffolk Co., Massachusetts. Son of Ezra Badlam and Mary Lovis. Married Mary Ann Brannan, ca. 1833, near Saco, York Co., Maine. Participant in Zion's Camp expedition to Missouri, 1834. Ordained an elder, 28 Feb. 1835. Appointed member of First Quorum of the Seventy, Feb. 1835. Lived at Daviess Co. and Caldwell Co., Missouri. Fled Missouri to Illinois, 1839. Presided over Boston branch of church. Sailed for California from Boston on ship *Corsair* with two hundred passengers, 1849. Lived at Sacramento, Sacramento Co., California. Migrated to Utah Territory, 1850. Served mission to California, 1852. By 1872, had left LDS church. Died at San Francisco.

Bailey, Lydia Goldthwaite. See Knight, Lydia Goldthwaite.

Baker, Elizabeth (Betsey). See Carrico, Elizabeth (Betsey) Baker.

Barnard, John Porter (28 Jan. 1804–27 July 1874), farmer, blacksmith; born at New Hartford, Oneida Co., New York. Son of Ezra Barnard and Diadema Porter. Married Eliza Ann Wycoff, 31 Aug. 1826, at Ulysses, Tompkins Co., New York. Baptized, June 1835. Migrated to Far West, 1836. Exiled from Missouri; first located at Pike Co., Illinois, and then Nauvoo. Ordained a seventy, June 1839. Migrated to Salt Lake Valley, 1848. Died at Harper, Box Elder Co., Utah Territory.

Beemer, Philip (ca. 29 Jan. 1789–ca. 18 Sept. 1846); born at Grimsby, Province of Quebec. Son of John Beemer and Hannah Lewis. Served in War of 1812. Married Mary Ann Bloomfield, 1816. JS held a meeting in home of a Mr. Beamer at Colborne, Norfolk Co., Upper Canada, 1833. In December, Moses Nickerson informed Sidney Rigdon that a "Mr. and Mrs. Beamer are seriously enquiring after the truth." A "Beamer" is listed as being baptized in Colborne, 1833. These accounts appear to be associated with Philip Beemer. Buried at Simcoe, Norfolk Co., London District, Canada West.

Beman (Beaman), Alvah (22 May 1775–15 Nov. 1837), farmer; born at New Marlboro, Berkshire Co., Massachusetts. Son of Reuben Beman and Mariam. Married Sarah (Sally) Burt, 18 Aug. 1796. Moved to Avon, Livingston Co., New York, 1831. Among first to be acquainted with JS and his work at Palmyra, Wayne Co., New York. Assisted JS in concealing Book of Mormon plates from Palmyra mob and in fashioning box to contain plates. Appointed to preside over Kirtland elders quorum, 1836. Died at Kirtland.

Beman (Beaman), Sarah (Sally) Burt (27 Apr. 1775–29 Aug. 1840); born at Lyme, New London Co., Connecticut. Daughter of Joseph Burt and Elizabeth Peck. Married Alvah Beman, 18 Aug. 1796. Baptized, by 1835, in New York. Moved to Kirtland after Oct. 1835. Died at Nauvoo.

Bierce, Lucius Verus (4 Aug. 1801–11 Nov. 1876), lawyer; born at Cornwall, Litchfield Co., Connecticut. Son of William Bierce and Abigail Bell. District attorney, 1825–1836, and county prosecuting attorney, 1829–1839, in Portage Co., Ohio. Married first Frances C. Peck, 1836, in Ohio. Lived in Akron, Portage Co., from 1836. Brigadier general in Ohio militia, 1837. Akron mayor, 1839, 1841, 1844, 1849, 1867, 1868. Married second Sophronia Ladd, 1 Jan. 1840, in Portage Co. Master of Masonic lodge; and Grand Master of Ohio Masons, 1853–1859. State senator, 1862–1864. Died at Akron.

Bishop, Francis Gladden (19 June 1809–30 Nov. 1864), watchmaker; born at Livonia, Ontario Co., New York. Son of Isaac Gates Bishop and Mary Hyde. Served as minister in Freewill Baptist Church, by 1831. Baptized into LDS church, July 1832, in Olean Point, Cattaraugus Co., New York. Engaged in extensive missionary work from North Carolina to Upper Canada, 1833–1840. Organized schismatic movement called "Kingdom of God," 1842. Lived at Kirtland, 1850. Instrumental in eight religious movements, 1847–ca. 1860. Migrated to Utah Territory, 1864. Died in Salt Lake City.

Bissell (Bissel), Benjamin (1805–13 Oct. 1878), lawyer, judge; born at Hartwick, Otsego Co., New York. Son of Benjamin Bissell and Elizabeth Heath. Married Sarah

Bright, 10 Apr. 1829, at Painesville, Geauga Co., Ohio. Defended JS in variety of lawsuits during Kirtland period and helped him escape from Painesville mob in 1837.

Black, Adam (11 Sept. 1801–14 July 1890), farmer, judge; born at Henderson Co., Kentucky. Son of William Black and Jane Wilson. Moved near Booneville, Copper Co., Missouri Territory, 1819. Elected sheriff of Ray Co., Missouri, 1824. Married first Mary W. Morgan, 6 Sept. 1825, at Ray Co. Assessor, Ray Co., 1826. Served in Black Hawk War, 1832. Moved to what later became Daviess Co., Missouri, 1834. Served as justice of the peace and county judge in Daviess Co. Moved to Gentry Co., Missouri, 1844, where he served as justice of the peace and judge. Married second Margaret Grooms, ca. 1847. Married third Sallie Kelley, 15 Oct. 1857. Moved to Livingston Co., Missouri, 1861, where he served as county judge. Died in Livingston Co.

Boggs, Lilburn W. (14 Dec. 1796–14 Mar. 1860), bank cashier, merchant, Indian trader, lawyer, doctor, postmaster, politician; born at Lexington, Fayette Co., Kentucky. Son of John M. Boggs and Martha Oliver. Served in War of 1812. Moved to St. Louis, ca. 1816, and engaged in business. Married first Julia Ann Bent, July 1817, at St. Louis. Married second Panthea Grant Boone, July 1823. Located at Independence, Jackson Co., Missouri, 1826; elected to state senate on Democratic ticket, 1826. Elected lieutenant governor, 1832. Became governor upon resignation of predecessor, Daniel Dunklin, 1836. Played prominent role in 1838 expulsion of Mormons from Missouri under what was termed his "extermination order." Severely wounded by assassin, 1842; accused JS of complicity with Orrin Porter Rockwell in perpetrating the crime. Served in state senate, 1842–1846. Migrated to California, 1846. Died at Napa Valley, Napa Co., California.

Bond, Ira (19 Jan. 1798–30 Nov. 1887); born at Caldwell, Essex Co., New Jersey. Married Charlotte Wilcox of Mendon, Monroe Co., New York. Baptized by Joseph Young, at Mendon. Appointed to preside over Kirtland deacons quorum, 1836. Affiliated with RLDS church. Died in Kirtland.

Boosinger, George (1784–28 Feb. 1862), farmer; born in Pennsylvania. Son of Conrad Boosinger and Catharine Barbara Yancer. Journeyed to Trumbull Co., Northwest Territory, ca. 1801. Married first Nancy Simcox, ca. 1807. Enlisted in War of 1812. Resident of Tallmadge, Portage Co., Ohio, 1820. Married second Mary Ann Workinger, 21 Aug. 1822, in Wayne Co., Ohio. Performed baptisms for LDS church near Middlebury, Portage Co., 1836. Ordained to high priesthood at Kirtland, 29 Mar. 1836. Made substantial loans to church presidency, 1836. Moved to Ray Co., Missouri, 1836. Moved during exodus of Saints to Smooth Prairie, Madison Co., Illinois, 1839. In Madison Co. swore affidavit against state of Missouri for damages suffered in Ray Co. from 1836 to 1839. Lived in Macoupin Co., Illinois, in 1840. Retained some ties with church, as he baptized Joel Ricks, who lived on Silver Creek, Madison Co., 6 June 1841, and received letter from JS on a tithing matter, 1842. Lived in Macoupin Co. in 1850 and 1860. Died in Macoupin Co.

Bosier, Squire. See Bozarth (Bosier, Bozorth), Squire.

Bosley, Edmund/Edmond (25 June 1776–15 Dec. 1846); born at Northumberland, Northumberland Co., Pennsylvania. Son of John P. Bosley and Hannah Bull. Married Ann Kelly of Northumberland Co. Lived at Livonia, Livingston Co., New York, 1822–1834. Gristmill owner in Livonia, 1822. Moved to Kirtland. Excommunicated, July 1835. Apparently reinstated. Served as second counselor in Kirtland elders quorum, 1837. Moved to Missouri, by 1838. Located at Adams Co., Illinois, 1839. Ordained a high priest, 1844, at Nauvoo. Died at Winter Quarters during Mormon exodus to Salt Lake Valley.

Bosworth, Joseph Bucklin (6 Mar. 1790–16 July 1850); born at Scituate, Providence Co., Rhode Island. Son of Benajah Bosworth. Married Lucina Hopkins, 17 May 1815. Baptized, by 1834. Lived in Hancock Co., Illinois, 1843. Joined Sidney Rigdon's Church of Christ for brief period, 1845. Died at Peoria, Peoria Co., Illinois.

Boynton, John Farnham (20 Sept. 1811–20 Oct. 1890), merchant, lecturer, scientist, inventor; born at East Bradford, Essex Co., Massachusetts. Son of Eliphalet Boynton and Susanna Nichols. Baptized by JS, Sept. 1832. Ordained member of Quorum of the Twelve, 15 Feb. 1835. Married to Susannah (Susan) Lowell by JS, 20 Jan. 1836, at Kirtland. Dissented over handling of temporal matters associated with Kirtland Safety Society; disfellowshipped from Quorum of the Twelve, 3 Sept. 1837. Reinstated to church and membership in Quorum of the Twelve, 10 Sept. 1837. Excommunicated, Dec. 1837. Settled at Syracuse, Onondaga Co., New York. Assisted in running boundary line between U.S. and Mexico. Died at Syracuse.

Boynton, Susannah (Susan) Lowell (20 Aug. 1816–6 Aug. 1859); born at Buxton, Cumberland Co., Maine. Daughter of Samuel Lowell and Sarah Hayes. Baptized, 1833. Married to John F. Boynton by JS, 20 Jan. 1836, at Kirtland. Lived at Syracuse, Onondaga Co., New York, and Saco, York Co., Maine. Died at Syracuse.

Bozarth (Bosier, Bozorth), Squire (11 Jan. 1792–16 Mar. 1853); born at Nelson Co., Virginia (later in Kentucky). Son of John Bozarth and Sarah Shaw. Married Mildred (Milly) Hoard Willis at Litchfield, Grayson Co., Kentucky, 11 July 1816. Baptized by George M. Hinkle and Elisha Groves in Lewis Co., Missouri, ca. 1835–1836. Moved to Clay Co., Missouri, 1836. Moved with many Latter-day Saints to Caldwell Co., Missouri, ca. 1836. Owned property near Commerce, including large house, by 1839, when Heber C. Kimball built house nearby. Lived in Lee Co., Iowa Territory, 1841. Died at Woodland, Washington Territory.

Brannan, Samuel (ca. Mar. 1819–5 May 1889), printer, miner, businessman, land developer; born at Saco, York Co., Maine. Son of Thomas Brannan and Sarah Emery. Moved to Kirtland, 1833. Baptized, 1833, in Kirtland. Printer's apprentice for three years; reportedly resided with family of JS. Ordained an elder, 1838, in Kirtland. Married Ann Eliza Corwin, ca. 1842, in New York. Led group of 238 Latter-day Saints from New York to San Francisco via Hawaii by ship, 1846. Died at Escondido, San Diego Co., California.

Brewer, Nancy Jane Carter (26 Feb. 1827–1 Feb. 1904); born at Benson, Rutland Co., Vermont. Daughter of John S. Carter and Elizabeth Kenyon. Lived at Kirtland, by 1833. Father died of cholera, 24 June 1834, on Rush Creek, Clay Co., Missouri. Received patriarchal blessing from Joseph Smith Sr., 29 Jan. 1836, at Kirtland. Located at Far West, 1838. Lived in Nauvoo, 1840s. Married first William S. Clapp, 2 Dec. 1846, at Whiteside Co., Illinois. Married second William H. Brewer, 12 May 1868, at Diamond Springs, El Dorado Co., California. Died at Ringgold, El Dorado Co.

Brown, Eliza. See Perry, Eliza Brown.

Brunson, Seymour (1 Dec. 1798–10 Aug. 1840); born at Plattsburgh, Clinton Co., New York. Son of Reuben Brunson and Sally Clark. Married Harriet Gould of Hector, Tompkins Co., New York, ca. 1823. Baptized, Jan. 1831, at Strongsville, Cuyahoga Co.,

Ohio. Moved to Caldwell Co., Missouri. In 1839, located at Quincy, Adams Co., Illinois. Located at Commerce, 1839, and appointed to Commerce high council, Oct. 1839. Died at Nauvoo.

Bump, Jacob (1791–before 1865), craftsman; born at Butternuts, Otsego Co., New York. Son of Asa Bump and Lydia Dandley. Married Abigail Pettingill of Butternuts, ca. 1811. Participant in Zion's Camp expedition to Missouri, 1834. Labored on Kirtland temple, 1835. Joined dissenters in Kirtland to depose JS. Used influence with dissenters to prevent mob violence against Mormons leaving Kirtland, 1838. Appointed bishop in Kirtland stake of James J. Strang's organization, 7 Aug. 1846. Broke with Strang and reconstituted Church of Christ with William E. McLellin, Jan. 1847. Lived at Kirtland, 1860.

Burch, Thomas C. (ca. 1803–Sept. 1839); born in Tennessee. Married first Ann Ross, 20 Jan. 1824, at Howard Co., Missouri. Began law practice, 1831, at Richmond, Ray Co., Missouri. Married second Celenary (Selinary) Jacobs, 23 Jan. 1834, at Ray Co. Circuit attorney for Ray Co., 1838. Appointed judge of Eleventh Judicial Circuit, 1838. On 15 Apr. 1839, JS and other prisoners with him secured change of venue to Columbia, Boone Co., Missouri, because of Burch's new judicial appointment. His office posed conflict of interest, as he had been prosecuting attorney for state at hearing in Richmond, Nov. 1838. Died at Keytesville, Chariton Co., Missouri.

Burdick, Thomas (17 Nov. 1795–6 Nov. 1877), farmer, teacher, judge, postmaster; born at Canajoharie, Montgomery Co., New York. Son of Gideon Burdick and Catherine Robertson. Married Anna Higley, 1828, at Jamestown, Chautauque Co., New York. Appointed church clerk to record membership licenses, Feb. 1836. Member of Kirtland high council, 1837. Bishop at Kirtland, 22 May 1841. Located at Montrose, Lee Co., Iowa Territory, Oct. 1846. Crossed plains; located at San Bernardino, San Bernardino Co., California, 1853. Died at Los Angeles.

Butler, John Lowe (8 Apr. 1808–10 Apr. 1860); born at Warren Co., Kentucky. Son of James Butler and Charity Lowe. Married Caroline Farzine Skeen, 3 Feb. 1831, at Sumner Co., Tennessee. Baptized, 9 Mar. 1835, possibly in Drake's Creek area of Simpson Co., Tennessee. In fall 1836, moved to Missouri. Lived at Marrowbone Creek settlement, Daviess Co., Missouri, by summer 1838. One of principal participants in election day fight at Gallatin, Daviess Co., 6 Aug. 1838. Fled Far West for Quincy, Adams Co., Illinois, Dec. 1838. Lived at Nauvoo, 1840. Assisted James Emmett to establish Camp Vermillion in present-day South Dakota for Latter-day Saint immigrants, 1845. Migrated to Utah Territory, 1852. Settled at Spanish Fork, Utah Co., Utah Territory, where he was bishop from 1856 until his death.

Butterfield, Josiah (13 Mar. 1795–3 Mar. 1871); born at Dunstable, Middlesex Co., Massachusetts. Son of Abel Butterfield and Mary Farnsworth. Married first Polly Moulton, 30 Oct. 1819. Baptized by John F. Boynton, 1 Oct. 1833, in Maine. Appointed a president of the Seventy, 6 Apr. 1837. Assisted in migration of Kirtland Camp to Missouri, 1838. Following expulsion of Mormons from Missouri, settled at Bear Creek, Adams Co., Illinois, 1839. Married second Margaret Lawrence. Baptized into RLDS church by Glaud Rodger, 1 May 1865, at Watsonville, Santa Cruz Co., California. Died at Watsonville.

Cahoon, Lerona. See Stanley, Lerona Cahoon.

Cahoon, Nancy Miranda Gibbs (27 July 1817–6 Oct. 1867); born at Benson, Rutland Co., Vermont. Daughter of Aaron Gibbs and Prudence Carter. Married to William F. Cahoon by JS, 17 Jan. 1836, at Kirtland. Lived in Far West, 1838, and moved to Montrose, Lee Co., Iowa Territory, fall 1839. Migrated to Salt Lake Valley, 1849. Died at Salt Lake City.

Cahoon, Reynolds (30 Apr. 1790–29 Apr. 1861), farmer, tanner, builder; born at Cambridge, Washington Co., New York. Son of William Cahoon Jr. and Mehitable Hodges. Married Thirza Stiles, 11 Dec. 1810. Baptized, Oct. 1830. Ordained a high priest by JS, 3 June 1831, at Kirtland; had been ordained an elder previously. Appointed counselor to Bishop Newel K. Whitney at Kirtland, 10 Feb. 1832. Member of committee to oversee building of Kirtland temple. Member of Kirtland stake presidency. Moved to Missouri; arrived by 24 May 1838. Appointed counselor to stake president John Smith at Adam-ondi-Ahman, Daviess Co., Missouri, 28 June 1838. Located at Lee Co., Iowa Territory, following exodus from Missouri. Appointed counselor to John Smith in Iowa stake, Lee Co., 1839. Served on building committees for Nauvoo House, Mansion House, and Nauvoo temple. Member of Council of Fifty, 11 Mar. 1844. Participated in plural marriage during JS's lifetime. Migrated to Salt Lake Valley, 1848. Died at South Cottonwood Ward, Salt Lake Co., Utah Territory.

Cahoon, William Farrington (7 Nov. 1813–6 Apr. 1893); born at Harpersfield, Ashtabula Co., Ohio. Son of Reynolds Cahoon and Thirza Stiles. Baptized, 16 Oct. 1830, at Kirtland. Married to Nancy Miranda Gibbs by JS, 17 Jan. 1836, at Kirtland. Moved to Far West, spring 1838. Located at Montrose, Lee Co., Iowa Territory, fall 1839. Migrated to Salt Lake Valley, 1849. Died at Salt Lake City.

Capron, Henry (14 Mar. 1815–18 Jan. 1865); born in New York. Son of Joseph Capron and Sabra Avery. Moved to Perinton, Ontario Co., New York, by 1820. Lived next to JS's family at Manchester, Ontario Co., by 1830. Visited JS, 30 Nov. 1835, in Kirtland. Married Laura Brown. Died in Auburn, Cayuga Co., New York.

Carrico, Elizabeth (Betsey) Baker (4 Dec. 1811–2 May 1883); born at Bethlehem, Grafton Co., New Hampshire. Married to Thomas Carrico Jr. by JS, 14 Jan. 1836, at Kirtland. Baptized at Kirtland. Moved to Missouri with husband. Located at Nauvoo, 1840s. Later affiliated with RLDS church. Died near Logan, Harrison Co., Iowa.

Carrico, Thomas, Jr. (20 Sept. 1801–22 Feb. 1882); born at Beverly, Essex Co., Massachusetts. Son of Thomas Carrico and Deborah Wallis. Married first Mary E. Raymond, 30 Aug. 1827. Baptized, ca. 1832, at New Rowley, Essex Co., Massachusetts. Married second to Elizabeth (Betsey) Baker by JS, 14 Jan. 1836, at Kirtland. Lived in Missouri and then settled at Nauvoo, where appointed counselor to Bishop Jonathan H. Hale. Later baptized into RLDS church. Died near Logan, Harrison Co., Iowa.

Carter, Angeline Sarah. See Johnson, Angeline Sarah Carter.

Carter, Gideon Hayden (Haden) (1798–25 Oct. 1838); born at Killingworth, Middlesex Co., Connecticut. Son of Gideon Carter and Johanna Sims. Married first Hilah (Hilda) Burwell, 1822, at Benson, Rutland Co., Vermont. Baptized by JS and ordained a priest by Oliver Cowdery, 25 Oct. 1831, at Orange, Cuyahoga Co., Ohio. Married second Charlotte Woods, ca. 1833. Migrated to Far West, 1838. Killed in Battle of Crooked River, near Ray Co., Missouri.

Carter, Jared (14 June 1801–6 July 1849), cordwainer (shoemaker); born at Killingworth, Middlesex Co., Connecticut. Son of Gideon Carter and Johanna Sims. Married Lydia Ames, 20 Sept. 1825, at Benson, Rutland Co., Vermont. Baptized by Hyrum Smith, ca. 20 Feb. 1831. Migrated with Colesville, Broome Co., New York, branch to Kirtland, Apr.–May 1831. Ordained an elder, by Sept. 1831. Member of Kirtland temple building committee, 1833. Appointed to first Kirtland high council, 17 Feb. 1834. Removed family to Far West, 1837. Member of Far West high council, 1838. Moved from Far West to Illinois, 1839. Affiliated with James J. Strang's Church of Jesus Christ of Latter Day Saints, 1846. Died at De Kalb, De Kalb Co., Illinois.

Carter, Johanna. See Roundy, Johanna Carter.

Carter, Marietta. See Holmes, Marietta Carter.

Carter, Nancy Jane. See Brewer, Nancy Jane Carter.

Carter, Simeon (7 June 1794–3 Feb. 1869); born at Killingworth, Middlesex Co., Connecticut. Son of Gideon Carter and Johanna Sims. Married Lydia Kenyon, 2 Dec. 1818, at Benson, Rutland Co., Vermont. Baptized and ordained an elder, 1831, at Kirtland. President of Big Blue River, Kaw Township, Jackson Co., Missouri, branch, 1833. Member of Clay Co., Missouri, high council, 1834, and Far West high council, 1836. Exiled from Missouri, 1839. Located at Lee Co., Iowa Territory. Arrived at Salt Lake Valley, 1849. Died at Brigham City, Box Elder Co., Utah Territory.

Clark, Josiah (ca. 1794–Aug. 1869), farmer; born in New Jersey. Married Parthenia. Lived at Columbia, Hamilton Co., Ohio, 1830. Subscriber to *LDS Messenger and Advocate,* 1836. Represented Cincinnati branch of church at conference held at Springdale, Hamilton Co., Ohio, 4 Sept. 1841. Died at Dayton Precinct, Campbell Co., Kentucky.

Cleminson (Clemenson), John James (28 Dec. 1798–28 Dec. 1879); born at Lancaster, Lancashire, England. Married Lydia Lightner, 5 Jan. 1823, at Lafayette Co., Missouri. Was Latter-day Saint at Far West by 1838. Testified against JS at hearing in Richmond, Ray Co., Missouri, Nov. 1838. Lived at Montrose, Lee Co., Iowa Territory, 1842. Lived at New Town, Monterey Co., California, 1852. Died at El Monte, Los Angeles Co., California.

Coe, Joseph (12 Nov. 1784–17 Oct. 1854); born at Cayuga Co., New York. Son of Joel Coe and Huldah Horton. Married first Pallas Wales, 12 Jan. 1816. Married second Sophia Harwood, ca. 1824. Baptized and ordained an elder before 1831. Kirtland high council member, 1834–1837. Provided one-third of money for purchase of mummies and papyri associated with JS translation of book of Abraham, 1835, at Kirtland. Died at Kirtland.

Coltrin, Zebedee (7 Sept. 1804–21 July 1887); born at Ovid, Seneca Co., New York. Son of John Coltrin and Sarah Graham. Belonged to Methodist church. Married Julia Ann Jennings. Baptized into LDS church, 1831. Ordained a high priest by Hyrum Smith and Reynolds Cahoon, 22 July 1832, at Kirtland. Participant in Zion's Camp expedition to Missouri, 1834. Appointed a president of First Quorum of the Seventy, 1835. Located at Commerce, 1839, but soon after moved to Kirtland. Appointed second counselor to Almon W. Babbitt in Kirtland stake, 1841. Migrated to Salt Lake Valley with Brigham Young pioneer company, 1847. Died at Spanish Fork, Utah Co., Utah Territory.

Comer, John Baker (1814–ca. 1867); born in Ohio. Son of John Comer and Mary Baker. Lived in Missouri by 1837. With two others, attempted to illegally transport state firearms from Richmond, Ray Co., Missouri, to arm mob in Daviess Co., Missouri, for use against Mormons. Apprehended in Caldwell Co., Missouri, by William Allred and others. Released by order of circuit judge Austin A. King, Sept. 1838. Participated in massacre at Haun's Mill, Caldwell Co., 30 Oct. 1838. Daviess Co. deputy sheriff, 1839, 1852. Married Ann Caroline Estes of Kentucky, 23 Jan. 1848, in Daviess Co. Lived in Ray Co., by 1867.

Copley, Leman (ca. 1781–ca. 22 May 1862); christened at New Preston, Litchfield Co., Connecticut. Son of Samuel Copley and Rhoda Parmalee. Married Salley. Joined United Society of Believers in Christ's Second Appearing (Shakers). Moved to Thompson, Geauga Co., Ohio, by 1820. Baptized into LDS church, 1831. Allowed Latter-day Saints from Colesville, Broome Co., New York, to settle on his land under law of consecration, but then rescinded his agreement, June 1831. Remained in Ohio when body of Latter-day Saints went to Missouri, 1838. In 1849, joined James Brewster's Church of Christ; later joined Austin Cowles's Church of Christ. Died at Thompson.

Corrill, John (17 Sept. 1794–26 Sept. 1842), carriage builder; born near Barre, Worcester Co., Massachusetts. Married Margaret, ca. 1830. Lived at Harpersfield, Ashtabula Co., Ohio, 1830. Baptized, 10 Jan. 1831, at Kirtland. Ordained an elder, Jan. 1831, at Kirtland. Ordained a high priest, 3 June 1831, at Kirtland. Counselor to Bishop Edward Partridge in Jackson Co., Missouri, and also presided over Independence, Jackson Co., branch of church. Forced from Jackson Co. and located at Clay Co., Missouri, Nov. 1833, where he continued as counselor to Bishop Partridge. Returned to Kirtland and labored on temple, 1834–1836. Returned to Missouri and became a founder of Far West, after Mar. 1836. Appointed "Keeper of the Lord's store House," Far West, May 1837. Released as counselor to Bishop Partridge, Aug. 1837. Elected state representative from Caldwell Co., Missouri, 1838. Appointed church historian, 1838. Testified for state at JS's hearing in Richmond, Ray Co., Missouri, Nov. 1838. Moved to Illinois, 1839. Excommunicated, 17 Mar. 1839, at Quincy, Adams Co., Illinois. Published *A Brief History of the Church of Christ of Latter Day Saints, (Commonly Called Mormons),* 1839. Died in Adams Co.

Covey, Almira Mack (28 Apr. 1805–10 Mar. 1886); born at Tunbridge, Orange Co., Vermont. Daughter of Stephen Mack and Temperance Bond. Cousin of JS. Baptized by David Whitmer and confirmed by JS, 1830. Married first William Scobey, 7 Aug. 1831. Moved to Clay Co., Missouri, 1835. Married second Benjamin Covey, Oct. 1836, at Kirtland. Moved to Far West; part of forced exodus from Missouri. Migrated to Salt Lake Valley; arrived 21 Sept. 1848. Died at Salt Lake City.

Cowdery, Oliver (3 Oct. 1806–3 Mar. 1850), teacher, justice of the peace, lawyer, newspaper editor; born at Wells, Rutland Co., Vermont. Son of William Cowdery and Rebecca Fuller. Raised Congregationalist. Moved to western New York and clerked at a store, ca. 1825–1828. Taught term as local schoolmaster at Manchester, Ontario Co., New York, 1828–1829. Assisted JS as principal scribe in translation of Book of Mormon, 1829. Baptized, 1829. With JS, received Aaronic and Melchizedek priesthoods, 1829. One of the Three Witnesses of the Book of Mormon, June 1829. Helped oversee printing of Book of Mormon by E. B. Grandin, 1829–1830. Among six original members of church, 6 Apr. 1830. Led small group of missionaries through Ohio and to Missouri on mission to unorganized Indian Territory, 1830–1831. With John Whitmer, left Ohio to take revelations to Missouri for publication, Nov. 1831. Assisted William W. Phelps in setting up and conducting church's printing operations at Jackson Co., Missouri, 1832–1833. Married Elizabeth Ann Whitmer, 1832, in Jackson Co. Member of United Firm, Literary Firm, and Kirtland high council, 1832–1837. Edited Kirtland continuation of *The Evening and the Morning Star,* 1833–1834, and directed republication and revision of these volumes under modified title *Evening and Morning Star.* Edited *LDS Messenger and Advocate,* 1834–1835, 1836–1837, and *Northern Times,* 1835. Appointed assistant president of church, 5 Dec. 1834. Appointed church recorder, 1835. Elected justice of the peace in Kirtland, 1837. Moved to Far West, 1837. Excommunicated, 1838. Briefly practiced law at Kirtland and then moved to Tiffin, Seneca Co., Ohio, where he continued law practice and held political offices, 1840–1847. Helped incorporate and for a time attended Methodist Protestant Church at Tiffin. Moved to Elkhorn, Walworth Co., Wisconsin, 1847. Ran unsuccessfully for Wisconsin State Assembly, 1848. Coeditor of *Walworth County Democrat,* 1848. Requested readmission to LDS church and rebaptized, Kanesville, Pottawattamie Co., Iowa, 1848. Died at Richmond, Ray Co., Missouri.

Cowdery, Warren A. (17 Oct. 1788–23 Feb. 1851), physician, druggist, farmer, editor, justice of the peace, election judge; born at Wells, Rutland Co., Vermont. Son of William Cowdery and Rebecca Fuller. Raised Congregationalist. Married Patience Simonds, 22 Sept. 1814. Moved to Freedom, Cattaraugus Co., New York, ca. 1815–1816. Became first town postmaster of Freedom, 1824. Baptized into LDS church, 1834. Appointed presiding elder of church at Freedom, 1834. Moved to Kirtland, Feb. 1836. Involved in managing bookbindery and printing office. Assisted in writing dedicatory prayer delivered by JS in Kirtland temple, 1836. Editor of *LDS Messenger and Advocate* and clerk to JS, 1836–1837. Served on Kirtland high council, 1837. Became disaffected with church leadership, 1838. Served as justice of the peace, 1838–1840. Election judge in Kirtland, 1841–1842. In 1850, farmed at Kirtland, where he died.

Cowdery, William, Jr. (5 Sept. 1765–26 Feb. 1847); born at East Haddam, Middlesex Co., Connecticut. Son of William Cowdery and Hannah Emmons. Raised Congregationalist. Married first Rebecca Fuller, ca. 1787. After Rebecca's death married second Keziah Pearce, 1810. Moved to Williamson, Ontario Co., New York, 1810. Baptized into LDS church and moved to Kirtland. Served as president of Kirtland priests quorum. Remained at Kirtland after main body of Latter-day Saints departed, 1838. Died at Kirtland.

Crosby, Jonathan (20 July 1807–12 June 1892); born at Wendell, Franklin Co., Massachusetts. Son of Jonathan Crosby and Lois Barnes. Baptized, 2 Dec. 1833. Married Caroline Barnes, 25 Oct. 1834. Moved to Kirtland. Member of Kirtland Camp migration to Missouri, 1838. In 1838–1842, lived in Indiana, where he presided over Pleasant Garden branch, near Vincennes, Knox Co. Lived in Nauvoo. Migrated to Salt Lake Valley, 1848. Died at Beaver, Beaver Co., Utah Territory.

Cushman, Nathan (16 Dec. 1782–after Sept. 1866); born at Bennington, Bennington Co., Vermont. Son of Charles Cushman and Keziah Branch. Married Polly Weeks, 9 Dec. 1802, at Bennington. Lived at Rutland, Rutland Co., Vermont, 1820. Lived at Willoughby, Lake Co., Ohio, 1840–1860. Lived at East Cleveland, Cuyahoga Co., Ohio, 19 Sept. 1866.

Cutler, Louisa Elizabeth. See Rappleye, Louisa Elizabeth Cutler.

Daley, Moses (16 Apr. 1794–9 Dec. 1865); born at Walkill, Orange Co., New York. Son of John Daley and Amy Mapes. Married Almira Barber, 22 Jan. 1819, at Marcellus, Onondaga Co., New York. Served mission to Michigan Territory, 1832. Ordained a high priest by JS and Frederick G. Williams, 31 Mar. 1836. Settled at Adam-ondi-Ahman, Daviess Co., Missouri, 1838. Exiled from Missouri; located at Big Neck Prairie, Adams Co., Illinois. Migrated to Salt Lake Valley, 1849. Settled at San Bernardino, Los Angeles Co., California, 1851. Died at Riverside, Riverside Co., California.

Doniphan, Alexander William (9 July 1808–8 Aug. 1887); born near Maysville, Mason Co., Kentucky. Son of Joseph Doniphan and Ann Smith. Opened law office at Lexington, Lafayette Co., Missouri, 1830. In 1833, moved to Liberty, Clay Co., Missouri. Employed as legal counsel by Latter-day Saints during their expulsion from Jackson Co., Missouri, 1833. Elected to Missouri General Assembly representing Clay Co. as a Whig, 1836, 1840, 1854. Married Elizabeth Jane Thornton, 21 Dec. 1837. Appointed brigadier general in state militia. Refused order from Major General Samuel Lucas to execute JS and other church leaders at Far West, 1 Nov. 1838. Again defended JS and others in courts, 1838–1839. Served as colonel in Mexican War, 1846–1847. Died at Richmond, Ray Co., Missouri.

Dort, David (6 Jan. 1793–10 Mar. 1841); born at Surry/Gilsum, Cheshire Co., New Hampshire. Son of John Dort and Elishaba Briggs. Married first JS's cousin Mary (Polly) Mack, 2 June 1813. After Mary's death, married second her sister Fanny. Moved to Pontiac, Oakland Co., Michigan Territory. Baptized, 1831. Participant in Zion's Camp expedition to Missouri, 1834. Member of Kirtland high council, 1837. In 1838, moved to Far West, where he served on high council. Located at Nauvoo following exodus from Missouri, 1839, and became member of high council there. Died at Nauvoo.

Dunklin, Daniel (14 Jan. 1790–25 July 1844); born near Greenville, Greenville District, South Carolina. Son of Joseph Dunklin Jr. and Sarah Margaret Sullivan. Married Emily W. Haley, 1815. Sheriff of Washington Co., Missouri, 1815–1819. Served in Missouri House of Representatives, 1822–1823. Elected lieutenant governor of Missouri, 1828, and governor, 1832. Resigned as governor, 1836, to accept appointment as surveyor general of Missouri and Illinois. Moved to Herculaneum, Jefferson Co., Missouri, 1840. Died near Herculaneum.

Eaton, Frazier (23 Jan. 1780–ca. 1859); born at Goffstown, Hillsborough Co., New Hampshire. Son of Enoch Eaton and Esther Williams. Married Lucinda Metcalf, by 1800. By 1820, lived at Rushford, Allegany Co., New York. Donated substantial sum for building of Kirtland temple. Lived in Hancock Co., Illinois, 1840. Died at Rushford.

Elliott, David (18 Nov. 1799–2 Dec. 1855); born at Charleston, Montgomery Co., New York. Son of Peter Elliott and Phebe Holley. Married first Almira Holliday of Solon, Cortland Co., New York, ca. 1821. Baptized, 2 Jan. 1831, at Fayette, Seneca Co., New York. Married second Mary Cahoon, 21 May 1831, in Geauga Co., Ohio. Participant in Zion's Camp expedition to Missouri, 1834. Appointed member of First Quorum of the Seventy, 1835. Moved to Missouri with Kirtland Camp, 1838. Following exodus from Missouri, settled at Springfield, Sangamon Co., Illinois. Migrated to Salt Lake Valley, 1852. Died in Salt Lake City.

Emmett, James (22 Feb. 1803–28 Dec. 1852); born at Boone Co., Kentucky. Son of Silas Emmett and Elizabeth Trowbridge. Married Phebe Jane Simpson, 13 Apr. 1823. Baptized, 1831, in Illinois. Member of Far West high council, 1838. Participated in Battle of Crooked River, near Ray Co., Missouri, 25 Oct. 1838. Appointed to Iowa stake high council, Lee Co., Iowa Territory, 24 Apr. 1841. Led advance party of Latter-day Saint settlers from vicinity of Nauvoo to vicinity of present-day Vermillion, Clay Co., South Dakota, 1845–1846. Wintered on Niobrara River in present-day Knox Co., Nebraska, 1846–1847. Moved to Fremont Co., Iowa, 1847. Migrated from Iowa to the West, 1849. Located at San Bernardino, Los Angeles Co., California, where he died.

Follett, King (24 July 1788–9 Mar. 1844); born at Winchester, Cheshire Co., New Hampshire. Son of John Follett and Hannah Oaks. Married Louisa Tanner, by 1816. Lived at De Kalb, St. Lawrence Co., New York, where he was baptized, 1831. Member of Whitmer branch at Kaw Township, Jackson Co., Missouri, by 1833. Lived in Clay Co., Missouri, 1833. During difficulties in Missouri in 1838–1839, imprisoned at Richmond, Ray Co., Missouri, and Columbia, Boone Co., Missouri. Died at Nauvoo.

Fordham, Elijah (12 Apr. 1798–9 Sept. 1879); born at New York City. Son of George Fordham and Mary Baker. Married Jane Ann Fisher, 1822. Lived at Pontiac, Oakland Co., Michigan Territory, 1831–1833. Participant in Zion's Camp expedition to Missouri, 1834. Received elder's license at Kirtland, 1 Apr. 1836. Appointed to Iowa stake high council, Lee Co., Iowa Territory, 1839. Migrated to Utah Territory, 1850. Died at Wellsville, Cache Co., Utah Territory.

Foster, James (1 Apr. 1786–12 Dec. 1846); born at Hillsboro, Hillsboro Co., New Hampshire. Married Abigail Glidden in Maine. Baptized, by 1834. Participant in Zion's Camp expedition to Missouri, 1834. Set apart as a president of the Seventy, 6 Apr. 1837. One of leaders of Kirtland Camp migration to Missouri, 1838. After Latter-day Saints left Missouri, settled at Jacksonville, Morgan Co., Illinois. Died at Jacksonville.

Fullmer, John Solomon (21 July 1807–8 Oct. 1883); born at Huntington, Luzerne Co., Pennsylvania. Son of Peter Fullmer and Susannah Zerfass. Married Mary Ann Price, 1837, at Nashville, Davidson Co., Tennessee. Baptized, 1839, at Commerce. During exodus of Mormons from Nauvoo, appointed one of three trustees-in-trust to handle church business. Migrated to Salt Lake Valley, 1848. Died at Springville, Utah Co., Utah Territory.

Galland, Isaac (15 May 1791–27 Sept. 1858), merchant, tavern owner, postmaster, land speculator, doctor; born at Somerset Co., Pennsylvania. Son of Matthew Galland and Hannah Fenno. Married first Nancy Harris, 1811. Married second Margaret Knight, 1816. Moved to Washington Co., Indiana. Resident of Owen Co., Indiana, by 1820. Married third Hannah Kinney, 5 Oct. 1826. Moved to Oquawka, Henderson Co., Illinois, 1827. Established settlement of Nashville on west bank of Mississippi River, in unorganized territory, where he practiced medicine, established trading post, and founded first school in what later became Iowa Territory. Moved to Edgar Co., Illinois, about 1832. Served in Black Hawk War, 1832. Married fourth Elizabeth Wilcox, 25 Apr. 1833. Platted original town of Keokuk, Lee Co., Michigan Territory (later in Iowa Territory), 1837. Moved to Commerce, winter 1839. Purchased land in Half-Breed Tract in Lee Co., and sold some nineteen thousand acres of it to Latter-day Saints, 1839. Also sold properties in Commerce to Latter-day

Saints. Baptized, 1839. Ordained an elder, 1839. Acted as authorized agent for church in settling certain land transactions involving property exchanges by eastern Latter-day Saints moving to Nauvoo. Withdrew from church activity, 1842. Firm believer in Spiritualism during last ten years of life. Died at Fort Madison, Lee Co., Iowa.

Garrett, Henry Dwight (5 Sept. 1814–after 1843); born at Deerfield, Oneida Co., New York. Received patriarchal blessing from Joseph Smith Sr., 29 Jan. 1836, at Kirtland. Lived at Kirtland, 1836–1843.

Gause, Jesse (ca. 1784–ca. Sept. 1836), schoolteacher; born at East Marlborough, Chester Co., Pennsylvania. Son of William Gause (Goss) and Mary Beverly. Joined Society of Friends, 1806. Married first Martha Johnson, 1815, at Philadelphia. After Martha died, 1828, married second Minerva and joined United Society of Believers in Christ's Second Appearing (Shakers). Moved to Shaker community at North Union, Cuyahoga Co., Ohio, 1831. Baptized into LDS church, by Mar. 1832, when appointed counselor to JS. Began mission with Zebedee Coltrin to Shaker community at North Union; Thompson, Geauga Co., Ohio; and Rappite community of Economy near Pittsburgh, 1 Aug. 1832. Visited Minerva and tried to persuade her to leave Shakers. Parted company with Coltrin, 19 Aug. 1832. Apparently excommunicated, 3 Dec. 1832. Resided in Chester Co., Pennsylvania, at time of death.

Gaylord, John C. (12 July 1797–17 July 1874); born at Luzerne Co., Pennsylvania. Son of Chauncey John Gaylord and Dorithy Taylor. Married first Elizabeth Terry of East Palmyra, Wayne Co., New York, Apr. 1820. Baptized, 2 Aug. 1835, at Niagara, Niagara Co., New York. Appointed a president of First Quorum of the Seventy, 6 Apr. 1837, at Kirtland. Excommunicated, 13 Jan. 1838, at Kirtland. Moved to Commerce, 1839. Married second Elvira Edmonds, 31 Dec. 1840, in Walnut Grove, Knox Co., Illinois. Rebaptized, 4 Aug. 1841, at Nauvoo. Affiliated with James J. Strang at Voree, Walworth Co., Wisconsin. Received into RLDS church as a seventy, 6 Oct. 1858. Died near Burlington, Racine Co., Wisconsin.

Gee, Salmon (16 Oct. 1792–13 Sept. 1845); born at Lyme, New London Co., Connecticut. Son of Zopher Gee and Esther Beckwith. Married Sarah Watson Crane, 1814. Baptized, July 1832, Geauga Co., Ohio. Appointed a president of the Seventy, 6 Apr. 1837. Member of Kirtland high council under Almon W. Babbitt, 1841–1844. Died at Ambrosia, Lee Co., Iowa Territory. Buried at Nauvoo.

Gibbs, Nancy Miranda. See Cahoon, Nancy Miranda Gibbs.

Gilbert, Algernon Sidney (28 Dec. 1789–29 June 1834), merchant; born at New Haven, New Haven Co., Connecticut. Son of Eli Gilbert and Lydia Hemingway. Married Elizabeth Van Benthusen, 30 Sept. 1823. Merchant at Mentor, Geauga Co., Ohio. Partner with Newel K. Whitney in N. K. Whitney & Co. store at Kirtland, by 1827. Baptized by missionaries to unorganized Indian Territory under Oliver Cowdery, Nov. 1830, at Kirtland. Ordained an elder, 6 June 1831, by JS, in Kirtland. Ordained a high priest, 26 Apr. 1832, by JS, in Kirtland. Acted as church agent in operating Gilbert, Whitney & Co. store at Independence, Jackson Co., Missouri, 1831–1833. Among Latter-day Saints driven from Jackson Co. into Clay Co., Missouri, Nov. 1833. Hosted men of Zion's Camp expedition to Missouri, 1834. Died of cholera near Rush Creek, Clay Co.

Gould, Dean C. (ca. 1810/1820–after 1840); participant in Zion's Camp expedition to Missouri, 1834. Baptized during expedition by Lyman Wight, 15 June 1834, in Chariton River, Missouri. Member of elders quorum in Kirtland, 1836. Lived at Kirtland, 1839–1840.

Gould, John (11 May 1808–9 May 1851), pastor; born in Upper Canada. Son of Seth Gould and Hannah Sager. Married Abigail (Aby) Harrington. Baptized, Dec. 1832, at Chautauque Co., New York. Ordained an elder by David W. Patten, 17 Dec. 1832. Traveled from Kirtland with Orson Hyde to inform church leaders in Missouri that they must obtain redress through legal channels for their impending eviction from Jackson Co., Missouri, Aug. 1833. Assisted JS in recruitment of volunteers for Zion's Camp expedition to Missouri, 1834. Appointed a president of the Seventy, 1837. Ordained a high priest, 1844. Migrated to Salt Lake Valley, 1847. Returned to Winter Quarters, 1847. Died at Cooley's Mill, Pottawattamie Co., Iowa.

Granger, Oliver (7 Feb. 1794–25 Aug. 1841), sheriff, church agent; born at Phelps, Ontario Co., New York. Son of Pierce Granger and Clarissa Trumble. Married Lydia Dibble, 8 Sept. 1818, in Ontario Co. Member of Methodist church and licensed exhorter. Sheriff of Ontario Co. and colonel in militia. Nearly blind from 1827 onward. Lived at Phelps, 1830. Baptized into LDS church and ordained an elder by Brigham and Joseph Young, ca. 1832–1833, at Sodus, Wayne Co., New York. Moved to Kirtland, 1833. Ordained a high priest, 29 Apr. 1836. Appointed to Kirtland high council, 1837. Appointed to settle JS's business affairs in Kirtland, Jan. 1838. Left Kirtland for Far West, possibly to confer regarding JS's Kirtland business affairs. Directed in July 1838 revelation to move to Far West. Returned to Kirtland to settle his and JS's affairs and move family to Far West. Left Kirtland for Far West in Oct. 1838 with family, but turned back by mob in Missouri and returned to Kirtland. Following Mormon exodus from Missouri, moved from Kirtland to Commerce. Acted as agent in securing lands in Lee Co., Iowa Territory, 1839. Appointed to preside over church in Kirtland, 4 May 1839. Died at Kirtland.

Greene, Evan Melbourne (22 Dec. 1814–2 May 1882); born at Aurelius, Cayuga Co., New York. Son of John Portineus Greene and Rhoda Young. Baptized, 1832. Married Susan Kent, 1835. Clerk of Kirtland elders quorum, 1836–1837. Ordained a high priest. Postmaster at Kanesville, Pottawattamie Co., Iowa, and recorder and treasurer of Pottawattamie Co., 1848–1852. Migrated to Salt Lake Valley, 1852. Member of Utah territorial legislature. Died at Clover Flat, Sevier Co., Utah Territory.

Greene, John Portineus (3 Sept. 1793–10 Sept. 1844), farmer, shoemaker; born at Herkimer, Herkimer Co., New York. Son of John Coddington Greene and Anna Chapman. Married Brigham Young's sister Rhoda Young, 11 Feb. 1813. Baptized by Eleazer Miller, 13 Apr. 1832, at Mendon Township, Monroe Co., New York. Organized branch of church at Warsaw, Genesee Co., New York, 1832. Migrated from New York to Kirtland, Oct. 1832. Member of Kirtland high council, then Far West high council. Participated in Battle of Crooked River, near Ray Co., Missouri, 25 Oct. 1838. Elected to Nauvoo City Council, 1841, and became city marshal, 1843. Carried out orders of JS and city council to suppress *Nauvoo Expositor* press, 10 June 1844. Died at Nauvoo.

Grover, Thomas (22 July 1807–20 Feb. 1886); born at Whitehall, Washington Co., New York. Son of Thomas Grover and Polly Spaulding. Married Caroline Whiting of

Whitehall, 1828. Baptized by Warren A. Cowdery, Sept. 1834, at Freedom, Cattaraugus Co., New York. Appointed to Kirtland high council, 1836. Removed his family to Far West, where he served on high council, 1837. Located at Commerce, 1839. Appointed to Commerce high council, 1839. Member of Brigham Young pioneer company, 1847. Died at Farmington, Davis Co., Utah Territory.

Guymon, Thomas (10 Mar. 1787–20 Oct. 1855); born in Surry Co., North Carolina. Son of Isaiah Guymon and Elizabeth Flynn. Married Sarah Gordon, 23 Feb. 1809, in Stokes Co., North Carolina. Lived near Paris, Edgar Co., Illinois. Baptized by "Brother Rathburn" (Robert Rathbun Jr.?), by 9 June 1835. Selected to lead branch of church near Guymon's horse mill, Caldwell Co., Missouri, 21 June 1835. Migrated to Utah Territory, 1850. Died at Springville, Utah Co., Utah Territory.

Hancock, Levi Ward (7 Apr. 1803–10 June 1882); born at Springfield, Hampden Co., Massachusetts. Son of Thomas Hancock III and Amy Ward. Baptized, 16 Nov. 1830, at Kirtland. Married Clarissa Reed, 1833. Participated in Zion's Camp expedition to Missouri, 1834. Appointed a president of First Quorum of the Seventy, 28 Feb. 1835. Moved to Missouri, 1838. Located at Commerce, 1839. Enlisted in Mormon Battalion at Council Bluffs, Iowa Territory; served 1846–1847. Only general authority of church on march; served as unofficial chaplain for battalion. Arrived in Salt Lake Valley, 1847. Member of Utah territorial legislature for three terms, beginning in 1851. Died at Washington, Washington Co., Utah Territory.

Hancock, Solomon (14/15 Aug. 1793/1794–2 Dec. 1847); born at Springfield, Hampden Co., Massachusetts. Son of Thomas Hancock III and Amy Ward. Married first Alta Adams, 12 Mar. 1815. Baptized, 16 Nov. 1830, in Ohio. Lived in Jackson Co., Missouri. Appointed to Clay Co., Missouri, high council, 1834. Married second Phebe Adams, 28 June 1836. Member of Far West high council, 1838. Exiled from Missouri, spring 1839; located at Adams Co., Illinois. Presided over Yelrome (Morley's Settlement) branch of church, Hancock Co., Illinois, 1844. Died near Council Bluffs, Pottawattamie Co., Iowa, during exodus from Nauvoo.

Harriman, Henry (9 June 1804–17 May 1891); born at Bradford, Essex Co., Massachusetts. Son of Enoch Harriman and Sarah Brockbank. Married Clarissa Boynton, 26 Apr. 1827. Baptized by Orson Hyde, 29 Aug. 1832. Ordained an elder, 8 June 1833, at Bath, Grafton Co., New Hampshire. Moved to Kirtland, 1834. Participated in Zion's Camp expedition to Missouri, 1834. Member of First Quorum of the Seventy, 1835. Appointed a president of the Seventy, 6 Feb. 1838. An organizer of Kirtland Camp migration from Kirtland to Missouri, 1838. Lived at Adam-ondi-Ahman, Daviess Co., Missouri, Oct. 1838. Expelled from Missouri, spring 1839; located at Commerce that same year. Migrated to Salt Lake Valley, 1848. Died at Huntington, Emery Co., Utah Territory.

Harris, Emer (29 May 1781–28 Nov. 1869); born at Cambridge, Washington Co., New York. Son of Nathan Harris and Rhoda Lapham. Married first Roxana Peas, 22 July 1802. Married second Deborah Lott, 16 Jan. 1819. Married third Parna Chapell, 29 Mar. 1826. Baptized by Hyrum Smith and Newel Knight while living near Windham, Luzerne Co., Pennsylvania, 10 Feb. 1831. Moved to Kirtland, 1831. Migrated to Missouri, Oct. 1838; exiled to Quincy, Adams Co., Illinois, and then Commerce, 1839. Migrated to Utah Territory, 1852. Died at Logan, Cache Co., Utah Territory.

Harris, George Washington (1 Apr. 1780–1857); born at Lanesboro, Berkshire Co., Massachusetts. Son of James Harris and Diana (Margaret) Burton. Married first Elizabeth, ca. 1800. Married second Margaret, who died in 1828. Married third Lucinda Pendleton, 30 Nov. 1830, at Batavia, Genesee Co., New York. Moved to Terre Haute, Vigo Co., Indiana, where baptized in 1834. Moved to Missouri and appointed to Far West high council, 1838. Owned land at Adam-ondi-Ahman, Daviess Co., Missouri, 1838. Exiled from Far West. Appointed to Commerce high council, 1839. Elected alderman, 1841. President of Nauvoo Coach and Carriage Manufacturing Association. Started west with Mormon exodus from Nauvoo, 1846. Bishop at Council Bluffs, Iowa Territory, 1846. Lived at Council Bluffs until death.

Harris, Martin (18 May 1783–10 July 1875), farmer; born at Easton, Albany Co., New York. Son of Nathan Harris and Rhoda Lapham. In 1793, moved with parents to Swift's Landing, Ontario Co., New York, area. Married his first cousin Lucy Harris at Palmyra, Ontario Co., New York, 1808. Served in War of 1812 in New York militia. Became landowner of some 320 acres at Palmyra. Reportedly investigated the Quakers, Universalists, Restorationists, Baptists, Methodists, and Presbyterians. Took transcript of Book of Mormon characters to Charles Anthon and Samuel Latham Mitchill at New York City, Feb. 1828. Assisted JS as scribe during translation of first 116 manuscript pages of Book of Mormon, ca. 12 Apr.–14 June 1828. One of the Three Witnesses of the Book of Mormon, June 1829. Baptized by Oliver Cowdery, 6 Apr. 1830. Ordained a priest, by 9 June 1830. Paid printing costs for publication of Book of Mormon through sale of 151 acres. Led members of Manchester, Ontario Co., New York, branch from Palmyra, Wayne Co., New York, to Kirtland, May 1831. Ordained a high priest, 6 June 1831, at Kirtland. Participant in Zion's Camp expedition to Missouri, 1834. Member of Kirtland high council, 1834. Excommunicated, Dec. 1837. Rebaptized, 1842, at Kirtland. Member of high council of James J. Strang's Church of Jesus Christ of Latter Day Saints at Kirtland, 7 Aug. 1846. Joined with William E. McLellin's religious movement, 1847. Joined with William Smith to organize a church at Kirtland, 1858. Migrated to Salt Lake Valley, 1870. Rebaptized into LDS church, 1870. Died at Clarkston, Cache Co., Utah Territory.

Harris, Preserved (8 May 1785–18 Apr. 1867); born at Easton, Albany Co., New York. Son of Nathan Harris and Rhoda Lapham. In 1793, moved with parents to Swift's Landing, Ontario Co., New York, area. Married Nancy Warren, by 1811. Baptized, ca. 1831. Located at Mentor, Geauga Co., Ohio. Member of high council of James J. Strang's Church of Jesus Christ of Latter Day Saints at Kirtland. Died at Mentor.

Hedlock, Reuben (1809–5 July 1869); son of Jonathan Hedlock and Betty. Married Susan Wheeler, 12 Feb. 1827, at Bath, Grafton Co., New Hampshire. Lived at Avon, Livingston Co., New York, 1830. Received elder's license in LDS church, 1 Apr. 1836. Counselor to Alvah Beman in presidency of elders quorum in Kirtland; appointed president, 27 Nov. 1837, after Beman's death. Moved to Missouri with Kirtland Camp, 1838. Settled family in Commerce, Sept. 1839. Presided over British mission, Nov. 1843–6 Apr. 1845. Excommunicated at Manchester, England, 17 Oct. 1846. Lived in Marylebone, London, England, 1851, and Croydon, Sussex Co., England, 1861. Died at Gravesend, Kent Co., England.

Higbee, Elias (23 Oct. 1795–8 June 1843); born at Galloway, Gloucester Co., New Jersey. Son of Isaac Higbee and Sophia Somers. Moved to Clermont Co., Ohio, 1803. Married Sarah Elizabeth Ward, 10 Sept. 1818. Lived at Tate, Clermont Co., 1820. Located at Fulton, Hamilton Co., Ohio, 1830. Baptized, spring 1832, at Cincinnati. Ordained an elder by Isaac Higbee, Feb. 1833, at Cincinnati. Migrated to Jackson Co., Missouri, ca. 1833. Driven from Jackson Co., Nov. 1833. Ordained a high priest by Orson Pratt, 7 Aug. 1834, in Clay Co., Missouri. Member of Clay Co. high council, 1836. Presiding judge of Caldwell Co., Missouri. Appointed to Far West high council, 1837. With John Corrill, appointed church historian, 6 Apr. 1838, at Far West. Participated in Battle of Crooked River, near Ray Co., Missouri, 25 Oct. 1838. Fled Missouri; located at Quincy, Adams Co., Illinois, 1839. Member of committee that investigated lands offered for sale by Isaac Galland, 1839. Settled at Commerce, 1839. Traveled to Washington DC with JS to seek redress for Missouri grievances, Oct. 1839–Mar. 1840. Member of Nauvoo temple committee. Died at Nauvoo.

Hill, Isaac (28 Sept. 1806–25 June 1879), blacksmith, brick maker; born near Brighton, Beaver Co., Pennsylvania. Son of John Hill and Nancy Warrick. Married Mary Bell, 7 June 1827, at East Liverpool, Columbiana Co., Ohio. Baptized, Aug. 1833, at Liverpool. Lived at Kirtland, 1834. With Latter-day Saints in Missouri. Ordained a high priest by Isaac Higbee, 8 Dec. 1844, at Nauvoo. Migrated to Utah Territory, 1850. Bishop of Salt Lake City Second Ward, 1854–1864. Died at Fish Haven, Bear Lake Co., Idaho Territory. Buried at Saint Charles, Bear Lake Co.

Hillman, Mayhew (Mahew) (4 Mar. 1793–2 Nov. 1839); born at Chilmark, Dukes Co., Massachusetts. Son of Samson Hillman and Damaris Look. Married Sarah King, ca. 1818. Baptized, 1832. Lived at Kirtland, 1834–1838. Appointed to Kirtland high council, 3 Sept. 1837. Member of Adam-ondi-Ahman high council, 1838. Died at Commerce.

Hinkle, George M. (13 Nov. 1801–14 Nov. 1861), merchant, physician, minister, farmer; born in Jefferson Co., Kentucky. Son of Michael Hinkle and Nancy Higgins. Married first a Miss Starkey. Married second Mary Loman Hartman. Baptized, 1832. Served on high councils at Clay Co. and Caldwell Co., Missouri, 1836–1838. Commissioned colonel in Missouri state militia. During Missouri conflict in 1838, directed defense of De Witt, Carroll Co., Missouri, and commanded Mormon militia defending Far West. While assisting in negotiation of truce between state militia and Latter-day Saints at Far West, surrendered church leaders to General Samuel Lucas. Excommunicated, 17 Mar. 1839, at Quincy, Adams Co., Illinois. Organized religious society named The Church of Jesus Christ, the Bride, the Lamb's Wife at Moscow, Muscatine Co., Iowa Territory, 24 June 1840. Affiliated briefly with Sidney Rigdon and Church of Christ, 1845. Died at Decatur, Decatur Co., Iowa.

Hitchcock, Jesse (10 Aug. 1801–1846); born in Ashe Co., North Carolina. Son of Isaac Hitchcock and Elizabeth Wheeler. Married Mary Polly Hopper, 4 July 1821, at Lafayette Co., Missouri. Baptized by Oliver Cowdery, 20 July 1831. Located with Colesville, Broome Co., New York, branch in Jackson Co., Missouri, 1831–1833. Ordained a high priest, 26 Sept. 1833, in Jackson Co. Fled Jackson Co., Nov. 1833. Member of Missouri high council, 1836–1837. Served mission in Illinois to "disabuse the public mind" over arrest of JS, 1843. Member of the Seventy at Nauvoo. Died at Mount Pisgah, Union Co., Iowa Territory, en route to Salt Lake Valley.

Holbrook, Joseph (16 Jan. 1806–14 Nov. 1885), farmer, teacher, carpenter, miner, probate judge; born at Florence, Oneida Co., New York. Son of Moses Holbrook and Hannah Lucretia Morton. Married Nancy Lampson, 30 Dec. 1830, at Western, Worcester Co., Massachusetts. Baptized by Leonard C. Rich, 6 Jan. 1833, at Warsaw, Genesee Co., New York, and ordained a teacher, 7 Jan. 1833. Ordained an elder by Reynolds Cahoon, 12 Apr. 1833. Participated in Zion's Camp expedition to Missouri, 1834. Lived at Clay Co. and Caldwell Co., Missouri, 1836–1839. Commissioned a first lieutenant in Missouri state militia. Participated in Battle of Crooked River, near Ray Co., Missouri, 25 Oct. 1838. First counselor to President Joel Hills Johnson in Ramus stake, Macedonia, Hancock Co., Illinois, 1840. Commissioned a captain in Nauvoo Legion, 1841. Arrived in Salt Lake Valley, 20 Sept. 1848. Served as Davis Co., Utah Territory, judge, 1851–1859. Elected to Utah territorial legislature, 1857 and 1859. Served as a bishop's counselor. Died at Bountiful, Davis Co.

Hollister, John (12 Oct. 1792–1839); born at Marbletown, Ulster Co., New York. Son of Isaac Hollister and Elizabeth Newcomb. Married Lavina (Vina) Clearwater, ca. 1817, at Marbletown. Lived at Caroline, Tompkins Co., New York. Baptized at Portage Co., Ohio. Died in Illinois.

Holmes, Erastus (12 Oct. 1800–26 Aug. 1863); born at Salisbury, Litchfield Co., Connecticut. Son of George Holmes and Elizabeth (Betsy) Ball. Married Mary Ann Leming, after Jan. 1823, in Clermont Co., Ohio. Visited JS at Kirtland to inquire about LDS church, 14–16 Nov. 1835. Served as postmaster at Miami, Clermont Co., 1839–1846. Buried at Miami.

Holmes, Marietta Carter (4 Apr. 1820–20 Aug. 1840); born at Benson, Rutland Co., Vermont. Daughter of John S. Carter and Elizabeth Kenyon. Lived at Kirtland, by 1833. Father died of cholera, 24 June 1834, on Rush Creek, Clay Co., Missouri. Received patriarchal blessing from Joseph Smith Sr., 29 Jan. 1836, at Kirtland. Married to Jonathan Harriman Holmes by Frederick G. Williams, 13 Apr. 1837, at Kirtland. Exiled from Missouri; located at Nauvoo. Died at Nauvoo.

Holmes, Milton (16 Jan. 1811–30 Apr. 1881); born at Rowley, Essex Co., Massachusetts. Son of Nathaniel Holmes and Sarah Harriman. Lived at Napoli, Cattaraugus Co., New York, 1830. Assigned proselytizing mission to Upper Canada with Lyman E. Johnson, 20 Feb. 1834. Participated in Zion's Camp expedition to Missouri, 1834. Member of Wilford Woodruff company traveling from Fox Islands to Kirtland, 6 Oct. 1838. Married Aphia S. Woodman of Wilton, Kennebec Co., Maine, 25 Jan. 1846. Lived near Boston, 1847, when affiliated with James J. Strang's Church of Jesus Christ of Latter Day Saints. Died in Franklin Co., Maine.

Howe, Eber Dudley (9 June 1798–10 Nov. 1885), newspaper editor and publisher, farmer, manufacturer; born at Clifton Park, Saratoga Co., New York. Son of Samuel William Howe and Mabel Dudley. Enlisted with New York Volunteers in War of 1812 at Batavia, Genesee Co., New York, 1814. A founder of *Cleveland Herald,* 1819, at Cleveland, Cuyahoga Co., Ohio. Publisher of *Painesville Telegraph,* Painesville, Geauga Co., Ohio, beginning 1822. Married Sophia Hull of Clarence, Erie Co., New York, June 1823. An abolitionist; his house was a station on Underground Railroad to assist runaway slaves. Published anti-Mormon articles in *Painesville Telegraph* from 1831 to 1835, when he sold paper to his brother Asahel Howe. His *Mormonism Unvailed,* 1834, was first major anti-Mormon book published. With Doctor Philastus Hurlbut, advanced Rigdon-Spaulding theory of origin of Book of Mormon. Believer in Spiritualism at time he wrote his autobiography, 1878. Died at Painesville.

Howe, Harriet (ca. 1796–1856); born at Clifton Park, Saratoga Co., New York. Daughter of Samuel William Howe and Mabel Dudley. Sister of Eber D. Howe. Baptized, 1832, at Painesville, Geauga Co., Ohio. Died at Akron, Summit Co., Ohio.

Howe, Sophia Hull (1800–1866); of Clarence, Ontario Co., New York. Daughter of Warren Hull and Polly Gillet. Married Eber D. Howe, June 1823. Baptized, by 1834. Died at Painesville, Lake Co., Ohio.

Hubbell, Laura Fuller (1797–11 Apr. 1850); born at Granville, Washington Co., New York. Daughter of Willard S. Fuller and Tryphena Dryer. Married Adoniram Hubbell at Whitehall, Saratoga Co., New York, 2 Feb. 1819. Moved to Newburgh, Cuyahoga Co., Ohio, before June 1820; to Chagrin, Cuyahoga Co., by June 1826; and back to Newburgh in 1827. At Kirtland, Feb. 1831, professed to be a "prophetess" and to believe in Book of Mormon. Moved to Hartland Township, Livingston Co., Michigan Territory, Oct. 1835. Died at Hartland Township.

Humphrey, Solomon, Jr. (23 Sept. 1775–Sept. 1834); born in Canton, Hartford Co., Connecticut. Son of Solomon Humphrey and Lucy Case. Married Ursula Andrews. Baptized, presumably by JS, when he visited JS at Palmyra, Wayne Co., New York, in fall 1830. Accompanied Lucy Mack Smith company from Seneca Co., New York, to Kirtland, May 1831. Participated in Zion's Camp expedition to Missouri, 1834. Died in Clay Co., Missouri.

Hunt, Jefferson (22 Jan. 1804–11 May 1879), farmer, colonizer, scout; born at Edwards, Bracken Co., Kentucky. Son of John Hunt and Martha Jenkins. Married Celia Mounts, 1823. Baptized, ca. 1834. Moved to Clay Co., Missouri. Member of Far West elders quorum, 1838. Participated in Battle of Crooked River, near Ray Co., Missouri, 25 Oct. 1838. Moved to Illinois following extermination order of Governor Lilburn W. Boggs. Senior Mormon officer in Mormon Battalion in U.S. war with Mexico, 1846–1847. Migrated to Salt Lake Valley, Oct. 1847. Assisted in founding settlements that would become Provo, Utah Co., Utah Territory, 1849, and San Bernardino, San Bernardino Co., California, 1851–1857. Member of California legislature. Participated in Utah War as member of territorial Nauvoo Legion, 1857–1858. Died in Oxford, Bannock Co., Idaho Territory.

Hunt, Susanna (Susan) Bailey Smith (27 Oct. 1835–14 Dec. 1905); born at Kirtland. Daughter of Samuel H. Smith and Mary Bailey. Located at Marrowbone, Daviess Co., Missouri, 1838. Located at Macomb, McDonough Co., Illinois, Mar. 1839, and Commerce later that year. Orphaned, 1844; lived with mother's sister in Wisconsin. Married Alonzo A. Hunt, ca. 1852. Died at Dell Rapids, Minnehaha Co., South Dakota.

Huntington, Dimick Baker (26 May 1808–1 Feb. 1879), farmer, blacksmith, shoemaker, constable, deputy sheriff, Indian interpreter; born at Watertown, Jefferson Co., New York. Son of William Huntington and Zina Baker. Married first Susan Maria Cardin of Watertown, ca. 1823. Married second Fannie Maria Allen, 1830, at Lorraine, Jefferson Co.,

New York. Baptized, 1 Aug. 1835. Constable at Far West and later deputy sheriff. Participated in Battle of Crooked River, near Ray Co., Missouri, 25 Oct. 1838. Coroner and constable at Nauvoo. Arrived in Salt Lake Valley, July 1847. Served as interpreter in meetings between Indian tribes and LDS church leaders. Died at Salt Lake City.

Hurlbut, Doctor Philastus (3 Feb. 1809–16 June 1883), clergyman, farmer; born at Chittenden Co., Vermont. "Doctor" was his given name. Baptized, 1832/1833. Ordained an elder by Sidney Rigdon, 18 Mar. 1833. Excommunicated, June 1833. Married Maria Sheldon Woodbury, 29 Apr. 1834, in Ashtabula Co., Ohio. Employed by Geauga Co., Ohio, citizens to collect information about Smith family and origin of Book of Mormon. Findings were published in Eber D. Howe's *Mormonism Unvailed,* 1834. Arrested for allegedly threatening JS's life, 1834, and ordered to enter into recognizance to keep the peace. Lived at Elk Creek, Erie Co., Pennsylvania. Moved to Mentor, Geauga Co. Lived at Bedford, St. Laurence Co., Michigan, where he became United Brethren minister. Settled at Sandusky Co., Ohio. Died at Madison/Gibsonburgh, Sandusky Co.

Hyde, Heman Tilton (18 June 1812–26 May 1842); born at Strafford, Orange Co., Vermont. Son of Heman Hyde and Polly Wyman Tilton. Baptized by JS or Parley P. Pratt, 11 Mar. 1834, at Freedom, Cattaraugus Co., New York. Participated in Zion's Camp expedition to Missouri, 1834. Married Eunice Sawyer, 13 Oct. 1835, at Freedom. Moved to Kirtland, Feb. 1836. Attempted to migrate to Far West, but compelled by mob action to settle in Quincy, Adams Co., Illinois, 1838. Died at Payson, Adams Co.

Hyde, Orson (8 Jan. 1805–28 Nov. 1878), clerk, storekeeper, schoolteacher, editor, businessman, lawyer; born at Oxford, New Haven Co., Connecticut. Son of Nathan Hyde and Sally Thorpe. Joined Methodist church, ca. 1827. Later affiliated with Reformed Baptists (later Disciples of Christ or Campbellites). Baptized into LDS church by Sidney Rigdon, 2 Oct. 1831, at Kirtland. Baptized many during proselytizing mission with Samuel H. Smith to eastern states, 1832. Appointed clerk to First Presidency, 1833. Member of Kirtland high council, 1834. Participated in Zion's Camp expedition to Missouri, 1834. Married to Marinda Nancy Johnson by Sidney Rigdon, 4 Sept. 1834, at Kirtland. Member of Quorum of the Twelve, 1835. Served mission to western New York and Upper Canada, 1836. Served mission to England with Heber C. Kimball, 1837–1838. Sided with dissenters against JS, 1838. Lived at Howard Co., Missouri, winter 1838–1839. Restored to church and to Quorum of the Twelve at Commerce, 27 June 1839. Served mission to Palestine to dedicate land for gathering of Israel, 1840–1842. Member of Nauvoo City Council, 1843–1844. Participated in plural marriage during JS's lifetime. Departed Nauvoo during exodus to the West, mid-May 1846. Served mission to Great Britain, 1846–1847. Presided over Latter-day Saints in Iowa before migrating to Utah Territory. Published *Frontier Guardian* at Kanesville, Pottawattamie Co., Iowa, 1849–1852. Migrated to Utah Territory, 1852. Elected to Utah territorial legislature, 27 Nov. 1852. Presided over church in Carson Co., Utah Territory, 1855–1856. Moved to Sanpete Co., Utah Territory, 1860; presiding ecclesiastical authority there, 1860–1877. Died at Spring City, Sanpete Co.

Jackman, Levi (28 July 1797–23 July 1876); born at Vershire, Orange Co., Vermont. Son of Moses French Jackman and Elizabeth Carr. Married Angeline Myers Brady, 13 Nov. 1817, at Alexander, Genesee Co., New York. Baptized by Harvey G. Whitlock, 7 May 1831, in Portage Co., Ohio. Left for Jackson Co., Missouri, 2 May 1832. Member of

Clay Co., Missouri, high council, 3 June 1834. Moved to Kirtland, July 1835. Returned to Clay Co., 1836. Appointed to Far West high council, Nov. 1837. Obtained land at Commerce, 1839. Migrated with Brigham Young pioneer company to Salt Lake Valley, 1847. Died at Salem, Utah Co., Utah Territory.

Jackson, Henry (?–before 1850?); married Sarah. Disciplined at church conference at Winchester, Randolph Co., Indiana; subsequently reordained an elder, Nov.–Dec. 1831. Attended special conference held at Big Blue settlement, Kaw Township, Jackson Co., Missouri, Sept. 1832. Plaintiff in church disciplinary proceeding near Guymon's horse mill, Caldwell Co., Missouri, which was appealed to Far West high council, 28 Apr. 1838.

Jackson, Sarah (1815–after 1860); born in Kentucky. Married first Henry Jackson. Henry disciplined at church conference at Winchester, Randolph Co., Indiana, Nov.–Dec. 1831. Lived at Kaw Township, Jackson Co., Missouri, Sept. 1832. Present with husband during appeal heard before Far West high council, 28 Apr. 1838. Married second James Lipstrap, 28 May 1853, in Jackson Co. Lived at Kansas City, Jackson Co., 1860.

Jackson, Truman (ca. 1802?–after 1880); born in Vermont. Lived in Verona, Oneida Co., New York, 1820–1830. Evidently baptized in Ohio. Member of Kirtland elders quorum, 27 Feb. 1836. Married to Ann Brown by Oliver Cowdery, 10 Sept. 1837, at Kirtland. Lived at Greenville, Bureau Co., Illinois, 1880.

James, Samuel (1814–Apr. 1876); born in Washington Co., Pennsylvania. Ordained a high priest and appointed to Kirtland high council, 13 Jan. 1836. Married Marian Evans, 6 Jan. 1841, at Montrose, Lee Co., Iowa Territory. Appointed to serve mission in England, 11 May 1843. Followed Sidney Rigdon after death of JS. Lived at Jefferson Co., Ohio, 1850–1870. Died at Steubenville, Jefferson Co.

Johnson, Angeline Sarah Carter (26 Aug. 1823–1888); born at Benson, Rutland Co., Vermont. Daughter of John S. Carter and Elizabeth Kenyon. Lived at Kirtland, by 1833. Father died of cholera, 24 June 1834, on Rush Creek, Clay Co., Missouri. Received patriarchal blessing from Joseph Smith Sr., 29 Jan. 1836, at Kirtland. Lived at Upper Alton, Madison Co., Illinois, following exile from Missouri. Married John S. Johnson, 27 June 1849, in Whiteside Co., Illinois. Buried at Oakfield Cemetery at Brayton, Exira Township, Audubon Co., Iowa.

Johnson, Ezekiel (12 Jan. 1773–13 Jan. 1848); born at Uxbridge, Worcester Co., Massachusetts. Son of Ezekiel Johnson and Bethia Gurnsey. Married Julia Ellis Hills, 12 Jan. 1801, at Grafton, Worcester Co. Moved to Vermont, and to Fredonia, Pomfret Township, Chautauque Co., New York, 1813. Opposed baptism of family into LDS church. Followed Julia and their children to Kirtland, spring 1833. Located with a daughter at Mentor, Geauga Co., Ohio. Lived with Latter-day Saints at Nauvoo. Died at Nauvoo.

Johnson, John (11 Apr. 1779–30 July 1843); born at Chesterfield, Cheshire Co., New Hampshire. Son of Israel Johnson and Abigail Higgins. Married Elsa Jacobs, 22 June 1800. Settled at Hiram, Portage Co., Ohio, 1818. Baptized, ca. 1831. JS lived at Johnson home, Sept. 1831–Apr. 1832 and June 1832–Sept. 1832. Moved to Kirtland, 1833. Provided funds to church for purchase of Peter French properties and other properties. Member of Kirtland high council, 1834–1837. Disaffected from church, 1837–1838. Died at Kirtland.

Johnson, Luke (3 Nov. 1807–9 Dec. 1861), farmer, teacher, doctor; born at Pomfret, Windsor Co., Vermont. Son of John Johnson and Elsa Jacobs. Lived at Hiram, Portage Co.,

Ohio, when baptized by JS, 10 May 1831. Ordained a priest by Christian Whitmer shortly after baptism. Ordained an elder, by Oct. 1831. Ordained a high priest, 25 Oct. 1831. Served missions to Pennsylvania, Virginia, and Kentucky, 1831–1833. Married Susan Harminda Poteet, 1 Nov. 1833, in Cabell Co., Virginia. Appointed to Kirtland high council, 17 Feb. 1834. Participated in Zion's Camp expedition to Missouri, 1834. Member of Quorum of the Twelve, 1835–1837. Served mission to eastern states with Twelve, 1835, and to New York and Upper Canada, 1836. Constable in Kirtland. Disfellowshipped, 3 Sept. 1837. Reinstated to church and membership in Quorum of the Twelve, 10 Sept. 1837. Excommunicated, Dec. 1837. Taught school in Virginia and also studied medicine, which he practiced at Kirtland. Rebaptized into LDS church by Orson Hyde, 8 Mar. 1846, at Nauvoo. Following exodus from Nauvoo in 1846, became member of Brigham Young pioneer company; arrived in Salt Lake Valley, July 1847. Bishop at St. John, Tooele Co., Utah Territory, 1858. Died at Salt Lake City.

Johnson, Lyman Eugene (24 Oct. 1811–20 Dec. 1856), merchant, lawyer; born at Pomfret, Windsor Co., Vermont. Son of John Johnson and Elsa Jacobs. Baptized by Sidney Rigdon, Feb. 1831. Ordained an elder by Oliver Cowdery, 25 Oct. 1831. Ordained a high priest, 1 Nov. 1831. Served missions with Orson Pratt to eastern states and New England, 1832–1833, and Upper Canada, 1834. Participated in Zion's Camp expedition to Missouri, 1834. Member of Quorum of the Twelve, 1835–1838. Married Sarah Lang, by 1836. Disfellowshipped, 3 Sept. 1837, but restored to fellowship, 10 Sept. 1837. Migrated to Far West. Excommunicated, 13 Apr. 1838. Lived in Iowa Territory by 1842. Remained friendly to church. Practiced law at Davenport, Scott Co., and Keokuk, Lee Co., Iowa. Died near Prairie du Chien, Crawford Co., Wisconsin.

Johnson, Orson (15 June 1803–23 Mar. 1883); born at Bath, Grafton Co., New Hampshire. Son of Thomas Johnson and Elizabeth (Betsey) Smith. Married Nancy Mason, 24 Oct. 1827, at Bath. Baptized by Orson Pratt and Lyman E. Johnson, 1832. Participated in Zion's Camp expedition to Missouri, 1834. Member of Kirtland high council, 28 Aug. 1834. Excommunicated, 1837. Lived at Peoria, Peoria Co., Illinois, 1840, 1850; and at Altona, Knox Co., Illinois, 1880. Died at Riverside, San Bernardino Co., California.

Johnson, Susan Ellen (16 Dec. 1814–16 Mar. 1836); born at Pomfret Township, Chautauque Co., New York. Daughter of Ezekiel Johnson and Julia Ellis Hills. Baptized, ca. 1833, and moved to Kirtland. Died of "consumption" at Kirtland.

Kimball, Heber Chase (14 June 1801–22 June 1868), blacksmith, potter; born at Sheldon, Franklin Co., Vermont. Son of Solomon Farnham Kimball and Anna Spaulding. Married Vilate Murray, 22 Nov. 1822, at Mendon, Monroe Co., New York. Member of Baptist church at Mendon, 1831. Baptized into LDS church by Alpheus Gifford, 15/16 Apr. 1832, at Mendon. Ordained an elder by Joseph Young, 1832. Moved to Kirtland, 1833. Participated in Zion's Camp expedition to Missouri, 1834. Ordained member of Quorum of the Twelve, 1835. Served mission to the East with Quorum of the Twelve, 1835. Presided over first Latter-day Saint missionaries to British Isles, 1837–1838. Moved from Kirtland to Far West, 1838. Worked closely with Brigham Young and others in supervising removal of Latter-day Saints from Missouri, 1838–1839. Present at Far West temple site on 26 Apr. 1839, when members of Quorum of the Twelve formally began their missionary assignment to British Isles. In removing from Missouri, initially located at Quincy, Adams Co., Illinois, and then Commerce, May 1839. Served mission with Quorum of the Twelve to British Isles, 1839–1841. Elected to Nauvoo City Council, 1841. Participated in plural marriage during JS's lifetime. Served mission to eastern states, 1843. Labored on Nauvoo temple. Joined exodus from Illinois into Iowa Territory, Feb. 1846. Member of Brigham Young pioneer company to Salt Lake Valley; arrived July 1847. Sustained as first counselor to Brigham Young in First Presidency at Council Bluffs, Pottawattamie Co., Iowa, 27 Dec. 1847. Elected lieutenant governor in provisional State of Deseret. Served in Utah territorial legislature. Died at Salt Lake City.

King, Austin Augustus (21 Sept. 1802–22 Apr. 1870), attorney, judge; born at Sullivan Co., Tennessee. Son of Walter King and Nancy Sevier. Married Nancy Harris Roberts, May 1828, at Jackson, Madison Co., Tennessee. Moved to Missouri in 1830, where he practiced law at Columbia, Boone Co. Elected to state legislature as Jacksonian Democrat from Boone Co., 1834 and 1836. In 1837, removed to Richmond, Ray Co., Missouri, where he received appointment as circuit judge in northwestern Missouri by Governor Lilburn W. Boggs. Between 1837 and 1848, served as judge of Missouri's Fifth Judicial Circuit, consisting of counties of Clinton, Ray, Caldwell, Clay, Daviess, Carroll, and Livingston. In Nov. 1838, presided at preliminary hearing of JS and other Mormons at Richmond. Committed them to jail pending trials to be held following March. Governor of Missouri, 1848–1852. Represented Missouri in U.S. Congress, 1862–1864. Died at St. Louis. Buried in Richmond.

Kingsbury, Horace (1798–12 Mar. 1853); born in New Hampshire. Married Dianthe Stiles, 20 July 1826. In 1827, moved to Painesville, Geauga Co., Ohio. Died at Painesville.

Kingsbury, Joseph Corrodon (2 May 1812–15 Oct. 1898); born at Enfield, Hartford Co., Connecticut. Son of Solomon Kingsbury and Bathsheba Amanda Pease. Moved from Enfield to Painesville, Geauga Co., Ohio, ca. 1813. Baptized by Burr Riggs, 15 Jan. 1832, at Kirtland. Appointed to Kirtland high council, 1835. Married to Caroline Whitney by JS, 3 Feb. 1836, at Kirtland. Moved to Far West, May–Sept. 1838. Joined exodus from Missouri, Jan. 1839, and finally located at Montrose, Lee Co., Iowa Territory. Clerk in JS's red brick store at Nauvoo, 1842. Entered Salt Lake Valley, Sept. 1847. Died at Salt Lake City.

Knight, Lydia Goldthwaite (9 June 1812–3 Apr. 1884); born at Sutton, Worcester Co., Massachusetts. Daughter of Jesse G. Goldthwaite and Sally Burt. Married first Calvin Bailey, fall 1828, but deserted by him, 1831. Moved to home of Eleazer Freeman Nickerson at Mount Pleasant, Brantford Township, Wentworth Co., Gore District, Upper Canada, Feb. 1833. Baptized by JS, 27 Oct. 1833, at Mount Pleasant. Moved to Kirtland, 1835. Married second to Newel Knight by JS, 24 Nov. 1835, at Kirtland. Moved to Missouri, 1836, and Illinois, 1839. Left Nauvoo with Mormon exodus, 1846. Traveled with Newel Knight and others to Camp Ponca on Niobrara River in what is now Knox Co., Nebraska, 1846. Migrated to Salt Lake Valley as widow, 1850. Died at St. George, Washington Co., Utah Territory.

Knight, Newel (13 Sept. 1800–11 Jan. 1847), miller, farmer; born at Marlborough, Windham Co., Vermont. Son of Joseph Knight Sr. and Polly Peck. Moved to Colesville, Broome Co., New York, 1811. Married first Sally Coburn, 7 June 1825. Became acquainted with JS when Knight's father hired JS as farmhand, 1826. Baptized by David Whitmer, last week of May 1830, at Seneca Lake, Seneca Co., New York. Branch president who led Colesville branch from Broome Co. to Thompson, Geauga Co., Ohio, 1831. Colesville branch again moved, this time to Kaw Township, Jackson Co., Missouri, June–July 1831. Ordained a high priest, by July 1832. Expelled from Jackson Co., 1833. Member of Clay Co., Missouri, high council, 1834. Married second to Lydia Goldthwaite Bailey by JS, 24 Nov. 1835, at Kirtland. Lived at Clay Co., 1836–1838. Located at Far West, Feb. 1838. Member of Far West high council, 1837–1838. Left Far West during exodus. Commerce high council member, 1839–1845. Left Nauvoo, 18 Apr. 1846. Directed by Brigham Young to assist intended advance party to Rocky Mountains, 1846. Died at Camp Ponca on Niobrara River in what is now Knox Co., Nebraska.

Knight, Vinson (14 Mar. 1804–31 July 1842), farmer, druggist; born at Norwich, Hampshire Co., Massachusetts. Son of Rudolphus Knight and Rispah (Rizpah) Lee. Married Martha McBride, 1826, at Perrysburg, Cattaraugus Co., New York. Owned farm at Perrysburg when baptized, spring 1834. Moved to Kirtland, by 1835. Ordained an elder, 2 Jan. 1836. Ordained a high priest and appointed counselor to Bishop Newel K. Whitney, 13 Jan. 1836, at Kirtland. Located at Adam-ondi-Ahman, Daviess Co., Missouri, summer 1838. Appointed acting bishop at Adam-ondi-Ahman. Exiled from Missouri; located at Quincy, Adams Co., Illinois, 1839. Church land agent; with others purchased approximately nineteen thousand acres in Half-Breed Tract in Lee Co., Iowa Territory, from Isaac Galland, and about 190 acres in Hancock Co., Illinois, from Galland and from Hugh White, 1839. Appointed bishop of Lower Ward at Commerce, 5 Oct. 1839. Elected to Nauvoo City Council, 1 Feb. 1841. Died at Nauvoo.

Lewis, Job L. (10 Sept. 1776–after 1848); born at Exeter, Washington Co., Rhode Island. Son of Joseph Lewis and Mary Stanton. Married Margaret Lowers, New York, ca. 1807. Lived at Westfield, Chautauque Co., New York, 1830. Baptized, by 1833. Excommunicated, 1836.

Lewis, Lloyd L. (18 July 1807–24 Dec. 1902); born at Onondaga Co., New York. Son of Job L. Lewis and Margaret Lowers. Baptized, 1835, at Westfield, Chautauque Co., New York. Disaffected from church, by Nov. 1835. Married first Lucy, ca. 1837, in Illinois. Married second Elizabeth Donnelly, 23 Sept. 1848, at Knoxville, Knox Co., Illinois. Died at Minong, Washburn Co., Wisconsin.

Lewis, Lorenzo L. (ca. 1812–ca. May 1897); born in New York. Son of Job L. Lewis and Margaret Lowers. Probably baptized at Westfield, Chautauque Co., New York. Excommunicated, 28 Sept. 1835. Married Mandana Isabel Gould, ca. 1836, in Illinois. Died at Salem, Marion Co., Oregon. Buried at Gervais, Marion Co.

Lightner, Adam, Jr. (14 Apr. 1810–29 Aug. 1885); born at Lancaster, Lancaster Co., Pennsylvania. Son of Adam Lightner and Mary Trout. Married Mary Elizabeth Rollins, 11 Aug. 1835, at Liberty, Clay Co., Missouri. Never member of LDS church. Lived in Far West, 1837. Defense witness in JS preliminary hearing, 7 Sept. 1838. Lived at Montrose, Lee Co., Iowa Territory, 1840. Migrated from Wisconsin to Salt Lake Valley, 1863. Located at Minersville, Beaver Co., Utah Territory, 1863.

Littlefield, Waldo (24 May 1797–29 Jan. 1879); born at Petersburg, Rensselaer Co., New York. Son of Josiah Littlefield and Eunice Hunt. Married Mercy Higgins, 18 May 1817. Baptized and ordained a deacon by Jared Carter, 1832. Participated in Zion's Camp expedition to Missouri, 1834, and remained in Clay Co., Missouri, until 1836. Removed to Caldwell Co., Missouri, and was part of forced exodus from Missouri during winter 1838–1839. Lived at Quincy, Adams Co., Illinois, 1839. Ordained an elder, 1840. Appointed a president of Eleventh Quorum of the Seventy, 8 Oct. 1844, at Nauvoo. Migrated to Utah Territory, 1852. Died at Cannonville, Garfield Co., Utah Territory.

Loud, Austin (3 Nov. 1797–10 Feb. 1852), builder, millwright; born at Westhampton, Hampshire Co., Massachusetts. Son of Caleb Loud Jr. and Jerusha Clark. Married Mehetable Bartlett, 11 Dec. 1821. Moved to Kirtland, 1832. Built gristmill and sawmill there. Died at Huntsburg, Geauga Co., Ohio.

Lowell, Susannah (Susan). See Boynton, Susannah (Susan) Lowell.

Lyman, Amasa Mason (30 Mar. 1813–4 Feb. 1877); born at Lyman, Grafton Co., New Hampshire. Son of Roswell Lyman and Martha Mason. Baptized by Lyman E. Johnson, 27 Apr. 1832, at Lyman. Moved to Kirtland, 1832. Participated in Zion's Camp expedition to Missouri, 1834. Married Maria Louisa Tanner, 10 June 1835, at Kirtland. Moved to Far West, 1837; to Walnut Grove, McDonough Co., Illinois, 1839; and to Nauvoo, 1840. Ordained member of Quorum of the Twelve, 20 Aug. 1842, at Nauvoo. Counselor in First Presidency, 1843–1844. Captain of wagon companies to Salt Lake Valley, 1847, 1848. Appointed to establish colony of San Bernardino, Los Angeles Co., California, 1851. Migrated to Salt Lake Valley, 1858. President of European Mission, 1860–1862. Moved to Fillmore, Millard Co., Utah, 1862. Deprived of apostleship, 6 Oct. 1867, and excommunicated, 12 May 1870. President of Godbeite Church of Zion, 1870. Died at Fillmore.

Lyon, Aaron Child (ca. 1781–30 Sept. 1839); born in Holland, Hampton Co., Massachusetts. Married Roxana Palmer, 15 July 1806. Baptized, ca. 1831. Labored on Kirtland temple. Acquired land at Caldwell Co., Missouri, including town lot at Far West, 1836–1837. Used claims of revelation to attempt to coerce Sarah Jackson to marry him. Jackson's husband brought charges. Far West high council stripped him of high priest office, 28 Apr. 1838. Died on Bear Creek, Hancock Co., Illinois.

Lyon, Windsor Palmer (8 Feb. 1809–Jan. 1849); born at Orwell, Addison Co., Vermont. Son of Aaron Child Lyon and Roxana Palmer. Baptized, 1832, in New York. Lived at Willoughby, Cuyahoga Co., Ohio, 1835, where he owned a store. Owned land in Far West, 1836. Married Sylvia Porter Sessions, Mar. 1838, at Far West. Opened drug and variety store at Nauvoo. Died at Iowa City, Johnson Co., Iowa.

Markham, Stephen (9 Feb. 1800–10 Mar. 1878); born at Avon, Livingston Co., New York. Son of David Markham and Dinah Merry. Married Hannah Hogaboom of Manchester, Bennington Co., Vermont. Baptized, July 1837, at Chester, Geauga Co., Ohio. Led company of sixty Latter-day Saints to Far West, 1838. Escorted family of JS from Far West to Quincy, Adams Co., Illinois, 1839. Returned to Far West and assisted in disposal of Mormon properties. Moved to Illinois, 1839. Appointed counselor to Nauvoo priests quorum president Samuel Rolfe, 1841. Captain in Brigham Young pioneer company migrating to Salt Lake Valley, 1847. Died at Spanish Fork, Utah Co., Utah Territory.

Marks, William (15 Nov. 1792–22 May 1872); born at Rutland, Rutland Co., Vermont. Son of Cornell (Cornwall) Marks and Sarah Goodrich. Married Rosannah R. Robinson, 2 May 1813. Lived at Portage, Allegany Co., New York, where he was baptized, by Apr. 1835. Moved to Kirtland, by Sept. 1837. Appointed as member of Kirtland high council and as agent to Bishop Newel K. Whitney, 1837. President of Kirtland stake, 1838. While at Kirtland, appointed stake president at Far West, 8 July 1838. Did not reach Far West before expulsion of Latter-day Saints from Missouri. Located with Latter-day Saints at Quincy, Adams Co., Illinois, 1839. Commerce stake president, 5 Oct. 1839. Elected alderman of Nauvoo, 1841. Appointed a regent of University of Nauvoo, 1841. Member of Council of Fifty, 1844. Aligned himself with leadership claims of Sidney Rigdon following death of JS, 1844. Counselor to James J. Strang, 16 Dec. 1846. Affiliated with Charles B. Thompson, 1852–1853, and John E. Page, 1855, in leadership of new religious movements. Baptized into RLDS church, 10 June 1859, at Amboy, Lee Co., Illinois. Ordained a counselor in RLDS church presidency, 1863. Died at Plano, Kendall Co., Illinois.

Marsh, James G. (31 May 1823–7 May 1838); probably born at Charlestown, Middlesex Co., Massachusetts. Son of Thomas B. Marsh and Elizabeth Godkin. Moved to Palmyra, Wayne Co., New York, by Sept. 1830. Migrated to Kirtland, May 1831. Baptized, early spring 1832, at Kirtland. Arrived at Jackson Co., Missouri, 10 Nov. 1832. Died at Far West.

Marsh, Thomas Baldwin (1 Nov. 1800–25 Jan. 1866), farmer, hotel worker, waiter, horse groom, grocer, type foundry worker, teacher; born at Acton, Middlesex Co., Massachusetts. Son of James Marsh and Molly Law. Married Elizabeth Godkin, 1 Nov. 1820, at New York City. Joined Methodist church at Boston. Migrated to Palmyra, Wayne Co., New York, by Sept. 1830. Baptized into LDS church by David Whitmer, 3 Sept. 1830, at Cayuga Lake, Seneca Co., New York. Ordained an elder by Oliver Cowdery, Sept. 1830. Moved to Kirtland with Manchester, Ontario Co., New York, branch of church, May 1831. Ordained a high priest by Lyman Wight, 6 June 1831, at Kirtland. Served mission to Missouri, June–Aug. 1831. Moved to Jackson Co., Missouri, 10 Nov. 1832. Appointed president of Big Blue River, Jackson Co., branch. Expelled from Jackson Co., 1833. Member of Clay Co., Missouri, high council, 1834. Ordained member of Quorum of the Twelve, 26 Apr. 1835, at Kirtland. Sustained as president of Quorum of the Twelve, 2 May 1835. Served mission with the Twelve to eastern states and Upper Canada, 1835. President pro tempore of church in Far West, 5 Feb. 1838. Withdrew from church at Far West, 22 Oct. 1838. Excommunicated in absentia, 17 Mar. 1839, at Quincy, Adams Co., Illinois. Sought readmittance, Jan. 1857. Rebaptized into LDS church at Florence, Douglas Co., Nebraska, 16 July 1857. Migrated to Utah Territory in 1857. Settled at Spanish Fork, Utah Co., Utah Territory. Moved to Ogden, Weber Co., Utah Territory, latter part of 1862. Died at Ogden.

Matthews, Robert, aliases Matthias the Prophet and Joshua the Jewish Minister (1788–1841), carpenter, joiner, merchant; born at Cambridge, Washington Co., New York. Raised in Anti-Burgher Secession Church. Married Margaret Wright, 1813, at New York City. Adopted beliefs of Methodism and then Judaism. Lived at Albany, Albany Co., New York, 1825. Claimed to be God the Father reincarnated in body of Matthias, the ancient apostle. Prophesied destruction of Albany, 1830. Left Albany and his family to embark on grand apostolic preaching tour through eastern and southern U.S. Upon his return to New York, recruited local religious figures Elijah Pierson and Benjamin Folger. Committed to hospital for the insane at Bellevue, New York City, for a time. Little is known of Matthias after his 1835 visit with JS at Kirtland. Reported to have died in Iowa Territory.

McAlister, Samuel (ca. 1758–21 Feb. 1846); born in Ireland. Married Elizabeth Salmond of Rhode Island, ca. 1790. Early resident of Mount Pleasant, Brantford Township, Wentworth Co., Gore District, Upper Canada; operated inn there for many years. Baptized by JS, 27 or 28 Oct. 1833, at Mount Pleasant. Died at Mount Pleasant.

McBride, Reuben (16 June 1803–26 Feb. 1891); born at Chester, Washington Co., New York. Son of Daniel McBride and Abigail Mead. Married Ann Anderson, 16 June 1833, at Villanova, Chautauque Co., New York. Baptized, 4 Mar. 1834, in Villanova. Participated in Zion's Camp expedition to Missouri, 1834. Ordained a seventy, 1836, in Kirtland. Lived at Kirtland, ca. 1836–1848. Assigned to oversee church interests there after departure of main body of Latter-day Saints in 1838. Appointed counselor in Kirtland bishopric, 22 May 1841. Migrated to Salt Lake Valley, by 1852. Returned to Kirtland, 1851, and led company of Latter-day Saints from there to Utah Territory, 1858. Died at Fillmore, Millard Co., Utah Territory.

McCleary, Sophronia Smith (16 May 1803–22 July 1876); born at Tunbridge, Orange Co., Vermont. Daughter of Joseph Smith Sr. and Lucy Mack. Married first Calvin W. Stoddard, 30 Dec. 1827, at Palmyra, Wayne Co., New York. Lived at Macedon, Wayne Co., 1830. Lived at Kirtland, by 1832. Married second William McCleary, 11 Feb. 1838, at Kirtland. Left Kirtland for Far West, May 1838. Fled to Illinois, Feb. 1839. Lived at Ramus, Hancock Co., Illinois, 1843. Lived at Tennessee, McDonough Co., Illinois, 1860. Received into RLDS church, 8 Apr. 1873. Died at Fountain Green, Hancock Co. Buried at Colchester, McDonough Co.

McCleary, William (9 Oct. 1793–ca. 1847); born at Rupert, Bennington Co., Vermont. Married Sophronia Smith Stoddard, 11 Feb. 1838, at Kirtland. Ordained an elder by Reuben Hedlock, 26 Feb. 1838, at Kirtland. Left Ohio for Caldwell Co., Missouri, May 1838. Exiled from Missouri, Feb. 1839, and located initially at Quincy, Adams Co., Illinois. Lived at Kirtland, Mar. 1841. Lived at Ramus, Hancock Co., Illinois, when appointed to conduct election for board of trustees for that community, 3 Mar. 1843. Built wagons in Nauvoo in preparation for Mormon exodus, 1845–1846, but remained in Illinois.

McCown, Marcellus (9 Sept. 1807–1881); born at Pompey, Onondaga Co., New York. Married first Phebe Weston of Freeport, Cumberland Co., Maine. Lived at Farmersville, Cattaraugus Co., New York, 1830. Lived at Quincy, Adams Co., Illinois, 1840. Married second Susan Ann Lamoreaux in Adams Co., 1843. Lived at Yelrome (Morley's Settlement), Hancock Co., Illinois, 1845. A Latter-day Saint by 1846. Died in Mills Co., Iowa.

McLellin, William E. (18 Jan. 1806–24 Apr. 1883), farmer, schoolteacher, physician, publisher; born at Smith Co., Tennessee. Son of Charles McLellin. Married first Cynthia Ann, 30 July 1829. Baptized by Hyrum Smith, 20 Aug. 1831, in Jackson Co., Missouri. Ordained an elder by Hyrum Smith and Edward Partridge, 24 Aug. 1831. Served two short-term missions. Married second Emeline Miller, 26 Apr. 1832, at Ravenna, Portage Co., Ohio. Left Ohio for Independence, Jackson Co., Missouri, 2 May 1832. Served mission to Missouri and Illinois with Parley P. Pratt, Jan.–June 1833. Fled with fellow Latter-day Saints from Jackson Co. into Clay Co., Missouri, Nov. 1833. Proselytized in Indiana on way to Kirtland, 1834. Appointed instructor in Kirtland School, 1834–1835. Appointed and ordained member of Quorum of the Twelve, 15 Feb. 1835. Disfellowshipped over difficulties arising during eastern mission with Quorum of the Twelve; reinstated 26 Sept. 1835. Wrote letter of withdrawal from church, Aug. 1836. Again sustained to Quorum of the Twelve, 3 Sept. 1837, at Kirtland. In Far West, commissioned captain in First Company, Fifty-Ninth Regiment, Second Brigade, Third Division of Missouri state militia, 22 Nov. 1837. Associated with factions organized under leadership of George M. Hinkle, William Law, Sidney Rigdon, James J. Strang, David Whitmer, and Granville Hedrick. Broke with all organized religion, 1869. Died at Independence.

McWethy (McWithey), Eliza Ann. See Webb, Eliza Ann McWethy (McWithey).

McWithy, Isaac (13 Feb. 1776–4 June 1851); born in New York. Married Hannah Taylor of Vermont. Lived at Bennington, Genesee Co., New York, with family of five, 1830. Ordained an elder, 15 Feb. 1833. Lived at Kirtland, 1835. Died at Kirtland.

Middleton, Julia M. Smith (30 Apr. 1831–12 Sept. 1880); born in Warrensville, Cuyahoga Co., Ohio. Daughter of John Murdock and Julia Clapp. Adopted by JS and Emma Smith at age of nine days, after death of her mother. Lived in Hiram, Portage Co., Ohio, 1831. Moved to Kirtland, 1832; to Far West, 1838; to Quincy, Adams Co., Illinois, 1839; and to Commerce later that year. Married first Elisha Dixon, by 1850. Moved to Galveston, Galveston Co., Texas, ca. 1851. Moved back to Nauvoo, 1853, following husband's death. Married second John Jackson Middleton, 19 Nov. 1856, in Hancock Co., Illinois. Converted to Catholicism. Died at Sonora, Hancock Co. Buried at Nauvoo.

Miles, Daniel Sanborn (23 July 1772–12 Oct. 1845); born at Sanbornton, Belknap Co., New Hampshire. Son of Josiah Miles and Marah Sanborn. Married Electa Chamberlin, 30 Sept. 1813. Baptized by Orson Pratt and Lyman E. Johnson, Apr. 1832, at Bath, Grafton Co., New Hampshire. Moved to Kirtland, 1836. Appointed a president of the Seventy, 6 Apr. 1837. Arrived at Far West, ca. 1838. Early settler at Commerce. Died in Hancock Co., Illinois.

Miller, Allen (?–?); apprehended at Caldwell Co., Missouri, for illegally transporting state firearms from Richmond, Ray Co., Missouri, to arm vigilantes in Daviess Co., Missouri, for use against Mormons, 1838. Arraigned before Justice Albert Petty at Far West; charged and found guilty but released by order of circuit judge Austin A. King of Richmond, Sept. 1838.

Millet, Artemus (11 Sept. 1790–19 Nov. 1874); born at Westmoreland, Cheshire Co., New Hampshire. Son of Ebenezer Millet and Catherine Dryden. Married Ruth Grannis of Milton, Chittenden Co., Vermont, 17 May 1815. Baptized by Brigham Young and confirmed by Joseph Young, Jan. 1833, at Loughborough, Upper Canada. Moved to Kirtland, Oct. 1833, where he supervised construction of temple. Moved back to Upper Canada, ca. 1837. Returned to body of church at Nauvoo, Apr. 1843. Migrated to Utah Territory, 1850. Died at Scipio, Millard Co., Utah Territory.

Millikin, Lucy Smith (18 July 1821–9 Dec. 1882); born at Palmyra, Ontario Co., New York. Daughter of Joseph Smith Sr. and Lucy Mack. Baptized, possibly 1830. Migrated from Seneca Falls, Seneca Co., New York, to Kirtland, May 1831. Moved to Far West, summer 1838. Migrated to Quincy, Adams Co., Illinois, Feb. 1839. Located at Commerce, May 1839. Married to Arthur Millikin by JS, 4 June 1840, at Nauvoo. Cared for Lucy Mack Smith for several years. Settled at Colchester, McDonough Co., Illinois, early 1850s.

Received into RLDS church, 8 Apr. 1873, based on original baptism. Died near Colchester.

Millikin, Nathaniel (25 Dec. 1793–Aug. 1874); born at Buxton, York Co., Maine. Son of Nathaniel Millikin and Mary Lord. Married Mary Fairfield Hayes, 22 Apr. 1819. Died in Ohio.

Morey, George (30 Nov. 1803–15 Dec. 1875), farmer; born at Pittstown, Rensselaer Co., New York. Son of William Morey and Anda Martin. Married Sylvia Butterfield, 29 Oct. 1825, at Butler Co., Ohio. In Clay Co., Missouri, 1834. In Kirtland, 1835–1836. Member of Far West high council, 1837–1838. Participated in Battle of Crooked River, near Ray Co., Missouri, 25 Oct. 1838. Constable at Nauvoo, 1841. Supported Sidney Rigdon as successor to JS. Settled at Hamilton, Decatur Co., Iowa, 1852. Presided over Little River branch of RLDS church, Decatur Co., 1859. Died at Hamilton.

Morin, Josiah (179?–after 1840), farmer, merchant, judge; probably born at Bourbon Co., Kentucky. Son of John Morin and Sarah Fishback. Married Harriet Barnet, 26 Feb. 1831, in Missouri. A pioneer settler of Millport, in unorganized area of Missouri (later Daviess Co.), 1831. Appointed county judge of Daviess Co., 1837. Helped to mediate peace between Mormons and Missourians in Daviess Co., Aug. 1838. Participated in court hearing at Gallatin, Daviess Co., for JS, Hyrum Smith, Lyman Wight, Caleb Baldwin, and Alexander McRae, 9–11 Apr. 1839. After they were granted change of venue to stand trial in Columbia, Boone Co., Missouri, JS and his party stayed evening of 14–15 Apr. 1839 in home of Judge Morin, who seemed at least partially sympathetic to Mormon cause. Lived at Gallatin, 1840.

Morley, Isaac (11 Mar. 1786–24 June 1865), farmer, cooper; born at Montague, Hampshire Co., Massachusetts. Son of Thomas Morley and Editha (Edith) Marsh. Married Lucy Gunn, June 1812, at Montague. Baptized by Parley P. Pratt, 15 Nov. 1830. Latter-day Saints migrating from New York settled on his farm at Kirtland, 1830. Counselor to Bishop Edward Partridge at Kirtland, 1831, and in Missouri, 1831–1838. Lived at Independence, Jackson Co., Missouri, 1831. Driven from Jackson Co. into Clay Co., Missouri, Nov. 1833. Ordained a patriarch by JS, Sidney Rigdon, and Hyrum Smith, Nov. 1837. President of church branch at Lima, Adams Co., Illinois, 1840. Migrated to Salt Lake Valley, 1848. Led initial settlement of Latter-day Saints at Sanpete Valley, unorganized U.S. territory (later in Sanpete Co., Utah Territory), 1849, and presided at Manti, Sanpete Co., 1849–1853. Member of Utah territorial legislature, 1851–1855. Died at Fairview (formerly North Bend), Sanpete Co. Buried at Manti.

Morton, John (31 Jan. 1790–1 Jan. 1858); born at Portsmouth, Rockingham Co., New Hampshire. Son of Isaac Morton and Anna Barber. Married Elizabeth Stimson, ca. 1812, at Batavia, Genesee Co., New York. Baptized, ca. 1832, at Mendon, Monroe Co., New York. Counselor in Kirtland elders quorum, 1836, and president of that quorum, 1838–1840. Died at Akron, Summit Co., Ohio.

Mulholland, James (1804–3 Nov. 1839); born at Armagh, Ireland. Family migrated to Halton Co., Upper Canada. Baptized in Upper Canada. Married Sarah Scott, 8 Feb. 1838, at Far West. Engaged in clerical work for JS, 1838, at Far West. Ordained a seventy, 28 Dec. 1838. After expulsion from Missouri, lived at Quincy, Adams Co., Illinois, spring 1839. Relocated at Commerce, May 1839. Scribe for two of JS's journals, fall 1838 and 1839.

Scribe in dictation of JS's personal history, beginning 11 June 1839. Appointed clerk for land contracts and subtreasurer of church at Commerce, 20 Oct. 1839. Died at Commerce.

Murdock, John (15 July 1792–23 Dec. 1871), farmer; born at Kortright, Delaware Co., New York. Son of John Murdock Sr. and Eleanor Riggs. Married Julia Clapp of Mentor, Geauga Co., Ohio, 14 Dec. 1823. Baptized by Parley P. Pratt, 5 Nov. 1830, at Kirtland. Ordained an elder by Oliver Cowdery, 7 Nov. 1830, at Mayfield, Cuyahoga Co., Ohio. Organized branches of church at Orange and Warrensville, Cuyahoga Co. Julia died following birth of twins, 30 Apr. 1831, at Warrensville. JS and Emma Smith adopted the twins, Joseph and Julia. Ordained a high priest by JS, 1831, at Kirtland. Participated in Zion's Camp expedition to Missouri, 1834. Member of Clay Co., Missouri, high council. President of Far West high council. With George M. Hinkle, purchased large number of lots for Mormon settlement in De Witt, Carroll Co., Missouri, 23 June 1838. Forced out of De Witt by vigilantes in Oct. 1838; returned to Far West, 1838. Left Far West for Quincy, Adams Co., Illinois, 4 Feb. 1839. Lived at Lima, Adams Co., 1839–1841. Moved to Nauvoo, spring 1841. Bishop of Nauvoo Fifth Ward, 1842–1844. Arrived in Salt Lake Valley, 24 Sept. 1847. Member of Salt Lake high council beginning in 1847 and appointed bishop of Salt Lake City Fourteenth Ward, 1849. Served in Utah territorial legislature. Moved to Beaver, Beaver Co., Utah Territory. Died at Beaver.

Myers, Jacob, Sr. (11 Aug. 1782–17 Oct. 1867), millwright; born at Pence, Northumberland Co., Pennsylvania. Son of Frederick Myers and Elizabeth Wirick. Married Sarah Colman, 5 Jan. 1804, at Jefferson Co., Ohio. Lived in Richland Co., Ohio, 1804–1836. Baptized, 29 Jan. 1834. Presiding elder of Worthington branch, Richland Co., 1836. Led company from southern Richland Co. to Missouri, 1836. Built mill at Haun's Mill settlement on Shoal Creek, Caldwell Co., Missouri. Wounded during attack at Haun's Mill, 1838. Presiding elder of church branch at Freedom, Adams Co., Illinois, 1842. Appointed bishop to watch over families left behind in Iowa Territory when Mormon Battalion volunteers left for U.S. war with Mexico, 16 July 1846. Lived in Michigan, 1857.

Nelson, Hiram (12 Nov. 1797–27 July 1862); born at Orange Co., North Carolina. Son of Thomas Burton Nelson and Martha Williams. Married Mary (Polly) B. Roundtree, 4 July 1825, in Illinois. Baptized by 1838, when he moved to Daviess Co., Missouri. Involved in election day brawl at Gallatin, Daviess Co., 6 Aug. 1838. Died at Spring Creek, Kerr Co., Texas.

Nickerson, Eleazer (12 Aug. 1776–23 Sept. 1856); born at South Dennis, Barnstable Co., Massachusetts. Son of Eleazer Nickerson and Thankful Chase. Married Mercy Taylor Weldon, 7 Dec. 1801. Lived at Yarmouth, Barnstable Co., 1830.

Nickerson, Eleazer Freeman (2/12 Apr. 1806–16/14 Sept. 1862), merchant, farmer; born at Cavendish, Windsor Co., Vermont. Son of Freeman Nickerson and Huldah Chapman. Moved from Dayton, Cattaraugus Co., New York, to Mount Pleasant, Brantford Township, Wentworth Co., Gore District, Upper Canada, 1830. Married Eliza McAlister, 9 Feb. 1831, at Woodhouse, Norfolk Co., Upper Canada. Baptized by JS, 27 Oct. 1833, at Mount Pleasant, and set apart as branch president. Migrated to Missouri, 1838. Returned to Upper Canada, settling at Colborne, Norfolk Co., 1840. Listed faith as Latter-day Saint in Canadian census, 1851. Died at Colborne.

Nickerson, Eliza McAlister (12 Sept. 1812–16 Aug. 1835); born at Burford, Upper Canada. Daughter of Samuel McAlister and Elizabeth Salmond. Married Eleazer Freeman Nickerson, 9 Feb. 1831, at Woodhouse, Norfolk Co., Upper Canada. Baptized by JS, 27 Oct. 1833, at Mount Pleasant, Brantford Township, Wentworth Co., Gore District, Upper Canada. Died at Mount Pleasant.

Nickerson, Freeman (5 Feb. 1779–12/22 Jan. 1847), farmer; born at (South) Dennis, Barnstable Co., Massachusetts. Son of Eleazer Nickerson and Thankful Chase. Moved to Windsor Co., Vermont, 1800. Married Huldah Chapman, 10 Jan. 1801, at Cavendish, Windsor Co. Served as officer in Vermont infantry in War of 1812. Located at South Dayton, Perrysburg, Cattaraugus Co., New York, 1825. Baptized by Zerubbabel Snow, Apr. 1833, at Dayton, Perrysburg, Cattaraugus Co., and soon after ordained a deacon. Visited JS, Sept. 1833, at Kirtland, and persuaded JS and Sidney Rigdon to accompany him to Mount Pleasant, Brantford Township, Wentworth Co., Gore District, Upper Canada, to proselytize among his children. Along with two sons, Chittenden and Levi, participated in Zion's Camp expedition to Missouri, 1834. Member of elders quorum. Journeyed to Missouri, 1839, only to find that Latter-day Saints had been driven out. Located first at Quincy, Adams Co., Illinois, and then Commerce, 1839. Served mission to Vermont and Massachusetts, 1841. With Erastus Snow, organized branch of church at Boston, Mar. 1842. Left Nauvoo for the West during Mormon exodus, Sept. 1846. Died on Chariton River, Iowa Territory.

Nickerson, Moses Chapman (9 Mar. 1804–4 Mar. 1871); born at Cavendish, Windsor Co., Vermont. Son of Freeman Nickerson and Huldah Chapman. Moved to Mount Pleasant, Brantford Township, Wentworth Co., Gore District, Upper Canada, 1831. Baptized by JS, 27 Oct. 1833, at Mount Pleasant. Married widow Mary Boss Colver, 10 Feb. 1834. Expelled from Missouri. Appointed counselor to John Smith in presidency of stake in Iowa Territory, 1841. Moved to Port Dover, Norfolk Co., Canada West, 1842. Lived at Woodhouse, Norfolk Co., 1851, listing himself as Methodist. Baptized into RLDS church. Died in Jackson Co., Missouri.

Olney, Oliver H. (11 Aug. 1796–by 1850), woolen manufacturer and farmer; born at Eastford, Windham Co., Connecticut. Son of Ezekiel Olney and Lydia Brown. Married Alice (Elsa) Johnson, daughter of John Johnson and Elsa Jacobs, 14 Sept. 1820, at Hiram, Portage Co., Ohio. President of Kirtland teachers quorum, 1836. Ordained a seventy, 1836, at Kirtland. Driven out of De Witt, Carroll Co., Missouri, into Caldwell Co., Missouri, 1838. Excommunicated, 1842, at Nauvoo. Printed anti-Mormon tract titled *The Absurdities of Mormonism Portrayed,* spring 1843. In St. Louis, published exposé on polygamy titled *Spiritual Wifery at Nauvoo Exposed,* 1845. Apparently died in Iowa.

Orton, Roger (1799–1851); born in New York. Son of Roger Orton and Esther Avery. Married Clarissa Bicknell, ca. 1822. Baptized, ca. 1833. Appointed to Kirtland high council, 1835. Excommunicated, 1837, at Kirtland; restored to membership. Lived in Augusta, Hancock Co., Illinois. Died in Lee Co., Iowa.

Packard, Noah (7 May 1796–17 Feb. 1860), farmer, miner; born at Plainfield, Hampshire Co., Massachusetts. Son of Noah Packard and Molly Hamblin. Married Sophia Bundy, 29 June 1820, at Parkman, Geauga Co., Ohio. Baptized by Parley P. Pratt, June 1832. Ordained a priest by JS, 1832, at Kirtland. Ordained an elder by John Gould, 1833, at

Westfield, Chautauque Co., New York. Appointed president of Parkman branch, 1833. Moved to Kirtland, 1835. Ordained a high priest, 13 Jan. 1836. Member of Kirtland high council, 1836. Left Ohio for Missouri, late fall 1838, but instead spent winter at Wellsville, Columbiana Co., Ohio. Located at Quincy, Adams Co., Illinois, 1839. Moved to Nauvoo, May 1840. Agent for church to collect funds in Michigan for Nauvoo temple, 1845. Migrated to Utah Territory, 1850. In 1851, settled at Springville, Utah Co., Utah Territory, where he was appointed first counselor in branch presidency. Alderman in Springville city government. Died at Springville.

Page, John Edward (25 Feb. 1799–14 Oct. 1867); born at Trenton, Oneida Co., New York. Son of Ebenezer Page and Rachel Hill. Married first Betsey Thompson, 1831, in Huron Co., Ohio. Baptized by Emer Harris, 18 Aug. 1833, at Brownhelm, Lorain Co., Ohio. Ordained an elder by Ebenezer Page, 12 Sept. 1833, at Florence, Erie Co., Ohio. Married second Lavona Stephens, 26 Dec. 1833, in Huron Co. Moved to Kirtland, 1835. Proselytized in Upper Canada, 1836–1837, and led company of converts from Upper Canada to Missouri, 1838. Located at De Witt, Carroll Co., Missouri, and then Far West. Ordained member of Quorum of the Twelve, 19 Dec. 1838, at Far West. Married third Mary Judd, ca. Jan. 1839. With others of the Twelve, returned to Far West to fulfill revelatory directive, 26 Apr. 1836. Preached in eastern U.S., 1841–1842. Presided over church in Pittsburgh and published *The Gospel Light*, 1843. Labored in Washington DC, 1843–1844. Supported James J. Strang's claim as successor to JS. Affiliated with faction led by James C. Brewster, 1849. Held own religious services with William Marks and other friends, by 1855. Joined the Church of Christ (Hedrickites), ca. 1863. Died near Sycamore, De Kalb Co., Illinois.

Palmer, Ambrose (15 Sept. 1784–before Sept. 1837); born at Winchester, Litchfield Co., Connecticut. Married Lettis (Lettice) Hawkins of Castleton, Rutland Co., Vermont, ca. 1810. Justice of the peace in New Portage, Medina Co., Ohio. Baptized, early 1830s. Presiding elder at New Portage, 1835. Died at Far West.

Parrish, Martha H. Raymond (1 Dec. 1804–14 July 1875); born in Massachusetts. Married to Warren F. Parrish by JS, 3 Dec. 1835, at Kirtland. Lived at Emporia, Lyon Co., Kansas, 1870. Died at Emporia.

Parrish, Warren Farr (10 Jan. 1803–3 Jan. 1877), clergyman, gardener; born in New York. Son of John Parrish and Ruth Farr. Married first Elizabeth (Betsey) Patten of Westmoreland Co., New Hampshire, 1826. Lived at Alexandria, Jefferson Co., New York, 1830. Purchased land at Chaumont, Lyme Township, Jefferson Co., 1831. Baptized by Brigham Young, 20 May 1833, at Theresa, Jefferson Co. Participated in Zion's Camp expedition to Missouri, 1834. Betsey died of cholera at Rush Creek, Clay Co., Missouri, while accompanying Warren on expedition, 27 June 1834. Served mission to Missouri, Kentucky, and Tennessee with David W. Patten, 1834–1835. Appointed member of First Quorum of the Seventy, 1835. Served mission to Kentucky and Tennessee with Wilford Woodruff, Mar.–July 1835. Started clerical work and engaged as scribe for JS, 29 Oct. 1835. Married second to Martha H. Raymond by JS, 3 Dec. 1835, at Kirtland. Appointed secretary and treasurer of Kirtland Safety Society, 2 Jan. 1837. Found guilty of speculation, costing bank estimated $25,000 in 1837. Led movement of reformers opposed to JS. Excommunicated, ca. Dec. 1837. Lived at Chardon, Geauga Co., Ohio, 1840. Baptist clergyman in Fox River area of Wisconsin/Illinois, 1844. Clergyman at Mendon, Monroe Co., New York, 1850.

Lived at Rockford, Winnebago Co., Illinois, 1860. Lived at Emporia, Lyon Co., Kansas, 1870. Died at Emporia.

Partridge, Edward (27 Aug. 1793–27 May 1840), hatter; born at Pittsfield, Berkshire Co., Massachusetts. Son of William Partridge and Jemima Bidwell. Married Lydia Clisbee, 22 Aug. 1819, at Painesville, Geauga Co., Ohio. Initially a Universal Restorationist but adhered to Reformed Baptist (later Disciples of Christ or Campbellite) faith when first contacted by Mormon missionaries in Nov. 1830. With Sidney Rigdon, visited JS at Waterloo, Seneca Co., New York. Baptized by JS, 11 Dec. 1830, in nearby Seneca River. Ordained an elder by Sidney Rigdon, Dec. 1830. Named first bishop in church, 1831, at Kirtland. Accompanied JS to Missouri and called to oversee settlement of Latter-day Saints in Missouri, summer 1831. Heavily involved in acquisition of lands and administering stewardships under law of consecration. Tarred and feathered during mob violence in Jackson Co., Missouri, July 1833. Fled with family to Clay Co., Missouri, Nov. 1833. Served as bishop in Clay Co. Involved in unsuccessful negotiations to restore Mormons to their Jackson Co. lands and obtain redress. Served mission to New York and New England, 1835. Forced to move from Clay Co. to what soon became Caldwell Co., Missouri, fall 1836, where he continued to serve as bishop. Jailed at Richmond, Ray Co., Missouri, Nov. 1838. Exiled from state. Appointed bishop of Upper Ward at Commerce, 1839. Died at Nauvoo.

Patten, David Wyman (14 Nov. 1799–25 Oct. 1838), farmer; born in Vermont. Son of Benoni Patten and Edith Cole. Lived at Monroe Co., Michigan Territory, 1828, when he married Phoebe Ann Babcock. Affiliated with the Methodists. Baptized into LDS church by his brother John Patten, 15 June 1832, at Fairplay, Greene Co., Indiana, and ordained an elder by Elisha Groves, 17 June 1832. Served mission to Michigan Territory, 1832. Ordained a high priest by Hyrum Smith, 2 Sept. 1832. Served mission to eastern states, 1832–1833. Moved family from Michigan Territory to Florence, Erie Co., Ohio, 1833. With William Pratt, carried dispatches from JS to church leaders in Clay Co., Missouri, Dec. 1833. Served mission to Tennessee with Warren F. Parrish, 1834–1835. Ordained member of Quorum of the Twelve, 15 Feb. 1835, at Kirtland. Moved from Kirtland to Far West, 1836. Member of presidency pro tempore of church in Far West, 1838. Captain, Missouri state militia. Mortally wounded during Battle of Crooked River, near Ray Co., Missouri, 25 Oct. 1838. Died near Far West.

Peck, Hezekiah (19 Jan. 1782–25 Aug. 1850); born at Guilford, Windham Co., Vermont. Son of Joseph Peck and Elizabeth Read. Married Martha Long of Guilford, ca. 1805. Baptized by Oliver Cowdery, 28 June 1830, at Joseph Knight Sr. farm, Colesville, Broome Co., New York. Moved from New York to Thompson, Geauga Co., Ohio, Apr.–May 1831. Migrated to Jackson Co., Missouri, June–July 1831. Relocated at Clay Co., Missouri, Nov. 1833. Located in Caldwell Co., Missouri, 1838. Located at Adams Co., Illinois, 1840. Counselor in Nauvoo priests quorum, 1841. Bishop of Nauvoo Tenth Ward, 1844. Served as bishop at Winter Quarters, 1847–1848. Lived at Jackson, Andrew Co., Missouri, June 1850. Died in Andrew Co.

Peck, Reed (1814–23 Aug. 1894); born in New York. Son of Hezekiah Peck and Martha Long. Baptized, ca. 1830. Moved from New York to Ohio and then Kaw Township, Jackson Co., Missouri, Apr.–July 1831. Married Clarissa Melissa Chapin, ca. Aug. 1837.

Member of Mormon delegation that attempted to negotiate equitable solution to Mormon War with General Samuel Lucas, 31 Oct. 1838. Disaffected from church. Wrote extended account of his Missouri experience. Died at Afton, Chenango Co., New York.

Peixotto, Daniel Levy Maduro (18 July 1800–13 May 1843), physician, author, linguist; born at Amsterdam, Holland. Son of Moses Peixotto. Married Rachel M. Seixas, 19 Mar. 1823. Pioneer in field of preventive medicine. Physician at New York City Dispensary. President of New York County Medical Society, 1830–1832. Editor of *New-York Medical and Physical Journal,* first quarterly medical journal printed in English language. Revised George Gregory's medical textbook, *Elements of the Theory and Practice of Physic,* 1830. Moved to Ohio, ca. 1835. Was appointed professor of "Theory and Practice of Medicine and Obstetrics" at newly established Willoughby Medical College of Lake Erie in Willoughby, Cuyahoga Co., Ohio—the only institution for regular medical training in Western Reserve. Later returned to New York City, where he resumed his practice. Died at New York City.

Peniston, William Poitras (ca. 1811–ca. 1850); born at Jessamine Co., Kentucky. Son of Robert Peniston and Nancy Nuttle. Married Mary Walls. A founder of Millport, in what would become Daviess Co., Missouri, where family built mill, 1832. Appointed deputy sheriff for Daviess Co., 1837. Candidate for Missouri legislature, 1838. Tried to prevent Mormons from voting at Gallatin, Daviess Co., 6 Aug. 1838, which precipitated a riot. Moved to California, 1850. Died at Sacramento, Sacramento Co., California.

Perkins, Ute, Sr. (16 July 1761–11 Mar. 1844); born at Lincoln Co., North Carolina. Son of Robert Biggan Perkins and Elizabeth Lollar. Married Sarah (Sally) Gant, 15 July 1781, at Asheville, Buncombe Co., North Carolina. First permanent settler of what became Fountain Green, Hancock Co., Illinois, 1826. Member of LDS church, 1839. Died at Nauvoo.

Perry, Eliza Brown (5 Oct. 1808–after 1846); born at Sherburne, Chenango Co., New York. Daughter of George Brown and Sally Burniss. Received patriarchal blessing, 12 Mar. 1835, at Kirtland. Married William C. Perry, 25 Oct. 1835, at Kirtland. Lived among Latter-day Saints in Missouri and Illinois. Lived near Quincy, Adams Co., Illinois, 15 Feb. 1841.

Perry, William Chadwick (26 Jan. 1812–9 May 1893); born at Madison, Madison Co., New York. Son of Asahel Perry and Polly Chadwick. Lived at Middlebury, Genesee Co., New York, 1815–1830. Baptized, 1832. Married Eliza Brown, 25 Oct. 1835, at Kirtland. Migrated to Missouri with Kirtland Camp, 1838. Located at Quincy, Adams Co., Illinois, by May 1839. At time of death, resided at Stewartsville, De Kalb Co., Missouri.

Petty, Albert (10 Aug. 1795–19 June 1869); born at Bourbon Co., Kentucky. Son of Ralph Petty and Isabelle McClure. Married Catherine Petty (no relation), 2 June 1829, at Henry Co., Tennessee. Baptized, 1835, at Benton Co., Tennessee. Teachers quorum president in Far West, 1838. Justice of the peace in Far West, Sept. 1838. Exiled from Far West to Illinois. Arrived in Salt Lake Valley, 24 Sept. 1848. Helped establish Manti, unorganized U.S. territory (later in Sanpete Co., Utah Territory), 1849. In fall 1862, was a founder of Springdale, Washington Co., Utah Territory, where he died.

Phelps, William Wines (17 Feb. 1792–7 Mar. 1872), newspaper editor; born at Hanover, Morris Co., New Jersey. Son of Enon Phelps and Mehitabel Goldsmith. Married

Sally Waterman, 1815. Founding member of Anti-Masonic Party in New York, ca. 1828. Edited Anti-Masonic newspapers *Lake Light* at Trumansburg, Thompkins Co., New York, and *Ontario Phoenix* at Canandaigua, Ontario Co., New York. Obtained copy of Book of Mormon, 1830. Met JS, 24 Dec. 1830, at Peter Whitmer Sr. farm, Fayette, Seneca Co., New York. Migrated to Kirtland, 1831. Baptized and ordained an elder by JS, 16 June 1831, at Kirtland. Moved to Jackson Co., Missouri, Oct. 1831. Became editor of *The Evening and the Morning Star* and *Upper Missouri Advertiser,* published 1832–1833 at Independence, Jackson Co. Published Book of Commandments, but most copies destroyed by mob action when printing office razed, 20 July 1833. Exiled from Jackson Co. to Clay Co., Missouri, Nov. 1833. Appointed counselor/assistant president to David Whitmer, president of church in Missouri, 3 July 1834. Appointed to return to Kirtland to assist with printing. Helped compile Doctrine and Covenants and first Latter-day Saint hymnal, 1835, at Kirtland. Prolific writer of hymns. Acted as scribe for JS in translation of book of Abraham. Returned from Kirtland to Clay Co., where he resumed duties with Missouri presidency, 1836. Excommunicated, 10 Mar. 1838. Reconciled with church, July 1840; joined Latter-day Saints at Nauvoo, 1841. Acted as clerk to JS and assisted John Taylor in editing *Times and Seasons* and *Nauvoo Neighbor.* Migrated to Salt Lake Valley, 1848. Admitted to Utah territorial bar, 1851. Member of territorial legislative assembly, 1851–1857. Died at Salt Lake City.

Pickett, Agnes Moulton Coolbrith (11 July 1811–26 Dec. 1876); born at Scarborough, Cumberland Co., Maine. Daughter of Joseph Coolbrith and Mary Foss. Baptized by Orson Hyde or Samuel H. Smith, 30 July 1832, at Boston. Moved to Kirtland, summer 1833. Married first Don Carlos Smith, 30 July 1835, at Kirtland. Moved to Far West, summer 1838. Soon afterward located at Millport, Daviess Co., Missouri, near Adam-ondi-Ahman. Left Missouri, Feb. 1839, and found refuge at Quincy, Adams Co., Illinois. Relocated first at Macomb, McDonough Co., Illinois, and then Commerce, late summer 1839. Married second William Pickett, 1846, presumably at Nauvoo or St. Louis. Moved to St. Louis, 1846–1851. Moved to California, 1851. Lived at Marysville, Yuba Co.; Los Angeles; San Bernardino, San Bernardino Co.; San Francisco; and Oakland, Alameda Co., California. Died at Oakland.

Pratt, Orson (19 Sept. 1811–3 Oct. 1881), farmer, writer, teacher, merchant, surveyor; born at Hartford, Washington Co., New York. Son of Jared Pratt and Charity Dickinson. Baptized by Parley P. Pratt, 19 Sept. 1830, at Canaan, Columbia Co., New York. Ordained an elder by JS, 1 Dec. 1830, in New York, and appointed to mission to Colesville, Broome Co., New York. With Samuel H. Smith, traveled from New York to Kirtland; arrived on 27 Feb. 1831. Served mission with Lyman E. Johnson to the East from Kirtland, Feb. 1832. Participated in Zion's Camp expedition to Missouri, 1834. Ordained member of Quorum of the Twelve, 26 Apr. 1835, at Kirtland. Married Sarah Marinda Bates, 4 July 1836, at Henderson, Jefferson Co., New York. Served mission to Upper Canada, 1836. Served mission to Great Britain with other members of Quorum of the Twelve, 1839–1841. Excommunicated, 20 Aug. 1842, at Nauvoo. Rebaptized, 20 Jan. 1843, and ordained to his former office in Quorum of the Twelve. Participated in plural marriage during JS's lifetime. Elected to Nauvoo City Council, 1843. Entered Salt Lake Valley with Mormon pioneers, 1847. Presided over church in Great Britain, 1848. Member of Utah territorial legislature. Appointed church historian, 1874. Died at Salt Lake City.

Pratt, Parley Parker (12 Apr. 1807–13 May 1857), farmer, editor, legislator; born at Burlington, Otsego Co., New York. Son of Jared Pratt and Charity Dickinson. Affiliated with Baptist church at age eighteen. Married first Thankful Halsey, 9 Sept. 1827, at Canaan, Columbia Co., New York. Proselytized to Reformed Baptist (later Disciples of Christ or Campbellite) faith by Sidney Rigdon, 1829. Baptized into LDS church and ordained an elder by Oliver Cowdery, 1 Sept. 1830, at Seneca Lake, Seneca Co., New York. Served mission to unorganized Indian Territory and Missouri with Oliver Cowdery and others, 1830–1831. Stopped at Kirtland and vicinity en route; missionaries baptized some 130 individuals. Participated in Zion's Camp expedition to Missouri, 1834. Ordained member of Quorum of the Twelve, 1835. Married second Mary Ann Frost Stearns, 9 May 1837, at Kirtland. First lieutenant in Missouri state militia, 1838. Participated in Battle of Crooked River, near Ray Co., Missouri, 25 Oct. 1838. Jailed at Richmond, Ray Co., and Columbia, Boone Co., Missouri, 1838–1839. Served mission to England, 1839–1842. Edited first number of *LDS Millennial Star* published in Manchester, England, 27 May 1840. President of British Mission, 1841–1842. Participated in plural marriage during JS's lifetime. Directed affairs of church in New York City, 1844–1845. Migrated to Salt Lake Valley, 1847. Led exploration party into southern Utah Territory, 1850. Served mission to Chile, 1851–1852. Murdered at Van Buren, Crawford Co., Arkansas.

Pratt, William Dickinson (3 Sept. 1802–15 Sept. 1870); born at Worcester, Otsego Co., New York. Son of Jared Pratt and Charity Dickinson. Lived in Ohio, 1830. Baptized, 1831. Participated in Zion's Camp expedition to Missouri, 1834. Married first Hannah Ward, 1 Jan. 1837, at Kirtland. Among exiles forced from Missouri to Illinois during winter 1838–1839. Located at Nauvoo, Aug. 1840. Married second Wealthy Eddy, 1 Mar. 1841. Migrated to Utah Territory; arrived 7 Oct. 1851. Died at Salt Lake City.

Raglin (Raglan), John Thomas (ca. 1800–after 1874); born in Virginia. Married first Flora Storm of Missouri, by 1825. A pioneer settler in what later became Caldwell Co., Missouri, 1831. At his home in Daviess Co., Missouri, JS and Lyman Wight were brought before Judge Austin A. King for preliminary hearing on charges brought by William P. Peniston, 7 Sept. 1838. Married second Cynthia Anne Maupin, 23 Apr. 1851, in Daviess Co. Lived in Tehama Co., California, as early as 1858. Married third Nellie M. Williams, 6 July 1872, in Tehama Co.

Rappleye, Louisa Elizabeth Cutler (16 May 1816–9 Mar. 1854); born at Lisle, Broome Co., New York. Daughter of Alpheus Cutler and Lois Lathrop. Baptized at Kirtland. Married to Tunis Rappleye by JS, 17 Jan. 1836, at Kirtland. Moved to Crooked River near Ray Co., Missouri, 1836. When driven from Missouri, located in Hancock Co., Illinois. Migrated to Council Bluffs, Iowa Territory, 1846, and to Utah Territory, 1853. Died at Lehi, Utah Co., Utah Territory.

Rappleye, Tunis (2 Feb. 1807–25 Dec. 1883); born at Ovid, Seneca Co., New York. Son of John Ransom Rappleye and Margaret (Peggy) Tillier. Married to Louisa Elizabeth Cutler by JS, 17 Jan. 1836, at Kirtland. Moved to Crooked River near Ray Co., Missouri, 1836. Lived at Macedonia, Hancock Co., Illinois, 1842–1844. Member of Brigham Young pioneer company to Salt Lake Valley, 1847. Died at Kanosh, Millard Co., Utah Territory.

Rathbun, Robert, Jr. (16 Mar. 1798–14 Apr. 1856); born at Cayuga Co., New York. Son of Robert Rathbun and Anna Allen. Married Hannah Warner, 1817, in Wayne Co., Ohio. Baptist minister at Mantua, Portage Co., Ohio, 1830, when Latter-day Saint missionaries to unorganized Indian Territory preached at his house. Among first Latter-day Saints to migrate to Independence, Jackson Co., Missouri. His blacksmith shop ransacked by vigilantes, 20 July 1833. Driven out of Jackson Co. into Clay Co., Missouri, Nov. 1833. Member of the Seventy, 1836. Lived at Haun's Mill, Caldwell Co., Missouri, at time of massacre, in which his son Hiram Rathbun was wounded, 30 Oct. 1838. Died in Van Buren Co., Iowa.

Raymond, Martha H. See Parrish, Martha H. Raymond.

Redfield, David Harvey (31 Aug. 1807–27 Dec. 1879); born at Herkimer, Herkimer Co., New York. Son of Samuel Russell Redfield and Sarah Gould. Baptized, by 1831. Lived at Independence, Jackson Co., Missouri, at time Mormons were expelled, 1833. Married Frances (Fanny) Atherton, 27 Oct. 1837, at Kirtland. Migrated from Ohio to Missouri with Kirtland Camp, 1838. Moved to Commerce, 1839. Migrated to Salt Lake Valley, 1849. In winter 1851, settled at Nicolaus, Sutter Co., California. Died near Nicolaus.

Redfield, Levi Harlow (25 Sept. 1801–3 Aug. 1866); born at Chestnut Hill, Killingworth Township, Middlesex Co., Connecticut. Son of Levi Redfield and Weltha Stevens. Married Caroline Foster, 1824. Baptized, 1831. Appointed to Kirtland high council. Moved from Kirtland to Far West, May 1838. Forced to flee Far West, Feb. 1839. Lived at Pittsfield, Pike Co., Illinois, 1840. Migrated to Utah Territory, Sept. 1850. Died at Salt Lake City.

Rich, Leonard (1800–1856); born in New York. Married Keziah. Lived at Warsaw, Genesee Co., New York, 1830. Participated in Zion's Camp expedition to Missouri, 1834. A president of First Quorum of the Seventy, 1835–1837. Sustained in Sidney Rigdon's Church of Christ as president of Quorum of the Seventy, 15 Mar. 1845, at Pittsburgh. Lived in Kirtland, 1845. With William E. McLellin and Jacob Bump, organized the Church of Christ at Kirtland, Jan. 1847. Died at Kirtland.

Richards, Levi (14 Apr. 1799–18 June 1876); born at Hopkinton, Middlesex Co., Massachusetts. Son of Joseph Richards and Rhoda Howe. Married first Sarah Shipley of Hopkinton, ca. 1824. Baptized, 1836. Migrated to Missouri; resident of Far West, 1838. Fled from Missouri to Adams Co., Illinois, by May 1840. Served mission to England, 1840–1843. Married second Sarah Griffith, 25 Dec. 1843, at Nauvoo. Member of Nauvoo City Council; physician. Served mission to Great Britain, 1848–1853. In 1853, settled in Salt Lake Valley. Died at Salt Lake City.

Richards, Phineas (15 Nov. 1788–25 Nov. 1874); born at Framingham, Middlesex Co., Massachusetts. Son of Joseph Richards and Rhoda Howe. Married Wealthy Dewey, 1818. Baptized by Brigham Young, 13 June 1837, at Kirtland. Served on Kirtland high council. Appointed to Nauvoo high council. Migrated to Salt Lake Valley in Willard Richards company, 1848. Member of Salt Lake high council and of Utah territorial legislature. Died at Salt Lake City.

Richards, Willard (24 June 1804–11 Mar. 1854), medical doctor; born at Hopkinton, Middlesex Co., Massachusetts. Son of Joseph Richards and Rhoda Howe. Baptized, 1836.

Served mission to England, 1837–1841. Married Jennetta Richards, 1838, in England. Ordained member of Quorum of the Twelve, 14 Apr. 1840, at Preston, Lancashire, England. Served as temple recorder, recorder of city council, clerk of municipal court, church historian, and private secretary to JS. Before death of JS, completed personal history of JS up to Aug. 1838. Elected to Nauvoo City Council, 1841. Participated in plural marriage during JS's lifetime. With JS in jail in Carthage, Hancock Co., Illinois, 1844, when JS and Hyrum Smith were murdered. Migrated to Salt Lake Valley, 1847. Appointed second counselor to Brigham Young in church presidency, Council Bluffs, Pottawattamie Co., Iowa, 1847. Secretary of Utah Territory, postmaster of Salt Lake City, and editor of *Deseret News*. Died at Salt Lake City.

Rigdon, Sidney (19 Feb. 1793–14 July 1876), tanner, farmer, minister; born at St. Clair, Allegheny Co., Pennsylvania. Son of William Rigdon and Nancy Gallaher. In 1817, joined United Baptists. Preached at Warren, Trumbull Co., Ohio, and vicinity, 1819–1821. Married Phoebe Brook, 12 June 1820, at Warren. Minister of First Baptist Church of Pittsburgh, 1821–1824. Later joined Reformed Baptist (later Disciples of Christ or Campbellite) movement and was influential preacher. Introduced to Mormonism by his former proselyte to Reformed Baptist faith, Parley P. Pratt, who was en route with Oliver Cowdery and others on mission to unorganized Indian Territory. Baptized into LDS church, Nov. 1830, by Oliver Cowdery. Scribe for JS, 1830. Accompanied JS to Upper Canada on proselytizing mission and helped keep JS's diary during trip, 1833. Counselor/assistant president in church presidency, 1832–1844. Arrived at Far West from Kirtland, 4 Apr. 1838. With JS in jail at Liberty, Clay Co., Missouri, Nov. 1838–Feb. 1839. After release, found refuge at Quincy, Adams Co., Illinois. Accompanied JS to Washington DC to seek redress for Missouri grievances, 1839–1840. Member of Nauvoo City Council; postmaster of Nauvoo. Claimed right to lead church after death of JS; excommunicated, 1844. Moved to Pittsburgh to lead schismatic Church of Jesus Christ of Latter Day Saints, 1844; name of church changed to Church of Christ, 1845. Located near Greencastle, Antrim Township, Franklin Co., Pennsylvania, 1845. Removed to Friendship, Allegany Co., New York, where he died.

Ripley, Alanson (8 Jan. 1798–11 July 1880); born at Livonia, Livingston Co., New York. Son of John Ripley. Married first Sarah Finkle. Member of LDS church in Ohio. Participated in Zion's Camp expedition to Missouri, 1834. Landholder in Caldwell Co., Missouri, 1837. Ordained a seventy, 7 July 1838, at Far West. Surveyed Adam-ondi-Ahman, Daviess Co., Missouri. One of the committee for removing the poor from Missouri in 1839. Bishop in Lee Co., Iowa Territory, 1839–1841. Appointed Nauvoo city surveyor, 1841. Married second Eliza Morse, 2 July 1846. Died in Morgan Co., Illinois.

Robinson, Angelina (Angeline) Eliza Works (22 Aug. 1814–8 Apr. 1880); born at Aurelius, Cayuga Co., New York. Daughter of Asa Works and Abigail Marks. Sister of Brigham Young's first wife, Miriam Works Young. Baptized, 1835, at Kirtland. Married Ebenezer Robinson, 13 Dec. 1835, at Kirtland. Moved to Far West, 1837. Lived at Commerce, 1839. Joined with Sidney Rigdon at Pittsburgh following death of JS, 1844. Lived at Greencastle, Franklin Co., Pennsylvania, 1846–1855. Moved to Iowa, 1855. Baptized into RLDS church. Died near Pleasanton, Decatur Co., Iowa.

Robinson, Ebenezer (25 May 1816–11 Mar. 1891), farmer, printer, editor, publisher; born in Oneida Co., New York. Son of Nathan Robinson and Mary Brown. Moved to Kirtland, May 1835, and worked as typesetter in printing office. Baptized, Oct. 1835. Married Angelina (Angeline) Eliza Works, 13 Dec. 1835, at Kirtland. Ordained an elder, 29 Apr. 1836. Member of the Seventy, 1836. Moved to Far West, spring 1837. Church clerk and recorder and clerk of Missouri high council, 1838. Member of Far West high council, Dec. 1838. Justice of the peace, 1839. When driven from Missouri, became a publisher, coeditor, and editor of *Times and Seasons,* 1839–1842, at Commerce. Justice of the peace in Hancock Co., Illinois, 1842. Affiliated with Sidney Rigdon and served as his counselor. Moved to Greencastle, Franklin Co., Pennsylvania, May 1846, where he edited Rigdonite *Messenger and Advocate of the Church of Christ.* Moved to Decatur Co., Iowa, Apr. 1855. Baptized into RLDS church by William W. Blair, 29 Apr. 1863, at Pleasanton, Hamilton Township, Decatur Co. Affiliated with David Whitmer's Church of Christ, 1888. Edited Whitmerite periodical *The Return,* 1889–1891. Died at Davis City, Decatur Co.

Robinson, George W. (14 May 1814–10 Feb. 1878), merchant, clothier, miller, banker; born at Pawlet, Rutland Co., Vermont. Son of Ephraim Robinson and Mary Upham. Member of the Seventy, 1836. Lived at Kirtland, 1837–1838. Married Athalia Rigdon, oldest daughter of Sidney Rigdon. In Sept. 1837, appointed general church recorder to replace Oliver Cowdery. Sustained as general church recorder and clerk to First Presidency at Far West, Apr. 1838. Imprisoned with JS and other church leaders in Missouri, Nov. 1838. First postmaster at Commerce, 1839. Affiliated with Sidney Rigdon's Church of Christ as an apostle. Moved to Friendship, Allegany Co., New York, 1847. Charter member of Masonic lodge in that community. Founder and president of First National Bank, 1 Feb. 1864. Died at Friendship.

Rogers, Jacob S. (1814–before 14 Oct. 1914); born in Kentucky. Lived in northern Ray Co., Missouri, by 1831. Married Elizabeth Talbert Scott, 5 June 1834. Lived at Gallatin, Daviess Co., Missouri, Oct. 1838. Participated in Haun's Mill massacre, Caldwell Co., Missouri. Died in Daviess Co.

Rolfe, Samuel Jones (26 Aug. 1794–July 1867); born at Concord, Merrimack Co., New Hampshire. Son of Benjamin Rolfe and Mary (Molly) Swett. Married Elizabeth Hathaway, 4 Mar. 1818/1819. Lived at Rumford, Oxford Co., Maine, when baptized, 1835. Moved to Kirtland, 1835. Lived in Caldwell Co., Missouri, 1837. Following expulsion from Missouri, located at Adams Co., Illinois. President of Nauvoo priests quorum, 1841. Bishop at Winter Quarters, 1846–1847. Arrived in Salt Lake Valley, Sept. 1847. Settled at San Bernardino, Los Angeles Co., California, 1851. Died at Lehi, Utah Co., Utah Territory.

Root, Henry (14 June 1813–9 Apr. 1895); born at Clinton, Upper Canada. Son of Henry Ruth and Marie Overholt. Purchased interest in town of De Witt (first called Eldersport), Carroll Co., Missouri, 1837. Sold lots to Latter-day Saints. Married Sarah Ann Miller, 1844. Prominent banker at Quincy, Adams Co., Illinois. Died at Quincy.

Roundy, Johanna Carter (26 Nov. 1824–5 Feb. 1847); born at Benson, Rutland Co., Vermont. Daughter of John S. Carter and Elizabeth Kenyon. Lived at Kirtland, by 1833. Father, a member of Zion's Camp expedition, died of cholera, 24 June 1834, on Rush Creek, Clay Co., Missouri. Received patriarchal blessing from Joseph Smith Sr., 29 Jan. 1836, at

Kirtland. Married to Lauren Hotchkiss Roundy by John Taylor, 16 Oct. 1842, at Nauvoo. Baptized at Nauvoo, 1843. Died at Winter Quarters.

Roundy, Shadrach (1 Jan. 1789–July 1872); born at Rockingham, Windham Co., Vermont. Son of Uriah Roundy and Lucretia Needham. Married Betsy Quimby, 22 June 1814, at Rockingham. Lived at Spafford, Onondaga Co., New York. There are two versions of story of his baptism: first, that he sought out JS at Fayette, Seneca Co., New York, and was baptized by JS following their first interview, winter 1830–1831 (reportedly 23 Jan. 1831); second, that William E. McLellin baptized him, as reported in McLellin's journal entry for 30 Jan. 1832. Ordained an elder by Orson Hyde and Samuel H. Smith, 16 May 1832. Lived at Elk Creek, Erie Co., Pennsylvania. Moved to Willoughby, Cuyahoga Co., Ohio, 1834. Member of the Seventy, 1836. Migrated to Far West. Located at Warsaw, Hancock Co., Illinois, 1839. Member of a bishopric in Nauvoo, 1841. In Brigham Young pioneer company, arriving in Salt Lake Valley July 1847. Bishop of Salt Lake City Sixteenth Ward, 1849–1856. Died at Salt Lake City.

Rudd, John, Jr. (16 June 1779–after 1835); born at Bennington, Bennington Co., Vermont. Son of John Rudd and Chloe Hills. A pioneer settler of Springfield, Erie Co., Pennsylvania, 1802. Married Rosanna Jackson of Bennington, ca. 1804. Baptized by Samuel H. Smith, ca. 22 Feb. 1832, at Springfield. JS stayed at Rudd home while traveling to and from the East, 1833. Gave small sum of money to assist JS in meeting his obligations, Dec. 1835.

Salisbury, Katharine Smith. See Younger, Katharine Smith.

Salisbury, Wilkins Jenkins (6 Jan. 1809–28 Oct. 1853), lawyer, blacksmith; born at Rushville, Yates Co., New York. Son of Gideon Salisbury and Elizabeth Shields. Baptized in New York. Married JS's sister Katharine Smith, 8 June 1831, at Kirtland. Settled at Chardon, Geauga Co., Ohio. Participated in Zion's Camp expedition to Missouri, 1834. Appointed member of First Quorum of the Seventy, 1835. Left Ohio for Far West, May 1838. Exiled from Missouri; located at Plymouth, Hancock Co., Illinois, 1839. Lived at Webster, Hancock Co., 1847. Died at Plymouth.

Scobey, Almira Mack. See Covey, Almira Mack.

Seixas, Joshua (4 June 1802–187?), Hebraist, textbook writer; probably born at New York City. Son of Gershom Seixas and Hannah Manuel. Married Henrietta Raphael of Richmond, Henrico Co., Virginia. Taught Hebrew at New York and Charlestown, Massachusetts. His work *Manual Hebrew Grammar for the Use of Beginners* was published at Andover, Essex Co., Massachusetts, 1833. Taught at Oberlin College, Ohio, 1835. Among his students was Lorenzo Snow, whose sister Eliza was a Latter-day Saint and lived in JS household at Kirtland. (JS possibly first heard of Seixas from this source or from Daniel Peixotto, whose wife, Rachel, was Seixas's cousin.) Taught private course in Hebrew for six weeks at Western Reserve College at Hudson, Portage Co., Ohio, beginning in Dec. 1835 and ending 23 Jan. 1836. On 26 Jan. 1836, arrived at Kirtland, where he taught Hebrew from 26 Jan. to 29 Mar. 1836. Taught second course of Hebrew lessons at Kirtland, summer 1836. Returned to New York by 1838.

Sherman, Lyman Royal (22 May 1804–ca. 15 Feb. 1839); born at Monkton, Addison Co., Vermont. Son of Elkanah Sherman and Asenath Hurlbut. Married Delcena Didamia Johnson, 16 Jan. 1829, at Pomfret, Chautauque Co., New York. Baptized,

Jan. 1832. Located at Kirtland, 1833. Participated in Zion's Camp expedition to Missouri, 1834. Appointed a president of First Quorum of the Seventy, 28 Feb. 1835. Appointed to Kirtland high council, 2 Oct. 1837. Moved to Far West, by Oct. 1838. Appointed member of Quorum of the Twelve, 16 Jan. 1839, but died at Far West before notified and ordained.

Sherwood, Henry Garlie (20 Apr. 1785–24 Nov. 1867); born at Kingsbury, Washington Co., New York. Son of Newcomb Sherwood and a woman whose maiden name was Tolman (first name unidentified). Married Jane J. McManagal (McMangle) of Glasgow, Lanark, Scotland, ca. 1824. Lived at Bolton, Warren Co., New York, 1830. Baptized, by Aug. 1832. Moved to Kirtland, ca. 1834. Appointed to Kirtland high council, 9 Sept. 1837. Migrated to Missouri; located at De Witt, Carroll Co., and then Daviess Co., 1838. Exiled from Missouri and located at Commerce, 1839. Member of Commerce high council, 6 Oct. 1839. Elected Nauvoo city marshal, 1841. Member of Brigham Young pioneer company to Salt Lake Valley, 1847. Moved to San Bernardino, Los Angeles Co., California, 1852. Died at San Bernardino.

Singley, Margaret Leasure (22 Dec. 1791–4 Oct. 1874); born at Unity, Westmoreland Co., Pennsylvania. Daughter of John Leasure (Lasure) and Sarah Crow. Married Nicholas Singley Sr. of Lehigh Co., Pennsylvania. Baptized, 1833. Left Kirtland for Caldwell Co., Missouri, May 1838. Located at Nauvoo after exodus from Missouri. Migrated to Salt Lake Valley, 1847, and to California, 1849. Baptized into RLDS church, 1866. Died at Eureka, Humboldt Co., California.

Smith, Agnes Moulton Coolbrith. See Pickett, Agnes Moulton Coolbrith.

Smith, Alexander Hale (2 June 1838–12 Aug. 1909); born at Far West. Son of JS and Emma Hale. Moved to Commerce, 1839. Married Elizabeth Agnes Kendall, 23 June 1861, at Nauvoo. Baptized into RLDS church by Joseph Smith III, 25 May 1862, at Nauvoo. Ordained an apostle in RLDS church 10 Apr. 1873 at Plano, Kendall Co., Illinois. Ordained president of RLDS church Quorum of the Twelve, 15 Apr. 1890, at Lamoni, Decatur Co., Iowa. Appointed counselor to RLDS church president, 12 Apr. 1897; RLDS patriarch, 12 Apr. 1897. Died at Nauvoo. Buried at Lamoni.

Smith, Alvin (11 Feb. 1798–19 Nov. 1823), farmer, carpenter; born at Tunbridge, Orange Co., Vermont. Son of Joseph Smith Sr. and Lucy Mack. Moved from Norwich, Windsor Co., Vermont, to Palmyra, Ontario Co., New York, 1816. Played prominent role in family economy, working to pay for 99.5-acre farm at Manchester, Ontario Co., jointly articled for with his father, 1820. Supervised construction of Smiths' frame home in Manchester. Supporter of JS's claims of heavenly manifestations. Experienced severe stomach cramps, perhaps caused by appendicitis, 15 Nov. 1823. Situation was apparently complicated by overdose of calomel. Died at Palmyra, Wayne Co., New York.

Smith, Asahel (21 May 1773–21 July 1848); born at Windham, Rockingham Co., New Hampshire. Son of Asael Smith and Mary Duty. Married Elizabeth Schellenger of Royalton, Windsor Co., Vermont, 21 Mar. 1802. Moved to Stockholm, St. Lawrence Co., New York, 1809. Baptized by Lyman E. Johnson, 26 June 1835, at Stockholm. Migrated to Kirtland, 1836. Appointed to Kirtland high council, 3 Sept. 1837. Appointed to Iowa stake high council, 5 Oct. 1839. Served on Nauvoo high council. Died at Iowaville, Van Buren Co., Iowa.

Smith, Charles H. (16 Apr. 1817–after 1850); born at Potsdam, St. Lawrence Co., New York. Son of Samuel Smith and Frances R. Wilcox. Baptized. Lived at Kirtland, 1836. Received patriarchal blessing from Joseph Smith Sr., 29 Jan. 1836. Served mission to Ohio with cousin George A. Smith, 1836. Reportedly left church, 1836. Lived at Cincinnati, 1850.

Smith, Don Carlos (25 Mar. 1816–7 Aug. 1841), farmer, printer; born at Norwich, Windsor Co., Vermont. Son of Joseph Smith Sr. and Lucy Mack. Baptized by David Whitmer, ca. 9 June 1830, at Seneca Lake, Seneca Co., New York. Accompanied his father on mission to Asael Smith family in St. Lawrence Co., New York, Aug. 1830. Migrated from Seneca Falls, Seneca Co., to Kirtland, with Lucy Mack Smith company of Fayette, Seneca Co., branch Latter-day Saints, May 1831. Employed by Kirtland printing shop under Oliver Cowdery, fall 1833. Married Agnes Moulton Coolbrith, 30 July 1835, at Kirtland. President of Kirtland high priests quorum, 15 Jan. 1836. Assumed editorial management of expiring *LDS Messenger and Advocate* and first issues of *Elders' Journal,* published first in Kirtland under editorship of JS with Thomas B. Marsh as publisher, Oct.–Dec. 1837. Left Ohio for Far West, May 1838. Soon located at Millport, Daviess Co., Missouri. Served mission to Kentucky and Tennessee, 1838. Expelled from Far West, Feb. 1839; moved to Quincy, Adams Co., Illinois. Lived at Macomb, McDonough Co., Illinois, and then Commerce, 1839. President of high priests in Commerce, 1839. Editor and publisher of *Times and Seasons,* with Ebenezer Robinson, 1839–1841, at Nauvoo. Member of Nauvoo City Council, 1841. Died at Nauvoo.

Smith, Elijah (1776–1855); born at Derby, New Haven Co., Connecticut. Married Rachel Webster of Otis, Crawford Co., Pennsylvania, 1812. Lived in Massachusetts, 1813. Lived at Kirtland, by Sept. 1824. Died at Kirtland.

Smith, Emma Hale (10 July 1804–30 Apr. 1879); born at Harmony, Susquehanna Co., Pennsylvania. Daughter of Isaac Hale and Elizabeth Lewis. Member of Methodist church at Harmony. Married first to JS by Zachariah Tarble, 18 Jan. 1827, at South Bainbridge, Chenango Co., New York. Assisted JS as scribe during translation of Book of Mormon at Harmony, 1828, and joined him during completion of translation at Peter Whitmer Sr. farm, Fayette, Seneca Co., New York. Baptized by Oliver Cowdery, 28 June 1830, at Colesville, Broome Co., New York. Migrated from New York to Kirtland, Jan.–Feb. 1831. Moved to John Johnson home at Hiram, Portage Co., Ohio, while JS worked on revision of Bible, 1831–1832. Edited *A Collection of Sacred Hymns, for the Church of the Latter Day Saints,* published 1835, at Kirtland. Fled Ohio persecution for Far West, Jan.–Mar. 1838. Exiled from Missouri, Feb. 1839; located near Quincy, Adams Co., Illinois. Moved to Commerce, 10 May 1839. Appointed president of Female Relief Society at Nauvoo, 17 Mar. 1842. Fled to Fulton, Fulton Co., Illinois, Sept. 1846–Feb. 1847. Married second Lewis C. Bidamon, 23 Dec. 1847, at Nauvoo. Affiliated with RLDS church, 1860. Died at Nauvoo.

Smith, Frederick Granger Williams (20 June 1836–13 Apr. 1862); born at Kirtland. Son of JS and Emma Hale. Married Anna Marie Jones, 1857, in Hancock Co., Illinois. Died at Nauvoo.

Smith, George Albert (26 June 1817–1 Sept. 1875); born at Potsdam, St. Lawrence Co., New York. Son of John Smith and Clarissa Lyman. Baptized by Joseph H. Wakefield, 10 Sept. 1832, at Potsdam. Moved to Kirtland, 1833. Labored on Kirtland temple. Participated in Zion's Camp expedition to Missouri, 1834. Appointed member of First

Quorum of the Seventy, 1 Mar. 1835. Arrived at Far West, from Kirtland, 16 June 1838, and soon located at Adam-ondi-Ahman, Daviess Co., Missouri. Member of Adam-ondi-Ahman high council. In exodus from Missouri, located north of Quincy, Adams Co., Illinois. Ordained member of Quorum of the Twelve by Heber C. Kimball, 26 Apr. 1839, at Far West. Married to Bathsheba W. Bigler by Don Carlos Smith, 25 July 1841, at Nauvoo. Member of Brigham Young pioneer company to Salt Lake Valley, 1847. Appointed church historian and recorder, 1854. Member of Utah territorial supreme court, 1855. First counselor to Brigham Young in church presidency, 1868. Died at Salt Lake City.

Smith, Hyrum (9 Feb. 1800–27 June 1844), farmer, cooper; born at Tunbridge, Orange Co., Vermont. Son of Joseph Smith Sr. and Lucy Mack. Moved from Norwich, Windsor Co., Vermont, to Palmyra, Ontario Co., New York, 1816. Member of Western Presbyterian Church of Palmyra, 1820. Lived at Manchester, Ontario Co., 1820–1826. Married first Jerusha Barden, 2 Nov. 1826, at Manchester. Baptized by JS, June 1829, at Seneca Lake, Seneca Co., New York. One of the Eight Witnesses of the Book of Mormon, June 1829. Assisted in arrangements for publication of Book of Mormon, Palmyra, Wayne Co., New York, 1829–1830. Among six original members of church, 6 Apr. 1830. Presided over Colesville, Broome Co., New York, branch, 1830–1831. Migrated to Kirtland, 1831. Member of committee to supervise construction of Kirtland temple, 1833–1836. Participated in Zion's Camp expedition to Missouri, 1834. Appointed as an assistant president of church, 6 Dec. 1834. Sustained as assistant counselor in presidency of church, 3 Sept. 1837. Appointed counselor in First Presidency, 7 Nov. 1837. Married second Mary Fielding, 24 Dec. 1837, at Kirtland. Imprisoned at Liberty, Clay Co., Missouri, with his brother JS, 1838–1839. Allowed to escape, 16 Apr. 1839, while en route from trial in Gallatin, Daviess Co., during change of venue to Columbia, Boone Co. Arrived at Quincy, Adams Co., Illinois, 22 Apr. 1839. Ordained church patriarch by his father, Sept. 1840. Sustained as patriarch of church and assistant president on 19 Jan. 1841. Member of Nauvoo City Council. Participated in plural marriage during JS's lifetime. Murdered at Carthage, Hancock Co., Illinois.

Smith, John (16 July 1781–23 May 1854), farmer; born at Derryfield, Rockingham Co., New Hampshire. Son of Asael Smith and Mary Duty. Member of First Congregational Church. Appointed overseer of highways, Potsdam, St. Lawrence Co., New York, 3 Mar. 1810. Married Clarissa Lyman, 11 Sept. 1815. Baptized into LDS church by Solomon Humphrey, 9 Jan. 1832, at Potsdam. Confirmed and ordained an elder by Joseph Wakefield, 9 Jan. 1832. Moved to Kirtland, 1833. Ordained a high priest by Lyman Wight, 3 June 1833. President of Kirtland high council. Served mission to eastern states with his brother Joseph Smith Sr., 1836. Appointed assistant counselor in First Presidency, 1837; member of Kirtland stake presidency, 1838. Left Kirtland for Far West, 5 Apr. 1838. Appointed president of stake in Adam-ondi-Ahman, Daviess Co., Missouri, 28 June 1838. Expelled from Missouri; arrived in Illinois on 28 Feb. 1839. Moved to Commerce, June 1839. Appointed president of stake in Lee Co., Iowa Territory, 5 Oct. 1839. Appointed to preside at Macedonia, Hancock Co., Illinois, 1843–1844. Ordained stake patriarch, 10 Jan. 1844. Appointed Nauvoo stake president, 7 Oct. 1844. Joined westward exodus of Latter-day Saints into Iowa Territory, 9 Feb. 1846. Arrived in Salt Lake Valley, 23 Sept. 1847. Presided over Salt Lake stake until 1 Jan. 1849. Ordained patriarch of church, 1 Jan. 1849. Died at Salt Lake City.

Smith, Joseph, Sr. (12 July 1771–14 Sept. 1840), cooper, farmer, schoolteacher, merchant; born at Topsfield, Essex Co., Massachusetts. Son of Asael Smith and Mary Duty. Nominal member of Congregationalist church at Topsfield. Married Lucy Mack, 24 Jan. 1796, at Tunbridge, Orange Co., Vermont. Joined Universalist Society at Tunbridge, 1797. Entered mercantile business at Randolph, Orange Co., Vermont, ca. 1802, and lost all in a ginseng root investment. Lived at Sharon, Windsor Co., Vermont. Moved from Norwich, Windsor Co., to Palmyra, Ontario Co., New York, 1816. One of the Eight Witnesses of the Book of Mormon, June 1829. Baptized by Oliver Cowdery, 6 Apr. 1830, at Fayette, Seneca Co., New York. Served mission to family of his father in St. Lawrence Co., New York, Aug. 1830. Moved to Kirtland, Mar. 1831. Ordained a high priest, 3 June 1831. Ordained patriarch of church and assistant president, 6 Dec. 1834. Member of Kirtland high council, 1834. Labored on Kirtland temple. Served mission to eastern states with his brother John Smith, 1836. Sustained as assistant counselor to First Presidency, 1837. Moved to Far West, summer 1838. Fled from Far West to Quincy, Adams Co., Illinois, Feb. 1839. Located at Commerce, May 1839. Died at Nauvoo.

Smith, Joseph, III (6 Nov. 1832–10 Dec. 1914); born at Kirtland. Son of JS and Emma Hale. Moved to Far West, 1838; to Quincy, Adams Co., Illinois, 1839; and to Commerce, 1839. Baptized by JS, Nov. 1843, at Nauvoo. Married first Emmeline Griswold, 22 Oct. 1856, at Nauvoo. Appointed president of RLDS church, 6 Apr. 1860, in Amboy, Lee Co., Illinois. Moved to Plano, Kendall Co., Illinois, 1865. Married second Bertha Madison, 12 Nov. 1869, at Sandwich, Kendall Co. Moved to Lamoni, Decatur Co., Iowa, 1881. Founded Graceland College in Lamoni and served as chairman of board of trustees, 1893–1898. Married third Ada Rachel Clark, 12 Jan. 1898, at Amaranth, Dufferin Co., Ontario, Canada. Moved to Independence, Jackson Co., Missouri, 1906. Died at Independence.

Smith, Julia M. See Middleton, Julia M. Smith.

Smith, Katharine. See Younger, Katharine Smith.

Smith, Lucy. See Millikin, Lucy Smith.

Smith, Lucy Mack (8 July 1775–14 May 1856); born at Gilsum, Cheshire Co., New Hampshire. Daughter of Solomon Mack Sr. and Lydia Gates. Married to Joseph Smith Sr. by Seth Austin, 24 Jan. 1796, at Tunbridge, Orange Co., Vermont. Lived at Sharon, Windsor Co., Vermont, when she gave birth to JS, 23 Dec. 1805. Migrated to Palmyra, Ontario Co., New York, from Norwich, Windsor Co., winter of 1816–1817. Member of Western Presbyterian Church of Palmyra, 1820. Lived at Manchester, Ontario Co., ca. 1825–1830. Baptized into LDS church, Apr. 1830. Lived at The Kingdom, unincorporated settlement at Seneca Falls, Seneca Co., New York, 1830–1831. Led company of approximately eighty Fayette, Seneca Co., branch members from Seneca Co. to Kirtland, May 1831. Migrated to Far West, summer 1838. Fled to Quincy, Adams Co., Illinois, during exodus from Missouri, Feb. 1839. Died at Nauvoo. Her narrative history of Smith family, published as *Biographical Sketches of Joseph Smith*, 1853, has been an invaluable resource for study of JS and early church.

Smith, Lyman (ca. 1817–1837); born at Potsdam, St. Lawrence Co., New York. Participated in Zion's Camp expedition to Missouri, 1834. Appointed member of First Quorum of the Seventy, 1835. Married Clarissa Lyman, 4 Nov. 1835, at Kirtland. Reportedly died in Illinois, 1837.

Smith, Mary Bailey (20 Dec. 1808–25 Jan. 1841); born at Bedford, Hillsborough Co., New Hampshire. Daughter of Joshua Bailey and Susannah Boutwell. Baptized by Samuel H. Smith, June 1832, at Boston. Migrated from Boston to Kirtland, 1833. Married Samuel H. Smith, 13 Aug. 1834, at Kirtland. Moved to Missouri, 1838. Located at Commerce, 1839. Died at Nauvoo.

Smith, Samuel Harrison (13 Mar. 1808–30 July 1844); born at Tunbridge, Orange Co., Vermont. Son of Joseph Smith Sr. and Lucy Mack. Moved from Norwich, Windsor Co., Vermont, to Palmyra, Ontario Co., New York, 1816. Member of Western Presbyterian Church of Palmyra, 1820. Baptized by Oliver Cowdery, 25 May 1829, at Harmony, Susquehanna Co., Pennsylvania. One of the Eight Witnesses of the Book of Mormon, June 1829. Probably among six original members of church, 6 Apr. 1830. Served mission to Ontario, Monroe, and Livingston counties, New York, 1830. Ordained an elder, 9 June 1830, at Fayette, Seneca Co., New York. Migrated from New York to Kirtland; arrived Feb. 1831. Ordained a high priest by Lyman Wight, 3 June 1831. Served mission to Missouri with Reynolds Cahoon, 1831. Served mission with Orson Hyde to eastern states, 1832. Member of first Kirtland high council, 1834. Married first Mary Bailey, 13 Aug. 1834, at Kirtland. Committee member and general agent for Literary Firm in Kirtland, 1835. Moved to Far West, where he lived briefly before moving to Marrowbone, Daviess Co., Missouri, 1838. Participated in Battle of Crooked River, near Ray Co., Missouri, 25 Oct. 1838. Among first Latter-day Saints to seek refuge at Quincy, Adams Co., Illinois, 1838. Hired to farm for George Miller near Macomb, McDonough Co., Illinois, Mar. 1839. Appointed a bishop at Nauvoo, 1841. Nauvoo city alderman and member of Nauvoo Legion, 1841. Married second Levira Clark, 1841. Moved to Plymouth, Hancock Co., Illinois, 1842. Died at Nauvoo.

Smith, Sophronia. See McCleary, Sophronia Smith.

Smith, Susanna (Susan) Bailey. See Hunt, Susanna (Susan) Bailey Smith.

Smith, Sylvester (28 Mar. 1806–22 Feb. 1880), farmer, carpenter, lawyer, realtor; born at Tyringham, Berkshire Co., Massachusetts. Son of Chileab Smith and Nancy Marshall. Married Elizabeth (Betsey) Frank, 27 Dec. 1827, in Chautauque Co., New York. Lived at Amherst, Lorain Co., Ohio, 1828–1834. Baptized, 1831. Ordained a high priest by Oliver Cowdery, 25 Oct. 1831. Served mission to New England with Gideon Carter, 1832. Member of Kirtland high council, 1834. Participated in Zion's Camp expedition to Missouri, 1834. Tried by Kirtland high council for making false charges against JS, confessed, and retained his membership, 1834. Lived at Kirtland, 1835–1853. Appointed a president of First Quorum of the Seventy, 1835. Temporary scribe to JS during illness of Warren F. Parrish, 1836. Left church, 1838. Sold land in Kirtland and moved to Council Bluffs, Pottawattamie Co., Iowa, Apr.–June 1853. Practiced law and bought and sold real estate. Served as Pottawattamie Co. school fund commissioner and justice of the peace, 1850s–1860s. Died at Council Bluffs.

Smith, William B. (13 Mar. 1811–13 Nov. 1893), farmer, newspaper editor; born at Royalton, Windsor Co., Vermont. Son of Joseph Smith Sr. and Lucy Mack. Moved from Norwich, Windsor Co., Vermont, to Palmyra, Ontario Co., New York, winter 1816–1817. Baptized by David Whitmer, 9 June 1830, at Seneca Lake, Seneca Co., New York. Lived at The Kingdom, unincorporated settlement in Seneca Falls, Seneca Co., Oct. 1830. Moved to

Kirtland, May 1831. Married first Caroline Amanda Grant, 1833, at Kirtland. Participated in Zion's Camp expedition to Missouri, 1834. Appointed member of Quorum of the Twelve, 14 Feb. 1835. Left Kirtland for Far West, May 1838. Disfellowshipped, 4 May 1839. Settled at Plymouth, Hancock Co., Illinois, 1839, where he kept a tavern. Restored to fellowship. Elected to Nauvoo City Council, 1842. Represented Hancock Co. in Illinois House of Representatives, 1842–1843. Editor of Nauvoo newspaper *The Wasp,* 1842. Ordained patriarch of church, 24 May 1845. Married second Mary Jane Rollins, 22 June 1845, in Hancock Co. Excommunicated, 12 Oct. 1845. Sustained James J. Strang as successor to JS, 1 Mar. 1846. Married third Roxey Ann Grant, 19 May 1846, in Knox Co., Illinois. Ordained Strangite patriarch, 11 June 1846, at Voree, Walworth Co., Wisconsin Territory. Excommunicated from Strangite movement, 8 Oct. 1847. Affiliated briefly with Lyman Wight, 1850–1851. Initiated a new movement with Martin Harris and Chilton Daniels, 1 Nov. 1855. Married fourth Eliza Elsie Sanborn, 12 Nov. 1857, in Lake Co., Ohio. Enlisted in U.S. Army during Civil War and apparently adopted middle initial *B* at this time. Spent active duty time in Arkansas. Joined RLDS church, 1878. Married fifth Rosanna Jewitt Surprise, 21 Dec. 1889, at Clinton, Clinton Co., Iowa. In 1890, moved to Osterdock, Clayton Co., Iowa, where he died.

Snow, Erastus (9 Nov. 1818–27 May 1888); born at St. Johnsbury, Caledonia Co., Vermont. Son of Levi Snow and Lucina Streeter. Baptized by William Snow, 3 Feb. 1833, at Charleston, Orleans Co., Vermont. Arrived at Kirtland, Dec. 1835. Located with Latter-day Saints in Missouri, Aug. 1838. Married Artimesia Beman, 3 Dec. 1838. Located at Montrose, Lee Co., Iowa Territory; appointed to high council of Iowa stake, Lee Co., Iowa Territory, 1839. Served mission to Pennsylvania, New Jersey, and Massachusetts, 1840–1843. Participated in plural marriage during JS's lifetime. Member of Brigham Young pioneer company to Salt Lake Valley, 1847. Ordained member of Quorum of the Twelve, 12 Feb. 1849. Established Scandinavian Mission, 1850. Published and edited *St. Louis Luminary* in Missouri, 1854. Founded St. George, Washington Co., Utah Territory, 1861. Died at Salt Lake City.

Snow, Zerubbabel (29 Mar. 1809–27 Sept. 1888); born at St. Johnsbury, Caledonia Co., Vermont. Son of Levi Snow and Lucina Streeter. Baptized by Orson Pratt or Lyman E. Johnson, 1832. Married first Susan Slater Lang, Oct. 1833. Migrated to Kirtland, 1834. Participated in Zion's Camp expedition to Missouri, 1834. Appointed member of First Quorum of the Seventy, 1835, at Kirtland. Practiced law in Ohio, 1839–1850. Married second Mary Augusta Hawkins at Streetsboro, Portage Co., Ohio, 25 Aug. 1841. Appointed associate justice for Utah Territory, 1850; migrated to Utah Territory, 1851, and served 1851–1854. Served mission to Australia, 1856–1858. Attorney general of Utah Territory, 1869–1874. Died at Salt Lake City.

Squires, Andrew Jackson (17 Sept. 1815–3 Sept. 1897); born at Aurora, Portage Co., Ohio. Son of Ezekiel Squires and Clarissa Stuart. Ordained an elder in LDS church. Left church and joined briefly with the Methodists. Returned to LDS church, 1835. Ordained a seventy, 1836. Practiced medicine at Mantua, Portage Co., Ohio, 1843–1864. Married Martha Wilmot, 1850. Served in Ohio state legislature, 1859–1861. Died at Hiram, Portage Co., Ohio.

Stanley, Harvey (ca. Dec. 1811–16 Feb. 1862); born in New York. Son of Benjamin Stanley. Participated in Zion's Camp expedition to Missouri, 1834. Labored on Kirtland temple. Married to Lerona Cahoon by JS, 17 Jan. 1836, at Kirtland. Property holder in Kirtland, 1837. Lived at Nauvoo, 1843. Lived at Keokuk, Lee Co., Iowa, 1850. Migrated to Petaluma, Sonoma Co., California, by 11 Nov. 1853. Died at San Antonio, Marin Co., California.

Stanley, Lerona Cahoon (25 Oct. 1817–18 June 1840); born at Harpersfield, Ashtabula Co., Ohio. Daughter of Reynolds Cahoon and Thirza Stiles. Married to Harvey Stanley by JS, 17 Jan. 1836, at Kirtland. Charged and forgiven in disciplinary case before Kirtland high council, 1 Nov. 1837. Died at Nauvoo and buried at Montrose, Lee Co., Iowa Territory.

Stoddard, Calvin W. (7 Sept. 1801–19 Nov. 1836); born at Palmyra, Ontario Co., New York. Son of Silas Stoddard and Bathsheba Sheffield. Lived at Ontario Co., New York, 1810. Married Sophronia Smith, 30 Dec. 1827, at Palmyra, Wayne Co., New York. Solicited sales of Book of Mormon, 1830. Migrated to Kirtland with Lucy Mack Smith company of Fayette, Seneca Co., New York, branch members, 1831. Ordained a priest by JS at Orange, Cuyahoga Co., Ohio. Ordained an elder, 1832. Became estranged from church. Died at Macedon, Wayne Co.

Stoddard, Sophronia Smith. See McCleary, Sophronia Smith.

Strobridge, Richard Ransom (6 June 1815–ca. 1870); born at Solon, Cortland Co., New York. Son of James Gordon Strobridge and Nancy Maybury. Baptized by JS, 27 Oct. 1833, at Mount Pleasant, Brantford Township, Wentworth Co., Gore District, Upper Canada. Purchased Eleazer Freeman Nickerson's mercantile store in Mount Pleasant, 1837, before Nickerson family moved to Missouri. Lived at Brantford, Brant Co., Canada West, 1851, when he and family were listed as Methodists.

Strong, Elial (ca. 1810–26 June 1834); born at Sullivan, Tioga Co., Pennsylvania. Married Martha Curtis of Columbia, Bradford Co., Pennsylvania, ca. 1827. Baptized, June 1831, at Kirtland. Late 1831, proselytized in Monroe and Ontario counties, New York, where he and others from Columbia, Bradford Co., branch were instrumental in eventual conversion of Brigham Young, Heber C. Kimball, and others. Participated in Zion's Camp expedition to Missouri, 1834, and died of cholera on Rush Creek, Clay Co., Missouri.

Strong, Ezra (26 June 1788–2 Apr. 1877); born at Philipstown, Albany Co., New York. Son of Ezra Strong and Nancy Gates. Married Olive Lowell, 19 Nov. 1814. Baptized and ordained a priest, by 1833. Moved to Rockport, Allen Co., Ohio, by Oct. 1834. Ordained a high priest at Kirtland, 1836. Moved to Nauvoo area by 1842. Migrated to Salt Lake Valley by 1848. Baptized into RLDS church, 12 Oct. 1862, at Santaquin, Utah Co., Utah Territory. Died at Woodland, Cowlitz Co., Washington Territory.

Tanner, John (15 Aug. 1778–13 Apr. 1850); born at Hopkinton, Washington Co., Rhode Island. Son of Joshua Tanner and Thankful Tefft. Married first Tabitha Bentley, about Jan. 1800. Married second Lydia Stewart, fall 1801. Married third Elizabeth Beswick, 1825. Baptized by Simeon Carter, 17 Sept. 1832, at Bolton's Landing, Warren Co., New York. Moved to Kirtland, Dec. 1834. Loaned and donated substantial monies to JS and church. Left Kirtland for Far West, Apr. 1838. Severely beaten during conflict between Latter-day Saints and other Missourians, fall 1838. Located near Montrose, Lee Co., Iowa

Territory, Mar. 1840. Materially assisted in building of Nauvoo temple. Member of Amasa M. Lyman pioneer company to Salt Lake Valley; arrived 13 Oct. 1848. Died at South Cottonwood, Salt Lake Valley, unorganized U.S. territory. Buried at Salt Lake City.

Taylor, John (1 Nov. 1808–25 July 1887), wood turner, editor, publisher; born at Milnthorpe, Westmoreland Co., England. Son of James Taylor and Agnes Taylor, members of Church of England. At age fifteen, joined Methodists and was local preacher. Migrated from England to York, Upper Canada, 1829. Married Leonora Cannon, 28 Jan. 1833, at York. Baptized into LDS church by Parley P. Pratt, 9 May 1836, near Downsview, northwest of Toronto. Appointed to preside over churches in that district of Upper Canada. Ordained a high priest by JS and others, 21 Aug. 1837. Moved to Far West, fall 1838. Ordained member of Quorum of the Twelve by Brigham Young and Heber C. Kimball, 19 Dec. 1838, at Far West. Served mission to England, 1839–1841. Member of Nauvoo City Council, judge advocate of Nauvoo Legion, and editor of *Times and Seasons* and *Nauvoo Neighbor.* Participated in plural marriage during JS's lifetime. With JS when JS and Hyrum Smith were murdered in jail at Carthage, Hancock Co., Illinois, 27 June 1844. Served mission to England, 1846–1847. Arrived in Salt Lake Valley, 1847. Served mission to France and Germany, 1850–1852; arranged for translation of Book of Mormon into French and published *L'Etoile du Deseret* (The Star of Deseret). In Germany, supervised translation of Book of Mormon into German and published *Zions Panier* (Zion's Banner). Editor of *The Mormon,* New York City, 1855–1857. Member of Utah territorial legislature, 1857–1876. Following death of Brigham Young, presided over church from 1877 to 1887. Ordained president of church, 10 Oct. 1880. Died at Kaysville, Davis Co., Utah Territory. Buried in Salt Lake City.

Taylor, Jonathan (6 June 1793–after 1846); born at Burlington, Hartford Co., Connecticut. Son of Eliza Taylor. Married first Lydia Azula Taylor, 12 June 1828. Lived at Norton, Medina Co., Ohio, 1830. Visited by JS at his home at Norton, 1834. Baptized. Sold Medina Co. land holdings, 1838. Listed in Nauvoo Third Ward, 1842. Married second Martha Pierce at Nauvoo, 22 Jan. 1846. Sold land at Nauvoo, 14 May 1846.

Thayer, Ezra (1793–6 Sept. 1862); born in New York. Married Elizabeth Frank of New York, 1810. Baptized by Parley P. Pratt and confirmed by JS, Oct. 1830, at Ontario Co., New York, or Palmyra, Wayne Co., New York. With JS, departed New York for Kirtland, Jan. 1831. Commissioned to superintend land purchases in Kirtland, 1833. Participated in Zion's Camp expedition to Missouri, 1834. Ordained a seventy, 1 Mar. 1835, at Kirtland. Church membership suspended, 2 May 1835, at Kirtland. Apparently reinstated. Member of high council, Adam-ondi-Ahman, Daviess Co., Missouri, 28 June 1838. Lived at Brighton, Monroe Co., New York, 1840. Present at church conference at Comstock, Kalamazoo Co., Michigan, 1 June 1844. Lived at Chili, Monroe Co., 1850. Affiliated briefly with James J. Strang at Voree, Walworth Co., Wisconsin, but soon returned to New York. Rebaptized into LDS church, Sept. 1854, in New York. Lived at Jefferson, Cass Co., Michigan, 1860. Baptized into RLDS church at Galien, Berrien Co., Michigan. Died in Cass Co.

Thomas, David (12 Mar. 1797–25 Apr. 1845); born at Flat Rock District, Bourbon Co., Kentucky. Son of Richard Thomas and Elizabeth Bowles. Married Martha Parker of Bourbon Co., Kentucky, 1816. Migrated to Carrollton, Carroll Co., Missouri, 1833. With Henry Root, landowner at De Witt, Carroll Co., successfully solicited some seventy families of Latter-day Saints to purchase land and settle there in 1838. Died in Carroll Co.

Tippets, John Harvey (5 Sept. 1810–14 Feb. 1890); born at Wilton, Rockingham Co., New Hampshire. Son of John Tippets and Abigail Pearce. Lived at Lewis, Essex Co., New York, 1813–1834. Baptized by Elijah Collins, July 1832. Married first Abigail (Abby) Jane Smith, Oct. 1834, at Bolton, Washington Co., New York. Lived at Kirtland, 1834–1835; Missouri, 1835–1839; and Adams Co., Illinois, 1839–1840. Lived at Nauvoo, 1840–1846. Married second Caroline Fidelia Calkins Pew, 25 Sept. 1840, at Nauvoo. Member of Mormon Battalion in U.S. war with Mexico, 1846–1847. Helped lead Pueblo detachment of battalion and Mississippi Latter-day Saints to Salt Lake Valley, 1847. Served mission to England, 1856–1857. Died at Farmington, Davis Co., Utah Territory.

Tippets, Joseph Harrison (4 June 1814–12 Oct. 1868); born at Lewis, Essex Co., New York. Son of Joseph Tippets and Abigail Lewis. Baptized, Apr. 1832, in New York. Moved to Kirtland, 1834. Married first Rosalia Elvira Perry, 1 Jan. 1837, in Clinton Co., Missouri. After Missouri expulsion, moved to Quincy, Adams Co., Illinois, and later Nauvoo, 1840. Married second Amanda Melvina Perry, 26 June 1842, at Nauvoo. Lived in Pottawattamie Co., Iowa, 1848–1850. Traveled west to Utah Territory, 1852. Married third Rose Wickham, 10 May 1865, in Utah Territory. Died at Brigham City, Box Elder Co., Utah Territory.

Tippets, William Plummer (26 June 1812–29 Mar. 1877); born at Groton, Grafton Co., New Hampshire. Son of John Tippets and Abigail Pearce. Baptized, May 1832. Lived at Kirtland, 1834–1835. Married first Caroline Tippets, his cousin, 30 July 1835. Lived at Liberty, Clay Co., Missouri. Married second Jeanette Stebbins or Styles, ca. 1838–1840, in Missouri. Married third Sophia Burnham Mead, 1 Jan. 1842, at Liberty. Migrated to Utah Territory, 1850. Died at Three Mile Creek, Box Elder Co., Utah Territory. Buried at Brigham City, Box Elder Co.

Turley, Theodore (10 Apr. 1801–12 Aug. 1871); born at Birmingham, Warwickshire, England. Son of William Turley and Elizabeth Yates. Married Frances Amelia Kimberley, 26 Nov. 1821, at Harborne, Staffordshire, England. Migrated to Upper Canada, 1825. Purchased land at Churchville, Toronto Township, Upper Canada, 1834. Baptized by Isaac Russell, 1 Mar. 1837, at Churchville. Migrated from Upper Canada to Missouri in Almon W. Babbitt company, July 1838. Member of Far West high council. Appointed member of committee on removal from Missouri under Brigham Young, 29 Jan. 1839. Accompanied Quorum of the Twelve on mission to Great Britain, 1839–1840. Served as officer of Nauvoo Legion. Participated in plural marriage during JS's lifetime. Left Nauvoo during exodus, Feb. 1846. Member of Winter Quarters high council. Arrived in Salt Lake Valley, 1849. Settled at San Bernardino, Los Angeles Co., California, 1851. Returned to Utah Territory, 1857/1858. Died at Beaver, Beaver Co., Utah Territory.

Turner, James B. (1815–ca. 1864); born in Tennessee. County clerk, 1837, and clerk of Daviess Co., Missouri, circuit court, 1838. Ray Co., Missouri, probate judge, 1853–1864. Died in Ray Co.

Waterman, John O. (16 May 1797–5 Mar. 1876); born at Richfield, Otsego Co., New York. Son of Zebulon Waterman and Elizabeth. Married Emeline Shepard, ca. 1825, at Hartford, Hartford Co., Connecticut. Lived among Latter-day Saints in Ohio, 1836.

Emeline received endowment in Nauvoo temple, 18 Dec. 1845. Died at Moline, Rock Island Co., Illinois.

Weaver, Russell (27 July 1788–24 Apr. 1865); born at Shaftsbury, Bennington Co., Vermont. Son of Thomas Weaver and Lois Greene. Married Lydia Cowell, 1 June 1808. Lived at Cambria, Niagara Co., New York, by 1809. A preacher for Christian or Unitarian church. Introduced to JS by Joseph Rose, 12 Jan. 1836, while visiting at Kirtland. Died at Cambria.

Webb, Catherine Noramore (17 Dec. 1809–11 July 1884); born at Staco, New Baltimore Township, Greene Co., New York. Daughter of John Noramore and Lydia Hoag. Married first Eber Edward Wilcox, 14 Sept. 1826. Baptized and moved to Kirtland. Eber died of cholera in Clay Co., Missouri, 25 June 1834, while participating in Zion's Camp expedition. Married second to John Webb by JS, 14 Jan. 1836, at Kirtland. Lived at Adams Co., Illinois, in early 1840s. Arrived in Utah Territory, 1850. Died at Coyote Creek, Garfield Co., Utah Territory.

Webb, Edwin Densmore (16 Dec. 1813–ca. 1887); born at Hanover, Chautauque Co., New York. Son of James Webb and Hannah Griswold. Married first Eliza Ann McWethy (McWithey), 13 Dec. 1835, at Kirtland. Member of the Seventy in Kirtland, 1836. Lived at Kirtland, 1837–1842. Lived in Nauvoo, 1842, and in Wisconsin, 1842–1850. Migrated to Utah Territory, 1853. Married second Jane H., by 1870. Lived at Sacramento, Sacramento Co., California, 1870–1880. Registered voter in Sacramento, 1882–1886.

Webb, Eliza Ann McWethy (McWithey) (1817–before 1860); born in New York. Daughter of Isaac McWithy and Hannah Taylor. Married Edwin Densmore Webb, 13 Dec. 1835, at Kirtland. Lived in Nauvoo, 1842. Lived at Marquette Co., Wisconsin, 1850. Migrated to Utah Territory, 1853. Died in Utah Territory.

Webb, John (2 May 1808–3 May 1894); born at Manheim, Herkimer Co., New York. Son of James Webb and Betsy Faville or Caville. Married to Catherine Noramore Wilcox by JS, 14 Jan. 1836, at Kirtland. Baptized, 1839. Lived in Adams Co., Illinois, early 1840s. Arrived in Salt Lake Valley in 1848. Died at Coyote Creek, Garfield Co., Utah Territory.

Whitlock, Harvey Gilman (1809–ca. 1885), physician; born in Massachusetts. Son of Jack Whitlock. Married Minerva Abbott, 21 Nov. 1830. Baptized. Ordained an elder, by June 1831. Ordained a high priest, 3 June 1831. Moved his household to Jackson Co., Missouri, and became member of Whitmer branch at Kaw Township, Jackson Co., 1831. Victim of expulsion from Jackson Co., 1833; located at Clay Co., Missouri. Petitioned JS requesting forgiveness, Nov. 1835. Conference of First Presidency recommended he be rebaptized and reordained, 30 Jan. 1836. Withdrew from church, 1838. Baptized into Rigdonite Church of Christ by William E. McLellin at West Buffalo, Scott Co., Iowa Territory, 1845. Member of grand council of Rigdonite church. Migrated to Salt Lake Valley, 1849. By 1864, moved to California, where he was baptized into RLDS church that year. President of Pacific Slope area of RLDS church, 1866. Excommunicated from RLDS church, 1868. Lived in Bishop Creek, Inyo Co., California, 1870. Died at Watsonville, Santa Cruz Co., California.

Whitmer, David (7 Jan. 1805–25 Jan. 1888); born near Harrisburg, Dauphin Co., Pennsylvania. Son of Peter Whitmer Sr. and Mary Musselman. Arranged for completion of translation of Book of Mormon in his father's home, Fayette, Seneca Co., New York, June

1829. Baptized by JS, June 1829, in Seneca Lake, Seneca Co. One of the Three Witnesses of the Book of Mormon, June 1829. Among six original members of church, 6 Apr. 1830. Married Julia Ann Jolly, 9 Jan. 1831, at Seneca Co. Migrated from Fayette to Kirtland, 1831. Ordained a high priest, 25 Oct. 1831, at Orange, Cuyahoga Co., Ohio. Served mission to Jackson Co., Missouri, with Harvey G. Whitlock, 1831. Located in Whitmer branch at Kaw Township, Jackson Co., 1831. Driven from county by vigilantes, Nov. 1833; located in Clay Co., Missouri. Appointed president of church in Missouri, 3 July 1834. Left for Kirtland, Sept. 1834. Moved to Far West, summer 1837. Rejected as president in Missouri at meetings in Caldwell Co., Missouri, 5–9 Feb. 1838. Excommunicated, 13 Apr. 1838, at Far West. Moved to Richmond, Ray Co., Missouri, where he operated a livery stable. Ordained by William E. McLellin to preside over McLellinite Church of Christ, Sept. 1847, but later rejected that movement. Elected mayor of Richmond, 1867–1868. Formed a church with emphasis on return to "original Mormonism," 1875–1876. Later set forth his claims in *An Address to All Believers in Christ, by a Witness to the Divine Authenticity of the Book of Mormon,* 1887. Died at Richmond.

Whitmer, John (27 Aug. 1802–11 July 1878), farmer, stock raiser, newspaper editor; born in Pennsylvania. Son of Peter Whitmer Sr. and Mary Musselman. Member of German Reformed Church, Fayette, Seneca Co., New York. Evidently baptized by Oliver Cowdery, June 1829, in Seneca Lake, Seneca Co. Acted as scribe during translation of Book of Mormon at Whitmer home, June 1829. One of the Eight Witnesses of the Book of Mormon, June 1829. Ordained an elder by 9 June 1830. Copied revelations as scribe to JS, beginning July 1830. Sent by JS to Kirtland, Jan. 1831. Appointed church historian, 8 Mar. 1831. Wrote a church history covering 1831–1838. Ordained a high priest, 3 June 1831, at Kirtland. With Oliver Cowdery, left Ohio to take revelations to Missouri for publication, Nov. 1831. Member of Whitmer branch at Kaw Township, Jackson Co., Missouri. Married to Sarah Maria Jackson by William W. Phelps, 10 Feb. 1833, at Kaw Township. Forced to remove from Jackson Co. to Clay Co., Missouri, Nov. 1833. Appointed an assistant to his brother David Whitmer in Missouri church presidency, 3 July 1834. Editor of *LDS Messenger and Advocate,* Kirtland, 1835–1836. Lived in Clay Co., 1836. Helped establish Latter-day Saints at Far West. Excommunicated, 10 Mar. 1838, at Far West. Left Far West for Richmond, Ray Co., Missouri, June 1838. Returned to Far West after departure of Latter-day Saints. In Sept. 1847, met with his brother David Whitmer and William E. McLellin at Far West in an attempt to reconstitute Church of Christ under presidency of David Whitmer. Died at the site of Far West. Buried at Kingston, Caldwell Co., Missouri.

Whitmer, Peter, Jr. (27 Sept. 1809–22 Sept. 1836); born at Fayette, Seneca Co., New York. Son of Peter Whitmer Sr. and Mary Musselman. Baptized, June 1829, in Seneca Lake, Seneca Co. One of the Eight Witnesses of the Book of Mormon, June 1829. Among six original members of church, 6 Apr. 1830. Served mission to unorganized Indian Territory on western border of Missouri, 1830–1831. Married to Vashti Higley by Oliver Cowdery, 14 Oct. 1832, at Jackson Co., Missouri. Appointed to Clay Co., Missouri, high council, Jan. 1836. Died near Liberty, Clay Co.

Whitney, Elizabeth Ann Smith (26 Dec. 1800–15 Feb. 1882); born at Derby, New Haven Co., Connecticut. Daughter of Gibson Smith and Polly Bradley. Married Newel K. Whitney, 20 Oct. 1822, at Kirtland. Baptized by missionaries to unorganized Indian

Territory under Oliver Cowdery, Nov. 1830. Left Kirtland for Far West, fall 1838, but at St. Louis learned that Latter-day Saints were being driven from Missouri. Located at Carrollton, Greene Co., Illinois, winter 1838–1839. Moved to Quincy, Adams Co., Illinois, and then Commerce. Migrated to Salt Lake Valley, arriving 8 Oct. 1848. Second counselor to Eliza R. Snow in presidency of Relief Society, 1866–1882. Died at Salt Lake City.

Whitney, Newel Kimball (5 Feb. 1795–23 Sept. 1850), trader, merchant; born at Marlborough, Windham Co., Vermont. Son of Samuel Whitney and Susanna Kimball. Merchant at Plattsburg, Clinton Co., New York, 1814. Mercantile clerk for Algernon Sidney Gilbert at Mentor, Geauga Co., Ohio, ca. 1820. Opened a store in Kirtland, by 1822. Married Elizabeth Ann Smith, 20 Oct. 1822, at Kirtland. Unitarian and then member of Reformed Baptist (later Disciples of Christ or Campbellite) faith. Entered partnership with Algernon Sidney Gilbert in N. K. Whitney & Co. store, by 1827. Baptized into LDS church by missionaries to unorganized Indian Territory under Oliver Cowdery, Nov. 1830. Appointed bishop at Kirtland, 1831. Traveled with JS to Missouri and then to New York City, Albany, and Boston, 1832. Member of United Firm in Kirtland. En route to Missouri, fall 1838, when difficulties in that state were confirmed at St. Louis. Located his family temporarily at Carrollton, Greene Co., Illinois, and returned to Kirtland to conduct business. Moved family from Carrollton to Quincy, Adams Co., Illinois, and then Commerce. Appointed bishop of Middle Ward at Commerce, Oct. 1839. Alderman for Nauvoo, 1841. Member of Council of Fifty, 1844. Joined exodus of Latter-day Saints into Iowa Territory and Winter Quarters, 1846. Sustained as presiding bishop of church at Council Bluffs, Pottawattamie Co., Iowa, 6 Apr. 1847. Migrated to Salt Lake Valley, Oct. 1848. Bishop of Salt Lake City Eighteenth Ward, 1849, concurrently with service as presiding bishop. Died at Salt Lake City.

Wight, Lyman (9 May 1796–31 Mar. 1858), farmer; born at Fairfield, Herkimer Co., New York. Son of Levi Wight Jr. and Sarah Corbin. Married Harriet Benton, 5 Jan. 1823, at Henrietta, Monroe Co., New York. Baptized into Reformed Baptist (later Disciples of Christ or Campbellite) faith by Sidney Rigdon in Warrensville, Cuyahoga Co., Ohio, area, May 1829. Moved to Isaac Morley homestead at Kirtland and joined with other Reformed Baptist families having all things in common, Feb. 1830. Lived at Mayfield, Cuyahoga Co., Ohio, when baptized into LDS church in Chagrin River, 14 Nov. 1830, and confirmed by Oliver Cowdery at Kirtland, 18 Nov. 1830. Ordained an elder by Oliver Cowdery, 20 Nov. 1830. Ordained a high priest by JS, 3 June 1831. Ordained JS and Sidney Rigdon high priests, 3 June 1831. Served mission to Jackson Co., Missouri, via Detroit and Pontiac, Michigan Territory, June–Aug. 1831. Joined by family at Jackson Co., Sept. 1831; located at Prairie branch, Jackson Co., where he presided over that settlement. Moved to and presided over Big Blue settlement, Jackson Co. Driven from Jackson Co. into Clay Co., Missouri, Nov. 1833. Recruited volunteers for Zion's Camp expedition to Missouri, 1834. Member of Clay Co. high council, 1834. Moved to what became Caldwell Co., Missouri, 1836. Elected colonel at organization of Caldwell Co. militia, Aug. 1837. Lived at Adam-ondi-Ahman, Daviess Co., Missouri, 1837–1838. Member of Adam-ondi-Ahman stake presidency, 1838. Imprisoned with JS at Richmond, Ray Co.; Liberty, Clay Co.; and Gallatin, Daviess Co., Missouri, 1838–1839. Allowed to escape Missouri imprisonment during change of venue to Columbia, Boone Co., Missouri, and fled to Quincy, Adams Co., Illinois, Apr. 1839.

Counselor in Zarahemla stake presidency, Lee Co., Iowa Territory, Oct. 1839. Ordained member of Quorum of the Twelve, 8 Apr. 1841, at Nauvoo. Elected to Nauvoo City Council, 1842. Leader in development of Mormon settlements in Wisconsin pineries on Black River, Wisconsin Territory, 1843–1844. Served mission to eastern states to campaign for JS as candidate for U.S. president, 1844. Returned to Wisconsin Territory, 1844–1845. Led company of some 150 Latter-day Saints from Wisconsin Territory to Republic of Texas, arriving in Nov. 1845. Established a settlement at Zodiac, Gillespie Co., Texas. Excommunicated, 3 Dec. 1848. Elected chief justice of Gillespie Co., 1850. Died at Dexter, Medina Co., Texas. Buried at Zodiac.

Wilcox, Benjamin (23 Aug. 1796–4 Oct. 1870); born at Tiverton, Newport Co., Rhode Island. Son of Edward Wilcox and Anna. Married Mary McOmber of New York, 18 Mar. 1818. Lived at Elk Creek, Erie Co., Pennsylvania, 1830. Baptized by Evan M. Greene or John F. Boynton. Sold Erie Co. property, 1837. A son, Benjamin Cyrus Wilcox, was born in Illinois, 29 Sept. 1839. Captain in Willard Richards pioneer company to Salt Lake Valley, 1848. Died at San Juan Bautista, San Benito Co., California.

Wilcox, Catherine Noramore. See Webb, Catherine Noramore.

Williams, Frederick Granger (28 Oct. 1787–10 Oct. 1842), farmer, ship's pilot, teacher, physician, justice of the peace; born at Suffield, Hartford Co., Connecticut. Son of William Wheeler Williams and Ruth Granger. Practiced Thomsonian botanical system of medicine as physician. Married Rebecca Swain, Dec. 1815. Lived at Warrensville, Cuyahoga Co., Ohio, by 1816. Worshipped with Sidney Rigdon's Reformed Baptist (later Disciples of Christ or Campbellite) congregation. Baptized into LDS church, confirmed, and ordained an elder, Nov. 1830, at Kirtland, by missionaries under leadership of Oliver Cowdery who were en route to Missouri and unorganized Indian Territory. Accompanied Cowdery to Missouri frontier on mission. Appointed clerk and scribe to JS, 20 July 1832. Assistant president/counselor in presidency of church, 1833–1837. Consecrated by deed to JS about 142 prime acres in Kirtland, 1834. Participated in Zion's Camp expedition to Missouri, 1834. Editor of *Northern Times* and member of publications committee that printed Doctrine and Covenants and Emma Smith's *A Collection of Sacred Hymns, for the Church of the Latter Day Saints* under auspices of firm F. G. Williams & Co., 1835. Helped organize and was a trustee of School of the Prophets. Elected justice of the peace, Kirtland, 1837. Officer in Kirtland Safety Society, 1837. Removed from church presidency, 7 Nov. 1837. Moved to Far West, late 1837. An 8 July 1838 JS revelation directed Williams to be ordained an elder and preach abroad. Rebaptized by 5 Aug. 1838. Excommunicated, 17 Mar. 1839, at Quincy, Adams Co., Illinois. Restored to fellowship at Commerce, 8 Apr. 1840. Died at Quincy.

Williams, John A. (1805–30 Apr. 1884), merchant, farmer, politician; born in Kentucky. Married first Nancy. Moved to Millport, Daviess Co., Missouri, 1836. Elected Daviess Co. treasurer, 29 May 1837; member of Missouri House of Representatives, 1838, 1842. Appointed presiding judge of Daviess Co. court, Sept. 1851. Moved from Daviess Co. during 1852. Resident of Clark Co., Washington Territory, June 1860. Moved to Sandy, Multnomah Co., Oregon, by 28 July 1860, and to Polk Co., Oregon, before Nov. 1867. Married second Eliza A. Gardner, 17 Nov. 1867, in Polk Co. Resident of Bridgeport, Polk Co., June 1880. Died in Polk Co.

Williams, Joseph Swain (1819–May 1838); born at Warrensville, Cuyahoga Co., Ohio. Son of Frederick G. Williams and Rebecca Swain. Evidently a lifelong invalid. Died at Far West.

Williams, William Wheeler, Jr. (29 June 1790–19 Dec. 1852); born at Suffield, Hartford Co., Connecticut. Son of William Wheeler Williams and Ruth Granger. Married first Lovina Dibble, 25 Dec. 1814, at Cleveland, Cuyahoga Co., Ohio. Married second Nancy Sherman, 27 Aug. 1817, at Cleveland. Died at Newburgh, Cuyahoga Co., Ohio.

Wilson, John (28 Jan. 1790–2 Feb. 1877); born in Virginia. Son of William Wilson and Catharine Yancey. Married first Percilla (Priscilla) McGowen/McCoun. Married second Martha Woods, 24 June 1817, at Augusta Co., Virginia. Married third Ann Robertson Pulliam/Pullian, 27 Nov. 1823/1824, in Saline Co., Missouri. Circuit attorney, 1828, at Howard Co., Missouri. Ran for U.S. representative from Missouri, 1838; defeated. Appointed Indian agent; moved briefly to Salt Lake City. Appointed naval agent for West Coast, 1849; moved to San Francisco. Died at Suisun, Solano Co., California.

Woodruff, Wilford (1 Mar. 1807–2 Sept. 1898), farmer, miller; born at Farmington, Hartford Co., Connecticut. Son of Aphek Woodruff and Beulah Thompson. Baptized by Zera Pulsipher, 31 Dec. 1833, near Richland, Oswego Co., New York. Ordained a teacher, 25 Jan. 1834, at Richland. Participated in Zion's Camp expedition to Missouri, 1834. Served mission to southern Missouri, northern Arkansas, and western Tennessee, 1834–1836. Appointed member of the Seventy, 1836. Married to Phoebe Carter by Frederick G. Williams, 13 Apr. 1837, at Kirtland. Served missions to New England and Fox Islands off coast of Maine, 1837–1838. Ordained member of Quorum of the Twelve by Brigham Young, 26 Apr. 1839, at Far West. Served mission to Great Britain, 1839–1841. Served mission to eastern states and Province of Canada to raise funds for building Nauvoo temple, 1843. Served mission to eastern states to campaign for JS as candidate for U.S. president, 1844. Member of Brigham Young pioneer company to Salt Lake Valley, 1847. Appointed to mission to eastern states and Province of Canada, 1848–1850. Member of Utah territorial legislature. Appointed assistant church historian, 7 Apr. 1856. First president of St. George temple, Utah Territory, 1877. President of Quorum of the Twelve, 1880. Sustained as church historian and general church recorder, 1883. President of church, 7 Apr. 1889–2 Sept. 1898. Died at San Francisco.

Works, Angelina (Angeline) Eliza. See Robinson, Angelina (Angeline) Eliza Works.

Young, Brigham (1 June 1801–29 Aug. 1877), carpenter, painter, glazier; born at Whitingham, Windham Co., Vermont. Son of John Young and Abigail (Nabby) Howe. Brought up in Methodist Episcopal household; later joined Reformed Methodist Church. Moved from Whitingham to Sherburne, Chenango Co., New York, 1804. Married first Miriam Angeline Works of Aurelius, Cayuga Co., New York, 8 Oct. 1824. Lived at Mendon, Monroe Co., New York, when baptized into LDS church, 15 Apr. 1832, by Eleazer Miller at Mendon. Served missions to New York and Upper Canada, 1832–1833. Migrated to Kirtland, 1833. Labored on Kirtland temple. Married second Mary Ann Angell, 18 Feb. 1834, at Kirtland. Participated in Zion's Camp expedition to Missouri, 1834. Ordained member of Quorum of the Twelve, 14 Feb. 1835. Served missions to New York, Upper Canada, and New England, 1835–1837. Fled Kirtland, 22 Dec. 1837. Joined JS near Quincy, Adams Co., Illinois, en route to Far West; arrived with him 14 Mar. 1838. Member of presidency pro tempore of church in Far West, 1838. Directed Mormon evacuation from Missouri. Forced to leave Far West; reached Quincy, 14 Feb. 1839. Served mission to England, 1839–1841, departing from Commerce. Elected to Nauvoo City Council, 1841. Participated in plural marriage during JS's lifetime. Officiator in proxy baptisms for the dead in Nauvoo, 1843. Served mission to campaign for JS as candidate for U.S. president, 1844. With the Twelve, sustained to administer affairs of church after JS's death, 8 Aug. 1844, at Nauvoo. Directed Mormon migration from Nauvoo to Salt Lake Valley, 1846–1848. Appointed president of church, Dec. 1847. Governor of Utah Territory, 1850–1858; superintendent of Indian affairs for Utah Territory, 1851–1857. Directed establishment of hundreds of communities in western U.S. Died at Salt Lake City.

Young, Joseph (7 Apr. 1797–16 July 1881); born at Hopkinton, Middlesex Co., Massachusetts. Son of John Young and Abigail (Nabby) Howe. Baptized by Daniel Bowen, 6 Apr. 1832, at Columbia, Bradford Co., Pennsylvania, and ordained an elder by Ezra Landon, Apr. 1832. Married Jane Adeline Bicknell, 18 Feb. 1834, at Geneseo, Livingston Co., New York. Participated in Zion's Camp expedition to Missouri, 1834. Appointed a president of First Quorum of the Seventy, 1 Mar. 1835. During exodus from Missouri, located temporarily at Quincy, Adams Co., Illinois. Moved to Nauvoo, 1840. Migrated to Utah Territory, 1850. Died at Salt Lake City.

Young, Lorenzo Dow (19 Oct. 1807–21 Nov. 1895); born at Smyrna, Chenango Co., New York. Son of John Young and Abigail (Nabby) Howe. Married Persis Goodall, 26 June 1826, at Watertown, Jefferson Co., New York. Baptized, 1832. Participant in Battle of Crooked River, near Ray Co., Missouri, 25 Oct. 1838. Participated in plural marriage during JS's lifetime. In Brigham Young pioneer company to Salt Lake Valley, 1847. Bishop of Salt Lake City Eighteenth Ward, 1851–1878. Died at Salt Lake City.

Young, Phineas Howe (16 Feb. 1799–10 Oct. 1879); born at Hopkinton, Middlesex Co., Massachusetts. Son of John Young and Abigail (Nabby) Howe. Married first Clarissa Hamilton, 28 Sept. 1818, at Auburn, Cayuga Co., New York. Baptized by Ezra Landon, 5 Apr. 1832, at Columbia, Bradford Co., Pennsylvania. Married second Lucy Pearce Cowdery, half sister of Oliver Cowdery, 28 Sept. 1834, at Kirtland. Purchased land at Caldwell Co., Missouri, and then moved to Clinton Co., Missouri. Forced to flee to Adam-ondi-Ahman, Daviess Co., Missouri, by Clinton Co. mob, fall 1838. Lived at Morgan Co., Illinois, for about one year. Member of Brigham Young pioneer company, 1847. Bishop of Salt Lake City Second Ward, 1861–1871. Died at Salt Lake City.

Younger, Katharine Smith (28 July 1813–2 Feb. 1900); born at Lebanon, Grafton Co., New Hampshire. Daughter of Joseph Smith Sr. and Lucy Mack. Reported hearing JS's recitals concerning heavenly visitations and reported actually lifting gold plates. Baptized by David Whitmer, 9 June 1830, at Seneca Lake, Seneca Co., New York. Migrated to Kirtland from Seneca Co., May 1831. Married first to Wilkins Jenkins Salisbury by Sidney Rigdon, 8 June 1831, at Kirtland. After marriage, settled at Chardon, Geauga Co., Ohio, 1831. Left Ohio for Far West, May 1838. After expulsion from Missouri, located at Plymouth, Hancock Co., Illinois, 1839. Moved to Nauvoo, by 1845. Lived at Webster, Hancock Co., fall 1847. Husband died 28 Oct. 1853 in Plymouth. Married second Joseph Younger, 1857. Received into RLDS church, 1873, based on original baptism. Died at Fountain Green, Hancock Co. Buried in Webster Cemetery, Fountain Green.

Ecclesiastical Organizational Charts

In spring 1830, JS organized the Church of Christ with elders, priests, and teachers. Over the next five years, he developed and adapted church organization to a growing membership, adding the offices of high priest, deacon, bishop, patriarch, apostle, and seventy and organizing quorums, councils, presidencies, and bishoprics. The first chart that appears below, titled "Church Structure, 1835–1839," outlines the ecclesiastical structure that emerged by 1836. The three subsequent charts supply the names of church officers in Kirtland, Ohio; Missouri; and the Commerce (later Nauvoo), Illinois, area. They also track major changes in personnel. Because of the constant change in church organization between 1832 and 1834—the period covered in JS's first journal—a chart showing officers for that period is not supplied. During 1835–1836, the period covered in JS's second journal, JS worked to refine organizational structure and fully staff church positions in preparation for the solemn assembly to be held in the House of the Lord in Kirtland. The chart dated March 1836 presents the resulting organization. The next chart, dated spring–summer 1838, approximates church organization and officers named in JS's two 1838 Missouri journals. The final chart, dated October 1839, reflects the early reorganization efforts that followed the Mormon exodus from Missouri to Illinois. It presents church organization and leadership as it existed by the conclusion of JS's first Illinois journal in 1839. Readers wishing to conduct further research may consult the documented organizational charts posted on the Joseph Smith Papers website.

Church Presidencies and Councils

At the church's organization in April 1830, JS was recognized as first elder and Oliver Cowdery as second elder. On 8 March 1832, JS was "president of the high priesthood," and Jesse Gause and Sidney Rigdon were his "councellers of the ministry of the presidency of th[e] high Pri[e]sthood." The term "counsellor" was still used in a revelation of 8 March 1833 designating these officers—by now Sidney Rigdon and Frederick G. Williams—as being equal with JS in holding the keys of the kingdom.

Beginning in June 1830, JS used gatherings or "conferences" of church officers as deliberative bodies in which to conduct the business of the church, including disciplinary proceedings. In time, "general conferences" involving a substantial proportion of church officers were supplemented by more frequent ad hoc, or "special," conferences. Beginning in 1832, the term "council" was used interchangeably with "conference" for these smaller, ad hoc meetings. JS and his counselors played leading roles in the proceedings.

JS formalized the practice by organizing in February 1834 at Kirtland "the high council of the Church of Christ," a standing body consisting entirely of high priests. Thereafter, the term "assistant president" was generally applied to those who had earlier been called counselors to JS, and members of the high council were called the presidency's counselors, thus avoiding confusion in the use of the term counselor. JS and his assistant presidents served as the presidency of the high council as well as the presidency of the high priesthood and therefore the presidency of the church. In July 1834, a similar high council was organized in Clay County, Missouri, which was designated the high council for Zion, and JS ordained David Whitmer president of the high council, with William W. Phelps and John Whitmer as David Whitmer's "assistants," after which JS ordained "their twelve Counsellors"—the members of the high council. Whitmer was recognized as "President, head and leader in Zion (in the absence of br. Joseph Smith jr.)."

In December 1834, JS reorganized the church presidency, adding Oliver Cowdery as an assistant president, ranking before the existing assistants, Rigdon and Williams. JS also ordained Hyrum Smith and Joseph Smith Sr. as assistant presidents.

During late 1835 and early 1836, while members of the Missouri presidency and most of their high council were temporarily residing in Kirtland preparing to receive the promised endowment of power, the configuration of church councils held in Kirtland varied. Frequently a "council of the Presidency" met, consisting of members of both the general church presidency based in Kirtland and the Zion presidency from Missouri. When the high council was convened, it might consist of any combination of twelve members taken from the Zion high council from Missouri, the high council of the Kirtland stake of Zion, or the traveling high council—the Quorum of the Twelve Apostles—with one to three members of the combined presidency serving as presidents of the high council for that particular meeting. Further complicating the scene, in addition to the presidencies of each high council, by 21 January 1836 one of the twelve regular members of each high council was designated its president. On that date, John Smith was recognized as "the president of the counsellors in Kirtland" and Simeon Carter as "the president, of the counsellors of Zion."

In late 1835 and early 1836, JS anticipated that he and his assistant presidents would move to Missouri by the following spring. Regulations for the approval of ordinations adopted in early 1836 seem to anticipate a level of interaction between Kirtland and Missouri church authorities that could take place only if they remained in close proximity—and it was anticipated that this would be in Missouri, not Ohio. However, the logistics of migration to Missouri and financial entanglements in Ohio precluded JS's relocation that year, and the presidency and high council of Zion eventually returned to Missouri without him and other leaders who continued to be based in Kirtland. The close working relationships, and indeed the interrelationships of 1835–1836, therefore never materialized again.

In 1837, contending with dissent in Kirtland and a perceived weakening of support among some church leaders in Missouri, JS reiterated his authority over the entire church. His 4 September letter to Saints in Missouri was headed "Joseph Smith J[r.] Pres[t] of the Church of Christ of Latter Day Saints in all the world." It also applied the term "first Presidency" to the presidency of the church who were then located at Kirtland. This was not a new position or assertion of authority for JS but clarified arrangements that may have seemed ambiguous. Some may have misinterpreted the earlier configuration of presidencies as a decentralized leadership with one presidency responsible for each of the church's two main divisions, Missouri and Ohio. JS's reassertion of churchwide leadership caused Hepzibah Richards to write from Kirtland in January 1838 that "the presidents, Joseph & Sidney & Hiram returned from Missouri a few weeks since. They are elected to the first presidency, or to preside over all the churches instead of this place only." The term "first presidency," first used officially in 1834, came into more general use during 1838 and eventually supplanted other nomenclature.

The September 1837 conference documents a transition in terminology and organization. In Kirtland in September, JS as president and Sidney Rigdon and Frederick G. Williams as his counselors constituted "the three first presidnts of the Church." Oliver Cowdery, Joseph Smith Sr., Hyrum Smith, and John Smith were now "assistant Councillors," and the seven were "to be concidered the heads of the Church." After this conference, use of the titles "assistant president" and "assistant counselor" diminished. The last known use of "assistant" in connection with the First Presidency during JS's lifetime was the temporary appointment of John C. Bennett as assistant president in Nauvoo, 1841.

Church Structure, 1835–1839

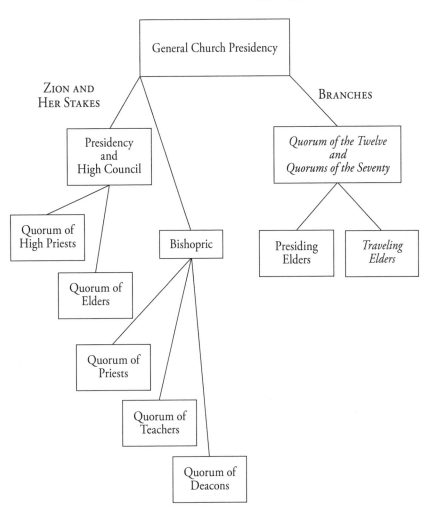

Key

MAJOR JURISDICTIONS
Standing organizations or officers
Traveling organizations or officers

March 1836

During the period covered in his 1835–1836 journal, JS worked to fully organize the priesthood units in preparation for the solemn assembly that was held in the House of the Lord in Kirtland, Ohio, on 30 March 1836. This organizational effort included staffing each quorum, council, or presidency; organizing each quorum with a presidency; and clarifying relations among groups.

GENERAL CHURCH OFFICERS

Presidency Joseph Smith Jr., president Oliver Cowdery, assistant president Sidney Rigdon, assistant president Frederick G. Williams, assistant president Hyrum Smith, assistant president Joseph Smith Sr., assistant president During the period in which Missouri officers were in Kirtland awaiting the solemn assembly, the general church presidency (based in Kirtland) and the Missouri church presidency often functioned as a general presiding council, to which JS referred as "my council of the presidency" or, more commonly, as simply "the presidency" or "the presidents." This council of nine men or an available subset functioned in Kirtland as a presiding council until the Missouri presidency returned to its local jurisdiction.	*Patriarch* Joseph Smith Sr.

OTHER OFFICERS

Zion (Clay County, Missouri) Officers	Kirtland Stake Officers	Traveling Officers
The Missouri Latter-day Saints, having been driven from their homes in Jackson County, were living primarily in Clay County in March 1836. *Presidency* David Whitmer, president William W. Phelps, assistant president John Whitmer, assistant president *High Council* The Missouri high council apparently retained its original order, based on the 7 July 1834 casting of lots, with replacement members taking the number of their predecessors. Although John Murdock was the president of the council in March 1836, he was still listed among the other members with his original number. Simeon Carter Elisha Groves Jesse Hitchcock Calvin Bebee Levi Jackman Solomon Hancock	*Presidency* The presidency of the church presided over the Kirtland stake and its high council. *High Council* John Smith, president John Johnson Orson Johnson Martin Harris Samuel Smith Jared Carter Joseph Coe John P. Greene Thomas Grover Noah Packard Joseph Kingsbury Samuel James *Bishopric* Newel K. Whitney, bishop Reynolds Cahoon, counselor Vinson Knight, counselor *Presidency of Quorum of High Priests* Don Carlos Smith, president *CHART CONTINUED ON NEXT PAGE*	*Quorum of the Twelve* Listed in order of seniority—that is, age at time of appointment of the original Twelve. Thomas B. Marsh, president David W. Patten Brigham Young Heber C. Kimball Orson Hyde William E. McLellin Parley P. Pratt Luke Johnson William Smith Orson Pratt John F. Boynton Lyman Johnson *Quorum of the Seventy, Presidents* The presidents of the Seventy presided over the Quorum of the Seventy. The presidents were apparently ordered by seniority of age. Hazen Aldrich Joseph Young Leonard Rich Levi Hancock

OTHER OFFICERS CONTINUED

Zion (Clay County, Missouri) Officers	Kirtland Stake Officers	Traveling Officers
Peter Whitmer Jr. Newel Knight George M. Hinkle Lyman Wight Elias Higbee John Murdock, president *Bishopric* Edward Partridge, bishop Isaac Morley, counselor John Corrill, counselor No evidence has been found of additional quorums functioning in Missouri at this time.	Unidentified counselors (Gideon Carter and Warren Cowdery in May 1837) *Presidency of Quorum of Elders* Alvah Beman, president Reuben Hedlock, counselor John Morton, counselor *Presidency of Quorum of Priests* William Cowdery Jr., president Unidentified counselors *Presidency of Quorum of Teachers* Oliver Olney, president Unidentified counselors *Presidency of Quorum of Deacons* Ira Bond, president Unidentified counselors	Zebedee Coltrin Lyman Sherman Sylvester Smith

Spring–Summer 1838

In the two years between spring 1836 and summer 1838, there were substantial changes in church leadership, the result of two principal factors. First, in response to dissent among church leaders in late 1837 and early 1838, JS oversaw or approved the removal and replacement of several officers. Second, other officers in Kirtland, Ohio, followed JS in migrating to Missouri in 1838. Some but not all Kirtland officers were replaced. A few leaders stayed behind to oversee stake matters, while most loyal Latter-day Saints prepared to move to Missouri. As Caldwell County, Missouri, filled with Latter-day Saints, immigration was steered northward to Adam-ondi-Ahman, Daviess County, Missouri, where a stake was organized on 28 June 1838.

GENERAL CHURCH OFFICERS

First Presidency	*Patriarch*
During a church conference held in Kirtland in September 1837, JS presented Sidney Rigdon, Frederick G. Williams, and himself as "the three first presidnts of the Church." He then presented Oliver Cowdery, Joseph Smith Sr., Hyrum Smith, and John Smith as "assistant Councillors." In a conference held in Missouri two months later, Williams was removed and replaced by Hyrum Smith. The assistant counselors were not presented for sustaining at this Missouri conference, and they were not again presented as such. Joseph Smith Jr., president Sidney Rigdon, counselor Hyrum Smith, counselor Joseph Smith Sr., assistant counselor John Smith, assistant counselor	Joseph Smith Sr.

OTHER OFFICERS

Zion (Far West, Missouri) Officers	Kirtland Stake Officers	Adam-ondi-Ahman Stake Officers	Traveling Officers
Presidency (Pro Tempore) Thomas B. Marsh David W. Patten Brigham Young *High Council* Simeon Carter Jared Carter Thomas Grover John P. Greene Levi Jackman Solomon Hancock George Morey Newel Knight George M. Hinkle George W. Harris Elias Higbee John Murdock, president *Patriarch* Isaac Morley *Bishopric* Edward Partridge, bishop Isaac Morley, counselor Titus Billings, counselor *President of Quorum of High Priests* Charles Rich Don Carlos Smith, the former president of the quorum of high priests in Kirtland, followed JS in migrating from Kirtland to Missouri but, according to JS's journal, had not yet arrived there as of 6 July 1838. He was later sustained in the same position in the central stake at Commerce, Illinois, which suggests the possibility that he replaced Rich after arriving. Smith served a fund-raising mission beginning 26 September 1838. *President of Quorum of Elders* Harvey Green *President of Quorum of Priests* As bishop, Edward Partridge presided over the quorum of priests. *President of Quorum of Teachers* Albert Petty *President of Quorum of Deacons* Unidentified	After JS's departure from Kirtland on 12 January 1838, a few leaders stayed behind to oversee stake matters while loyal Latter-day Saints prepared to move to Missouri. *Presidency* William Marks John Smith Reynolds Cahoon *Bishop* Newel K. Whitney Reynolds Cahoon and Vinson Knight served earlier as Whitney's counselors in Kirtland, but Cahoon was pressed into service in the temporary presidency of the stake in January 1838 shortly after JS's departure, and both apparently migrated to Missouri by summer 1838. *President of Quorum of High Priests* Hiram Kellogg *Presidency of Quorum of Elders* John Morton, president Hezekiah Fisk, counselor Lahasa Hollister, counselor	*Presidency* John Smith Reynolds Cahoon Lyman Wight *Bishop (Pro Tempore)* Vinson Knight *High Council* It is unclear whether there was an established order of counselors in the Adam-ondi-Ahman high council. John Lemon Daniel Stanton Mayhew Hillman Daniel Carter Isaac Perry Harrison Sagers Alanson Brown Thomas Gordon Lorenzo Barnes George A. Smith Harvey Olmstead Ezra Thayer	*Quorum of the Twelve* Quorum members held seniority according to age. Thomas B. Marsh, president David W. Patten Brigham Young Heber C. Kimball Orson Hyde Parley P. Pratt William Smith Orson Pratt Quorum members William E. McLellin, Luke Johnson, John F. Boynton, and Lyman Johnson had been excommunicated. An 8 July 1838 revelation appointed John E. Page, Wilford Woodruff, John Taylor, and Willard Richards to replace the former quorum members, but none were ordained to office before December 1838. *Quorum of the Seventy, Presidents* The presidents of the Quorum of the Seventy were reorganized in April 1837 amid confusion over the relationship between high priests and seventies. Presidents of the Seventy who had been previously ordained high priests were reassigned to the high priests quorum, and new presidents of the Seventy were appointed to replace the outgoing high priests. The presidents presided over three quorums of seventy. It is unclear whether there was an order of seniority among the presidents. Joseph Young Levi Hancock James Foster Daniel Miles Josiah Butterfield Henry Harriman Zera Pulsipher

October 1839

Following their forced expulsion from Missouri in spring 1839, the Latter-day Saints regrouped in Illinois. After JS's escape from incarceration in April 1839, he began to reorganize the Latter-day Saints at Commerce (later Nauvoo), Illinois, and across the river in Iowa. Banished from the land they considered Zion, the Latter-day Saints denominated Commerce, now the central church unit, a "stake" like other major church units.

GENERAL CHURCH OFFICERS

First Presidency Joseph Smith Jr., president Sidney Rigdon, counselor Hyrum Smith, counselor	*Patriarch* Joseph Smith Sr.

OTHER OFFICERS

Commerce Stake Officers	Iowa Stake Officers	Traveling Officers
President William Marks *High Council* It is unclear whether there was an established order of counselors in the Commerce high council. Samuel Bent, the oldest member of the council, may have been president. Samuel Bent George W. Harris Henry Sherwood David Fullmer Alpheus Cutler William Huntington Thomas Grover Newel Knight Charles Rich David Dort Seymour Brunson Lewis Wilson *Bishops* Newel K. Whitney, Middle Ward Edward Partridge, Upper Ward Vinson Knight, Lower Ward *President of Quorum of High Priests* Don Carlos Smith	*President* John Smith *High Council* It is unclear whether there was an established order of counselors in the Iowa high council. Asahel Smith John Burk Abraham Smoot Richard Howard Willard Snow Erastus Snow David Pettigrew Elijah Fordham Edward Fisher Elias Smith John Patten Stephen Chase *Bishop* Alanson Ripley	*Quorum of the Twelve* The original members continued in their age-based seniority; newer members followed, ordered by age amongst themselves. On 16 January 1839, the First Presidency instructed Heber C. Kimball and Brigham Young to appoint the oldest of the original members to be president of the quorum. Young was sustained as president on 14 April 1840. Brigham Young, president Heber C. Kimball Orson Hyde Parley P. Pratt William Smith Orson Pratt John E. Page John Taylor Wilford Woodruff George A. Smith A July 1838 revelation appointed John E. Page, Wilford Woodruff, John Taylor, and Willard Richards to replace excommunicated quorum members William E. McLellin, Luke Johnson, John F. Boynton, and Lyman Johnson. Page and Taylor were ordained 19 December 1838. Woodruff was ordained 26 April 1839, as was George A. Smith, the latter filling the vacancy left by the apostasy of Thomas B. Marsh. Richards,
	CHART CONTINUED ON NEXT PAGE	

OTHER OFFICERS *CONTINUED*

Commerce Stake Officers	Iowa Stake Officers	Traveling Officers
		still proselytizing in England, was not ordained until 14 April 1840. By this time, David W. Patten had been killed in the Missouri conflicts and Thomas B. Marsh had apostatized, as noted above, with Orson Hyde, who soon returned to the church. A conference held near Quincy, Illinois, on 4 May 1839 resolved that the apostolic privileges of Orson Hyde and William Smith be "suspended" until the next church conference, at which time they would be allowed to give an account of their conduct. Both were "restored" to their offices at a conference held in October 1839. The quorum reached a full contingent of twelve men with the appointment of Lyman Wight in 1841.

Presidents of the Seventy
The presidents of the Seventy presided over three quorums of seventy and a number of seventy not assigned to a specific quorum. It is unclear whether there was an established order of seniority among the presidents.

Joseph Young
Levi Hancock
James Foster
Daniel Miles
Josiah Butterfield
Henry Harriman
Zera Pulsipher

Glossary

This glossary defines particularly Mormon terms—especially ordinances, offices, and organizations—that appear in the texts of the journals. Terms are defined as they were used in the 1830s. Readers wishing to conduct further research may consult the fully documented glossary posted on the Joseph Smith Papers website.

Aaronic Priesthood. The lower or lesser of two orders of priesthood in the church. Sometimes called the "Levitical priesthood." It is named for Aaron, the brother of Moses, "because it was conferred upon Aaron and his seed" in antiquity (Revelation, ca. Apr. 1835, in Doctrine and Covenants 3:8, 1835 ed. [D&C 107:13]). This authority holds "the keys of the ministring of angels, and to administer in outward ordinances—the letter of the gospel—the baptism of repentance for the remission of sins" (Revelation, ca. Apr. 1835, in Doctrine and Covenants 3:10, 1835 ed. [D&C 107:20]). JS said that the Aaronic Priesthood was conferred upon Oliver Cowdery and himself by John the Baptist on 15 May 1829.

Adam-ondi-Ahman. See "Adam-ondi-Ahman," in Geographical Directory.

Anoint. Following a biblical pattern, JS on 21 January 1836 instituted the ordinance of anointing with oil on the head or body as a sign of sanctification and consecration in preparation for the endowment of "power from on high" (Prayer, 27 Mar. 1836, in *Prayer, at the Dedication of the Lord's House,* 1 [D&C 109:35]). This anointing was combined with the ordinance of washing of bodies. In addition, the ordinance of blessing of the sick included anointing with oil. Latter-day Saints also used the term *anointed* in the metaphorical sense to mean chosen, elected, or otherwise designated by God to some position or responsibility.

Apostle. JS's revelations first associated the term *apostle* with himself, Oliver Cowdery, and David Whitmer. When JS and Oliver Cowdery became holders of the Melchizedek Priesthood, they were called "apostles and especial witnesses" of Christ (Revelation, ca. Aug. 1830, in Doctrine and Covenants 50:3, 1835 ed. [D&C 27:12]). The term *apostle,* from the Greek for "envoy" or "messenger," was also used more generally to denote those with missionary duties. An 1829 revelation indicated that twelve disciples would be "called to go into all the world to preach my gospel" (Revelation, June 1829–B, in Doctrine and Covenants 43:5, 1835 ed. [D&C 18:28]). With the organization of the Quorum of the Twelve Apostles in February 1835, *apostle* became increasingly associated with the twelve men who held that specific priesthood office. These apostles had responsibility to act as "special witnesses of the name of Christ, in all the world" (Revelation, ca. Apr. 1835, in Doctrine and Covenants 3:11, 1835 ed. [D&C 107:23]). Nevertheless, a broader definition of *apostle* that included members of the Quorums of Seventy persisted for some time.

Baptism. Water baptism by immersion, an ordinance of salvation. New converts were to be received into the church by baptism after they "humble themselves before God and . . . witness before the church that they have truly repented of all their sins and are willing to take upon them the name of Jesus Christ" (Revelation, 10 Apr. 1830, in Doctrine and Covenants 2:7, 1835 ed. [D&C 20:37]). An early revelation directed that converts who had previously been baptized into other denominations must be rebaptized. Baptism was not to be performed for infants, but for those who had "arriven to the years of accountability" (Revelation, June 1829–B, in Doctrine and Covenants 43:6, 1835 ed. [D&C 18:42]).

Bishop. Priesthood office whose duties included caring for church members' material needs, acting as a "judge in Israel" in settling disputes, and sitting "in judgment upon transgressors" (Revelation, 11 Nov. 1831–B, in Doctrine and Covenants 3:32, 1835 ed. [D&C 107:72]). In 1831, JS appointed Bishop Edward Partridge to preside over the church in Missouri and Bishop Newel K. Whitney to preside over the church in Kirtland, Ohio. In early 1835, a revelation explained that the bishop was the highest office in the Aaronic, or lower, order of the priesthood and that bishoprics presided over the Aaronic Priesthood generally and over local priests in particular. Separate presidents of the priests quorums were sometimes called as well.

Bishopric, bishoprick. Eventually used to describe the ecclesiastical body comprising the bishop and his counselors, the term was also used in the 1830s to describe priesthood positions generally, as in, for example, the idea that one could have his "bishoprick" taken from him (see Acts 1:20).

Bishop's council. Used to designate a bishop and his assistants or counselors as they carried out ecclesiastical or administrative responsibilities. The term "bishop's council" also denoted the officers who served in a bishop's court.

Bishop's court. Official church proceedings convened to handle disputes or allegations of misconduct. The officers of the court were a bishop, his assistants or counselors, and additional high priests or elders assembled on an ad hoc basis. Until high councils were established in 1834, matters that could not be settled satisfactorily by the bishop's council were referred to a court, or council, of twelve high priests over which the president of the church presided. Thereafter, appeals of bishop's court decisions were directed to high councils or, if necessary, to the church's presidency. Allegations of misconduct against a president of the church were to be considered by a council consisting of a bishop and twelve high priests.

Blessing of the sick. JS's revelations instructed elders to lay their hands on those who were ill and offer a blessing of healing. Beginning in the mid-1830s, blessings usually included a preliminary anointing with oil. As in the New Testament, having faith was a necessary component of being healed.

Branch. See "Stake."

Celestial kingdom. Highest kingdom of glory among the multiple heavens described in a revelation dated 16 February 1832. According to this revelation, inheritors of the highest kingdom "are they who received the testimony of Jesus, and believed on his name, and were baptized . . . and receive the Holy Spirit by the laying on of the hands . . . who overcome by faith" (Vision, 16 Feb. 1832, in Doctrine and Covenants 91:5, 1835 ed. [D&C 76:51–53]). Those so qualified are "given all things," "are gods, even the sons of God," and "dwell in the presence of God and his Christ forever and ever" (Vision, 16 Feb. 1832, in Doctrine and Covenants 91:5, 1835 ed. [D&C 76:55, 58, 62]). Additionally, a 21 January 1836 revelation declared that all who had died without "knowledge of this gospel" could "be heirs of the celestial kingdom" if they would have received the gospel had they "been permited to tarry" (Vision, 21 Jan. 1836, in JS, Journal, 21 Jan. 1836 [D&C 137:7]).

Chapel. See "House of the Lord."

Church of Jesus Christ of Latter Day Saints. The first name used to denote the church JS organized on 6 April 1830 was "the church of Christ" (Revelation, 10 Apr. 1830, in Book of Commandments 24:1 [D&C 20:1]). At a 3 May 1834 conference, church leaders approved changing the name to "The Church of the Latter Day Saints" ("Communicated," *The Evening and the Morning Star,* May 1834, 160). A revelation dated 26 April 1838 incorporated both previous official names: "For thus shall my Church be called in the Last days even the Church of Jesus Christ of Latter Day Saints" (Revelation, 26 Apr. 1838, in JS, Journal, 26 Apr. 1838, p. 258 herein [D&C 115:4]). Usage during JS's lifetime varied.

Communion. See "Sacrament."

Conference. Most church business was transacted at meetings called conferences, originally to be held quarterly or as otherwise needed. Conferences were convened by church leaders and were attended by lay members and representatives of various church branches. Many meetings referred to as conferences in early church records were priesthood meetings for reports or for instruction and deliberation regarding policies, appointments, ordinations, and church discipline. Conferences provided an opportunity for decisions to be ratified by the general membership of the church according to the law of "common consent." Since they were also important occasions for preaching, conferences often included a meeting to which the general public was invited. Beginning in May 1835, the Quorum of the Twelve conducted a series of meetings in New York and New England at which branches of the church under their jurisdiction were incorporated into geographic areas for church governance, each of which was called a conference. "General" conferences held in May and October 1839 began the establishment of a pattern of semiannual meetings at which business was transacted for the entire church.

Confirmation. After baptism, new converts were "confirmed" members of the church and given the gift of the Holy Ghost in an ordinance by the laying on of hands. JS stated that the first confirmations were given at the organization of the church on 6 April 1830. The term *confirmation* was also used more generally to describe any bestowal of spiritual blessings, such as priesthood ordination by the laying on of hands.

Consecration. An 1831 revelation outlined a church law of community-based economic arrangements to provide for the poor and contribute to the building up of the church. In obedience to this law, individual church members would donate, or consecrate, their property to the church and receive back a "stewardship" based on their circumstances, needs, and wants. Local bishops were to oversee the application of the law. Initially, the church sought to retain ultimate ownership rights for the church and provide usage rights for individual stewards, but JS eventually directed that each steward would own his or her property, whether or not he or she remained in the church. After the initial consecration of property, it was expected that each steward would contribute any yearly surplus to a bishop's storehouse, from which the needy could be supported. A revelation dated 8 July 1838 did away with the initial consecration of property but instructed Latter-day Saints to give "all their surplus property" to the bishop and then a "tenth of all their interest annually" thereafter (Revelation, 8 July 1838–C, in JS, Journal, 8 July 1838, p. 288 herein [D&C 119:1, 4]). The system was thus significantly adjusted during JS's ministry, but the principles continued to guide church efforts to cooperatively share resources in building up communities and the church.

Danites. The common name for the "Daughter of Zion," a military society organized among the Mormons in Missouri in June 1838 to defend the church from both internal and external opposition. The official name was apparently derived from Micah 4:13: "Arise and thresh, O daughter of Zion: for I will make thine horn iron, and I will make thy hoofs brass: and thou shalt beat in pieces many people: and I will consecrate their gain unto the Lord, and their substance unto the Lord of the whole earth." The more common nickname was derived from the Israelite warrior tribe of Dan. JS later indicated that the nickname originated with him. The society began in connection with the effort to intimidate dissenters into leaving Far West, Missouri. It promoted political candidates favored by the First Presidency and facilitated the economic program of consecration. The Danites were organized into companies of tens and fifties led by captains, modeling the structure of the Israelite armies of the Old Testament. Parallel to state militia organization, the hierarchy also included generals, colonels, and other officers. According to its constitution, the society sought to protect the God-given rights of the Latter-day Saints and to resist oppression. Its constitution vested executive authority in JS and his counselors in the First Presidency. JS attended at least one of the society's meetings and reportedly expressed approval of its aims, but the precise nature of his involvement with and approval of the organization is unclear. The society's activity in the summer of 1838 included participation in the Independence Day commemoration at Far West on 4 July, in the election-day brawl in Daviess County on 6 August, and in the party that afterwards demanded a statement of neutrality from local justice of the peace Adam Black. As troubles with other Missourians mounted, the Danites were apparently absorbed into the larger Mormon militia that conducted Mormon military operations during September and October 1838. Following the surrender of Far West and the ensuing court hearing, JS wrote on 16 December that he had only recently learned that Sampson Avard, one of the Danite generals, had presented "false and pernicious" teachings as having come from the First Presidency. While there is no credible evidence that the Danite society outlived the Mormon War in Missouri, its brief existence contributed to widespread and lasting rumors of an enduring secret society of Mormon avengers.

Deacon. An office in the Aaronic Priesthood. Deacons were "to warn, expound, exhort, and teach, and invite all to come unto Christ" (Revelation, 10 Apr. 1830, in Doctrine and Covenants 2:11, 1835 ed. [D&C 20:59]). The first known deacon ordinations occurred by 1831.

Dispensation. A period of God's work on earth, such as the "dispensation of the gospel of Abraham" (Vision, 3 Apr. 1836, in JS, Journal, 3 Apr. 1836 [D&C 110:12]). The phrase "dispensation of the fulness of times" appears often in the writing of early Latter-day Saints; they typically used it to describe the final dispensation, the "last times" "wated [awaited] with anxious expectation" when God would bring together the work of all dispensations and complete his earthly work (Revelation, ca. Aug. 1830, in Doctrine and Covenants 50:3, 1835 ed. [D&C 27:13]; JS et al., Liberty, MO, to the church members and Edward Partridge, Quincy, IL, 20 Mar. 1839, in Revelations Collection, CHL [D&C 121:27]). Revelations stated that JS had been given "the Keys of this dispensation" (Vision, 3 Apr. 1836, in JS, Journal, 3 Apr. 1836 [D&C 110:16]).

Elder. An office in the Melchizedek Priesthood signifying general leadership and carrying no age requirement. The founding articles of the church outlined the duty of elders "to baptize, and to ordain other elders, priests, teachers, and deacons, and to administer bread and wine . . . to teach, expound exhort, . . . and watch over the church; and to confirm the church . . . and to take the lead of all meetings" (Revelation, 10 Apr. 1830, in Doctrine and Covenants 2:8, 1835 ed. [D&C 20:38–44]). JS and Oliver Cowdery were designated the "first" and "second" elders respectively at the church's organizational meeting in 1830, indicative not only of their being the first ordained elders but also of their serving as the infant church's presiding officers. The term also had more general usages. All bearers of the Melchizedek Priesthood could be referred to as elders, regardless of the specific priesthood office they held. The term was also used to signify proselytizing missionaries generally.

Elders School. See "School of the Prophets."

Endow, endowment. The terms *endow, endowed,* and *endowment*—as well as *endued* and *enduement*—were used to describe the bestowal of spiritual blessings upon the Latter-day Saints. In common usage, these terms meant essentially the same thing: to clothe, to put on, to furnish, or to supply with. In revelations in 1831, Latter-day Saints were promised an endowment "with power from on high" (Revelation, 2 Jan. 1831, in Doctrine and Covenants 12:7, 1835 ed. [D&C 38:32]), and by 1833 the promises were associated with the House of the Lord, then under construction in Kirtland, Ohio. In one reference, the promises were made analogous to the New Testament instruction to the apostles that they should tarry at Jerusalem until they were "endued with power from on high" (Luke 24:49). Many Latter-day Saints considered the outpouring of spiritual power, including speaking in tongues, visions, and prophesying, that they experienced in Kirtland in March 1836 to be their endowment with power. Church members later referred to a specific temple ordinance introduced in 1842 in Nauvoo, Illinois, as an endowment.

Endue. See "Endow, endowment."

F. G. Williams & Co. After the destruction of the church printing press in Missouri in 1833, the United Firm formed F. G. Williams & Co. as a commercial entity in Kirtland, Ohio, with publishing as its primary purpose. Following the dissolution of the United Firm in 1834, F. G. Williams & Co. continued as a stewardship assigned to Oliver Cowdery and Frederick G. Williams. Its financial books show that the company contributed support to the whole church presidency. The business's church printing projects included publication of the first edition of the Doctrine and Covenants, the first hymnbook, and church and local newspapers. The partnership was dissolved 7 June 1836.

First elders. In 1830, JS was designated by revelation as the "first elder" in the specific sense of his authority as the church's presiding priesthood officer. During the period before the elaboration of church offices, he functioned in this role with Oliver Cowdery as "second elder," or second presiding officer. The term "first elders" in later records generally meant "leading elders," especially in reference to those who were to prepare for the endowment of power in the House of the Lord.

First Presidency. The presiding body of the church. From the day of the church's organization on 6 April 1830, JS and Oliver Cowdery led the church in their capacity as elders. An 11 November 1831 revelation directed that "the duty of the president of the office of the high priesthood is to preside over the whole church" (Revelation, 11 Nov. 1831–B, in Doctrine and Covenants 3:42, 1835 ed. [D&C 107:91]). JS was ordained to that office on 25 January 1832. A presidency of the church was first organized 8 March 1832 when JS selected Jesse Gause and Sidney Rigdon as his counselors in the presidency of the high priesthood. Gause served only briefly, and by March 1833 Frederick G. Williams was appointed his successor. The term "first presidency of the church," used first in 1834 (Minutes, 17 Feb. 1834, in Doctrine and Covenants 5:11, 14, 1835 ed. [D&C 102:26, 33]), did not become standard until 1838. The presidency consisted of a president (JS) and two or more counselors or assistant presidents. After standing high councils were organized in 1834 and the quorums of the Twelve Apostles and the Seventy were organized in February 1835, revelation indicated that those bodies were each nominally equal in authority to the presidency of the church, but the Seventy were to officiate under the direction of the Twelve and the Twelve under the direction of the presidency. The presidency's jurisdiction included the entire church, and they were to "preside in counsel and set in order all the affairs of this church" (Revelation, 8 Mar. 1833, in Doctrine and Covenants 84:5, 1835 ed. [D&C 90:16]), whereas the jurisdiction of the Twelve and the Seventy was primarily outside Zion and its stakes, and the high councils were responsible for Zion and the stakes, respectively. For several months in 1835 and 1836 when Missouri church officers were visiting Kirtland, Ohio, while preparing for the solemn assembly in the House of the Lord, the Missouri church presidency were incorporated into the general church presidency in what was sometimes called a council, or quorum, of presidents. After the Missouri presidency's departure from Kirtland, a 3 September 1837 conference sustained JS, Sidney Rigdon, and Frederick G. Williams as "the three first presidnts of the Church" and Oliver Cowdery, Joseph Smith Sr., Hyrum Smith, and John Smith as "assistant Councillors." The minutes of the meeting explained, "These last four are allso, together with the first three to be concidered the heads of the Church" (Minute Book 1, 3 Sept. 1837). By 7 November 1838 only the three members of the First Presidency were mentioned in official records as the presidency of the church.

Fulness of times. See "Dispensation."

Gathering. As directed by early revelations, Latter-day Saints "gathered" in communities. In December 1830, Latter-day Saints living in New York were commanded to "assemble together" with the church members in Ohio (Revelation, 30 Dec. 1830, in Doctrine and Covenants 58:2, 1835 ed. [D&C 37:3]). In July 1831, "Zion" in western Missouri was designated as a gathering place. Along with receiving the practical benefits of living among fellow believers, the Latter-day Saints considered this assembling to be critical to the church in the "last days." A revelation dated September 1830, for instance, instructed elders "to bring to pass the gathering of [the] elect" who would "be gathered in unto one place, upon the face of this land" (Revelation, Sept. 1830–A, in Doctrine and Covenants 10:2, 1835 ed. [D&C 29:7–8]). Proselytizing efforts of missionaries gained converts who converged at these points of gathering. Those so concentrated together would "prepare their hearts, and be prepared in all things, against the day when tribulation and desolation are sent forth upon the wicked" (Revelation, Sept. 1830–A, in Doctrine and Covenants 10:2, 1835 ed. [D&C 29:8]). Even after repeated friction with neighbors caused some Latter-day Saints to question the wisdom of gathering together, the majority of the Saints continued in building up "gathered" communities. JS taught that ultimately Latter-day Saints gathered for the same reason Israel gathered anciently—to build a temple where God could reveal knowledge and ordinances. Latter-day Saints also anticipated a gathering, or restoration, of scattered Israel to the Holy Land.

Hebrew School. Educational program instituted by JS in Kirtland, Ohio, in January 1836 for the study of the Hebrew language. Class was usually held in the westernmost room in the third, or attic, story of the House of the Lord in Kirtland. Under the tutelage of Joshua Seixas, a Hebraist and language scholar, at least eighty students gained a basic knowledge of Hebrew in sessions that met regularly until the end of March of that year. Seixas apparently conducted an additional term of the Hebrew School in Kirtland in the summer of 1836. See also "Hebrew School," in Geographical Directory.

High council. Although JS utilized councils of elders and high priests earlier in church government, the first standing high council of the church was organized in Kirtland, Ohio, on 17 February 1834. The second high council was organized a few months later in Clay County, Missouri. These high councils ultimately consisted of twelve high priests and were organized "for the purpose of settling important difficulties, which might arise in the church, which could not be settled by the church, or the bishop's council, to the satisfaction of the parties" (Minutes, 17 Feb. 1834, in Doctrine and Covenants 5:1, 1835 ed. [D&C 102:2]). In addition to providing a judicial function, high councils played an important administrative role in the church. For congregations outside the jurisdiction of the standing high councils in Zion and her stakes, the Quorum of the Twelve constituted a traveling high council to regulate church affairs.

High priest. An office in the Melchizedek Priesthood, first instituted on 3 June 1831 with several ordinations to the high priesthood. Revelations set forth that high priests had "a right to officiate in their own standing, under the direction of the presidency, in administering spiritual things" (Revelation, ca. Apr. 1835, in Doctrine and Covenants 3:5, 1835 ed. [D&C 107:10]) and that they could serve as bishops or bishops' counselors, officiate in all lesser offices, constitute high councils, and serve in the church's presidency. High priests were organized into a quorum by January 1836, at which time JS's brother Don Carlos Smith was sustained as president of the high priests, an office distinct from JS's role as "president of the high priesthood."

High priesthood. Variously used to denote the authority held by individuals ordained to the office of high priest, the high priests as a body, the presidents or presidency of the high priesthood, and the Melchizedek Priesthood.

Hosanna. A Hebrew cry to God for help also used in the New Testament to give acclaim. An exultant, formulaic "Hosanna Shout," uttered in unison by all present, occurred several times in the House of the Lord in Kirtland, Ohio, both in meetings leading up to and during the dedication of the edifice.

House of the Lord. The sacred edifice in Kirtland, Ohio, since known as the Kirtland temple. Although the term *temple* in the early days of the church designated a category of buildings, the proper name applied to the structure in Kirtland was "House of the Lord."

JS and the Latter-day Saints also referred to it as "the chapel" and, in rare instances, "the temple." Revelations relating to the construction of the House of the Lord in Kirtland made clear that it would serve as a place of religious instruction and a place of God's presence, where he would manifest himself to faithful Latter-day Saints and endow his servants "with power from on high" (Revelation, 1 June 1833, in Doctrine and Covenants 95:2, 1835 ed. [D&C 95:8]). The building became a focal point for the religious community, providing a place for church meetings, office space for church leaders, rooms for schools, and sacred space for ordinances and revelation. The term "House of the Lord" was intended to be used more widely than just in Kirtland. In June 1833, JS and the presidency directed that twenty-four temples were to be built in Independence, Missouri, eighteen of which would bear proper names beginning with "House of the Lord."

Keys. Early revelations equated "keys" with authority, which paralleled biblical use of the term. Keys were often associated with the presiding officers of the church. Revelation described JS as having the "keys of the kingdom" of heaven on earth (Revelation, 15 Mar. 1832, in Doctrine and Covenants 79:1, 1835 ed. [D&C 81:2]). He stated that he received the several keys that constituted the authority necessary to lead the church from divine messengers. The imagery of a key was especially powerful with respect to the Quorum of the Twelve, upon whom were conferred the keys "to unlock the door of the kingdom" to the nations of the earth (Revelation, 23 July 1837, in JS, Journal, 23 July 1837, p. 307 herein [D&C 112:17]). JS's revelations also connected the idea of keys to essential knowledge or understanding.

Laying on of hands. A ritual bestowing power, authority, or other blessings. One holding priesthood authority placed his hands upon another's head to confer the gift of the Holy Ghost, confer the priesthood, set apart to an office or calling, or offer a blessing for counsel, comfort, or healing. JS stated that John the Baptist appeared to Oliver Cowdery and JS in May 1829 to confer the Aaronic Priesthood upon them by the laying on of hands.

License. The founding articles of the church instructed each holder of the priesthood to keep a certificate from the person who ordained him which "shall authorize him to perform the duties of his calling" (Revelation, 10 Apr. 1830, in Doctrine and Covenants 2:15, 1835 ed. [D&C 20:64]). Licenses were routinely issued to those ordained to the priesthood to certify their standing and authority in the church and could be revoked as a measure of church discipline. Church licensing practices were standardized in March 1836.

Lord's Supper. See "Sacrament."

Melchizedek Priesthood. The greater or higher of two orders of priesthood in the church. Also known as "the holy priesthood, after the order of the Son of God" (Revelation, ca. Apr. 1835, in Doctrine and Covenants 3:1, 1835 ed. [D&C 107:3]), "the high priesthood," and "the high and holy priesthood." This priesthood held the "right of presidency," the responsibility "to administer in spiritual things," and the "keys of all the spiritual blessings of the church" (Revelation, ca. Apr. 1835, in Doctrine and Covenants 3:3, 9, 1835 ed. [D&C 107:8, 18]). The name honors the Old Testament priest Melchizedek, to whom Abraham paid tithes, and was also used to respectfully avoid too frequent repetition of the name of Deity. Those holding offices in the Melchizedek Priesthood were to preside over the church and its stakes and branches as well as to officiate in ordinances. Those holding the Aaronic

Priesthood could also perform some ordinances, but JS's revelations stipulated that only in the ordinances of the higher priesthood was "the power of godliness . . . manifest" (Revelation, 22 and 23 Sept. 1832, in Doctrine and Covenants 4:3, 1835 ed. [D&C 84:19–20]). Latter-day Saints believed that both the Aaronic and Melchizedek priesthoods were held anciently but that the higher priesthood was taken away from ancient Israel. Peter, James, John, and other members of Christ's early church were understood to have held the Melchizedek Priesthood, which had again been taken from the earth after the time of Christ and had been later restored to JS after a similar restoration of the Aaronic Priesthood.

New and everlasting covenant. This phrase and a shortened version, "everlasting covenant," appeared in JS's revelations as synonymous with the "fulness of [the] gospel"—the sum total of the church's message—or with individual elements of it (Revelation, 1 Nov. 1831–B, in Doctrine and Covenants 1:3–4, 1835 ed. [D&C 1:15, 22]; Revelation, 29 Oct. 1831, in Doctrine and Covenants 74:1, 1835 ed. [D&C 66:2]). Baptism by priesthood authority, for instance, was identified as a "new and an everlasting covenant" in an early revelation (Revelation, 16 Apr. 1830, in Doctrine and Covenants 47:1, 1835 ed. [D&C 22:1]). The phrase was later used with reference to marriage sealings by church priesthood authority.

Official member. Common term for church members who were also officials; men who held priesthood offices.

Ordain, ordination. Priesthood offices were conferred on males, primarily adults, by the laying on of hands "by those who are in authority" (JS, "Church History," *Times and Seasons,* 1 Mar. 1842, 3:709 [Articles of Faith 1:5]; see also 1 Timothy 4:14). This conferral was frequently referred to as an *ordination.* The term was also occasionally used in the generic sense, meaning to appoint, decree, or establish.

Ordinance. Religious rituals that early Latter-day Saints believed God had instituted for the blessing of humanity. Ordinances were performed by priesthood authority, were generally authorized by presiding officers, and often involved the making or renewing of covenants with God. A September 1832 revelation stated that in the ordinances of the Melchizedek Priesthood "the power of godliness is manifest" (Revelation, 22 and 23 Sept. 1832, in Doctrine and Covenants 4:3, 1835 ed. [D&C 84:19–20]). Revelations singled out some ordinances, such as baptism and bestowal of the gift of the Holy Ghost, as necessary for eternal glory.

Patriarch. An office in the Melchizedek Priesthood with the authority and responsibility to give inspired blessings similar to those given by the Old Testament patriarchs. Joseph Smith Sr. was the first appointed patriarch, ordained in December 1834. According to the Book of Patriarchal Blessings, he held "the keys of the patriarchal priesthood over the Kingdom of God on earth" (Patriarchal Blessings, 1:9). Additional patriarchs were called thereafter. Joseph Smith Sr. periodically held "patriarchal meetings" or "blessing meetings" to administer such blessings. JS sometimes referred to patriarchs as "evangelical ministers" or "evangelists." The blessings they gave were recorded and preserved as church records.

Patriarchal blessing. See "Patriarch."

Presidency. Priesthood quorums and various bodies of Latter-day Saints were overseen by presidencies. As early as November 1831, a revelation outlined the need for the organization of a formal church presidency, and by 1832, JS and two counselors constituted the general presidency over the church. In the years that followed, other individuals were called as counselors—or sometimes assistant presidents—in this presidency. A local presidency was formed in 1834, when David Whitmer, William W. Phelps, and John Whitmer were appointed to serve as the presidency of the church in Missouri under the direction of the general presidency of the church. In Kirtland, Ohio, in 1835–1836, in preparation for the solemn assembly in the House of the Lord, the Missouri group frequently joined the church presidency to function as a unit, designated variously as the "quorem of the presidency" and the "council of the presidency" (JS, Journal, 28 Jan. 1836). During this period, this council consisted of some or all of nine individuals: JS, Oliver Cowdery, Sidney Rigdon, Frederick G. Williams, Hyrum Smith, Joseph Smith Sr., David Whitmer, William W. Phelps, and John Whitmer. That combination ended with the departure of the Missouri presidency from Kirtland. In the aftermath of the dissension and apostasy that disrupted the church in 1837 and 1838, the general presidency of the church consisted of one president with two counselors. Presidencies of individual church stakes generally followed this same pattern of one president with two counselors, as did presidencies of quorums of high priests, elders, priests, teachers, and deacons. Bishops and their counselors were designated in revelation as presidencies of the Aaronic Priesthood. The Quorum of the Twelve was presided over by a single president, and the original Quorum of the Seventy was led by seven presidents.

Priest. An office in the Aaronic Priesthood. The founding articles of the church outlined the duties of the priest as including the following: "to preach, teach, expound, exhort, and baptize, and administer the sacrament, and visit the house of each member, and . . . ordain other priests, teachers, and deacons" (Revelation, 10 Apr. 1830, in Doctrine and Covenants 2:10, 1835 ed. [D&C 20:46–48]). Priests were to take charge of church meetings in the absence of elders.

Priesthood. Power and authority from God delegated to man to govern the church and perform ordinances. Priesthood officers held responsibility for administering the memorial sacrament of the Lord's Supper and other ordinances, overseeing pastoral duties, preaching, and proselytizing. JS oversaw the conferral of priesthood by the laying on of hands on ordinary adult male members of the church in good standing. No specialized training was required for ordination. Priesthood officers belonged to one of two general priesthood levels, which JS designated in 1835 as the Aaronic Priesthood and the higher Melchizedek Priesthood. Officers belonged to "quorums" organized by office. JS reported having received "keys," or governing authority in the priesthood, from resurrected biblical figures who appeared to himself and Oliver Cowdery.

Quorum. Refers especially to a group to which individuals ordained to the Aaronic or Melchizedek priesthoods belonged. Quorums were organized by office, such as an "elders quorum." The organization of quorums provided leadership and a manageable structure for varied priesthood responsibilities.

Redemption of Zion. See "Zion" and "Zion's Camp."

Sacrament. In Latter-day Saint usage, this term primarily applied to the sacrament of the Lord's Supper, or Communion, as opposed to other religious sacraments. An 1830 revelation directed "that the church meet together often to partake of bread and wine in remembrance of the Lord Jesus" (Revelation, 10 Apr. 1830, in Doctrine and Covenants 2:23,

1835 ed. [D&C 20:75]). A revelation later that year directed that the Latter-day Saints were to use only wine "made new among you" (Revelation, ca. Aug. 1830, in Doctrine and Covenants 50:1, 1835 ed. [D&C 27:4]); otherwise they were to resort to other, presumably nonalcoholic, beverages for the sacrament. During JS's lifetime, either wine or water was generally used.

School. See "Hebrew School" and "School of the Prophets."

School of the Prophets. In response to revelation, the Latter-day Saints established a "School of the Prophets" in Kirtland, Ohio, in January 1833 to prepare leading elders of the church for their ministry. Those who attended that winter and early spring were instructed in church doctrine and various secular topics. In accordance with the 1833 instructions, members were initiated into the school by the ordinance of the washing of feet and met each other with a formal, prescribed greeting at each school meeting. A similar school convened in Jackson County, Missouri, during summer 1833. In late 1834, ministerial training resumed under the name "Elders School" or "School of the Elders." Although it differed from the original School of the Prophets in that its attendance was expanded to include additional bearers of the priesthood beyond church leaders and did not include the foot-washing ordinance or the formal greeting, JS and others sometimes referred to the Elders School as the "School of the Prophets." Additional sessions of the Elders School were held in winter 1835–1836. See also "Elders School," in Geographical Directory.

Seal. To confirm, to solemnize, and to conclude. Early revelations adopted biblical usage of the term *seal;* for example, "seal up the testimony" referred to proselytizing and testifying of the gospel with finality with the approach of the end-time (Revelation, 27 and 28 Dec. 1832 and 3 Jan. 1833, in Doctrine and Covenants 7:23, 1835 ed. [D&C 88:84]). JS and other early Latter-day Saints also used forms of the word *seal* when describing confirmations of religious proceedings, prayers, blessings, anointings, or marriages. Such sealings were performed in many ways: by the laying of hands on the person's head, with uplifted hands, by prayer, by announcement, with hosannas or amens, or by combinations of these. *Sealing* was also used in connection with the notion of power sufficient to bind (or loose) on earth and be recognized in heaven, or to consign to God's punishment or to salvation. JS explained in October 1831 that high priests had authority to seal members to salvation.

Seventy. An office in the Melchizedek Priesthood patterned after the seventy envoys called by Jesus in the New Testament. The first members of the Quorum of the Seventy were called in February 1835. Revelation stipulated that "the seventy are also called to preach the gospel, and to be especial witnesses unto the Gentiles and in all the world" and "to act in the name of the Lord, under the direction of the twelve . . . in building up the church and regulating all the affairs of the same, in all nations: first unto the Gentiles and then to the Jews" (Revelation, ca. Apr. 1835, in Doctrine and Covenants 3:11, 13, 1835 ed. [D&C 107:25, 34]). JS occasionally referred to the Seventy as "seventy elders" or "seventy apostles." The Seventy were led by seven presidents, who could choose additional quorums of the Seventy "until seven times seventy, if the labor in the vineyard of necessity requires it" (Revelation, ca. Apr. 1835, in Doctrine and Covenants 3:43, 1835 ed. [D&C 107:96]).

Solemn assembly. Generally, a special church meeting, such as the meeting of the School of the Prophets on 23 January 1833 and the dedication of the House of the Lord in Kirtland, Ohio, on 27 March 1836. In particular, it referred to the meeting held in the

House of the Lord on 30 March 1836. A solemn assembly was promised in revelations as a time when faithful Latter-day Saints would receive an endowment "with power" (Revelation, 1 June 1833, in Doctrine and Covenants 95:2, 1835 ed. [D&C 95:8]) prior to going forth to preach. It was to be preceded by a period of preparation, which would include instructions, ordinances of washing and anointing, and renewals of commitment. Many people who were present during the dedication of the House of the Lord in Kirtland, the 30 March 1836 solemn assembly in that same structure, and related events reported having experienced manifestations of spiritual power, including speaking in tongues, seeing visions, and prophesying.

Stake. The ecclesiastical organization of Latter-day Saints in a particular locale. The terms *stake, branch,* and *church* were used in a roughly similar way, although the latter was also used to denote the church in its entirety or the Latter-day Saints generally in an area. Unlike smaller branches, which were headed by a presiding elder or a high priest, stakes were typically larger local organizations of church members ideally headed by a presidency, a high council, and a bishopric. Additionally, revelations dated January 1838 made clear that only the First Presidency could designate stakes and that such designation required prior recognition of the authority of the First Presidency by a vote of the members in that jurisdiction. Some revelations refer to stakes "to" or "of" Zion—places where substantial congregations of Latter-day Saints could be found outside the central place of gathering. This conceptualization drew on Old Testament imagery of the tent of Zion supported by cords fastened to stakes. During the years of gathering in Missouri, the term *stake* was not used in reference to the principal Mormon community in that state, which was "Zion" itself. However, several stakes were later planned for upper Missouri, and one in Adam-ondi-Ahman was operational before the forced exodus in 1838.

Teacher. An office in the Aaronic Priesthood. The founding articles of the church outlined the duties of a teacher as including the following: "to watch over the church, . . . see that there is no iniquity in the church, . . . see that the church meet together often, and also see that all the members do their duty . . . to take the lead of meetings in the absence of the elder or priest" (Revelation, 10 Apr. 1830, in Doctrine and Covenants 2:11, 1835 ed. [D&C 20:53–56]).

Temple. See "House of the Lord."

Twelve Apostles. The Quorum of the Twelve Apostles was organized in February 1835. Its members were to be "special witnesses of the name of Christ, in all the world" and to act "under the direction of the presidency of the church" in proclaiming the gospel and in building up and regulating the church (Revelation, ca. Apr. 1835, in Doctrine and Covenants 3:11–12, 1835 ed. [D&C 107:23, 33]). Initially, the Twelve constituted a "travelling, presiding high council" (Revelation, ca. Apr. 1835, in Doctrine and Covenants 3:12, 1835 ed. [D&C 107:33]) and had governing authority only outside of Zion and organized stakes, where local high councils had jurisdiction. An exception was the service of apostles Thomas B. Marsh, David W. Patten, and Brigham Young as the acting presidency of the church in Missouri after the removal of the existing presidency. At the dedication of the House of the Lord in Kirtland, Ohio, JS, "the Presidency," and the Twelve were presented and upheld as "Prophets and Seers" (JS, Journal, 27 Mar. 1836).

United Firm. An organization that supervised the management of church enterprises and properties, 1832–1834. A revelation of 1 March 1832 directed that the church's publishing and mercantile businesses in Kirtland and in Missouri were to be placed under a central leadership. Implementation began with the 27 April 1832 establishment at Independence, Missouri, of a mercantile branch of the Newel K. Whitney store. JS and nine other men were the original officers of the United Firm. Each property or enterprise under United Firm supervision was owned by individuals, rather than by the firm or by its officers as a group. Individual owners were to manage the various undertakings and make profits available to support church enterprises such as the publication of scriptures while also providing for the financial needs of the firm's officers. In addition to mercantile and publishing enterprises, officers of the United Firm supervised farms and residential real estate, an ashery, a tannery, a stone quarry, a sawmill, and a brick kiln. The firm's Missouri operations were halted by the November 1833 expulsion of the Saints from Jackson County, and the firm faced substantial indebtedness for mortgage payments and a printing press. After efforts to raise funds to repay the firm's debts failed, a revelation of 23 April 1834 directed that the United Firm in Kirtland be separated from that in Missouri, and called for a redistribution of the Kirtland firm's assets to its officers and cancellation of all debts they owed each other. In effect, this marked the end of the United Firm, since its supervisory function was largely assumed by the Kirtland high council.

Washing of feet. Ordinance symbolizing unity and cleanliness. Revelation directed that the "president, or presiding elder of the church" was to administer the ordinance "in the house of the Lord, in the school of the prophets" (Revelation, 27 and 28 Dec. 1832 and 3 Jan. 1833, in Doctrine and Covenants 7:44–46, 1835 ed. [D&C 88:136–141]), in accordance with the pattern set by Jesus at the Last Supper. It was initially performed in the School of the Prophets in 1833. As Latter-day Saints prepared for the endowment of power in the House of the Lord in Kirtland, Ohio, JS established the sequence of washings, anointings, blessings, and sealings, which culminated with the washing of feet of priesthood officers during the solemn assembly on 30 March 1836.

Washings. Washings of bodies as an ordinance began on 21 January 1836, when JS had priesthood holders wash to prepare for the endowment "with power from on high" connected with the dedication of the House of the Lord in Kirtland, Ohio (Revelation, 1 June 1833, in Doctrine and Covenants 95:2, 1835 ed. [D&C 95:8]). Biblical in origin, ritual washing symbolized a cleansing of body and spirit to be worthy of God's presence. It was performed in preparation for the ordinance of anointing with oil.

Zion. In JS's earliest revelations, *Zion* was a synonym for God's work generally, but it soon came to mean the ideal society that JS sought to establish mirroring Enoch's righteous, unified, poverty-free community also called Zion. It also came to mean the place where God's people were to establish a holy city. On 20 July 1831, JS designated Independence, Jackson County, Missouri, as the site for the city of Zion—and Missouri generally as the "land" of Zion. The term *Zion* was subsequently used for the Missouri church headquartered in Clay County and then Caldwell County. Ancillary communities of Latter-day Saints called "stakes," figuratively tethered to the tent of Zion, were to collectively sustain the center. See also "Zion," in Geographical Directory.

Zion brethren. Veterans of the spring 1834 expedition to Clay County, Missouri. A revelation of 22 June 1834 indicated that God had "a blessing and an endowment" for the members of the expedition (Revelation, 22 June 1834, in Doctrine and Covenants 102:3, 5, 1844 ed. [D&C 105:12, 18]). Veterans of the expedition met on 13 February 1835 at Kirtland to receive such a blessing, which was called a "Zion's blessing" (Kimball, "History," 27). Subsequently, other veterans of the expedition received their blessing individually from members of the church presidency.

Zion's Camp. The name by which the spring 1834 military expedition from Kirtland, Ohio, to Clay County, Missouri, came to be known. This relief expedition, appointed by revelation and led by JS, consisted of about two hundred armed but largely untrained men who hoped to reinstate the exiled Latter-day Saints to their lands in Jackson County, Missouri. Despite the sacrifice of the marchers in journeying on foot more than eight hundred miles under difficult circumstances, the expedition did not fulfill its ostensible mission. A revelation directed that Zion's Camp be disbanded and that its members "wait for a little season for the redemption of Zion" (Revelation, 22 June 1834, in Doctrine and Covenants 102:3, 1844 ed. [D&C 105:9]). Members of the original Quorum of the Twelve and the original Quorum of the Seventy were later selected primarily from those who made this trek to Missouri with JS.

Essay on Sources

The contemporaneous sources in this volume's annotation range from personal writings to institutional records to published books. Most sources are specific to certain time periods and therefore appear chiefly in the annotation to a specific journal. For all of JS's journals, especially the first three, the texts of his revelations are essential background sources. The revelations embodied JS's religious values, conveyed his sense of mission, and outlined his agenda for building Zion. Major sources for revelation texts are the journals themselves, other early manuscript sources, early church newspapers, and the church's published compilations of revelations and other authoritative material. The first attempt to publish such a compilation was the Book of Commandments. Church printer William W. Phelps had printed most of the projected contents of the Book of Commandments by July 1833 when the printing shop in Independence, Missouri, was destroyed by a mob. Several Latter-day Saints recovered complete sets of the sheets that had been printed up to that point and had them bound. A second effort was completed on a new church press in Kirtland, Ohio, in 1835. The new compilation, titled Doctrine and Covenants, contained two parts. The first part consisted of seven "Lectures" or essays on the subject of faith. The second part contained the texts of almost one hundred revelations, official statements on marriage and government, and other items.

JS's first journal (1832–1834) records his frequent travels and also church problems in Missouri, hundreds of miles from JS's Kirtland headquarters. Both sets of circumstances required letter writing. Letters that JS wrote to his wife Emma, to Missouri Latter-day Saint leaders William W. Phelps and Edward Partridge, and to various friends and acquaintances illuminate the content of the journal in many instances. Minute Book 1 (created 1832–1837) often supplies valuable information regarding meetings that are mentioned in the journal. Important contextual material is also found in the church's first newspaper, *The Evening and the Morning Star,* which was edited by Phelps in Independence, Missouri, from June 1832 to July 1833. Printing resumed in Kirtland in December 1833 under the editorship of Oliver Cowdery, who produced another ten issues. Beginning in January 1835, the entire run of twenty-four issues was reprinted with modifications under a shortened title, *Evening and Morning Star.*

JS's second journal (1835–1836) records meetings held in preparation for the completion of the House of the Lord in Kirtland and for the Pentecost that Latter-day Saints expected to experience therein. As with the 1832–1834 journal, Minute Book 1 augments the 1835–1836 journal's notes of meetings. The contemporaneous diaries of assistant president Oliver Cowdery and Missouri bishop Edward Partridge clarify some entries in the second half of the journal. Numerous reminiscent accounts add details of the dedication of the House of the Lord, the solemn assembly, and surrounding events recorded at the end of the journal. The King James Version of the Bible is particularly helpful in this journal for identifying JS's biblical paraphrasing and allusions. JS's 1835–1836 journal is also illuminated by a contemporaneous church history created from 1834 to 1836. In the spring of 1836, Warren

Cowdery and Warren Parrish recast the first-person narrative of the journal into a third-person historical narrative. For the most part the history follows closely the wording of the journal, but in occasional departures it clarifies the text of the journal. Additional contextual information can be found in the *Latter Day Saints' Messenger and Advocate,* which replaced *The Evening and the Morning Star* as the principal church periodical. Edited by Oliver Cowdery and others, it was published monthly in Kirtland from October 1834 to September 1837. The same press produced the *Northern Times,* Kirtland's Democratic Party–affiliated community newspaper, which was produced chiefly by Oliver Cowdery.

The first part of JS's principal Missouri journal (March–September 1838) consists of copied documents that manifest a central concern: to restore unity and order in the church by quelling dissent. Much helpful information relating to the perspective of JS and loyal church leaders is found in the minutes of the disciplinary councils in Far West, Missouri, recorded in Minute Book 2 (created 1838–circa 1839, 1842, 1844). The Oliver Cowdery correspondence of the period reveals the contrasting views and concerns of those who felt JS and his supporters had become despotic. The church's official periodical at the time, the *Elders' Journal of the Church of Latter Day Saints,* also supplies helpful information for this period. Two issues were published in Kirtland, with JS as editor and Thomas B. Marsh as publisher, for the months of October and November 1837. Two more issues bearing a revised title, *Elders' Journal of the Church of Jesus Christ of Latter Day Saints,* were published for July and August 1838 in Far West. The final portion of this JS Missouri journal, which covers the initial phase of Mormon conflict in northern Missouri, is illuminated by several Missouri newspaper accounts that describe the conflict and by the evidence that was later presented in the preliminary hearing for JS and other Latter-day Saints charged in connection with their participation in the conflict.

The record kept by James Mulholland of JS's comings and goings from his home at Far West (September–October 1838) is so terse that there is hardly any material to be elucidated. However, the partially overlapping March–September 1838 journal, kept by George W. Robinson, augments the first week covered by the journal Mulholland kept, and the history that JS started the same year sheds some light on the final days covered in the journal.

Mulholland's second journal for JS (1839), which he kept in Quincy and Commerce in Illinois, is complemented by the diary Mulholland kept for himself during the same time period. Mulholland's personal diary helps to distinguish whether he or JS is the protagonist in certain entries of the journal he kept for JS. The contemporaneous diary of apostle Wilford Woodruff and the "History of Brigham Young," based on contemporaneous Young diaries, also contextualize a number of the entries recording JS's endeavors to build the kingdom of God anew in Illinois and to prepare the apostles to take the Mormon gospel overseas.

Works Cited

This list of sources serves as a comprehensive guide to all sources cited in this volume (documentation supporting the reference material in the back of this volume may be found at josephsmithpapers.org). Annotation has been documented with original sources where possible and practical. In entries for manuscript sources, dates identify when the manuscript was created, which is not necessarily the time period the manuscript covers.

Most sources cited in this volume are referred to on first and subsequent occurrences by a conventional shortened citation. For convenience, some documents are referred to by editorial titles rather than by their original titles or by the titles given in the catalogs of their current repositories, in which case the list of works cited provides the editorial title followed by full bibliographic information.

Scriptural References

The annotation includes numerous references to works accepted as scripture by The Church of Jesus Christ of Latter-day Saints. The principal citations of Mormon scripture appearing in annotation are to JS-era published or manuscript versions. However, for reader convenience, these citations also include a bracketed reference to the current and widely available Latter-day Saint scriptural canon. All versions of scripture cited in this volume, early or modern, are identified in the list of works cited.

The church's current scriptural canon consists of the King James (or Authorized) Version of the Bible (KJV), plus three other volumes: the Book of Mormon, the Doctrine and Covenants, and the Pearl of Great Price. The following paragraphs provide more detailed information about uniquely Mormon scriptures and how they are cited in this volume.

Book of Mormon. The first edition of the Book of Mormon was printed for JS in 1830. He oversaw the publication of subsequent editions in 1837 and 1840. The Book of Mormon, like the Bible, consists of a number of shorter books. However, the present volume cites early editions of the Book of Mormon by page numbers because these editions were not divided into numbered verses. The bracketed references to the modern (1981) Latter-day Saint edition of this work identify the book name with modern chapter and verse.

Doctrine and Covenants. JS authorized publication of early revelations beginning in 1832 in *The Evening and the Morning Star,* the church's first newspaper, and initiated the publication of a compilation of revelations, which first appeared in 1833 under the title Book of Commandments. Revised and expanded versions of this compilation were published in 1835 and 1844 under the title Doctrine and Covenants. Since JS's time, The Church of Jesus Christ of Latter-day Saints has continued to issue revised and expanded versions of the Doctrine and Covenants, as has the Community of Christ (formerly the Reorganized Church of Jesus Christ of Latter Day Saints). The bracketed references to the modern (1981) Latter-day Saint edition of the Doctrine and Covenants, which cite by section number and verse, use the abbreviation D&C in the place of Doctrine and Covenants. A table titled Corresponding Section Numbers in Editions of the Doctrine and Covenants, which appears after the list of works cited, aligns the corresponding section numbers of the three JS-era compilations and the current editions of the Doctrine and Covenants published by The Church of Jesus Christ of Latter-day Saints and by the Community of Christ. For more information about the format of Doctrine and Covenants citations, see the Editorial Method.

Joseph Smith Bible revision. Beginning in June 1830, JS systematically reviewed the text of the KJV and made revisions and additions to it. JS largely completed the work in 1833, but only a few excerpts were published in his lifetime. The Reorganized Church of Jesus Christ of Latter Day Saints published the entire work in 1867 under the title Holy Scriptures and included excerpts from the writings of Moses in two sections of its Doctrine and Covenants. The Church of Jesus Christ of Latter-day Saints, which today officially refers to JS's Bible revisions as the Joseph Smith Translation, has never published the entire work, but two excerpts are canonized in the Pearl of Great Price and many other excerpts are included in the footnotes and appendix of the modern (1979) Latter-day Saint edition of the KJV. In the present volume, references to JS's Bible revision are cited to the original manuscripts, with a bracketed reference given where possible to the relevant book, chapter, and verse of the Joseph Smith Translation.

Pearl of Great Price. The Pearl of Great Price, a collection of miscellaneous writings that originated with JS, was first published in 1851 and was canonized by The Church of Jesus Christ of Latter-day Saints in 1880. The modern (1981) edition of this work consists of the following: selections from the book of Moses, an extract from JS's Bible revision manuscripts; the book of Abraham, writings that were translated from papyrus JS and others acquired in 1835 and that were first published in the *Times and Seasons* in 1842; Joseph Smith—Matthew, another extract from JS's Bible revision manuscripts; Joseph Smith—History, a selection from the history that JS began working on in 1838; and the Articles of Faith, a statement of beliefs included in a JS letter to Chicago newspaper editor John Wentworth that was published in the *Times and Seasons* in 1842. Except in the case of Joseph Smith—History, citations in this volume to early versions of each of these works also include a bracketed reference to the corresponding chapter and verse in the modern Latter-day Saint canon. The Pearl of Great Price is not part of the canon of the Community of Christ. References to the history JS began work on in 1838 are cited to the original manuscript of that history (see entry on "JS History" in the list of works cited).

Abbreviations for Frequently Cited Repositories

BYU   L. Tom Perry Special Collections, Harold B. Lee Library, Brigham Young University, Provo, Utah

CCLA   Community of Christ Library-Archives, Independence, Missouri

CHL   Church History Library, The Church of Jesus Christ of Latter-day Saints, Salt
        Lake City

FHL   Family History Library, The Church of Jesus Christ of Latter-day Saints, Salt Lake
        City

——————— ❧ ———————

Abraham (book of). See *Pearl of Great Price.*

Abzug, Robert H. *Cosmos Crumbling: American Reform and the Religious Imagination.* New
    York: Oxford University Press, 1994.

*Acts of a General Nature, Enacted, Revised and Ordered to Be Reprinted, at the First Session of
    the Twenty-ninth General Assembly of the State of Ohio.* Columbus: Olmsted and
    Bailhache, 1831.

Adams, Dale W. "Chartering the Kirtland Bank." *BYU Studies* 23 (Fall 1983): 467–482.

———. "Grandison Newell's Obsession." *Journal of Mormon History* 30 (Spring 2004):
    159–188.

Adler, Selig. "Backgrounds of American Policy toward Zion." In *Israel: Its Role in
    Civilization,* edited by Moshe Davis, 251–283. New York: The Seminary Israel Institute
    of the Jewish Theological Seminary of America, 1956.

Allen, James B., Ronald K. Esplin, and David J. Whittaker. *Men with a Mission, 1837–1841:
    The Quorum of the Twelve Apostles in the British Isles.* Salt Lake City: Deseret Book,
    1992.

Allred, William Moore. Reminiscences and Diary, 1885–1887. CHL.

*An American Dictionary of the English Language; Exhibiting the Origin, Orthography,
    Pronunciation, and Definitions of Words.* Edited by Noah Webster. New York: Harper
    and Brothers, 1845.

Ames, Ira. Autobiography and Journal, 1858. CHL.

Anderson, Lavina Fielding, ed. *Lucy's Book: A Critical Edition of Lucy Mack Smith's Family
    Memoir.* Salt Lake City: Signature Books, 2001.

Anderson, Richard Lloyd. "The Alvin Smith Story: Fact and Fiction." *Ensign,* Aug. 1987,
    58–72.

———. "Clarifications of Boggs's 'Order' and Joseph Smith's Constitutionalism." In
    Regional Studies in Latter-day Saint Church History: Missouri, edited by Arnold K. Garr
    and Clark V. Johnson, 27–83. Provo, UT: Department of Church History and
    Doctrine, Brigham Young University, 1994.

———. "I Have a Question: What Changes Have Been Made in the Name of the Church?"
    Ensign, Jan. 1979, 13–14.

———. *Joseph Smith's New England Heritage: Influences of Grandfathers Solomon Mack and
    Asael Smith.* Rev. ed. Salt Lake City: Deseret Book; Provo, UT: Brigham Young
    University Press, 2003.

Angell, Truman O. Autobiography, 1884. CHL. Also available in Archie Leon Brown and
    Charlene L. Hathaway, *141 Years of Mormon Heritage: Rawsons, Browns, Angells—
    Pioneers* (Oakland, CA: By the authors, 1973), 119–135.

The Articles of Faith of the Church of Jesus Christ of Latter-day Saints. See *Pearl of Great
    Price.*

Avery, Elroy McKendree. *A History of Cleveland and Its Environs: The Heart of New Connecticut.* 3 vols. Chicago: Lewis, 1918.

Bachman, Danel W. "New Light on an Old Hypothesis: The Ohio Origins of the Revelation on Eternal Marriage." *Journal of Mormon History* 5 (1978): 19–32.

Backman, Milton V., Jr. *The Heavens Resound: A History of the Latter-day Saints in Ohio, 1830–1838.* Salt Lake City: Deseret Book, 1983.

———, comp. *A Profile of Latter-day Saints of Kirtland, Ohio, and Members of Zion's Camp, 1830–1839: Vital Statistics and Sources.* 2nd ed. Provo, UT: Department of Church History and Doctrine and Religious Studies Center, Brigham Young University, 1983.

Bagley, Will, ed. *Scoundrel's Tale: The Samuel Brannan Papers.* Kingdom in the West: The Mormons and the American Frontier 3. Spokane, WA: Arthur H. Clark, 1999.

Baugh, Alexander L. "A Call to Arms: The 1838 Mormon Defense of Northern Missouri." PhD diss., Brigham Young University, 1996. Also available as *A Call to Arms: The 1838 Mormon Defense of Northern Missouri,* Dissertations in Latter-day Saint History (Provo, UT: Joseph Fielding Smith Institute for Latter-day Saint History; BYU Studies, 2000).

Benjamin Brown Family Collection, 1835–1983. CHL.

Bennett, Richard E. "A Study of the Church of Jesus Christ of Latter-day Saints in Upper Canada, 1830–1850." Master's thesis, Brigham Young University, 1975.

Bercovitch, Sacvan, and Cyrus R. K. Patell, eds. *The Cambridge History of American Literature.* Vol. 2, *Prose Writing, 1820–1865.* Cambridge: Cambridge University Press, 1995.

Berrett, LaMar C., ed. *Sacred Places: A Comprehensive Guide to Early LDS Historical Sites.* 6 vols. Salt Lake City: Deseret Book, 1999–2007.

Best, Christy. "Register of the Revelations Collection in the Church Archives, the Church of Jesus Christ of Latter-day Saints," July 1983. CHL.

Bible. See *Holy Bible.*

Blessing of Alvin Winegar, 7 Feb. 1836. Private possession. Copy in CHL.

Blocker, Jack S., Jr. *American Temperance Movements: Cycles of Reform.* Boston: Twayne, 1989.

Bloom, Harold. *The American Religion: The Emergence of the Post-Christian Nation.* New York: Simon and Schuster, 1992.

Bode, Carl. *The American Lyceum: Town Meeting of the Mind.* New York: Oxford University Press, 1956.

The Book of Abraham. See *Pearl of Great Price.*

Book of Abraham Manuscripts, ca. 1835–1838, ca. 1841–1843. CHL.

A Book of Commandments, for the Government of the Church of Christ, Organized according to Law, on the 6th of April, 1830. Zion [Independence], MO: W. W. Phelps, 1833. The copy used for this volume is available at CHL.

Book of Doctrine and Covenants: Carefully Selected from the Revelations of God, and Given in the Order of Their Dates. Independence, MO: Herald Publishing House, 2004.

The Book of Mormon: An Account Written by the Hand of Mormon, upon Plates Taken from the Plates of Nephi. Palmyra, NY: E. B. Grandin, 1830. The copy used for this volume is available at CHL.

The Book of Mormon: Another Testament of Jesus Christ. Salt Lake City: The Church of Jesus Christ of Latter-day Saints, 1981.

The Book of Moses (selections from). See *Pearl of Great Price.*

Bradshaw, M. Scott. "Joseph Smith's Performance of Marriages in Ohio." *BYU Studies* 39, no. 4 (2000): 23–69.

Brodie, Fawn M. *No Man Knows My History: The Life of Joseph Smith, the Mormon Prophet.* New York: Knopf, 1945.

Buell, Lawrence. *New England Literary Culture: From Revolution through Renaissance.* Cambridge: Cambridge University Press, 1986.

Burgess, Harrison. Autobiography, ca. 1883. CHL. Also available as "Sketch of a Well-Spent Life," in *Labors in the Vineyard,* Faith-Promoting Series 12 (Salt Lake City: Juvenile Instructor Office, 1884), 65–74.

Burnett, Peter H. *Recollections and Opinions of an Old Pioneer.* New York: D. Appleton, 1880.

Bushman, Richard L. *Joseph Smith and the Beginnings of Mormonism.* Urbana: University of Illinois Press, 1984.

———. "Joseph Smith's Family Background." In *The Prophet Joseph: Essays on the Life and Mission of Joseph Smith,* edited by Larry C. Porter and Susan Easton Black, 1–18. Salt Lake City: Deseret Book, 1988.

Butler, John. Autobiography, ca. 1863. CHL.

Cahoon, William F. Autobiography, 1878. CHL.

Call, Anson. Autobiography and Journal, ca. 1857–1883. CHL.

———. Statement, 30 Dec. 1885. CHL.

Campbell, Alexander. *Delusions. An Analysis of the Book of Mormon; with an Examination of Its Internal and External Evidences, and a Refutation of Its Pretences to Divine Authority.* Boston: Benjamin H. Greene, 1832.

Carlyle, Gavin, ed. *The Prophetical Works of Edward Irving.* 2 vols. London: Alexander Strahan, 1867–1870.

Chambers, J. S. *The Conquest of Cholera: America's Greatest Scourge.* New York: Macmillan, 1938.

Chardon Spectator and Geauga Gazette. Chardon, OH. July 1833–Nov. 1835.

Clayton, William. Journals, 1842–1845. CHL.

A Collection of Sacred Hymns, for the Church of the Latter Day Saints. Edited by Emma Smith. Kirtland, OH: F. G. Williams, 1835.

Compton, Todd. *In Sacred Loneliness: The Plural Wives of Joseph Smith.* Salt Lake City: Signature Books, 2001.

Cook, Lyndon W. "Isaac Galland—Mormon Benefactor." *BYU Studies* 19 (Spring 1979): 261–284.

———. *Joseph Smith and the Law of Consecration.* Provo, UT: Grandin Book, 1985.

Cook, Lyndon W., and Milton V. Backman Jr., eds. *Kirtland Elders' Quorum Record, 1836–1841.* Provo, UT: Grandin Book, 1985.

Coray, Howard. Reminiscences, ca. 1883. BYU.

Coray, Martha Jane Knowlton. Notebook, ca. 1850. CHL.

Corrill, John. *A Brief History of the Church of Christ of Latter Day Saints, (Commonly Called Mormons;) Including an Account of Their Doctrine and Discipline; with the Reasons of the Author for Leaving the Church.* St. Louis: By the author, 1839.

Cowdery, Oliver. Diary, Jan.–Mar. 1836. CHL. Also available as Leonard J. Arrington, "Oliver Cowdery's Kirtland, Ohio, 'Sketch Book,'" *BYU Studies* 12 (Summer 1972): 410–426.

———. Letter, Tiffin, OH, to Phineas Young, Nauvoo, IL, 23 Mar. 1846. CHL.

———. Letter with Joseph Smith postscript, Kirtland Mills, OH, to William W. Phelps, John Whitmer, Edward Partridge, Isaac Morley, John Corrill, and Sidney Gilbert, [Independence, MO], 10 Aug. 1833. CHL.

———. Letterbook, 1833–1838. Henry E. Huntington Library, San Marino, CA.

Crawley, Peter. *A Descriptive Bibliography of the Mormon Church.* Vol. 1, *1830–1847.* Provo, UT: Religious Studies Center, Brigham Young University, 1997.

Crawley, Peter, and Richard L. Anderson. "The Political and Social Realities of Zion's Camp." *BYU Studies* 14 (Summer 1974): 406–420.

Crosby, Caroline Barnes. Autobiography, 1832–1846. In Jonathan Crosby Papers, 1807–1882. Utah State Historical Society, Salt Lake City.

Crosby, Jonathan. Autobiography, 1850–1852. Jonathan Crosby Papers, 1807–1882. Utah State Historical Society, Salt Lake City.

Cumming, John, and Audrey Cumming. *The Pilgrimage of Temperance Mack.* Mount Pleasant, MI: By the authors, 1967.

D&C. See *Doctrine and Covenants of the Church of Jesus Christ of Latter-day Saints* (1981).

Daviess Co., MO, Circuit Court Record. Bk. A, 1837–1843. Daviess Co. Circuit Court, Gallatin, MO.

Davis, Matthew L. Letter, Washington DC, to Mary Davis, New York City, NY, 6 Feb. 1840. CHL.

Debate on the Evidences of Christianity; Containing an Examination of "the Social System," and of All the Systems of Scepticism of Ancient and Modern Times. Held in the City of Cincinnati, Ohio, from the 13th to the 21st of April, 1829; between Robert Owen, of New Lanark, Scotland, and Alexander Campbell, of Bethany, Virginia. Cincinnati: Robinson and Fairbank, 1829.

Deseret News. Salt Lake City. 1850–.

Dibble, Philo. "Philo Dibble's Narrative." In *Early Scenes in Church History,* Faith-Promoting Series 8, pp. 74–96. Salt Lake City: Juvenile Instructor Office, 1882.

Doctrine and Covenants, 2004 Community of Christ edition. See *Book of Doctrine and Covenants.*

Doctrine and Covenants of the Church of the Latter Day Saints: Carefully Selected from the Revelations of God. Compiled by Joseph Smith, Oliver Cowdery, Sidney Rigdon, and Frederick G. Williams. Kirtland, OH: F. G. Williams, 1835. The copy used for this volume is available at CHL.

The Doctrine and Covenants of the Church of Jesus Christ of Latter Day Saints; Carefully Selected from the Revelations of God. Compiled by Joseph Smith. 2nd ed. Nauvoo, IL: John Taylor, 1844. The copy used for this volume is available at CHL.

The Doctrine and Covenants of the Church of Jesus Christ of Latter-day Saints: Containing Revelations Given to Joseph Smith, the Prophet, with Some Additions by His Successors in the Presidency of the Church. Salt Lake City: The Church of Jesus Christ of Latter-day Saints, 1981.

Document Containing the Correspondence, Orders, &c., in Relation to the Disturbances with the Mormons; and the Evidence Given before the Hon. Austin A. King, Judge of the Fifth Judicial Circuit of the State of Missouri, at the Court-House in Richmond, in a Criminal Court of Inquiry, Begun November 12, 1838, on the Trial of Joseph Smith, Jr., and Others, for High Treason and Other Crimes against the State. Fayette, MO: Boon's Lick Democrat, 1841.

Eighth Report of the American Temperance Society. Boston: American Temperance Society, 1836.

Eiserman, Rick. "Sterling Price: Soldier—Politician—Missourian." In *Missouri Folk Heroes of the 19th Century,* edited by F. Mark McKiernan and Roger D. Launius, 115–134. Independence, MO: Herald Publishing House, 1989.

Elders' Journal of the Church of Latter Day Saints. Kirtland, OH, Oct.–Nov. 1837; Far West, MO, July–Aug. 1838.

Encyclopedia of Mormonism. Edited by Daniel H. Ludlow. 5 vols. New York: Macmillan, 1992.

Encyclopedia of the History of Missouri, a Compendium of History and Biography for Ready Reference. Vol. 6. Edited by Howard L. Conard. New York: Southern History Co., 1901.

Erekson, Keith A., and Lloyd D. Newell. "The Conversion of Artemus Millet and His Call to Kirtland." *BYU Studies* 41, no. 2 (2002): 77–115.

Esplin, Ronald K. "The Emergence of Brigham Young and the Twelve to Mormon Leadership, 1830–1841." PhD diss., Brigham Young University, 1981. Also available as *The Emergence of Brigham Young and the Twelve to Mormon Leadership, 1830–1841,* Dissertations in Latter-day Saint History (Provo, UT: Joseph Fielding Smith Institute for Latter-day Saint History; BYU Studies, 2006).

———. "'Exalt Not Yourselves': The Revelations and Thomas Marsh, an Object Lesson for Our Day." In *The Heavens Are Open: The 1992 Sperry Symposium on the Doctrine and Covenants and Church History,* 112–129. Salt Lake City: Deseret Book, 1993.

The Evening and the Morning Star. Independence, MO, June 1832–July 1833; Kirtland, OH, Dec. 1833–Sept. 1834.

Far West Committee. Minutes, Jan.–Apr. 1839. CHL.

Faulring, Scott H., Kent P. Jackson, and Robert J. Matthews, eds. *Joseph Smith's New Translation of the Bible: Original Manuscripts.* Provo, UT: Religious Studies Center, Brigham Young University, 2004.

F. G. Williams and Company. Account Book, 1833–1835. In Patience Cowdery, Diary, 1849–1851. CHL.

Fielding, Joseph. Journals, 1837–1859. CHL.

Finney, Charles G. *Memoirs of Rev. Charles G. Finney. Written by Himself.* New York: A. S. Barnes, 1876.

Firmage, Edwin Brown, and Richard Collin Mangrum. *Zion in the Courts: A Legal History of the Church of Jesus Christ of Latter-day Saints, 1830–1890.* Urbana: University of Illinois Press, 1988.

Foote, Warren. Autobiography, not before 1903. CHL.

Ford, Thomas. *A History of Illinois, from Its Commencement as a State in 1818 to 1847. Containing a Full Account of the Black Hawk War, the Rise, Progress, and Fall of Mormonism, the Alton and Lovejoy Riots, and Other Important and Interesting Events.* Chicago: S. C. Griggs; New York: Ivison and Phinney, 1854.

Fullmer, Desdemona Wadsworth. Autobiography, 7 June 1868. Desdemona Wadsworth Fullmer, Papers, 1868. CHL.

Gates, Susa Young [Homespun, pseud.]. *Lydia Knight's History.* Noble Women's Lives Series 1. Salt Lake City: Juvenile Instructor Office, 1883.

Gee, John. "Eyewitness, Hearsay, and Physical Evidence of the Joseph Smith Papyri." In *The Disciple as Witness: Essays on Latter-day Saint History and Doctrine in Honor of Richard Lloyd Anderson,* edited by Stephen D. Ricks, Donald W. Parry, and Andrew H. Hedges, 175–217. Provo, UT: Foundation for Ancient Research and Mormon Studies, 2000.

General Church Minutes, 1839–1877. CHL.

General Public Acts of Congress, Respecting the Sale and Disposition of the Public Lands, with Instructions Issued, from Time to Time, by the Secretary of the Treasury and Commissioner of the General Land Office, and Official Opinions of the Attorney General on Questions Arising under the Land Laws. Vol. 2. Washington DC: Gales and Seaton, 1838.

Gentry, Leland Homer. "A History of the Latter-day Saints in Northern Missouri from 1836 to 1839." PhD diss., Brigham Young University, 1965. Also available as *A History of the Latter-day Saints in Northern Missouri from 1836 to 1839,* Dissertations in Latter-day Saint History (Provo, UT: Joseph Fielding Smith Institute for Latter-day Saint History; BYU Studies, 2000).

Givens, Terryl L. *The Viper on the Hearth: Mormons, Myths, and the Construction of Heresy.* New York: Oxford University Press, 1997.

[Goddard, William]. *A Brief Descriptive History of the Mormons in Mount Pleasant.* No publisher, [1980?]. Copy at BYU.

Goldman, Shalom. "Joshua/James Seixas (1802–1874): Jewish Apostasy and Christian Hebraism in Early Nineteenth-Century America." *Jewish History* 7 (Spring 1993): 65–88.

Gregg, Thomas. *History of Hancock County, Illinois, Together with an Outline History of the State, and a Digest of State Laws.* Chicago: Charles C. Chapman, 1880.

Grua, David W. "Joseph Smith and the 1834 D. P. Hurlbut Case." *BYU Studies* 44, no. 1 (2005): 33–54.

Hales, Kenneth Glyn, ed. *Windows: A Mormon Family.* Tucson, AZ: Skyline Printing, 1985.

Hamilton, C. Mark. *Nineteenth-Century Mormon Architecture and City Planning.* New York: Oxford University Press, 1995.

Hannibal Commercial Advertiser. Hannibal, MO. 1837–1839.

Hartley, William G. "'Almost Too Intolerable a Burthen': The Winter Exodus from Missouri, 1838–39." *Journal of Mormon History* 18 (Fall 1992): 6–40.

———. *My Best for the Kingdom: History and Autobiography of John Lowe Butler, a Mormon Frontiersman.* Salt Lake City: Aspen Books, 1993.

———. "Newel and Lydia Bailey Knight's Kirtland Love Story and Historic Wedding." *BYU Studies* 39, no. 4 (2000): 7–22.

Hicks, Michael. *Mormonism and Music: A History.* Urbana: University of Illinois Press, 1989.

Hill, Marvin S. *Quest for Refuge: The Mormon Flight from American Pluralism.* Salt Lake City: Signature Books, 1989.

Historian's Office. Catalogs and Inventories, 1846–1904. CHL.

———. Histories of the Twelve, ca. 1858–1880. CHL.

———. "History of Brigham Young." In Manuscript History of Brigham Young, ca. 1856–1860, vol. 1, pp. 1–104. CHL.

———. Joseph Smith History Documents, ca. 1839–1856. CHL.

History of Caldwell and Livingston Counties, Missouri, Written and Compiled from the Most Authentic Official and Private Sources. . . . St. Louis: National Historical Co., 1886.

The History of Clinton County, Missouri. Containing a History of the County, Its Cities, Towns, Etc., Biographical Sketches of Its Citizens. . . . St. Joseph, MO: National Historical Co., 1881.

The History of Daviess County, Missouri. An Encyclopedia of Useful Information, and a Compendium of Actual Facts. . . . Kansas City, MO: Birdsall and Dean, 1882.

History of Geauga and Lake Counties, Ohio, with Illustrations and Biographical Sketches of Its Pioneers and Most Prominent Men. Philadelphia: Williams Brothers, 1878.

The History of Lee County, Iowa, Containing a History of the County, Its Cities, Towns, &c., a Biographical Directory of Citizens. . . . Chicago: Western Historical Co., 1879.

History of the Church / Smith, Joseph, et al. *History of the Church of Jesus Christ of Latter-day Saints.* Edited by B. H. Roberts. Salt Lake City: Deseret News, 1902–1912 (vols. 1–6), 1932 (vol. 7).

History of the Lafayette Hinckley and Alsina Elisabeth Brimhall Families. No publisher, [1961?]. Copy at BYU.

The History of the Reorganized Church of Jesus Christ of Latter Day Saints. Vol. 6, *1903–1915.* Compiled by F. Henry Edwards. Independence, MO: Herald Publishing House, 1970.

Holt, Michael F. *The Rise and Fall of the American Whig Party: Jacksonian Politics and the Onset of the Civil War.* New York: Oxford University Press, 1999.

The Holy Bible, Containing the Old and New Testaments Translated Out of the Original Tongues: And with the Former Translations Diligently Compared and Revised, by His Majesty's Special Command. Authorized King James Version with Explanatory Notes and Cross References to the Standard Works of the Church of Jesus Christ of Latter-day Saints. Salt Lake City: The Church of Jesus Christ of Latter-day Saints, 1979.

Howe, Eber D. *Autobiography and Recollections of a Pioneer Printer: Together with Sketches of the War of 1812 on the Niagara Frontier.* Painesville, OH: Telegraph Steam Printing House, 1878.

————. *Mormonism Unvailed: Or, A Faithful Account of That Singular Imposition and Delusion, from Its Rise to the Present Time. With Sketches of the Characters of Its Propagators, and a Full Detail of the Manner in Which the Famous Golden Bible Was Brought before the World. To Which Are Added, Inquiries into the Probability That the Historical Part of the Said Bible Was Written by One Solomon Spalding, More Than Twenty Years Ago, and by Him Intended to Have Been Published as a Romance.* Painesville, OH: By the author, 1834.

Huntington, Oliver B. Diary and Reminiscences, 1843–1900. Typescript. CHL.

Hyde, Orson. *Ein Ruf aus der Wüste, eine Stimme aus dem Schoose der Erde: Kurzer Ueberblick des Ursprungs und der Lehre der Kirche "Jesus Christ of Latter Day Saints" in Amerika, gekannt von Manchen unter der Benennung: "Die Mormonen."* Frankfurt: Im Selbstverlage des Verfassers, 1842. Also available with English translation in Dean C. Jessee, ed., *The Papers of Joseph Smith* (Salt Lake City: Deseret Book, 1989), 1:402–425.

Jackson, Kent P., ed. *Manuscript Found: The Complete Original "Spaulding Manuscript."* Provo, UT: Religious Studies Center, Brigham Young University, 1996.

Jeffersonian Republican. Jefferson City, MO. 1831–1844.

Jennings, Warren A. "The Expulsion of the Mormons from Jackson County, Missouri." *Missouri Historical Review* 64 (Oct. 1969–July 1970): 41–63.

————. "Zion Is Fled: The Expulsion of the Mormons from Jackson County, Missouri." PhD diss., University of Florida, 1962.

Jessee, Dean C. "Joseph Knight's Recollection of Early Mormon History." *BYU Studies* 17 (Autumn 1976): 29–39.

————. "The Writing of Joseph Smith's History." *BYU Studies* 11 (Summer 1971): 439–473.

Jeter, Jeremiah B. *Baptist Principles Reset.* Richmond, VA: Religious Herald Co., 1901.

The Jewish Encyclopedia: A Descriptive Record of the History, Religion, Literature, and Customs of the Jewish People from the Earliest Times to the Present Day. Edited by Isidore Singer. 12 vols. New York and London: Funk and Wagnalls, 1901–1906.

Johnson, Benjamin Franklin. Papers, 1852–1911. CHL.

Johnson, Clark V., and Ronald E. Romig. *An Index to Early Caldwell County, Missouri, Land Records.* Rev. ed. Independence, MO: Missouri Mormon Frontier Foundation, 2002.

Johnson, Jeffery O. *Register of the Joseph Smith Collection in the Church Archives, the Church of Jesus Christ of Latter-day Saints.* Salt Lake City: Historical Department of the Church of Jesus Christ of Latter-day Saints, 1973.

Johnson, Paul E., and Sean Wilentz. *The Kingdom of Matthias.* New York: Oxford University Press, 1994.

Joseph Smith—Matthew. See *Pearl of Great Price.*

Joseph Smith Translation. See *Holy Bible.*

Journal of Discourses. 26 vols. Liverpool: F. D. Richards, 1855–1886.

JS. In addition to the entries that immediately follow, see entries under "Smith, Joseph."

JS History / Smith, Joseph, et al. History, 1839–1856. Vols. A-1–F-1 (originals), A-2–E-2 (early security copies). CHL. The history for the period after 5 Aug. 1838 was composed after the death of Joseph Smith. Also available as *History of the Church of Jesus Christ of*

Latter-day Saints, Period 1: History of Joseph Smith, the Prophet, by Himself, edited by B. H. Roberts, 6 vols. (Salt Lake City: Deseret News, 1902–1912).

JS History, 1832 / Smith, Joseph. "A History of the Life of Joseph Smith Jr," 1832. In Joseph Smith, "Letter Book A," 1832–1835, 1–[6] (earliest numbering). Joseph Smith Collection. CHL. Also available in Dean C. Jessee, ed., *The Papers of Joseph Smith* (Salt Lake City: Deseret Book, 1989), 1:1–10.

JS History, 1834–1836 / Smith, Joseph, et al. History, 1834–1836. In Joseph Smith et al., History, 1839–1856, vol. A-1, back of book (earliest numbering), 9–20, 46–187. CHL. Also available in Dean C. Jessee, ed., *The Papers of Joseph Smith* (Salt Lake City: Deseret Book, 1989), 1:15–209.

JS History, 1839 (draft) / Smith, Joseph. History, 1839. Draft. CHL. Also available in Dean C. Jessee, ed., *The Papers of Joseph Smith* (Salt Lake City: Deseret Book, 1989), 1:230–264.

JS Letterbook 1 / Smith, Joseph. "Letter Book A," 1832–1835. Joseph Smith Collection. CHL.

JS Letterbook 2 / Smith, Joseph. "Copies of Letters, &c. &c.," 1839–1843. Joseph Smith Collection. CHL.

Kansas City Daily Journal. Kansas City, MO. 1878–1891.

Kelly, Clyde. *United States Postal Policy.* New York: D. Appleton, 1932.

Kimball, Heber C. Collection, 1837–1898. CHL.

———. "History of Heber Chase Kimball by His Own Dictation," ca. 1842–1856. Heber C. Kimball, Papers, 1837–1866. CHL.

King, Austin A. Letter, Ray Co., MO, to William Morgan, Daviess Co., MO, 4 Sept. 1838. William Morgan, Papers, 1838–1839. CHL.

Kirtland Camp. Journal, Mar.–Oct. 1838. CHL.

Kirtland Egyptian Papers, ca. 1835–1836. CHL.

Kirtland Elders' Certificates / Kirtland Elders Quorum. "Record of Certificates of Membership and Ordinations of the First Members and Elders of the Church of Jesus Christ of Latter Day Saints Dating from March 21st 1836 to June 18th 1838 Kirtland Geauga Co. Ohio," 1836–1838. CHL.

Kirtland Elders Quorum. "A Record of the First Quorurum of Elders Belonging to the Church of Christ: In Kirtland Geauga Co. Ohio," 1836–1838, 1840–1841. CCLA.

Kirtland financial papers, ca. 1838. Temporary collection. CHL.

Knight, Newel. Autobiography and Journal, ca. 1846. CHL.

Lake County Historical Society. *Here Is Lake County, Ohio.* Cleveland: Howard Allen, 1964.

Latter Day Saints' Messenger and Advocate. Kirtland, OH. Oct. 1834–Sept. 1837.

Launius, Roger D. *Zion's Camp: Expedition to Missouri, 1834.* Independence, MO: Herald Publishing House, 1984.

The Law-Dictionary: Explaining the Rise, Progress, and Present State, of the English Law; Defining and Interpreting the Terms or Words of Art; and Comprising Copious Information on the Subjects of Law, Trade, and Government. Edited and compiled by Giles Jacob. 6 vols. 1st American ed.; edited by T. E. Tomlins from 2nd London ed. Philadelphia: P. Byrne; New York: I. Riley, 1811.

Laws of the State of Missouri, Passed at the First Session of the Ninth General Assembly, Begun and Held at the City of Jefferson, on Monday, the Twenty-first Day of November, in the

Year of Our Lord One Thousand Eight Hundred and Thirty-six. 2nd ed. St. Louis: Chambers and Knapp, 1841.

Laws of the State of Missouri, Passed at the First Session of the Twelfth General Assembly, Begun and Held at the City of Jefferson, on Monday, the Twenty-first Day of November, Eighteen Hundred and Forty-two, and Ended Tuesday, the Twenty-eighth Day of February, Eighteen Hundred and Forty-three. Jefferson City, MO: Allen Hammond, 1843.

Leonard, Glen M. *Nauvoo: A Place of Peace, a People of Promise.* Salt Lake City: Deseret Book; Provo, UT: Brigham Young University Press, 2002.

Leopard, John C., Buel Leopard, R. M. McCammon, and Mary McCammon Hillman. *History of Daviess and Gentry Counties, Missouri.* Topeka, KS: Historical Publishing Co., 1922.

LeSueur, Stephen C. *The 1838 Mormon War in Missouri.* Columbia: University of Missouri Press, 1987.

Library of Congress Collection. National Archives, Washington DC. Redress petitions from this collection are also available in Clark V. Johnson, ed., *Mormon Redress Petitions: Documents of the 1833–1838 Missouri Conflict,* Religious Studies Center Monograph Series 16 (Provo, UT: Religious Studies Center, Brigham Young University, 1992).

Lightner, Mary Elizabeth Rollins. "Mary Elizabeth Rollins Lightner." *Utah Genealogical and Historical Magazine* 17 (1926): 193–205, 250–260.

Littmann, Mark. *The Heavens on Fire: The Great Leonid Meteor Storms.* Cambridge: Cambridge University Press, 1998.

Lively, Robert L., Jr. "The Catholic Apostolic Church and the Church of Jesus Christ of Latter-day Saints: A Comparative Study of Two Minority Millenarian Groups in Nineteenth-Century England." PhD diss., University of Oxford, 1977.

Mace, Wandle. Autobiography, ca. 1890. CHL.

Madsen, Gordon A. "Joseph Smith and the Missouri Court of Inquiry: Austin A. King's Quest for Hostages." *BYU Studies* 43, no. 4 (2004): 93–136.

Mahoney, Timothy R. *Provincial Lives: Middle-Class Experience in the Antebellum Middle West.* Cambridge: Cambridge University Press, 1999.

Malone, Dumas. "Tapping the Wisdom of the Founding Fathers." *New York Times Magazine,* 27 May 1956.

Manuscripts about Mormons at Chicago History Museum, Research Center, ca. 1832–1954. Microfilm. Chicago Historical Society.

Maryland Gazette. Annapolis. Jan. 1827–Dec. 1839.

Matthews, Robert J. "Doctrinal Connections with the Joseph Smith Translation." In *The Doctrine and Covenants: A Book of Answers; The 25th Annual Sidney B. Sperry Symposium,* edited by Leon R. Hartshorn, Dennis A. Wright, and Craig J. Ostler, 27–42. Salt Lake City: Deseret Book, 1996.

McBride, Reuben, Sr. Reminiscences, no date. CHL.

McCabe, James M. "Early Ledgers and Account Books: A Source for Local Vermont History." *Vermont History* 37 (Winter 1969): 5–12.

McLellin, William E. Journal, Apr.–June 1836. William E. McLellin, Papers, 1831–1836, 1877–1878. CHL. Also available as Jan Shipps and John W. Welch, eds., *The Journals of William E. McLellin, 1831–1836* (Provo, UT: BYU Studies; Urbana: University of Illinois Press, 1994).

Messenger and Advocate of the Church of Christ. Pittsburgh. Apr. 1845–Sept. 1846.

Messinger, George, Jr. Letter, South Bainbridge, NY, to S. Presson Landers, Prompton, PA, 1 Aug. 1837. Andover-Harvard Theological Library, Cambridge, MA.

Millennial Harbinger. Bethany, VA. Jan. 1830–Dec. 1870.

Minute Book 1 / "Conference A," 1832–1837. CHL. Also available as Fred C. Collier and William S. Harwell, eds., *Kirtland Council Minute Book* (Salt Lake City: Collier's Publishing, 1996).

Minute Book 2 / "The Conference Minutes and Record Book of Christ's Church of Latter Day Saints," 1838–ca. 1839, 1842, 1844. CHL. Also available as Donald Q. Cannon and Lyndon W. Cook, eds., *Far West Record: Minutes of the Church of Jesus Christ of Latter-day Saints, 1830–1844* (Salt Lake City: Deseret Book, 1983).

Missouri Argus. St. Louis. 1835–1841.

Missouri Republican. St. Louis. 1822–1919.

Missouri, State of. "Copies of Part of the Evidence Taken in the Examination of the Mormon Prisoners before Judge King." Copy of Hearing Record, Richmond, MO, 12–29 Nov. 1838, *Missouri v. Joseph Smith et al. for Treason and Other Crimes.* Mormon War Papers, 1838–1841, Missouri State Archives, Jefferson City.

———. "Evidence." Hearing Record, Richmond, MO, 12–29 Nov. 1838, *Missouri v. Joseph Smith et al. for Treason and Other Crimes.* Eugene Morrow Violette Collection, 1806–1921, Western Historical Manuscript Collection, Ellis Library, University of Missouri, Columbia.

———. Recognizance of Joseph Smith and Lyman Wight, Daviess Co., MO, 7 Sept. 1838. Private possession. Copy in CHL.

———. Warrant for Joseph Smith and Lyman Wight, Ray Co., MO, 10 Aug. 1838. Private possession. Copy in CHL.

Mormon War Papers, 1838–1841. Missouri State Archives, Jefferson City.

Moses (selections from the book of). See *Pearl of Great Price.*

Mulholland, James. Journal, Apr.–Oct. 1839. In Joseph Smith, Journal, Sept.–Oct. 1838. Joseph Smith Collection. CHL.

Naked Truths about Mormonism: Also a Journal for Important, Newly Apprehended Truths, and Miscellany. Oakland, CA. Jan. and Apr. 1888.

Nauvoo City Council Minute Book / Nauvoo City Council. "A Record of the Proceedings of the City Council of the City of Nauvoo Handcock County, State of Illinois, Commencing A.D. 1841," ca. 1841–1845. CHL.

Nauvoo Municipal Court Docket Book / Nauvoo Municipal Court. "Docket of the Municipal Court of the City of Nauvoo," ca. 1841–1845. CHL.

Neibaur, Alexander. Journal, 1841–1862. CHL.

New Testament Revision 1 / "A Translation of the New Testament Translated by the Power of God," 1831. CCLA. Also available in Scott H. Faulring, Kent P. Jackson, and Robert J.

Matthews, eds., *Joseph Smith's New Translation of the Bible: Original Manuscripts* (Provo, UT: Religious Studies Center, Brigham Young University, 2004), 153–228.

New Testament Revision 2, part 2 / New Testament Revision Manuscript 2, part 2, 1831–1832. CCLA. Also available in Scott H. Faulring, Kent P. Jackson, and Robert J. Matthews, eds., *Joseph Smith's New Translation of the Bible: Original Manuscripts* (Provo, UT: Religious Studies Center, Brigham Young University, 2004), 299–581.

Niles' National Register. Washington DC. 1837–1849.

Noble, Mary A. Reminiscences, ca. 1836. In Joseph B. Noble, Reminiscences, ca. 1836. CHL.

Northern Times. Kirtland, OH. 1835–[1836?].

Oaks, Dallin H., and Marvin S. Hill. *Carthage Conspiracy: The Trial of the Accused Assassins of Joseph Smith.* Urbana: University of Illinois Press, 1975.

Ogden, D. Kelly. "The Kirtland Hebrew School (1835–36)." In *Regional Studies in Latter-day Saint Church History: Ohio,* edited by Milton V. Backman Jr., 63–87, 155–166. Provo, UT: Department of Church History and Doctrine, Brigham Young University, 1990.

Ohio Observer. Hudson. 1827–1855.

Ohio, State of. Marriage Licenses, Nov. 1835–Jan. 1836. Temporary collection. CHL.

Old Testament Revision 1 / "A Revelation Given to Joseph the Revelator June 1830," 1830–1831. CCLA. Also available in Scott H. Faulring, Kent P. Jackson, and Robert J. Matthews, eds., *Joseph Smith's New Translation of the Bible: Original Manuscripts* (Provo, UT: Religious Studies Center, Brigham Young University, 2004), 75–152.

Olsen, Steven L. "The Mormon Ideology of Place: Cosmic Symbolism of the City of Zion, 1830–1846." PhD diss., University of Chicago, 1985. Also available as *The Mormon Ideology of Place: Cosmic Symbolism of the City of Zion, 1830–1846,* Dissertations in Latter-day Saint History (Provo, UT: Joseph Fielding Smith Institute for Latter-day Saint History; BYU Studies, 2002).

Oration Delivered by Mr. S. Rigdon, on the 4th of July, 1838. Far West, MO: Journal Office, 1838. Also available in Peter Crawley, "Two Rare Missouri Documents," *BYU Studies* 14 (Summer 1974): 502–527.

Oswego Palladium. Oswego, NY. 1832–1852.

The Oxford Dictionary of the Christian Church. Edited by F. L. Cross and E. A. Livingstone. 3rd ed. New York: Oxford University Press, 1997.

Oxford English Dictionary. Compact ed. 2 vols. Oxford: Oxford University Press, 1971.

Painesville Republican. Painesville, OH. 1836–1841.

Painesville Telegraph. Painesville, OH. 1831–1838.

Parkin, Max H. "Conflict at Kirtland: A Study of the Nature and Causes of External and Internal Conflict of the Mormons in Ohio between 1830 and 1838." Master's thesis, Brigham Young University, 1966.

——. "A History of the Latter-day Saints in Clay County, Missouri, from 1833 to 1837." PhD diss., Brigham Young University, 1976.

——. "Joseph Smith and the United Firm: The Growth and Decline of the Church's First Master Plan of Business and Finance, Ohio and Missouri, 1832–1834." *BYU Studies* 46, no. 3 (2007): 5–66.

————. "Mormon Political Involvement in Ohio." *BYU Studies* 9 (Summer 1969): 484–502.

Partridge, Edward. Journal, Jan. 1835–July 1836. CHL.

Patriarchal Blessings, 1833–. CHL.

The Pearl of Great Price: A Selection from the Revelations, Translations, and Narrations of Joseph Smith, First Prophet, Seer, and Revelator to the Church of Jesus Christ of Latter-day Saints. Salt Lake City: The Church of Jesus Christ of Latter-day Saints, 1981.

Peck, Reed. Letter, Quincy, IL, to "Dear Friends," 18 Sept. 1839. Henry E. Huntington Library, San Marino, CA.

Peniston, William. Affidavit, Ray Co., MO, 10 Aug. 1838. Private possession. Copy in CHL.

Perkins, Keith W. "De Witt—Prelude to Expulsion." In *Regional Studies in Latter-day Saint Church History: Missouri,* edited by Arnold K. Garr and Clark V. Johnson, 261–280. Provo, UT: Department of Church History and Doctrine, Brigham Young University, 1994.

Peterson, Paul H. "An Historical Analysis of the Word of Wisdom." Master's thesis, Brigham Young University, 1972.

Phelps, William W. Letter, Kirtland Mills, OH, to Sally Phelps, Liberty, MO, 16 Sept. 1835. CHL.

————. Papers, 1835–1865. BYU.

Plan of the House of the Lord for the Presidency, 1833. CHL.

Plat of City of Zion, 1833. CHL.

Plat of Kirtland, OH, ca. 1833. CHL.

Plat of Kirtland, OH, ca. 1837. CHL.

Porter, Larry C. "Alvin Smith: Reminder of the Fairness of God." *Ensign,* Sept. 1978, 65–67.

————. "The Odyssey of William Earl McLellin: Man of Diversity, 1806–83." In *The Journals of William E. McLellin, 1831–1836,* edited by Jan Shipps and John W. Welch, 291–378. Provo, UT: BYU Studies; Urbana: University of Illinois Press, 1994.

————. "A Study of the Origins of the Church of Jesus Christ of Latter-day Saints in the States of New York and Pennsylvania, 1816–1831." PhD diss., Brigham Young University, 1971. Also available as *A Study of the Origins of the Church of Jesus Christ of Latter-day Saints in the States of New York and Pennsylvania, 1816–1831,* Dissertations in Latter-day Saint History (Provo, UT: Joseph Fielding Smith Institute for Latter-day Saint History; BYU Studies, 2000).

Post, Stephen. Journal, 1835–1839. Stephen Post, Papers, 1835–1921. CHL.

Pratt, Orson. Diaries, 1833–1837. CHL.

Pratt, Parley P. *The Autobiography of Parley Parker Pratt, One of the Twelve Apostles of the Church of Jesus Christ of Latter-Day Saints, Embracing His Life, Ministry and Travels, with Extracts, in Prose and Verse, from His Miscellaneous Writings.* Edited by Parley P. Pratt Jr. New York: Russell Brothers, 1874.

————. Letters, 1838–1839. CHL.

Prayer, at the Dedication of the Lord's House in Kirtland, Ohio, March 27, 1836—By Joseph Smith, Jr. President of the Church of the Latter Day Saints. Kirtland, OH: 1836.

The Public Statutes at Large of the United States of America, from the Organization of the Government in 1789, to March 3, 1845. . . . Vol. 4. Edited by Richard Peters. Boston: Charles C. Little and James Brown, 1846.

Quincy, Josiah. *Figures of the Past: From the Leaves of Old Journals.* Boston: Roberts Brothers, 1883.

Quincy Whig. Quincy, IL. 1838–1856.

Quinn, D. Michael. "The Evolution of the Presiding Quorums of the LDS Church." *Journal of Mormon History* 1 (1974): 21–38.

———. "Jesse Gause: Joseph Smith's Little-Known Counselor." *BYU Studies* 23 (Fall 1983): 487–493.

———. *The Mormon Hierarchy: Origins of Power.* Salt Lake City: Signature Books with Smith Research Associates, 1994.

Quorum of the Twelve Apostles, Record / Quorum of the Twelve Apostles. "A Record of the Transactions of the Twelve Apostles of the Church of the Latter Day Saints from the Time of Their Call to the Apostleship Which Was on the 14ᵗʰ Day of Feby. AD 1835," Feb.–Aug. 1835. In Patriarchal Blessings, 1833–, vol. 2. CHL.

Record of Seventies / First Council of the Seventy. "Book of Records," 1837–1843. Bk. A. In First Council of the Seventy, Records, 1837–1885. CHL.

The Return. Davis City, IA, 1889–1891; Richmond, MO, 1892–1893; Davis City, 1895–1896; Denver, CO, 1898; Independence, MO, 1899–1900.

Revelation Book 1 / "A Book of Commandments and Revelations of the Lord Given to Joseph the Seer and Others by the Inspiration of God and Gift and Power of the Holy Ghost Which Beareth Re[c]ord of the Father and Son Which Is One God Infinite and Eternal World without End Amen," 1831–1835. CHL.

Revelation Book 2 / "Book of Revelations," 1832–1834. Revelations Collection, 1831–ca. 1844, 1847, 1861, ca. 1876. CHL.

Revelations Collection, 1831–ca. 1844, 1847, 1861, ca. 1876. CHL.

The Revised Statutes of the State of Missouri, Revised and Digested by the Eighth General Assembly, During the Years One Thousand Eight Hundred and Thirty-four, and One Thousand Eight Hundred and Thirty-five. Together with the Constitutions of Missouri and of the United States. 3rd ed. St. Louis: Chambers and Knapp, 1841.

Richards, Hepzibah. Letter, Kirtland, OH, to Willard Richards, Bedford, England, 18–19 Jan. 1838. Willard Richards, Papers, 1821–1854. CHL.

Richards, Willard. "Willard Richards Pocket Companion Written in England," ca. 1838. Willard Richards, Papers, 1821–1854. CHL.

Ricks, Stephen D. "The Appearance of Elijah and Moses in the Kirtland Temple and the Jewish Passover." *BYU Studies* 23 (Fall 1983): 483–486.

Rigdon, John Wickliff. "Life Story of Sidney Rigdon," no date. CHL.

[Rigdon, Sidney]. *An Appeal to the American People: Being an Account of the Persecutions of the Church of Latter Day Saints; and of the Barbarities Inflicted on Them by the Inhabitants of the State of Missouri.* Cincinnati: Glezen and Shepard, 1840.

Rigdon, Sidney. Letter, Far West, MO, to Sterling Price, 8 Sept. 1838. Draft. CHL.

Riggs, Michael S. "The Economic Impact of Fort Leavenworth on Northwestern Missouri, 1827–1838. Yet Another Reason for the Mormon War?" In *Restoration Studies IV: A*

Collection of Essays about the History, Beliefs, and Practices of the Reorganized Church of Jesus Christ of Latter Day Saints, edited by Marjorie B. Troeh and Eileen M. Terril, 124–133. Independence, MO: Herald Publishing House, 1988.

Riley, I. Woodbridge. *The Founder of Mormonism: A Psychological Study of Joseph Smith, Jr.* New York: Dodd, Mead, 1902.

Robison, Elwin C. *The First Mormon Temple: Design, Construction, and Historic Context of the Kirtland Temple.* Provo, UT: Brigham Young University Press, 1997.

Rockwood, Albert Perry. Journal Entries, Oct. 1838–Jan. 1839. CHL.

Rorty, Richard. *Contingency, Irony, and Solidarity.* Cambridge: Cambridge University Press, 1989.

Saints' Herald. Independence, MO. 1860–.

School of the Prophets Provo Records, 1868–1872. CHL.

Seixas, Joshua. Letter, Charlestown, MA, to Elizabeth, 22 Feb. 1834. Papers of the Seixas Family, American Jewish Historical Society, New York City.

———. Letter, Utica, NY, to John J. Shipherd, Oberlin, OH, 29 May 1835. Office of the Treasurer Records, Oberlin College Archives.

———. *Manual Hebrew Grammar for the Use of Beginners.* 2nd ed., enl. and impr. Andover, MA: Gould and Newman, 1834.

Silverberg, Robert. *Mound Builders of Ancient America: The Archaeology of a Myth.* Greenwich, CT: New York Graphic Society, 1968.

"Sketch of an Elder's Life" (John Tanner). In *Scraps of Biography,* Faith-Promoting Series 10, pp. 9–19. Salt Lake City: Juvenile Instructor Office, 1883.

Skinner, Earnest M. "Joseph Smith, Sr.: First Patriarch to the Church." Master's thesis, Brigham Young University, 1958.

Smith, Elias. Journals, 1836–1888. CHL.

Smith, Emma. Letter, Nauvoo, IL, to Joseph Smith, Washington DC, 6 Dec. 1839. In Charles Aldrich Autograph Collection. State Historical Society of Iowa, Des Moines.

Smith, George A. Autobiography, ca. 1860–1882. George Albert Smith, Papers, 1834–1882. CHL.

Smith, Hyrum. "Book of Reckords," 1835–1838. BYU.

———. Letter, Kirtland, OH, to Elias Smith, East Stockholm, NY, 27 Feb. 1836. CHL.

Smith, James H. *History of Chenango and Madison Counties, New York, with Illustrations and Biographical Sketches of Some of Its Prominent Men and Pioneers.* Syracuse, NY: D. Mason, 1880.

Smith, Joseph. In addition to the entries that immediately follow, see entries under "JS."

Smith, Joseph. Collection, 1827–1846. CHL.

———. Letter, New York City, NY, to Emma Smith, Kirtland, OH, 13 Oct. 1832. CCLA.

———. Letter, Richmond, IN, to Emma Smith, Kirtland Mills, OH, 19 May 1834. CCLA.

———. Letter, Richmond, MO, to Emma Smith, Far West, MO, 12 Nov. 1838. CCLA.

Smith, Joseph, and Sidney Rigdon. Letter, Far West, MO, to Stephen Post, Bloomfield, PA, 17 Sept. 1838. Stephen Post, Papers, 1835–1921. CHL.

Smith, Lucy Mack. History, 1844–1845. 18 books. CHL. Also available in Lavina Fielding Anderson, ed., *Lucy's Book: A Critical Edition of Lucy Mack Smith's Family Memoir* (Salt Lake City: Signature Books, 2001).

————. History, 1845. CHL.

Snow, Erastus. Journal, 1836–1837. CHL.

Snow, LeRoi C. "Who Was Professor Joshua Seixas?" *Improvement Era,* Feb. 1936, 67–71.

Staker, Mark L. "'Thou Art the Man': Newel K. Whitney in Ohio." *BYU Studies* 42, no. 1 (2003): 75–138.

State of Missouri. See Missouri, State of.

State of Ohio. See Ohio, State of.

The Statutes of Ohio and of the Northwestern Territory, Adopted or Enacted from 1788 to 1833 Inclusive: Together with the Ordinance of 1787; the Constitutions of Ohio and of the United States, and Various Public Instruments and Acts of Congress: Illustrated by a Preliminary Sketch of the History of Ohio; Numerous References and Notes, and Copious Indexes. 3 vols. Edited by Salmon P. Chase. Cincinnati: Corey and Fairbank, 1833–1835.

Stern, Malcolm H., comp. *First American Jewish Families: 600 Genealogies, 1654–1977.* Cincinnati: American Jewish Archives; Waltham, MA: American Jewish Historical Society, 1978.

Stevens, Edward W., Jr. "Science, Culture, and Morality: Educating Adults in the Early Nineteenth Century." In *". . . Schools and the Means of Education Shall Forever Be Encouraged": A History of Education in the Old Northwest, 1787–1880,* edited by Paul H. Mattingly and Edward W. Stevens Jr., 68–83. Athens: Ohio University Libraries, 1987.

Stokes, Durward T., ed. "The Wilson Letters, 1835–1849." *Missouri Historical Review* 60, no. 4 (July 1966): 495–517.

Stone, William L. *Matthias and His Impostures: Or, The Progress of Fanaticism. Illustrated in the Extraordinary Case of Robert Matthews, and Some of His Forerunners and Disciples.* New York: Harper and Brothers, 1835.

Summerfield, Arthur E., with Charles Hurd. *U.S. Mail: The Story of the United States Postal Service.* New York: Holt, Rinehart, and Winston, 1960.

Swartzell, William. *Mormonism Exposed, Being a Journal of a Residence in Missouri from the 28th of May to the 20th of August, 1838, Together with an Appendix, Containing the Revelation concerning the Golden Bible, with Numerous Extracts from the 'Book of Covenants,' &c., &c.* Pekin, OH: By the author, 1840.

Tanner, Nathan. Autobiography, ca. 1854. BYU.

Thompson, Charles. *Evidences in Proof of the Book of Mormon, Being a Divinely Inspired Record, Written by the Forefathers of the Natives Whom We Call Indians, (Who Are a Remnant of the Tribe of Joseph,) and Hid Up in the Earth, but Come Forth in Fulfilment of Prophesy for the Gathering of Israel and the Re-establishing of the Kingdom of God upon the Earth.* Batavia, NY: D. D. Waite, 1841.

Thompson, Mercy R. "Recollections of the Prophet Joseph Smith." *Juvenile Instructor,* 1 July 1892, 398–400.

Times and Seasons. Commerce/Nauvoo, IL. Nov. 1839–Feb. 1846.

Todd, Jay M. *The Saga of the Book of Abraham.* Salt Lake City: Deseret Book, 1969.

Tuckett, Madge Harris, and Belle Harris Wilson. *The Martin Harris Story, with Biographies of Emer Harris and Dennison Lott Harris.* Provo, UT: Vintage Books, 1983.

Tullidge, Edward W. *The Women of Mormondom.* New York: Tullidge and Crandall, 1877.

Turley, Theodore. Reminiscences and Journal, Sept. 1839–July 1840. CHL.

Turner, James. *Without God, Without Creed: The Origins of Unbelief in America.* Baltimore: The Johns Hopkins University Press, 1985.

Tyler, Daniel. "Recollections of the Prophet Joseph Smith." *Juvenile Instructor,* 1 Feb. 1892, 93–95.

Tyler, Samuel D. "A Daily Journal of the Travelling of the Camp of Latter Day Saints Which Went Out from Kirtland for Zion, July 6th, 1838." CHL.

Underwood, Grant. *The Millenarian World of Early Mormonism.* Urbana: University of Illinois Press, 1993.

U.S. and Canada Record Collection. FHL.

U.S. Bureau of the Census. Population Schedules. Microfilm. FHL.

Van Wagoner, Richard S. *Sidney Rigdon: A Portrait of Religious Excess.* Salt Lake City: Signature Books, 1994.

Van Wagoner, Richard S., and Steven Walker. "Joseph Smith: 'The Gift of Seeing.'" *Dialogue: A Journal of Mormon Thought* 15 (Summer 1982): 49–68.

Vogel, Dan. *Joseph Smith: The Making of a Prophet.* Salt Lake City: Signature Books, 2004.

Waite, F. C. Letter, Cleveland, OH, to Joseph L. Rubin, Washington DC, 19 Oct. 1933. Copy in Milton V. Backman, Ohio Research Papers, ca. 1975. CHL.

Walker, Jeffrey N. "Mormon Land Rights in Caldwell and Daviess Counties and the Mormon Conflict of 1838: New Findings and New Understandings." Paper presented at the annual meeting of the Mormon History Association, Salt Lake City, 24–27 May 2007.

Walton, Michael T. "Professor Seixas, the Hebrew Bible, and the Book of Abraham." *Sunstone* 6, no. 2 (Mar.–Apr. 1981): 41–43.

Warsaw Message. Warsaw, IL. 1843–1844.

Warsaw Signal. Warsaw, IL. 1841–1853.

The Wasp. Nauvoo, IL. Apr. 1842–Apr. 1843.

Watson, Harry L. *Liberty and Power: The Politics of Jacksonian America.* Rev. ed. New York: Hill and Wang, 2006.

Western Historical Manuscript Collection. University of Missouri and State Historical Society of Missouri, Ellis Library, University of Missouri, Columbia.

Western Reserve Chronicle. Warren, OH. 1816–1854.

Whalen, Robert Kieran. "Millenarianism and Millennialism in America, 1790–1880." PhD diss., State University of New York at Stony Brook, 1971.

Wheeler, Robert A. "Medicine in the Western Reserve: 1820–1860." *Western Reserve Magazine,* 1979, 31–38.

Whitmer, History / Whitmer, John. "The Book of John Whitmer Kept by Commandment," ca. 1835–1846. CCLA. Also available as Bruce N. Westergren, ed., *From Historian to Dissident: The Book of John Whitmer* (Salt Lake City: Signature Books, 1995).

Whitmer, John. Daybook, 1832–1878. CHL.

———. Letter, Far West, MO, to Oliver Cowdery and David Whitmer, Kirtland Mills, OH, 29 Aug. 1837. Western Americana Collection, Beinecke Rare Book and Manuscript Library, Yale University.

Whitney, Newel K. Papers, 1825–1906. BYU.

Whitney, Orson F. "The Aaronic Priesthood." *Contributor,* Jan. 1885, 123–132.

———. "Newel K. Whitney." *Contributor,* Jan. 1885, 130–131.

Whittaker, David J. "The Book of Daniel in Early Mormon Thought." In *By Study and Also by Faith: Essays in Honor of Hugh W. Nibley on the Occasion of His Eightieth Birthday, 27 March 1990,* edited by John M. Lundquist and Stephen D. Ricks, 1:155–201. Salt Lake City: Deseret Book; Provo, UT: Foundation for Ancient Research and Mormon Studies, 1990.

Williams, Frederick G. "Frederick Granger Williams of the First Presidency of the Church." *BYU Studies* 12 (Spring 1972): 243–261.

Williams, Frederick G. Papers, 1834–1842. CHL.

Winchester, B[enjamin]. *The Origin of the Spaulding Story, concerning the Manuscript Found; with a Short Biography of Dr. P. Hulbert, the Originator of the Same; and Some Testimony Adduced, Showing It to Be a Sheer Fabrication, So Far as Its Connection with the Book of Mormon Is Concerned.* Philadelphia: Brown, Bicking, and Guilbert, 1840.

Woman's Exponent. Salt Lake City. 1872–1914.

Woodford, Robert J. "The Historical Development of the Doctrine and Covenants." 3 vols. PhD diss., Brigham Young University, 1974.

Woodruff, Wilford. Journals, 1833–1844. Wilford Woodruff, Journals and Papers, 1828–1898. CHL. Also available as *Wilford Woodruff's Journals, 1833–1898,* edited by Scott G. Kenney, 9 vols. (Midvale, UT: Signature Books, 1983–1985).

Woodward, Maria Jane Johnson. "Statement of Sister Maria Jane Woodward of Huntington, Emery County, Utah, Maiden Name, Maria J. Johnston." In George H. Brimhall, Provo, UT, to Joseph F. Smith, Salt Lake City, UT, 21 Apr. 1902. Joseph F. Smith, Papers, 1854–1918. CHL.

Zucker, Louis C. "Joseph Smith as a Student of Hebrew." *Dialogue: A Journal of Mormon Thought* 3 (Summer 1968): 41–55.

Corresponding Section Numbers
in Editions of the Doctrine and Covenants

The Book of Commandments, of which a number of partial copies were printed in 1833, was superseded by the Doctrine and Covenants. Because the numbering of comparable material in the Book of Commandments and different editions of the Doctrine and Covenants varies extensively, the following table is provided to help readers refer from the version of a canonized item cited in this volume to other published versions of that same item. This table includes revelations announced by JS—plus letters, records of visions, articles, minutes, and other items, some of which were authored by other individuals—that were published in the Book of Commandments or Doctrine and Covenants in or before 1844, the year of JS's death. The table also includes material originating with JS that was first published in the Doctrine and Covenants after 1844. Such later-canonized material includes, for example, extracts of JS's 20 March 1839 letter written from the jail in Liberty, Missouri. These extracts, first canonized in 1876, are currently found in sections 121 through 123 of the Latter-day Saint edition of the Doctrine and Covenants.

The 1835 and 1844 editions of the Doctrine and Covenants included a series of lectures on the subject of faith, which constituted part 1 of the volume. Only part 2, the compilation of revelations and other items, is represented in the table. Further, the table does not include materials originating with JS that were not canonized in his lifetime and that have never been canonized by The Church of Jesus Christ of Latter-day Saints or by the Community of Christ. As only one of many examples, the journal entry for 3 November 1835 in this volume contains a JS revelation concerning the Twelve. This revelation has never been canonized and therefore does not appear in the table. More information about documents not listed on the table below will be provided in other volumes of *The Joseph Smith Papers* and on the Joseph Smith Papers website.

Some material was significantly revised after its initial publication in the canon. For instance, the revelation in chapter 28 of the Book of Commandments included twice as much material when it was republished in the Doctrine and Covenants in 1835. As another example, chapter 65 of the Book of Commandments stops abruptly before the end of the revelation because publication of the volume was disrupted; the revelation was not published in its entirety until 1835. These and other substantial changes of greater or lesser significance are not accounted for in the table, but they will be identified in the appropriate volumes of the Documents series.

The far left column of the table gives the date of the canonized item, based on careful study of original sources. The date provides a way to identify each item and situate it chronologically with other documents, but it cannot be assumed that every date corresponds to the day an item was first dictated or recorded. In some cases, an item was recorded without a date notation. It is also possible that a few items were first dictated on a date other than the date surviving manuscripts bear. We have done our best to arrive at a date or approximate date using all available evidence, including later attempts by JS and his contemporaries to recover date, place, and circumstances.

Where surviving sources provide conflicting information about dating, editorial judgment has been exercised to select the most likely date (occasionally only an approximate month), based on the most reliable sources. In cases in which two or more items bear the same date, they have been listed in the order in which they most likely originated, and a letter of the alphabet has been appended, providing each item a unique editorial title (for example, May 1829–A or May 1829–B). Information on dating issues will accompany publication of these items in the Documents series.

The remaining five columns on the table provide the number of the chapter (in the case of the Book of Commandments) or section (in the case of editions of the Doctrine and Covenants) in which the item was published in one or more of five different canonical editions, the first three of which were initiated by JS. Full bibliographic information about these five editions is given in the list of works cited. See also the Scriptural References section in the introduction to Works Cited for more information about the origins of the Doctrine and Covenants and other Mormon scriptures.

Key to column titles

1833:   Book of Commandments
1835:   Doctrine and Covenants, 1835 edition, part 2
1844:   Doctrine and Covenants, 1844 edition, part 2[1]
1981:   Doctrine and Covenants, 1981 edition, The Church of Jesus Christ of Latter-day Saints[2]
2004: Doctrine and Covenants, 2004 edition, Community of Christ[3]

| Date | JS-Era Canon | | | | |
	1833	1835	1844	1981	2004
21 Sept. 1823				2[4]	
July 1828	2	30	30	3	2
Feb. 1829	3	31	31	4	4
Mar. 1829	4	32	32	5	5
Apr. 1829–A	5	8	8	6	6

---

1. The 1844 edition of the Doctrine and Covenants included one item written after the death of JS (section 111). That item is not included in this table.

2. The 1981 Latter-day Saint edition of the Doctrine and Covenants includes some items written after the death of JS. Those items are not included in this table. Any item for which information appears only in the "1981" column and in the "Date" column is a later-canonized JS item, as discussed in the first paragraph of the preceding introduction.

3. The 2004 Community of Christ edition of the Doctrine and Covenants includes two extracts from JS's Bible revision (sections 22 and 36) and items written after the death of JS. Neither the extracts nor the later items are included in this table.

4. This section, an extract from the history JS initiated in 1838, is here dated by the date of the event described in the section rather than the date of the document's creation.

	JS-Era Canon				
Date	1833	1835	1844	1981	2004
ca. Apr. 1829	9	36	36	10	3
Apr. 1829–B	7	34	34	8	8
Apr. 1829–C	6	33	33	7	7
Apr. 1829–D	8	35	35	9	9
15 May 1829				13[5]	
May 1829–A	10	37	37	11	10
May 1829–B	11	38	38	12	11
June 1829–A	12	39	39	14	12
June 1829–B	15	43	43	18	16
June 1829–C	13	40	40	15	13
June 1829–D	14	41	41	16	14
June 1829–E		42	42	17	15
Mar. 1830	16	44	44	19	18
6 Apr. 1830	22	46	46	21	19
Apr. 1830–A	17	45:1	45:1	23:1–2	21:1
Apr. 1830–B	18	45:2	45:2	23:3	21:2
Apr. 1830–C	19	45:3	45:3	23:4	21:3
Apr. 1830–D	20	45:4	45:4	23:5	21:4
Apr. 1830–E	21	45:5	45:5	23:6–7	21:5
10 Apr. 1830	24	2	2	20	17
16 Apr. 1830	23	47	47	22	20
July 1830–A	25	9	9	24	23
July 1830–B	27	49	49	26	25
July 1830–C	26	48	48	25	24
ca. Aug. 1830	28	50	50	27	26
Sept. 1830–A	29	10	10	29	28
Sept. 1830–B	30	51	51	28	27
Sept. 1830–C	31	52:1	52:1	30:1–4	29:1
Sept. 1830–D	32	52:2	52:2	30:5–8	29:2
Sept. 1830–E	33	52:3	52:3	30:9–11	29:3
Sept. 1830–F	34	53	53	31	30
Oct. 1830–A		54	54	32	31
Oct. 1830–B	35	55	55	33	32
Nov. 1830	36	56	56	34	33
ca. Dec. 1830		73	74	74	74

5. This section, an extract from the history JS initiated in 1838, is here dated by the date of the event described in the section rather than the date of the document's creation.

	JS-Era Canon				
DATE	1833	1835	1844	1981	2004
7 Dec. 1830	37	11	11	35	34
9 Dec. 1830	38	57	57	36	35
30 Dec. 1830	39	58	58	37	37
2 Jan. 1831	40	12	12	38	38
5 Jan. 1831	41	59	59	39	39
6 Jan. 1831	42	60	60	40	40
4 Feb. 1831	43	61	61	41	41
9 Feb. 1831[6]	44	13:1–19	13:1–19	42:1–73	42:1–19
Feb. 1831–A	45	14	14	43	43
Feb. 1831–B	46	62	62	44	44
23 Feb. 1831	47	13:21–23, 20	13:21–23, 20	42:78–93, 74–77	42:21–23, 20
ca. 7 Mar. 1831	48	15	15	45	45
ca. 8 Mar. 1831–A	49	16	16	46	46
ca. 8 Mar. 1831–B	50	63	63	47	47
10 Mar. 1831	51	64	64	48	48
7 May 1831	52	65	65	49	49
9 May 1831	53	17	17	50	50
20 May 1831		23	23	51	51
6 June 1831	54	66	66	52	52
8 June 1831	55	66[7]	67	53	53
10 June 1831	56	67	68	54	54
14 June 1831	57	68	69	55	55
15 June 1831	58	69	70	56	56
20 July 1831		27	27	57	57
1 Aug. 1831	59	18	18	58	58
7 Aug. 1831	60	19	19	59	59
8 Aug. 1831	61	70	71	60	60
12 Aug. 1831	62	71	72	61	61
13 Aug. 1831	63	72	73	62	62
30 Aug. 1831	64	20	20	63	63
11 Sept. 1831	65	21	21	64	64
29 Oct. 1831		74	75	66	66
30 Oct. 1831		24	24	65	65
1 Nov. 1831–A		22	22	68	68

6. See also the following entry for 23 Feb. 1831.

7. The second of two sections numbered 66. Numbering remains one off for subsequent sections within the 1835 edition.

	JS-Era Canon				
Date	1833	1835	1844	1981	2004
1 Nov. 1831–B	1	1	1	1	1
2 Nov. 1831		25	25	67	67
3 Nov. 1831		100	108	133	108
11 Nov. 1831–A		28	28	69	69
11 Nov. 1831–B[8]		3 (partial[9])	3 (partial[10])	107 (partial[11])	104 (partial[12])
12 Nov. 1831		26	26	70	70
1 Dec. 1831		90	91	71	71
4 Dec. 1831		89	90	72	72
10 Jan. 1832		29	29	73	73
25 Jan. 1832		87	88	75	75
16 Feb. 1832		91	92	76	76
ca. Mar. 1832				77	
1 Mar. 1832		75	76	78	77
7 Mar. 1832		77	78	80	79
12 Mar. 1832		76	77	79	78
15 Mar. 1832		79	80	81	80
26 Apr. 1832		86	87	82	81
30 Apr. 1832		88	89	83	82
29 Aug. 1832		78	79	99	96
22 and 23 Sept. 1832		4	4	84	83
27 Nov. 1832				85	
6 Dec. 1832		6	6	86	84
25 Dec. 1832				87	
27 and 28 Dec. 1832 and 3 Jan. 1833		7	7	88	85
27 Feb. 1833		80	81	89	86
8 Mar. 1833		84	85	90	87
9 Mar. 1833		92	93	91	88
15 Mar. 1833		93	94	92	89
6 May 1833		82	83	93	90
1 June 1833		95	96	95	92
4 June 1833		96	97	96	93
2 Aug. 1833–A		81	82	97	94

8. See also the following entry for ca. Apr. 1835.

9. Verses 31–33, 35–42, 44.

10. Verses 31–33, 35–42, 44.

11. Verses 59–69, 71–72, 74–75, 78–87, 89, 91–92, 99–100.

12. Verses 31–33, 35–42, 44.

	JS-Era Canon				
Date	1833	1835	1844	1981	2004
2 Aug. 1833–B		83	84	94	91
6 Aug. 1833		85	86	98	95
12 Oct. 1833		94	95	100	97
16 and 17 Dec. 1833		97	98	101	98
17 Feb. 1834		5	5	102	99
24 Feb. 1834			101	103	100
23 Apr. 1834		98	99	104	101
22 June 1834			102	105	102
25 Nov. 1834		99	100	106	103
ca. Apr. 1835[13]		3	3	107	104
ca. Aug. 1835 ("Marriage")		101	109		111
ca. Aug. 1835 ("Of Governments and Laws in General")		102	110	134	112
26 Dec. 1835				108	
21 Jan. 1836				137	
27 Mar. 1836				109	
3 Apr. 1836				110	
6 Aug. 1836				111	
23 July 1837			104	112	105
Mar. 1838				113	
11 Apr. 1838				114	
26 Apr. 1838				115	
19 May 1838				116	
8 July 1838–A				118	
8 July 1838–C[14]			107	119	106
8 July 1838–D				120	
8 July 1838–E				117	
20 Mar. 1839				121–123	
19 Jan. 1841			[103]	124	107[15]
Mar. 1841				125	
9 July 1841				126	

---

13. See also the preceding entry for 11 Nov. 1831–B.

14. This table skips from 8 July 1838–A to 8 July 1838–C because the revelation not shown here, 8 July 1838–B, has never been canonized.

15. The 2004 Community of Christ edition provides the following note regarding this section: "Placed in the Appendix by action of the 1970 World Conference: the Appendix was subsequently removed by the 1990 World Conference."

Date	JS-Era Canon			1981	2004
	1833	1835	1844	1981	2004
1 Sept. 1842			105	127	109[16]
7 Sept. 1842			106	128	110[17]
9 Feb. 1843				129	
2 Apr. 1843				130	
16–17 May 1843				131	
12 July 1843				132	

16. The 2004 Community of Christ edition provides the following note regarding this section: "Placed in the Appendix by action of the 1970 World Conference: the Appendix was subsequently removed by the 1990 World Conference."

17. The 2004 Community of Christ edition provides the following note regarding this section: "Placed in the Appendix by action of the 1970 World Conference: the Appendix was subsequently removed by the 1990 World Conference."

Acknowledgments

The Joseph Smith Papers Project is made possible by the help and cooperation of many people. The project has benefited from the guidelines and experience developed during the renaissance in editing historical and literary works in America since the 1940s. Administrators and officials at Brigham Young University, Provo, Utah, and The Church of Jesus Christ of Latter-day Saints, Salt Lake City, have provided support and resources that have facilitated this work. We give special acknowledgment to management and staff at the Church History Library, Salt Lake City, where the bulk of the Joseph Smith papers are housed. We also express special thanks to officials of the Community of Christ, Independence, Missouri, who have made many Joseph Smith documents available from their archives.

In addition to the Church History Library and the Community of Christ Library-Archives, other repositories have provided valuable material and assistance, including L. Tom Perry Special Collections, Harold B. Lee Library, Brigham Young University; the Chicago Historical Society; the Family History Library, The Church of Jesus Christ of Latter-day Saints, Salt Lake City; the Hancock County Historical Society, Carthage, Illinois; the Illinois State Historical Library, Springfield; the Lake County Genealogical Society, Painesville, Ohio; the Library of Congress, Washington DC; the Missouri Historical Society, St. Louis; the Montrose, Iowa, Public Library; the State Historical Society of Iowa, Des Moines; and the Utah State Historical Society, Salt Lake City.

The foundation for the present edition of Joseph Smith's journals was laid during work on the second volume of *The Papers of Joseph Smith,* which was published in 1992. During that time many individuals contributed their skills. These include Leonard J. Arrington, Maureen Ursenbach Beecher, William G. Hartley, Carol Cornwall Madsen, and Marilyn Rish Parks, all colleagues in the former Joseph Fielding Smith Institute for Latter-day Saint History at Brigham Young University; William W. Slaughter and Ronald G. Watt, Church History Library; Glen M. Leonard, Church History Museum, Salt Lake City; Glenn N. Rowe, Church History Department, The Church of Jesus Christ of Latter-day Saints; Chad J. Flake, Keith W. Perkins, and David J. Whittaker, Brigham Young University; Richard P. Howard and Ronald E. Romig, Community of Christ Library-Archives; Steven R. Thomas, University of Utah, Salt Lake City; Mary Alma Kay, Keokuk, Iowa; and Ronald A. Millett, Deseret Book Company, Salt Lake City. Adding further research assistance and technical help were many students at Brigham Young University, including David Brizee, Mark Davies, Carlos Domingues, Byron Ellenberg, Quinn Haddock, Craig Livingston, Michael Mitchell, Kurt Rowley, Drew Smith, and Elizabeth White.

This present edition of the Joseph Smith journals, enriching and revising the 1992 publication, has benefited from the more recent work of many of those whose names have been mentioned above. Of particular note are the contributions of Community of Christ archivist Ron Romig. Many other scholars, students, and specialists have also made significant contributions to the present edition of the journals. John W. Welch of *Brigham Young*

University Studies has provided invaluable editorial support, and many *BYU Studies* staff members assisted with source checking and other editorial tasks, including Becky Boyce, Erick Carlson, Maurianne Dunn, Stephen Fleming, Julie Geilman, Alison Kitchen, Kristine Lee, Kimberly Pace, and Anastasia Sutherland. The biographical directory was developed with the assistance of Raquel M. Lindaas, Stanley D. Lindaas, Wayne T. Morris, Nathaniel H. Wadsworth, and Elizabeth Watkins.

Isaac Montague, Brent Beck, Derek Farnes, and Kent Simons produced the maps that appear in the back of this volume under the direction of Brandon Plewe of the Department of Geography, Brigham Young University. John Hamer, co-executive director of the John Whitmer Historical Association, created the three illustrative maps that appear earlier in the volume. Welden C. Andersen, of the Audiovisual Department, The Church of Jesus Christ of Latter-day Saints, shot the textual photographs in this volume and helped prepare both textual and contextual images for the press. Steven W. Booras, Center for the Preservation of Ancient Religious Texts, and Gene A. Ware and Craig Livingston, Brigham Young University, applied multispectral imaging techniques to help recover badly faded text.

We extend special thanks for the consulting provided by John P. Kaminski, Martha J. King, Richard Leffler, and Sharon Ritenour Stevens as faculty of the Institute for the Editing of Historical Documents. We are indebted to Mark Staker, Church History Department, The Church of Jesus Christ of Latter-day Saints, for assisting in matters involving Kirtland, Ohio, and to David W. Grua for his dedicated research on Missouri-era issues. We thank the many volunteers with the Church History Department who assisted with research and other tasks. Management and staff at Deseret Book Company expertly assisted with the design, typesetting, proofreading, printing, and distribution of this volume. In particular, we thank Sheri L. Dew, Cory H. Maxwell, Anne Sheffield, Richard Erickson, Suzanne Brady, Laurie C. Cook, Gail Halladay, Rebecca B. Chambers, and Vicki Parry. We thank Scott Eggers for designing the dust jacket and cloth cover.

Other people whose work made important contributions include Linda Hunter Adams, Mary Teresa Anderson, Mike Atha, Douglas Atterberg, Charlie Baird, Ronald O. Barney, Alexander L. Baugh, Richard Bennett, Patrick A. Bishop, Tonya Boltz, Matthew Bowman, Deborah Bradford, Lyle Briggs, Lisse Brox, Kathryn Burnside, Jeffrey G. Cannon, Matthew B. Christensen, Justin Collings, Lia Suttner Collings, Renee Collins, Randy Dixon, Eric Dowdle, Steven R. Duke, Patrick C. Dunshee, Don Enders, Breck England, Barbara J. Faulring, J. Spencer Fluhman, Matthew J. Grow, Nathan Grow, Susan Hainsworth, Angella L. Hamilton, Rijen Hendrick, Sharalyn D. Howcroft, Susan Jellinger, Amy E. Jensen, Elizabeth L. Jensen, Emily W. Jensen, Michael Jensen, Robin Scott Jensen, Christopher C. Jones, Allan R. Loyborg, John D. Luke, Jenny Lund, Lachlan Mackay, Gordon A. Madsen, Julina A. Magnusson, Winston Matthews, Chris McAfee, Timothy G. Merrill, Crystal Moore-Walker, Scott M. Mooy, Pauline K. Musig, Amy Norton, Andrew D. Olsen, Benjamin E. Park, Sarah Gibby Peris, Jennifer Peters, Tadd R. Peterson, Elizabeth Pinborough, Josh E. Probert, Daren Ray, Ronald Read, Jedediah S. Rogers, Sandra Mason Roller, Ryan W. Saltzgiver, Gloria Scovill, Craig K. Sedgwick, Alex D. Smith, Emily Smith, Gina H. Smith, Todd M. Sparks, Virginia E. Stratford, Mia Strutenau, Jared Tamez, Lissa Thompson, Grant Underwood, Bethany Wadsworth, Jeffrey N. Walker, Kathryn Jensen Wall, Lorin Welker, Vivian Wellman, and Robert J. Woodford.

In addition to generous support from the Church History Library and Brigham Young University, our institutional sponsors, the project has been blessed by generous funding by Larry H. and Gail Miller. This funding has underwritten an expansion of personnel and infrastructure without which the project would have been of necessity less ambitious.

In acknowledging our indebtedness to many people for their help, the editors nevertheless remain solely responsible for the content.

The Journals series will be indexed cumulatively in the final volume of the series. A printable, searchable index for volume 1 is available at josephsmithpapers.org.